SHOPRITE

68-95

GRAHAMSTOWN REFLECTED

AN ALBANY MUSEUM PUBLICATION

All net income derived from the sale of this book is used to develop and maintain the work being done by the Albany Museum to foster an appreciation of our diverse South African heritage.

First edition, first impression 1995

ISBN 0-9583206-4-0 (Soft cover)
ISBN 0-9583206-5-9 (Hard cover)
ISBN 0-9583206-6-7 (Collectors' edition)

PLEASE NOTE

This book was hand-crafted in Grahamstown with love, care and human fallibility — which accounts for its character, charm and inevitable hiccups. The words were woven from many sources; the 800-plus specially taken photographs each pasted into position. All credit for the perfect high-tech printing goes to Cape Town, and is given with appreciative amazement.

Colour reproduction by Unifoto, Cape Town
Printed and bound by Creda Press (Pty)Ltd, Elliot Ave, Epping 2, Cape Town

GRAHAMSTOWN REFLECTED

By Emily O'Meara
Designed by Lyn Tyler
Photography by Duncan Greaves AIP

"The real voyage of discovery consists not in seeing new landscapes, but in having new eyes."
Marcel Proust, French writer
(1871 - 1922)

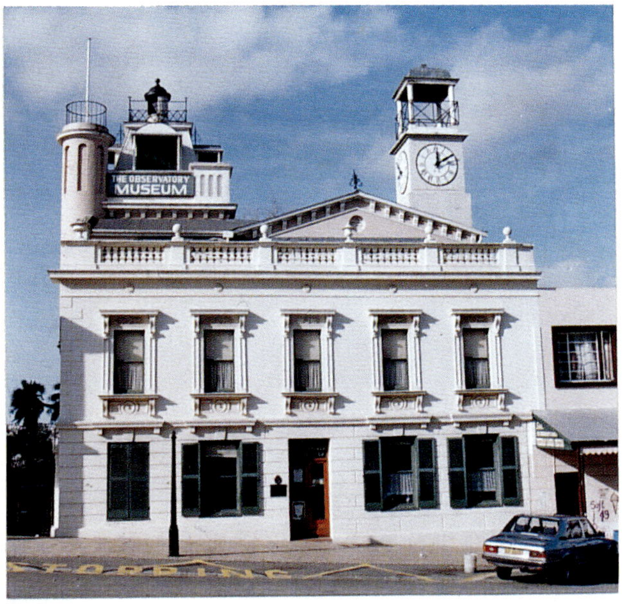

The Observatory Museum —where our story starts...

The creation and publication of this book was supported by the Standard Bank Foundation.

FORETHOUGHT

THERE is a fairy tale house in Bathurst Street with a magical mirror in the topmost turret which reflects Grahamstown onto a circular table below. Miniature moving pictures, glowingly colourful, true to life yet revealing unsuspected layers and links.

A time machine, an eye in the sky — the only Victorian camera obscura in the Southern Hemisphere, set up by the Wizard of "Obs", Henry Carter Galpin, in 1882. Just a small dark room at the top of the spiral stairs until the guide pulls a rope, the turret turns, and off you fly.

One moment you are hovering above a tangled back garden, the next high as the Cathedral spire. Up to the Township, down to the Market Square. Cars park, people pause. The past and present and glimpses of the future intermingle. All on a Lilliputian scale, intimate and accessible. A mosaic, a jigsaw puzzle, a kaleidoscope. The parts are greater than the whole.

Obviously the inspiration for the here, there and everywhere approach of this publication. An exploration, a celebration, not another predictably perfect place book. Because Grahamstown is unlike any other place. Perfectly enchanting but with obvious feet of clay. You can see the chalky kaolin deposits in the hills, the shacks on the Township slopes; the cultural crust and the poverty crunch, the past that is always present and the cracks in its facades. It is too small to hide its failings, so vulnerable that you want to — and almost can — put your arms around it.

Speed through via the N2 and Grahamstown is in one eye and out the other — a quick blur on the road between Port Elizabeth and East London. Linger longer and you may never leave. I didn't. In a previous incarnation as a jumpy Johannesburg journalist, I came for a conference and got back for good as soon as I could.

Caustic colleagues on the cutting edge confidently predicted I would soon turn into a museum piece. How right they were, how fortunate I am to be the curator of The Observatory Museum — familiarly dubbed "The Obs" — the most unusual home and business premises in the country, with the captivating camera the cherry on the top. Bric-à-brac galore, surprises on every floor.

"The Obs" started life as a humble structure bought by jeweller and clockmaker Henry Carter Galpin in 1850. With his additions it rose to great heights, but had hit such a low by the 1970s that it was doomed for demolition.

In true "Romancing the Stone" spirit, De Beers came riding to the restoration rescue because the Eureka — South Africa's first identified diamond — was conclusively authenticated on the premises in 1867.

So much has happened in Grahamstown, so much still does. Far too much to fit in through a glass lightly. Our book over-floweth! The little city's mood changes as often as its weather. Some days there is no place like it in the whole wide world. On others it is just a dorp, with a decided difference. But it is always a place in the heart.

Now — with a word of encouragement from Lewis Carroll's enterprising Alice — *"Let's pretend the glass has got all soft, like gauze, so that we can get through. Why, it's turning into a sort of mist now, I declare ..."* Step into Grahamstown and enjoy the adventure.

— **Emily O'Meara**

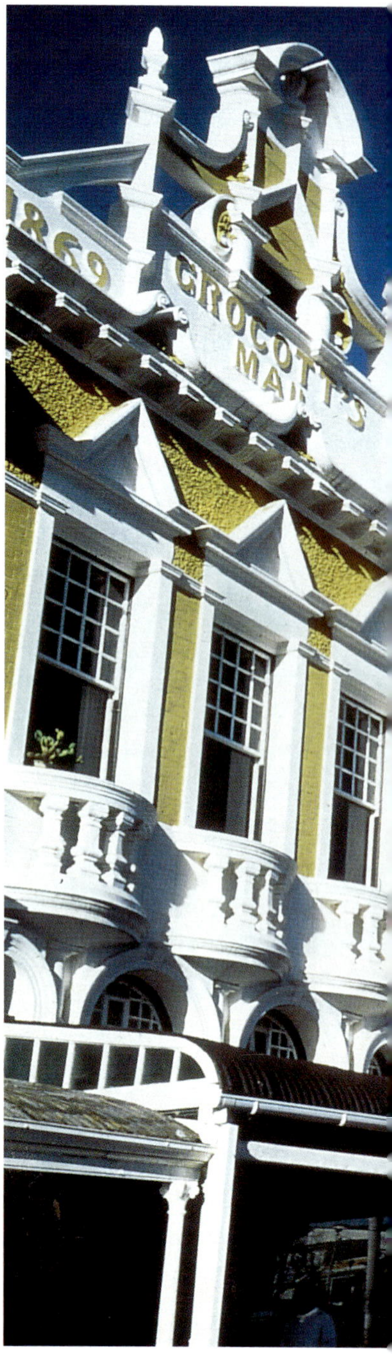

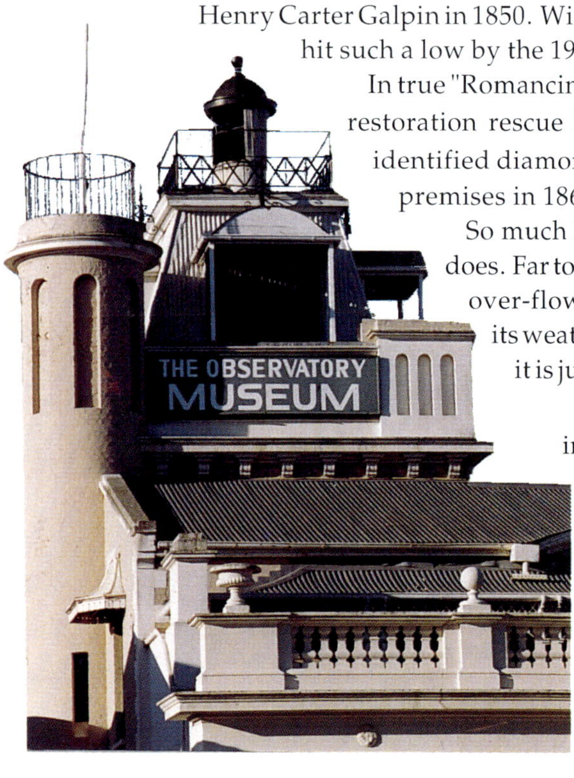

NO PLACE LIKE IT

"The local devotion of Grahamstown men is at once unique and admirable.

No other city, town or village in the colony is so rooted in the affections of its inhabitants, or stirs in them so superb a pride."

— *The Cape Times*, 1882

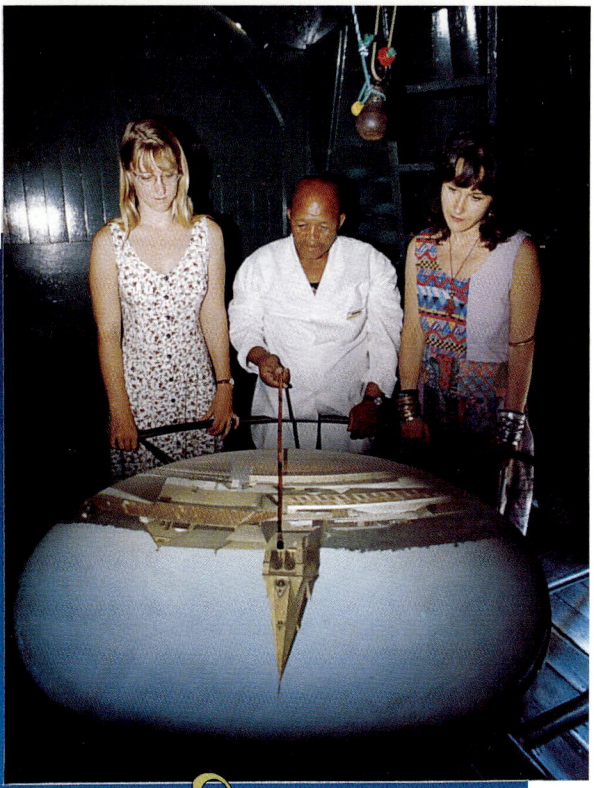

THROUGH THE LOOKING GLASS

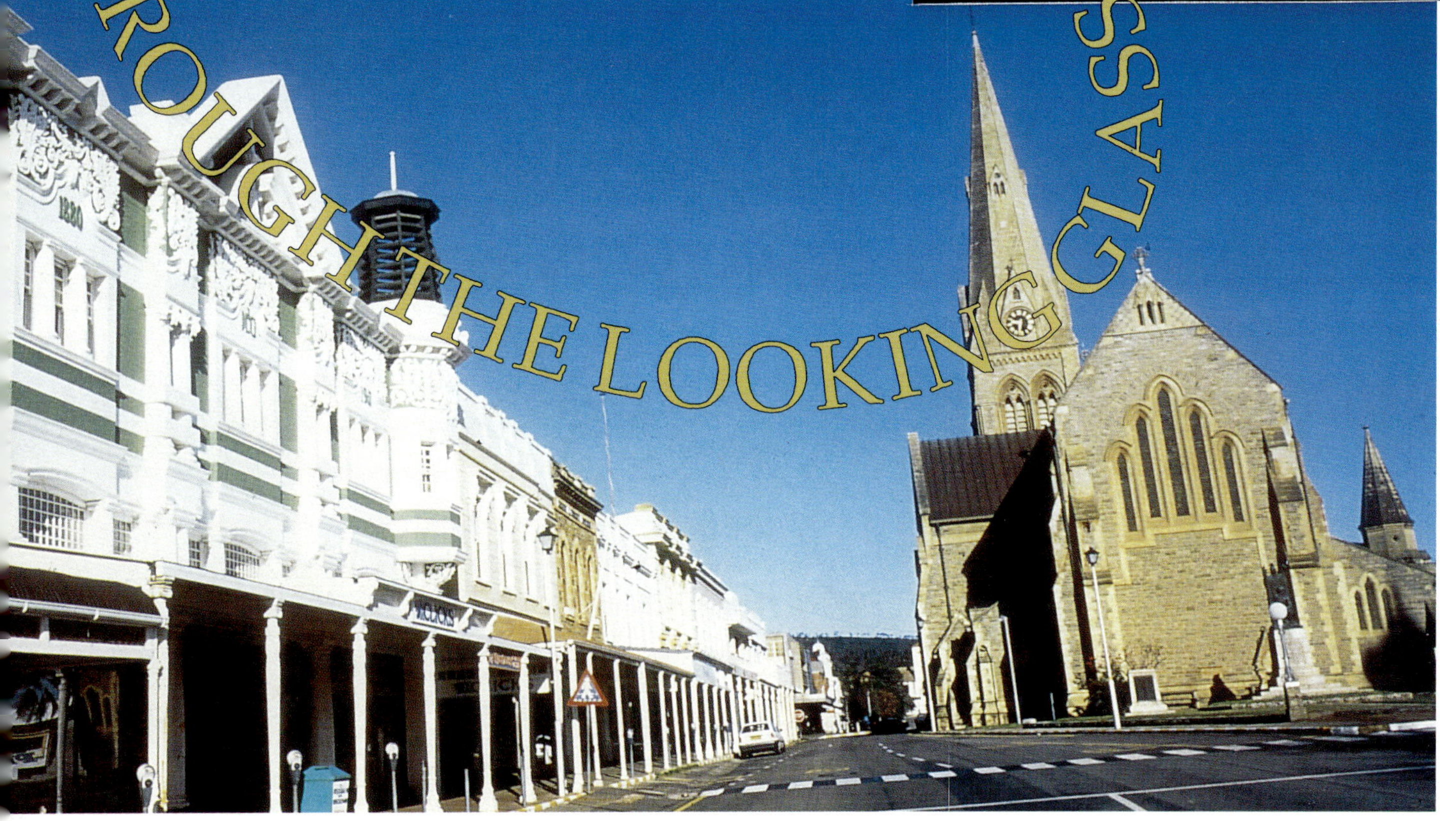

A DORP WITH A DIFFERENCE

"The Victorian Liberal statesman, John Bright, infuriated the Oxford of his day by describing it as 'provincial— with a difference'. One who knew South Africa well said of Grahamstown of this period that it was 'a dorp — with a difference'. There are those who would say that remains true today."

— **Ronald Currey, in his book on St Andrew's College, Grahamstown, 1955**

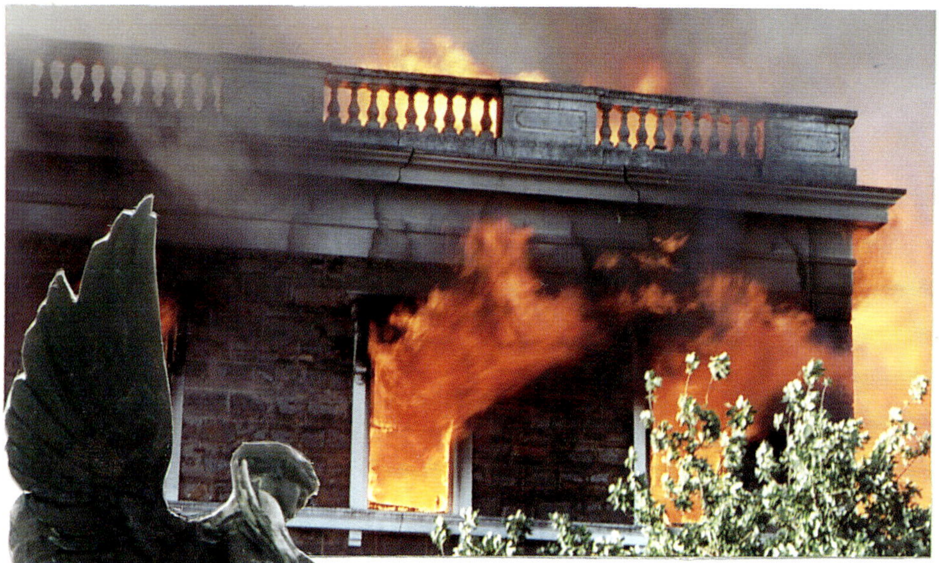

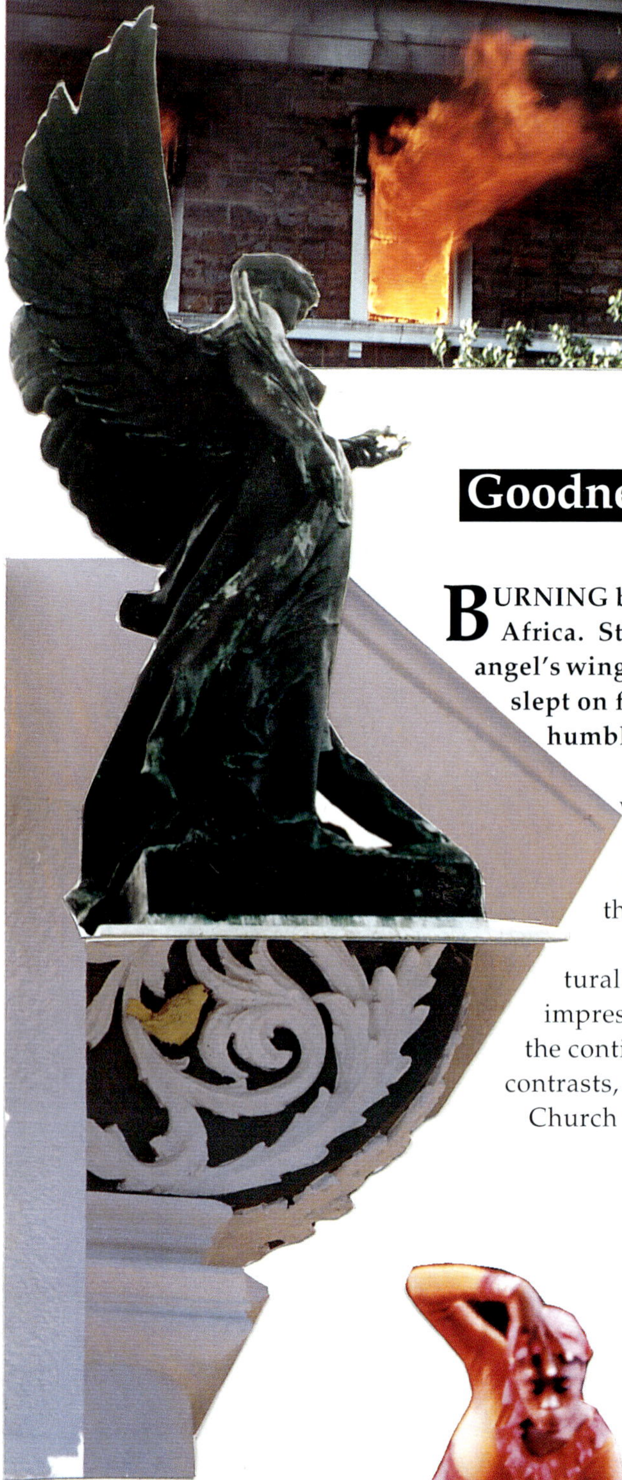

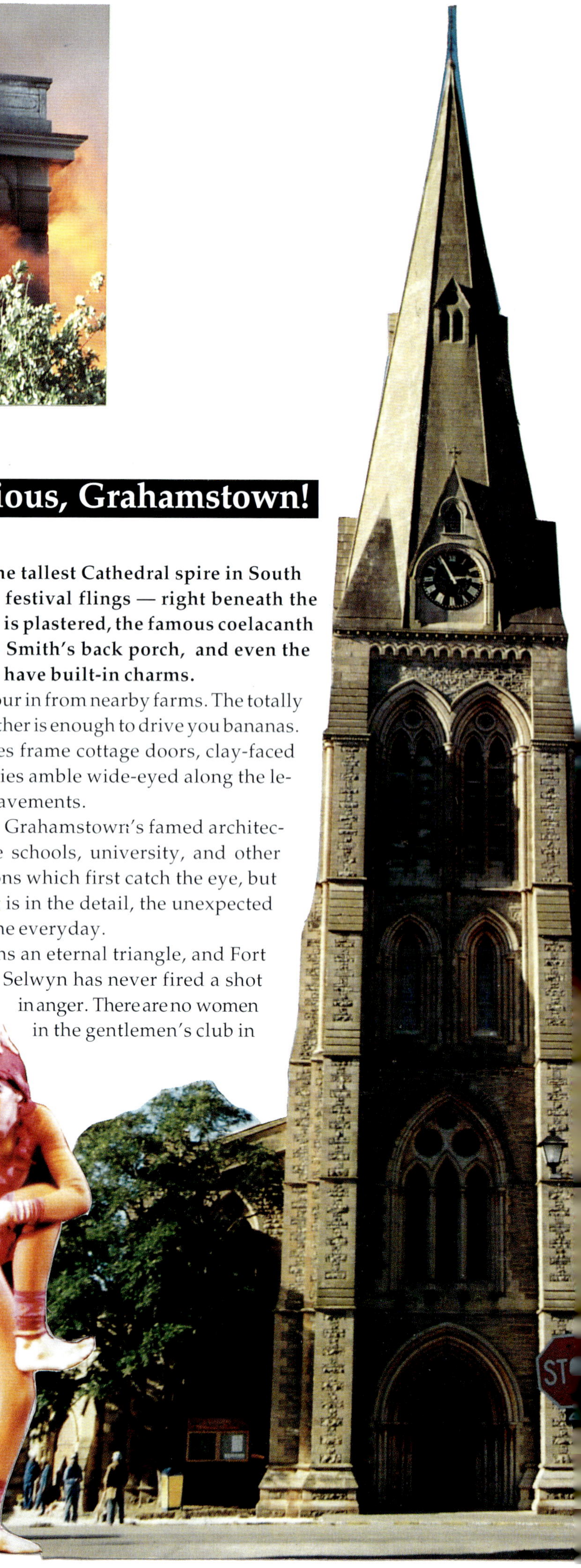

Goodness gracious, Grahamstown!

BURNING balustrades, the tallest Cathedral spire in South Africa. Student capers, festival flings — right beneath the angel's wings. The canary is plastered, the famous coelacanth slept on fish fundi JLB Smith's back porch, and even the humblest CBD sites have built-in charms.

Pineapples pour in from nearby farms. The totally wayward weather is enough to drive you bananas. Rambling roses frame cottage doors, clay-faced country beauties amble wide-eyed along the lethally uneven pavements.

Of course it is Grahamstown's famed architectural heritage, fine schools, university, and other impressive institutions which first catch the eye, but the continuing delight is in the detail, the unexpected contrasts, the magic of the everyday.

Church Square remains an eternal triangle, and Fort Selwyn has never fired a shot in anger. There are no women in the gentlemen's club in

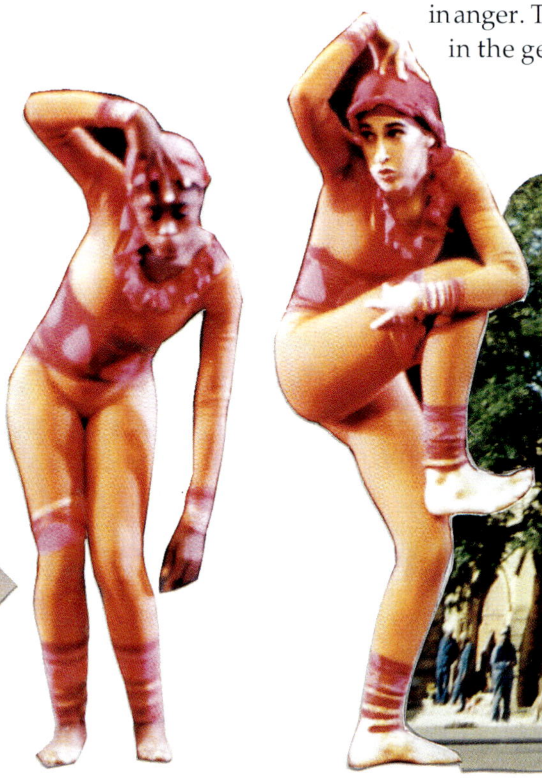

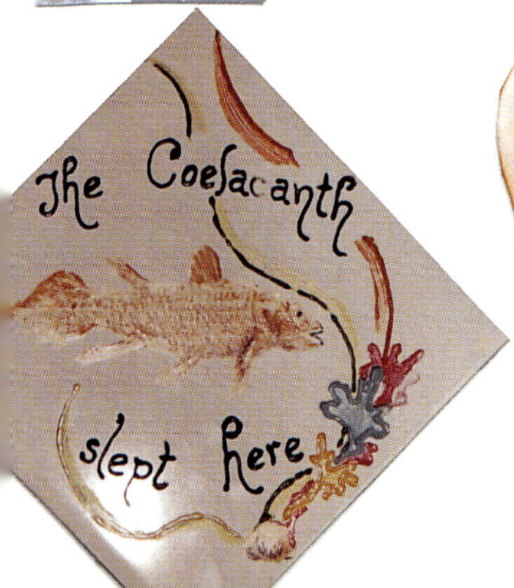

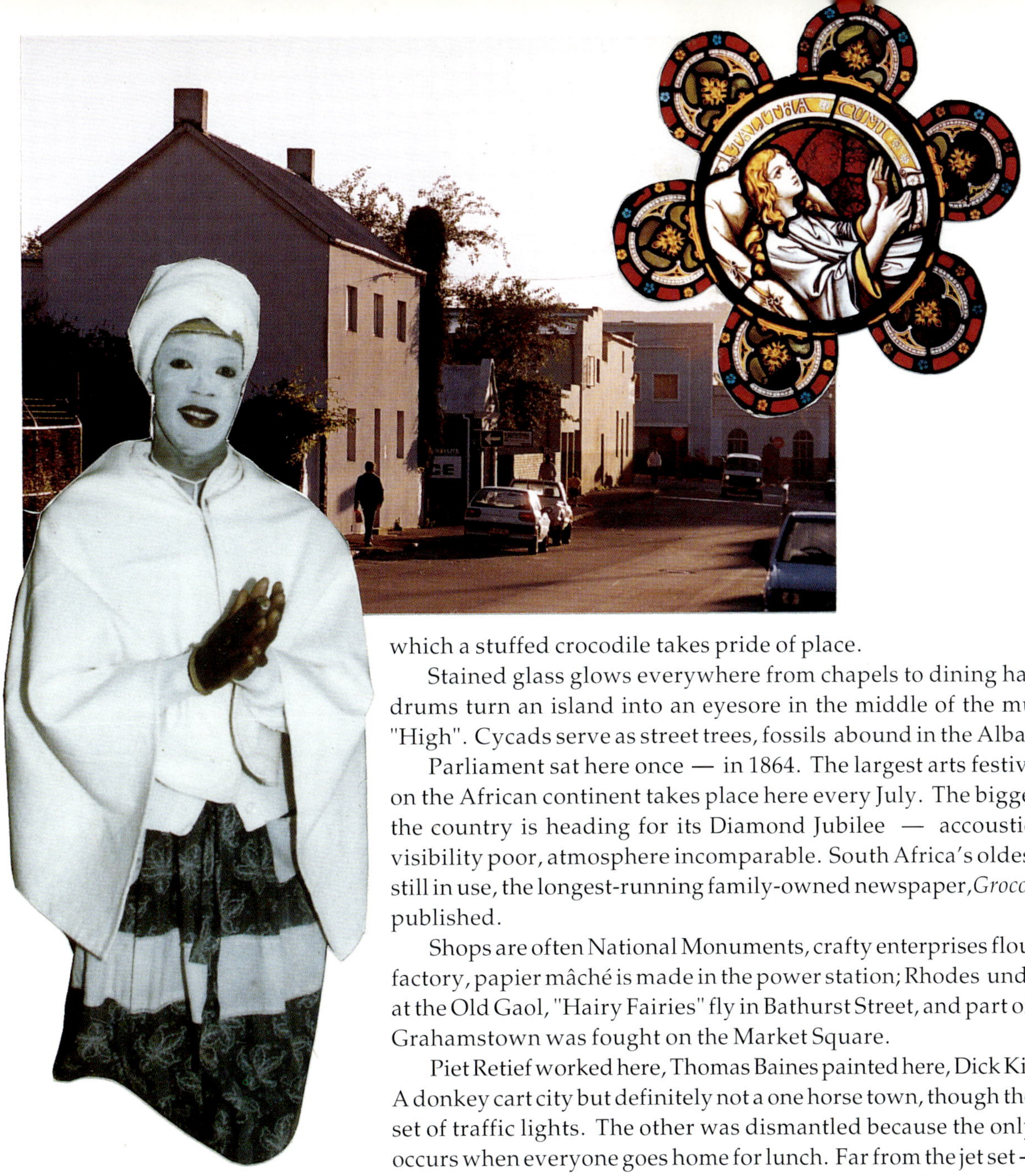

which a stuffed crocodile takes pride of place.

Stained glass glows everywhere from chapels to dining halls. Rubbish drums turn an island into an eyesore in the middle of the much-vaunted "High". Cycads serve as street trees, fossils abound in the Albany Museum.

Parliament sat here once — in 1864. The largest arts festival of its kind on the African continent takes place here every July. The biggest cinema in the country is heading for its Diamond Jubilee — accoustics atrocious, visibility poor, atmosphere incomparable. South Africa's oldest post-box is still in use, the longest-running family-owned newspaper, *Grocott's Mail*, still published.

Shops are often National Monuments, crafty enterprises flourish in an ice factory, papier mâché is made in the power station; Rhodes undergrads rave at the Old Gaol, "Hairy Fairies" fly in Bathurst Street, and part of the Battle of Grahamstown was fought on the Market Square.

Piet Retief worked here, Thomas Baines painted here, Dick King rode here. A donkey cart city but definitely not a one horse town, though there is just one set of traffic lights. The other was dismantled because the only traffic rush occurs when everyone goes home for lunch. Far from the jet set — unless you count the raucous hadedahs who make screech landings on their suburban roosts and often take off again in the middle of the night.

An endlessly surprising city in its own inimitable way. One of a kind. Come and explore the contents ...

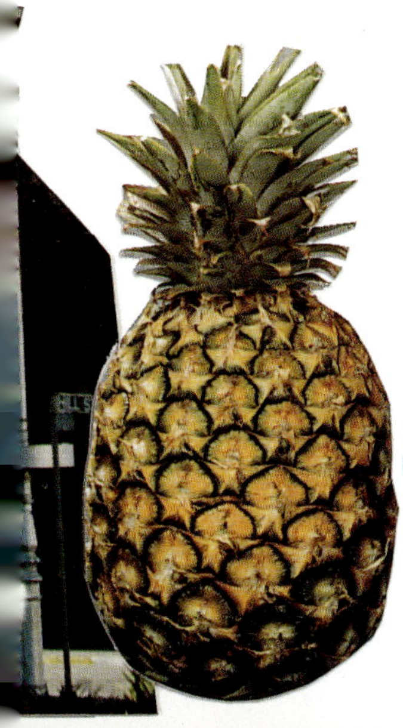

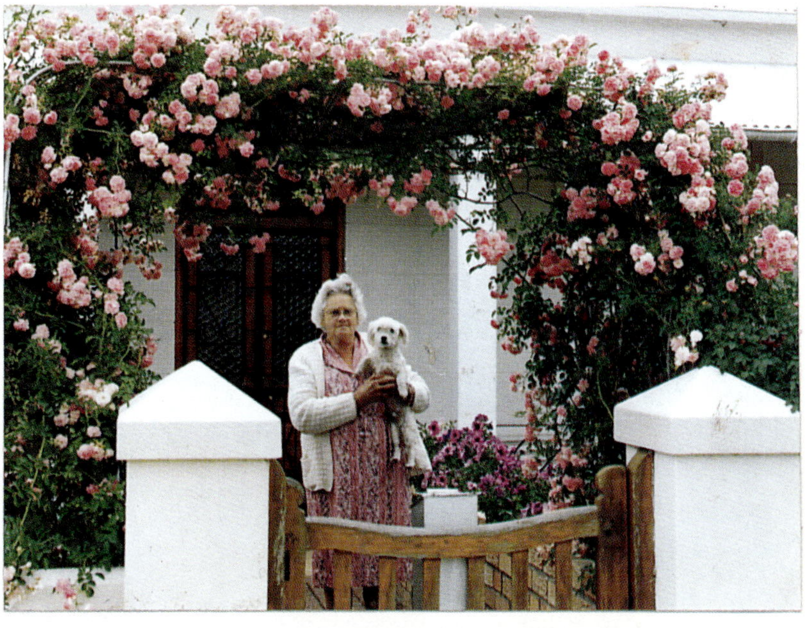

CONTENTS

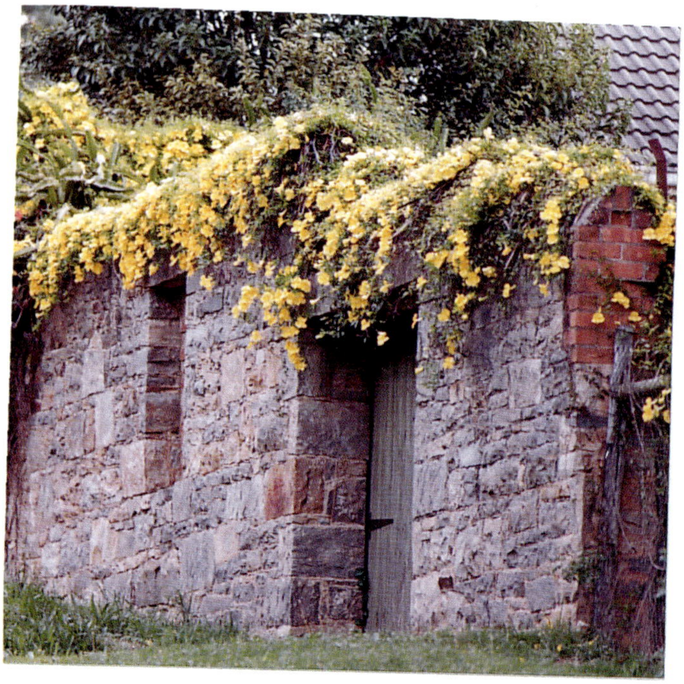

Poetry of the everyday...

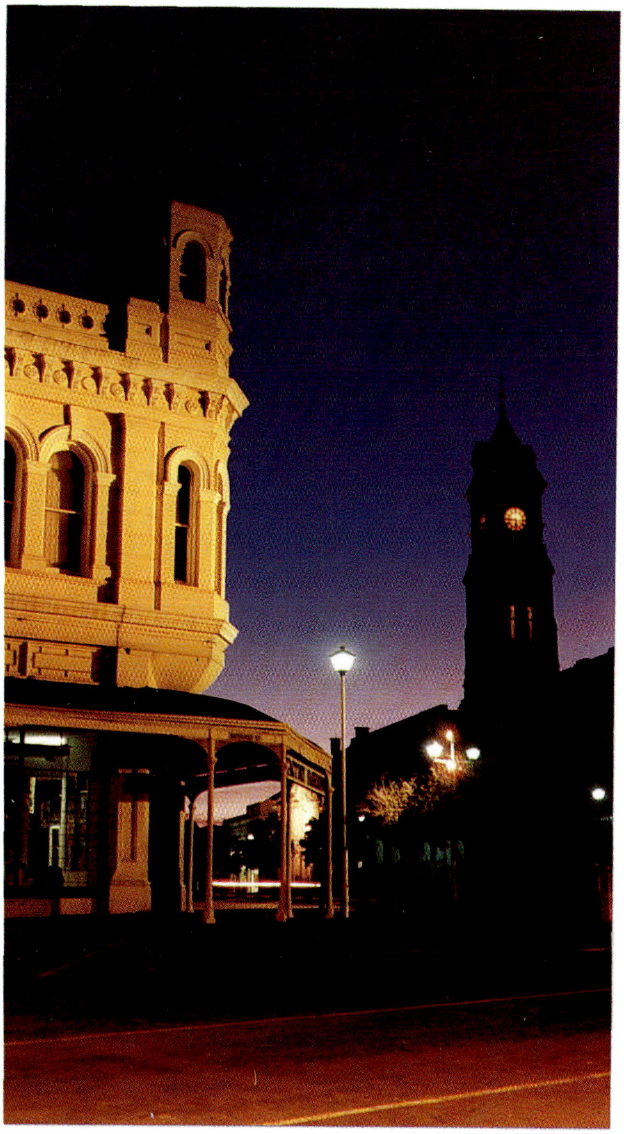

Magic of the night...

SPIRES DREAM, CLOCKS STOP

LIKE a heavenly exclamation mark, the soaring spire of the Cathedral of St Michael and St George — the highest in the land — hovers above the smallest of South Africa's 23 secondary cities as if in perpetual astonishment at its lofty aspirations.

Less ambitious steeples, towers and turrets punctuate the harmoniously low-rise lines of buildings which have grown old together and mellowed in the process. Clocks abound. Some definitely still ticking, others doddering along erratically, a few stopped dead in their tracks. Locals know them well, and make allowances for their idiosyncrasies.

In any event, with improved communications, the radio, and inexpensive watches, the need for public clocks has steadily diminished.

For many years during the last century, when time was not standard, local time was calculated by the military and announced by the firing of a 9am gun from Fort Selwyn on Gunfire Hill (next to the 1820 Monument).

This had obvious drawbacks. Even though the gun sounded like a thunder clap with a visible lightning flash, some inhabitants failed to "regulate, wind up or set going" their various timepieces, causing a general muddle. And the ancient artillery man who served as Old Father Time would occasionally subtract or add the odd half-hour to complete the confusion.

The absence of a public clock set to Grahamstown Mean Time, which could be seen throughout the day and be heard striking at night, made the establishment of an orderly communal life in the expanding settlement extremely difficult. In 1853 the idea of paying for a clock by public subscription was raised. Then as now, Grahamstonians were nice people with

Supreme Court at sunrise

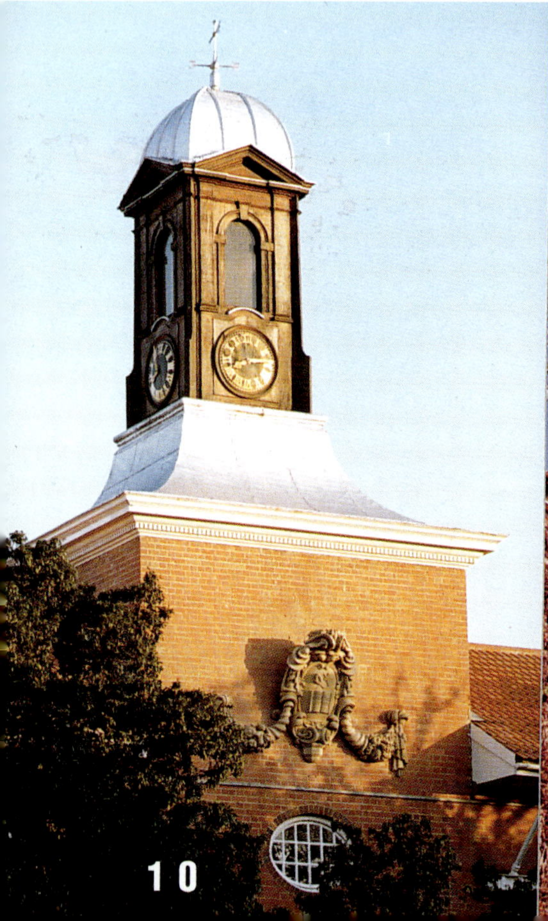

Rhodes University's ivory tower

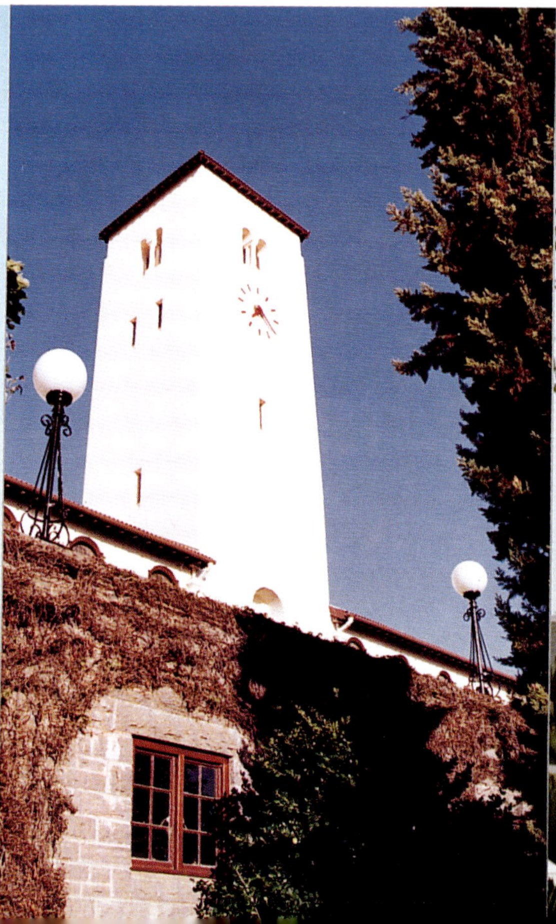

Observatory Museum's time warp

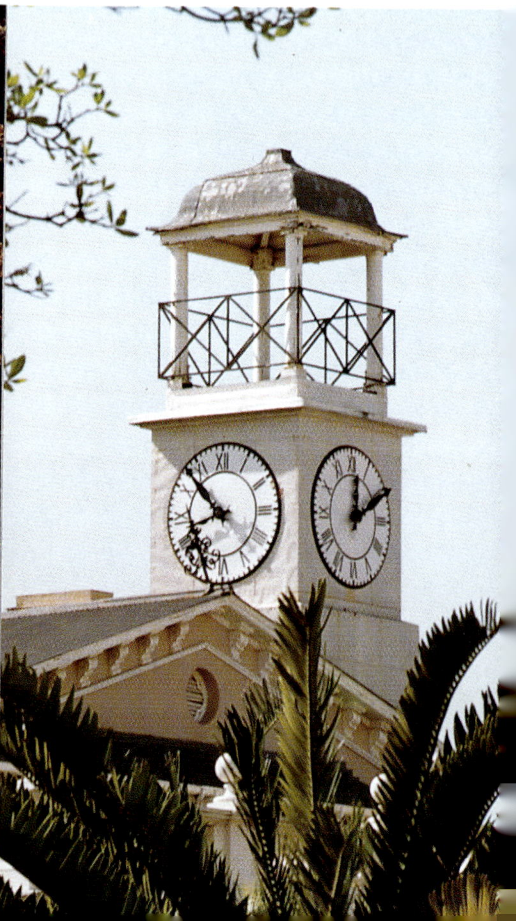

BUT TIME MARCHES ON

nice manners but just no money at all. It was 1873 before the first was installed at the Cathedral, followed in 1884 by a second in the Settler Memorial Tower which forms the entrance to the City Hall.

That same year, Henry Carter Galpin put a scaled down version of a clock in the new Royal Courts of Justice in London on the roof of the Observatory in Bathurst Street. The works are still on open view immediately below, while the ponderous pendulum swings down in the drawing room, emblazoned with the cautionary motto "Time runneth out, work is for aye". He also designed an ingenious Meridian Room with a north/south line on the floor to accurately ascertain Grahamstown time, which is 14 minutes behind SA Standard Time. Local noon occurs at 12h14.

Some may say Grahamstown is still behind the times, by considerably more than a scant quarter of an hour, and that nothing appears to change. Admittedly, change for the sake of change has never caught on here. We measure progress in different directions, mainly pushing forward the frontiers of knowledge; remembering that there is much to be learnt from the lessons of the past. Even in the carefully conserved historic heart, where change has been woven into the fabric rather than hastily applied to torn patches. Change and no change, change and continuity... The next 10 pages take you on a meandering march through time, past and present.

"Time present and time past
Are both perhaps present in time future,
And time future contained in time past."
— *Four Quartets*, TS Eliot (1888 - 1965)

City Hall and Cathedral spire — *Spire and DRC with weather vane* — *St Andrew's College Memorial Tower*

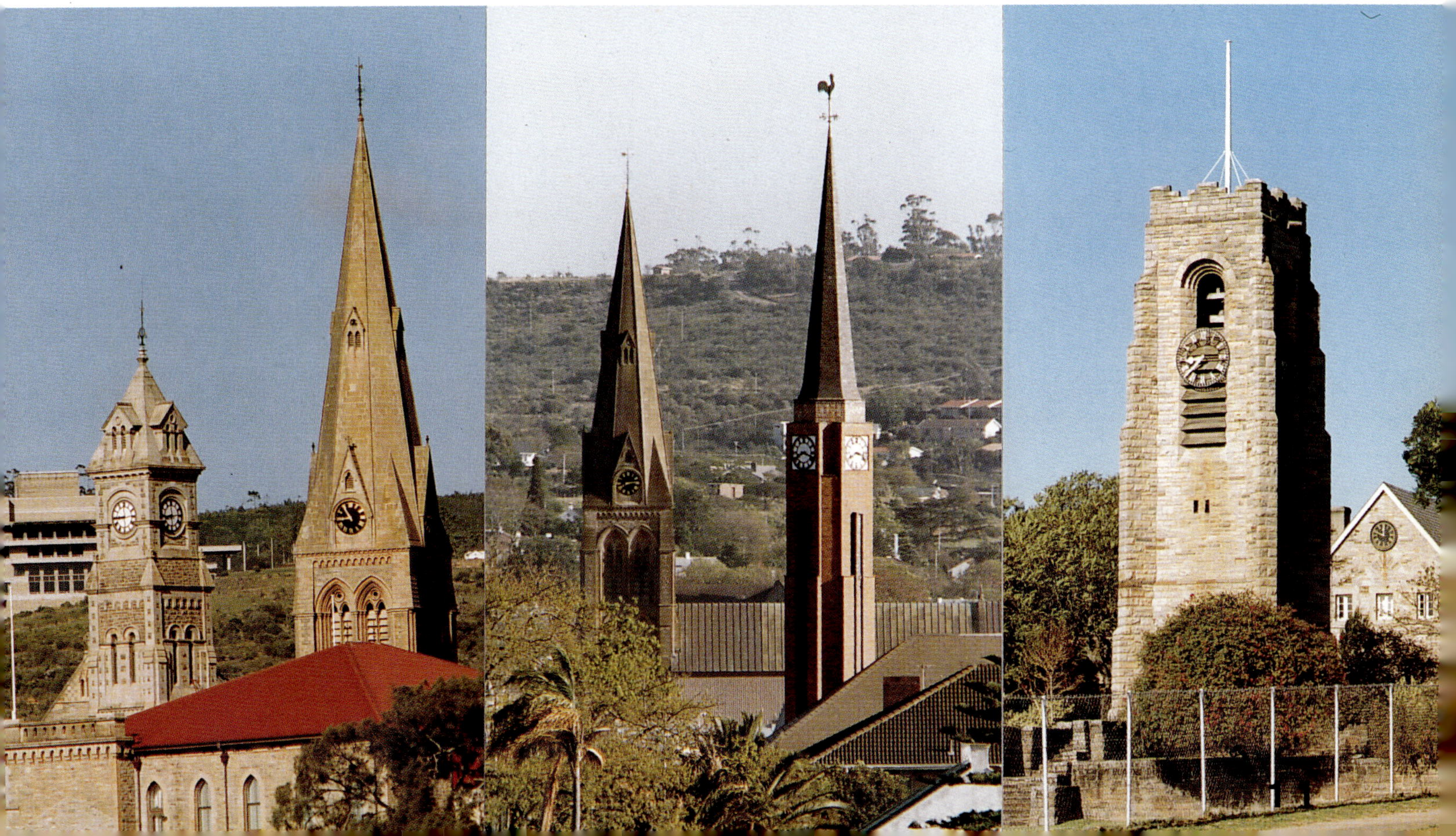

LIFE WAS A BEACH — AND THE REST IS HISTORY

"When you were a tadpole, and I was a fish,
In the Palaeozoic time,
And side by side in the ebbing tide
We sprawled through the ooze and slime..."
— ***Toast to a Lady,***
Langdon Smith (1858 - 1918)

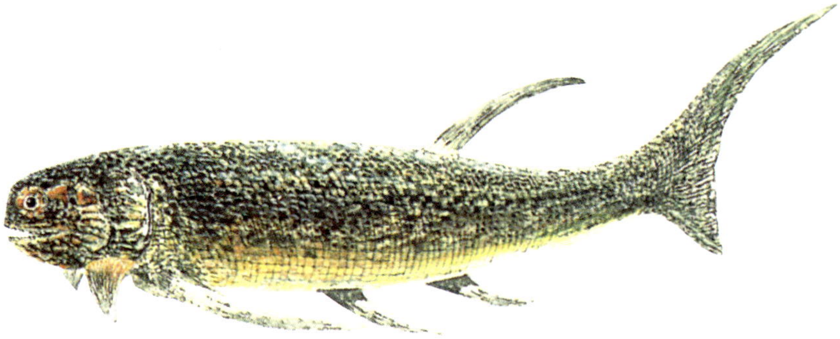

ABOVE: *Cyrancanthus specimen drawn from N2 fossil find*

SINCE early in the 19th century Grahamstown has been a meeting point for indigenous Xhosas and immigrant whites— explorers and traders, Boers and Brits, missionaries and military. A frontier town now mainly concerned with expanding the frontiers of knowledge in many different ways. An African village with a startlingly English edge, or vice versa, depending on where you stand.

"Grahamstown is as full of history as an egg is full of meat ..." wrote Prof George Cory of Rhodes University in a 1920 souvenir booklet. So many things have happened here that "to deal with them fully in this place could be productive of nothing but chronic mental indigestion".

Especially if you take the long view and start on the N2 road cutting near the 1820 Monument, site of a recent internationally significant find of fossil fish dating back 360 million years. They include the earliest remains in the world of *Holocephalans* — shark-like specimens — and sundry coelacanths. Supporting evidence suggests that the Grahamstown area was a seashore lagoon complex, sheltered by barrier islands and tidal channels.

Man put in an appearance approximately 1,5 million years ago, when Early Stone Age Hominids colonized the area. Artefacts from this period have been found scattered across the veld, the golf course included.

The San hunter-gatherers roamed for the past 10 000 years, the Khoi pastoralists for the last 2 000. The Iron Age forerunners of the present Xhosas had migrated in this direction along the coast from Natal by 800 AD.

Grahamstown in Xhosa is Rhini, the name of a Xhosa homestead head who once lived in the valley. It was in this area that the south-western migration of the Xhosas came into contact with the Dutch trekboers pushing forward from the Western Cape. Among the latter was Lucas Meyer. In 1812 his former farm was chosen as the site of the military garrison which grew into Grahams-town, named after Col John Graham.

The colonial government

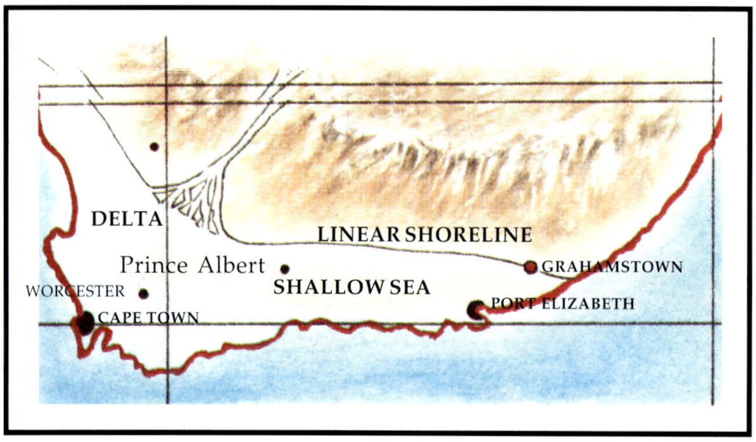

ABOVE: *Some 360-million years ago, Grahamstown was at the edge of a lagoon; now it is in the Eastern Cape, midway between Port Elizabeth and East London, approximately 40km from the coast*

RIGHT: *Grahamstown centenary monument, with steak house staff on steps*

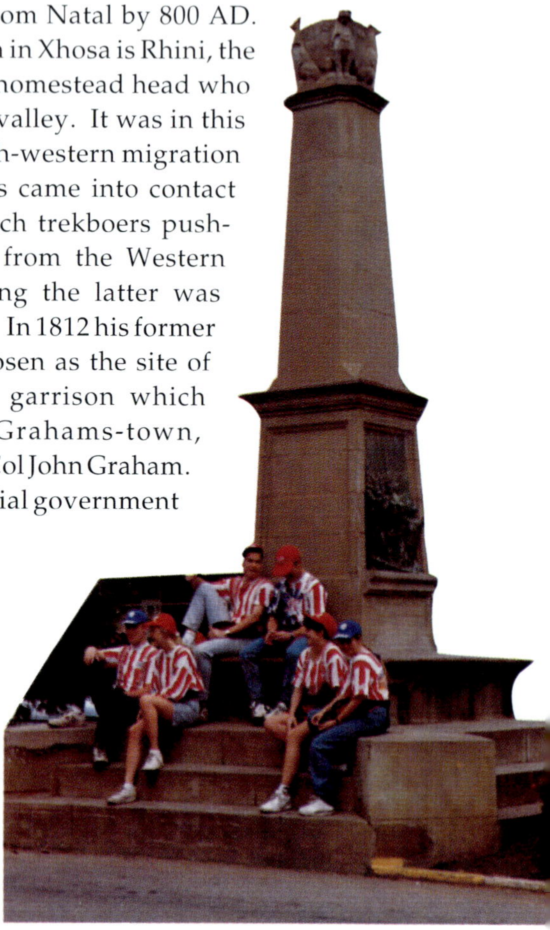

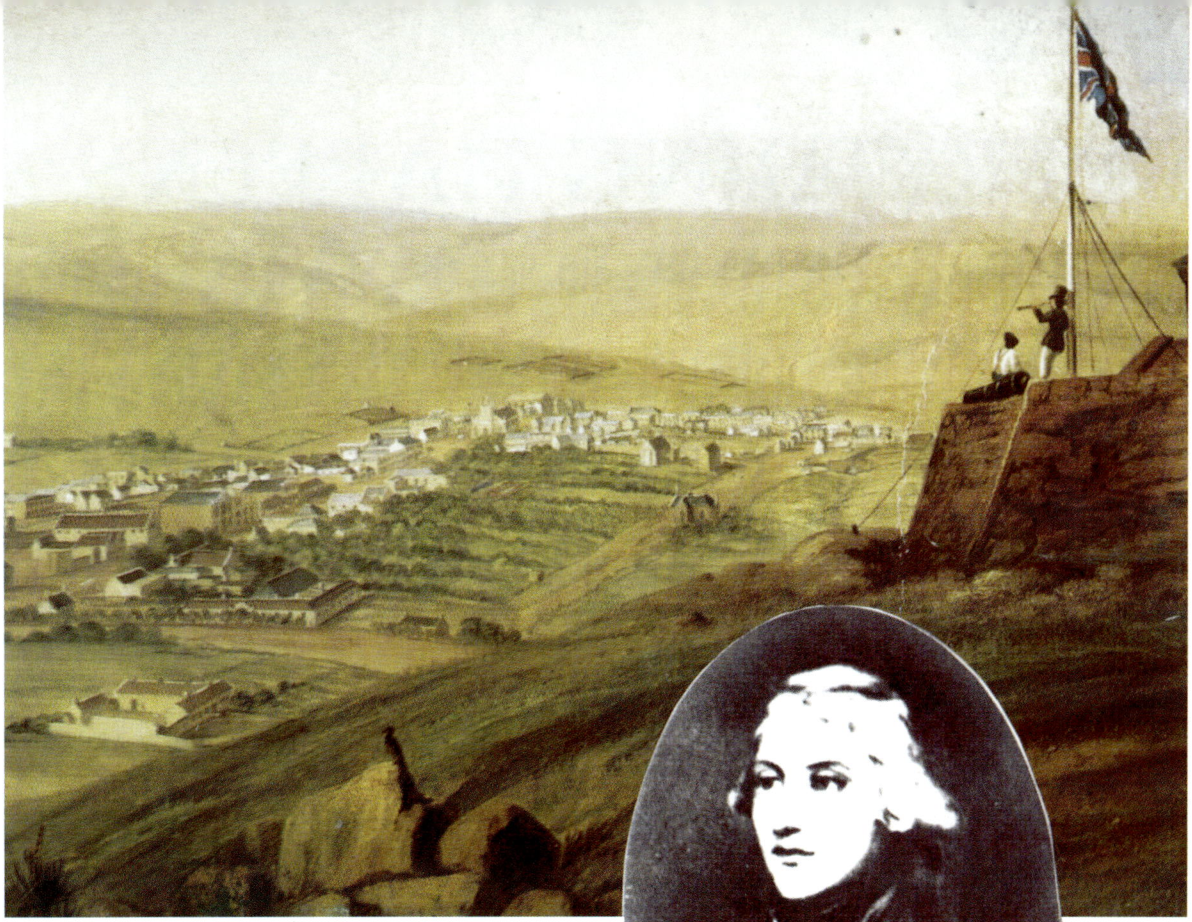

"If it's all the same to history it need not repeat itself any more." **— Bob Edwards, American editor**

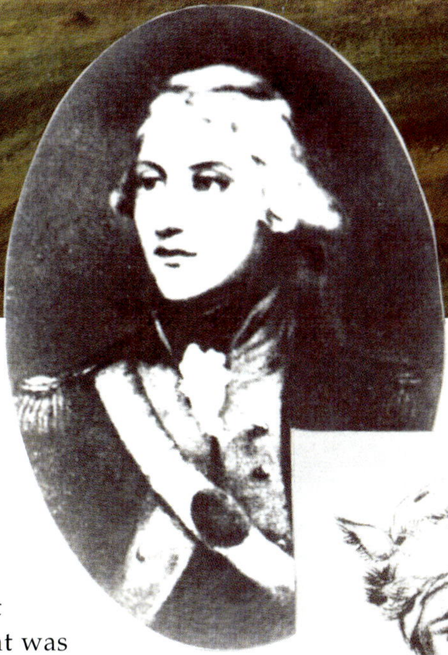

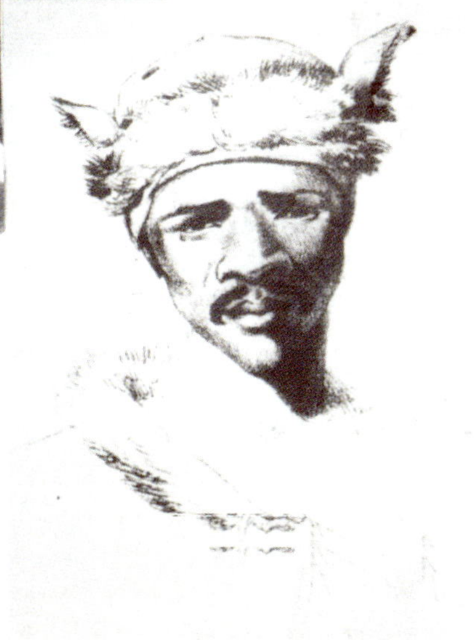

of the Cape Colony had appointed him to enforce the nearby Fish River as its eastern frontier with the Xhosa nation and curb growing friction over cattle and land. To supplement over-stretched military forces, the 1820 Settlers — close on 4 000 men, women and children — were brought from Britain. Attracted by the offer of farms in what was called the District of Albany, they were unaware that they were here to form a living chain of defence.

Harsh conditions forced many into Grahamstown, hence the strong British influence in buildings, institutions, and atmosphere.

By the time Grahamstown was designated the seat of administration for the Eastern Cape in 1836, it had grown into the largest centre in the colony outside Cape Town. However in the 1860s the tide of history started turning, and the action began shifting elsewhere.

The military importance of Grahamstown declined when the garrison moved forward to King William's Town, further into Xhosa territory. The discovery of diamonds — and later of gold — in the interior exacerbated the situation, and the rail link between Port Elizabeth and Kimberley left the little city stranded on a branch line. Not necessarily high and dry, but still surprisingly untouched by 20th century developments. The downside of its almost total lack of industry is a serious unemployment problem which increases steadily as the permanent population — in the region of 130 000 — does likewise...

Today Grahamstown is best known for its long-established schools, excellent university, many museums and numerous churches, as well as the Standard Bank National Arts Festival, which puts it in the spotlight every July.

CLOCKWISE: *Grahamstown from Fort Selwyn, painted in 1850 by Thomas Baines (original in Albany Museum); youthful portrait of Col John Graham, after whom the city was named; and a Khoi chief from the Eastern Cape, drawn c1820 by Samuel Daniell*

EVERYTHING HAPPENS IN HIGH STREET

"THERE is nothing like Grahamstown in Southern Africa and nothing more attractive, especially in those months of the year when the tower of the University and the spire of the Cathedral face each other down the length of the broad High Street over the heads of scarlet and purple flowering flame trees and jacarandas. Young people stroll about the streets of the old Frontier Post which, shed of its martial atmosphere, seems the epitome of peace as the summer mist rises over the spires of the 'City of Saints' amongst its surrounding hills."

— Joy Collier, *Frontier Post, The Story of Grahamstown,*

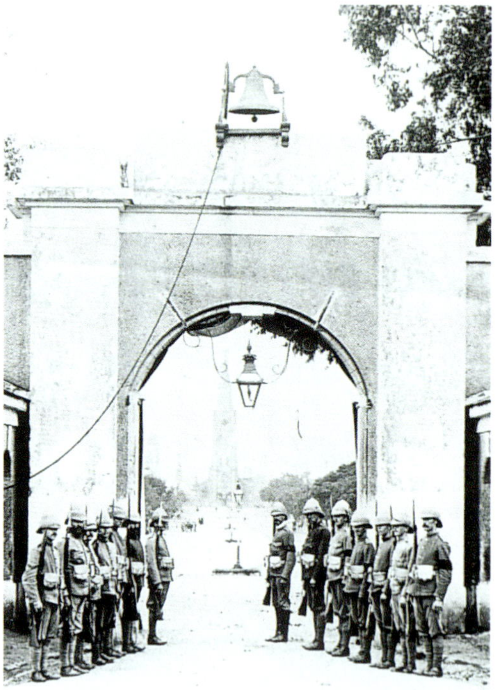

ABOVE: *Changing the Guard, Drostdy Gateway, 1902*

There you have our "High" in all its homespun glory. Splendour in the mist, heaven in the trees. A sight to remember. We could not have described it quite so glowingly ourselves without appearing boastful. Practically every town and village in England has a High Street.

Grahamstown's "High" is the only traditional one in South Africa. It is always bustling. Housewives, businessmen, legal eagles, secretary birds, students, schoolchildren, teachers, lecturers, clergymen, clerks, vegetable vendors, boerewors and broom sellers, farmers, bank managers, doctors, dentists... A pavement party where everyone meets everyone else during the course of the day.

The Drostdy Gateway at the top of upper High Street was completed in 1842, forming the entrance to a military parade ground. Stout sneezewood posts on either side protected the plaster from damage by gun carriages. Now pedestrians pass through to the rolling lawns of Rhodes University. The fire and curfew bell in the photograph on this page has gone into retirement behind an adjacent wall. It would certainly have come in handy when Blaine's Building went up in flames in December, 1992.

Completed in 1860 in time for a grand civic ball to celebrate the visit of Queen Victoria's second

BELOW: *High Street in 1877 by George Hawes (original watercolour in Albany Museum)*

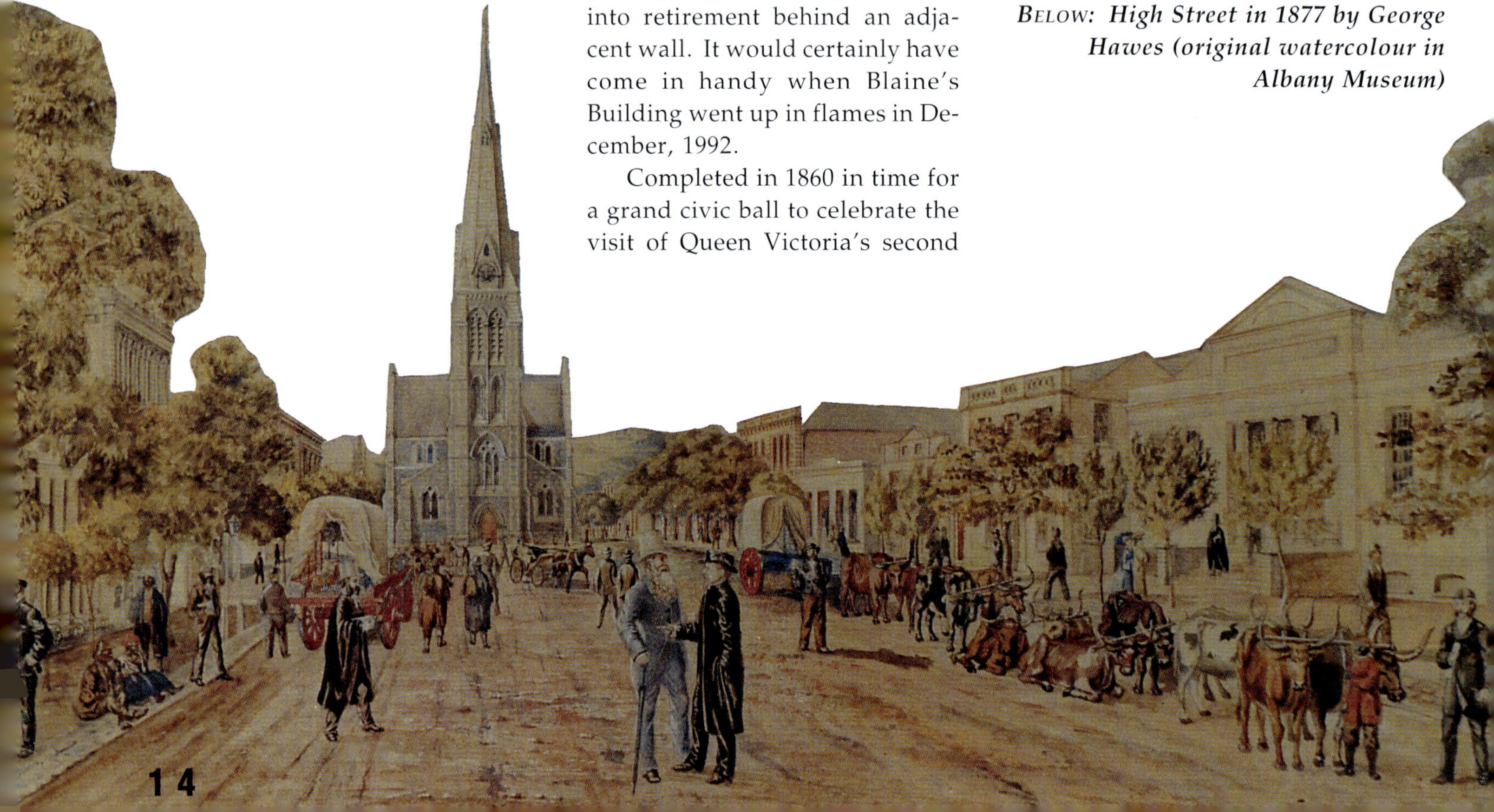

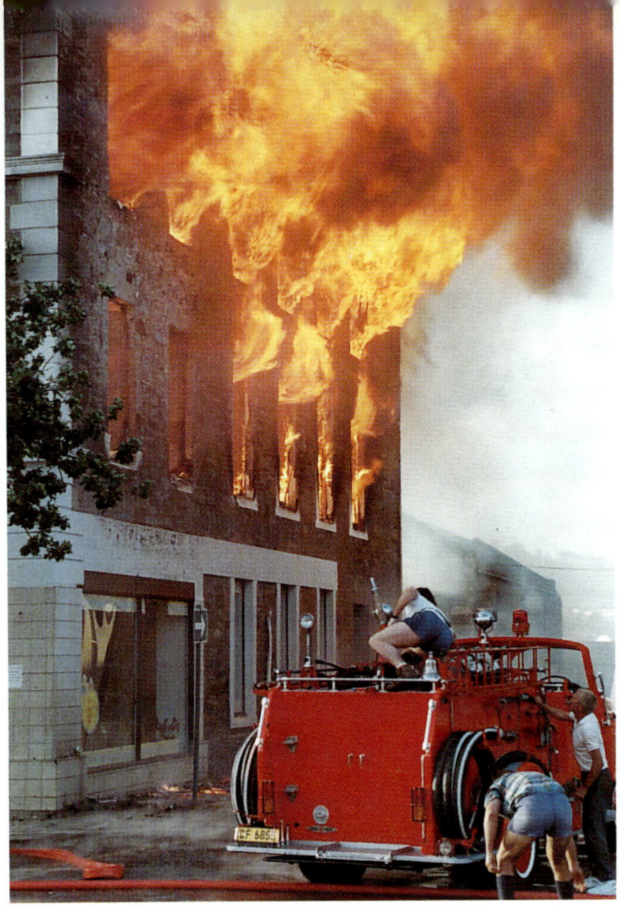

ABOVE: ***Blaine's Building burning, 1992***

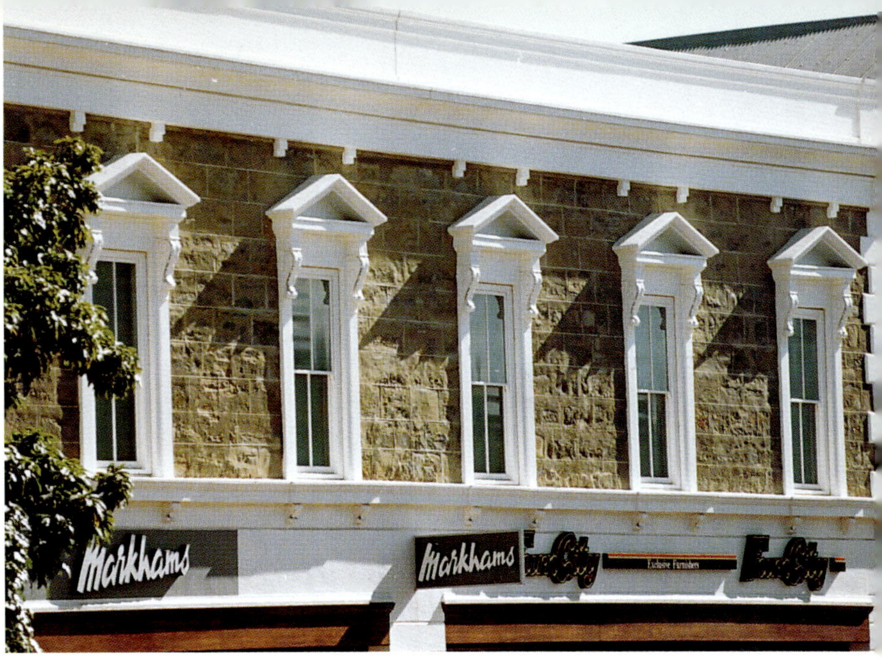

ABOVE: ***Blaine's Building up again, 1993***

son, Prince Alfred, it has been restored to look exactly as it did — minus its second storey because of current construction costs. This makes its contemporary, the three-tiered Hayton's diagonally across the road, the highest of the High.

There have, of course, been other changes since artist George Hawes took up his paint brush in 1877, carefully including a cast of characters of the time. Most noticeably the central islands, since ox-wagons are no longer about to make U-turns. They obviously prevent motorists from doing ditto. It is such a long stretch, and locals like to stop right where they shop, moving their vehicles as necessary. The resulting ins and outs often bring traffic to a sudden halt, especially as dreamy drivers often forget to indicate their intentions.

A few historic homes nestle neatly near the Rhodes end. The Courts command the middle ground. Businesses may come and businesses may go, but the trees keep blooming and the cycads look as if they have been there forever. They can live to be a hundred, and trace their ancestry back 50 million years. When they were planted in the High, an indignant reader wrote to *Grocott's Mail* complaining that the choice was typical of fossilized Grahamstown, and enquiring whether citizens should stand by for the return of the dinosaurs. Yes. The Albany Museum next to the Drostdy Gateway currently has Operation Dino well in hand. Stand by for the Stegosaurus!

BELOW: ***High Street in 1994; early morning, bins and all***

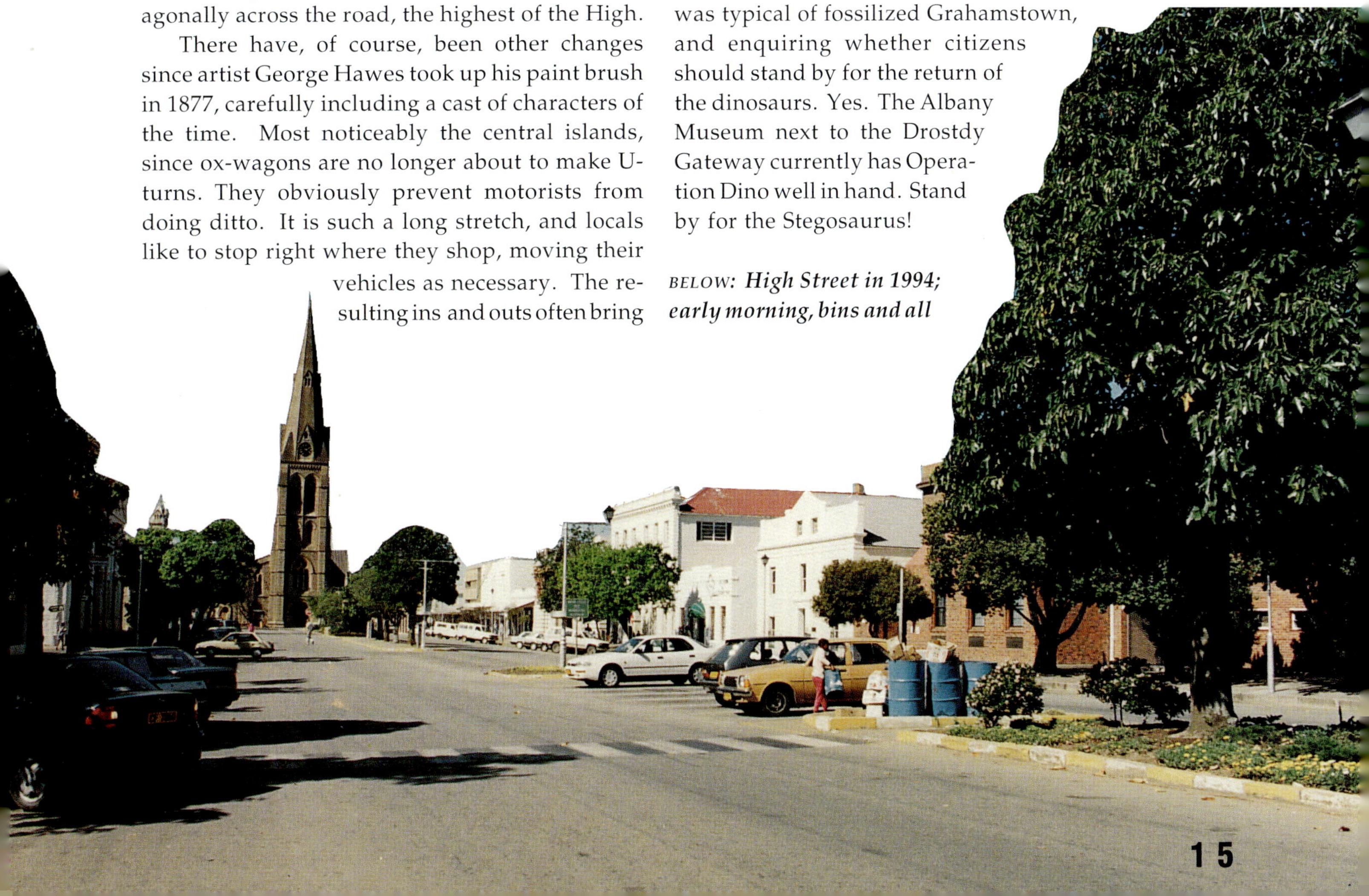

CHURCH SQUARE

WHEN is a Church Square not a square? When it is an eternal — traffic controllers would say infernal — triangle. Found in Grahamstown of course, and the natural centre of the city from its earliest beginnings. Slap in the middle of High Street, dividing it into upper and lower sections, a superb setting for the Cathedral of St Michael and St George. Created both by accident and design.

When Col John Graham selected the site for his military outpost early in 1812, the ruined homestead of Dutch pioneer farmer Lucas Meyer was restored as the officers' mess.

The building faced approximately due north by the compass, so it was natural for the officers to pitch their tents on a line parallel to their mess and facing it — the city hall side of today's triangle. Their permanent housing was built in the same position.

In 1814 surveyor J Knobel was sent to Graham's Town to plan the emerging settlement in an orderly fashion. Taking his line from the first gaol, he directed a broad street from west to east along the ridge — the High Street.

The officers' mess would have to go, but he tactfully recommended that their homes remain, declaring that "although a triangular space would be left open, that space having the most elevated ground in its centre, might allow a very convenient situation for a church or any other public building". Which is exactly what materialized.

In due course the military moved, commercial undertakings came in, and over the years the humble parish church gradually grew into the

BELOW: *Bank balance by night and the square in 1903*

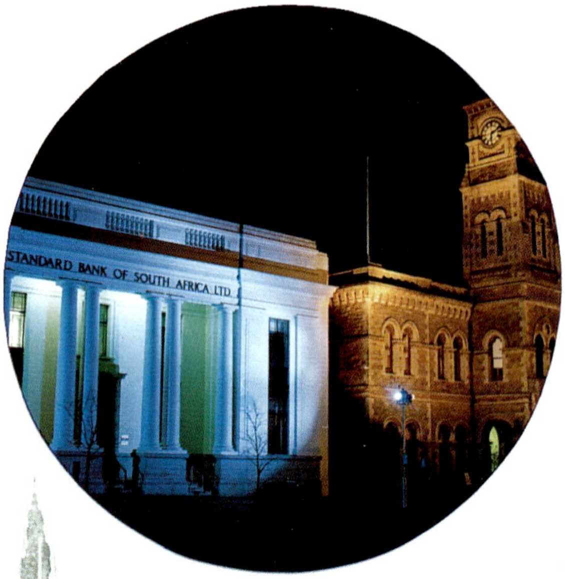

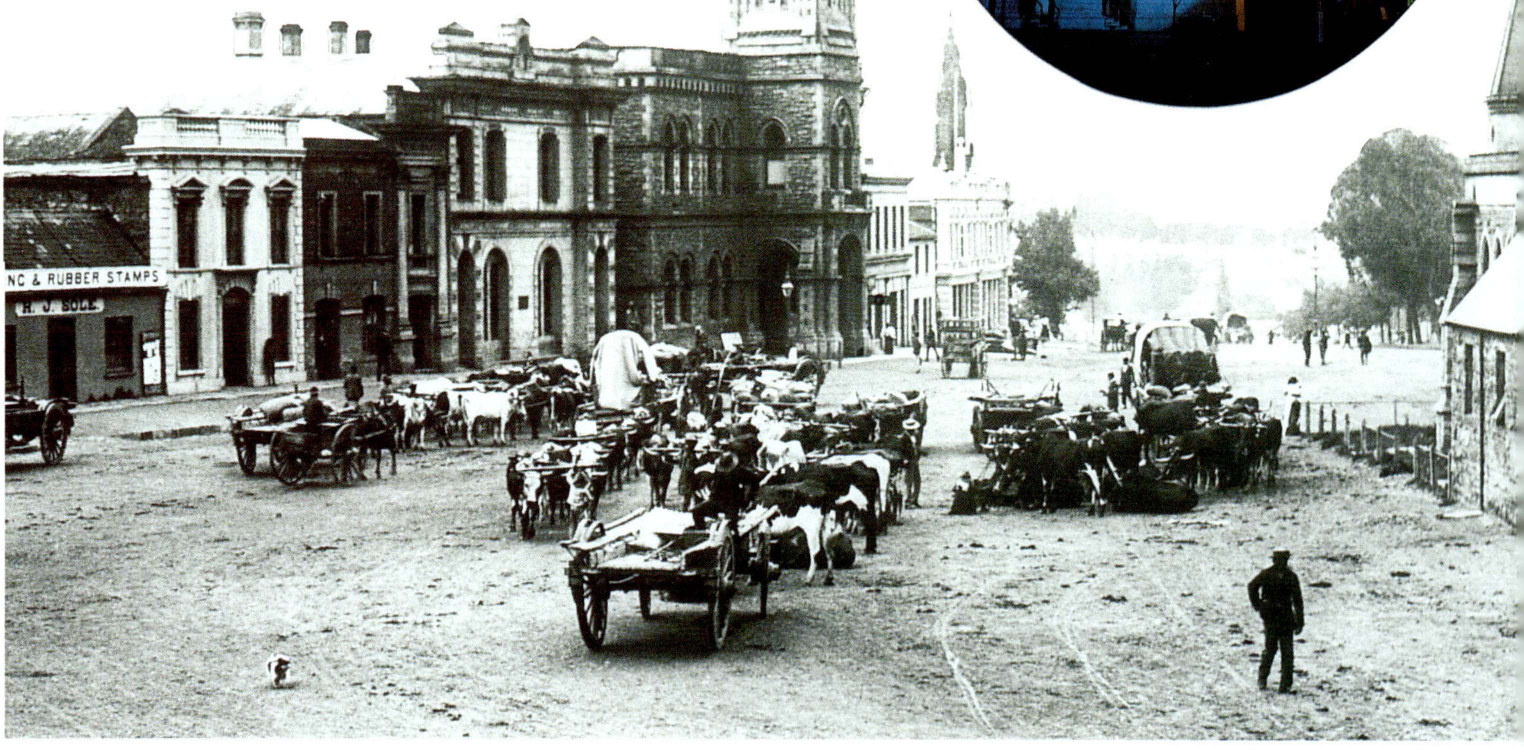

STILL THE ETERNAL TRIANGLE

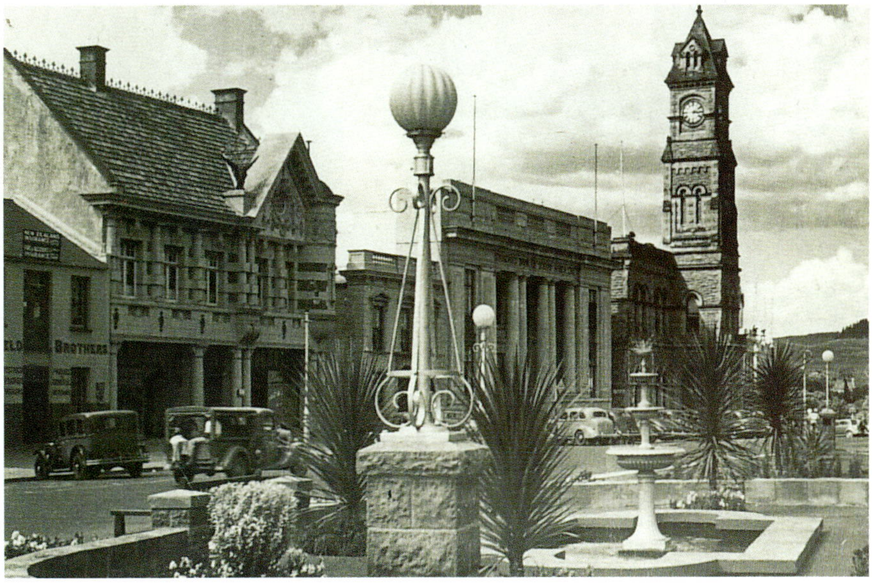

CLOCKWISE: *The latest lamps are based on this old design; bricks have replaced the grass, but the same buildings survey the work in progress...*

finest Gothic Revival cathedral in South Africa, the focal point of the country's best existing collective example of Victorian and early Edwardian architecture.

By the 1860s the "triangular square" was the central business district, complete with traffic problems — still unresolved in 1903, as the old photograph to the left indicates.

The most striking 20th century building on the northern side is the impressively pillared Standard Bank. Designed by the Port Elizabeth firm of Owen Eaton and Tait, it was awarded the Cape Province Institute of Architects' bronze medal in 1933. The natural stone finish has since been painted, altering its original subtle balance with the neighbouring City Hall. The Grahamstown branch of the Standard Bank dates back to 1864.

Over the years the Cathedral surround was increased. A pleasant park developed, incorporating a rosebed, fountain (usually dry), palms, and privet hedge borders. Rather old-fashioned and slightly scruffy, but with an evergreen charm.

Changing times have brought different requirements. The whole area was paved in 1994. New trees have taken root and a batallion of bollards guards the perimeter.

No opportunity to stop and smell the roses now, but the fragrant frangipani next to the Cathedral's north door is still there, as is the jacaranda which spreads a regal blue carpet near the main entrance to welcome the Christmas season.

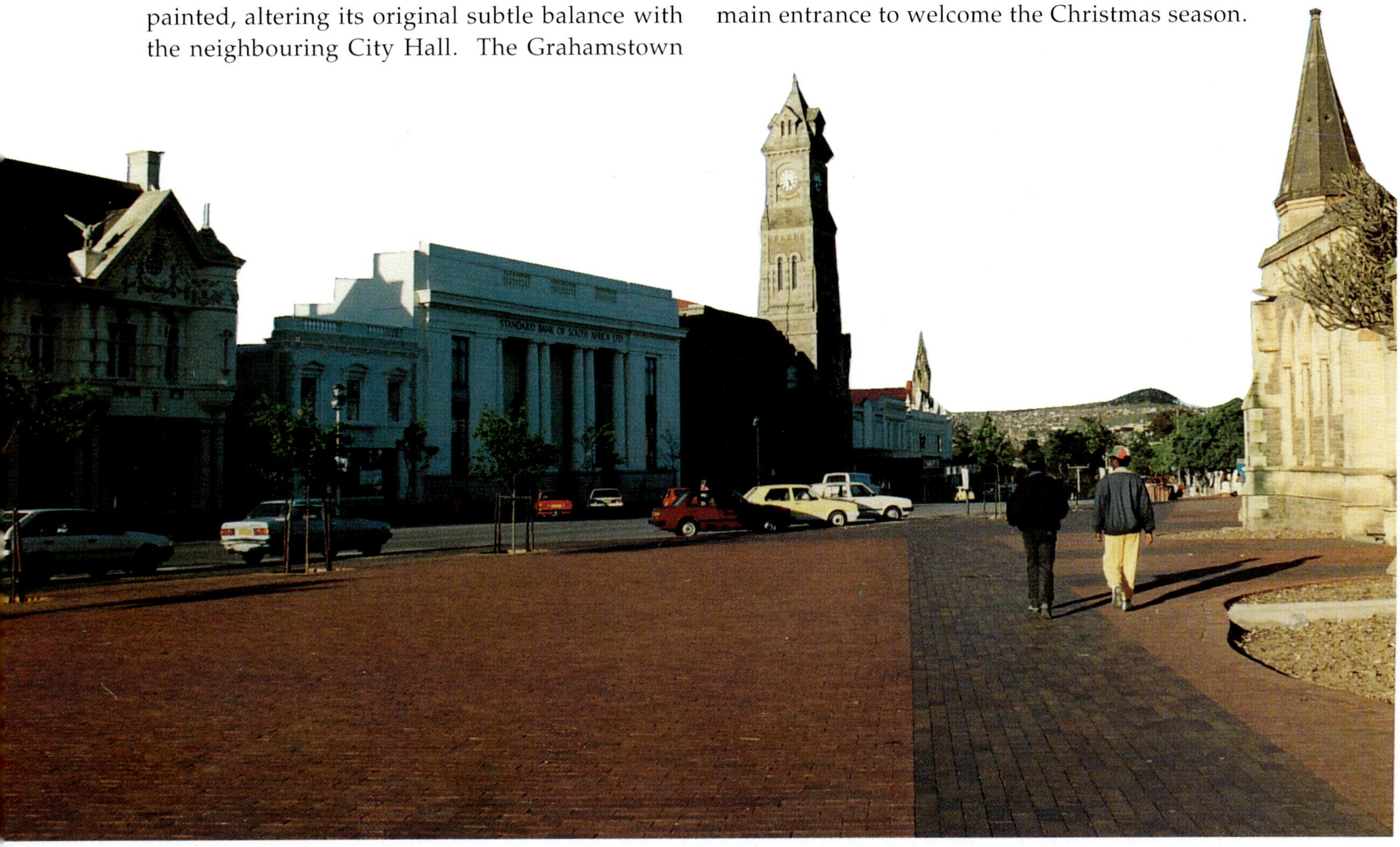

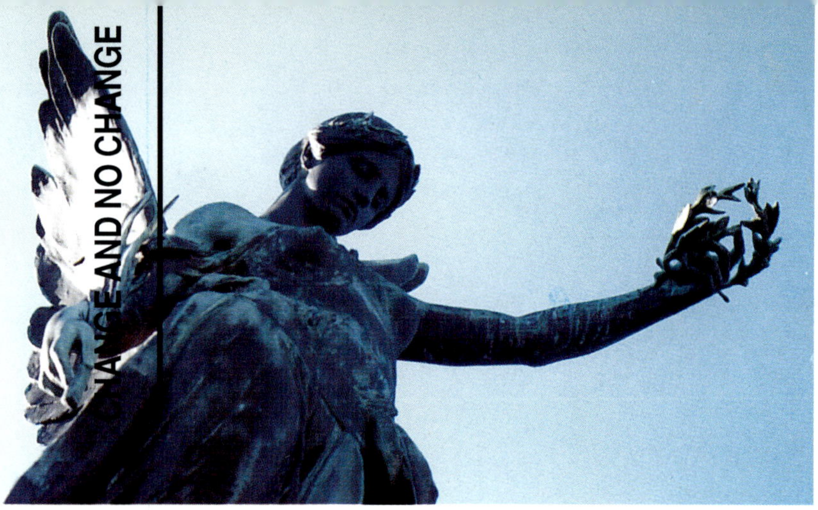

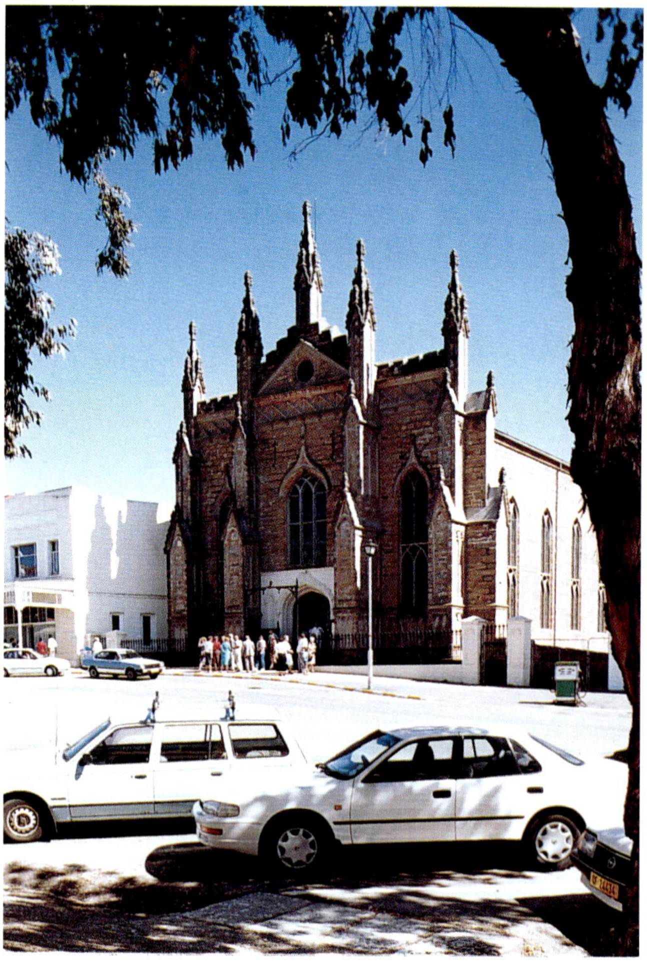

ABOVE: *Sheltering wings over Grahamstown; and Commem continues faithfully*

ALL CHANGE AT THE OLD WELL

GRAHAMSTOWN has its own guardian angel keeping a watchful eye on proceedings from a marble plinth on a little traffic island where Bathurst Street, the broadest street in the city, enters the narrow end of Church Square.

Decades before this heavenly body alighted there in 1906, the pivotal point was the site of a much-frequented public well — a traffic hazard in its own right because of milling crowds, one of the reasons for its eventual removal. Years later in the 1860s, frontier artist Frederick Timpson I'Ons nostalgically recreated the typical collection of "South African all-sorts" who frequented it in 1835, presided over by "jolly old Edwards seated on his water barrels like a temperance Bacchus" plus "the inevitable dogs a-fighting".

Allowing for artistic licence, the double-storey building in the background is where the Methodist Commemoration Church, the Mother Church of Methodism in SA, now stands. Built in a striking Gothic Revival style which once earned it the description of the Methodist Cathedral, it is affectionately known simply as "Commem".

The foundation stone was laid on April 10, 1845, the 25th anniversary of the arrival of the first party of British settlers — a noble memorial of gratitude for divine mercies. It also commemorates the preaching, translation scholarship, and missionary evangelism of its founding fathers. The dedication service was conducted by the Revd William Shaw on November 24, 1850.

Close on 1 200 people can be seated, and many special services have taken place there, among them the inauguration of Rhodes University. The splendid organ which dominates the interior is the third largest in SA, and was installed in 1875. It again made history on October 8, 1994, when the Grahamstown Massed Choirs raised their voices with thousands of others in more than 26 countries for the world's largest simultaneous singing event, a momentous performance of Handel's "Messiah" to raise funds for Hospice.

The original box pews rented by Victorian families are still in use, free of charge. It is, however, the simpler benches in the curved gallery which now attract the most attention. This has long been the preserve of lively lads, as witness a notice announcing the appointment in 1878 of a constable to control them. Here literally thousands of pupils from nearby Kingswood, the oldest Methodist school in the country, have carved their names, a tradition which continues even now that the school has its own chapel.

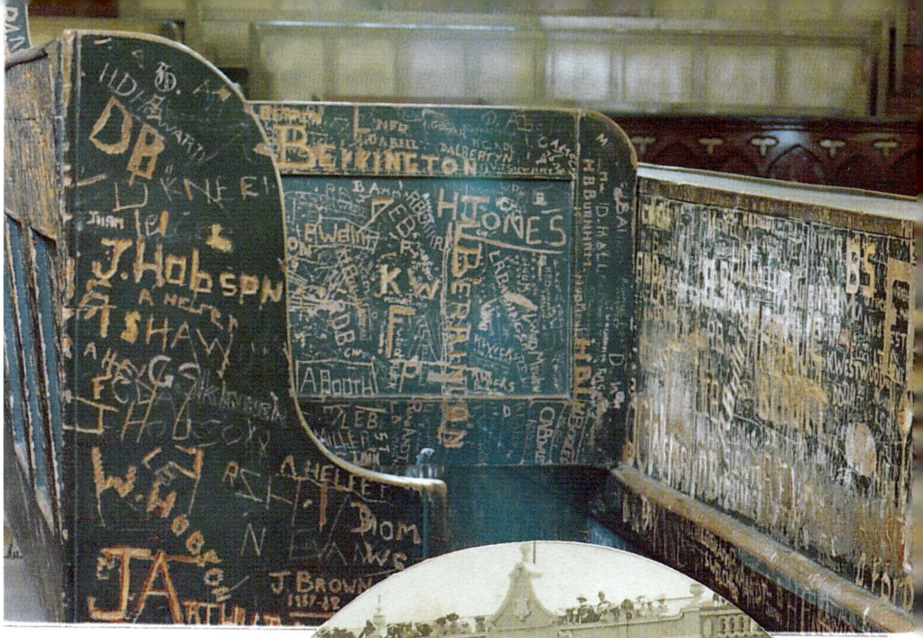

On the walls above are memorials to Old Kingswoodians killed in the two world wars. Many of the names listed are also among those of the young woodworkers below.

Which brings us back to the figure of Peace outside, who graces the monument "To the brave men of Albany, who died for the Empire, during the Anglo-Boer War, 1899-1902", perpetually proffering a laurel wreath to a dying soldier. The striking sculpture was made in London by Stanley Nicholson Babb. Rudyard Kipling specially wrote the patriotic inscription. The position was chosen as one which was "in the midst of our daily work and so would serve as a perpetual remembrance of the dead and be an inspiration for peace".

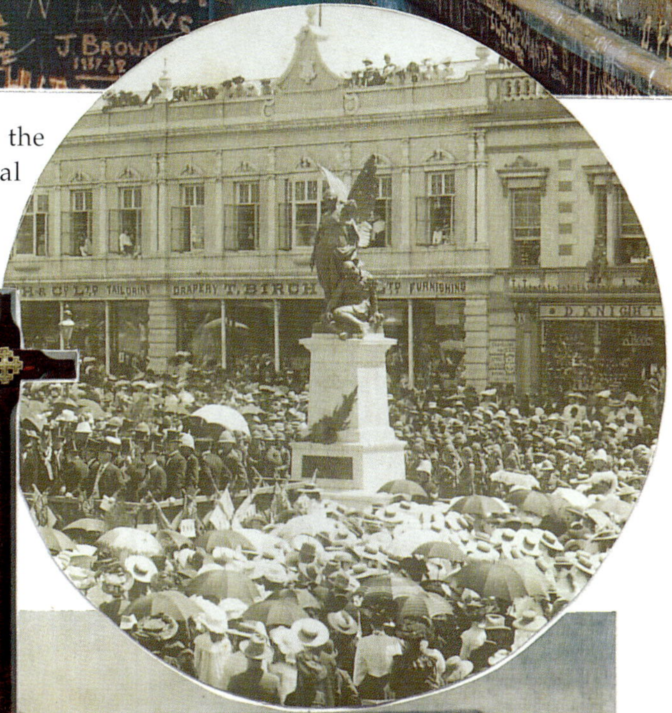

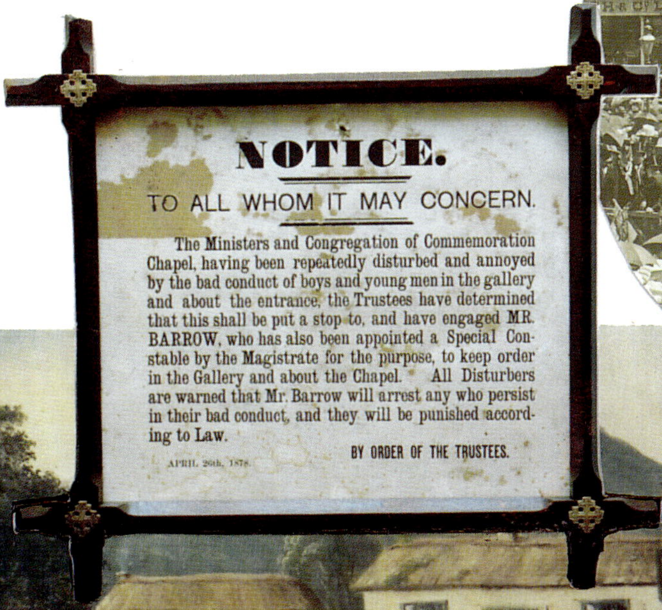

NOTICE.

TO ALL WHOM IT MAY CONCERN.

The Ministers and Congregation of Commemoration Chapel, having been repeatedly disturbed and annoyed by the bad conduct of boys and young men in the gallery and about the entrance, the Trustees have determined that this shall be put a stop to, and have engaged MR. BARROW, who has also been appointed a Special Constable by the Magistrate for the purpose, to keep order in the Gallery and about the Chapel. All Disturbers are warned that Mr. Barrow will arrest any who persist in their bad conduct, and they will be punished according to Law.

APRIL 26th, 1878. BY ORDER OF THE TRUSTEES.

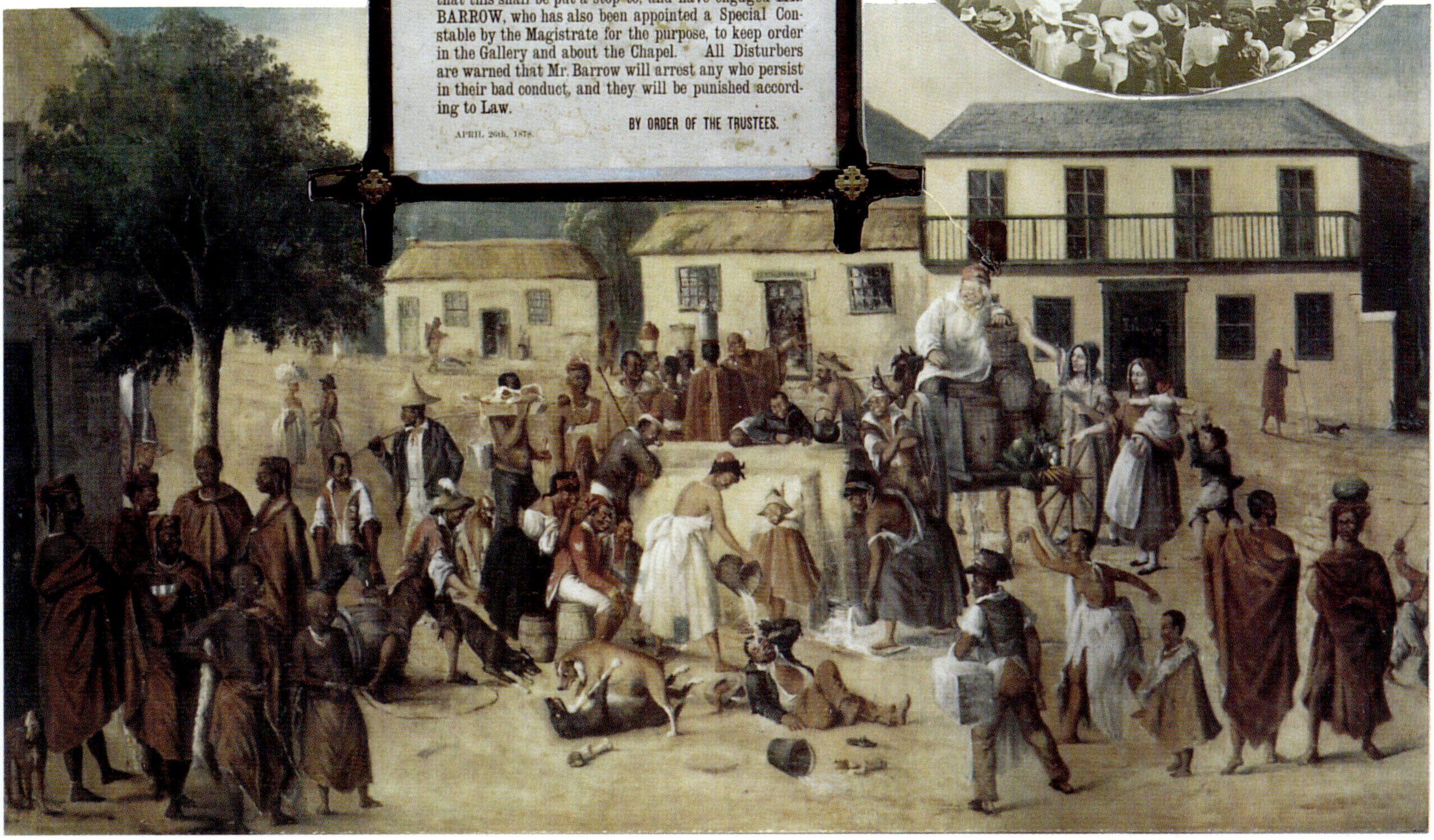

CLOCKWISE: *Pew carvers, undeterred by the moth-eaten notice; and the figure of Peace unveiled where the old well stood, as depicted by Frederick Timpson I'Ons*

BUSINESS AS USUAL
ON THE MARKET SQUARE

AS HARRASSED working wives sprint into the Market Square shopping complex to collect cold cuts, warm rolls and six bananas (everyone goes home to lunch — 12h55 is peak traffic time) the scene seems very different from "Mr Hume's wagons at the Grahamstown Market" painted by Thomas Baines on the selfsame spot in 1850.

Get a load of that merchandise! Enough to make a latterday conservationist collapse. Pile upon pile of ivory to be purchased by the merchants whose fine old homes still line the western side of the square. (Now the only tusks in town are at the Albany Museum, one magnificently carved by sculptor Ivan Mitford-Barberton to create a Rider Haggard-type trophy of the Dark Continent).

Leopard and crocodile skins, karosses and pelts of every description. Buffalo and buck horns. Ostrich feathers and eggs. Curiosities and marvels — mysterious pieces of wood or clay alleged to possess charmed powers, aromatic gum, intricately worked copper bracelets, Bushman bows and poison arrows...

For many years, anyone who wished to trade with the peoples inland had to pass through Grahamstown Market to obtain a permit. This, then, was the market from which European goods first penetrated the interior of southern Africa. The ox-wagons set out loaded with blankets, textiles, knives, beads, iron cooking pots, and sometimes guns (illegal cargo, hidden above the axle poles). On long, long journeys over the endless veld, bartering as they went. Eastward across the Great Fish River, northward as far as what is now Rustenburg, north-west towards Bechuanaland.

In different guises, trade is still the name of the game on this historic square, and business is

BELOW: *Gradwell's Mill, corner of Market and George Streets 1877, by Francis Lewin Dashwood*

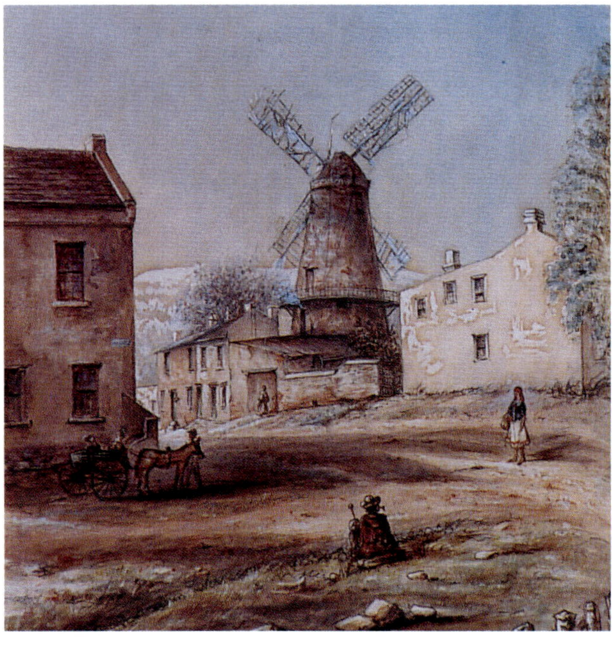

BELOW: *Today only Mill House remains, simple and unadorned*

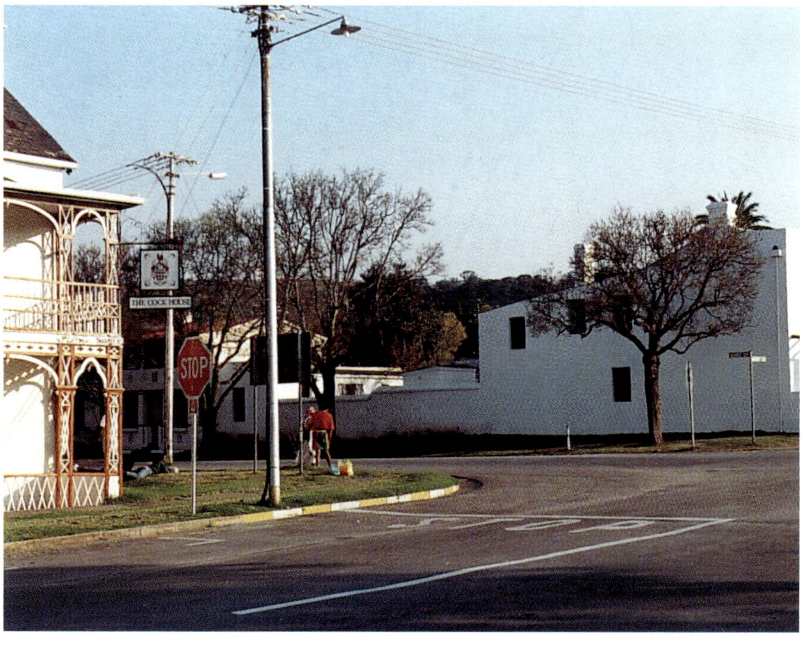

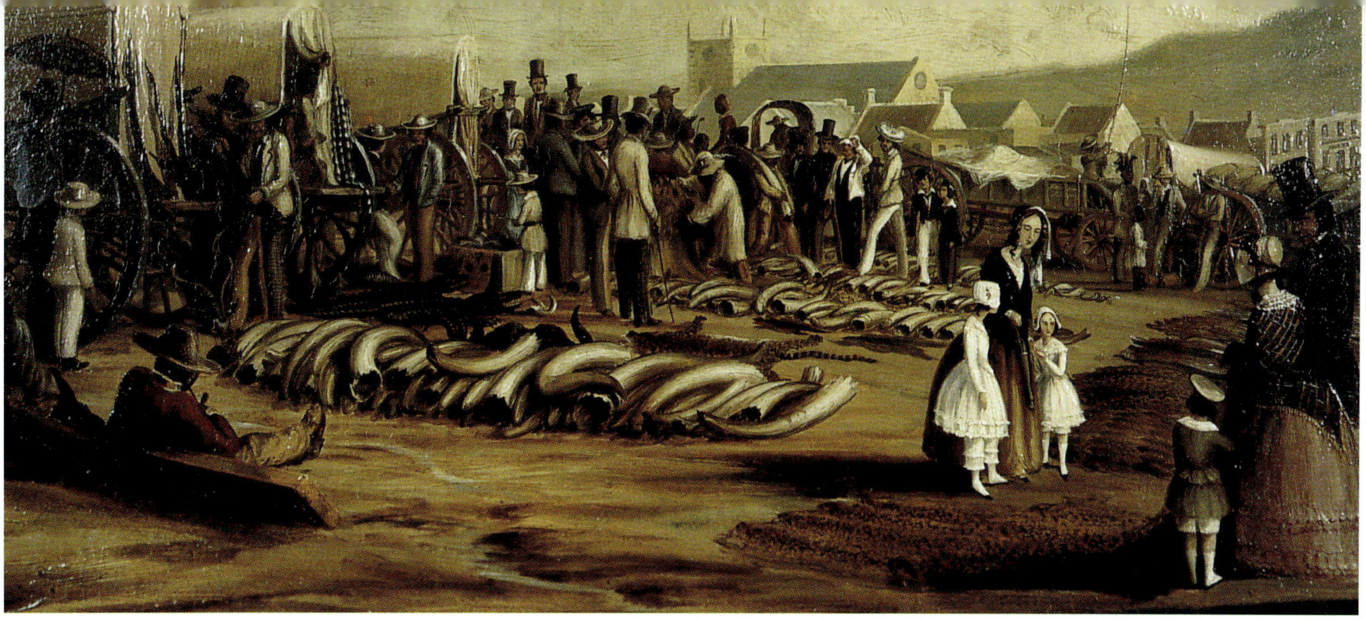

ABOVE: *Crinolines and crocodiles on the Market Square, circa 1850, a Baines painting in the Albany Museum*

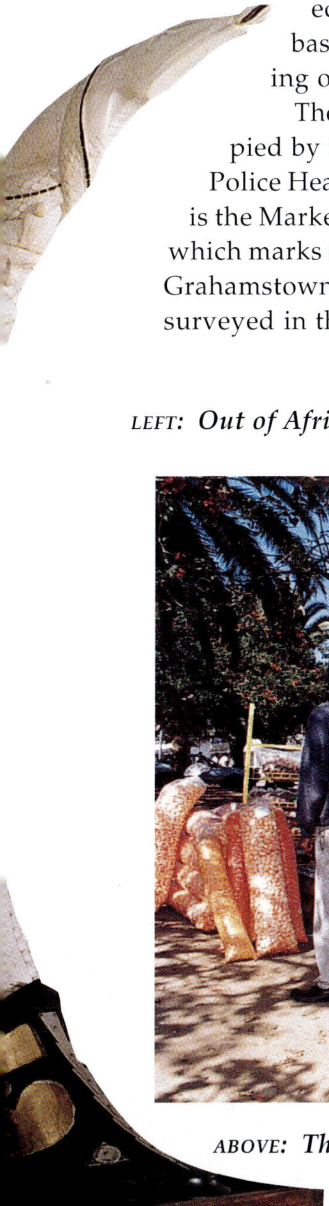

booming. Particularly in the dusty corner beneath the towering palms and flowering trees where the Mama Africas set out their wares. Pockets of sugar, samp, beans, rice, and mealie meal. See-through sacks of psychedelic orange puff snacks. Plastic basins and buckets, paraffin and cooking oil, cabbages and pineapples.

The other half of the square is occupied by the redbrick Grahamstown District Police Headquarters. Preserved *in situ* inside is the Market Stone — the original survey stone which marks one end of the base line from which Grahamstown and the surrounding district was surveyed in the early 1860s.

In Market Street overlooking the mall, Mill House stands staunchly, easily identified in Francis Lewin Dashwood's watercolour of 1877. Erected in the 1840s, it contained corn-cleaning, meal-sifting, and flour-dressing machines, powered by the huge wind-driven sails.

Opposite, an up-market restaurant runs in the house named after its third owner, 1820 Settler William Cock, developer of the harbour at Port Alfred. A more recent resident, distinguished author André Brink, restored it in the 1970s when the circus regularly raised its Big Top on the then largely undeveloped square. Lions — literary and lively — could be heard in the night.

LEFT: *Out of Africa — elephant's tusk transformed*

BELOW: *Market Square Mall, opened August, 1990*

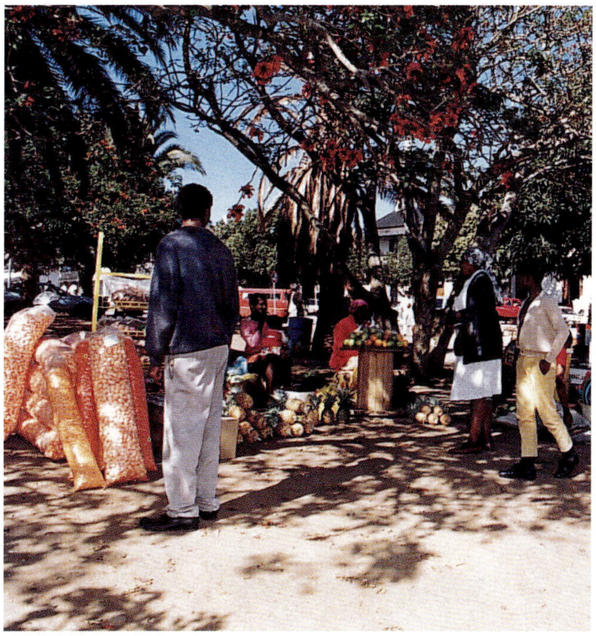

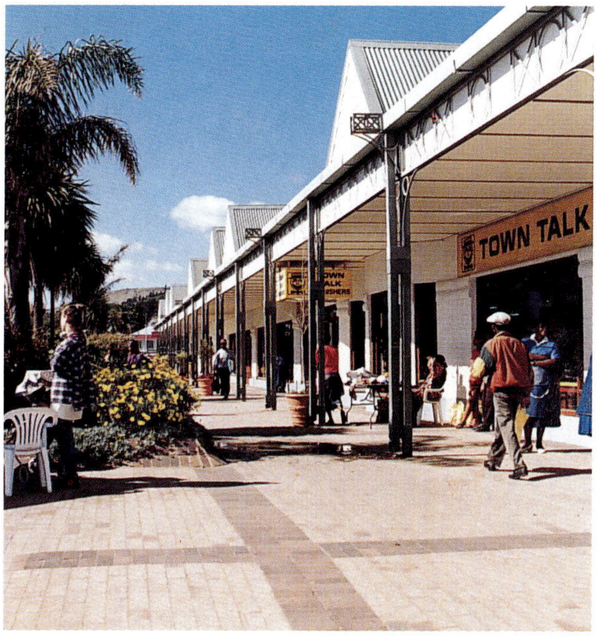

ABOVE: *The informal trading sector in full bloom*

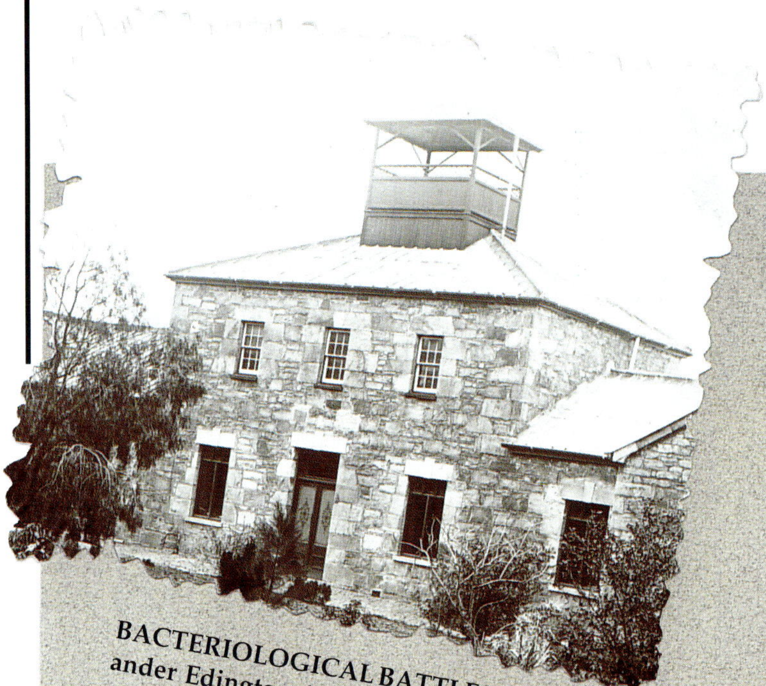

OUTCROP OF GEOLOGISTS The South African Geological Association (SAGA, 1888 - 1890) was the earliest scientific society in South Africa to devote its efforts entirely to geology and the related sciences. Dr WG Atherstone was the president during its brief existence in Grahamstown, and when the Geological Society of South Africa (GSSA) was founded in Johannesburg in 1895, he was elected first vice-president.

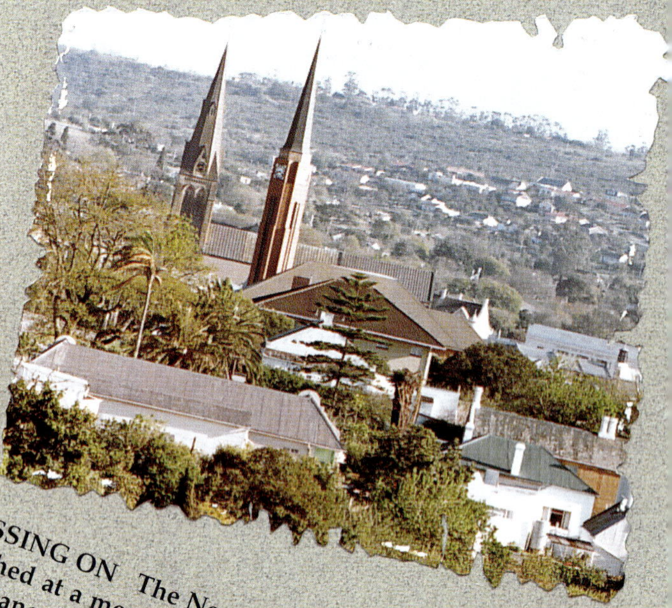

BACTERIOLOGICAL BATTLES In 1891, Dr Alexander Edington from Edinburgh established *"the most modern laboratory in the southern hemisphere"* — the first bacteriological laboratory of the Cape Colonial Government — in the former Royal Engineers Office and Stores (now the Department of Ichthyology and Fisheries Science at Rhodes University). Vaccines were produced to combat horse sickness, the catastrophic rinderpest cattle disease and the smallpox epidemic in Johannesburg in 1893/94.

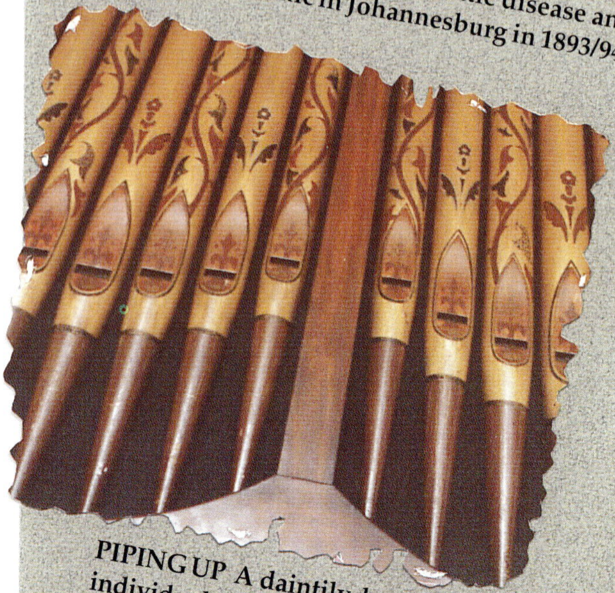

PRESSING ON The Newspaper Press Union of South Africa wa launched at a meeting in the City Hall on November 17, 1882. In Attendance were 26 newspaper editors from all over the country — among them TH Grocott, proprietor of the *Grocott's Penny Mail*, still published in Grahamstown and the oldest family-owned and managed paper in South Africa.

PIPING UP A daintily decorated pipe organ, the first and only individual musical instrument in South Africa to be proclaimed a National Monument, is still in regular use in the Wesley Methodist Church at the corner of Market and York Streets. Originally ordered during the mid-1830s by Lt Col Henry Somerset, commandant of the Eastern Frontier, for his Grahamstown home, *Oatlands House*, it was made by the celebrated William Hill of London.

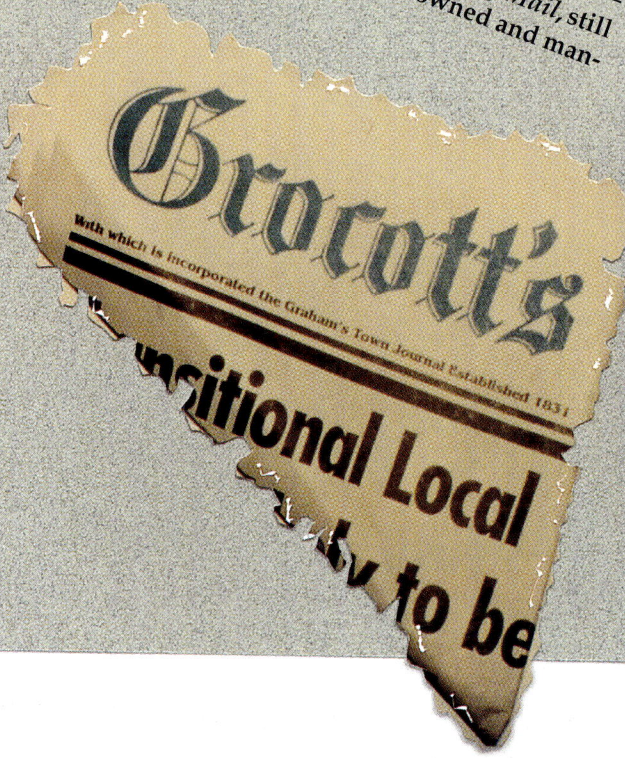

IS GRAHAMSTOWN TOO SMALL FOR ITS BOOT?

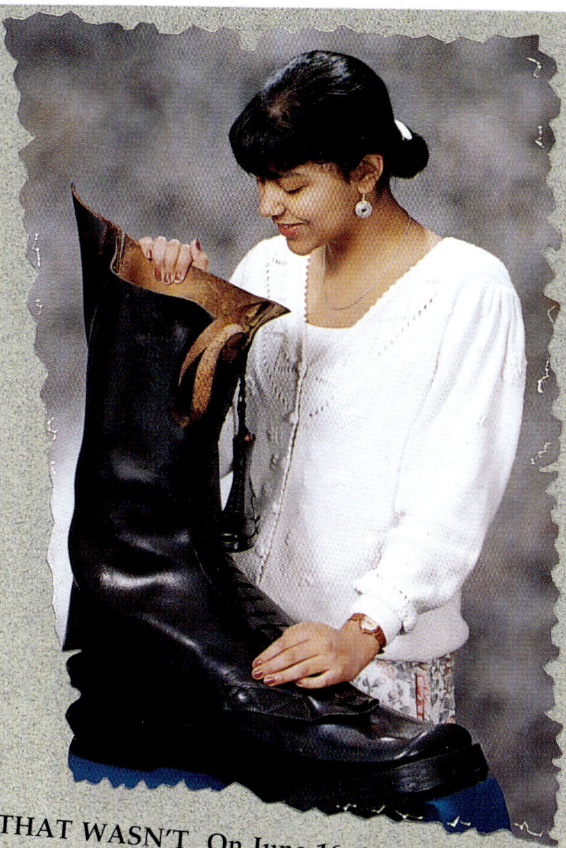

THE FIRST THAT WASN'T On June 16, 1847, Dr William Guybon Atherstone amputated Frederick Carlisle's gangrenous leg in what for close on 100 years was generally considered to be the first operation in South Africa using ether as an anaesthetic. However, in 1976 it was conclusively proved that he had been narrowly beaten to the scalpel by two Capetonians using more conventional apparatus than the home-made hubble-bubble shown in his original sketch. Though the Grahamstown first claim no longer has a leg to stand on, it refuses to lie down and is therefore included as advancing the Eastern frontiers of medical science...

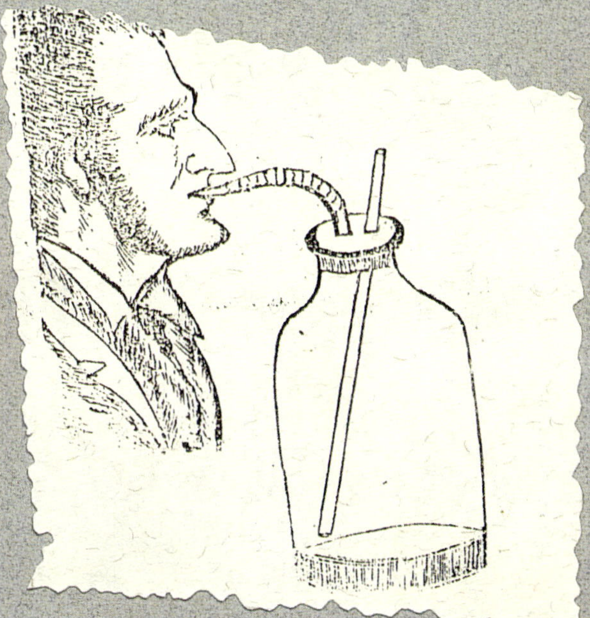

NOT A BIT OF IT. When it comes to first-footing, Grahamstown is in the big league. Just for starters, here is a round-up of some historical firsts both major and minor. More feature on the following eight pages. Others crop up throughout this essentially modest publication, like South Africa's First Industrial and Arts Exhibition held here in 1898, where the boot made its debut.

GT LAW The first law society in SA — the Eastern Districts Law Society—was established in Grahamstown on January 15, 1883. This pioneer body combined with Western Cape attorneys to form the Cape Law Society the next year.

FRONT LINES Harriet Ward, believed to have been the first professional woman journalist in SA and possibly also the world's first woman war correspondent, did much of her writing in Grahamstown when her officer husband was stationed here in the 1840s. She sent action-packed despatches to *The Cape Frontier Times* as well as *The London Times*, the latter rewarding her with two vases and a piano as it was not considered ladylike to accept a salary.

FIRST AID The St John Ambulance Association of SA was founded in Grahamstown on September 5, 1885, as part of the parent order in England's scheme to spread "general information as to the preliminary treatment of the Sick and Injured among all classes of society".

BELOW-RIGHT: *St John centenary souvenir plate*

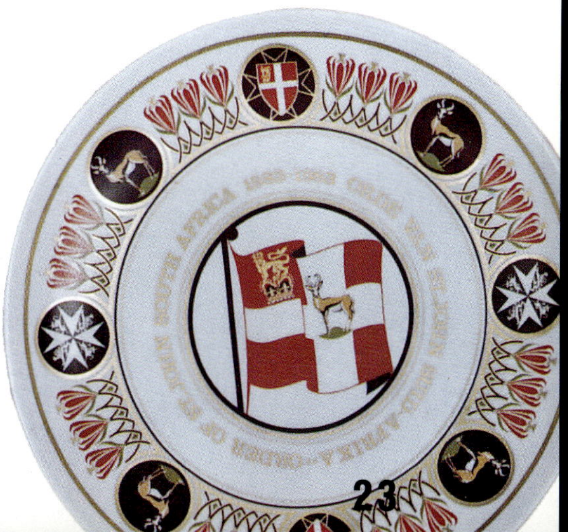

THE BOTANICAL GARDENS THROUGH VICTORIAN EYES

DEAR OLD "Bots"... Still rooted to its original spot, with the same affectionate nickname, but these days more visited down Memory Lane than up the garden path.

The first botanical garden to be established by the English in the Cape Colony, it started in 1853 and somehow managed to keep growing through disturbances, droughts, and depressions... Now it is getting back to grassroots level, as the winds of change whistle through the lofty trees, towering survivors of a past era, majestic in their maturity.

A very Victorian concept in the far-flung Empire, a botanical garden is an encyclopaedia of plants, a green atlas of foreign specimens, not just a pretty place. "Bots" made plant exchanges with India, Mauritius, New Zealand, Australia, and the Royal Botanic Gardens at Kew in England.

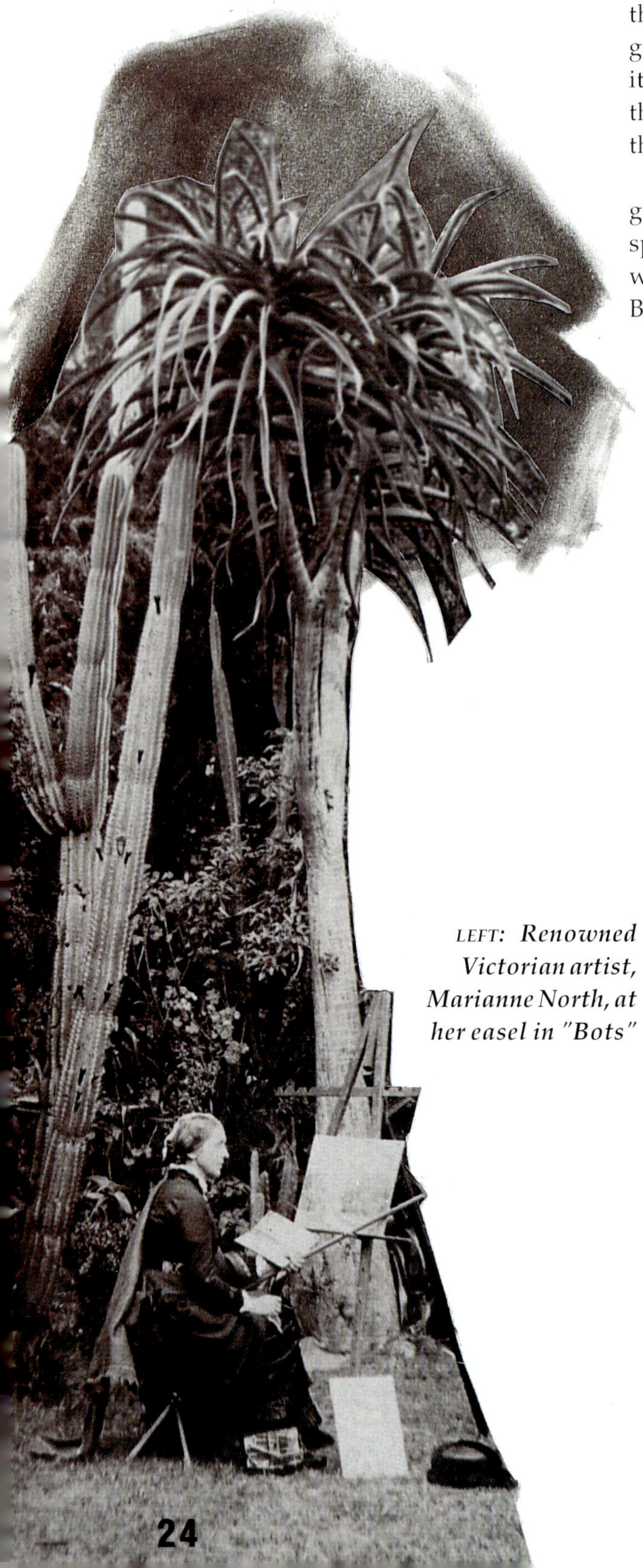

LEFT: *Renowned Victorian artist, Marianne North, at her easel in "Bots"*

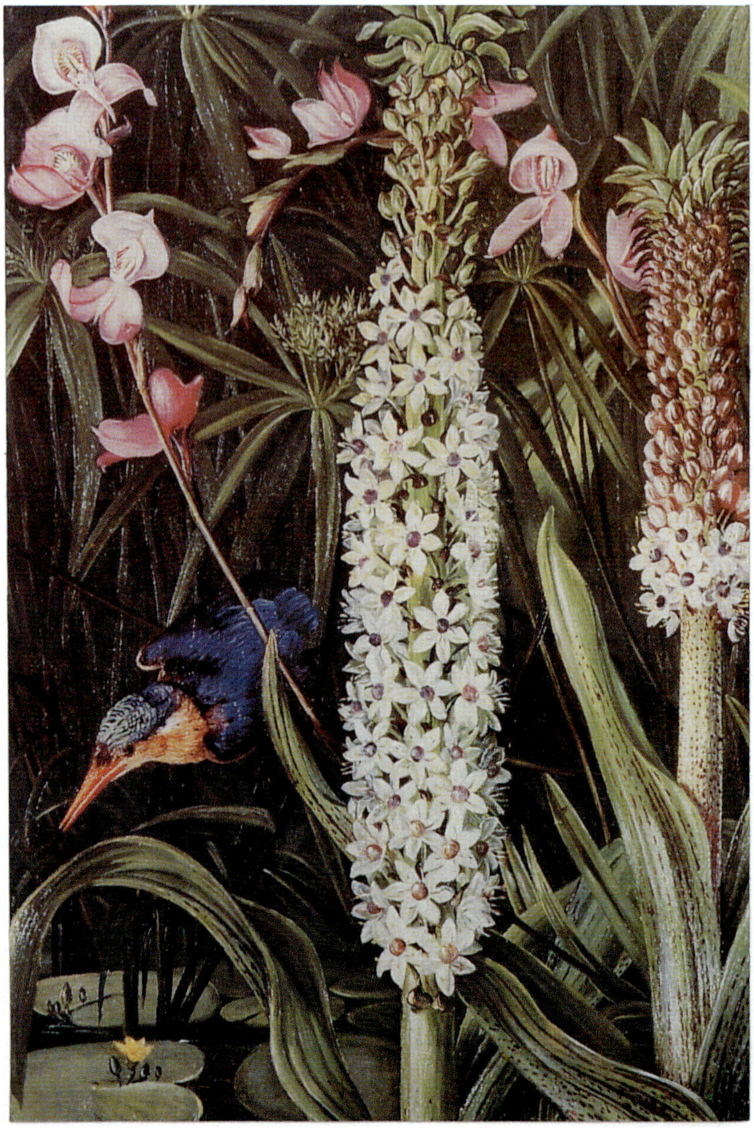

ABOVE: *One of her Grahamstown paintings, complete with kingfisher*

"To recline upon this delightful lawn on a bright summer's day, revelling in the glorious sunshine, listening to the warbling of the feathered songsters, and inhaling the delicious perfume from the flowers, is a blissful condition of things to which dwellers in the arid regions of the Colony are total strangers."

— Souvenir of Grahamstown, 1887

The newest roses were imported from Europe, and by the latter years of the 19th century everything in the garden was lovely. Regimental bands bashed; an ornamental fountain splashed. The Fordyce Conservatory — erected in memory of a courageous Colonel and since replaced by a languishing lily pond — was a fairyland of fragile winged cyclamens, calceolarias, primulas, cinerarias, and delicate maidenhair ferns trembling on the brink.

Developments continued sporadically through the decades. In 1965 it was incorporated in the 60 hectare wild flower reserve surrounding the 1820 Monument.

In 1984 the original tract of land, containing an enchanted Hansel and Gretel cottage at its heart, was declared a National Monument. The quaint cottage is now a flourishing restaurant named after the magnificent Monkey Puzzle trees nearby. A craft shop thrives in the Old Provost, which was built in 1838 as a military prison.

Pockets of early planting linger. The same prehistoric-looking dragon's blood trees still flank the original ornate iron entrance gates.

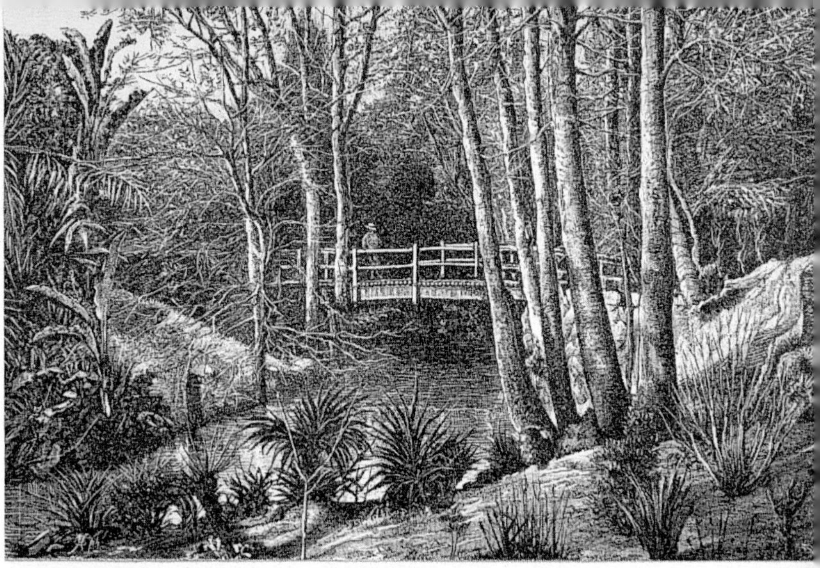

ABOVE: ***Bridge over murky waters in a tropical corner***

Marianne North would remember them well. A middle-aged spinster of comfortable means, she set off from England in 1871 on her first expedition to make a pictorial record of the tropical and exotic plants of the world. She toured South Africa in 1882-83, noting in her diary: "*The hills became very bare as we descended to Grahamstown, which is built in a perfect hole; but it was pretty inside, with many nice people with comfortable houses with lovely gardens. Its Botanical Garden was particularly well kept, full of interesting plants, the wild hillside and rocks coming down into it at the back.*" More than 800 of her paintings are housed in the Marianne North Gallery at Kew.

With "Bots" increasingly for the birds, Rhodes students recently undertook a sunbird survey. The iridescent green and coppery colours of their feathers are not produced by pigments, but are structural colours resulting from the reflection and diffraction of light. A rainbow is a familiar example of this phenomenon.

Flying rainbows in a Garden of Eden. All is not lost...

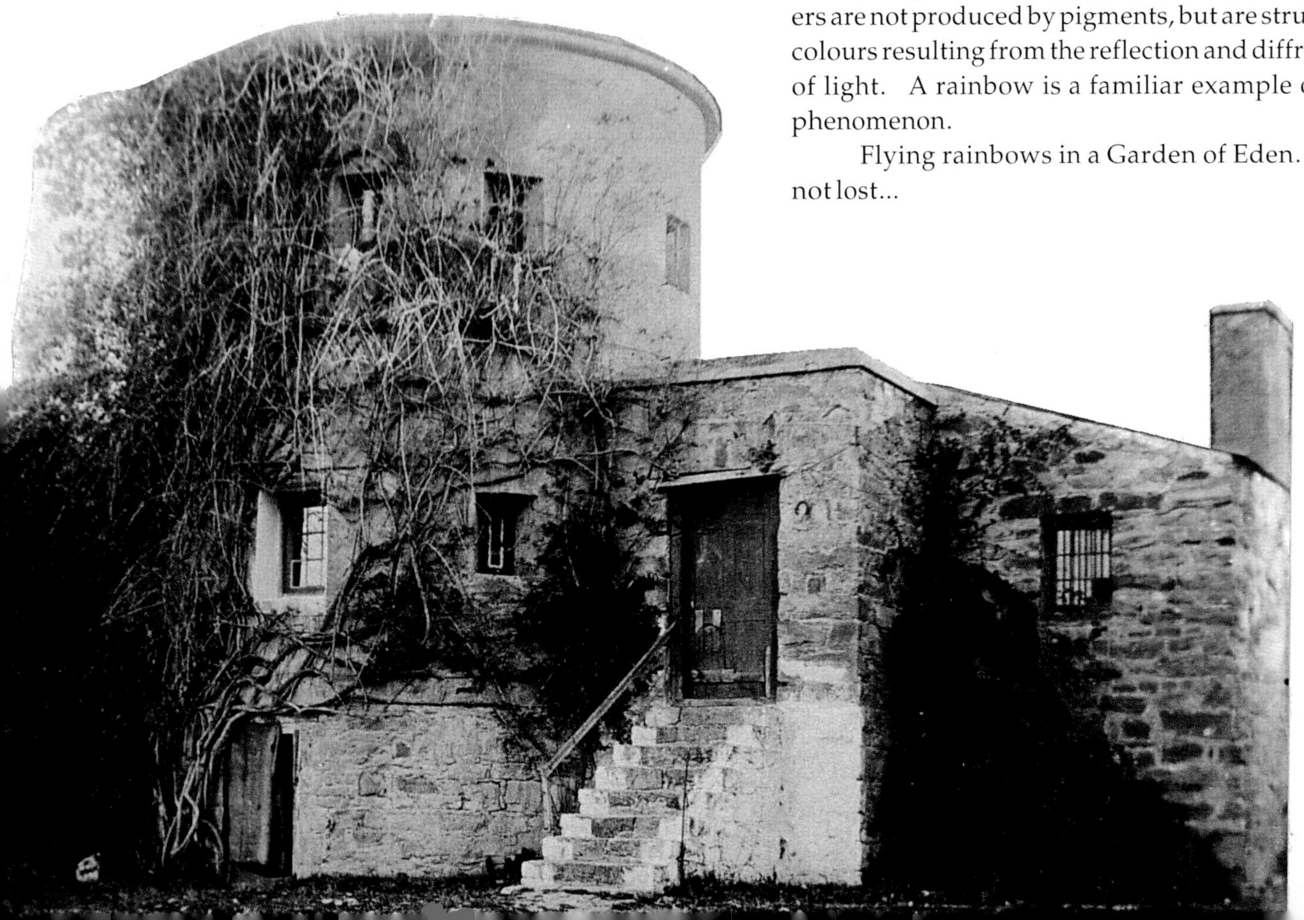

LEFT: ***Like something out of a Victorian novel, the Old Provost in the 19th century***

THE SEAT OF PARLIAMENT

WHERE *did* the Cape Parliament sit in Grahamstown the first and only time it met outside Cape Town? Symbolically speaking, the answer might well be the ornate chair specially carved by local coffin-maker and undertaker Joseph Hart, for the express use of the presiding Governor, Sir Philip Wodehouse.

But the back-benchers and forward-planners actually got down to deliberations in the Drostdy grounds. The 64 members of the House of Assembly met in the suitably renovated former military hospital opposite the Old Provost in Lucas Avenue, currently incorporated in the Department of Plant Sciences and Microbiology at Rhodes University. The smaller Legislative Council was cosily accommodated in three wooden Crimean War huts nearby.

Only the colourful opening ceremony on April 28, 1864, and the closing procedures 89 days later, took place at Shaw College (now Shaw Hall). In this respect the whole affair differed little from Cape Town (where the opening was performed in Government House and the two Houses met elsewhere, until the impressive Parliament building in the Gardens was completed in 1885).

Why did Parliament meet in Grahamstown? The Eastern and Western regions of the Cape Colony were vastly different areas in every way. The Easterns felt that their particular problems were often not understood. Over the years a strong movement developed which advocated a complete breakaway from the Western Province.

Eastern MPs had long urged that Parliament should at least occasionally convene in their part of the country. This eventually happened in 1864.

In typical City of Saints style, homely entertainment was offered throughout the three months — Xhosa choirs, dramatic performances, and numerous public lectures. These genteel diversions were perhaps more enjoyed by the populace than by the Parliamentarians.

When the singular session concluded at the end of July, both Houses met again in Shaw College and heard that the Governor considered the experiment a resounding success. The Westerns, however, had a different view. Those who still remained lost no time in getting back to their homes.

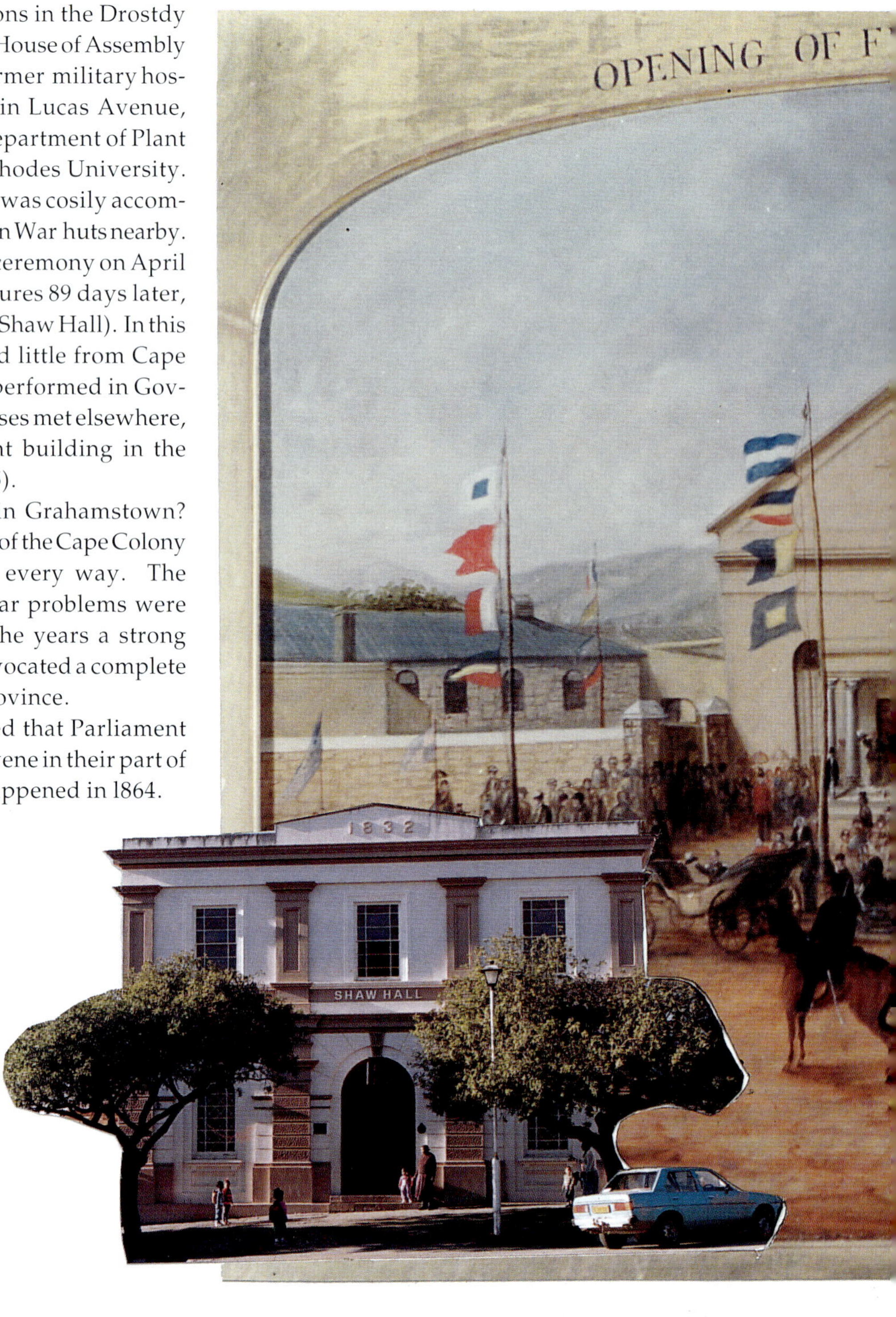

RIGHT: *Vivid portrayal of the great day by Charles Jay; Shaw Hall still survives, its facade much altered*

RIGHT: *The Wodehouse Chair and footstool, now in the Albany Museum, along with the painting below*

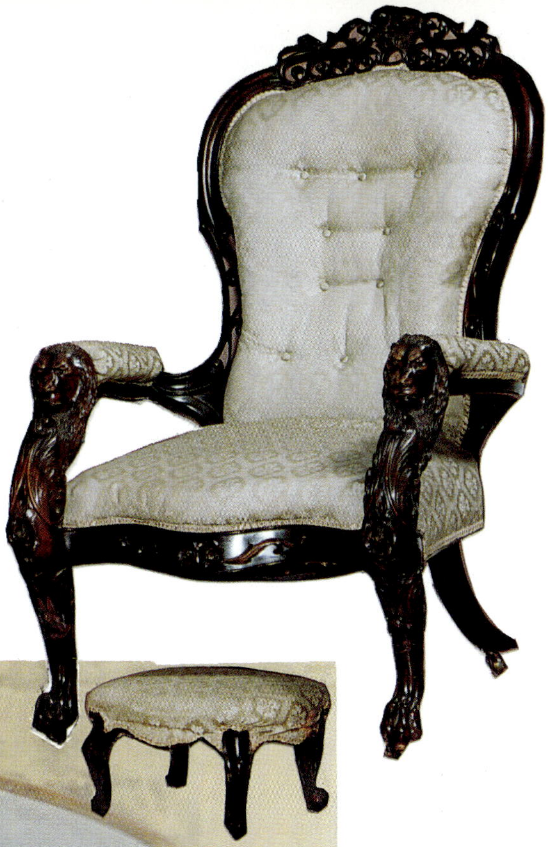

"Parliament opened yesterday by authority. His Excellency delivered his Speech. It was full of taxes. It announced measures of weighty importance. There was not a lively remark in its whole course. It was not relieved by humour or wit. There was no reason why it should have been."

— ***The Grahamstown Journal*, April 29, 1864**

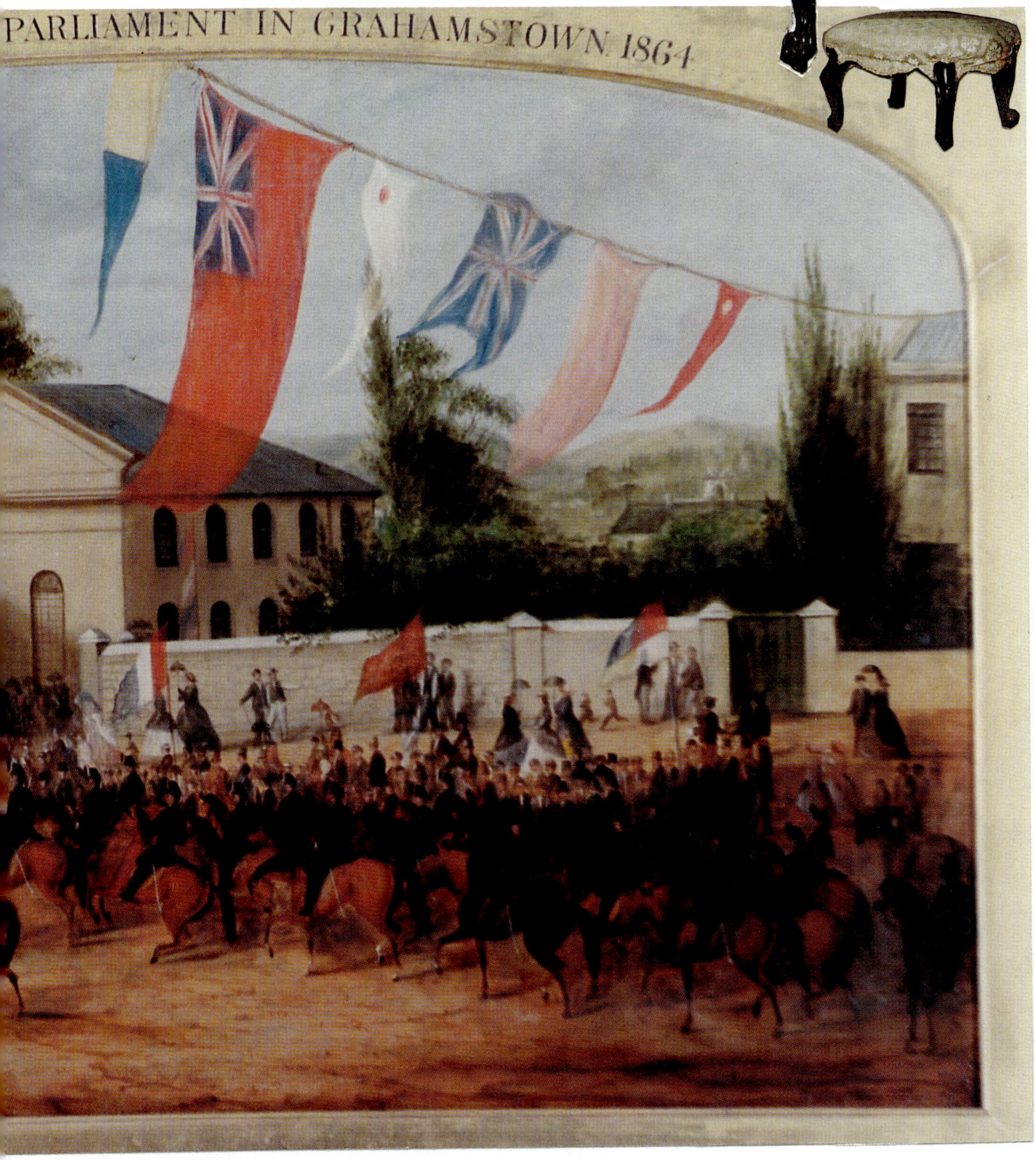

THE DIAMOND, THE DINOSAUR,

THE identification of the Eureka marked the beginning of South Africa's multi-million diamond industry. Picked up by children on a farm in the Hope Town district, 122kms from modern-day Kimberley in the Northern Cape, it was eventually despatched to Dr William Guybon Atherstone in Grahamstown. A multi-faceted medic and widely-known amateur geologist, he later vividly recalled its unheralded arrival:

"I was seated in my easy chair under the spreading branches of our giant pear tree in the garden of our home in Beaufort Street in the latter part of March 1867, when the postman handed me a letter which when I opened was from Mr Lorenzo Boyes, then the Clerk of the Peace at Colesberg . The envelope was just an ordinary looking one, with no seal or registration to arouse my curiosity. As I opened the envelope I sub-consciously realised that some-thing fell out onto the lawn but took no further notice of it until, after perusing the letter, I realised that what had dropped out of the envelope might be of considerable interest..."

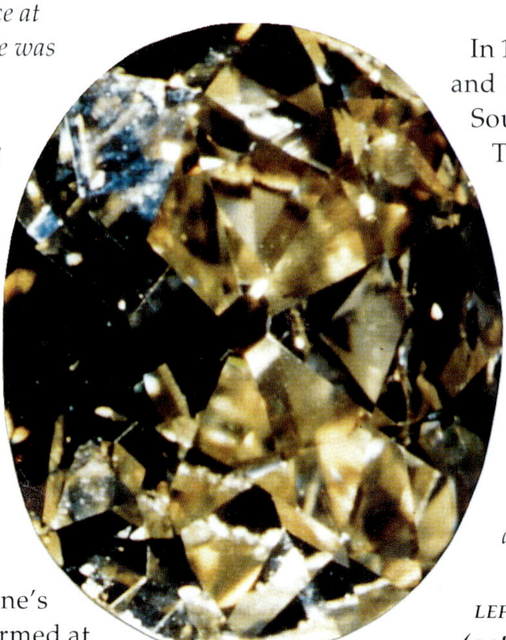

Dr Atherstone's diagnosis was confirmed at HC Galpin's premises in Bathurst Street, restored by De Beers as The Observatory Museum in 1982. A special display details the Diamond Story and the start of Kimberley's "Big Hole" diggings which changed South African history.

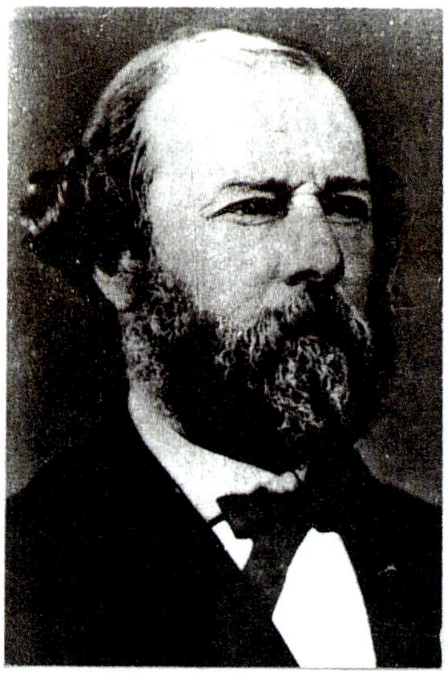

LEFT: The admirable Dr WG Atherstone, an expert on everything from astronomy to zoology

"The sun was high, our shirts were wet—our hands were sore — still no further advance beyond this, it was a reptile and was not a Dicynodon... My companions had already given up the hunt in despair, and were slowly sauntering homewards. I, too, was disappointedly lingering about when, giving a farewell blow to a dirty brown stone as I left, imagine my delight at perceiving it contained a portion of the lower jaw! The row of black serrated and fluted teeth proved it to belong to some creature allied to the Iguanodon. 'Hurrah!', I shouted, 'I've found him — Cape Iguanodon!' and back they all ran to examine it."

Dr WG Atherstone, *The Eastern Province Monthly Magazine*, 1857, Vol. 1.

In 1845, Dr William Guybon Atherstone and Dr Andrew Geddes Bain (father of South African geology, as well as of Thomas Bain, the Colossos of Roads) unearthed numerous fossil bones plus the jaw of "the Cape Iguanodon — a reptile bigger than an ox!" in the Bushman's River Valley near Grahamstown. Subsequent research has revealed that this was the first SA dinosaur discovery — a Stegosaurid from the lower Cretaceous period, *circa* 132 million years, later renamed *Paranthodon africanus* (Broom).

LEFT : The "Eureka" larger than life (actually 21,25 carats rough, 10,73 cut)

TOP-LEFT: J D R — his initials scratched on glass by James David Ricards to test the diamond's hardness

RIGHT: Stupendous Steg — how the fossil would have looked on its feet, 132 million years ago; the bones were sent from SA to London, but most went AWOL, never to be seen again

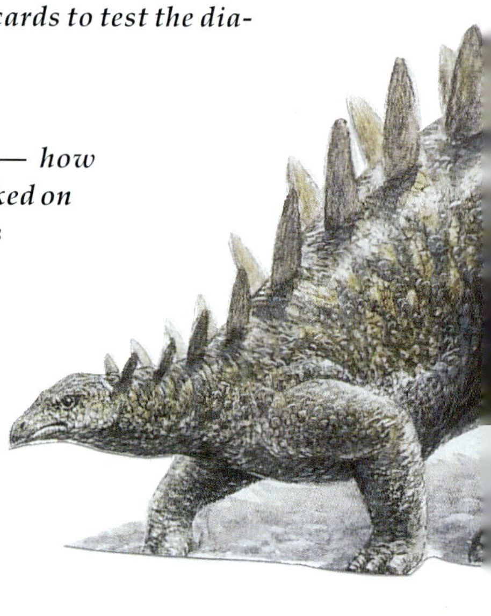

AND THE DEEPSEA MONSTER

"Miss Latimer's sketch and notes with that book left little doubt in my mind that if this fish of hers was not a Coelacanth, it was very like one. Just imagine: a Coelacanth, still living, and all the greatest authorities of the world would be prepared to swear that all Coelacanth fishes had died out about 50 million years ago (it is estimated at 70 million today). *Here was I in remote South Africa with the audacity to be convinced in my mind that this was a Coelacanthid fish. Even though I had done only spare-time work on fishes for less than ten years, I knew a good deal about them by then, and the careful and detailed papers I had published were known to scientists who worked on fishes all over the world; but I was still only on the way up. From almost every aspect it seemed impossible, the answer must be 'No'; and yet every time I took out that sketch, it said 'Yes', emphatically 'Yes'."*
— JLB Smith in *Old Fourlegs, the story of the Coelacanth.*

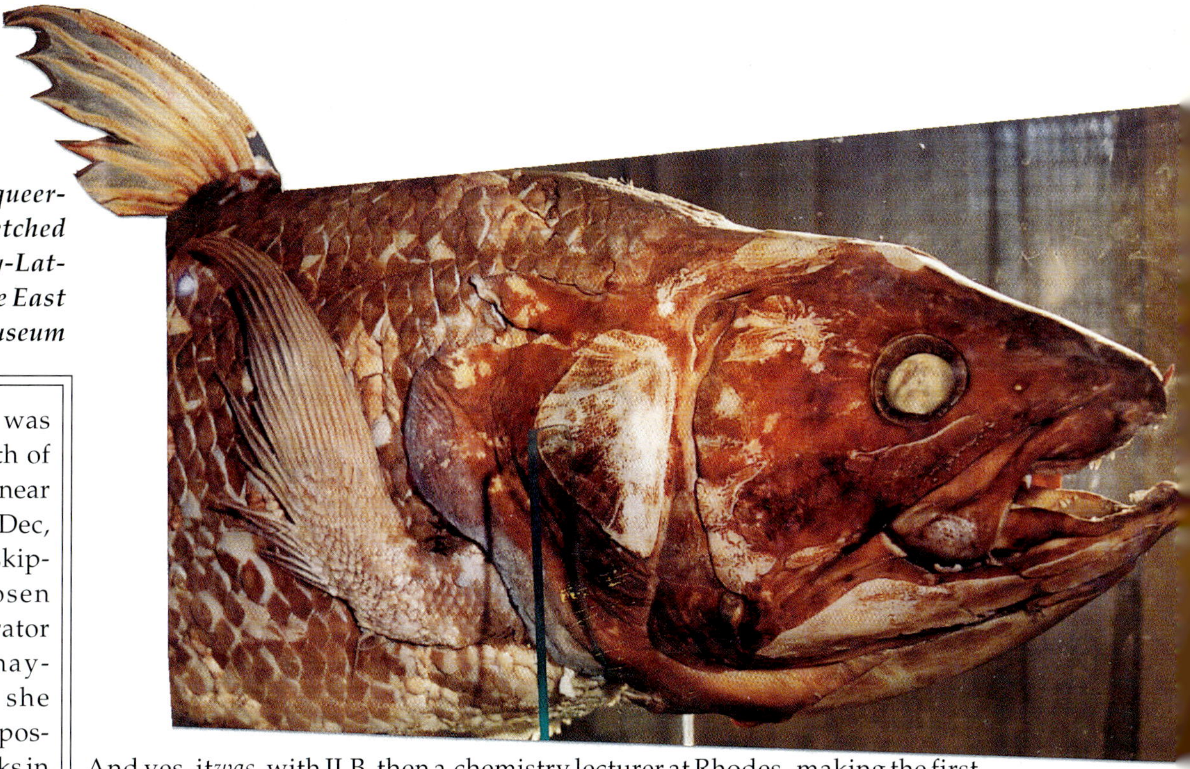

ABOVE: ***"The most queer-looking specimen" sketched by Marjorie Courtenay-Latimer, curator of the East London Museum***

The first coelacanth was caught off the mouth of the Chalumna River near East London on 21 Dec, 1938. Commercial skipper Hendrik Goosen alerted museum curator Marjorie Courtenay-Latimer, and she collected the decomposing fish from the docks in a taxi. Length: 1.4 metres, weight 57.6kg. It was later appropriately called *Latimeria chalumnae*.

And yes, it *was*, with JLB, then a chemistry lecturer at Rhodes, making the first positive identification of this living fossil which had drifted so far from — where? Finding the answer took till 1952, when the second living coelacanth surfaced. In an uncanny coincidence, scientists have recently unearthed the remains of several coelacanth fossils, dating back 360 million years, on the site of a prehistoric lagoon 3km outside Grahamstown. The Coelacanth Saga — set between East London and the Comoro Islands — is retold in the display area of the JLB Smith Institute in Somerset Street.

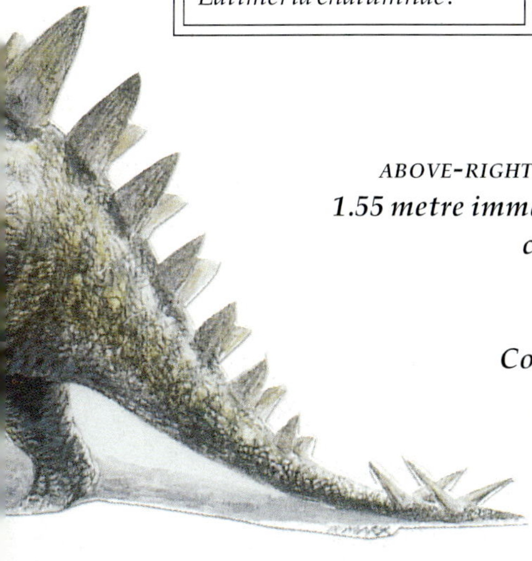

ABOVE-RIGHT: ***Perpetually pickled in propyl alcohol, this 1.55 metre immature male coelacanth gazes groggily at 20th century visitors to the JLB Smith Institute in Grahamstown***

RIGHT: ***The largest fish eggs ever seen. Coelacanths give birth to their young. Eggs are fertilized internally and the coelacanth pups (about 36cm long) develop in the oviduct of the female — as many as 26 full-termers at a time***

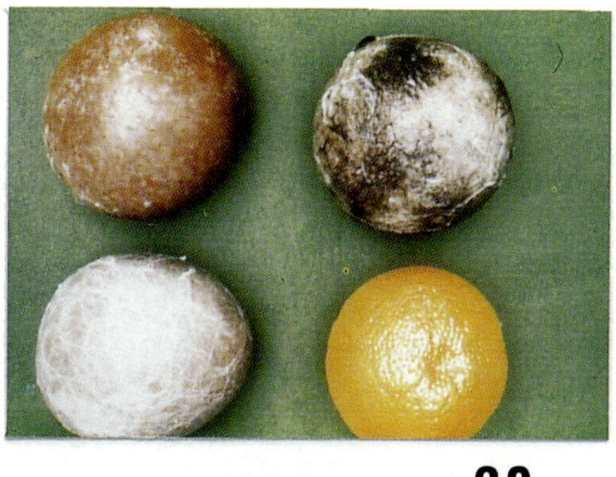

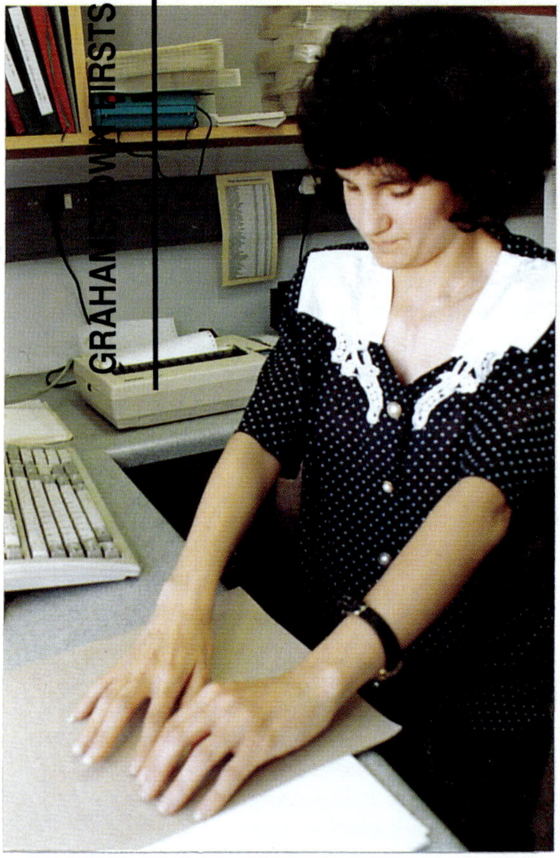

BLINDLIB

RECENT developments behind the sedate grey facades of the SA Library for the Blind in High Street are a real eye-opener. A Grahamstown "first" now past the 75-year mark, it has taken on a whole new lease on life — library liberation.

Blindlib for short, it includes Audiolib, Braillelib, Infolib and Techlib, spread over two buildings filled with the very latest equipment. Even the lift — a rarity in low-rise Grahamstown — has a set of braille buttons.

The audio and braille services it provides for the sight-impaired are many and varied. There are specially assembled picture stories for blind mothers to read with their young children, cookery books, braille world atlases which put sensitive fingertips on raised maps, dictionaries, encyclopaedias, non-fiction galore— and still more. Plus a braille correspondence course complete with instructor's manual.

Literature and novels range from Shakespeare to Agatha Christie, and include English, Afrikaans, and African titles— seven languages in all. Magazines too. An issue of *The Reader's Digest* can fill four large volumes. Even the British edition of *Cosmopolitan* is available on tape. So is *Bona*, the popular black SA monthly.

CLOCKWISE: *Braille proof check; getting Xhosa taped; the library's buildings; and founder Miss Josie Wood*

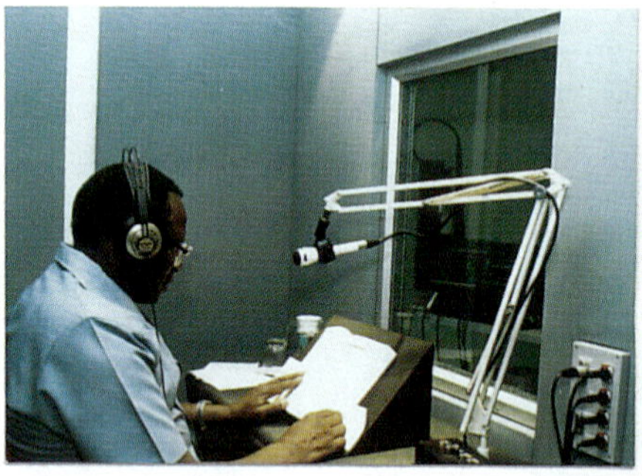

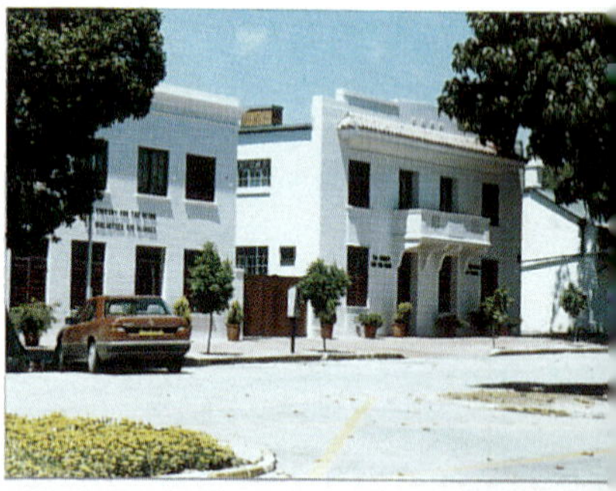

Braille versions are carefully packed to ensure that the dots will not flatten in transit, then placed in stout canvas bags and delivered free of charge by the Post Office to thousands of borrowers the length and breadth of southern Africa. Cassette players for audio books are provided at no cost.

Volunteers are extremely important to Blindlib. A dedicated Grahamstown contingent narrates books in the high-tech studios for the production of tapes. Similarly, books are transcribed into braille by volunteers round the country. They use a special computer programme, Edgar, and the disks come back to Blindlib for printing and proofreading.

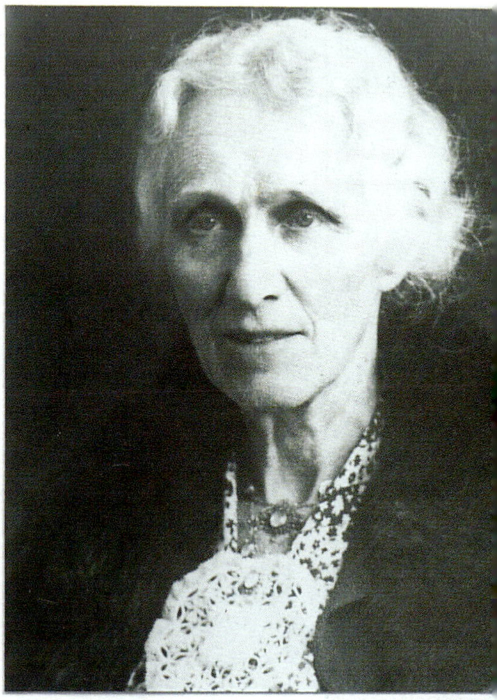

Now one of the world's "big five", the library had its beginnings back in 1919. The previous year, when the deadly Spanish influenza epidemic swept the land, Grahamstown was hard hit. Miss Josie Wood, with others, nursed people in the Township. It was there that she met an English missionary who persuaded her to take over one hundred braille books and circulate them from her home. This led to a lifetime of work for the blind, and many honours in recognition of it — including a visit from Helen Keller.

In 1962, she became the first Freeman of the City of Grahamstown. Nearing 90, frail and beautiful, at the civic ceremony she sat beneath the portrait of her father, who had been first mayor of the city exactly one hundred years before.

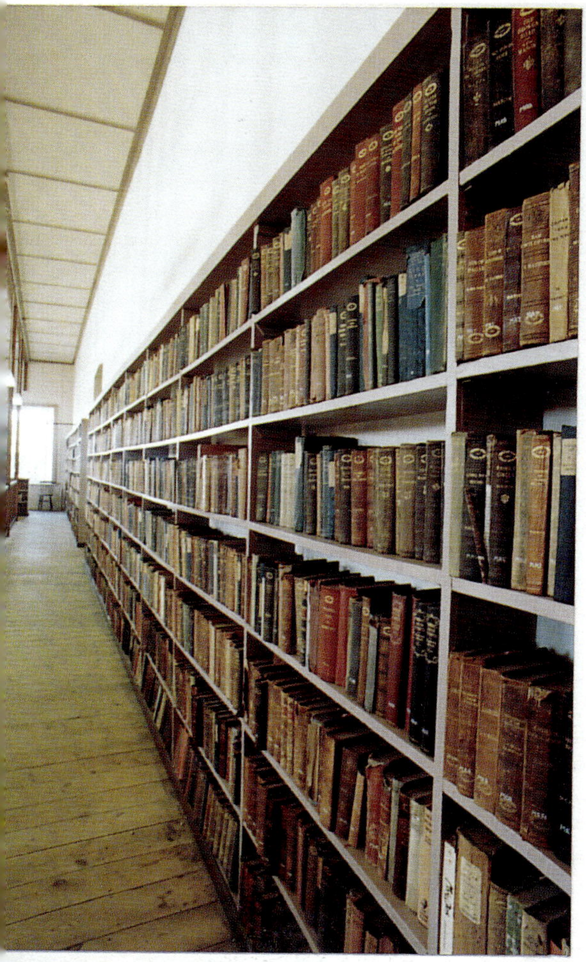

RUN OF THE MILL

ONCE inside the Grahamstown Public Library, you literally have the run of the mill — a converted steam rollermill. Dating back to the mid-19th century, it has been the library's permanent home from 1922, after a number of temporary resting spots since its start in 1842.

The solid 10m beams of yellowwood, 53 cm in width and thickness, are still visible. They supported the weight of piled flour bags when the massive stone walls vibrated to the roar of machinery, and the air was misty with meal.

Now all is hushed, especially upstairs in the gallery where the shelves are lined with ancient tomes— the old subscription library's stock, suspended in the amber of time.

It includes a demure selection of Victorian novels and improving literature. A reminder of the days when the chairman — an archdeacon— declared that the writings of Dickens and publications like *Punch* exercised an unfavourable influence on the mind and caused people to view all subjects, however grave, through the medium of ridicule. Therefore an overabundance of such light works should be carefully avoided, and books and papers selected which supplied not merely passing amusement but material for thought.

Downstairs, everything is thoroughly up-to-date (bestsellers too!). Only the antique chairs linger — bentwoods, straight-backed and grandfathers. Not another "first", but a first-class library in its own original way.

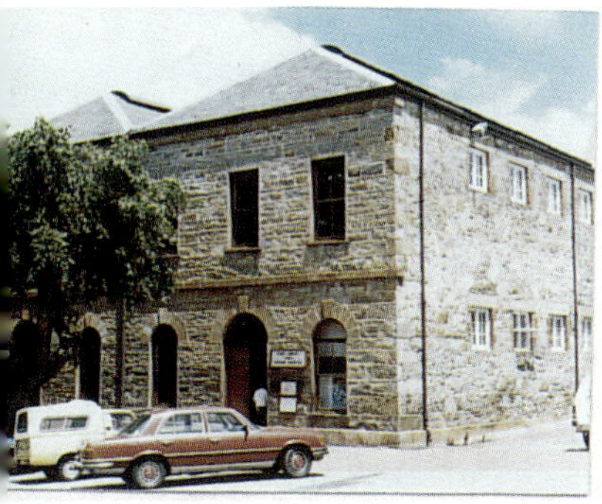

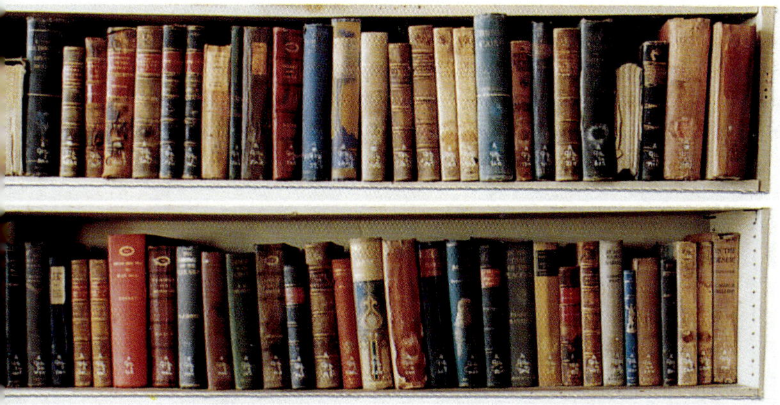

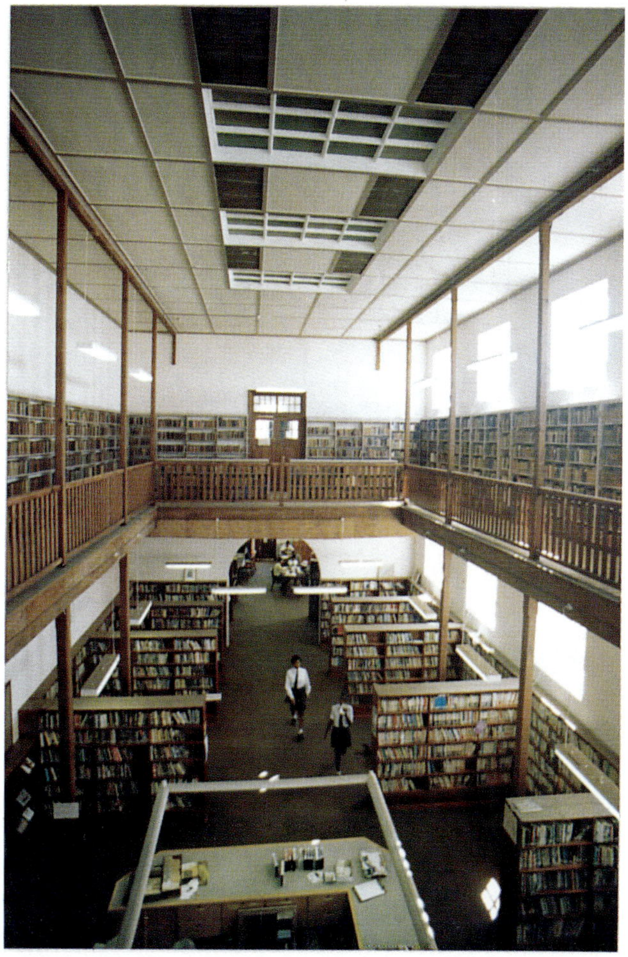

FROM TOP: *Vintage volumes pack gallery shelves; Public Library exterior and lofty interior*

CITY OF SAINTS, SINNERS, AND

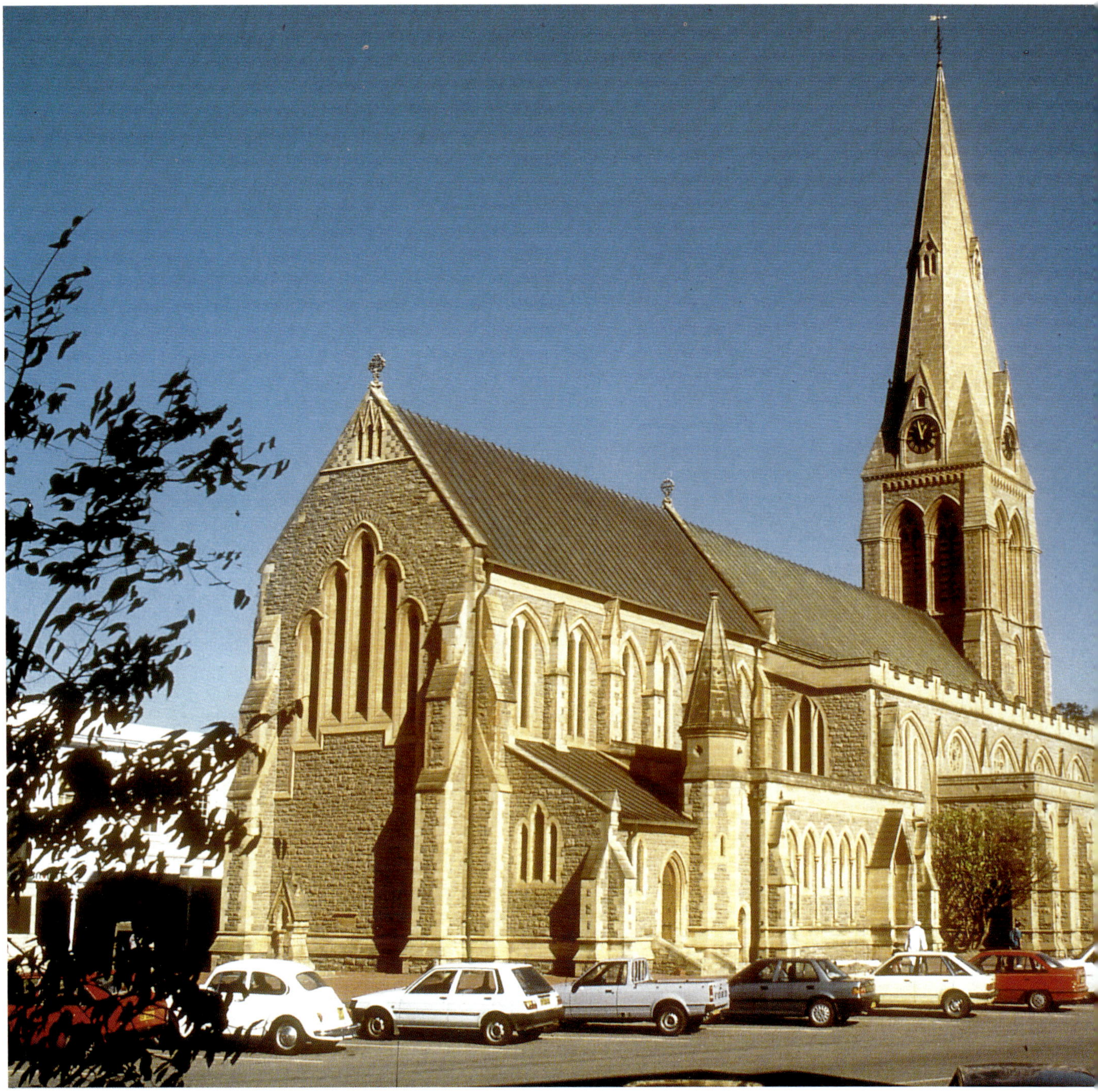

ABOVE: *The Anglican Cathedral of St Michael and St George — a positive presence right in the middle of Grahamstown*

STUDENTS

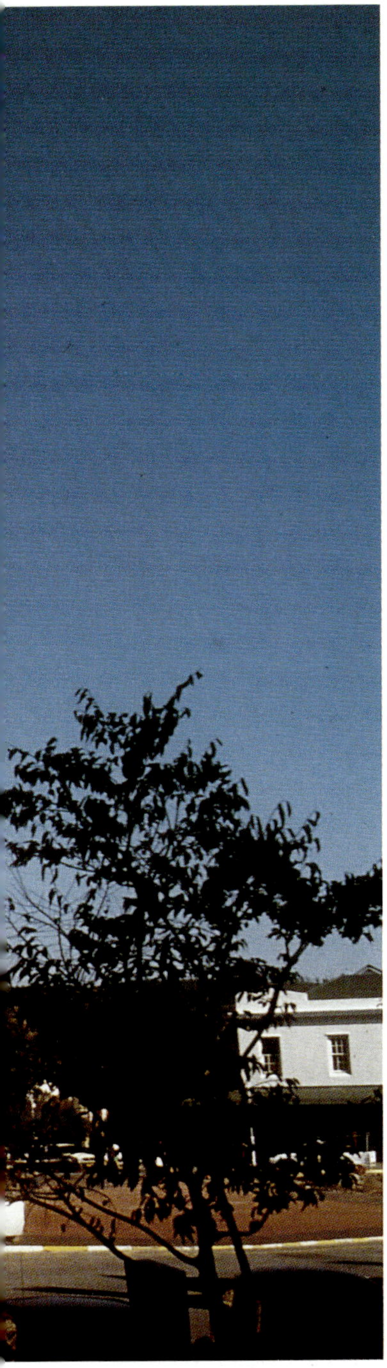

THERE *are* a lot of churches in Grahamstown. One for every week of the year, including school chapels and township sects, tabernacles and other temples of worship. Doubtless the origin of the 'City of Saints' tag, though locals favour the explanation that dates back to garrison days when a requisition for a vital piece of carpentry equipment met with the courteous reply: "We regret we have no vice in Grahamstown." Back bounced the obvious rejoinder : " Then you must all be saints."

Not all of us, though the centrally situated churches are inevitably part of everyone's daily scene, and always have been. Old familiars with affectionately shortened names — Commem, St Bart's, St Pat's and more recently, St Fig's (the College of the Transfiguration for the training of Anglican priests).

Inside, there is that almost palpable patina of devotion down the decades. The lovingly polished brass, needlework kneelers, fresh garden flowers ... Plus notices re fund-raising efforts to counteract the rising damp and falling roof, mixed with missions to the poor we have always with us.

Sinners amongst the supplicants of course, and elsewhere— as ever. The erstwhile gaols of Grahamstown are also very much part of the backdrop. Used for other purposes now, and concepts of crime and punishment much changed. The quality of mercy is not strained, and justice is firmly upheld in the Supreme Court of the Eastern Cape and the Magistrate's Court for the Albany District in Upper High Street.

Then there are the Rhodes University students, who feel the city revolves around them. Quite rightly. When they and their many mentors are away during the four "vacs", nothing moves. The proximity of the campus to the town makes for a convivially close relationship, but it is the Oppidans — those who live in digs which pop up here, there and everywhere—who really make their presence felt, usually audibly. Which brings in the other Grahamstown story. The one where an irate neighbour bellows: "Can't something be done about the music volume?", only to receive the politely shouted answer: "Sorry, no. It's turned up as high as it will go." A case of the sins of the young being visited on their elders.

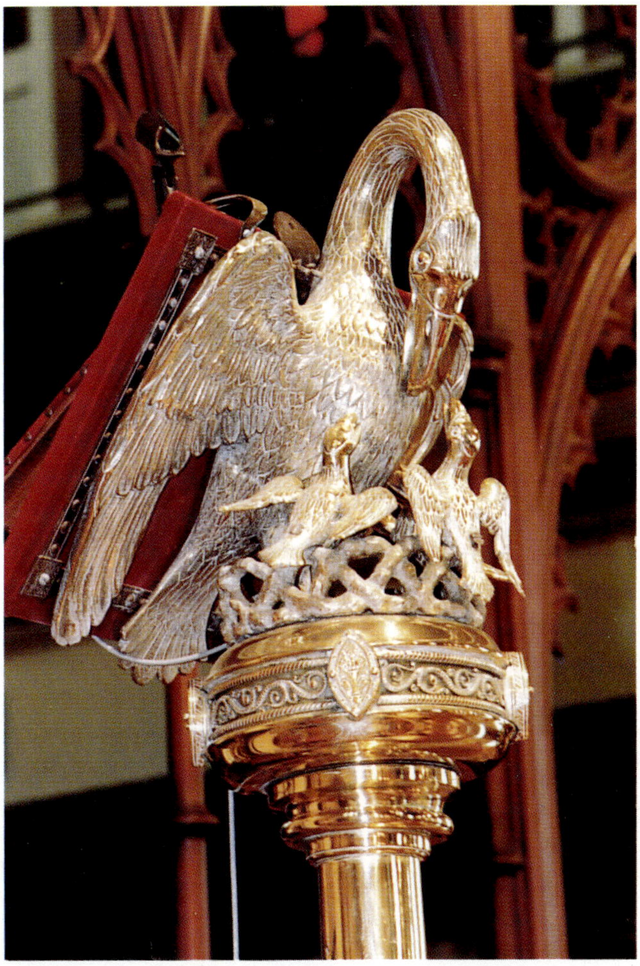

RIGHT: *Cathedral's symbolic pelican lectern*

Cathedral glory, human story

FOR ALL its outer magnificence and inner beauty, the Anglican Cathedral of St Michael and St George retains an essentially homely atmosphere. Welcoming rather than overwhelming. A legacy, perhaps, from its humble beginnings as a parish church.

Started in 1824 and opened in 1830, it was initially little more than a large room with a square tower at one end. "Church well situated, but miserable in point of architecture", noted Robert Gray, Bishop of Cape Town in 1848, an opinion echoed by many.

The Grahamstown Diocese was established in 1853, and the church became the seat of a bishop— a cathedral. Improvements were definitely called for.

In due course, the task of designing a new Grahamstown Cathedral went to no less a personage than Sir George Gilbert Scott in London, foremost exponent of the Victorian Gothic Revival style which swept all others before it. Knighted for his Albert Memorial in Kensington Gardens, Sir George never visited South Africa.

He laid down the main lines of the present building and designed the 150ft bell tower and spire which was completed in 1879 and remained the tallest structure in SA until 1923, when the 170ft campanile went up in Port Elizabeth. After Sir George's death, his son John Oldrid Scott designed the chancel (1893) and nave (1912). The final addition was the Lady Chapel in 1952. The south wall is the only remaining section of the original edifice, a National Monument in its own right as the oldest surviving part of an English church building in SA.

The two great arcades of the nave are supported by Belgian marble pillars. Like forest trees, they rise into the cool shadows of the timbered roof. Beyond, the altar is in a glade of light glowing through stained glass windows. Sacred and mysterious.

The graceful arched rood screen behind the pulpit was the work of black apprentice carvers at a local training institution. The pulpit itself is worth a closer look — especially the biblical scene on the side, which features four early Grahamstown bishops. Very Victorian gentlemen in spite of their eastern robes: one sports magnificent mutton chop whiskers.

Memorial plaques aplenty tell the tales of their times. All things bright and beautiful abound, as

"The real history of the Church in Grahamstown cannot be told, for it is known in its entirety only to God and includes the stories of the lives of his servants, clerical and lay, in this city of many denominations, and of the ways in which He has used them to serve and change their little bit of the world. At the same time, we are grateful to have such a beautiful temple for our worship and for the Bishop to keep his throne in."

— The Rt Revd Kenneth Oram, Bishop of Grahamstown 1974-1987

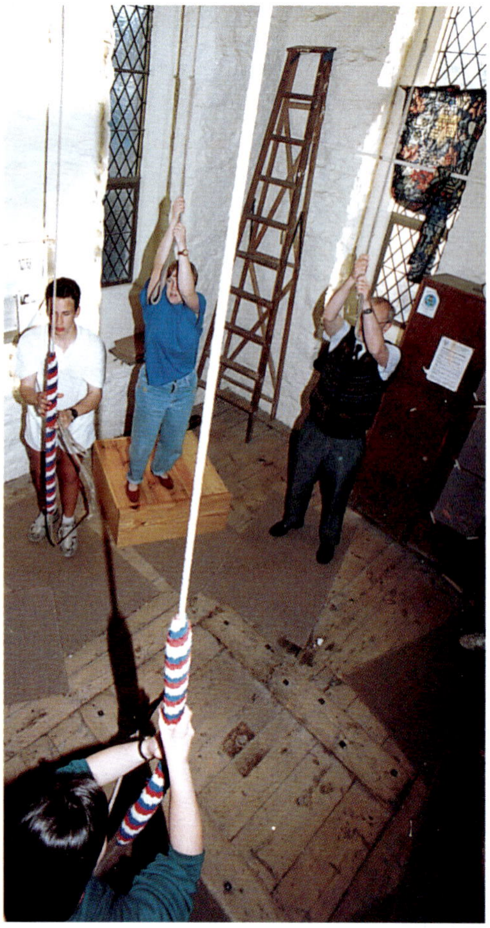

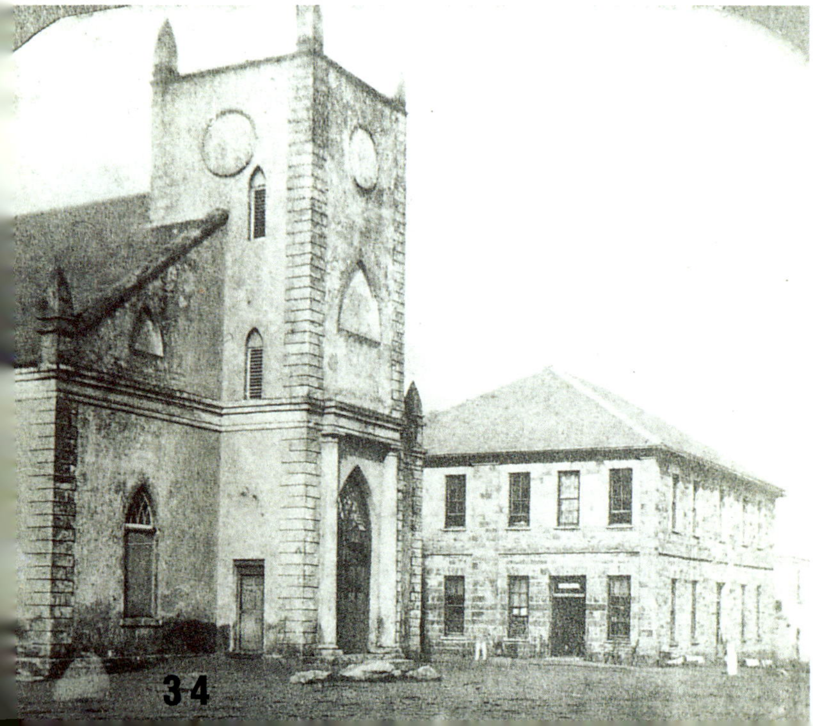

ABOVE: Bellringers in action
LEFT: Cathedral's predecessor, commenced in 1824

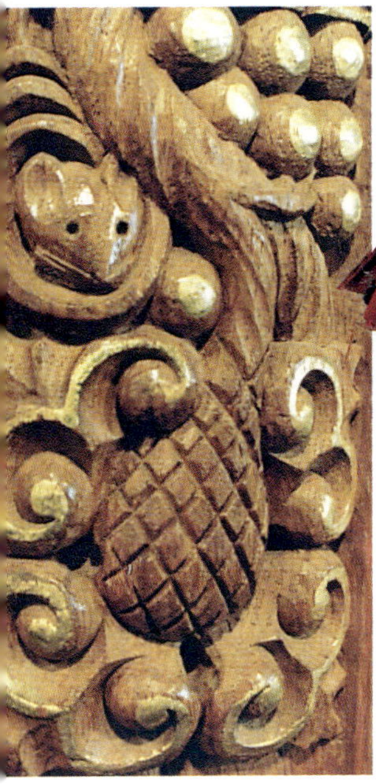

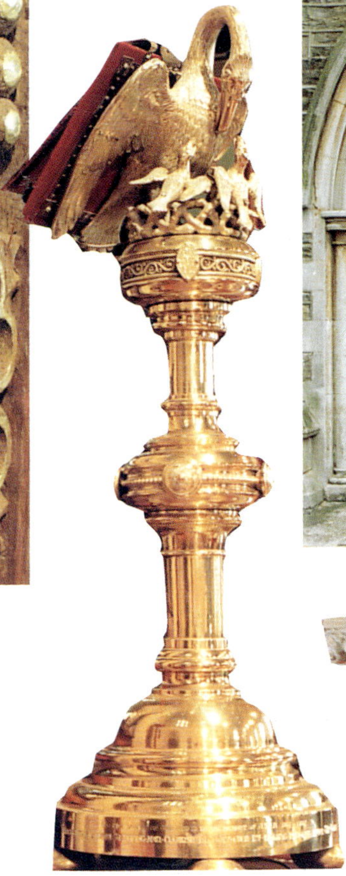

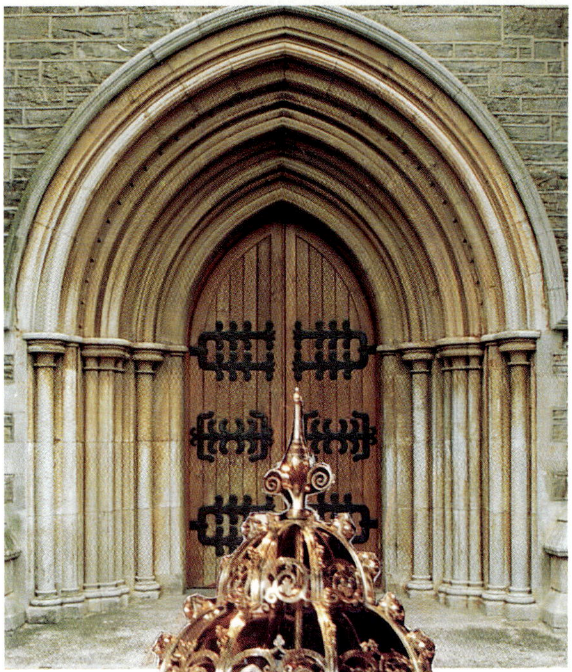

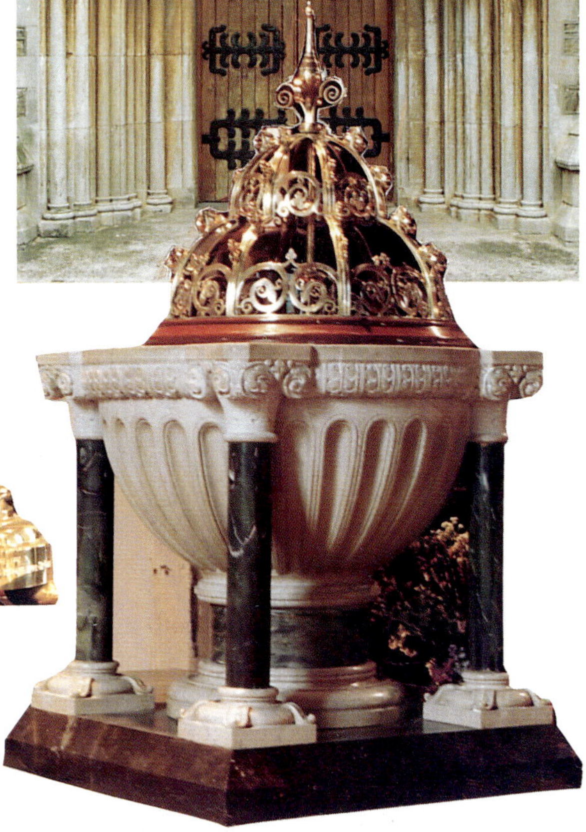

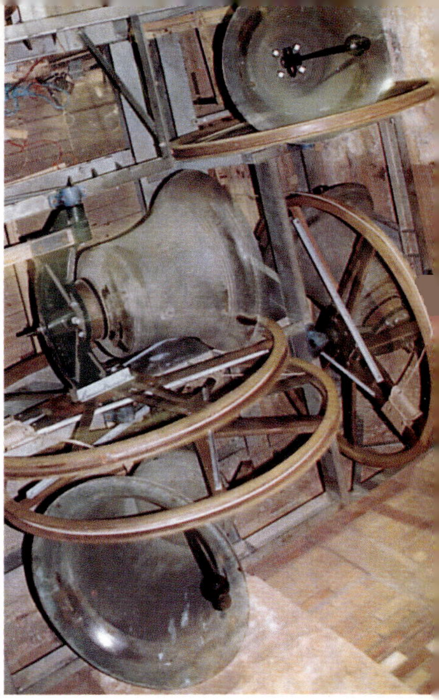

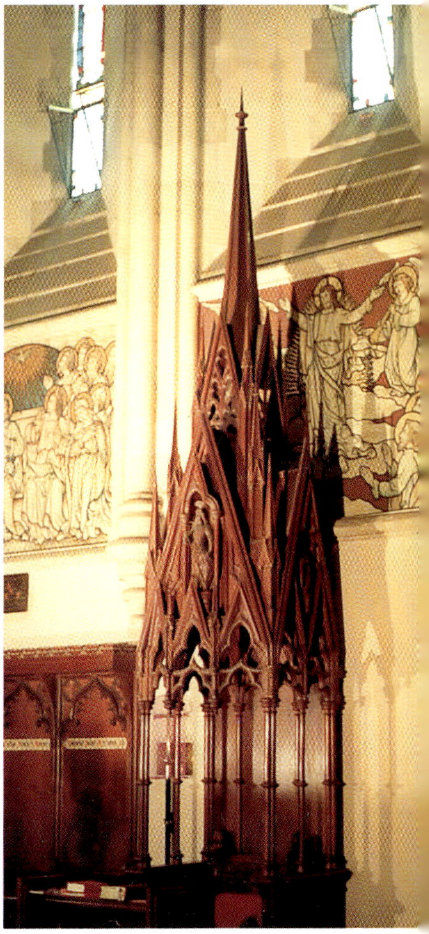

CLOCKWISE: ***Bellringers in action; church mouse in hiding; pelican lectern; the great west door; baptismal font with bowl of Shropshire stone; restored bells pealing; and the Bishop's throne plus frescoes***

well as some creatures great and small. The pelican lectern is a medieval symbol of Christ's self-giving, the Crucifixion and the Eucharist, since the pelican was said to feed her young with her blood. The World War II roll of honour was carved in England by Yorkshireman Robert Thompson, who signed his work with a mouse. The elaborate christening font near the door was erected by a daughter in memory of her mother, Elizabeth Owen-Smith, 1810 - 1892, whose 11 children were christened in this hallowed place.

The Bishop keeps his throne or *cathedra* in the cathedral. By ancient definition, the presence of a cathedral bestows city status, hence little Grahamstown's honorary title.

Then there is the first and heaviest ring of eight bells on the African continent. They were cast in London in 1878, hung in 1879, and finally dedicated 115 years later in July, 1994. This marked the successful conclusion of a mammoth five-year restoration effort which included the installation of a new steel frame.

Bell ringing now forms part of a course for BMus students at Rhodes University. Learning the ropes in the tower is not a simple undertaking, especially since the whole city hears any clangers. But nobody minds. A part of Grahamstown's soul was missing when the bells were sent overseas for repair. It is a blessing to have them back where they belong, making a joyful noise unto the Lord.

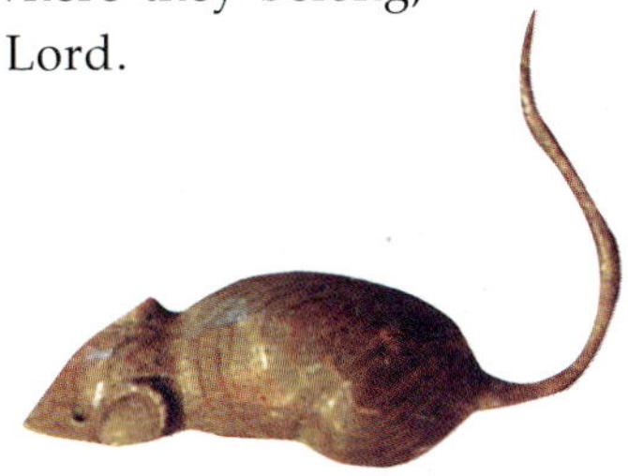

CITY AND SUBURBAN

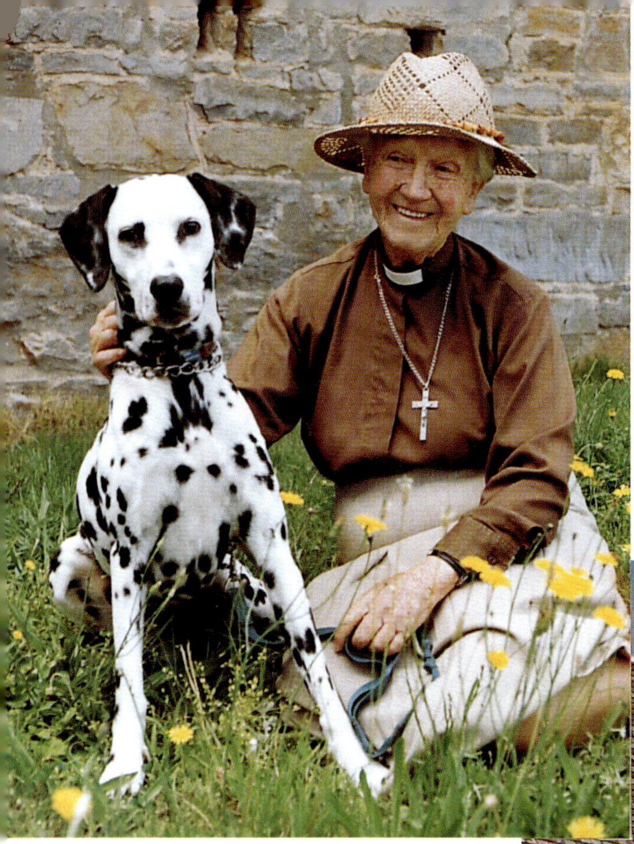

ABOVE: The Reverend Nancy and her dog with St Bartholomew's alongside

The Baptist

SANDWICHED between the worldly delights of the Odeon Cinema and the fleshly temptations of a livestock co-operative, (plus a touch of hellfire in the corner Curry Den) the oldest Baptist Church in South Africa steps back a bit. The year 1843 on its neo-classical facade clearly puts it in a completely different context.

Neighbouring 'coming attractions' posters alter twice a week. The biblical verses on its modest pavement textboard remain unchanged and unchallengeable.

The Baptist witness in SA began with the arrival of a few families in the predominantly Wesleyan 1820 Settler party aboard the *Brilliant*. They helped establish the nearby village of Salem, and a steadfast carpenter, William Miller, emerged as their spiritual leader.

Soon he was preaching in Grahamstown as well— covering the distance of some 48 kms to and fro on foot. Catastrophic farm-

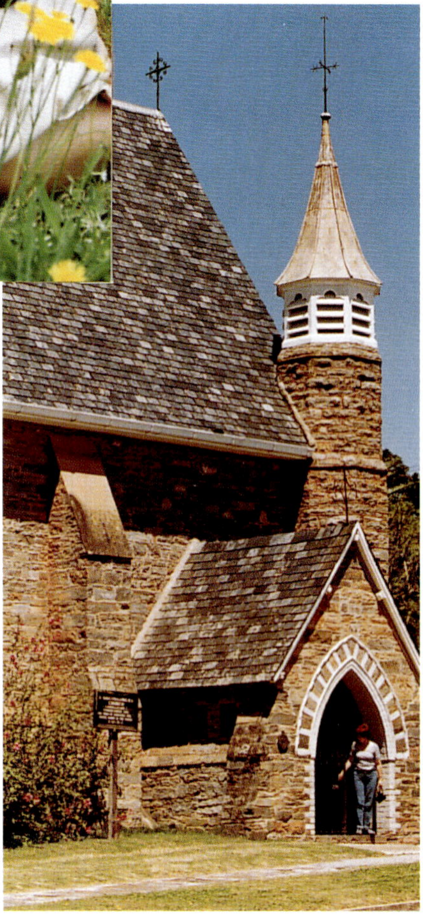

Simply St Bart's

ON the Market Street side of Artificers' Square, where 1820 Settler cottages mushroom white and small, St Bartholomew's Church stands perfectly in scale, St Bart's to one and all.

The first SA Anglican woman deacon "by about 24 hours" and — in alphabetical order — the first of the three women priests ordained in 1992, the Rev Nancy Charton cares for the parish and much else besides.

Often out and about in a broad-brimmed straw hat, she is by no means as indefatigable a walker as the church's first rector, Nathaniel James Merriman, father of John Xavier, last prime minister of the Cape (1908-10). In 1850 he walked to Bloemfontein, and in 1851 to Cape Town to attend synod, comfortably shod in boots he made himself.

The church's cornerstone was laid on August 24, 1857— the Feast of St Bartholomew. Soldiers supervised by Merriman and the Anglican Colonial Chaplain, the Rev John Heavyside, built the nave and chancel. The church was consecrated on June 24, 1860— the Feast of St John the Baptist.

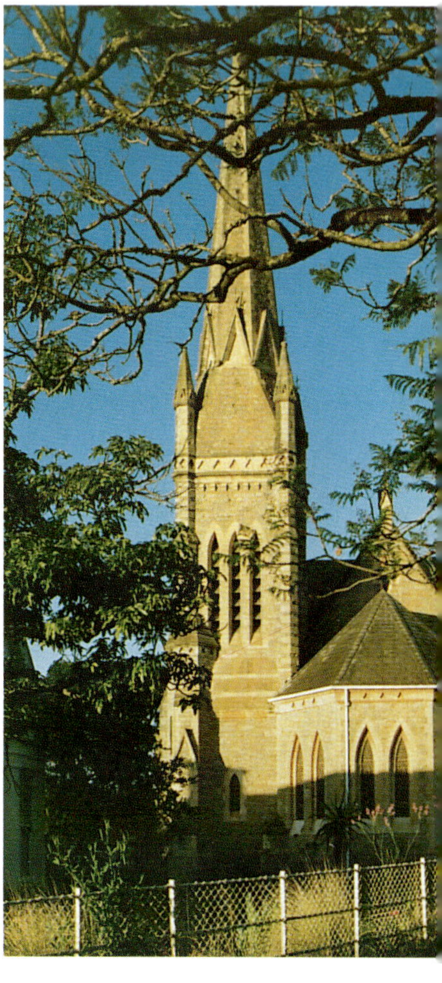

RIGHT: Baptist beginnings in Artificers' Square cottage led to a striking edifice in Bathurst Street (top left)

Mother Church

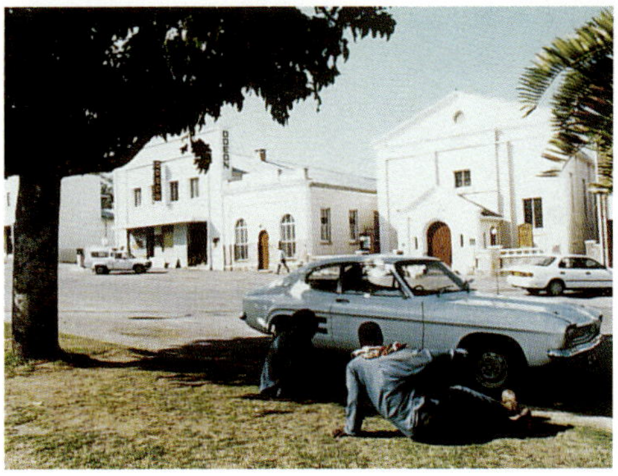

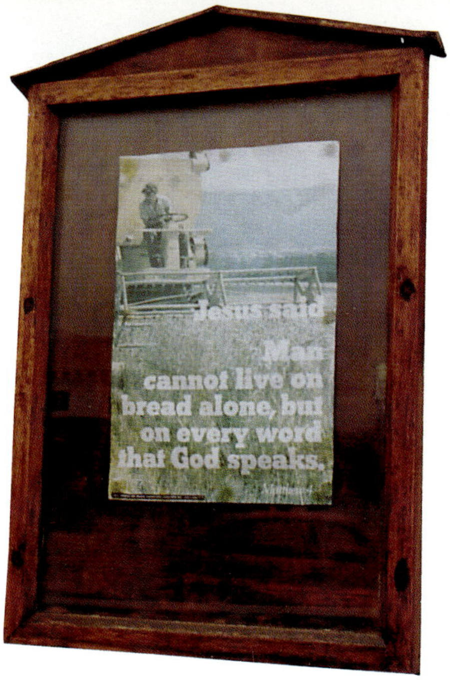

ing conditions forced him into town permanently, where he continued his ministry in a carpenter's shop.

Early in 1823 he joyfully recorded: "*My brother gave us the requisite ground and, as the great Master had honoured me in making me the instrument of establishing the Baptist Church, so was I requested to lay the foundation stone of the First Baptist Chapel.*"

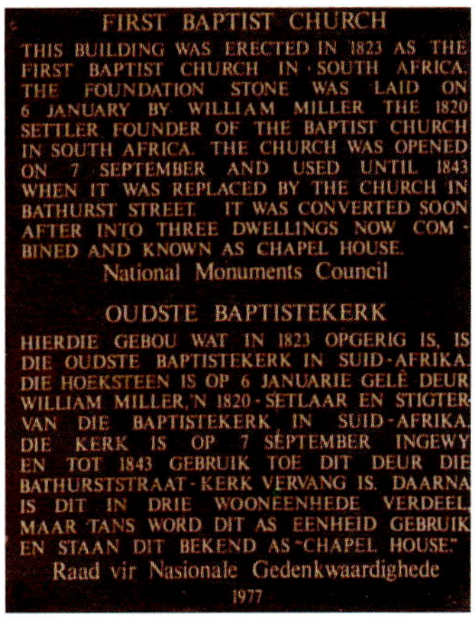

A solid double-storeyed Settler-style cottage in Bartholomew Street, it has long since been converted into two private homes with one name — Chapel House. A National Monuments Council plaque records the singular story for passers by wandering up from Artificers' Square. Twenty years later, the imposing edifice in Bathurst Street was opened on March 12, 1843, and there it remains come what may, the Mother Church of the Baptist Union of SA.

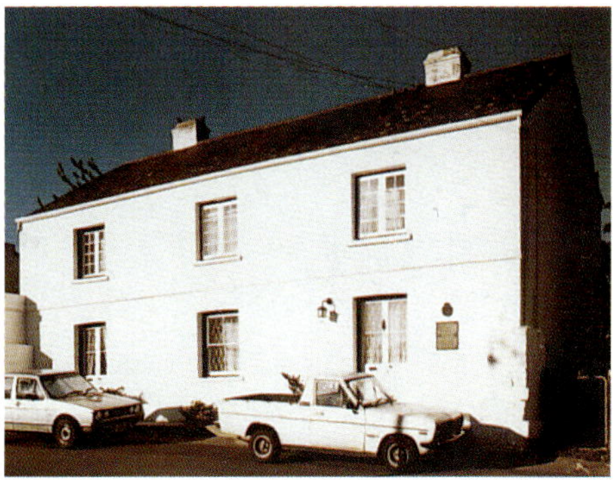

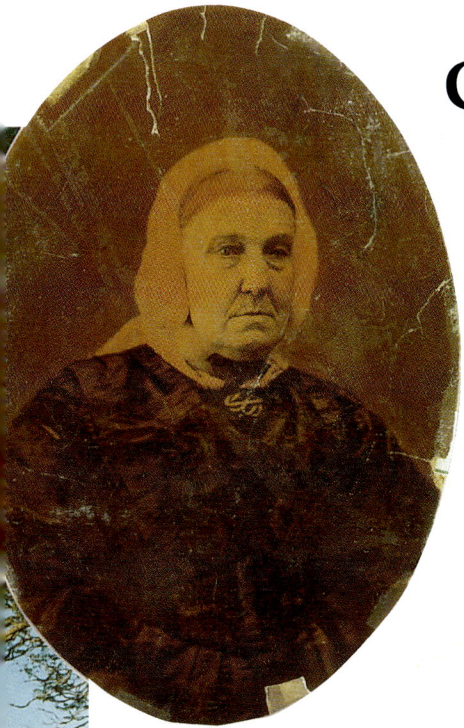

Christ Church grace

OATLANDS on the opposite side of town provides a garden suburb setting for another Gothic gem — Christ Church. A replica of an exquisite old church in Saxony, it was consecrated in 1876.

The windows are wonderful. Tall and narrow like illuminated bookmarks, radiantly bright inserts between plain white walls. All is beauty, all is light.

Among them is the first stained glass window to be made in South Africa. Designed and painted by Prof F W Armstrong, first head of the School of Art at Rhodes University, it is a glowing tribute to the memory of Julia Greathead (1824 - 1908).

Birds trill outside, bats chirrup within, especially at evensong. "Nothing is far from God", proclaims a window text. The organ has a particularly sweet tone and bears a wooden plaque commemorating Beryl MacKay, who served faithfully as organist for 50 years—from 1915 to 1965.

The church owes its existence to Mrs Rosa Wright, an 1820 Settler of evangelical principles, who left sufficient money in the hands of trustees to build and endow it as a thanks offering to God for the many blessings she had received in her adopted country. Although independent in some aspects, Christ Church has always been in communion with the Church of the Province of South Africa.

LEFT: A poem in stone made possible by Rosa Wright (insert)

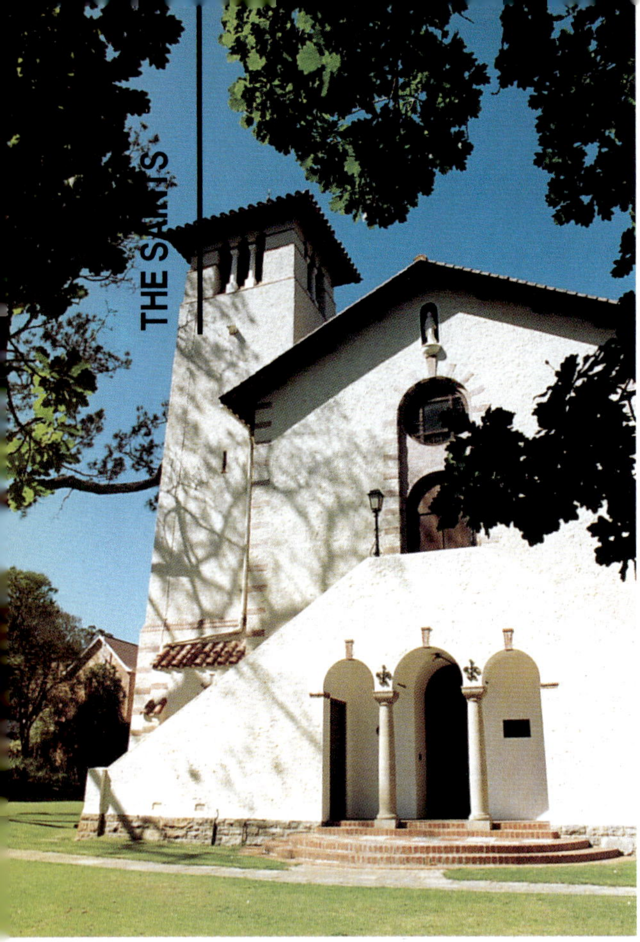

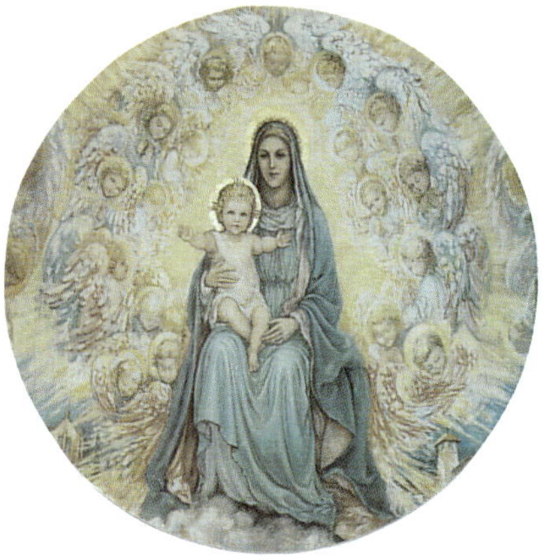

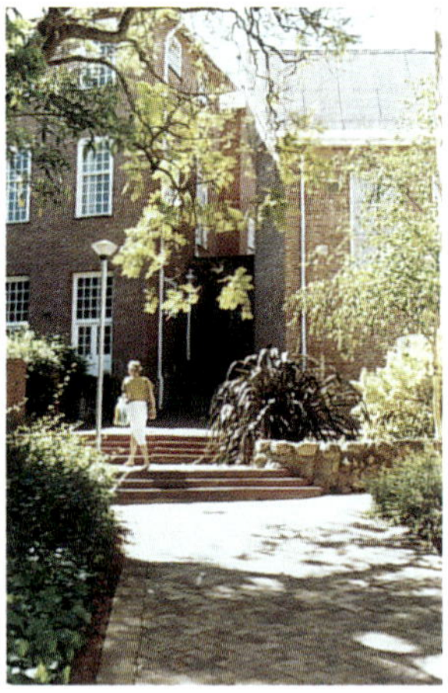

THE G

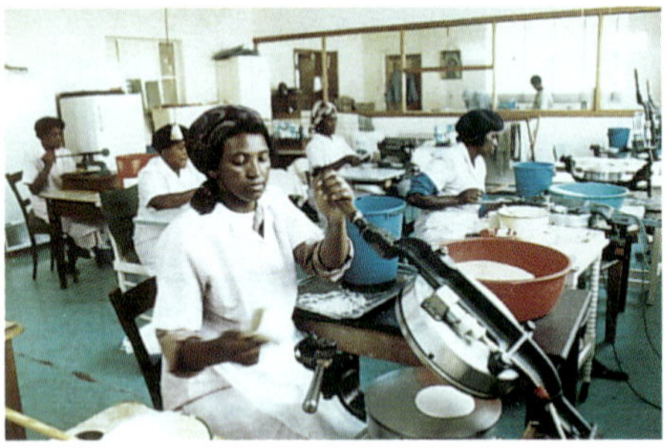

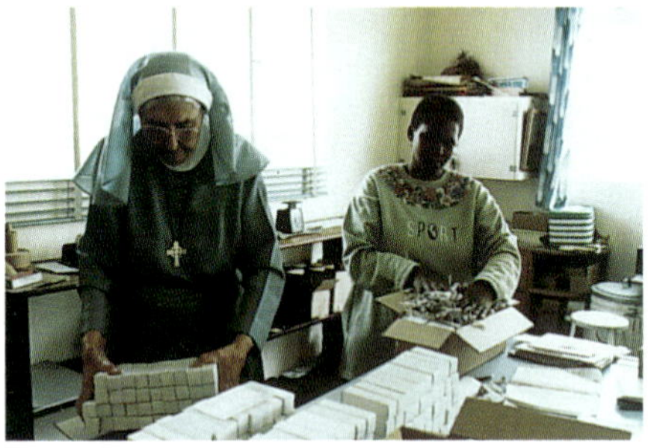

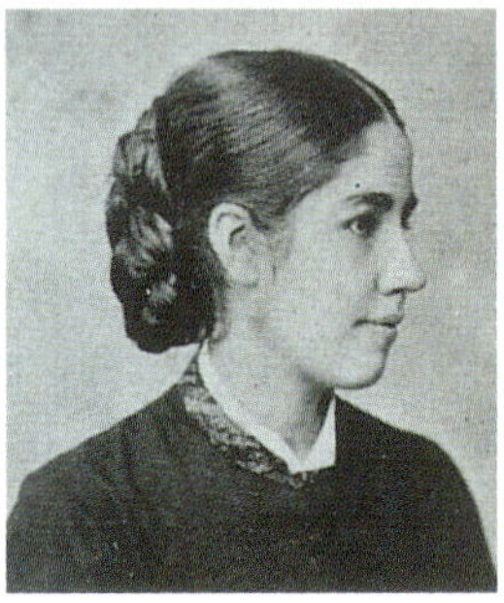

CLOCKWISE: Community of the Resurrection's Chapel exterior; angelic fresco within; Training College cameo; Communion wafer-making department still pressing on; and founder Mother Cecile at the time of her call

AS YOU enter the city from the N2 turn-off below the 1820 Monument, wending your way past the green depths of the Botanical Gardens, a russet brick village gently touched by time lies on your left. The former Grahamstown Training College complex, now St Peter's Campus and part of Rhodes University since 1975.

Straight on, at the corner of Hill Street, rock-solid reminders remain of the former Grahamstown Convent which closed its doors in 1982, after more than 130 years' service. It has since been incorporated into Victoria Primary School.

Two famed educational institutions of yesteryear, whose influence spread across the land. Both begun by intrepid young women of great faith. Mother Cecile — pioneer of teacher training in South Africa — was only 21 when she founded the Anglican Community of the Resurrection of Our Lord in Grahamstown in 1884.

Mother Gertrude — subsequently known far and wide as Notre Mère (Our Mother) — was 27 when she arrived to start the first Catholic convent school on SA soil, and in due course founded the Congregation of the Missionary Sisters of the Assumption.

Today, the drive from Port Elizabeth takes just over an hour. Notre Mère and her small band of Sisters landed at Algoa Bay on December 3, 1849, after a voyage from England lasting three miserable months, and set off in "chariots drawn by 16 oxen" on a jolting six-day journey.

Classes soon commenced, as did further frontier troubles. If direct attack threatened, Notre Mère led the orphans, boarders and Sisters

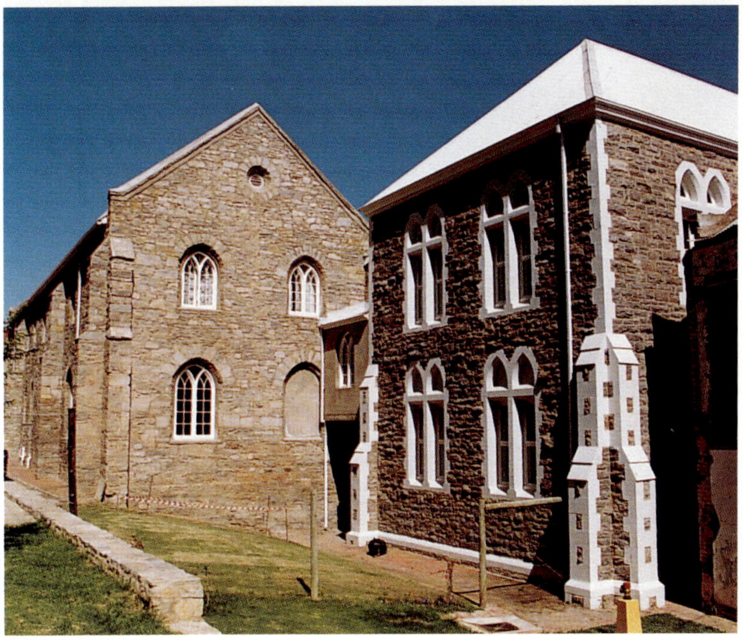

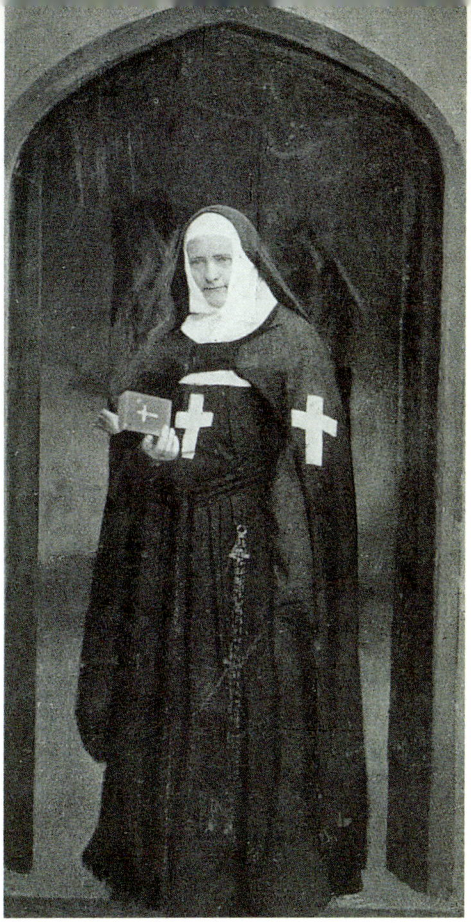

OOD SISTERS

to the fortified St Patrick's Church each night, brandishing a sword. When fuel ran out, the Sisters gathered cow dung from an abandoned kraal and baked bread "with a peculiar flavour" in a pot lid. Come what may, Notre Mère and her helpers persevered. It was they who first attracted to Grahamstown pupils from the furthest parts of SA, a major factor in its steady development as an educational centre.

Mother Cecile established St Peter's Home (the Gold Fields Centre for English at Rhodes from 1992) and in 1894 initiated the Grahamstown Training College, which grew into one of the community's biggest undertakings, producing thousands of primary school teachers during its long existence.

St Mary and All Angels at its heart has become the inter-denominational Rhodes Chapel. The fresco of the Madonna and Child above the altar was painted by Sister Margaret between 1924 and 1929, using pupils as heavenly models. When she expressed reservations about her artistic abilities, the Mother Superior pragmatically replied: "Well, we can always white-wash it over if we don't like it."

Both orders remain active in Grahamstown. Their ranks have dwindled and age has taken its inevitable toll, but their caring spirit remains undimmed. They continue their work in a number of spheres— most unusually at the Community of the Resurrection's Wafer Department, where millions of Communion wafers are made in special presses rather like giant waffle irons, and despatched to churches all over South Africa, Namibia, and Botswana.

CLOCKWISE: ***Convent core restored; Mother Gertrude, the nun who led the way; and a long-ago music lesson in the same setting***

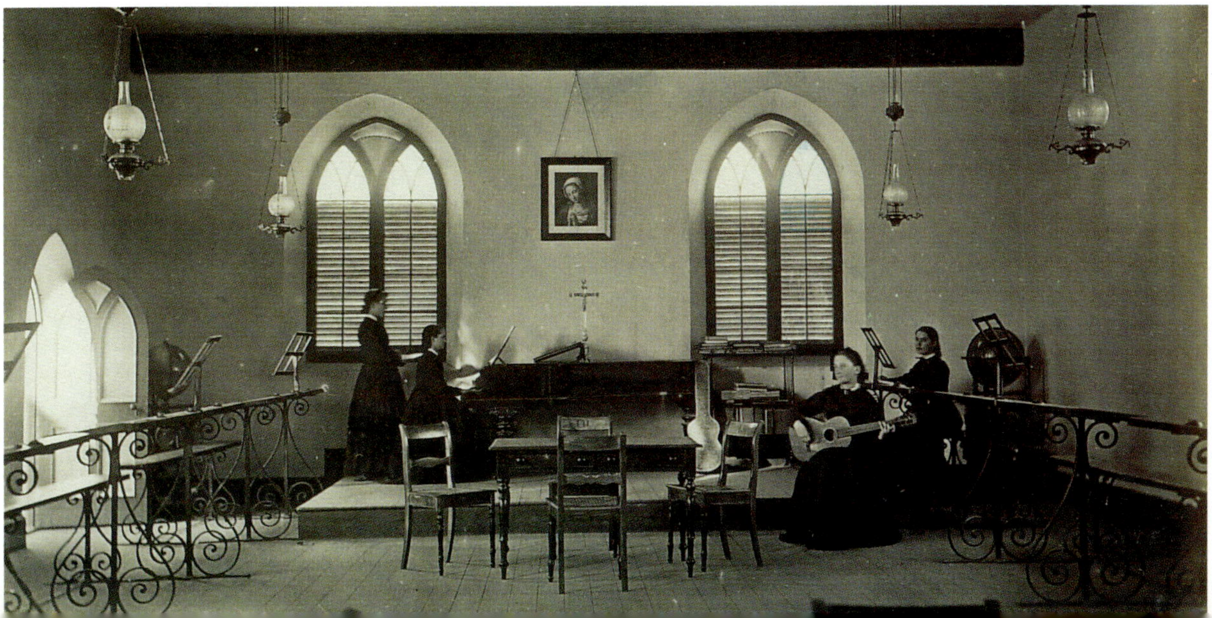

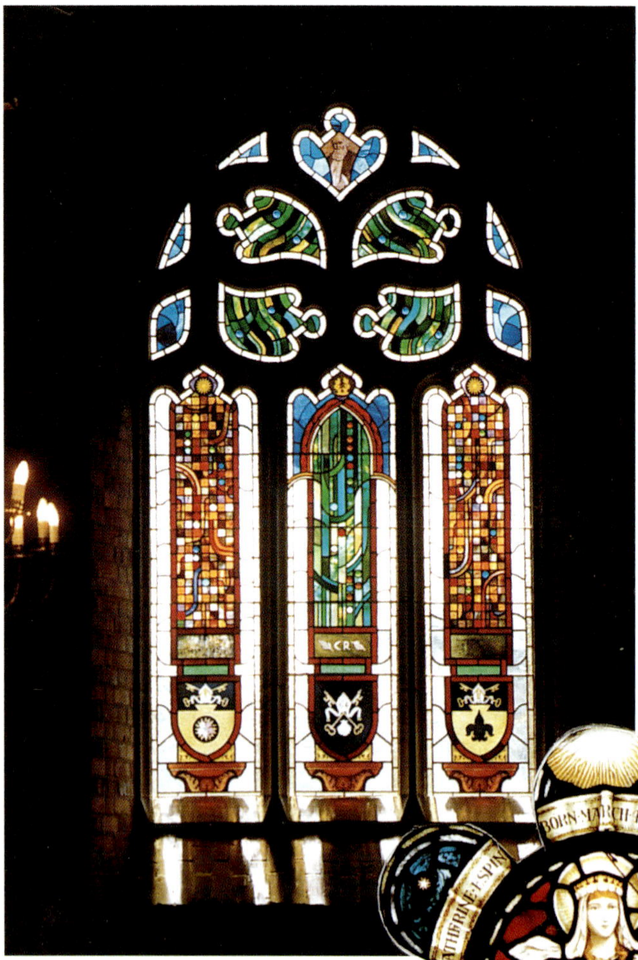

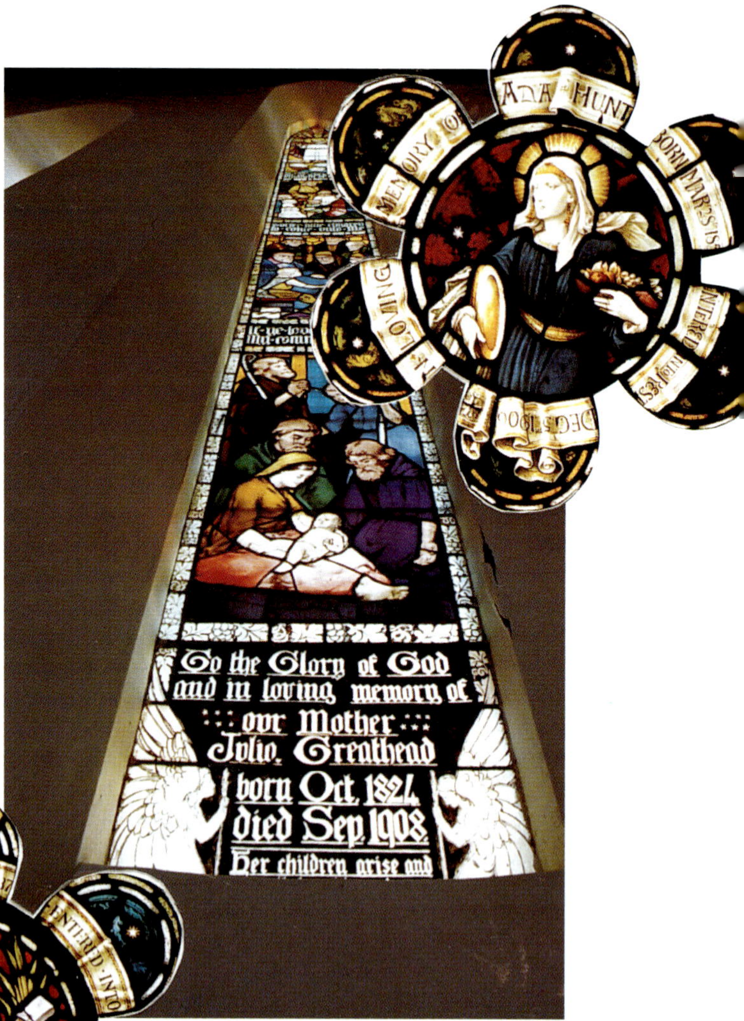
To the Glory of God
and in loving memory of
our Mother
Julia Greathead
born Oct 1824
died Sep 1908
Her children arise and
MEMORY OF
ADA HUNT
LOVING

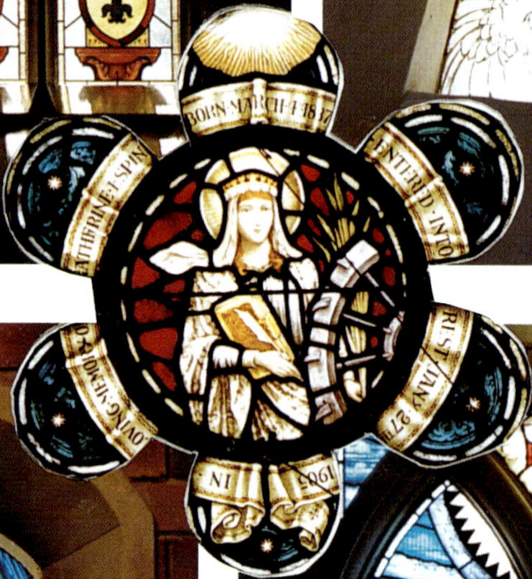

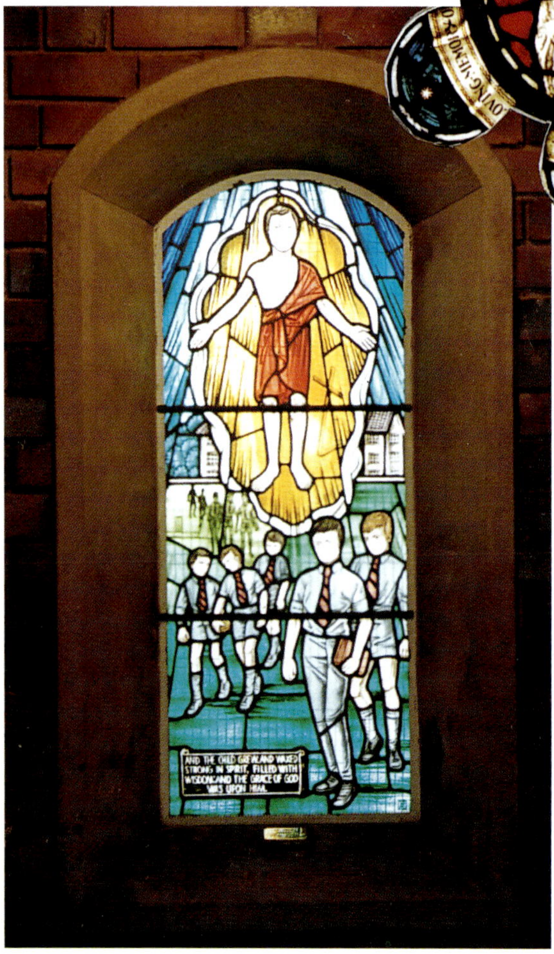
AND THE CHILD GREW AND WAXED
STRONG IN SPIRIT, FILLED WITH
WISDOM AND THE GRACE OF GOD
WAS UPON HIM.

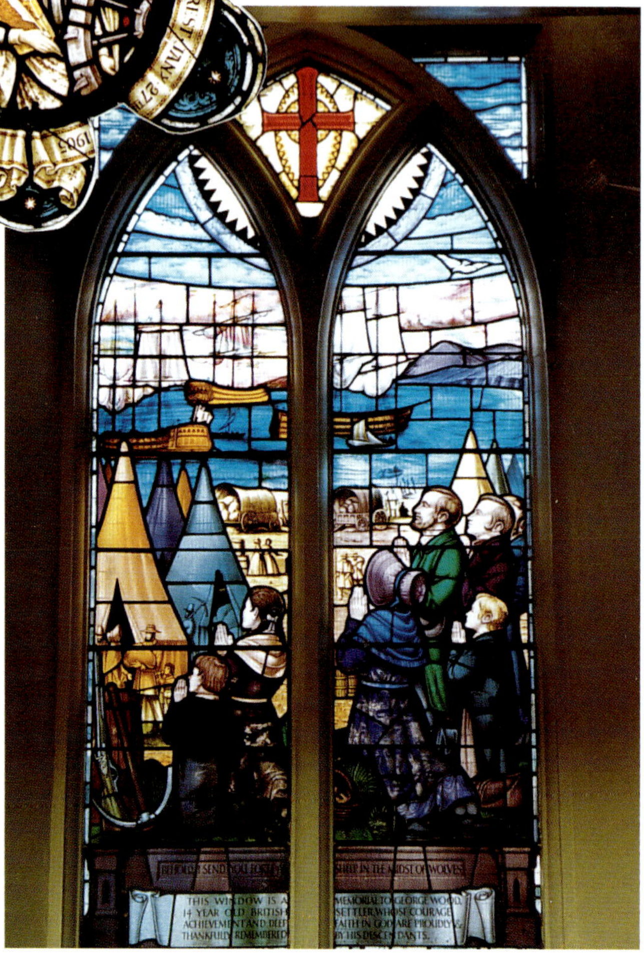
SHEEP IN THE MIDST OF WOLVES
THIS WINDOW IS A
MEMORIAL TO GEORGE WOOD
14 YEAR OLD BRITISH
SETTLER WHOSE COURAGE
FAITH IN GOD ARE PROUDLY &
THANKFULLY REMEMBERED
BY HIS DESCENDANTS.

WINDOWS OF THE SOUL

PRECIOUS jewels of Grahamstown, rich and rare. A wealth of wonderful windows radiate life and love in chapels and churches, illuminating the Cathedral's shadowy heights with their bright beauty. The Eastern Cape can justifiably claim to be the historical centre of stained glass in South Africa. The Calvinist ethic of the early Dutch Church in the Western Cape discouraged ornamentation in places of worship. It was the arrival of the 1820 Settlers which created a steady demand for these colourful creations — initially from British studios and later from Germany, France, Belgium, and Holland.

The first stained glass window made in South Africa was designed and painted by Prof F W Armstrong, former head of the Art School of Rhodes University, roundabout 1927. In memory of Julia Greathead, it shines out from the south wall of Christ Church in Speke Street.

This heavenly heritage has been added to over the years, and includes a number of variations on traditional religious themes. The latest major undertaking is a splendid work by the country's leading expert, Hunter Nesbit, dedicated in 1994. Not in a church but adorning Canterbury House at Rhodes University — in memory of the Sisters of the Community of the Resurrection of Our Lord who established the former Grahamstown Teachers Training College in this complex more than a century ago.

Shortly after mid-day, the sun catches little inserts of concave glass and the whole magnificent masterpiece dances with delight. A careful combination of traditional and modern styles, the central tree symbolises the past reaching into the present — new growth from deep roots — which is what Rhodes and Grahamstown are all about.

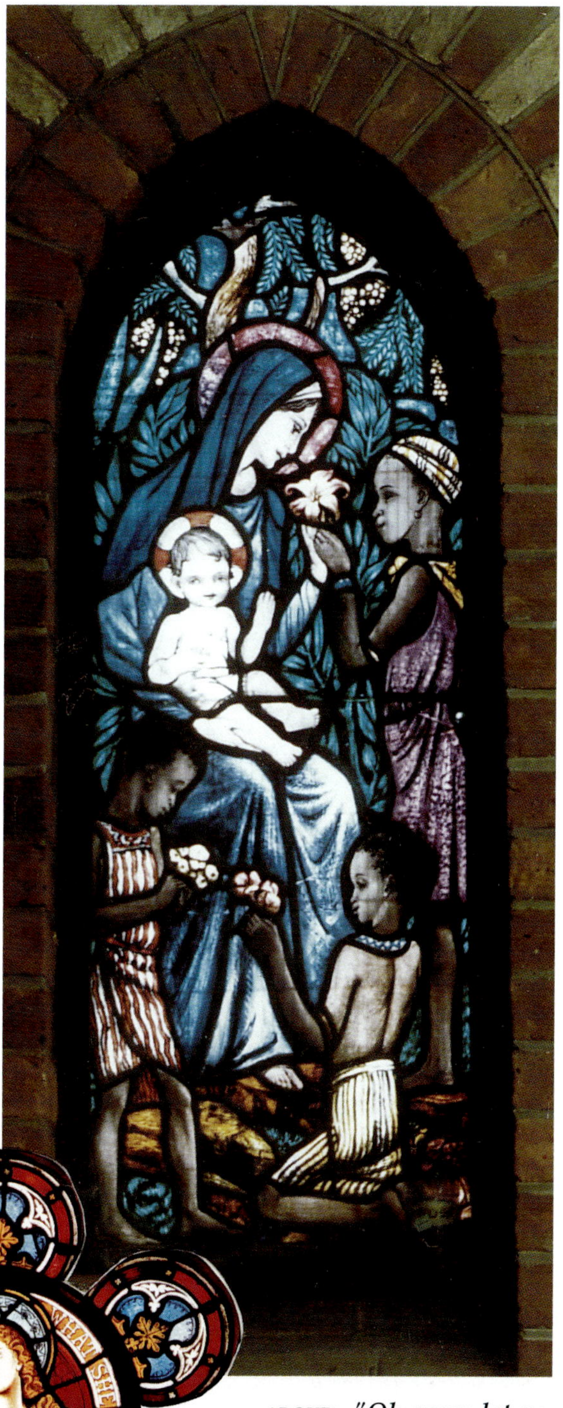

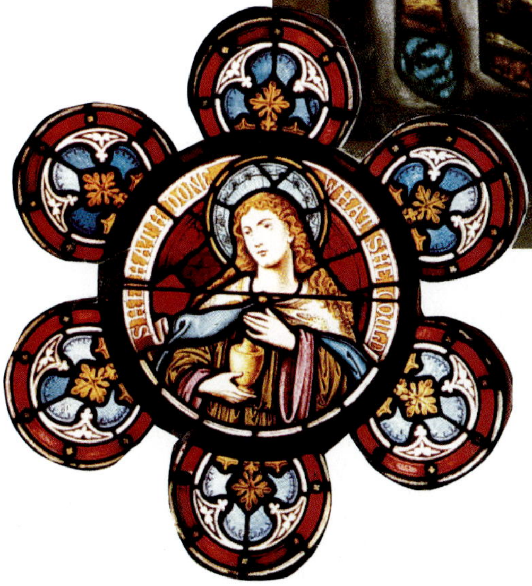

OPPOSITE PAGE FROM TOP LEFT: New glass in old setting at Canterbury House; first South African window; schoolboys in Kingswood Chapel; 1820 Settlers at Commemoration Church; and FLOATING: rare flower-like medallions in Diocesan School for Girls chapel

ABOVE: "Oh come let us adore him..." at St Philip's Anglican Church in Fingo Village

OTHER FAITHS — AND ST FIG'S

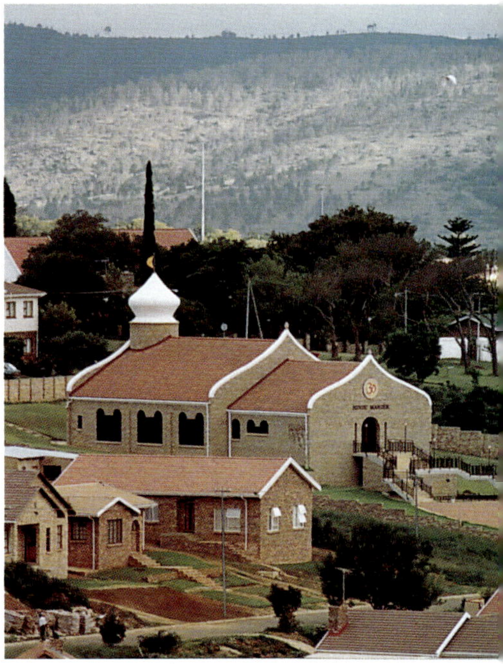

The dome of the new Hindu temple has joined Grahamstown's dreaming spires. Set in a hillside suburb, a saffron pennant emblazoned with the sign of the sound of the universe — AUM — flutters from the pinnacle to lift mundane minds to higher thoughts.

Inside, elaborate figures of the deities line the altar. Ganesha, the Elephant God; Shiva, the God of Destruction and his consort, Parvati; Radha and Krishna, and the Goddess Ambama. Central to the life of Grahamstown's small Indian community, colourful traditional ceremonies are faithfully observed, with Diwali— the Festival of Lights — the main event on the calendar.

It marks the beginning of the Hindu New Year in October or November, depending on the phases of the moon, celebrated over five days. Numerous lamps spread brightness, signifying the victory of light over darkness, knowledge over ignorance and good over evil.

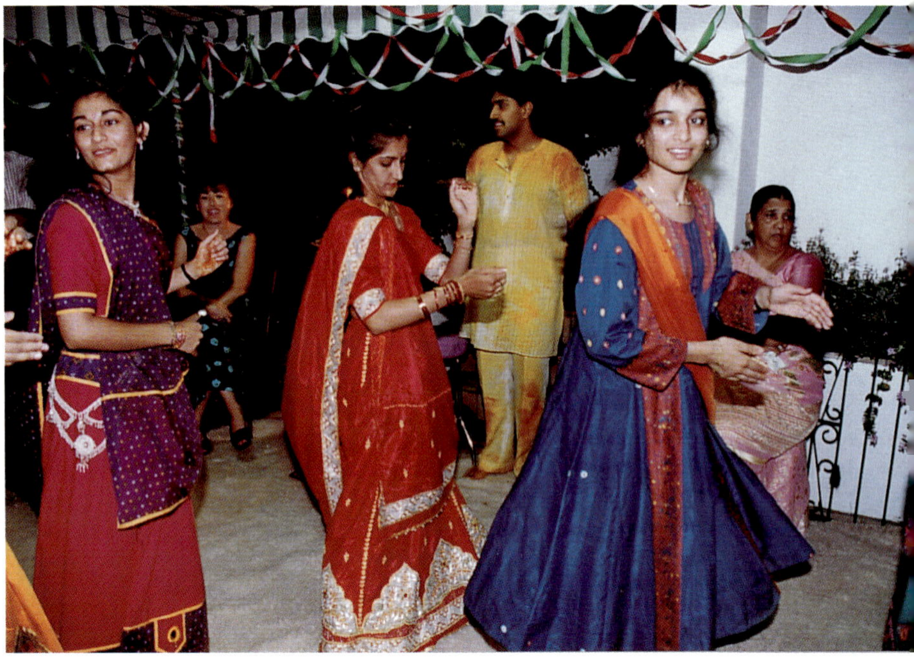

The most unusual sanctuary in Grahamstown is way down in York Street, in a rambling mansion that has seen many reincarnations. An upstairs meditation room contains the shrine from the Buddhist retreat centre which used to be in Nieu Bethesda, famous for the Owl House created there by Helen Martins.

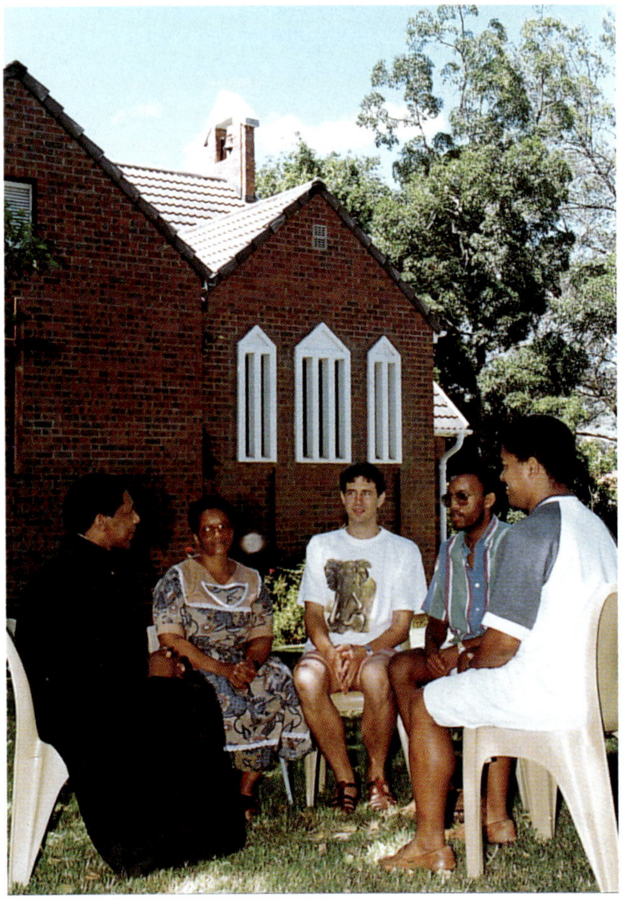

Dharma Arya Akong Rinpoche, widely revered teacher of the Karma Kagyu tradition of Tibetan Buddhism, inaugurated the shrine room one peaceful Grahamstown afternoon when only the sound of chirruping insects and the striking of a little brass gong interrupted the meditative silence. Cheerfulness keeps breaking through the group's activities, however. Particularly merry festivities welcome, the Tibetan New Year (Losa) near the beginning of March, each with an evocative name like Wood Hog Year, Fire Mouse Year or Wood Ox Year, and with a predominant female or male force.

Sadly, Grahamstown's Jewish community — never large — has now dwindled to such an extent that the traditional Friday Sabbath is only marked during Rhodes University terms, when students bolster the attendance, ensuring that there will be the 10 men required for the service.

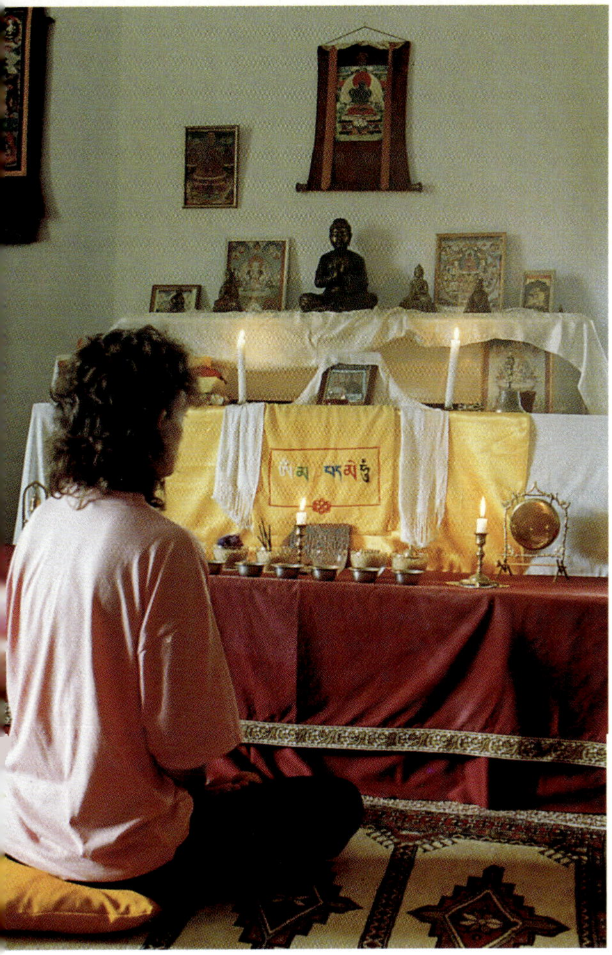

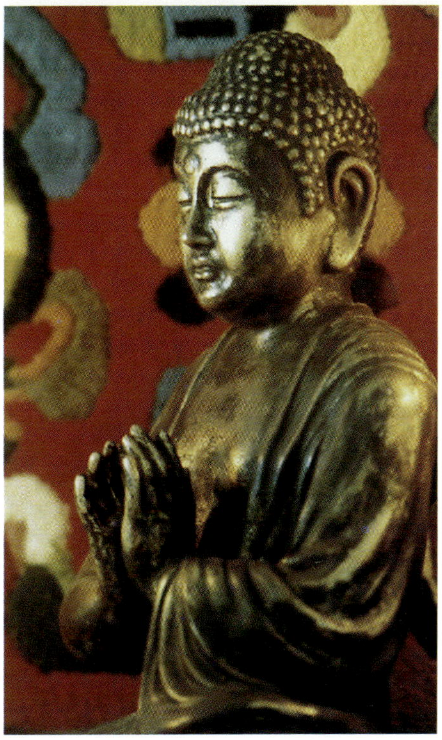

"Different creeds are but different paths to reach the Almighty. Various are the ways that lead to the house of the Lord. Every religion is but one such path that leads to God."

— **Sri Ramakrishna (1836-1886)**

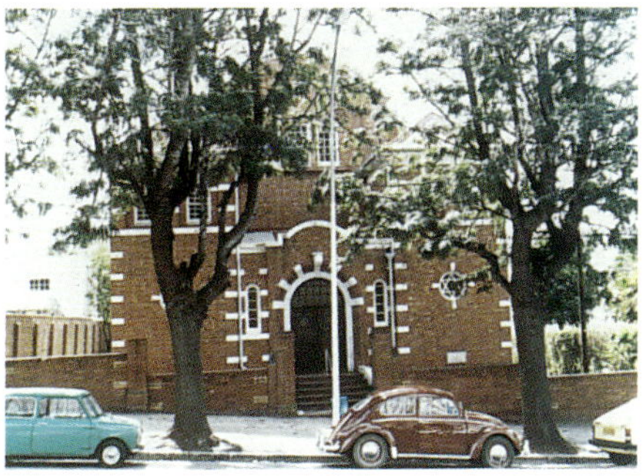

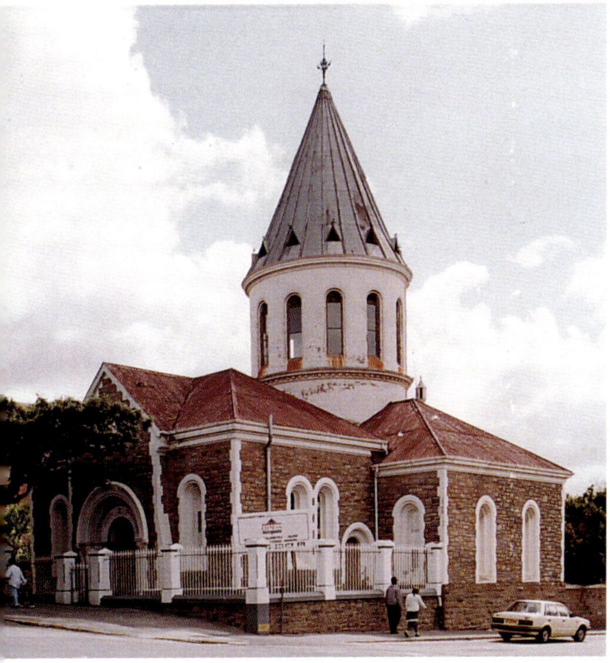

CLOCKWISE FROM TOP LEFT: ***Hindu temple amid modern homes, and traditional pre-wedding celebrations; meditative moods in Buddhist shrine; synagogue still serves but its former lantern-towered hall is now a fitness centre; and discussion at St Fig's***

The redbrick synagogue with Star of David windows in front was consecrated by Rabbi A Levy from Port Elizabeth on July 5, 1914. He took his text from Genesis Ch 28, v 17: "How awesome is this place! It is none other than a House of God, and this is a gate of Heaven."

As *The Grahamstown Journal* reported at the time, it was "*interesting to note, as showing the extent of religious tolerance and sympathy, that in the task of raising the necessary funds considerable assistance was rendered by non-Jewish citizens*". The building alongside served as the synagogue's hall for many years. Originally the St John's and Albany Masonic Lodge, its lantern tower symbolised the spread of the light of Freemasonry in South Africa.

Finally, St Fig's, as it is companionably called by locals. The College of the Transfiguration— the only provincial residential seminary in the Church of the Province of South Africa. Founded as St Paul's Theological College in 1903, it combined with St Bede's from Umtata in 1993 and the new name was chosen to indicate the change.

The atmosphere is relaxed and informal, as are teaching methods, but the end result is the same as it has been for more than 90 years. Every December, another group goes forward to become ordained ministers and spread the Word of Christ.

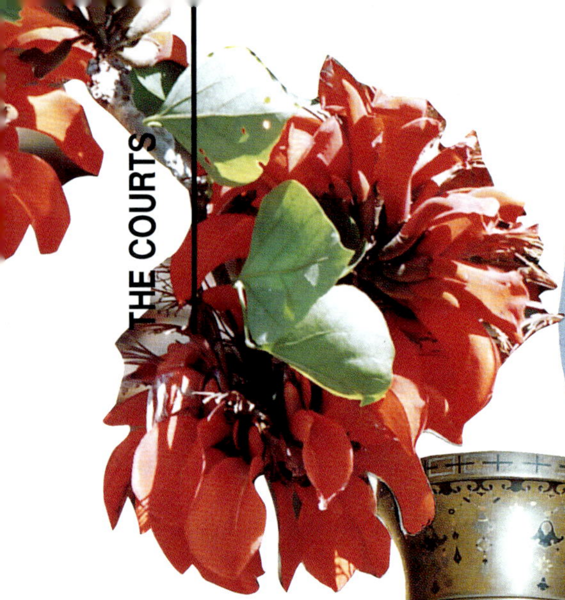

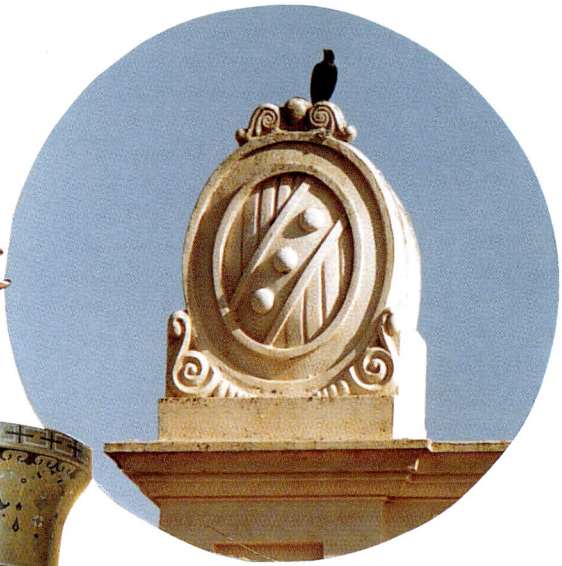

LEFT: Colourful combination — cora[...] trees frame traditional trimmings o[n] the old Magistrate's Court, while a new flag flies at its temporary quarters

ORDER IN THE COURTS

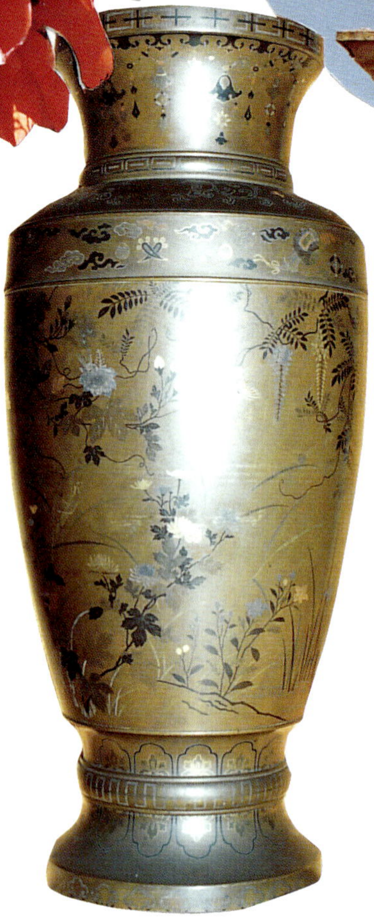

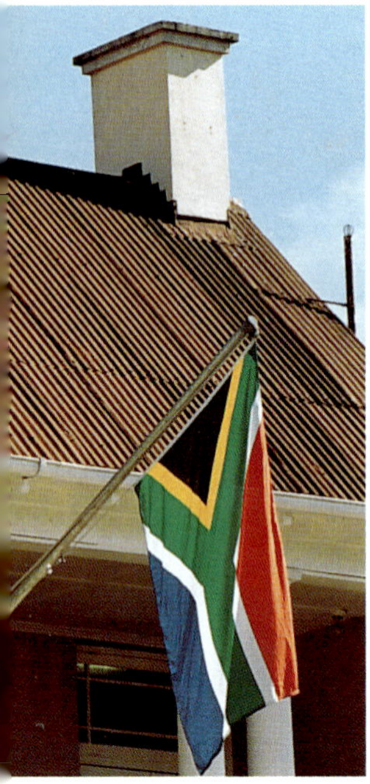

CENTRE: The Hay Vase, reminder of 1885 Supreme Court case

IN RECENT times the future of the Eastern Cape Division of the Supreme Court of South Africa has been hanging in the balance, if not the scales of Justice, with changing regional boundaries raising rumours of removal from Grahamstown. Whatever its future, its past record stands.

For more than 130 years it has served the wider community with distinction, including the Transkei and Ciskei until 1967 and 1981 respectively.

Latterly its extensive area of jurisdiction has stretched from the Storms River and Humansdorp, Uitenhage and Port Elizabeth to the south; to Graaff-Reinet and Murraysburg in the Karoo and Joubertina and Kareedouw in the Langkloof; north up to the Orange Free State, including Aliwal North and Colesberg; and west to the border areas of Queenstown, King William's Town, and East London.

Early records tell of the hazards which faced members of the court on circuit. Stormy weather in Tembuland and Griqualand East once caused a judge, who was travelling from Umtata to Kokstad via Port St John's and East Pondoland, to arrive after four days with no luggage and only the clothing he was wearing. Two of his staff who also braved the journey later surfaced to be told that they had been reported drowned.

The Eastern Districts Court was established in 1864. Proceedings originally took place in the Commercial Hall, opened in High Street in 1837 for civic occasions, theatrical presentations, balls and banquets. From the outside it looked most impressive, with four massive stone columns supporting a Greek pediment, but the amenities inside were limited, particularly the lighting. In 1891 *The Cape Law Journal* reported: "*The Eastern Districts is apparently presumed to be lit up when ten dip candles, in bedroom candlesticks, are placed in various positions... The effect at a recent evening sitting for the conclusion of a notorious murder case was quite ghostly.*" Part of this building is preserved in the structure of the present redbrick edifice erected in 1913.

Most citizens pass by, intent on their own affairs, totally unaware of the deliberations taking place within. An unusual tangible reminder of one of these courtroom dramas is in the Albany Museum — the Hay Vase presented to the editor of *The Cape Mercury*, George Hay, in 1885 by "*some of his fellow colonists to mark their appreciation of his conduct in publishing the facts and exposing the miscarriage in the Pelser case*", a vindication of the freedom of the Press, and of the right of free and honest

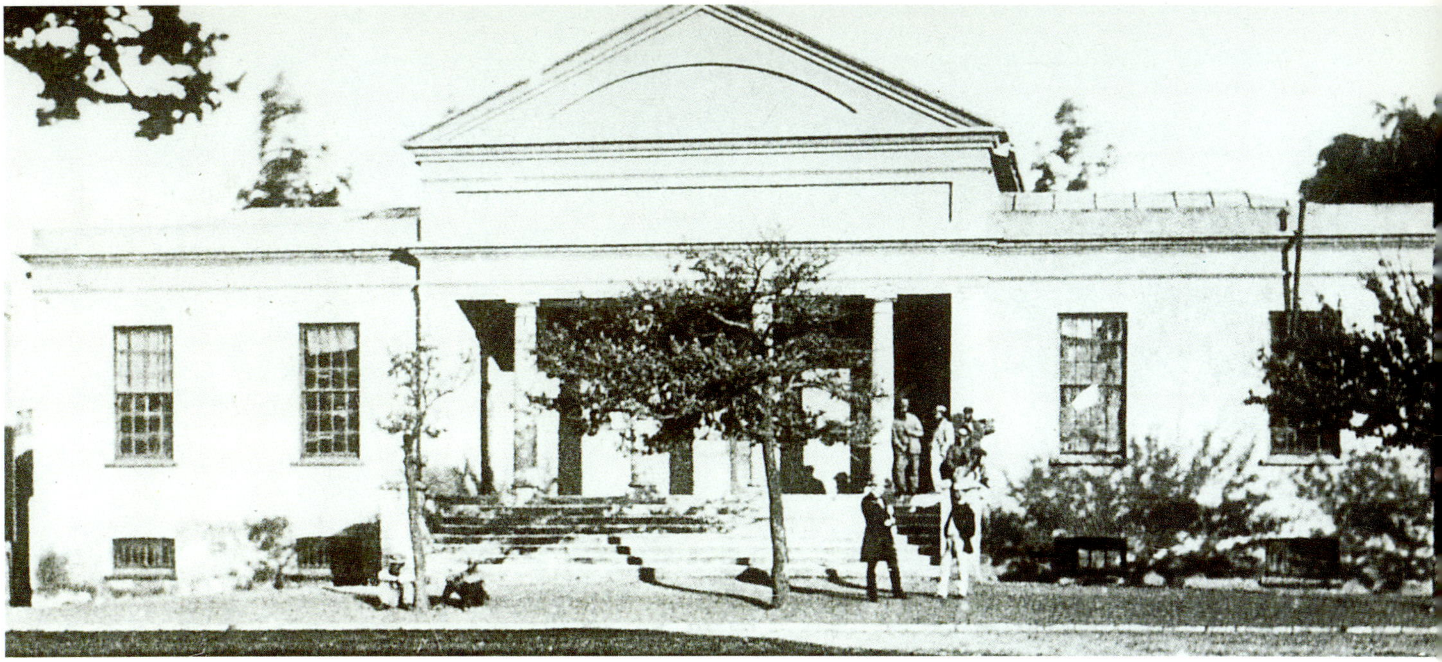

ABOVE: Commercial Hall 1837, where the Supreme Court started

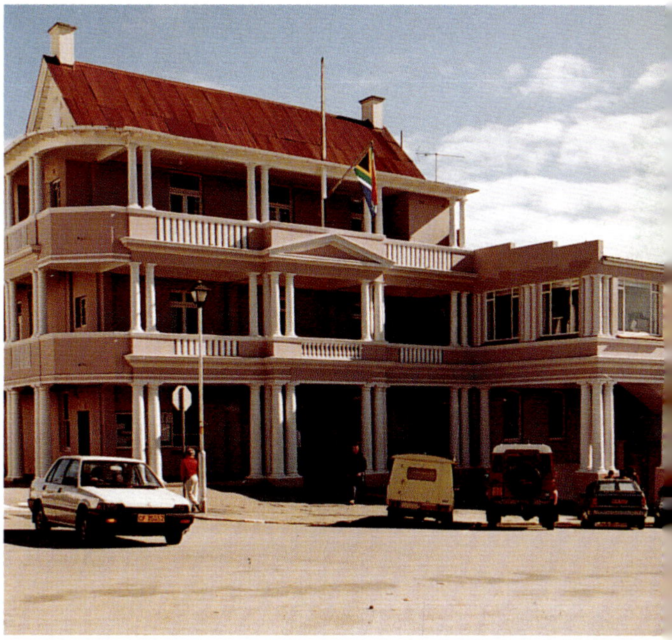

criticism of public officials, which continue to be of relevance some 100 years later.

Diagonally across the road, a stately trio of indigenous coral trees flourishes in front of the Magistrate's Court for the Albany District, a building of some magnificence designed by Sydney Stent, and completed in 1882 at a cost of sixpence a square foot.

In 1994 major additions, stretching right down to New Street, where the police station used to be, made a considerably larger hole in the budget. They necessitated the total relocation of the court to temporary accommodation in the old Grand Hotel, giving some offices the luxury of bathrooms *en suite*. The cash hall landed up in the lounge bar, with the actual courts designed to order in the former dining rooms and kitchen. Otherwise a case of business as usual, particularly in the bottle store below, which boasts one of the most extensive privately run cellars in South Africa.

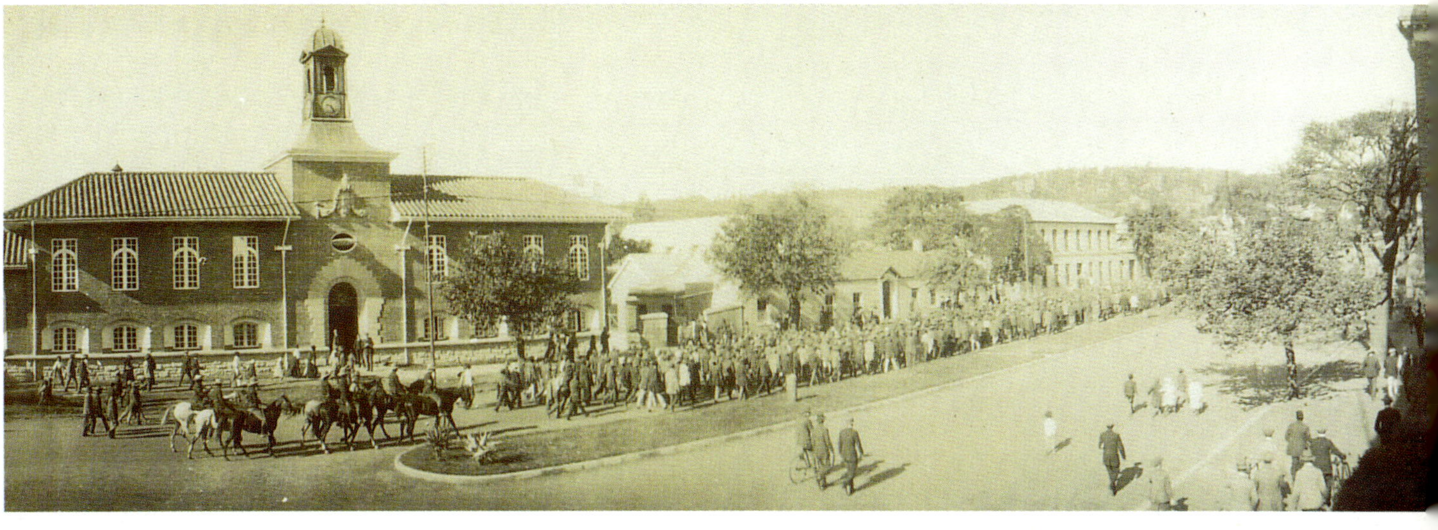

ABOVE-RIGHT: Five-star temporary accommodation for the Magistrate's Court in the old Grand Hotel in 1994

ABOVE: The 1917 township deputation to the Magistrate passing the newly built Supreme Court, now screened by trees

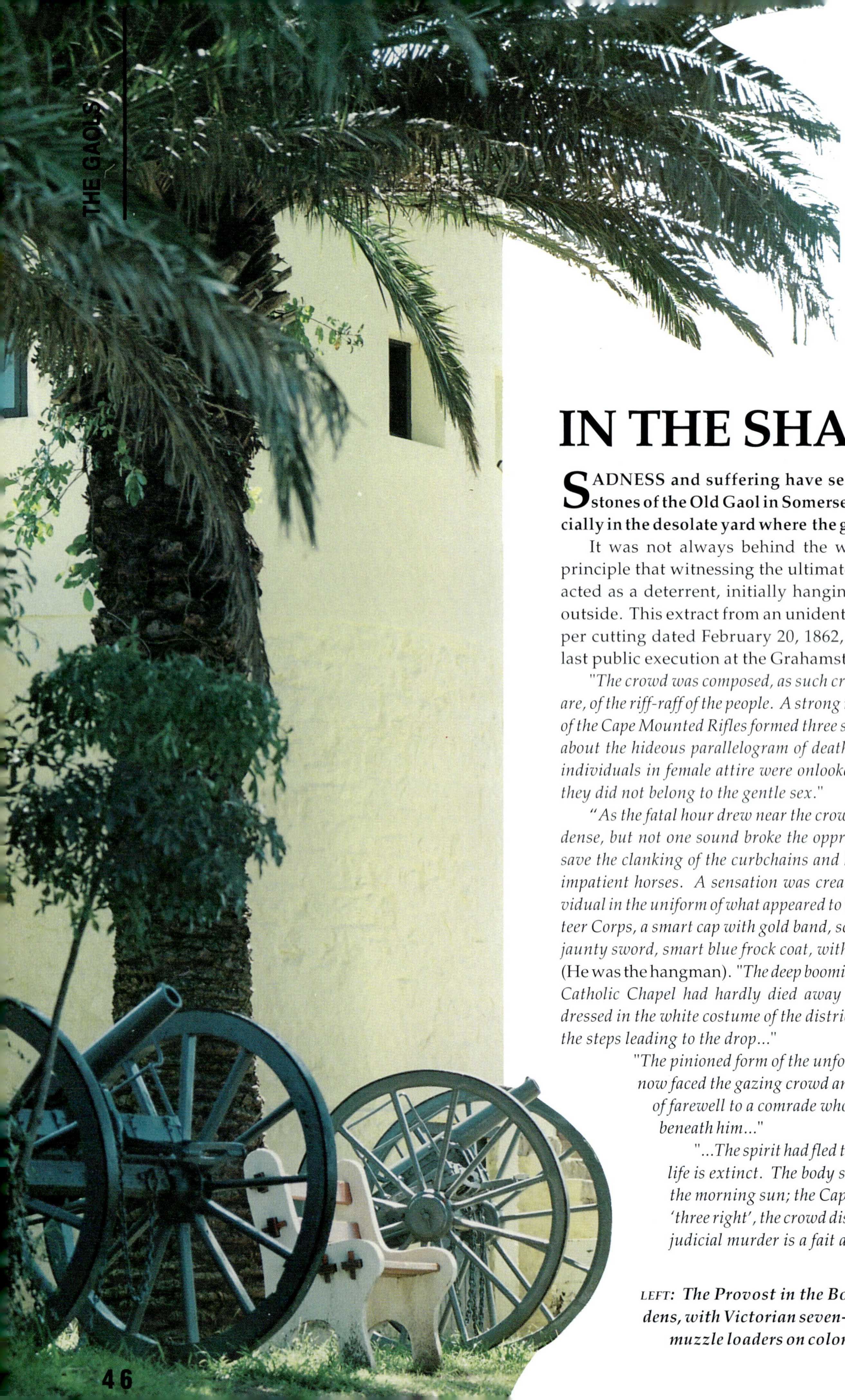

IN THE SHADOW

SADNESS and suffering have seeped into the stones of the Old Gaol in Somerset Street, especially in the desolate yard where the gallows stood.

It was not always behind the walls. On the principle that witnessing the ultimate punishment acted as a deterrent, initially hangings took place outside. This extract from an unidentified newspaper cutting dated February 20, 1862, describes the last public execution at the Grahamstown gaol:

"The crowd was composed, as such crowds generally are, of the riff-raff of the people. A strong mounted escort of the Cape Mounted Rifles formed three sides of a square about the hideous parallelogram of death. Two or three individuals in female attire were onlookers, but I think they did not belong to the gentle sex."

"As the fatal hour drew near the crowd became more dense, but not one sound broke the oppressive stillness save the clanking of the curbchains and headgear of the impatient horses. A sensation was created by an individual in the uniform of what appeared to be some Volunteer Corps, a smart cap with gold band, scarlet sash, and jaunty sword, smart blue frock coat, with red facings..." (He was the hangman). *"The deep booming from Roman Catholic Chapel had hardly died away when a figure dressed in the white costume of the district jail ascended the steps leading to the drop..."*

"The pinioned form of the unfortunate culprit now faced the gazing crowd and spoke a word of farewell to a comrade who was on sentry beneath him..."

"...The spirit had fled to its Maker, the life is extinct. The body sways slowly in the morning sun; the Cape Corps wheels 'three right', the crowd disperses, and the judicial murder is a fait accompli."

LEFT: ***The Provost in the Botanical Gardens, with Victorian seven-pounder rifle muzzle loaders on colonial carriages***

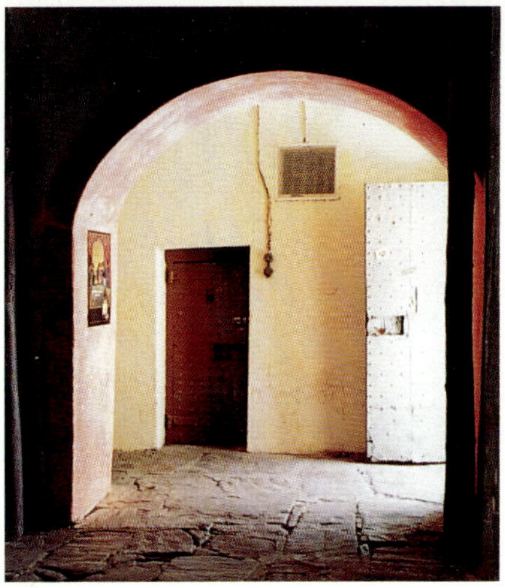

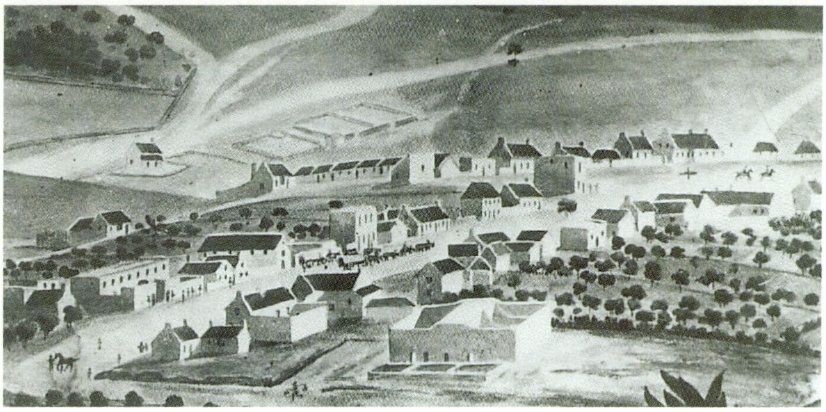

ABOVE: *Grahamstown, 1823, artist unknown; the Old Gaol, then brand new, is squarely upfront*

ABOVE: *Naught for your comfort in the Old Gaol*

OF THE GALLOWS

After 1862, a black flag was hoisted as a sign that the death sentence had been carried out within the prison walls. The Old Gaol was built in 1823, and was still in use as recently as the 1970s.

It was designed to hold 200, but numbers varied, rising to an unbelievable 2 748 in 1857. That same year, daily rations are recorded as including one pound of meat and one pound of bread per adult inmate, an interesting sidelight on the diet of the day.

Grahamstown's first gaol was the Yellow House, round the corner in High Street. Dating back to 1813, it is the city's longest surviving building, and the settlement was planned from it in 1814.

The Provost prison in the Botanical Gardens gets its name from the Provost-Marshal responsible for the maintenance of order in military camps. It was completed by the Royal Engineers in 1838 to an ingenious wheel-like design based on Jeremy Bentham's 18th century panopticon system for ceaseless surveillance of prisoners. Each window of the guardroom commands a view of at least two of the eight cells, complete with individual exercise yards.

Now part of the Albany Museum, the Old Provost has a craft shop at its hub. Previous voluntary occupants included a Rhodes student commune which declared it a republic and kept their own flag flying.

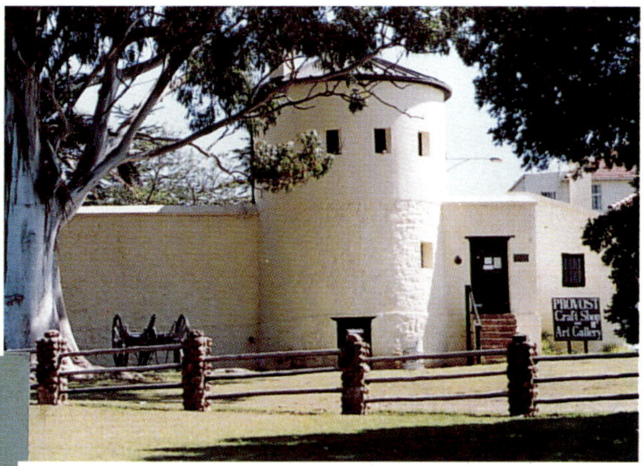

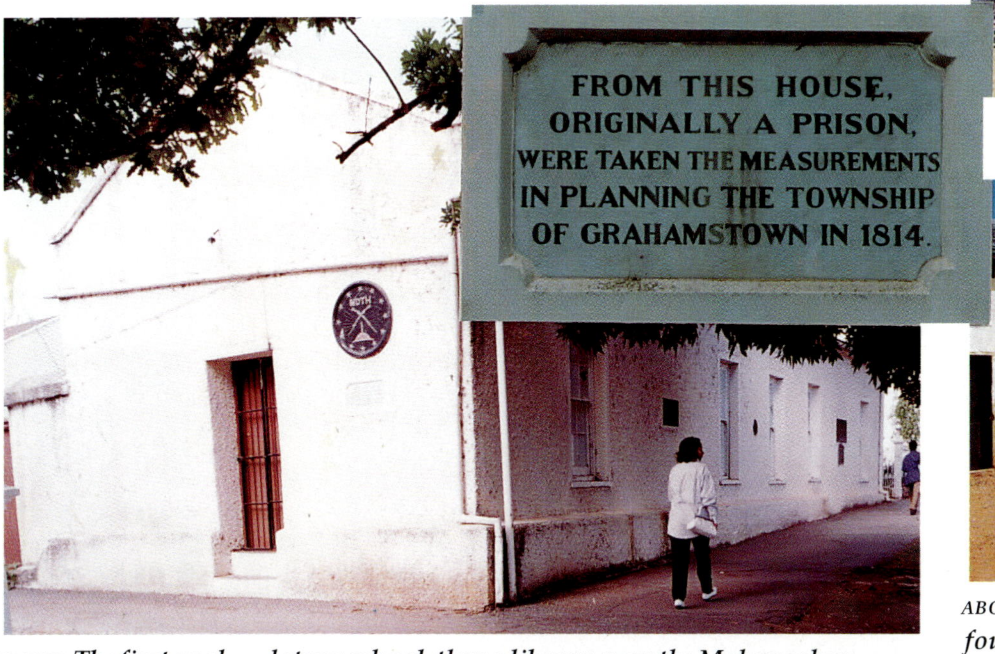

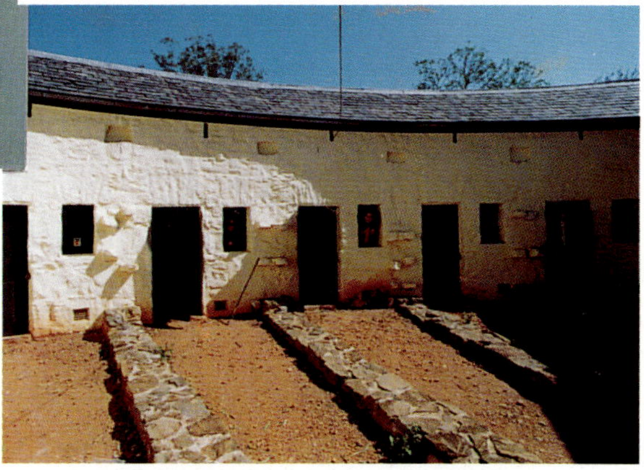

ABOVE: *The Old Provost outside; inside, foundations of cell-yard divisions remain*

ABOVE: *The first gaol — later a school, then a library, now the Makanaskop Shellhole of the Memorable Order of Tin Hats (MOTHS)*

DIG THIS!

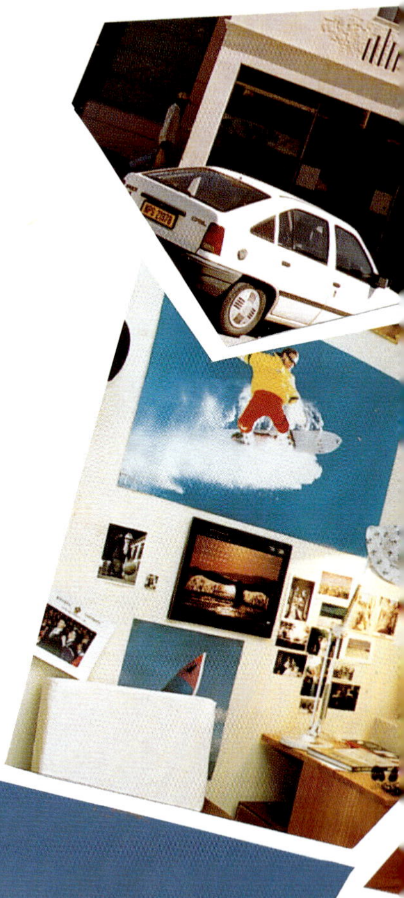

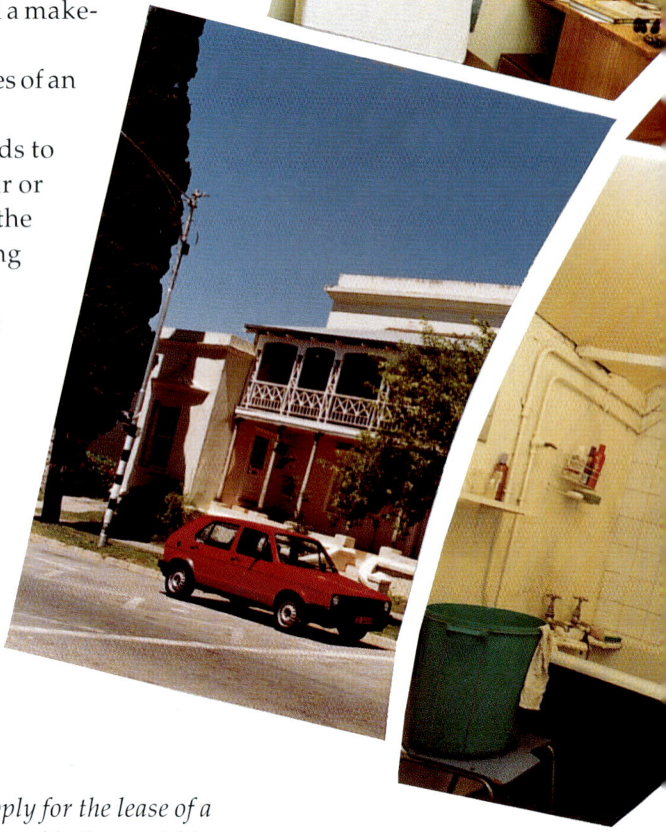

City of Saints, Sinners— and Students, springing fresh and green. Regular Rhodents hole up in residences on campus in comparative comfort and run with the pack. Others go for the independence gap and become Oppidans — Latin for those who live in the town.

Another breed entirely. Intrepid individualists, robust and resourceful — they have to be to cope with the rigours of life in Grahamstown's astonishing range of 'digs'.

Anything from a Victorian villa beneath burgeoning bougainvillea to an unrevived Gothic dive; a National Monument with pagoda windows to a settler cottage with wonky floorboards, bats in the leaking roof, and a make-shift shower in the outside storeroom.

Not to mention lurking landlords, many of whom are ladies of an uncertain age with Garfield cats.

The urge to move into a place of one's own generally leads to a close encounter of an unexpectedly intimate kind with four or five other free spirits who have to share everything from the telephone account to the kitchen sink, food shopping, cooking duty and getting the washing dry without it's being stolen.

Décor varies from traditional with a touch of tech to life *à La Bohème;* essential transport from bicycles to beat-up cars with character and class.

The pulsating parties of yore when whole neighbourhoods rocked round the clock are fewer and further between in the No Nonsense Nineties. But every now and then, especially in the carefree first term or on jasmine-scented spring nights, youthful spirits rejoice reverberatingly.

As one Oppidan puts it: "The fun about 'digs' life is that it spans a particularly crazy, spontaneous stage of your life, resulting in a kind of communal funny farm existence which one can only call experience."

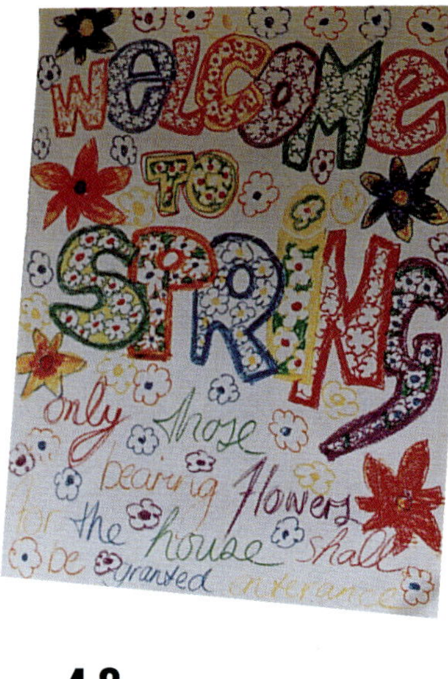

"Mature students are invited to apply for the lease of a four bedroomed residence with modern ablutions within several hundred paces of the Cathcart Arms. A monthly rental of R1500 includes the services of a gardener to tend to the spacious garden. Chars and stablehands will be for the tenant's own account. Kindly contact the advertiser during reasonable hours for an appointment to view. Livestock, excessive frivolity, and drama students will be frowned upon."

— Classified advertisement in *Grocott's Mail*, November 9, 1993

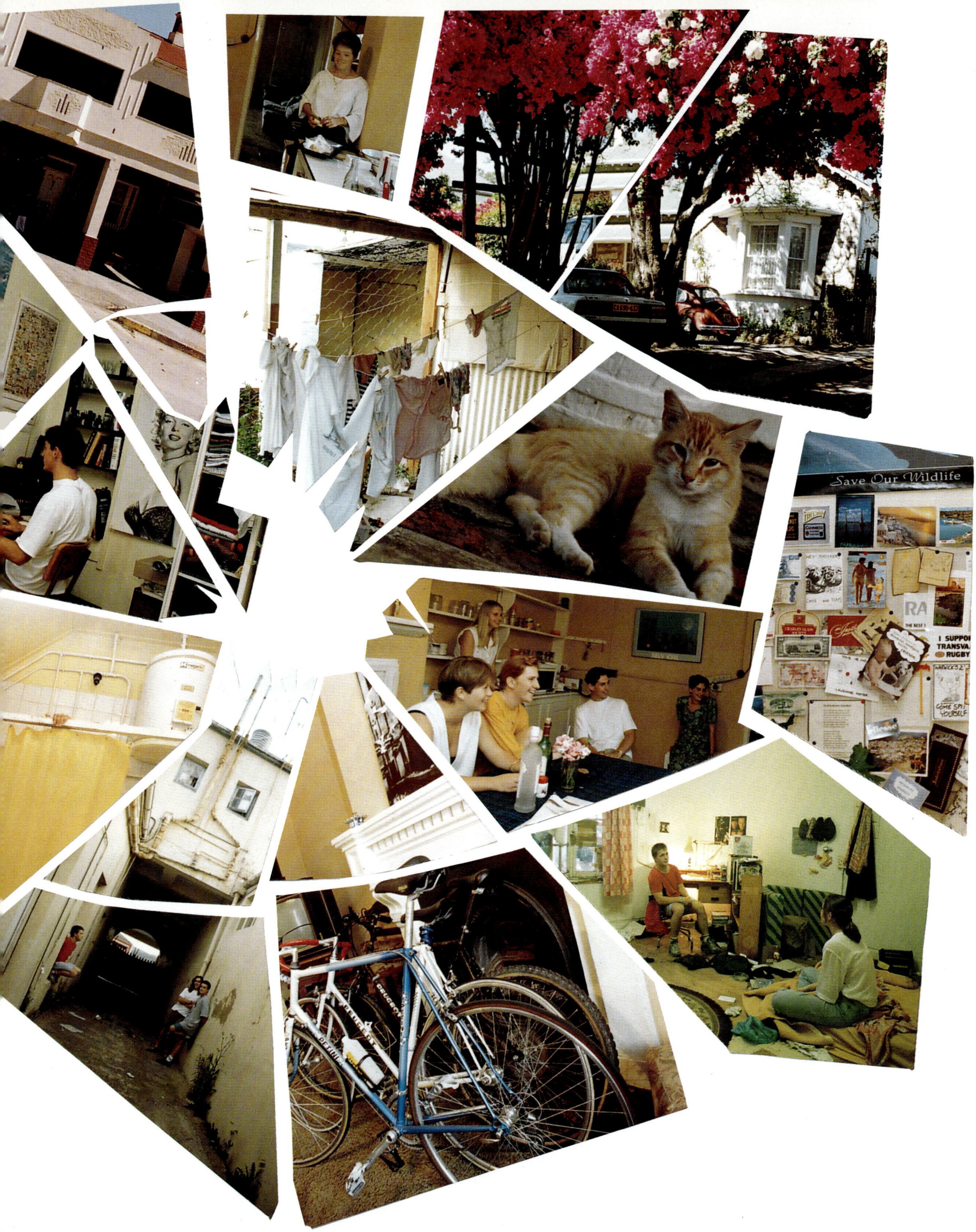
Save Our Wildlife

Enduring Old

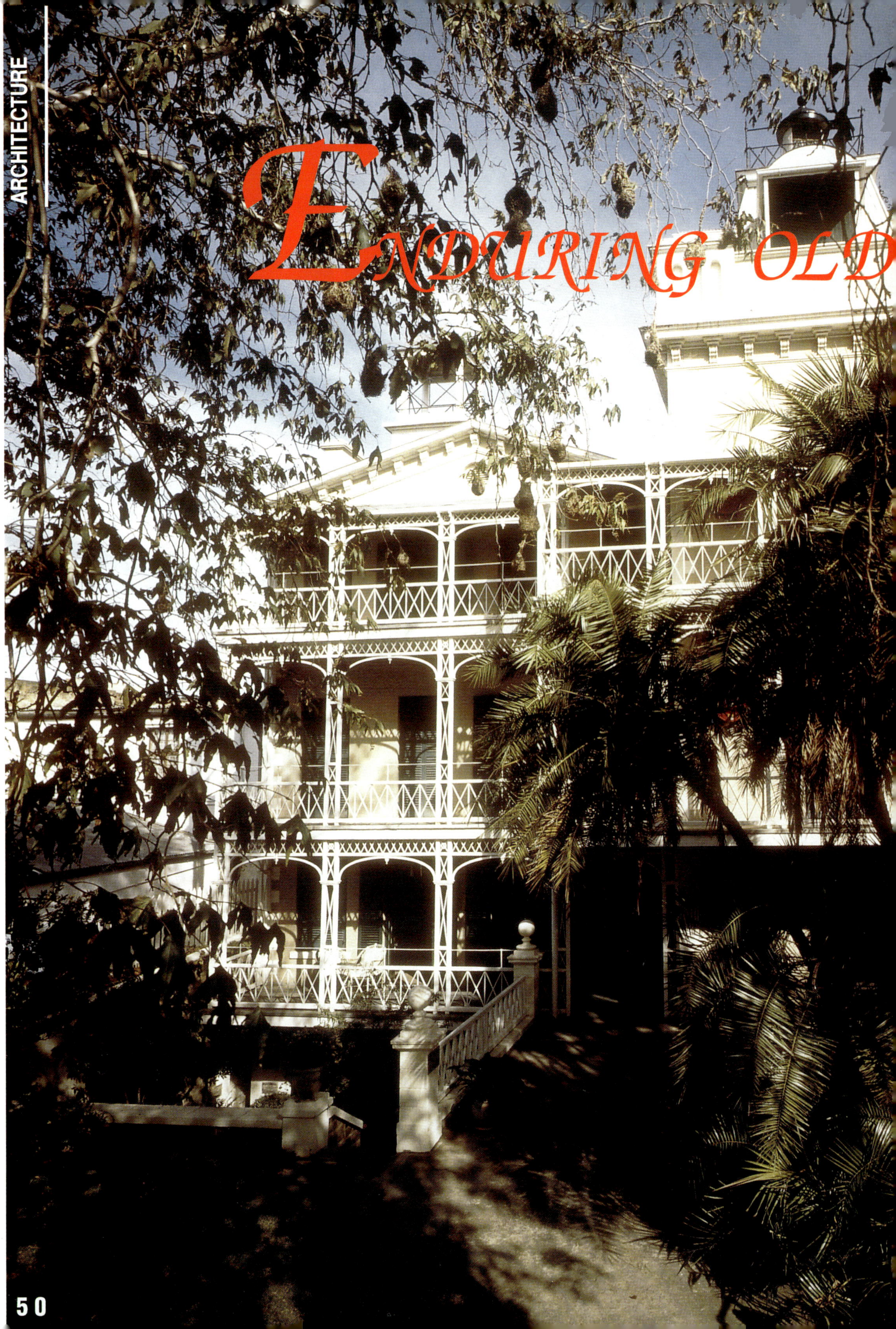

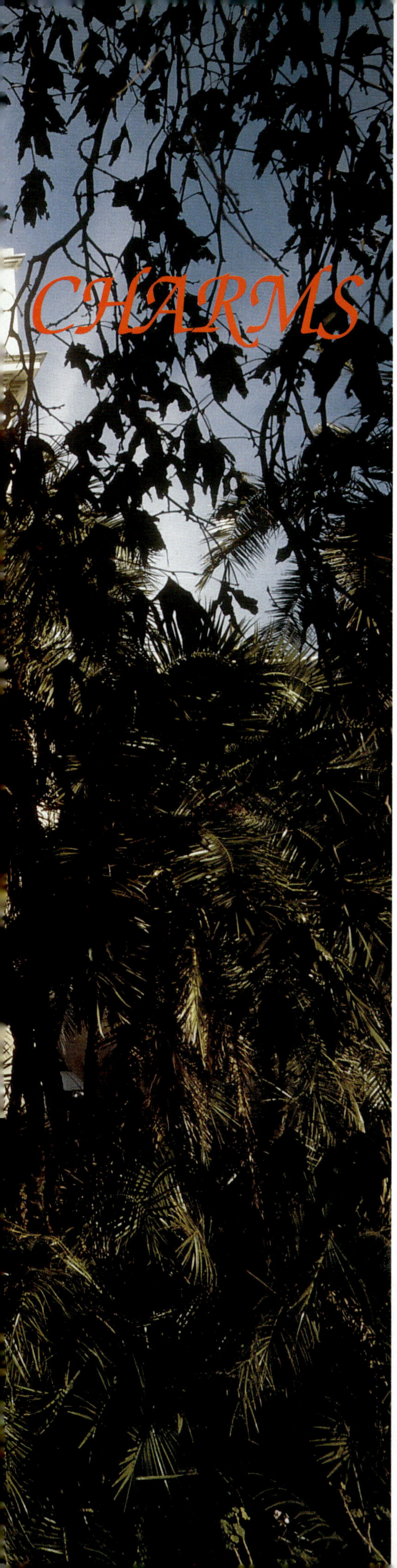

CHARMS

REAMS have been written about Grahamstown's unique architectural heritage. It is not that the individual buildings are such beauties — although there are some real stunners amongst them — but rather that so many are still here as their makers intended, toeing the street line on long narrow plots.

Together their enduring old charms are irresistible. Especially at night when shadows tactfully hide their inevitable wrinkles.

By day, a genteel shabbiness prevails. No glamorous facelifts and often in need of a touch of paint, which only makes them more appealing — for these are the genuine article. Not the Lost City, but a lost world of early Cape, Georgian, Victorian and Edwardian edifices with some grandly Gothic Revival churches — that 13th century ecclesiastical style which captured the 19th century imagination, and haunts us still.

Narrow lanes lead to unexpected vistas, arched entrances enchant. Trees uproot the pavements, frequently bringing the populace to grazed knees, but their spring finery, summer bloom, autumn gold, and stark winter silhouettes are worth falling for.

Gentle delights rather than sensational sights, radiating from the historic heart into tranquil suburbs, where Victorian villas and some surprisingly stately homes hold sway amid schools which are surrounded by the playing fields of this other Eton.

Queen of the scene is the Observatory Museum in raffish Bathurst Street, a dignified dowager with the prettiest backside in the country. Tiered like a wedding cake and fronded by an oasis of *Phoenix reclinata* palms flourishing in a slightly cracked well.

Yet ask most people which is their favourite and they will wax lyrical about some ancient stone wall they make a point of passing every day that speaks more eloquently of the past than any edifice. The National Monuments' Council has not put plaques on them — perhaps it should. The one below is on St Bartholomew's Church and there are some 70 like it scattered throughout the city. If you seek our monuments, look about you ...

LEFT: Sleeping Beauty — the Observatory Museum, Bathurst Street, viewed from the back garden, one of South Africa's magical places, and the first multi-storeyed building in the Eastern Cape

RIGHT: National Monuments' Council mark of approval

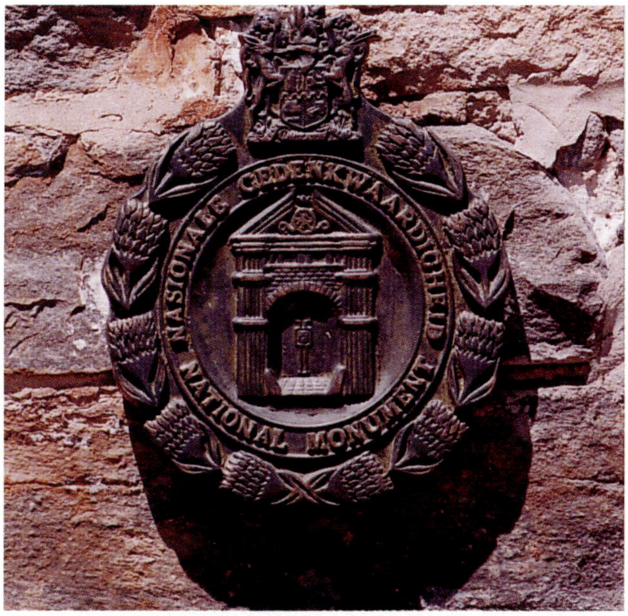

CLOCKWISE: *Muirhead and Gowie; Commemoration Church; super service station; masonic temple; Cathedral corner; and 1820 Settler's Memorial Tower in front of City Hall*

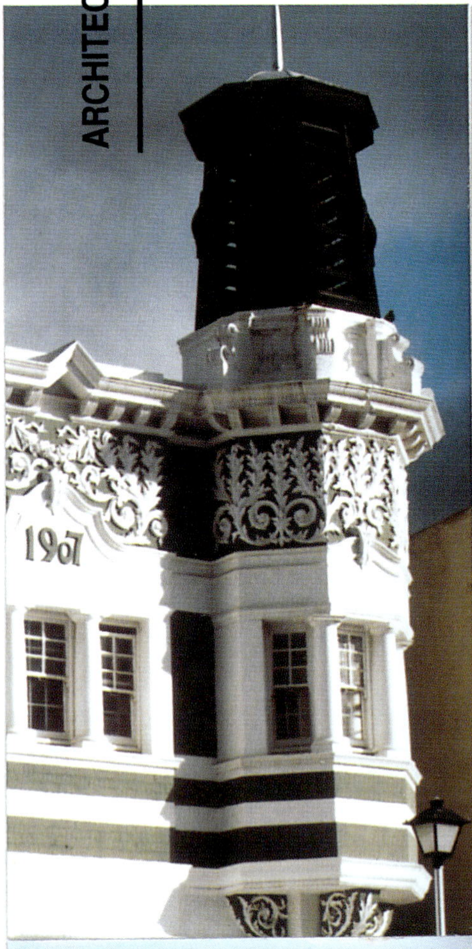

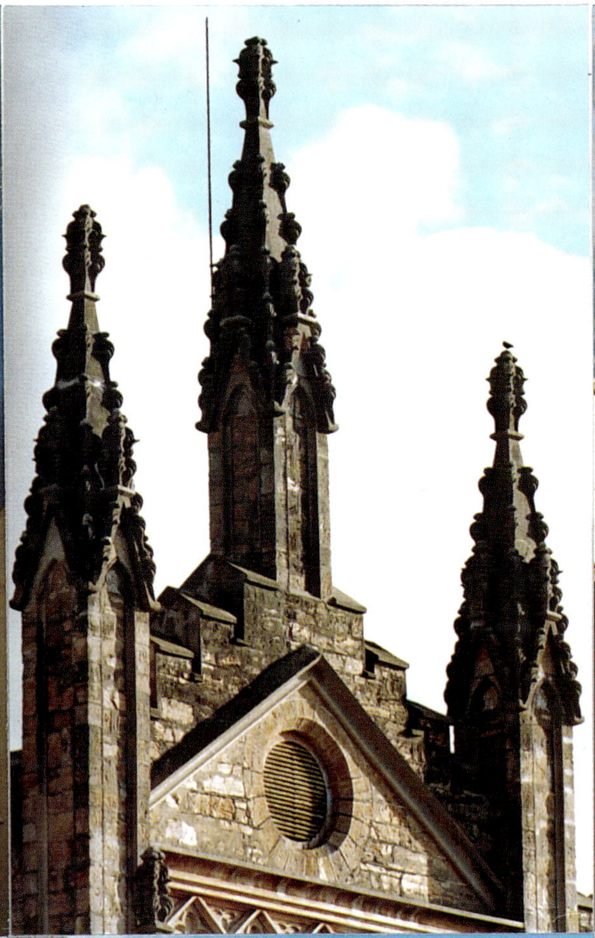

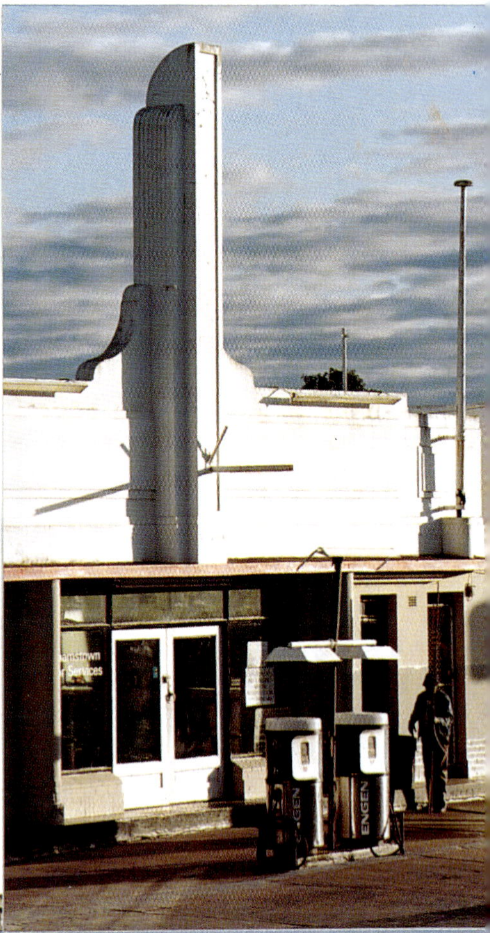

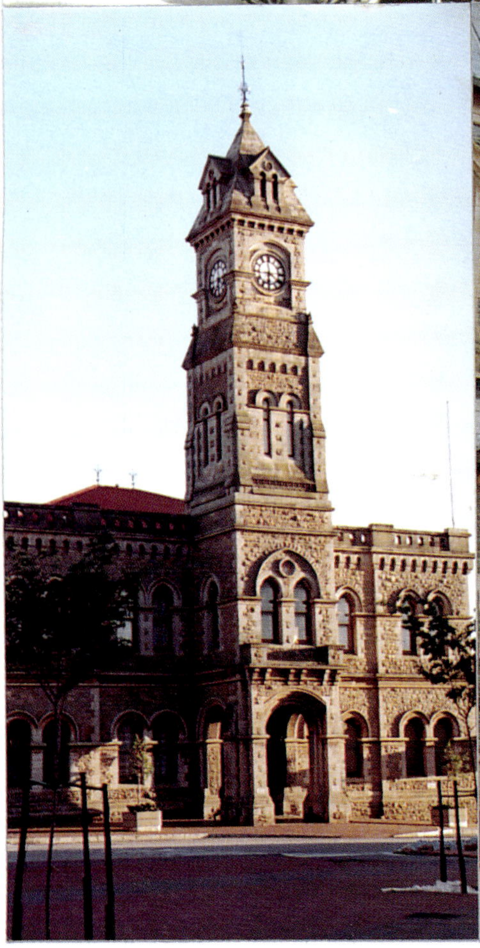

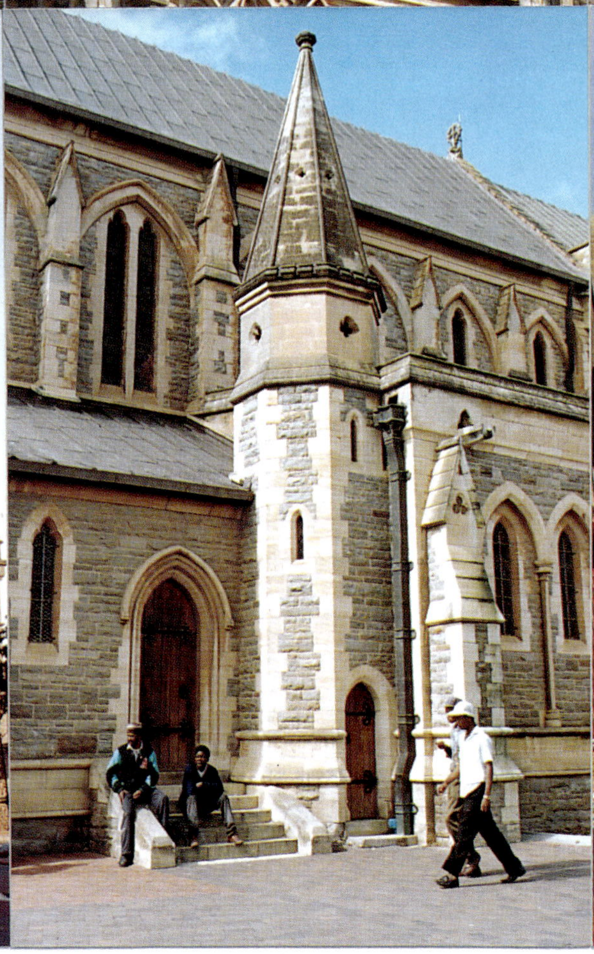

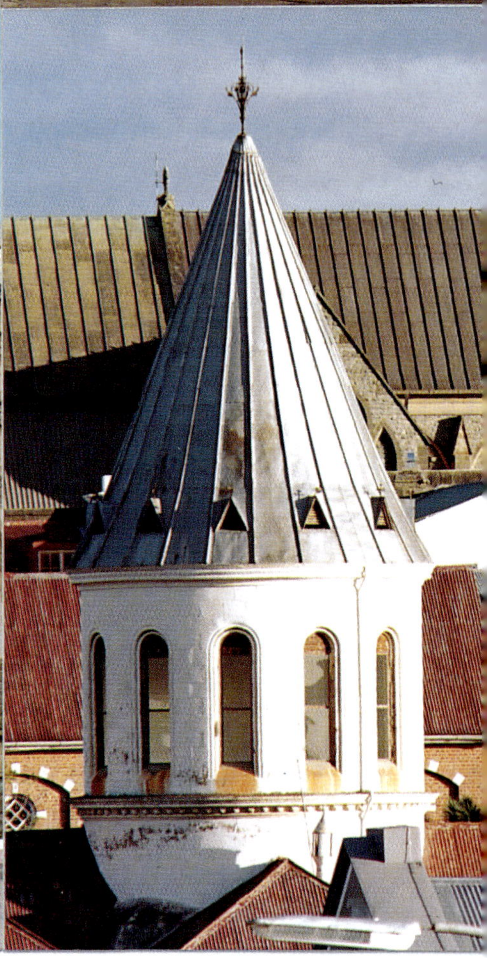

FAIRYTALE TURRETS AND TOWERS

EVEN the Grahamstown Motoring Services petrol station rises to unexpected heights with a distinctive Art Deco tower to fuel the imagination. From here, it is easy to set off on a turret trip, finding entrancing examples in the CBD— and a big surprise in the abandoned brickfields.

Making a firm stand on the Church Square, the Settlers' Memorial Tower initially almost did not get off the ground. The 50th anniversary of the 1820 Settlers' arrival was celebrated by the laying of its foundation stone, but it failed to rise as planned — tall, slender and alone.

Seven years later, the settlers' sons finally conceded that it never would, Grahamstown's imaginative reach having yet again exceeded its financial grasp. It was duly decided to incorporate it in the new town hall. This required some hasty redesigning to integrate the two, and explains why each has its own foundation stone bearing different dates.

Eventually the hall was publicly opened on May 4, 1882, and the tower inaugurated with due settler ceremony three weeks later, on May 24. Now in their second century, the odd couple's marriage of convenience has matured into a working relationship, not entirely harmonious, but totally inseparable.

Viewed from this vantage point, the Cathedral of St Michael and St George could be a little medieval hill village. Near the north-east corner is a fairytale tower with a little rounded door and quaint pepper-pot top. A traditional feature of Gothic cathedrals, it contains a staircase giving instant access to the Lady Chapel roof.

Across the square, the louvred black cupola on Muirhead & Gowie stands out starkly in the pastel parade. Missing for many years and carefully restored in the 1980s, it came as something of a shock to locals who had envisaged a romantically picturesque folly. It is in fact a ventilation duct — an early attempt at air conditioning.

More in the tradition of the Brothers Grimm is the conical silver roof of what started as a masonic temple, became the synagogue hall, was later a nursery school, and is now going strong as a fitness centre. Age obviously cannot dim nor custom stale its infinite variety.

The correct architectural description of the stalagmites on the Methodist Commemoration Church is "buttresses continuing through into highly decorated flèches".

The tower rearing up in the outback beyond West Hill on the other side of town, beyond the Rhodes University athletics track, is enough to bring anyone to a halt. A chimney erected in 1902 on a now defunct brickfield, it had its moment of international glory in the 1980s when it featured in *The Guinness Book of Records* as the tallest lavatory in the world. Those were the days of "Brickies", a student hot spot in an adjoining barrel-vaulted kiln where the accoustics were mind-blowing and the revels likewise.

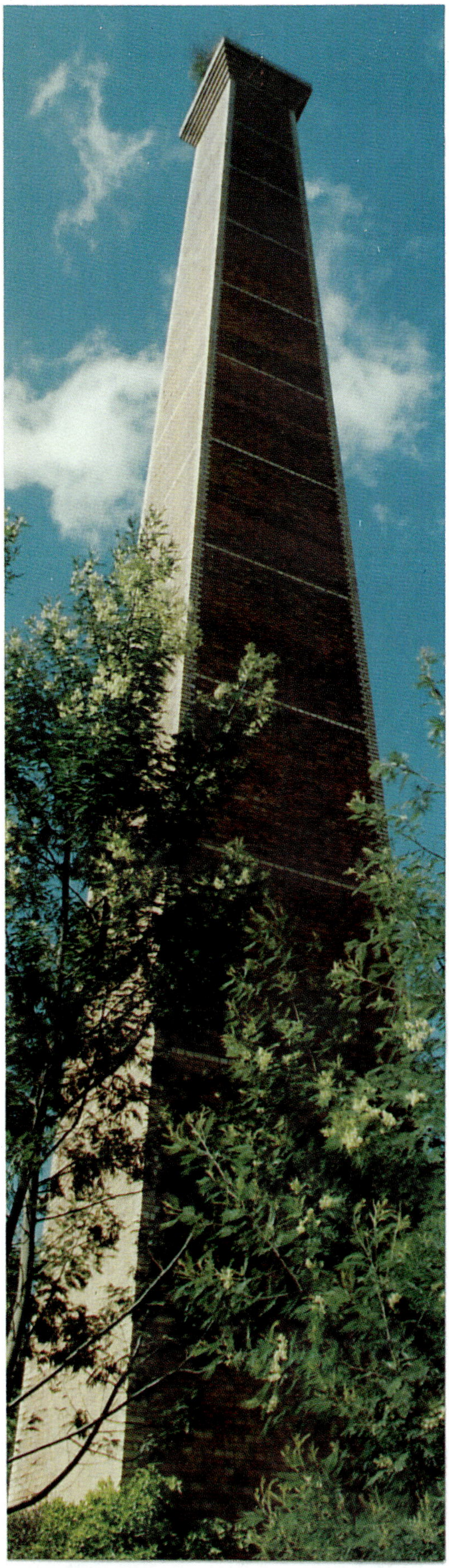

ABOVE: *The tallest toilet in the world*

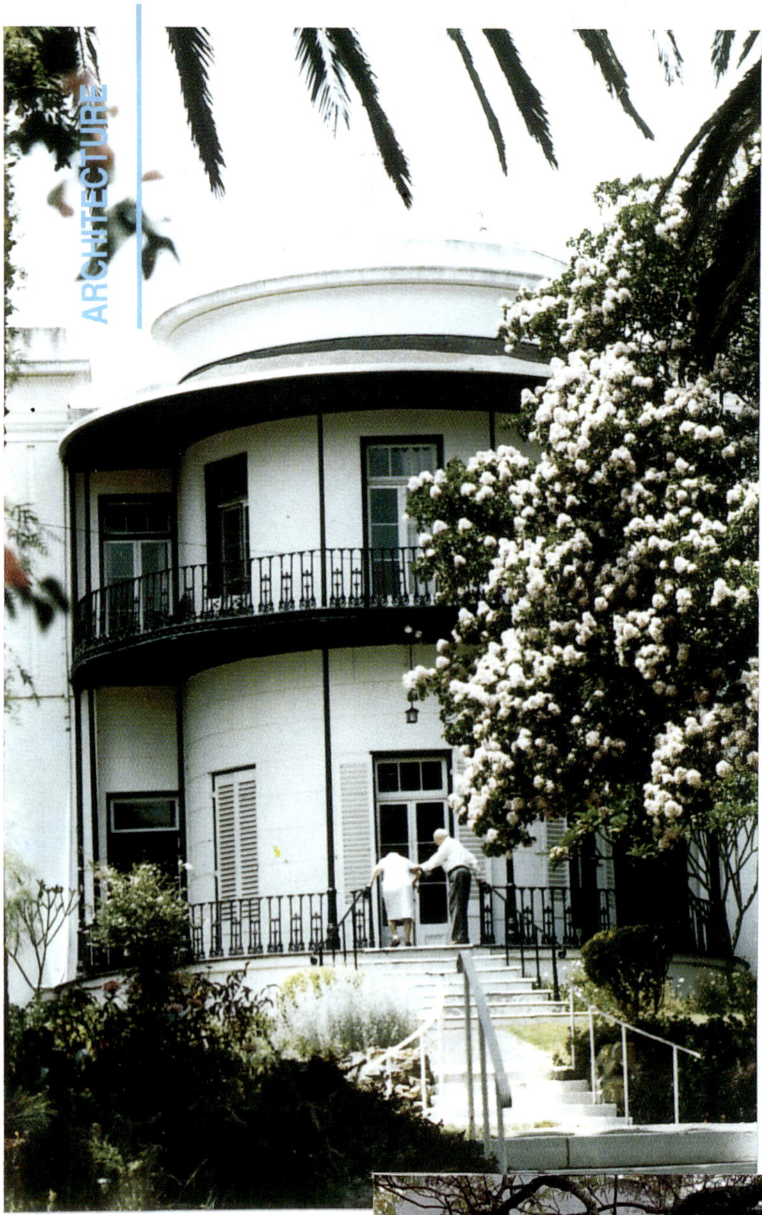

STATELY

DREAM houses ... The genuine article — not the all mod cons plus jacuzzi variety extolled by big city property supplements. In fact, modern conveniences are obviously afterthoughts, ingeniously added by plumbing the depths and other odd corners. Sing hey for the stately homes of Grahamstown!

Romantic beauties of generous proportions, some shielded by trees which have grown up with them, like trusted family retainers. Others gallantly adapting to new demands— divided into flats, merged with schools and Rhodes University, their grounds reduced; their croquet lawns, tennis courts and stables paved over.

Worcester Street on West Hill is graced by a number of noteworthy residences such as *Mayfield*, with its Gothic arches and Victorian bow windows screened by evergreens, and *The Hawthorns*, a stucco villa plus pillared portico inspired by the owner's grand tour of Italy. Alongside is a solid stone double-storey designed for Lady Maasdorp, wife of Sir Andries Maasdorp, liberally iced with imported white filigree cast-iron — an unusual luxury in Grahamstown, where decorative wooden verandahs are the more modest mode.

The two most written about are elsewhere, tucked out of sight on opposite sides of town. *Woodville* — now part of the Brookshaw Home for serene-agers — is still surrounded by a secret garden, though the waterfall of wistaria no longer cascades over the semi-circular Trafalgar balcony which puts it among South Africa's architectural gems.

Its first owner (1861) was the Hon George Wood, who had started out as a penniless 1820 Settler lad and rose to become a Member of the Legislative Council. Handicapped after a fall, he installed what is thought to be the first private lift in the country, a mechanical device to convey him to the upper floor. Downstairs, the lofty reception rooms, library, and conservatory retain their gracious atmosphere, though the butler's pantry and wine cellar are no more.

Oatlands House — hidden by the suburb which takes its name from the original estate — was built in 1823 for Lt Col Sir Henry

ABOVE: "Woodville" with balcony. Now part of Brookshaw Home, it has been an orphanage, college hostel, and haunted house in previous incarnations

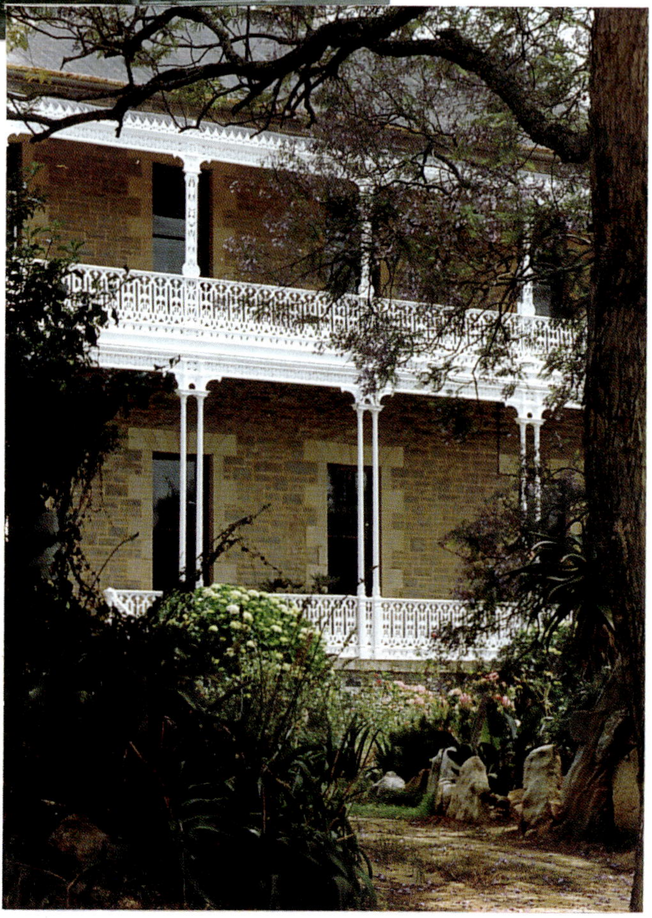

RIGHT: Lady Maasdorp's mansion in Worcester Street, a striking combination of stone and decorative cast-iron

Clockwise: Latterday Victorian Elaine Andrews completes the picture at Oatlands House; oak-shaded exterior; lamp-lit interiors

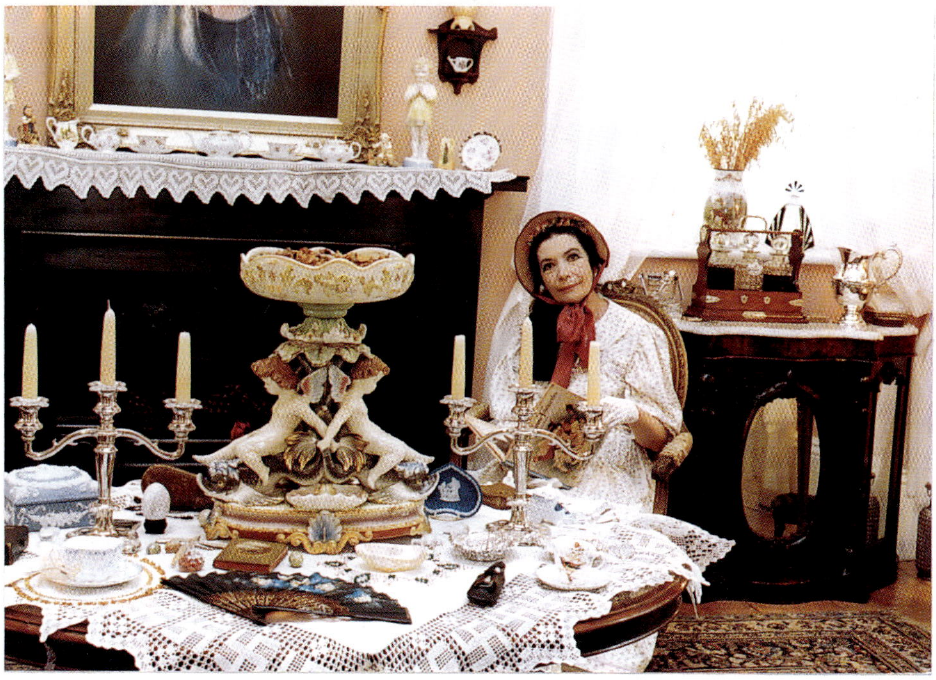

HOMES

Somerset, eldest son of the Cape Governor, Lord Charles Somerset, and commandant of the frontier forces for more than 30 years. He lived in it with his wife Frances and their 13 children until his posting to India in 1852.

It was the hub of the military and social world in the Eastern Province. All important visitors were entertained here, including Xhosa chiefs, who were accommodated in the guest cottages. One of them was much taken by the governess and asked if he could buy her as a wife. Since she was going back to England that week, Sir Henry unthinkingly agreed. This put him in an awkward spot a fortnight later, when the chief returned with 40 oxen in payment.

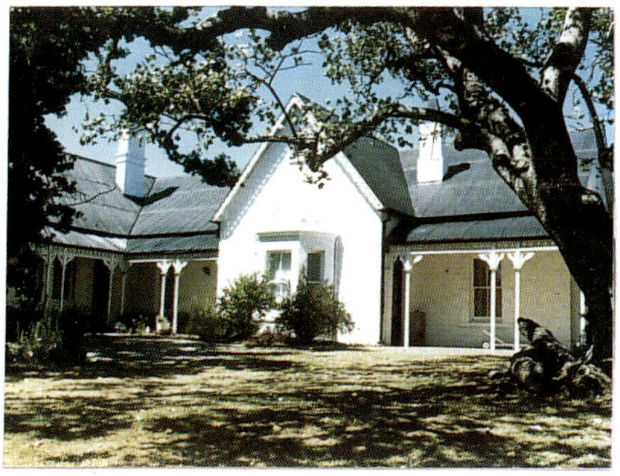

The current chatelaine, Elaine Andrews, has recreated the past so perfectly that it seems more real than the outside world. A Victorian gentlewoman personified, she has always worn the clothes of that period, and cares for her extensive collection herself, dusting and polishing, starching and ironing, on occasion sharing her exquisite retreat with those who appreciate the way of life she is trying to preserve. A national treasure in a proclaimed National Monument which continues to be a family home in the grand tradition.

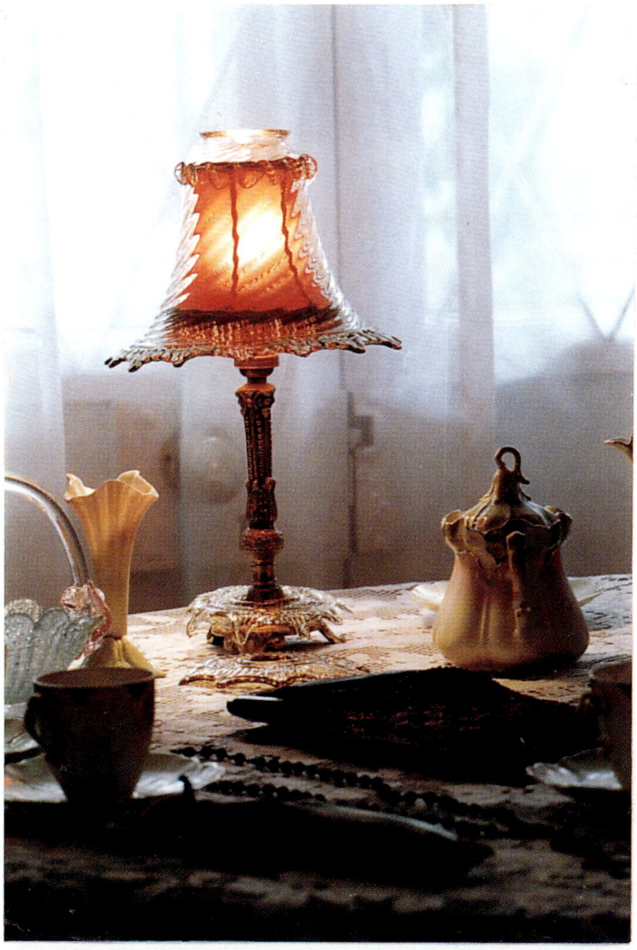

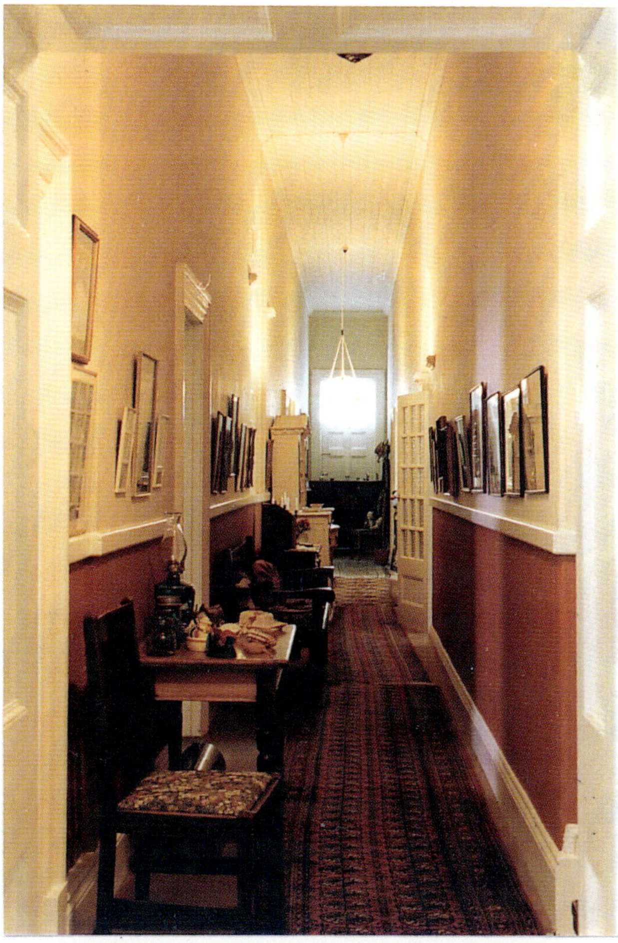

GRAHAMSTOWN has three castles to add to its straight-out-of-a-story-book atmosphere. The most imposing is St Patrick's Catholic Church in Hill Street.

It looked even more like something out of a medieval adventure saga when completed in 1844, with no trees to soften its strong Tudor Gothic Revival lines. Immediately called "The Castle" by locals, its stout stone walls made it an obvious place of refuge for many of them during the frontier disturbances of 1846 and 1851.

Its construction was largely due to the unflagging fund-raising of the Catholic military chaplain, Father Thomas Murphy, and the efforts of the Irish soldiers in the 27th Inniskilling Dragoons who gave their labour when free from military duty.

One of the men almost certainly connected with its design was Maj Charles Jasper Selwyn, appointed Commanding Royal Engineer on the Eastern frontier of the Cape of Good Hope in 1834.

CASTLES AND

"This castle hath a pleasant seat; the air nimbly and sweetly recommends itself unto our gentle senses."

— **Shakespeare, *Macbeth***

CLOCKWISE: ***St Patrick's Church all lit up for 150th anniversary; Selwyn Castle; and Salvation Army citadel***

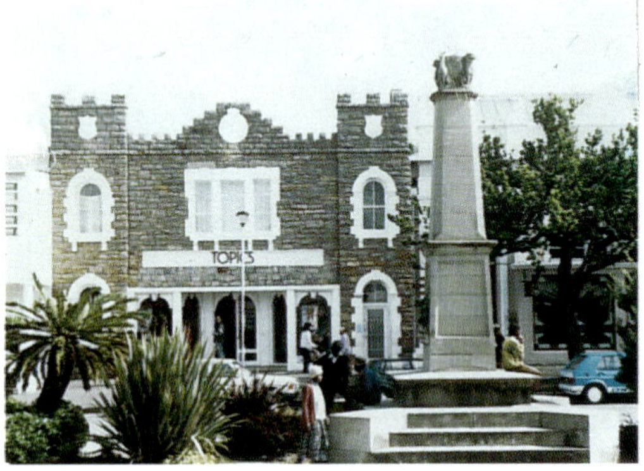

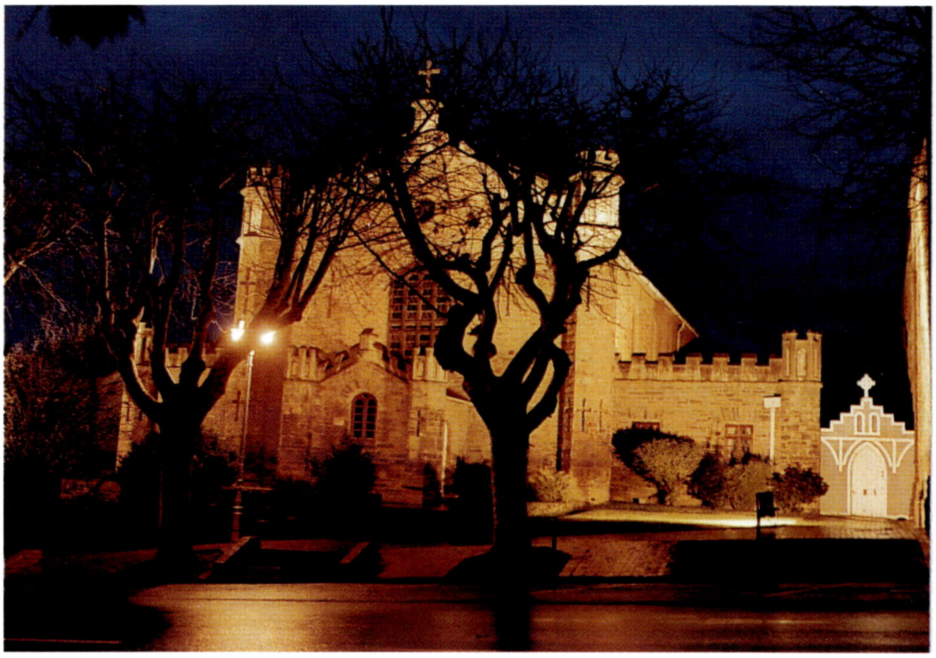

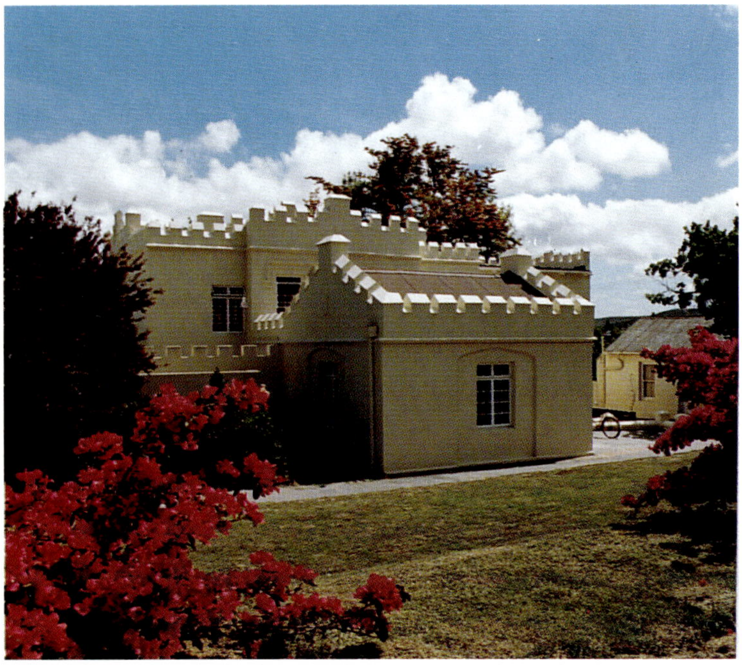

An Englishman's home is his castle, but not usually as literally as Selwyn Castle, which he built in Prince Alfred Street, heavily castellated and adorned with his family crest. It was so strongly criticized for its pretentiousness that it became an embarrassment to him and he moved out, offering it as the official residence of the new Lieutenant-Governor of the Eastern Province, Andries Stockenström, who entertained a number of black chiefs there during his two-year stay.

In the late 1890s it accommodated the overflow of boarders from Kingswood College, subsequently becoming an orphanage and then a Rhodes residence. It currently houses the Department of Anthropology.

The stone castle in High Street opposite the centenary monument was originally a Salvation Army citadel. Over the years it too has housed many different occupants, but continues to soldier on in its own dignified fashion.

PICTURE PALACES

"It is safe to say that, in recent years, no buildiing put up in Grahamstown has been more notable as a sign of definite advancement with the times as His Majesty's Theatre... Few, not even the most sanguine optimists, could have anticipated the sheer beauty and charm... Don't stand wonderingly outside. Come in and look over the building with me", invited the *Grocott's Mail* reporter in a feature to mark the gala opening on September 30, 1935.

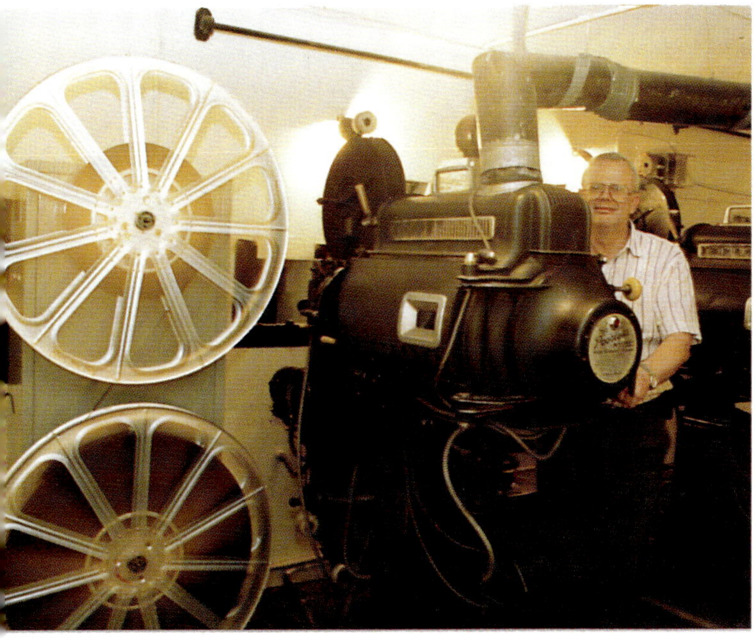

Off readers set, in mind's eye mounting the marble steps, pausing in the foyer "like a banking hall", marvelling at the rich crimson Arab velour plush seats, reverently treading aisles covered with soft-piled French grey carpet runners. Inspecting the orchestra pit in front of the stage and the talkie equipment of the most modern type, not forgetting the mechanical forced draught ventilation.

Some 60 years later, the right royal amenities have become distinctly pleb. The seats are covered with plastic, the aisles with linoleum. Regular write-ups still appear in *Grocott's* — in the Readers' Views columns. Plaintive moans about mixed reels, not being able to hear the dialogue, and the natural draught ventilation. In winter, woolly-hatted patrons arrive with blankets, even hot water bottles. Now its claim to fame is that with 1 002 seats it is the last of SA's big 'bioscopes' — possibly the largest in the southern hemisphere.

The Odeon in Bathurst Street also gives cause for occasional carping. Amazingly, it opened its doors as long ago as May 16, 1911, when it was called the Grand. Predictably, the Press was present: *"The new Bioscope House was originally a jam factory ... It is indeed a very roomy hall and possesses four exits, all opening outwards. Mr Chas Harris's cinematograph or bioscope machine is the latest pattern (the Maltese Cross) and the first machine of its kind in the country."* (Some of the present projection equipment dates back to the 1940s, but it has been modernized, as was the Odeon itself in the 1950s.)

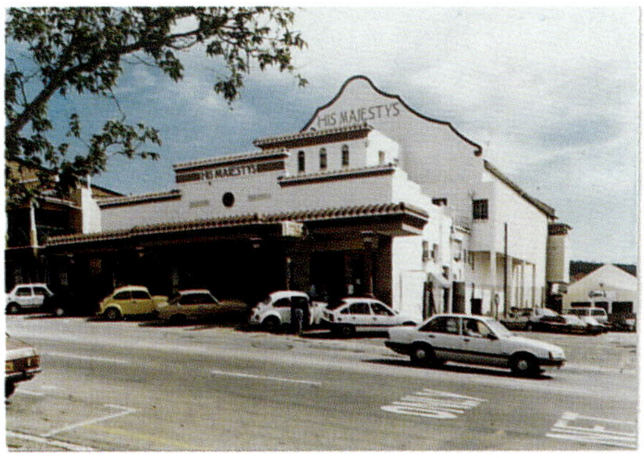

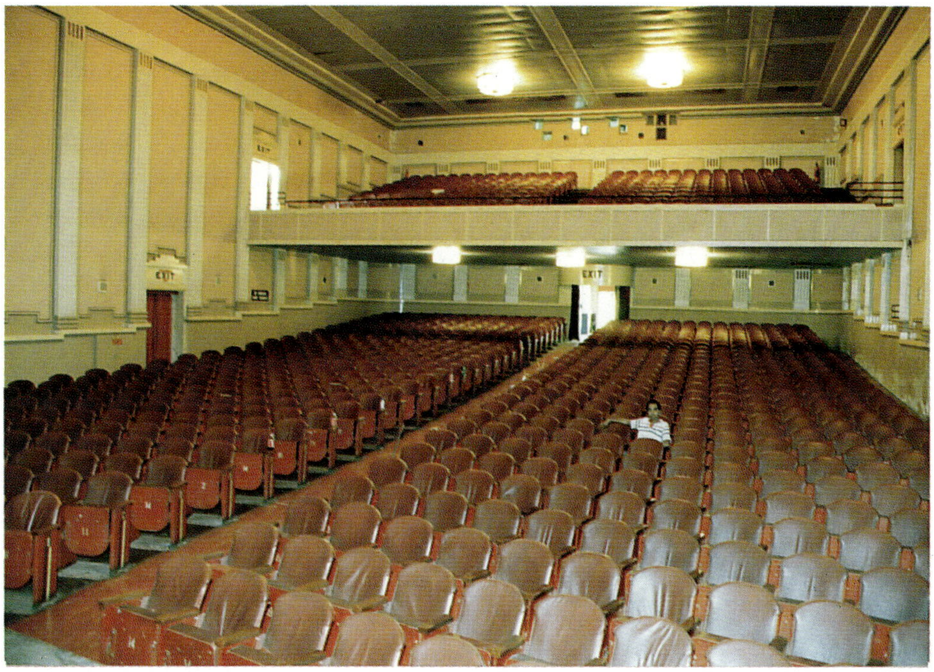

***TOP:* Projection equipment standing by at the Odeon since the 1940s**

***ABOVE:* His Majesty's, last of SA's big cinemas, has a style all of its own; and *RIGHT:* inside patrons can have their own space and plenty of it**

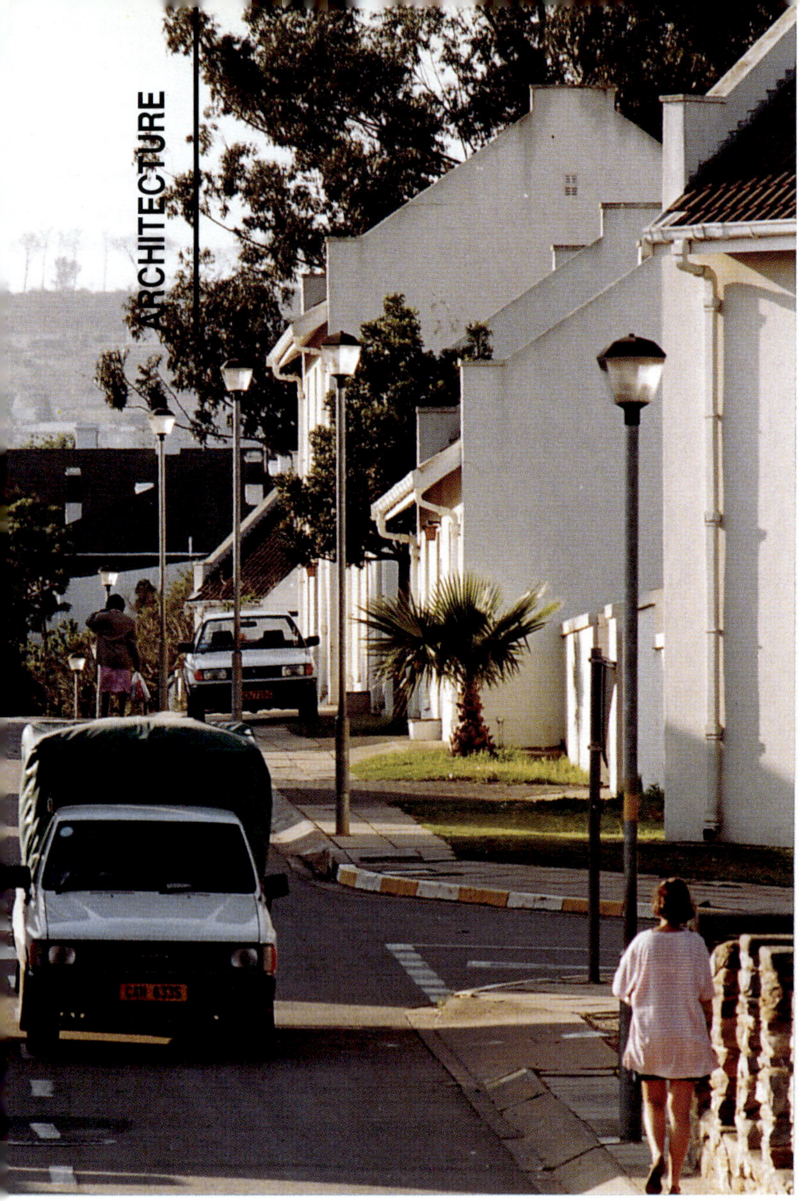

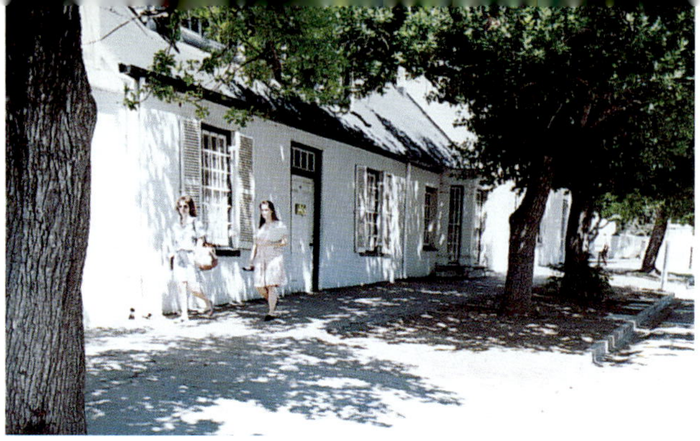

ABOVE: *Oldest cottage in town*
LEFT: *Stockenström Village — 1980's version of 1820's style*

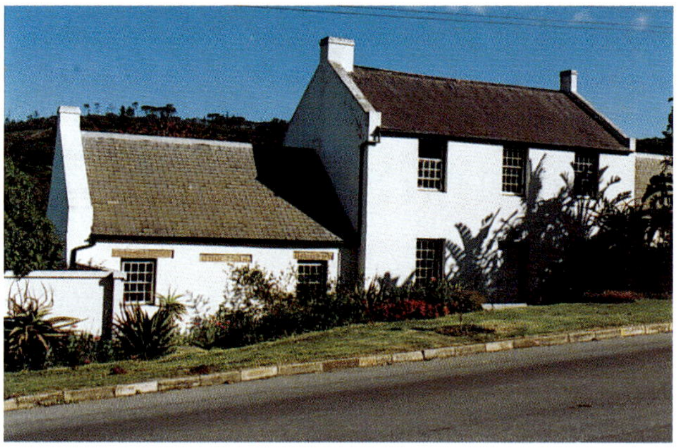

ABOVE: *Lawrance Street couple*

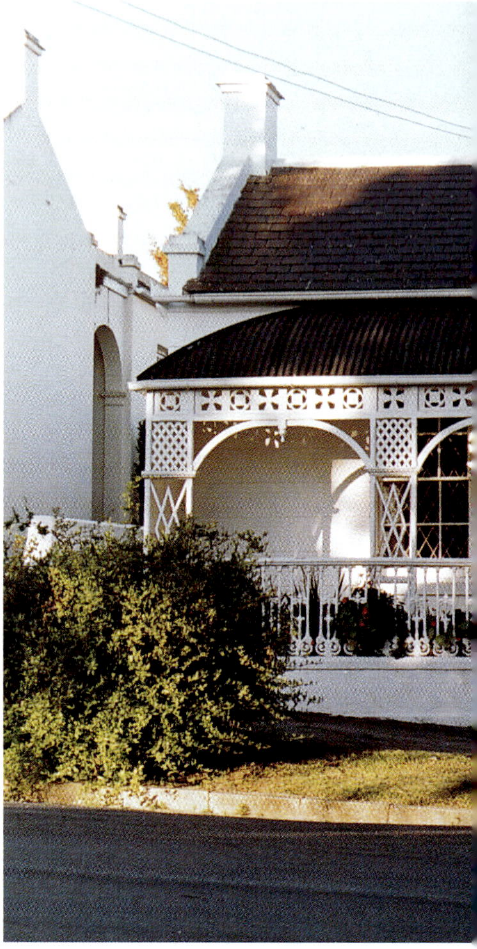

SETTLER COTTAGE PIE

THERE are as many types of architecture in Grahamstown as dishes on a fancy menu. But most people's favourite is still the settler cottage synonymous with the city. Totally endearing in its unpretentiousness, the eternal child's "two windows and a door" drawing, smoke spiralling comfortingly out of the gable chimney on a chilly winter's night.

Following the time-honoured pattern of the English country cottage, the simplest contained only two or three rooms whose width was determined by the length of the timber available for the construction of the roof. Most were bigger, but still mini-town scale.

The majority of these quaint little houses cluster in and about Artificers' — meaning artisans' — Square. From 1822 onwards, numbers of 1820 Settlers, overwhelmed by the harshness of life on inadequate farm allotments and in truth strangers to any form of agriculture, moved to town where their skills as masons, carpenters, and bricklayers could be put to better use.

They were permitted to take up residence on a portion of Settlers' Hill divided into four sections by two streets crossing at right angles, Artificers'

RIGHT: ***Simplicity and symmetry in George Street***
BELOW: ***Artificers' Square where wagon stones and 1820 Settler cottages converge***

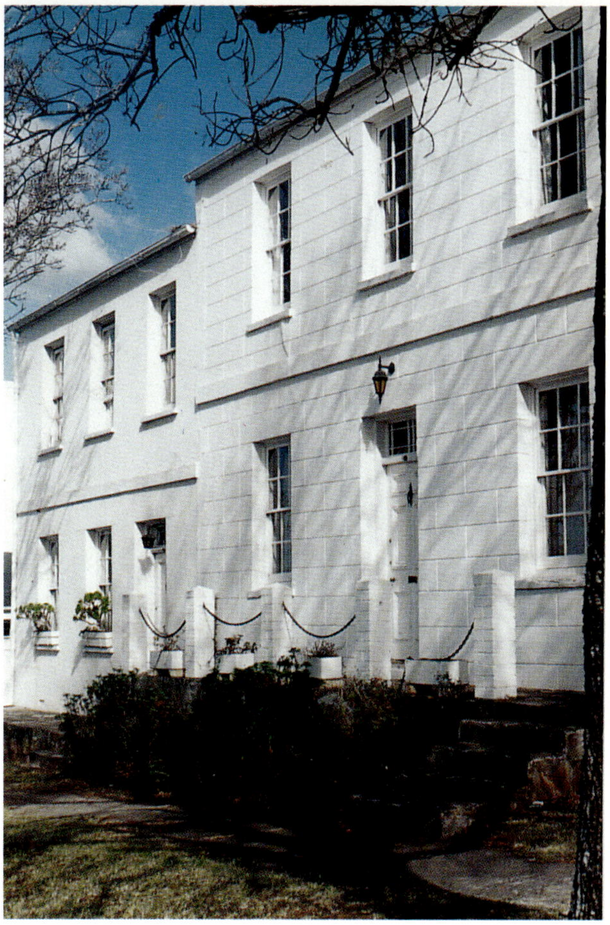

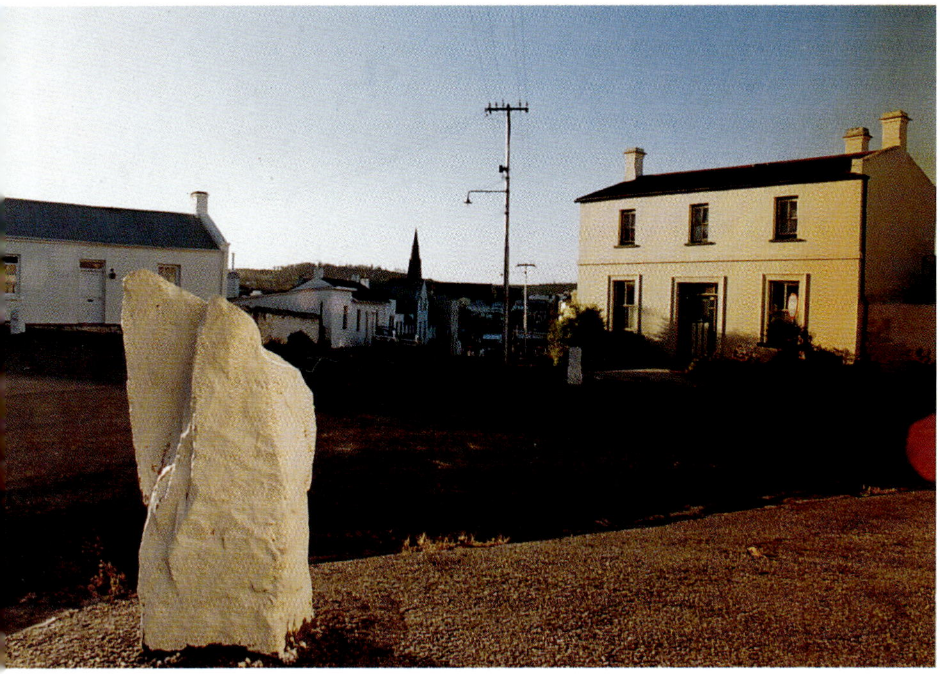

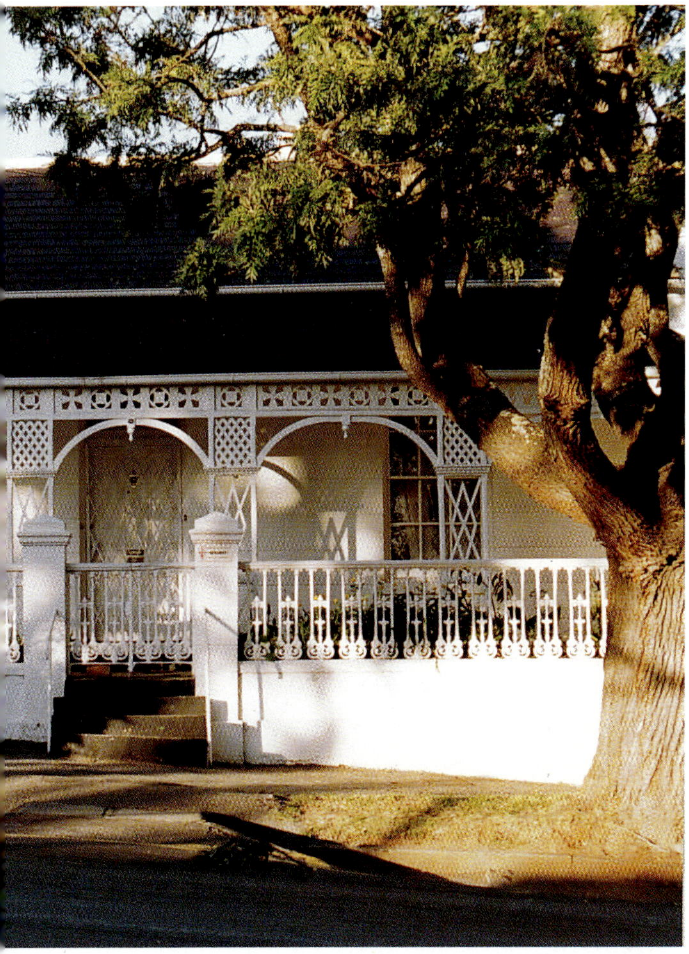

ABOVE: ***Lacy Victorian verandah, a later addition to Hill Street cottage***

Square in the centre being enlarged by cutting back the corners to form an octagon.

After a long period in the doldrums, the whole area was restored in the 1960s under the auspices of Historic Grahamstown.

Further downtown a whole new settler enclave developed in the 1980s, when the Cape Provincial Administration built 40 houses based on traditional designs for Roads Department staff. The development was called the Stockenström Village in honour of Andries Stockenström, co-founder of Grahamstown, who has tended to be unhonoured and unsung.

The more commodious homes in George Street have an appropriately Georgian look about them but are all cottages at heart, dating from between 1830 to the early 1840s.

The oldest cottage in Grahamstown is part of a row turned into a single residence at the Rhodes University end of High Street. Originally the court messenger's house, its frontage, together with that of the the first gaol nearby, was used to define the building line of High Street in 1814.

The little white houses of Grahamstown... How still we see them lie in early paintings of the fledgling settlement. A surprising number continue as comfortable homes, usually considerably extended. With mellow yellowwood floors and a sense of other lives lived behind their front doors, which usually open straight onto the pavement. Not much gentrification, but lots of tender loving care.

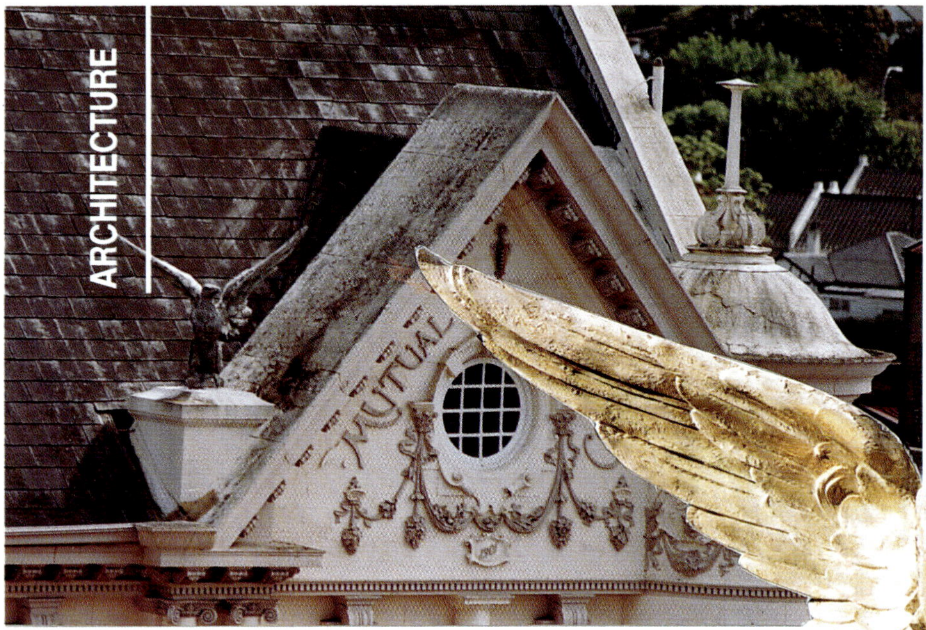

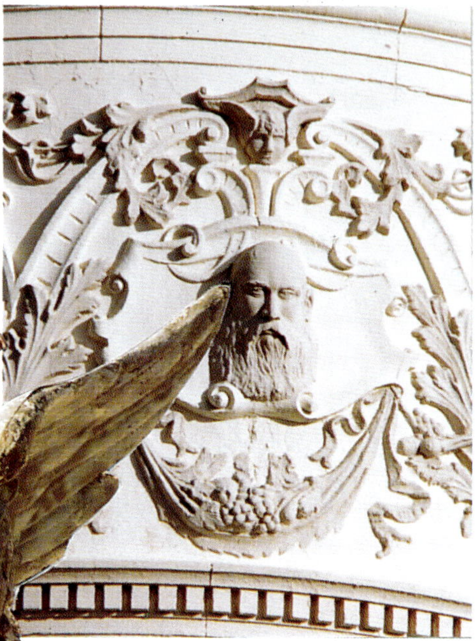

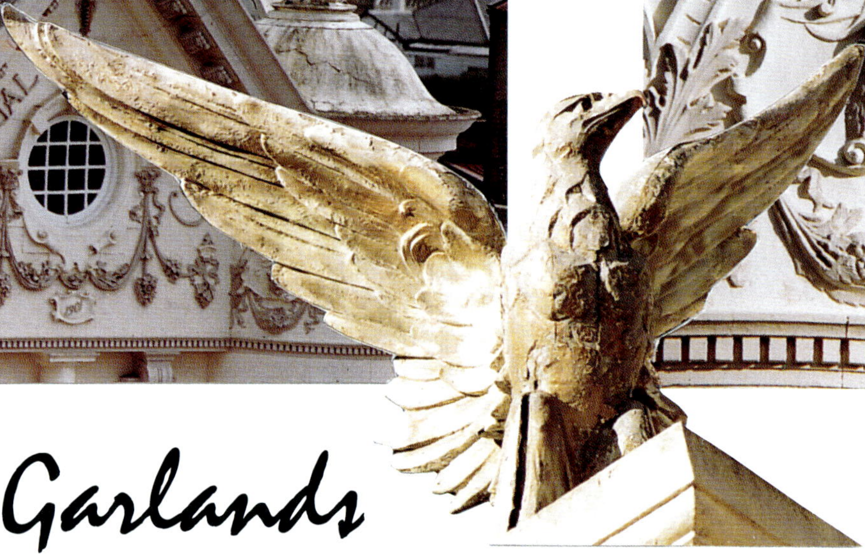

Elaborate Garlands

THE magical reality wrap-around in Church Square is so seamless that one is not in the least surprised to see a muscular eagle perched like Superman on the roof of the exuberantly ornate Mutual Building.

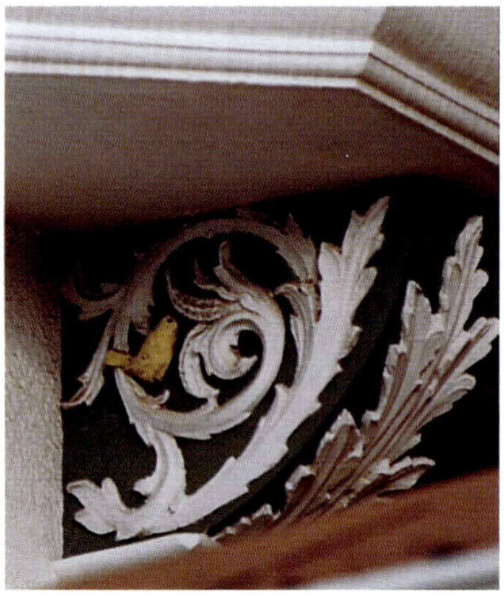

Distinctly larger than life, constantly ready for take-off, and completely plastered. So is the canary in the leafy scrolls at the base of Muirhead & Gowie's black tower, this particular little yellow bird being the plasterer's trademark.

Fine feathers make fabulous birds, as any envious passing pigeon will tell you. At the height of the ostrich feather vogue, the Grahamstown Feather Market was of such importance that in 1896 the greater part of the revenue received from letting the nearby City Hall was derived from this source alone. Frequently 1 500 lots were put up for sale in a single day.

A major buyer had his office in the frivolous Mutual mansion but his is not the face on the heavily festooned tower. That is reputed to be the architect's. Old Nick on the side is merely a bit of devilment, perhaps a dig at the sainted city. Inside the tower there is a strongroom which was not opened for over 40 years because nobody could find the key. And when they did, it was empty.

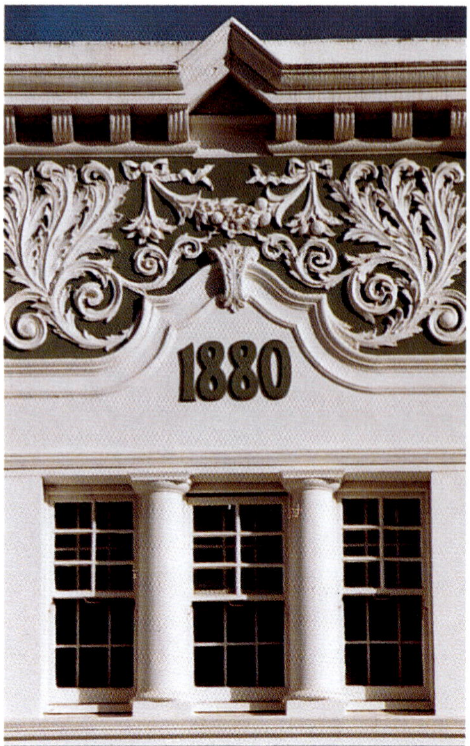

CLOCKWISE: Eagle's eye view of Church Square — Mutual Building swags, Muirhead & Gowie swirls: watch the canary!

Completely different from city skyscraper clones, the colourful characters in the vicinity are a real eyeful. The delight is in the detail, the swirls, curls and twirls of the famed south side facades, featured on the title page and long ago pronounced the finest line-up in the colonies. A theatrical backdrop for a Ruritanian operetta, astonishingly out of place but

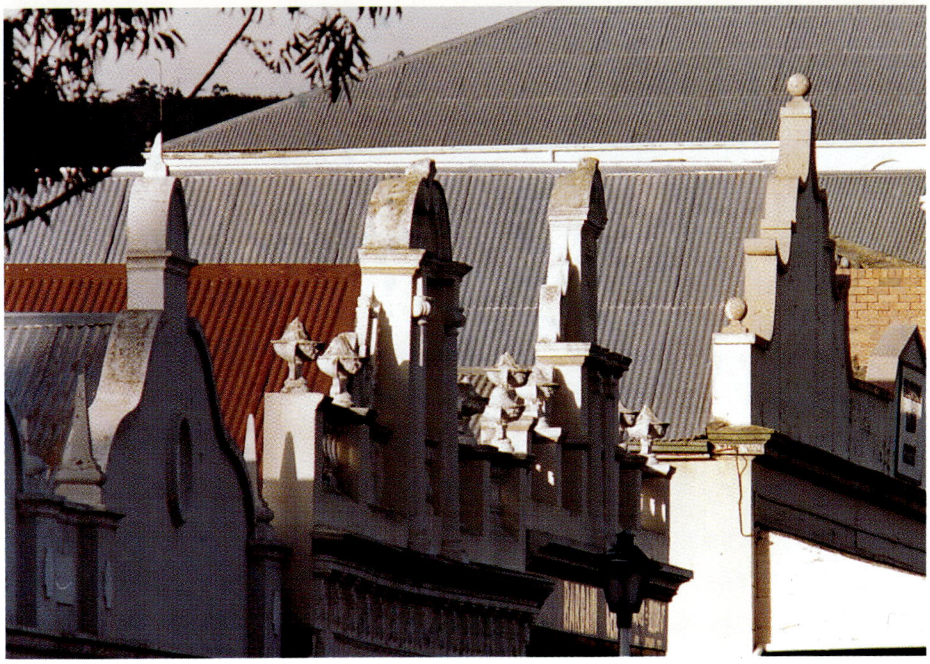

ABOVE: *Rising above the High Street dip*

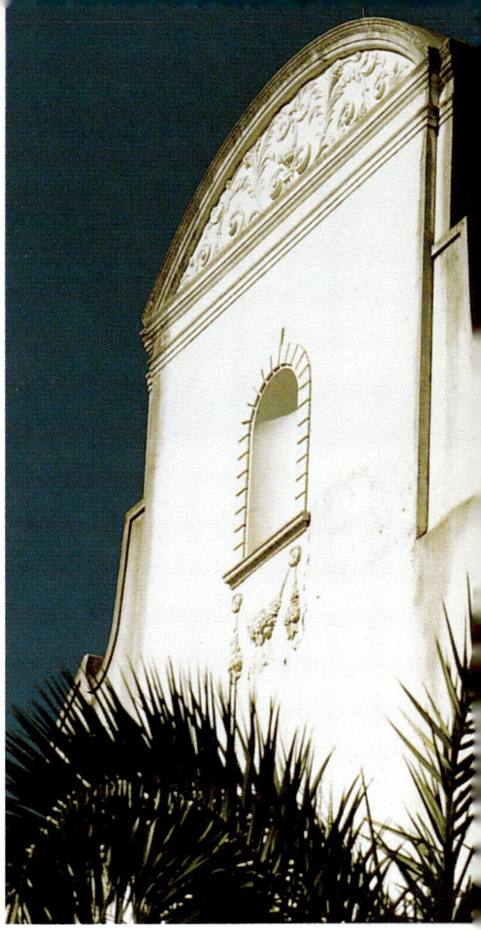

ABOVE: *Albany Museum classic*

Gracious Gables

totally at home beneath the blazingly blue African sky.

Show stopper Muirhead & Gowie was Grahamstown's most stylish shop in its heyday. Opened in 1880, burnt down in 1906, rebuilt with Edwardian elegance in 1907. A veritable Eastern Cape Harrod's. Imported ballgowns were displayed in a candlelit room so that the belles of the garrison could see how the colours of the shimmering silks and satins would change under night light. The best bonnet-maker in the entire Cape Colony presented regular seasonal collections. Now it is part of a national chain gang, handy for toothbrushes, tissues and toiletries.

Alongside, the home of good old *Grocott's Mail* with its flamboyantly gabled front, arches, false balconies and casement windows deserves a feature all to itself and that is what it gets towards the end of this book.

Gables gallivant throughout the town. Some wedding cake confections like those on the Lotus Fish Shop duo down in the lower High Street dip. Others sober-sided, such as the string on the Cawood Street extension of the Grand Hotel. Each indicates a self-contained suite for a commercial traveller — once the mainstay of small town hostelries — who could conveniently display his samples in a room with pavement access.

A dignified Cape Dutch gable graces the stately entrance to the Albany Museum. Unexpectedly, the Wesley Methodist Church near the Market Square is a rare example of the Cape Dutch revival style, compact and complete. A mini-*Constantia*, a diminutive *Nederburg*, it sits serenely behind a suburban brick wall. Part of the Lord's estate since 1913, and on the way to Fort England, South Africa's oldest functioning mental hospital, with which it has strong historic links. No vines, but many vintage years.

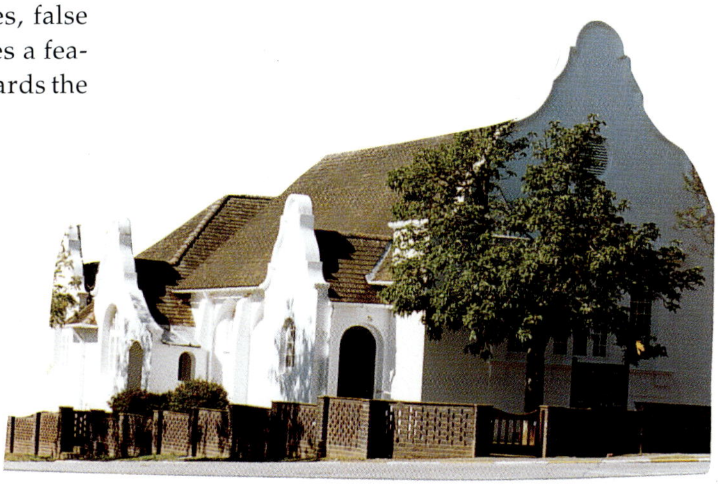

ABOVE: *Light and shade, Wesley Church*

HOTELS AND HOSTELRIES

OLD, older, oldest ... the list lengthens. The oldest existing hotel in South Africa, the Cathcart Arms, is situated in Grahamstown, under the shade of some Kurrajong trees — Australian evergreens which never lose their cool.

Alongside the Market Square, it was established by 1820 Settlers William and Ann Trotter in 1831 as a "brewery and house of accommodation". Its licence, granted by Cape Governor Lord Charles Somerset, was applied for much earlier — in 1825. The brewery was operated in the cavernous cellar (complete with well) below the present bar. Beer made from the clear pure water was popular among the thirsty frontier forces. Today, equally convivial customers down pints brewed further afield.

The only hostelry in the country to have been proclaimed a fort in which soldiers could be posted and a house of refuge for the local populace in event of attack. Loopholes cut in the thick stone walls during the seventh frontier war in 1846 can still be seen. The upstairs inner walls, surprisingly soundproof, are believed to be made of mud, goats' hair, and grass.

Stabling for horses and even kraals for cattle were in the big yard behind the premises. Two more exotic occupants arrived in 1844, when Mr Trotter purchased a pair of young female giraffes, brought from the interior by a Market Square trader, for the exorbitant sum of 80 pounds each, and charged the public a shilling per head to view them.

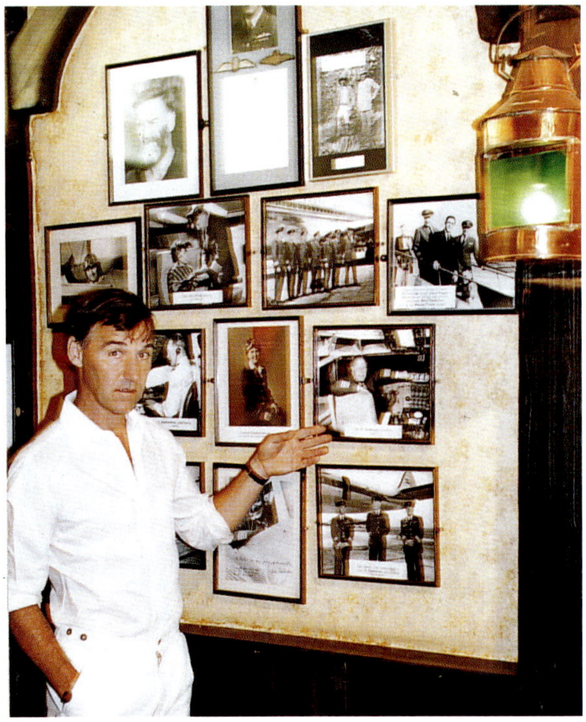

The name 'Cathcart Arms' dates back to the early 1850s when Sir George Cathcart was Governor of the Cape. He visited Grahamstown in May, 1852, but stayed at the Drostdy, not the inn on the square. The Cathcart family is Scottish in origin. The fact that the hotel's much-petted resident pooch is a particularly noble Scotty is purely coincidental.

Diagonally across the Market Square is another hospitable haven, The Cock House. Its original owner was Benjamin Norden, a member of the early Jewish community in Grahamstown. Later it became the residence of the Hon William Cock, after whom it is named. The leader of an 1820 Settler party, in 1847 he was a member of the first Legislative Assembly and much involved in the development of the Kowie harbour at what is now Port Alfred — in its formative years known by various names, including Port-o'-Grahamstown.

More than a century later, Afrikaans literary doyen André Brink — then lecturing at Rhodes — rescued the property from a downward slide. The former ballroom became a living room. Now it is the elegant restaurant of an atmospheric guesthouse, a proclaimed National Monument with generous helpings of history on the menu.

"All Rhodes lead to the Vic" declares a ubiquitous bumper sticker. The Hotel Victoria in New Street, scene of 1 001 nights of student roistering, more vividly recalled by some old Rhodians than the hallowed halls of their Alma Mater. Long a landmark in the street where once practically every other cottage was a pub because of the proximity of the Drostdy barracks, the angle of the corner wagon stone tends towards the horizontal.

Wot about the Mot? Indeed. Grahamstown's award-winning model "motel"— inevitably called the Settlers' Inn— nestling up near the 1820 Monument, more country club than car park. Ye olde English Flare Path Pub keeps the homefire burning in winter and is filled with photographs assembled by ex-Rhodian RAF pilot Bert Leach, who got the enterprise off the ground in 1968. Surprise, surprise! Something worth mentioning in Grahamstown that doesn't date back at least 100 years? Yes — but only just within the city limits!

LEFT: *Those magnificent men in their flying machines at the Flare Path Pub*

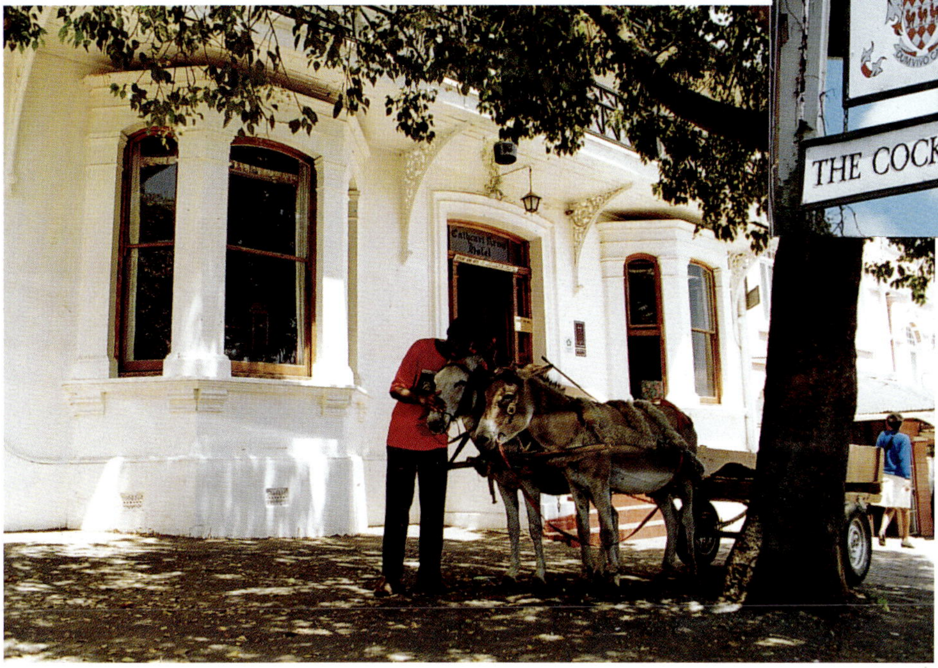

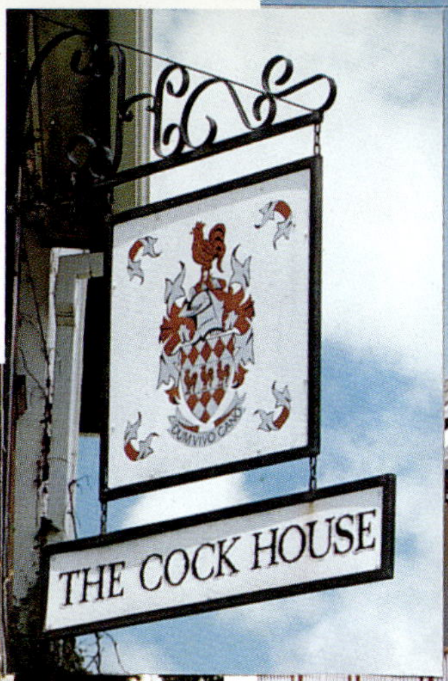

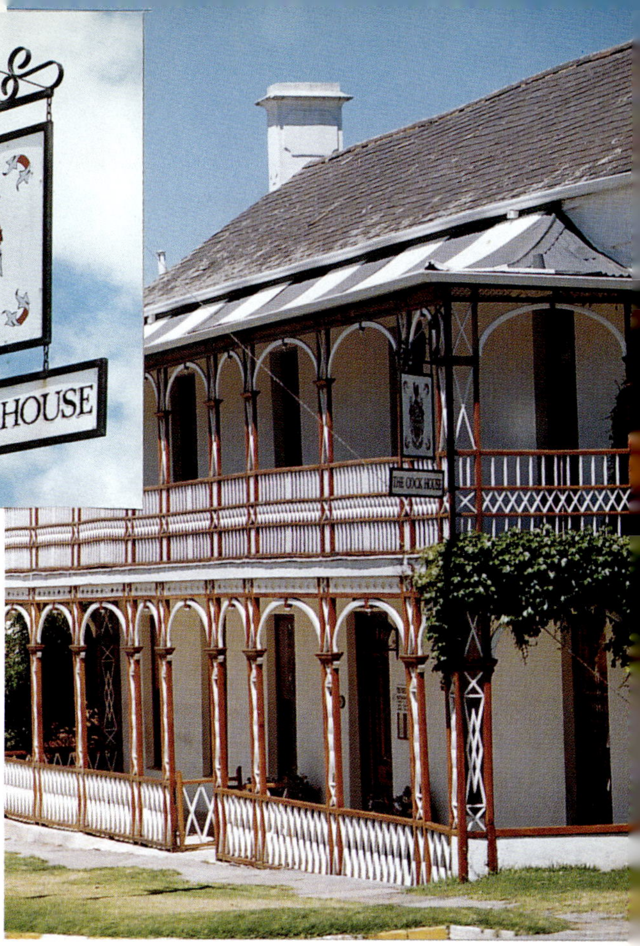

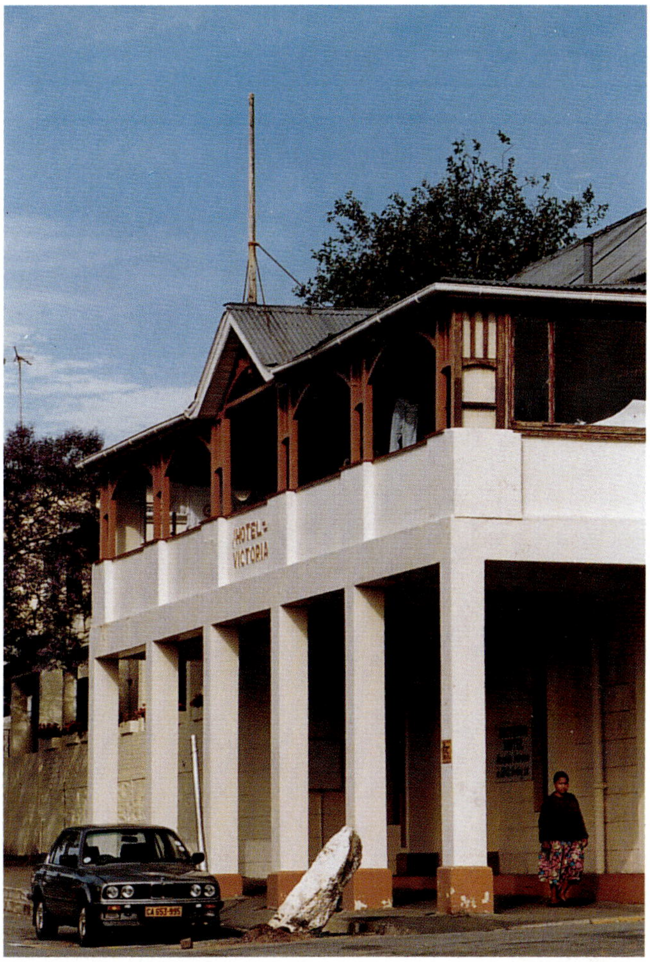

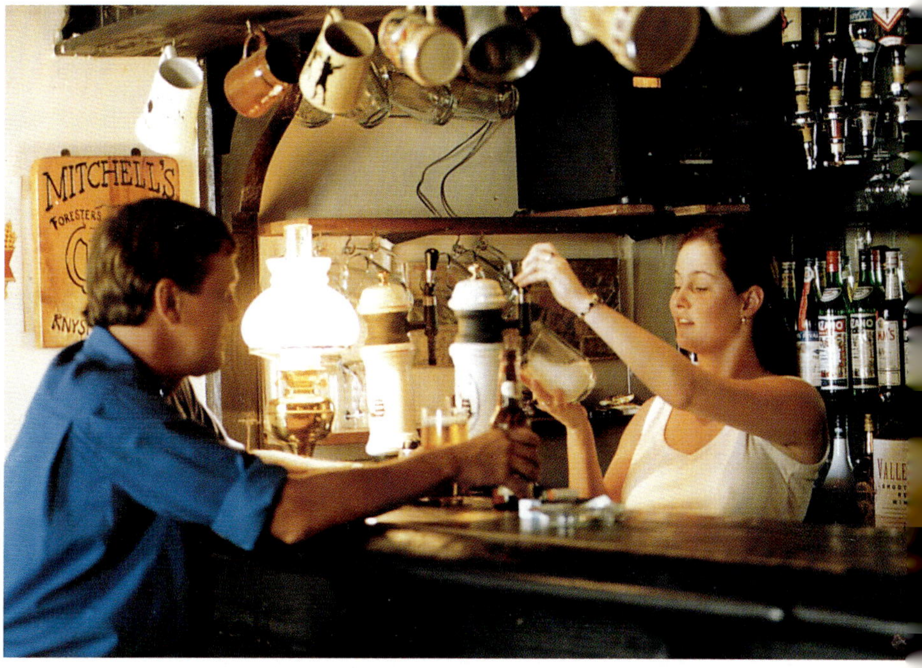

CLOCKWISE: *Light, shade, and donkey cart delivery at the Cathcart Arms (plus pub scene below); The Cock House verandah is an obvious afterthought; and the Hotel Victoria is still going strong*

TAILPIECE: *Dougall on duty at the Cathcart, ears up, eyes front*

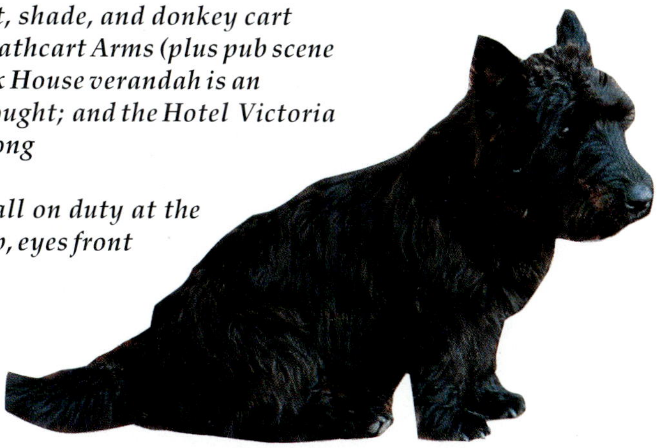

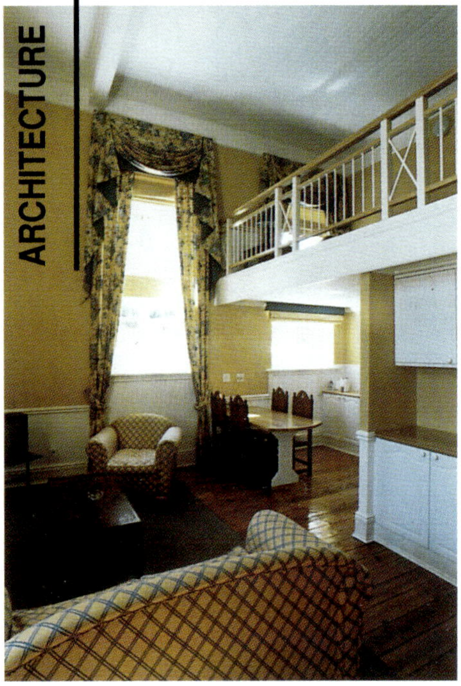

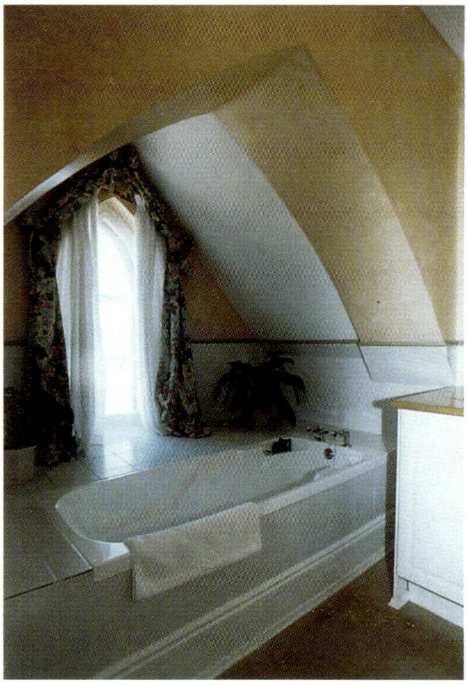

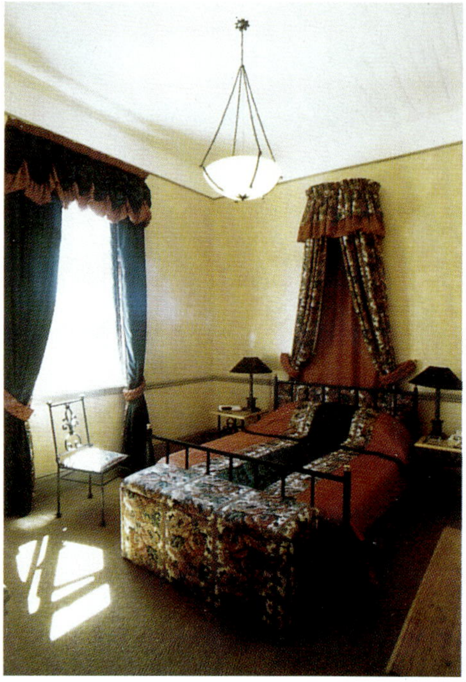

THE COURT OF ST AIDAN

SHADES of the Knights of the Round Table ... A vista out of a St Valiant adventure will widen your eyes when you glance left down the lane-like streets leading off "The High" near the Cathedral.

A medieval citadel with a colourful banner flying from the castle keep. Wend your way thither into the cobbled precinct where a fountain cascades, surrounded by iceberg roses in snowy bloom. Welcome to the Court of St Aidan — or rather, St Aidan's Court.

Story book stuff, written in stone. The largest group of Gothic Revival buildings in the country. Originally St Aidan's College, once the leading Roman Catholic college on the continent of Africa, it closed in 1973 after almost 100 years of noteworthy achievement. Reopened in February, 1994, as a hotel so different that it qualifies for comet rating rather than stars, on appearance alone. A Halley's hotel, in fact.

Recumbent stags recline on signs and portals. St Aidan was the patron saint of the Diocese of Fern in Ireland where all three founding Fathers (actually Bishops) of the college — Devereux,

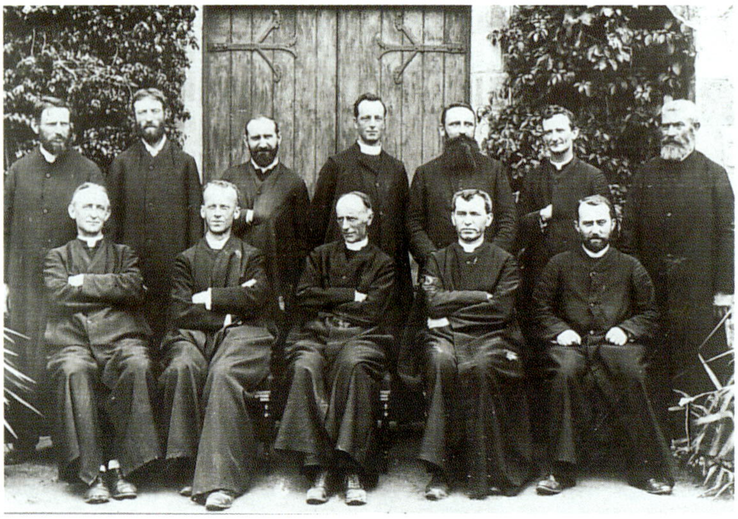

ABOVE: 1903 St Aidan's staff — Jesuit Fathers all, photographed by Father Marconnés (front right) using delayed action — a technique he utilized again in 1910 to capture Halley's Comet (opposite page)

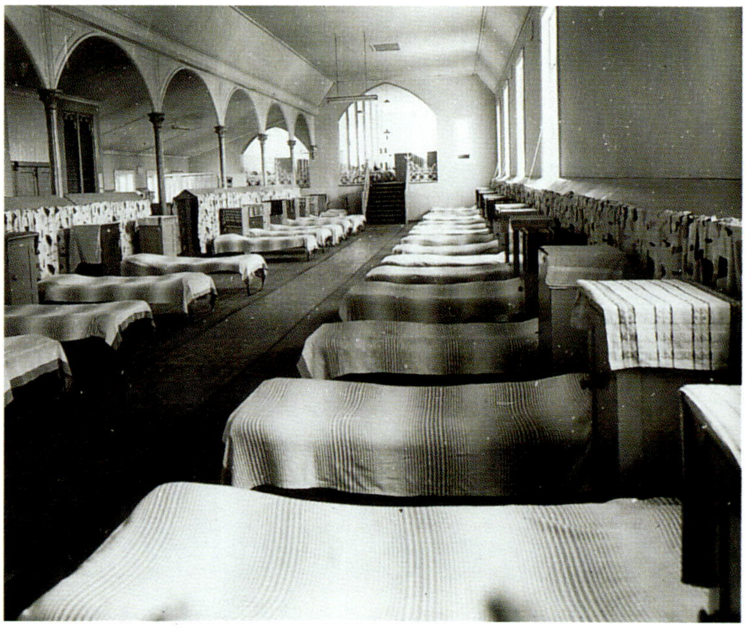

RIGHT: Middle dormitory, ready for inspection, a far cry from the luxurious accommodation of today (top of page) with suitably ecclesiastical bathroom en suite

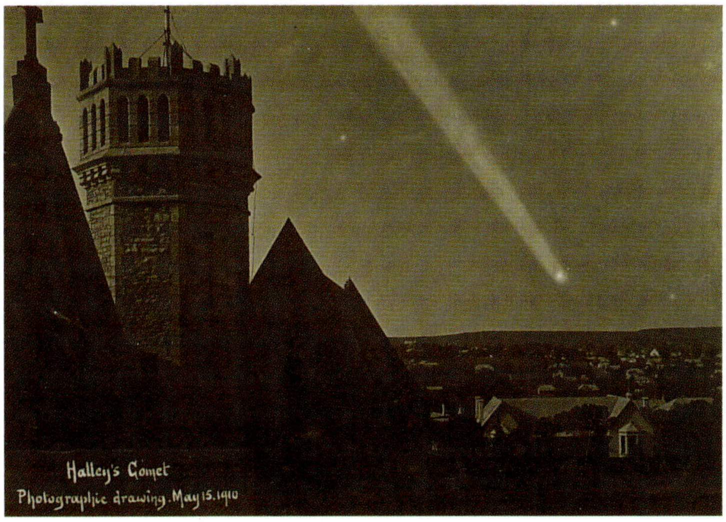

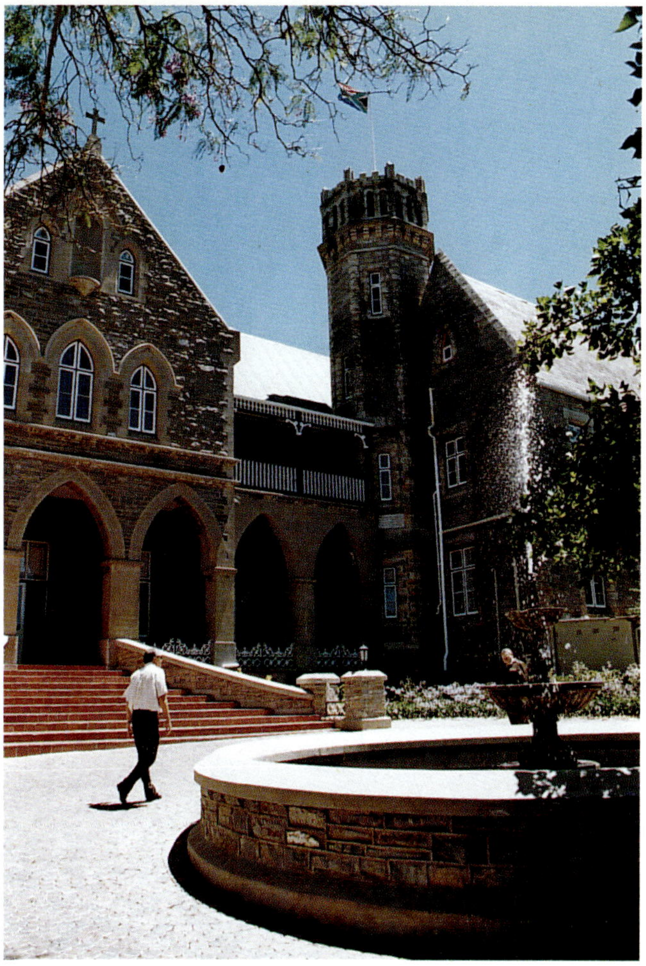

Moran and Ricards — had studied for the priesthood. Tradition has it that one day St Aidan was reading in a forest when a stag, hard pressed by huntsmen, appeared. He sprang to its rescue, hence his heraldic emblem— and the hotel's.

After the college's long educational service ended, the doors were locked and the entire complex went into the deep sleep of decline. Roofs leaked, vandals broke in and made fires on the wooden floors, mounds of abandoned books mouldered, pigeons roosted and owls hooted hopelessly.

Enter a man with a dream— Geoffrey Vetch, the moving force behind the rescue mission and subsequent transformation scene. Months turned into years. Renovations went on and on. Then suddenly, everything was perfectly in place.

Curtains up! And what curtains. Rich as papal robes — draped, flounced, swagged, tailed and tasselled. A dramatic touch which warms the lofty interiors as tapestries did the palaces of long ago.

Classrooms have been turned into suites, some with ceilings so high that mezzanine levels add extra dimensions. The junior dormitory is an art gallery, the original line of 20 Royal Doulton washbasins, back to back and cold water only, retained as an exhibit in its own right, the taps painted flaming flamingo to match the amazing walls.

The attic above is shaping up as a museum of St Aidan's memorabilia. Offers of blazers, ties, trophies and photographs from Old Boys, many of whom see this as "their hotel", are welcomed. The Old Aidanite reunion is a fixed date on the calendar each year.

And the chapel? The altar has been removed, the rest remains unchanged. The sublime space is still bathed in ethereal light shining through superb stained glass windows. A beautiful banqueting hall— a wonderful venue for weddings with a *Camelot* touch.

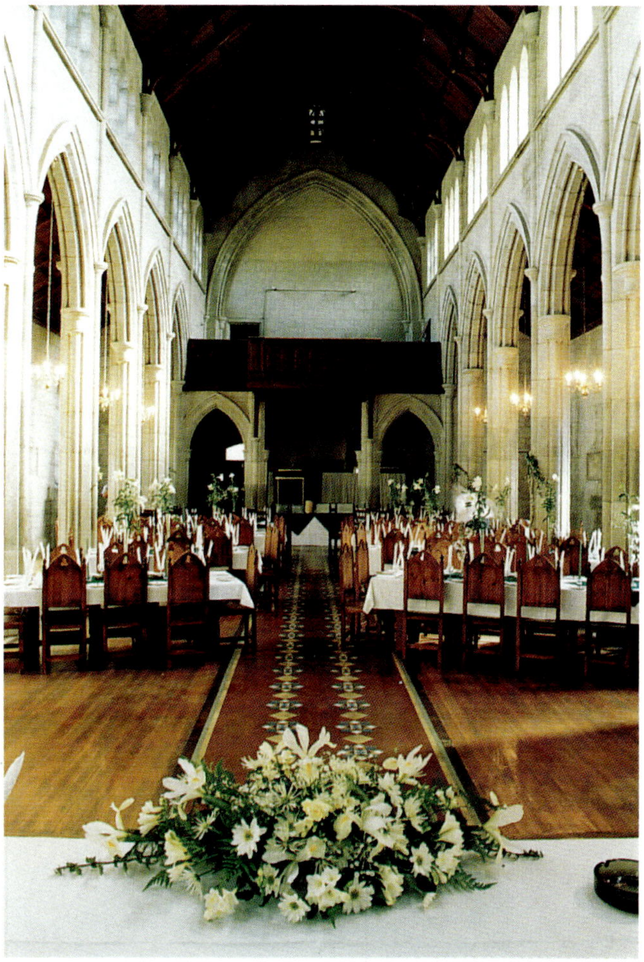

CLOCKWISE: ***Halley's Comet streaking past artistically in 1910; the main entrance; and chapel set for celebration***

PILLARS, PEDIMENTS

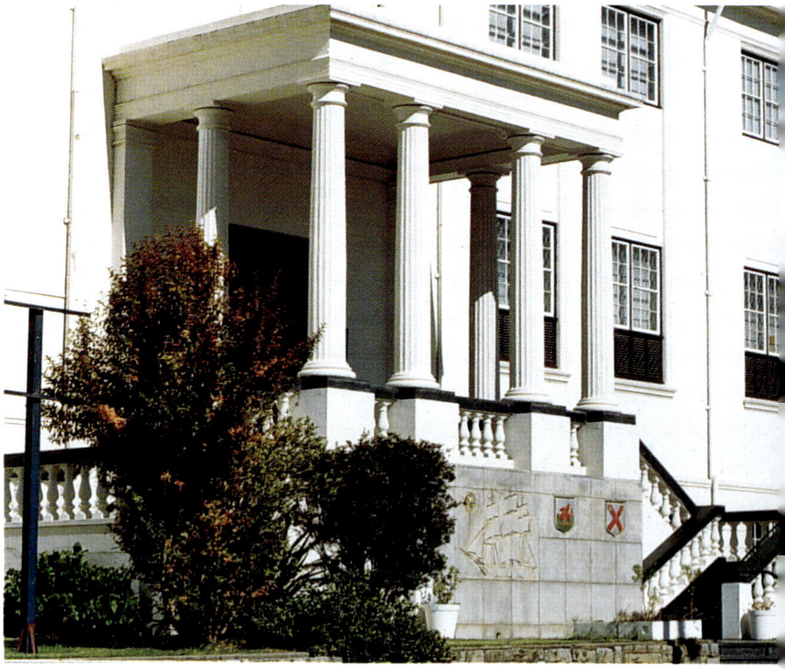

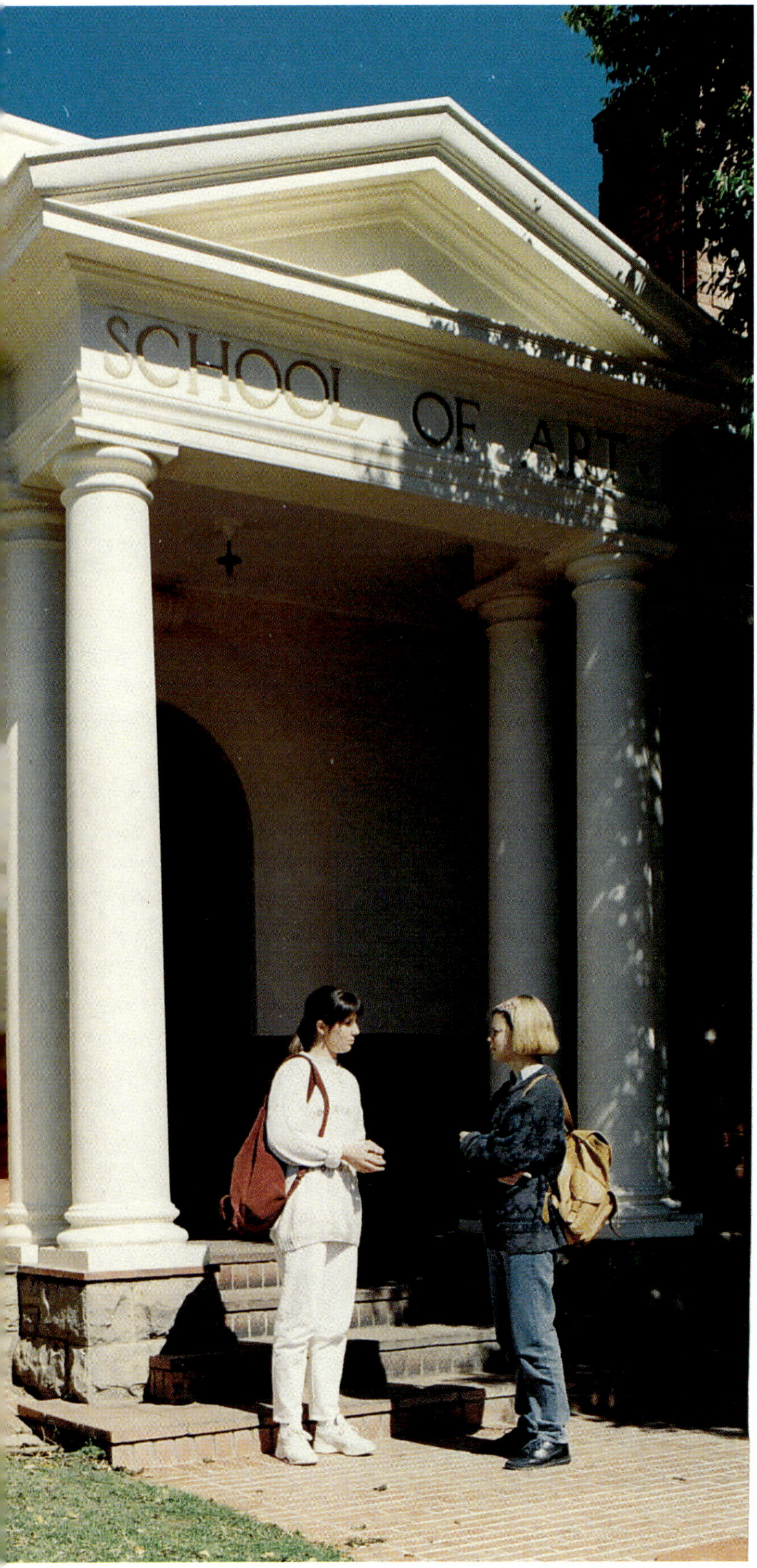

HARDLY the Athens of South Africa. A plenitude of pillars and pediments nonetheless lends a pleasingly classical air to places of worship, to the temples of learning and halls of commerce.

In a class and corner of its own, the Rhodes Art School is well to the fore on the campus, near the Drostdy Gateway.

As far back as 1881, some culturally oriented citizens had started a school of art which became part of Rhodes in 1925.

Today, graduates like David Champion, Cyril Coetzee, Jennifer Crooks, Hilary Graham, Noël Hodnett, Diane McLean, Hylton Nel, Neil Rodger, Dominic Thorburn, Penny Siopis, Jos Nel, and Tony Swift are national names in the art world. As is Robert Brooks, who was appointed head in 1980, and realized a long cherished dream when the Rhodes University Alumni Gallery was opened in 1993.

This is situated on the upper floor of the Albany Museum's history section — a pillared building of mixed architectural ancestry where the genealogical department's family trees are firmly rooted in the basement.

TOP AND LEFT: *Mixed history at the Albany Museum; architectural beauty at Rhodes*

The Trinity Presbyterian Church is a harmonious entity both inside and out, consecrated in 1842 and a proclaimed National Monument. Balm for the eyes and soul in tree-lined Hill Street.

Port Elizabeth architect John Rushmere's distinctively modern premises for a building society in High Street caused an outcry among traditionalists in 1986. Echoing elements of the past in a striking new way, it won him two major awards and has since mellowed into the cityscape as he intended, "telling the story of its own time instead of being a wimpish imitation". Message received!

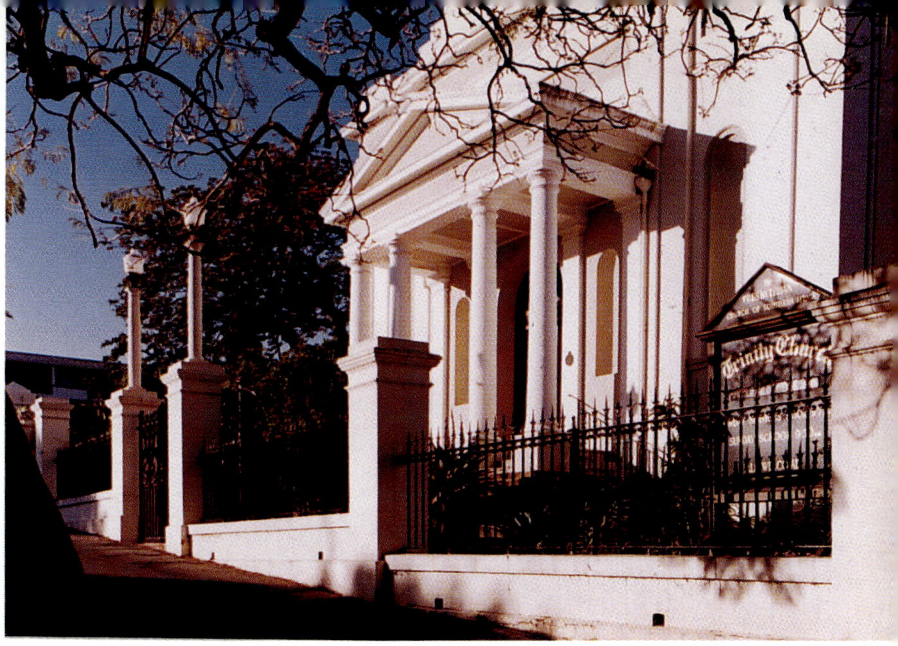

ABOVE: ***Trinity Church growing in grace***

...AND OLDEST POSTBOX

Painted pillar-box red and still in service, South Africa's oldest official letter box stands near St Andrew's College at the corner of Worcester Street.

It belongs to the flute type, one of the earliest styles supplied by the British Post Office between 1852 and 1859, and once proudly sported "VR" in curling script, denoting the reigning monarch, Queen Victoria.

To find its exact age would require some excavation. The box has been *in situ* so long — probably since 1860— that disturbing the soil which has built up over its base could cause it to collapse. Perish the thought! A venerable contender for a position among the world's "top twenty" red box survivors, it is definitely something to write home about.

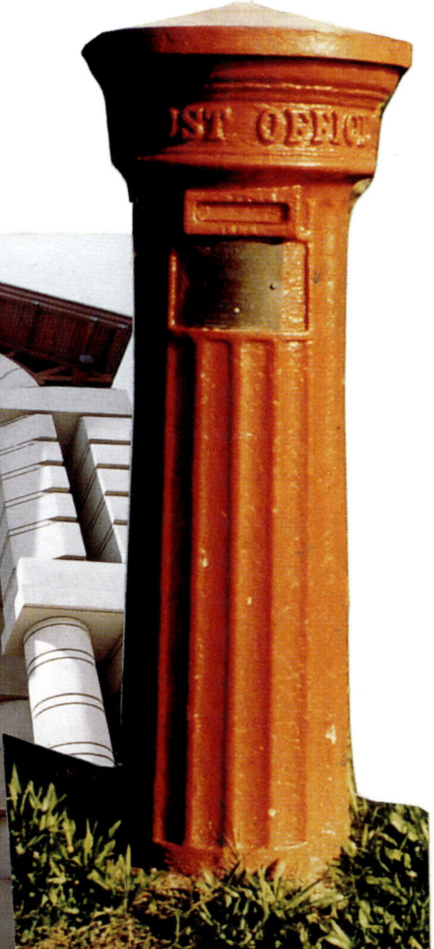

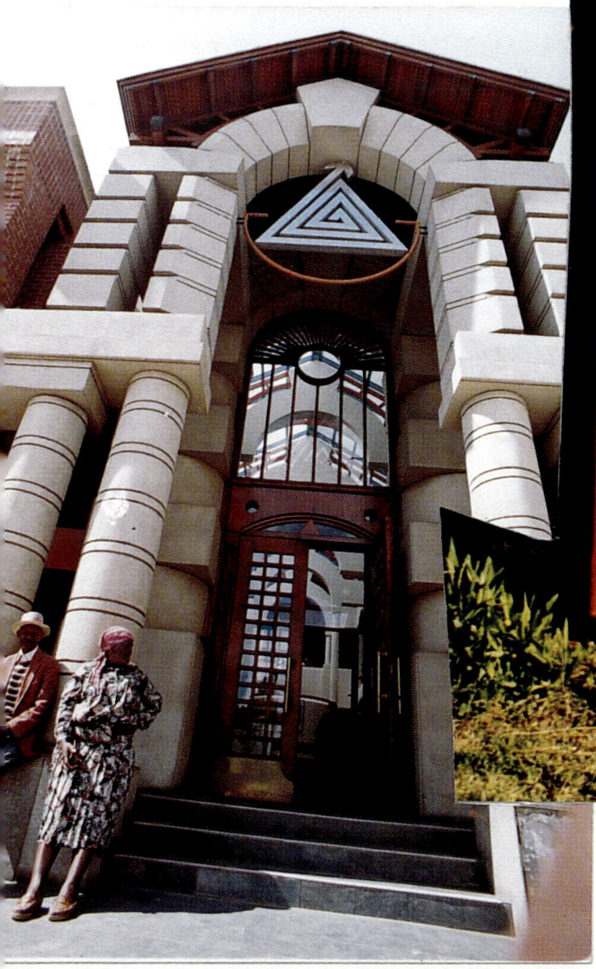

LEFT: ***Building for the future in High Street***

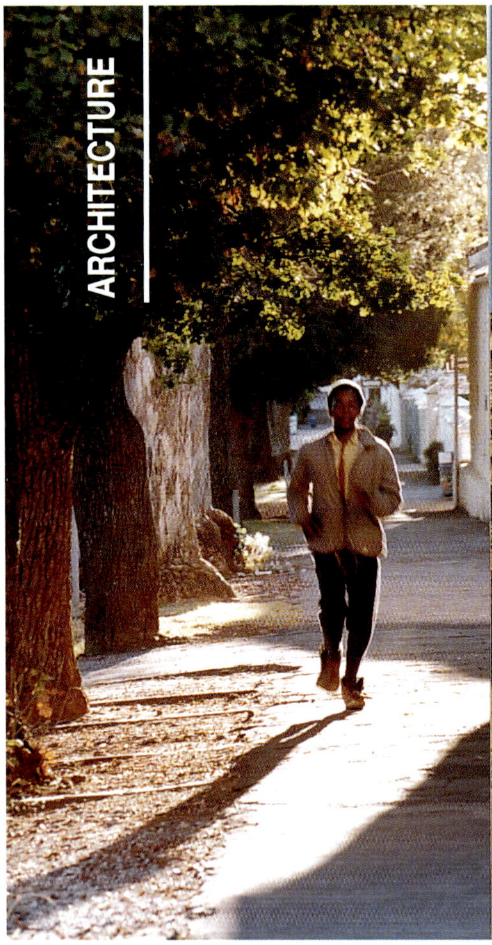

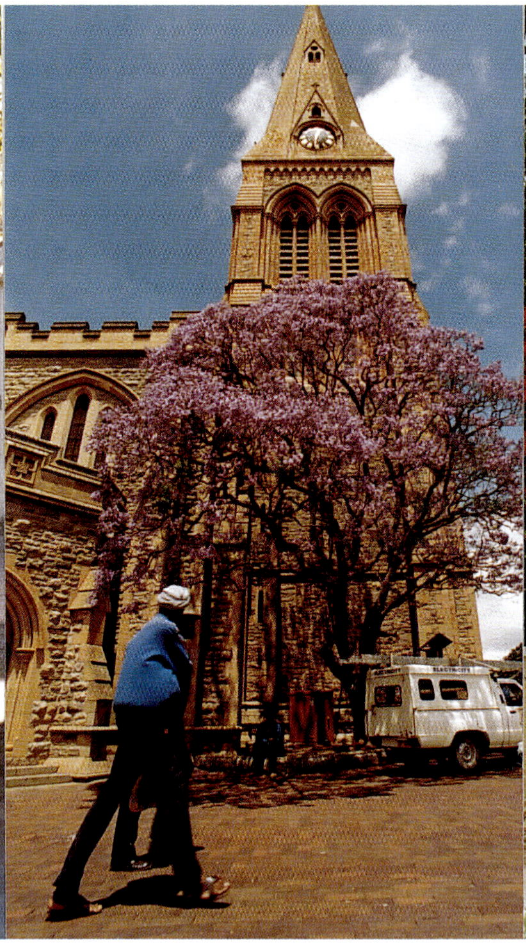

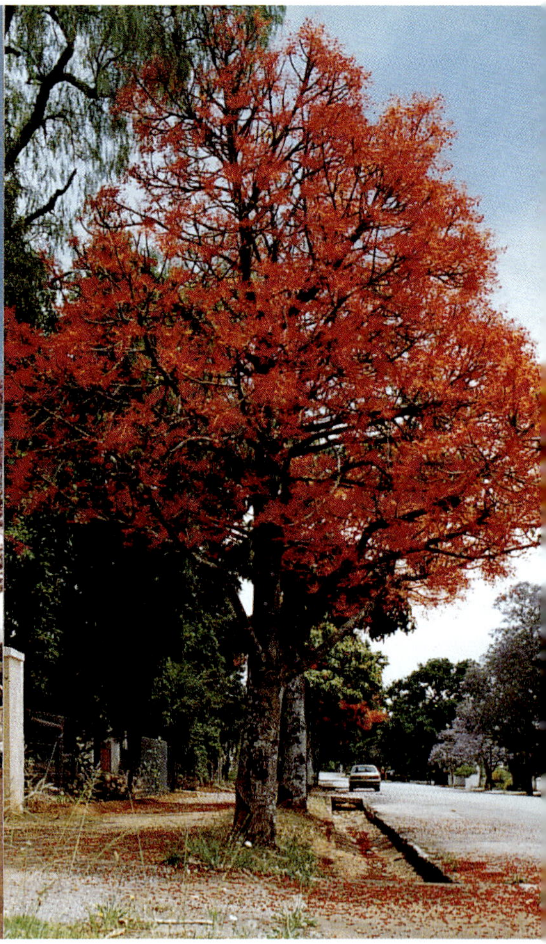

Green peace up "High"

Cathedral's heavenly blues

Oatlands Road aflame

TREES OF LIFE

IN DAYS long gone an old tree stood in the middle of High Street. A thorny *Acacia Karroo*, more romantically called a mimosa. It was believed to be the very tree beneath which Col John Graham and Capt Andries Stockenström founded Grahamstown in June, 1812.

An object of veneration but also a nuisance, as a local newspaper report indicated after it blew down on the wild and stormy night of August 25, 1843: "*It was broken short off at the butt which was found to be in a state of rapid decay. To those who delight in omens, this circumstance has afforded a fertile theme for conjecture... However this may be, it seems to be the general opinion that the destruction of the tree in question has rid the main street of an eyesore, as well as removed a great encumbrance from our most public thoroughfare.*"

The die-hards were determined to perpetuate the memory of the tree, which some even thought Col Graham had planted. A much criticized fountain made a brief appearance, and eventually the present centenary memorial rose after the inevitable Grahamstown grumbles and rumbles.

Some considered the obelisk more suitable for a cemetery. The cuddly heraldic beasts on top — two little leopards who look like furry puppies and a pair of even smaller giraffes seated similarly on their haunches — add a quirky touch. Symbols of the city, they flank the quartet of crowning crests, one of which features a broken stump putting forth a new shoot.

Today, trees of every description branch out in all directions. As the settlement grew, so did the saplings. Regulations of 1820 ruled that anyone found damaging them would be fined — or even imprisoned and flogged.

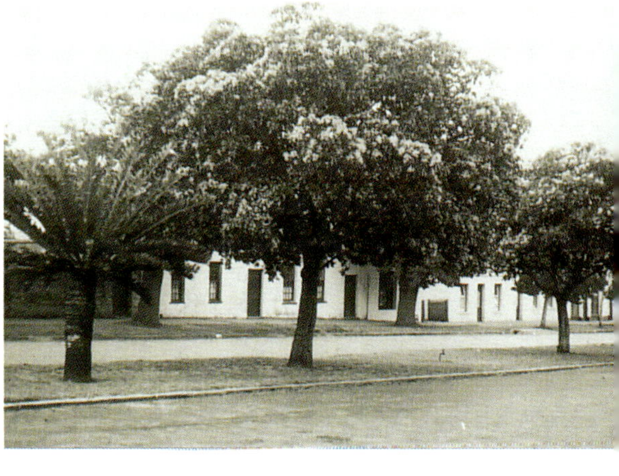

RIGHT: *High Street island duo, 1948*

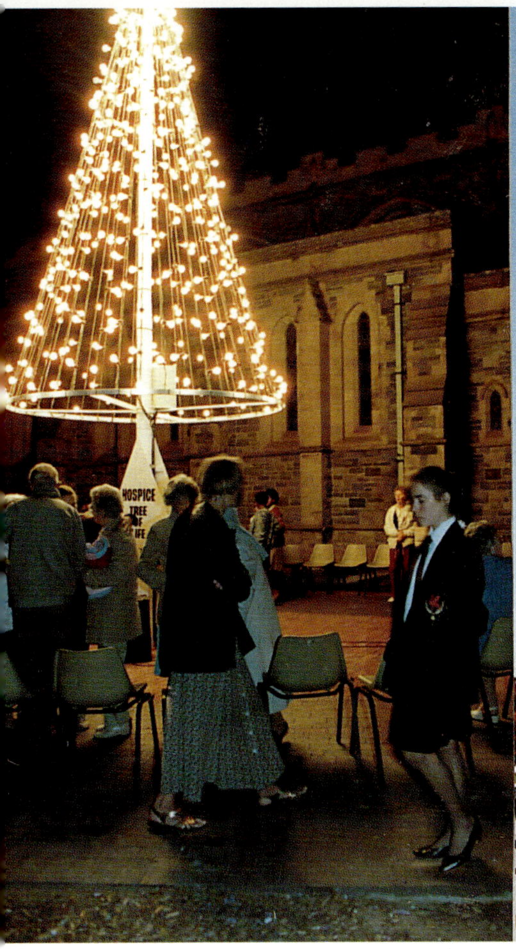

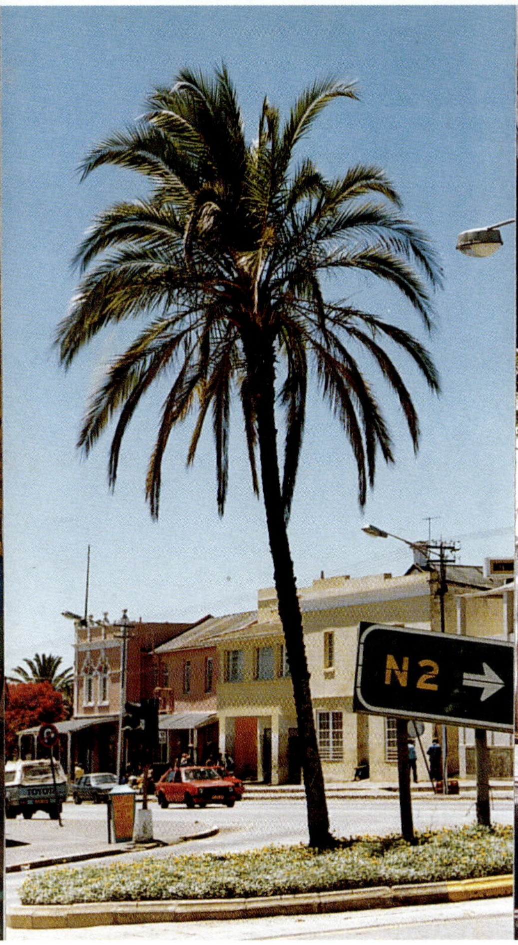

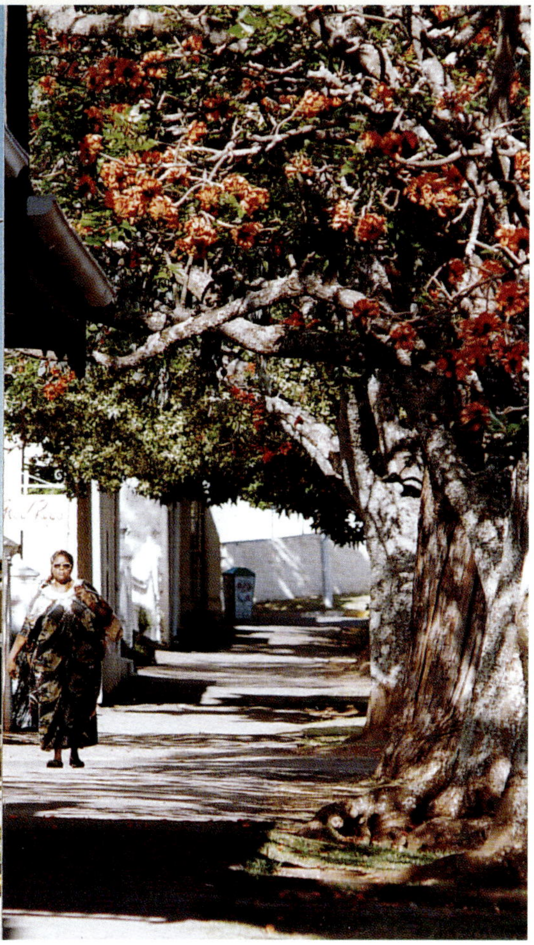

Hospice lights the way *Bathurst Street sentinel* *Coral tree coolth*

Once the Botanical Gardens, established in the early 1850s, got growing, an impressive list of exotics was available. Many thrived in local conditions. Planting has gone on through the decades, and this green heritage is as intrinsic a part of the cityscape as the buildings.

The Hanging Gardens of Grahamstown are a joyous sight from September when High Street bursts into successive waves of bloom. First the sizzling scarlet blossoms of the coral trees, followed by the Australian flame trees' brilliant blaze. Interspersed with foaming pink Cape chestnuts — this being the only city where they are used as street trees. Later there are the flowering gums.

Cycads by the dozen, their long yellow cones breaking open to reveal ruby seeds. And the oaks, stark and gnarled with age in winter, translucent with tender young leaves in spring. Their unfurling signals the start of swotting time for Rhodes students. If they delay till the violet-blue jacarandas burgeon, it will be too late for anything but tears.

The golden silver oaks of Hill Street, the plane trees outside the Public Library, the indigenous plums in front of the Albany Museum which produce a bountiful harvest of sweet fruit quickly collected by sharp-eyed youngsters.

The row of eucalyptus near Church Square where the egrets often roost, the lone palm in Bathurst Street, the ancient line-up outside the doctors' rooms in the Upper High with bunion-like bases and occasional strange growths... Shady characters, rooted to the spot.

At Christmas time, the Hospice Tree of Life shines out on Church Square, lightening the darkness of loss with loving memories. Trees for all seasons — and reasons.

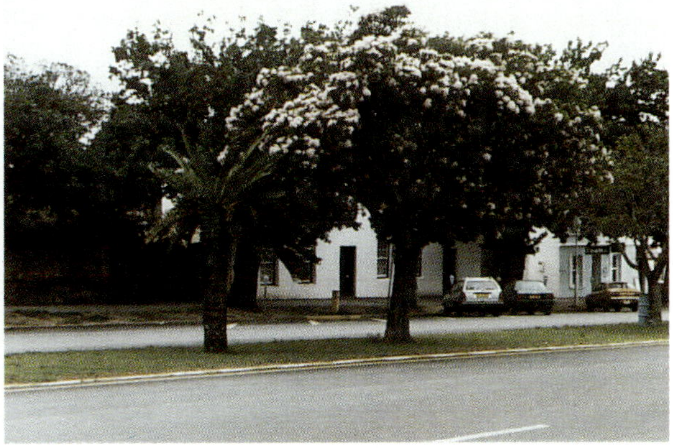

LEFT: *Same scene almost 50 years later ...*

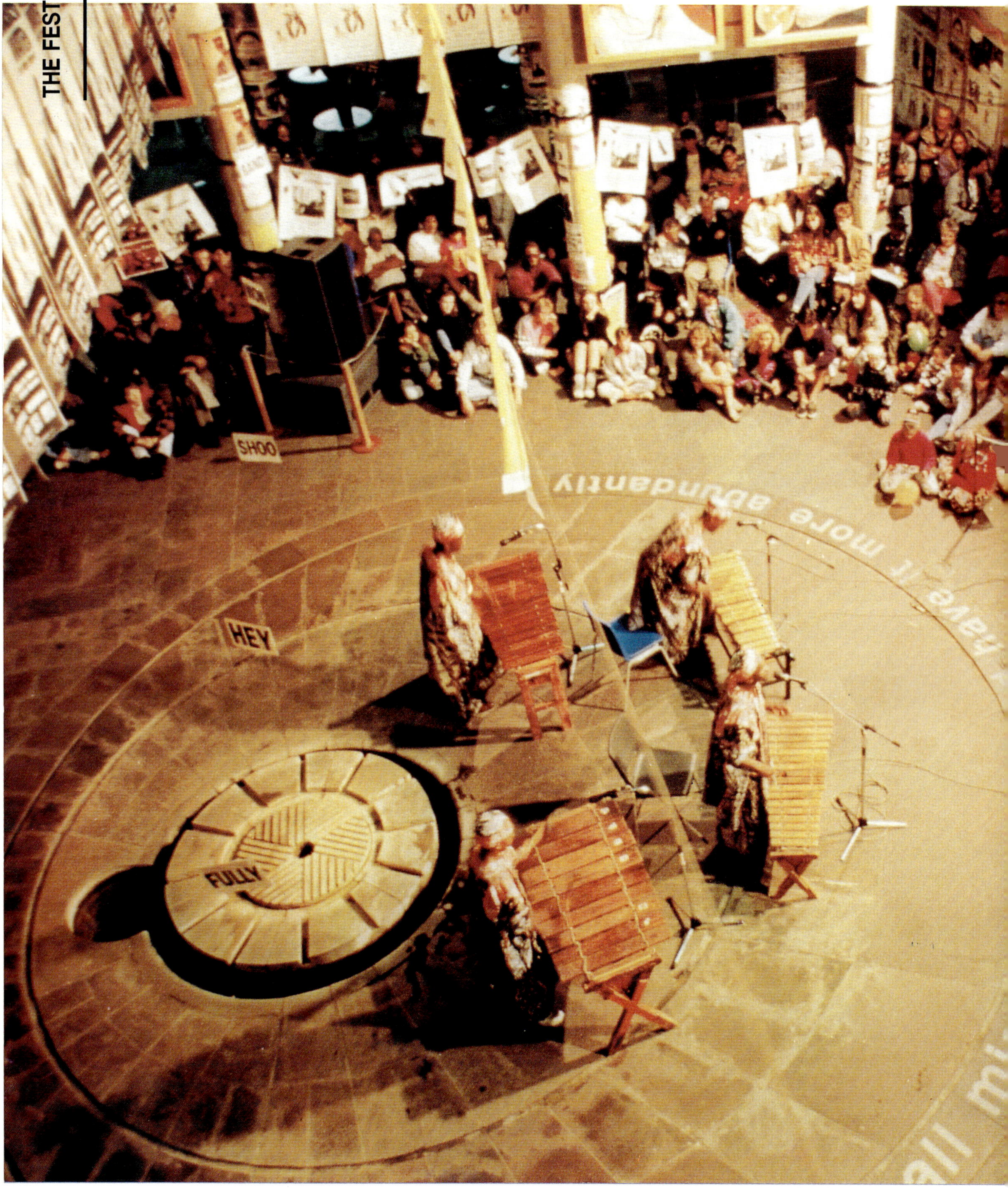

ABOVE: *The warm heart of the Standard Bank National Arts Festival beats in the 1820 Monument*

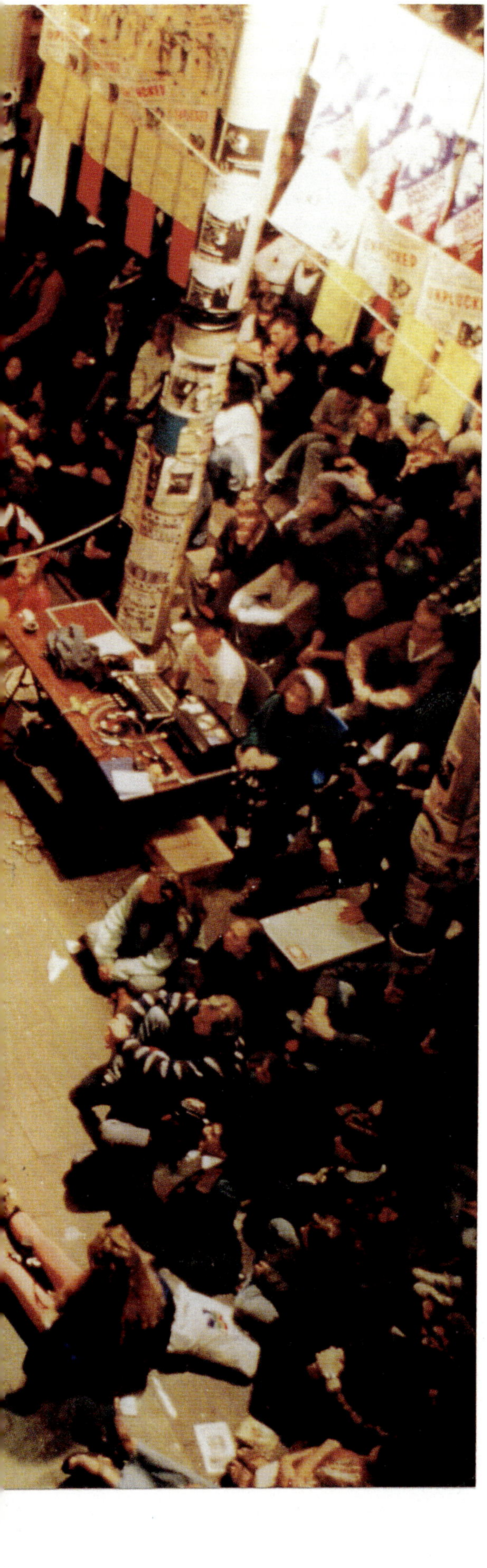

THE STANDARD BANK NATIONAL ARTS FESTIVAL

FUNNY, even peculiar, that isolated little Grahamstown should have such a flair for festivals. A sort of natural phenomenon which bursts briefly through the mundane daily crust like a great geyser, sinks totally out of sight while everybody takes a breather, then suddenly surges up again.

This is by no means a recent development. Way back in 1845 the 1820 Settlers marked the 25th anniversary of their arrival with much innocent revelry, and their 50th likewise. Though the Press did report a hitch at the grand banquet due to "*the forks being made of some metal which had the peculiarity of bending double on the slightest pressure... These were regarded as trifles, however, the Jubilee good humour being proof against anything*".

It continues to be so to this very day at the annual Standard Bank National Arts Festival. Come hellfire or high winds; power cuts or power plays; no more rooms at the inns and no more parking anywhere: locals combine forces in a by now legendary alliance. Together they get it all together. You do not come to Grahamstown to see The Festival, but to be part of it.

The Festival Spirit is alive and well and bubbling out of the 1820 Monument fountain deep in the central gathering place, "that all might have life and have it more abundantly" (John 10, Verse 10).

A quick double back to make mention of two particularly ambitious 19th century efforts that set the pattern for things to come — Queen Victoria's Golden Jubilee, a month-long exhibition visited by 86 892 people at the end of 1887, which paved the way for South Africa's first Great Exhibition at the end of the next decade, described in detail overleaf.

The 20th century has seen one celebration leading to another, culminating in the annual arts jamboree, the largest happening of its kind on the African continent. Changing with the challenges, but always maintaining that inimitable Grahamstown flavour. Festivals unlimited in every sense.

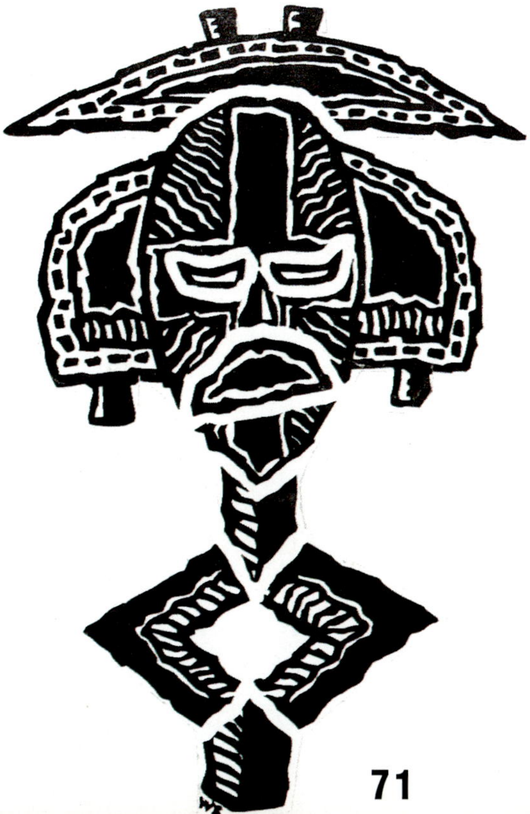

THE GREAT EXHIBITION

5 WEEKS OF GLORY

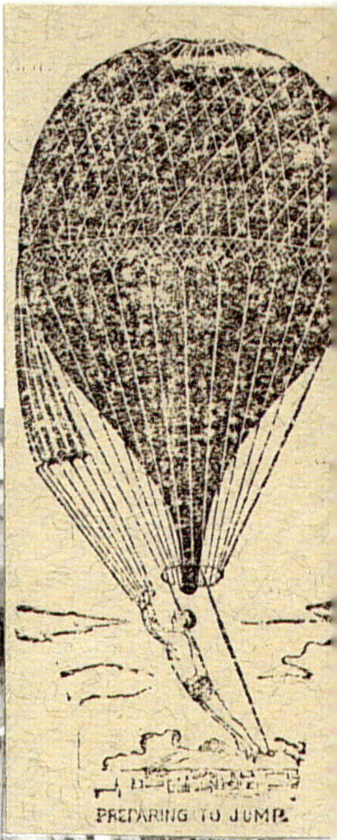

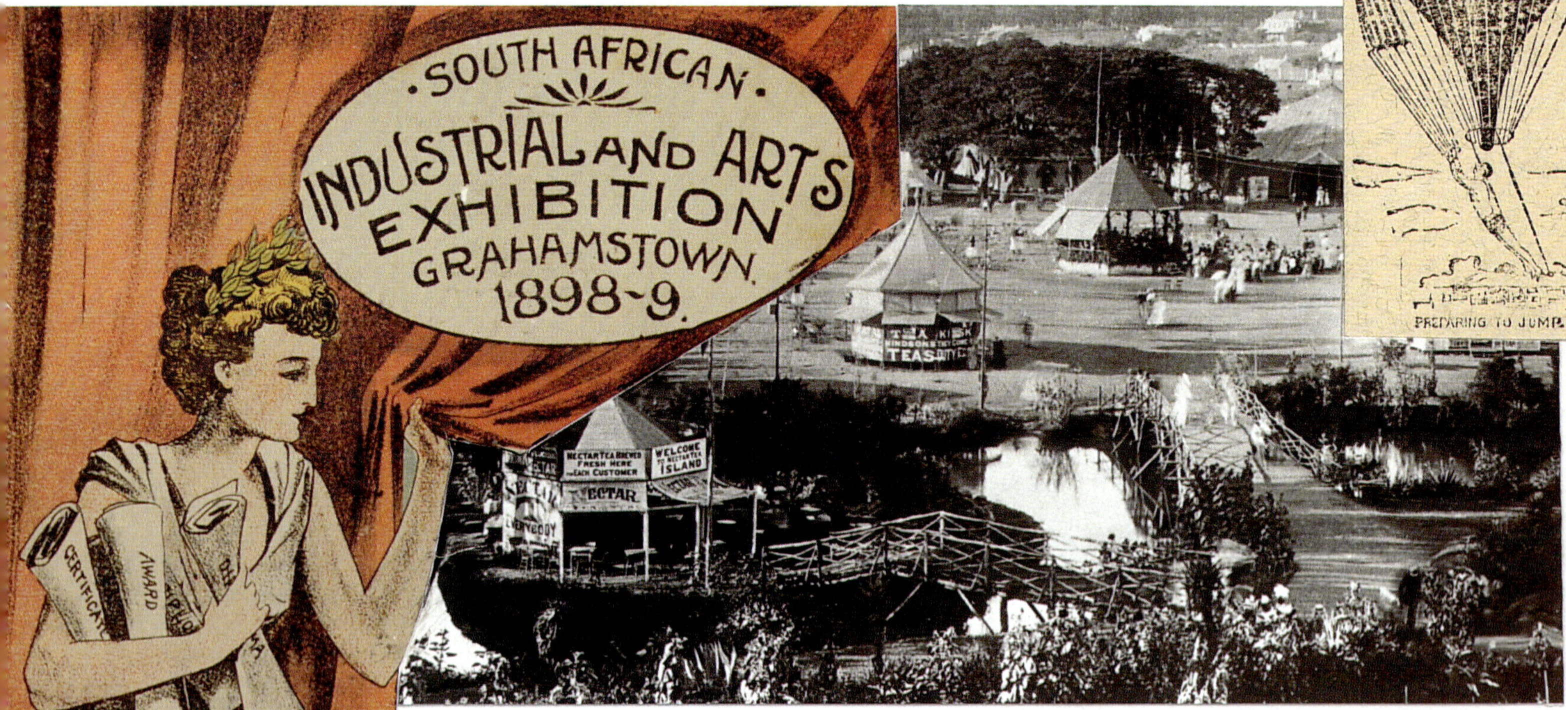

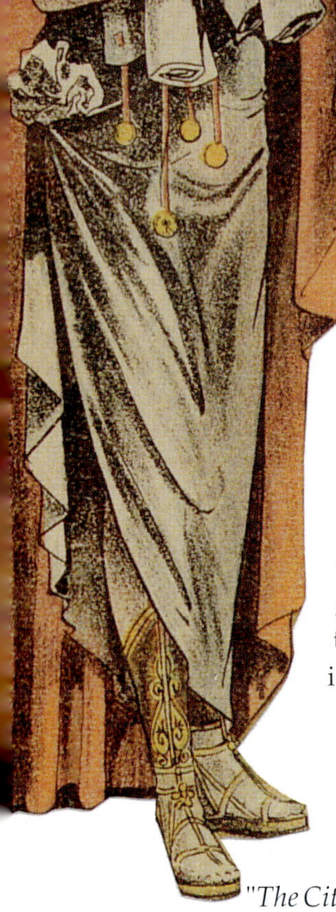

THE rarified Roman matron carefully lifting the curtain on the cover of the official catalogue for South Africa's first Great Exhibition reflects the lofty aspirations of the entire undertaking.

No simpering village maiden she; no small town hotchpotch this. Rather, an imaginative practical gesture towards building a united South Africa through commercial co-operation and tolerance in turbulent times. (So what's new? You might well ask...). A bit like today's Rand Show in general concept, with all the South African territories represented, and surprisingly impressive displays.

During the five week exhibition, which opened on December 15, 1898, some 160 000 people were counted through the newly-patented turnstiles. Visitors poured in from near and far, many on special 10-day excursion tickets issued by the Cape, Transvaal, Orange Free State, Natal, and Lourenco Marques railways respectively.

The main venue was the City Hall. A vast temporary wood and iron exhibition hall was constructed behind it, linked by terraces to Fiddler's Green, where the refreshment kiosks, bandstand, and entertainment pavilions were situated. Today the marquees of the National Arts Festival craft fair rise there annually.

Natal showed everything bar the kitchen sink. Dingaan, King of the Zulus' throne (lent by the Imperial Hotel, Pietermaritzburg), to coal, tins of fruit, vitrified bricks, bark, and rum, plus 28 rickshaws to help solve transport problems. The Matabeleland Jungle set up by Messrs C Wilde and K Offinke, Naturalists and Taxidermists, Bulawayo,

"The City of Saints is not living up to its reputation for sanctity....
Gay little rickshaws are shooting about in all directions."

— ***Grocott's Penny Mail*, December, 1898**

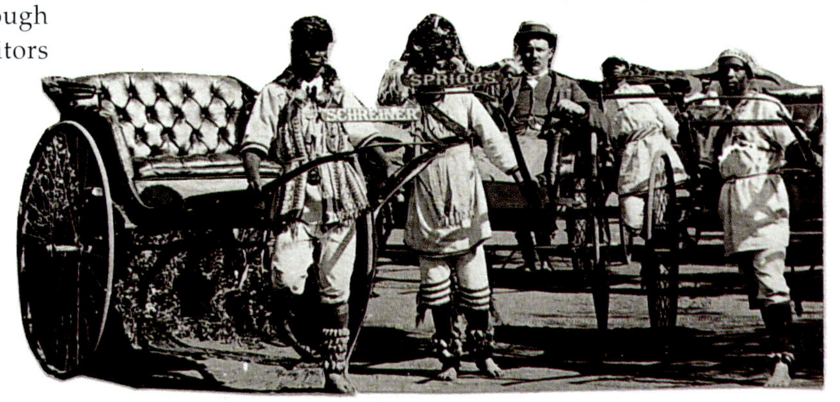

aroused enormous interest. For an extra shilling three live lions could be inspected — Lobengula and the five-month-old twin cubs, Oom Paul and Cecil John Rhodes.

The band of the Royal Berkshire Regiment played daily. Miss Florence Fraser, the Bloemfontein Nightingale, trilled. The Exhibition Waltz penned by Basil Scholefield (composer of the Hamba Suka Barn Dance) was an instant hit.

In the final week Professor Price, billed as the world's champion aeronaut, was about to make a record parachute descent for the benefit of a huge audience when disaster struck. *Grocott's Penny Mail* told the tale: "*Towards 9.30 the balloon, filled to its utmost capacity, was straining and swaying about, struggling for freedom, when the summit was seen to be belching forth clouds of smoke. In a few seconds the flimsy fabric collapsed, and yawing over on one side, an immense hole, 20 or more feet in diameter, was disclosed, ripped and torn by the pressure of the hot air within.*"

The intrepid Prof and his assistant took just 47 hours to sew up another monster sphere, aptly christened Vesuvius, and a spectacularly successful attempt was completed.

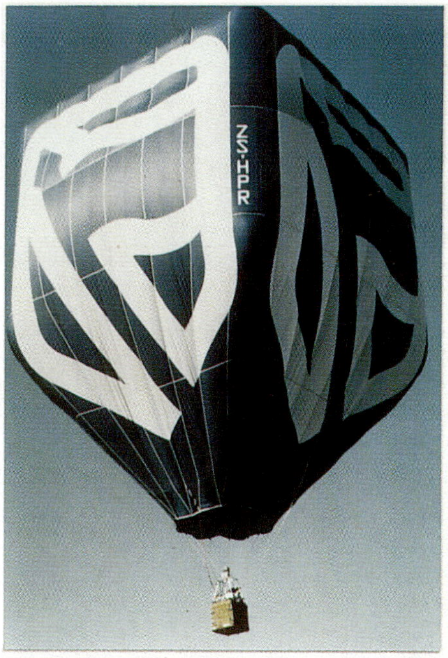

On this soaring note — and a rousing rendition of the Hallelujah Chorus — the extraordinary exhibition drew to a close. Like the Prof's initial balloon, the peaceful ideals (and deals) it had promoted sadly never got off the ground: the Anglo-Boer War started that October.

When the giant blue and white Standard Bank hot air balloon drifts serenely overhead during the National Arts Festival, it symbolizes another great Grahamstown get-together with high-flying hopes: unity through the Arts. And so far it has risen to new heights every year.

ALL AROUND: ***The 1890s and the 1990s — the marquees are in the same position, with a balloon way over the top; modern fashions have gone likewise***

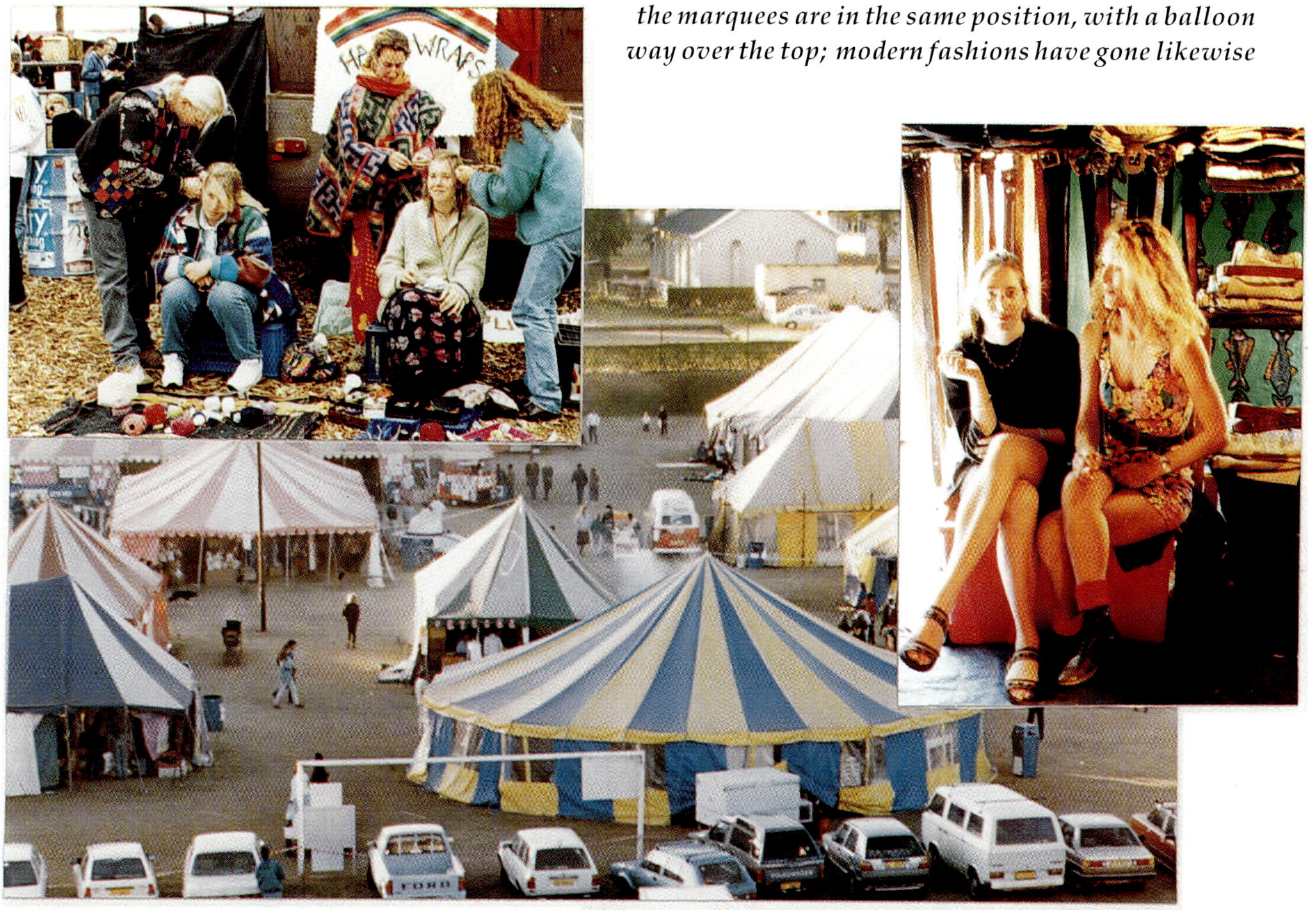

STANDARD BANK NATIONAL ARTS FESTIVAL

MIRACLE

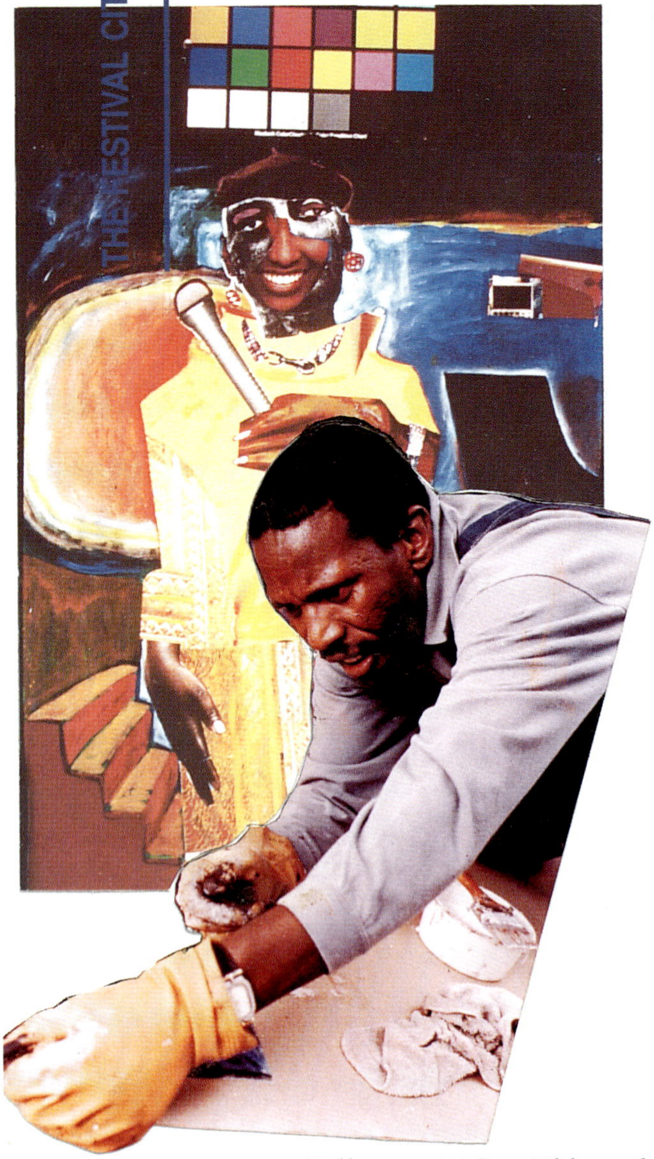

DOES it really happen? More than 20 years on, the annual transformation of the Sleeping Beauty city into the country's creative powerhouse for 11 heady days each July still never ceases to amaze.

Especially now that the Standard Bank National Arts Festival has grown to be one of the largest and most diverse of its kind in Africa. Some say the world. Like a child who suddenly towers over its parents, it seems totally unbelievable that those innocent

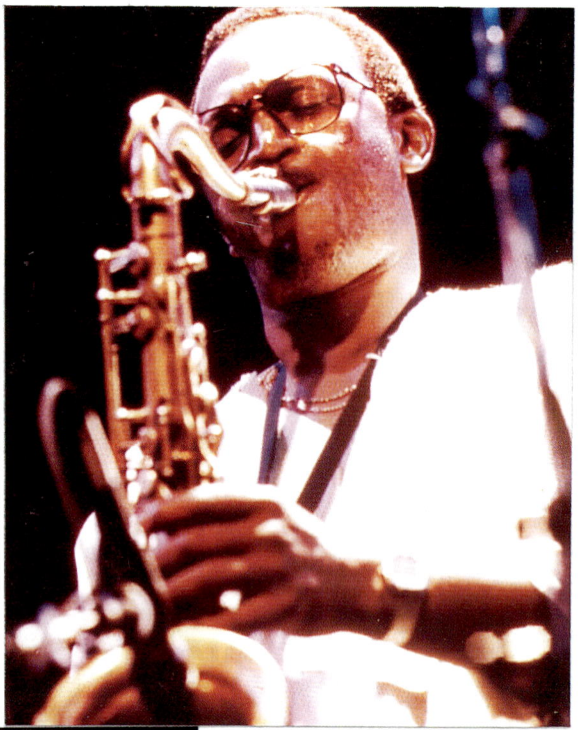

ABOVE: *Collage artist Sam Nhlengethwa at work*

RIGHT: *Blues on the Smirnoff Jazz Festival*

BELOW: *City nights — the perfect backdrop*

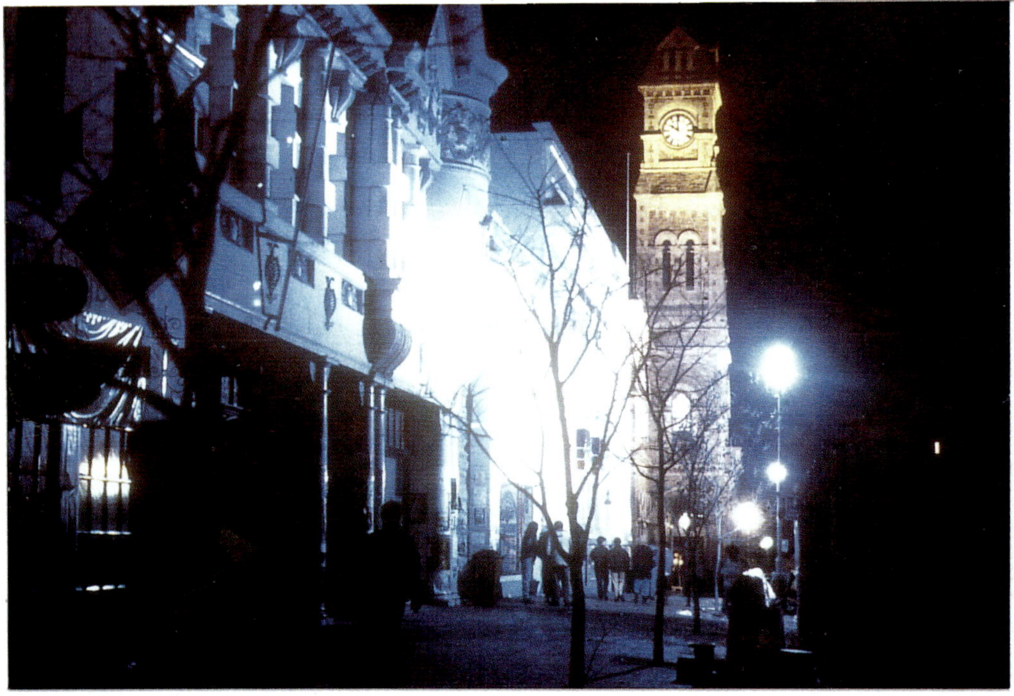

*"**Be prepared!** This refers to absolutely every type of art form, entertainment, behaviour and weather pattern you've ever encountered! Bring an open mind; a carry-all for your programme, souvenirs, vitamin C and tissues; comfortable walking shoes; warm clothes and a light T-shirt; hot water bottle; tanning lotion and your sense of humour because at Festival time Grahamstown has it all."*

— **Festival programme**

OF THE ARTS

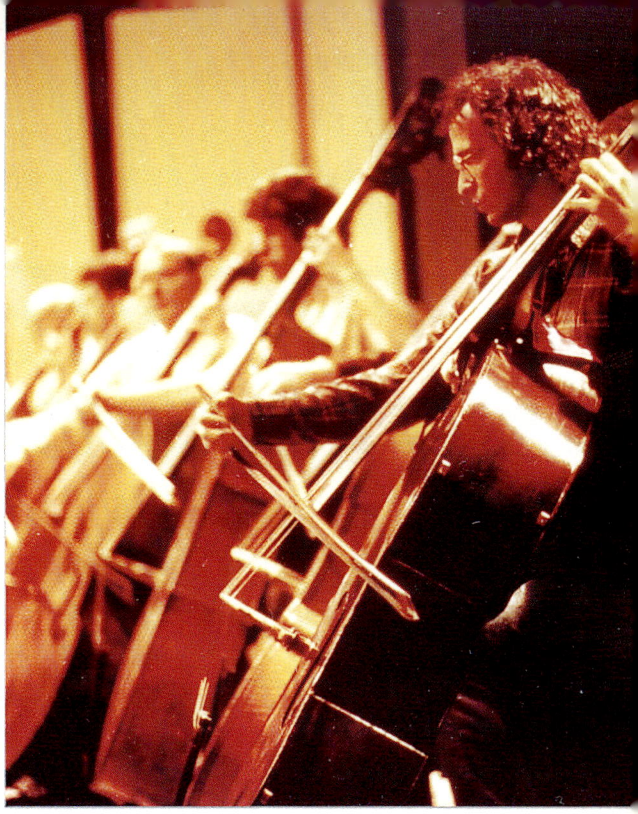

ABOVE: *Music in the classic mode*

early get-togethers "Boldly Beethoven" and "Mostly Mozart" could have produced this multi-cultural colossus. But here it is, right on our doorstep — vital, viable, and very 'Viva'!

Once upon a time you could see everything. Now you need a computer to help co-ordinate your complicated booking manoeuvres. There are literally hundreds of plays, scores of music recitals, dance presentations, films, lectures, art exhibitions, award ceremonies, opening parties, gala performances... It never stops.

The historic city centre vanishes beneath a blanket of posters. For weeks ahead, the media are filled with information on what to see, where to go, how to survive. Most people continue to arrive without a clue and rely on *Cue*, the Festival daily filled with reviews from SA's leading critics, who also occasionally confess to being a trifle overwhelmed.

Established talents are lauded, new faces applauded; trends spotted, contracts signed and dotted. All the stars come out to play, on stage and off, in an astonishing variety of venues.

BELOW: *All the town's a stage and everyone's a star*

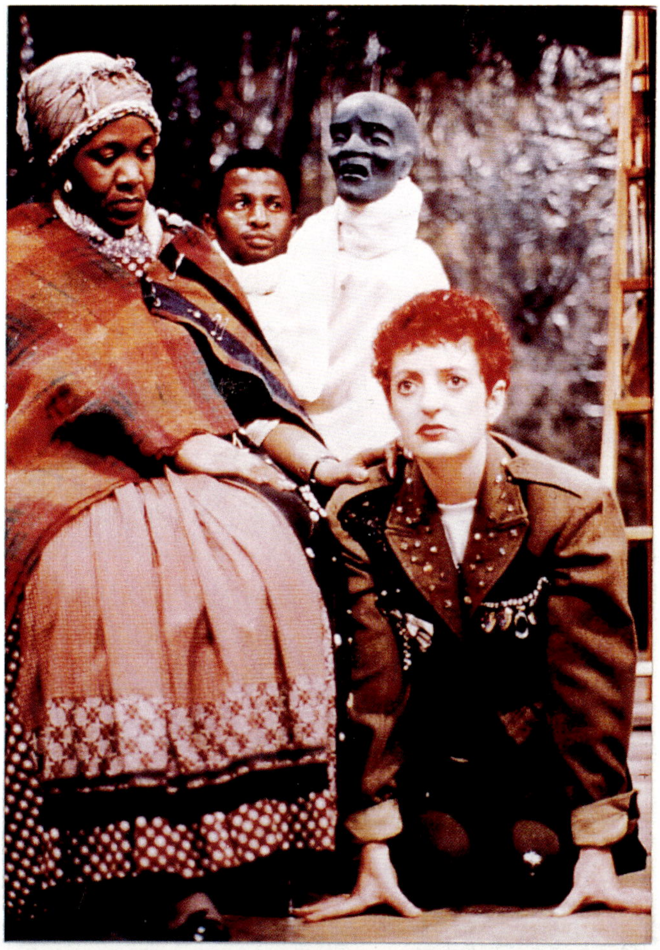

Basically there are two Festivals. The Main Events where the seats are softer, the prices higher, the proceedings prestigious and predictable. Carefully planned by the Grahamstown Foundation Festival Committee. Then there's The Fringe, where you need a cushion and an open mind; where the fix is in the mix described on the next two pages.

In a class of its own, the Smirnoff Jazz Festival blows hot and cool; the weather does likewise. Transnet has gone full steam ahead and turned the old station into a first-class platform for the arts with top-liners in the loco shed. St Aidan's Festival Club is modelled on Edinburgh's, and there's more, much more in store.

Although the Festival is masterminded by the Grahamstown Foundation up in the 1820 Monument, now only 10 percent of the action actually takes place there: it radiates to the valley below. A temporary central one-way street pattern is imposed downtown to accommodate the huge traffic inflow, totally bewildering locals who are in turn trying to accommodate thousands of visitors in their own homes, in caravans on sports fields, University residences, boarding school dormitories, and tents.

Somehow, somewhere, everybody fits in. Then suddenly, the party's over and they all disappear. Just like that. The poster removal squad sweeps through, no trace remains. Grahamstown snuggles back under its duvet of downy winter clouds. It *was* only a dream. It couldn't possibly have happened. Not HERE. Just too good to be true.

ON THE FRINGE and over the top

RIGHT: *Wherefore art thou, Romeo?*

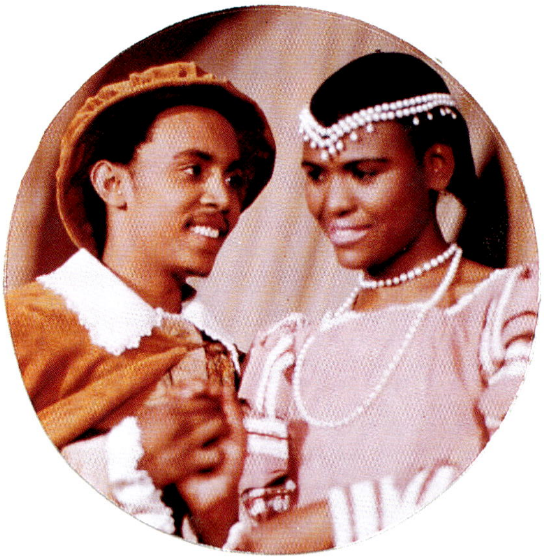

"The freedom of artists (and audiences) at the Fringe is utterly unrestrained. Festival staff organize this 'feast of culture' but all exhibitions and productions are created by the artists themselves. So speak to other Festival-goers, artists and performers to find out what the signals are on the network."
— **Official Festival programme**

TRULY Fully Hey Shoo-Wow... The wrap-around label of the UCT jazz band pretty well sews up the Standard Bank National Arts Fest Fringe — the anything goes, everything shows side of the annual July jamboree. To get the full flavour, add a generous dash of the "Doo Bee Boobies" by courtesy of Intimate Gorilla Theatre: "Doo-bee rude, Doo-bee trashy, Doo-bee fabulous. Doo-bee there!!"

What's in a name? Possibly more than you bargained for, if you read between the lines of the frankly freaky Fringe programme. From a recent lengthy list, "Where Do We Go From Here?" seems an appropriate place to start, especially if you land up at "Stalin — the World's Most Dangerous Band", "Psychedelic Cowboy & Sis-

BELOW: *Crowds at a standstill in City Hall lane*

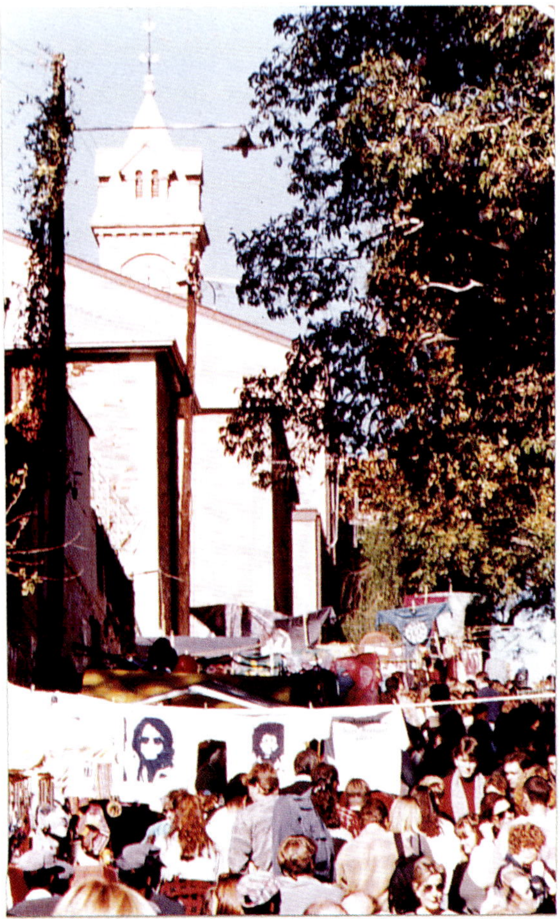

BELOW: *Garden pots for Africa at PX Village*

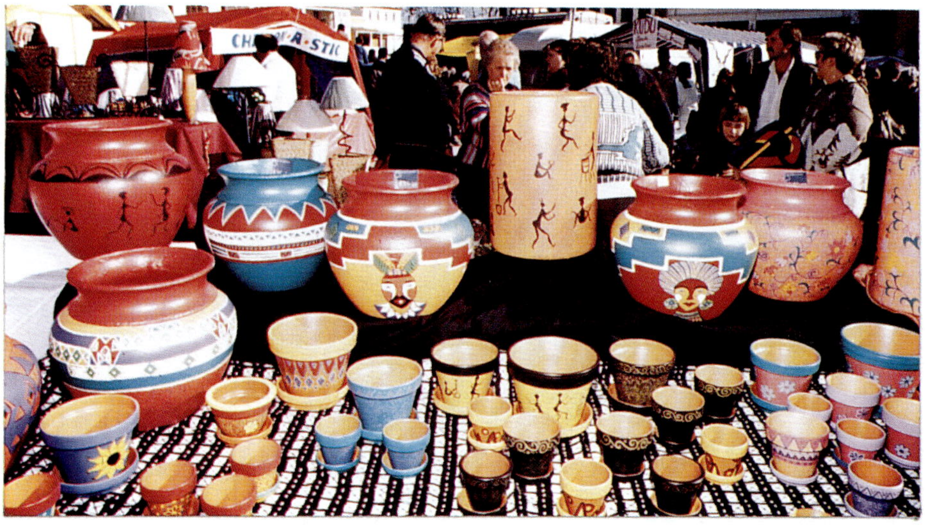

ter Nun" or "Pure as the Driven Slush". Talk about "Oops, Nasty Moments". More like "Nog 'n Potjiekos". No wonder most Festivalgoers soon have an air of "Ek Weet Nie So Mooi Nie".

Then there's "Emakhishini" (kitchen sink drama from the SA Domestic Workers Union), the Matlakeng-Zastron Passion Play, a depiction of the life and death of Jesus Christ from the Maluti Mountains with haunting melodies and songs featuring Mahlo Mlungwana and Tshidiso Laballo; not forgetting "Alice in Welwitschialand" (National Theatre of Namibia) and "Uitgefriekte Fractelina" (one woman's journey through her handbag with Toni Morkel).

Just working out what to see is a full-time occupation, never mind tracking down the venue in the Boy Scouts' Hall, high school gymnasium, Gothic chapel, or circus tent. When you do arrive, scaling the rickety stands may call for mountaineering skills, and whatever happens on stage, you're likely to be on the edge of your seat, hoping neither it nor you will fall down.

Hoo, boy! That's only for starters. Onwards, ever on... Christfest, kiddies' capers, rock round the clock, lute songs and love songs, city tours on foot or bicycles made for two, poetry readings, technoraves, even a fullscale Medieval banquet as a break from boerewors rolls and the shebeen in the Old Gaol.

In between, you shop till you drop at the Village Green Craft Fair, the PX Village, the Provost and the City Hall lane, with buskers, pavement artists and open air-concerts going for the gaps.

It should be total chaos. It almost is— frazzled, razzled, dazzled. But there are also oases of unexpected calm, enriching encounters with artists and actors, coffee with newfound friends, the delight of discovering Grahamstown's enduring old charms in out-of-the-way corners. It is this feeling of personal involvement that keeps confirmed Festinos coming back year after year. The Fringe— nothing like it. Truly Fully Hey Shoo-Wow...

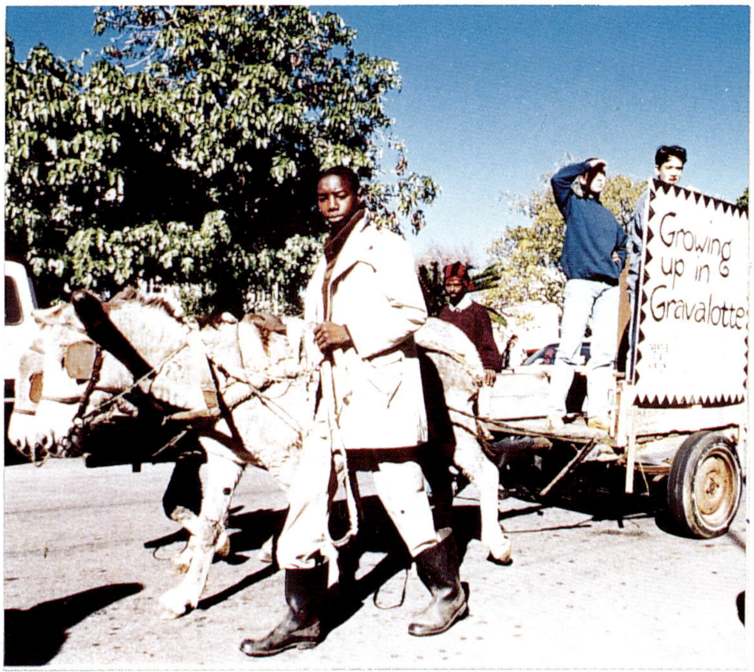

ABOVE: *Climbing on the donkey wagon to publicize a show*

BELOW: ***Baubles, beads and bright shining bells, a real eyeful— plus bags of bargains***

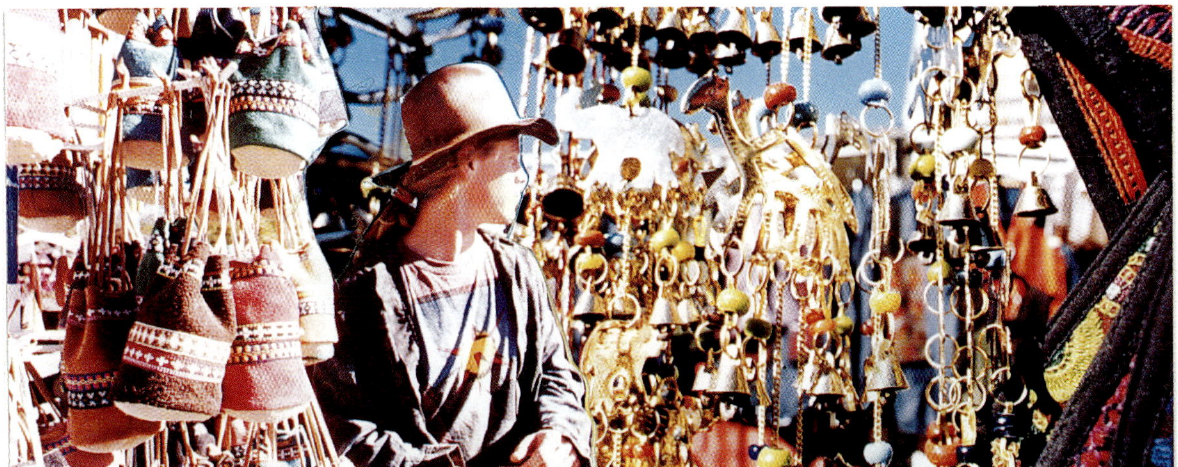

LESSONS THEY'LL NEVER FORGET

"Hi, Folks! Just a few lines. Arrived in Grahamstown safely. First talk this morning was "Getting away with it" by Evita Bezuidenhout — I mean Pieter Dirk-Uys. Then a hysterical bike tour through the historical village (which is called a city). THREE plays, plus a "Shutterbugs" session before supper and "The African Axemen" after. Great stuff — music and sort of poetry ... "axeman climbs to the mountain top of his mind to unleash lightning guitar licks spinning fire rhythms around gathering attack speed sky to ground volcanic eruptions dimensions of sound ...". Ended up at a rave round Monument fountain. Lots of new friends. As the programme says: And now, SLEEP.

G'night,
Pete"

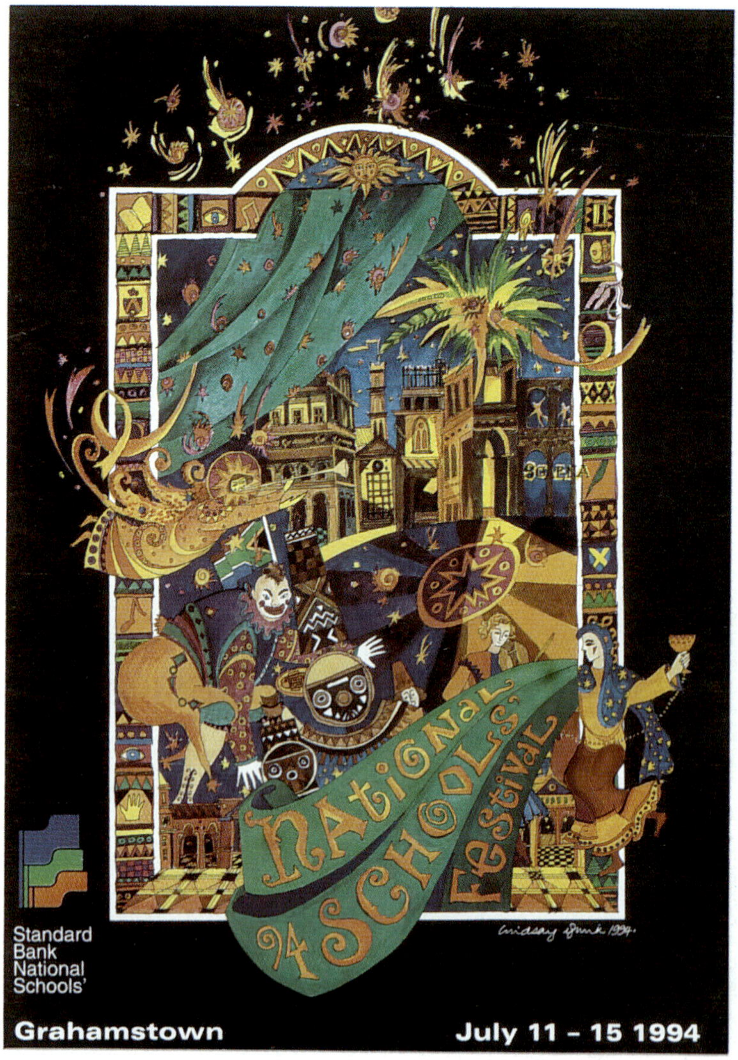

School was never like this, but then the Standard Bank National Schools' Festival is in a class of its own when it comes to making a week of mind-expanding work only a pleasure.

No sooner has the annual Arts Festival ended than close on 1 000 final year high school pupils arrive. They barely have time to don their blazers before embarking on an exciting exploration of English as an international language. An enriching trip through the creative arts organized by the Grahamstown Foundation.

No place for passengers, however. Everyone is pulled in, drawn out. Especially at the workshops where scholars devise their own cabarets on topical issues, shoot and edit videos, get with the beat of African dance and generally shake up their ideas. "*You have shown me the world to which I long to belong—a New World. Nothing can compare*", enthused one participant. Mind-stretching lectures like "King Lear as early striptease artist"; "Lekker accents, lekker okes!"— a look at language attributes; "Kitsch, comics and communications" and "Subliminal Seduction: a study of emotive techniques in advertising broadens horizons beyond the banal."

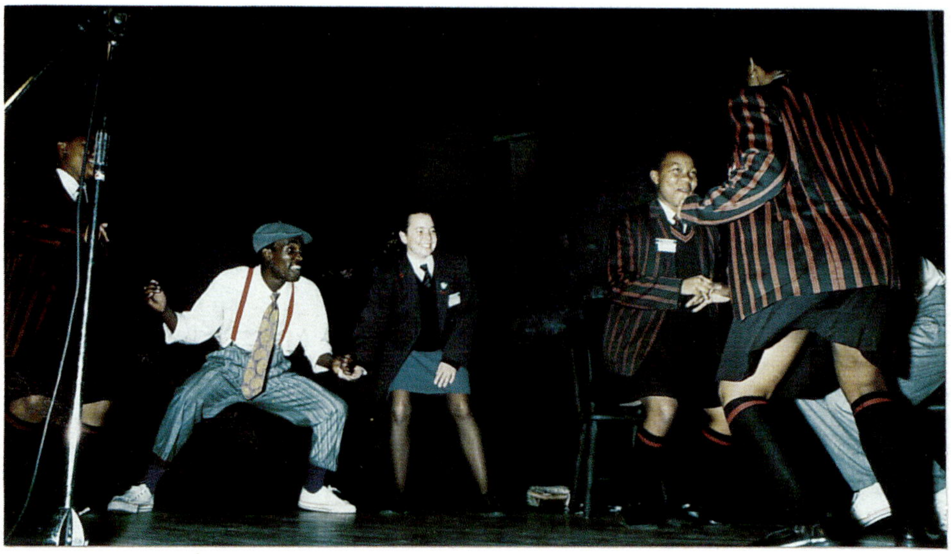

ABOVE: "Wow, look at me now!" Experiencing the lively arts at the National Schools Festival; poster by Lindsay Quirk

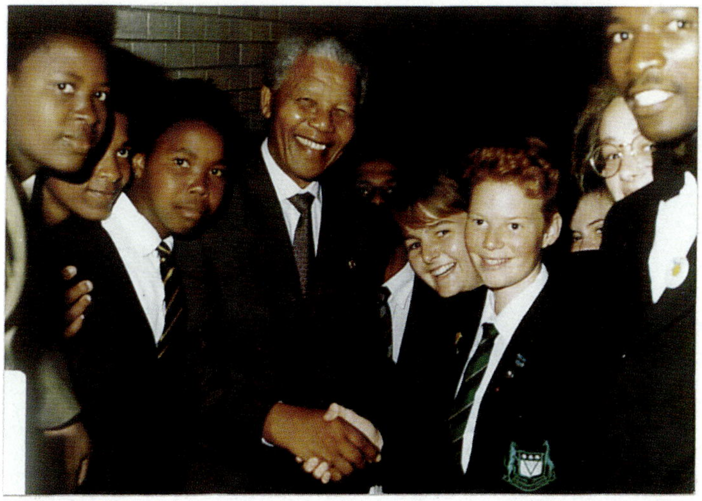

RIGHT: *Monumental welcome for President Nelson Mandela*

The response is such that the Foundation now arranges additional regional schools' festivals backed by other sponsors in the Highveld, Orange Free State, Western Cape and KwaZulu-Natal. This enables many more youngsters to benefit, cutting travelling and accommodation costs.

One of the highlights of the Grahamstown programme is the presentation of the Anglo-De Beers English Olympiad Award, a joint venture of the Foundation and the SA Council for English Education. Close on four thousand entrants wrestle with a thought-provoking open book exam and the three winners go on a fortnight's tour of England's literary shrines. In 1991, the triumphant trio included Jacques Coetzee, an Afrikaans-speaking blind matriculant who did the required reading in braille and typed his answers.

"I like your Monument", declared President Nelson Mandela when he attended the prizegiving of the Gold Shield Youth Education Support Programme—since renamed the President's Award Programme. "To be chosen for a Gold Shield", he told his audience, "reflects attributes that our country sorely needs— responsibility, commitment, dedication and the will to succeed". Originally a Foundation project based on the Duke of Edinburgh's Award Scheme, it has become a separate national undertaking which encourages the development of youthful potential in many different ways.

As does the Grahamstown Eisteddfod in the performing, written, and fine arts — ranging from rap to tap, Xhosa speech and drama to choral singing, photography, and classical ballet.

It is less a competition than a constructive assessment of progress. Approximately 70 percent of the entrants come from Port Elizabeth, East London, and other Eastern Cape centres. Staged by the Foundation shortly before the July Arts Festival, it helps to ensure that a healthy crop of talent is being nurtured in the wings, ready to shine in the spotlight in due season.

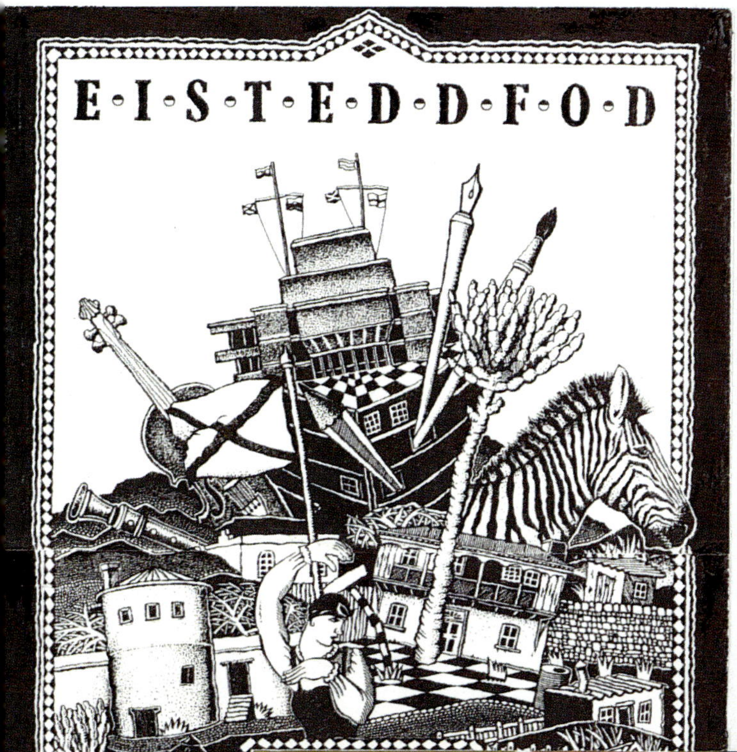

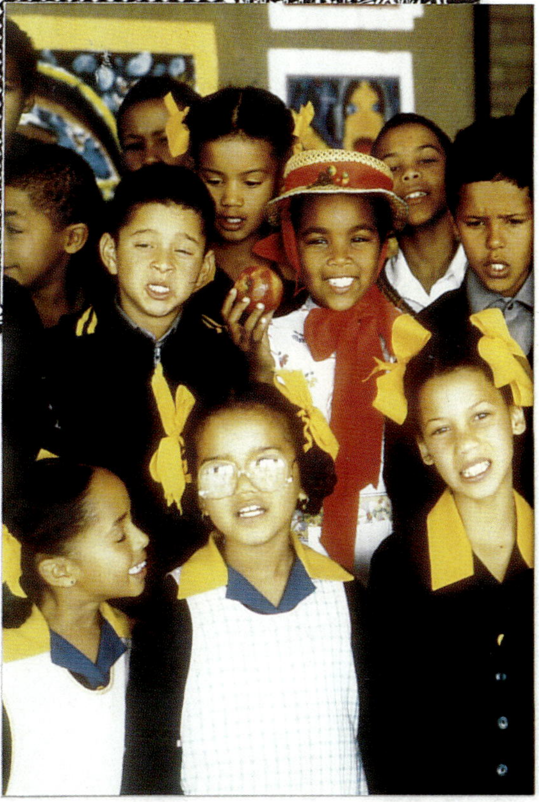

LEFT: *Group action at the Eisteddfod from pupils of St Mary's Primary School, Grahamstown; poster by William Steyn*

AFTER THE FIRE, THE PHOENI

THE LIVING MONUMENT

NOBODY could — or wanted to— believe their eyes. Almost total burnout inside the 1820 Settlers National Monument, the inspiration of the vibrant events on the preceding pages, and headquarters of the Grahamstown Foundation. Destruction on such a scale hardly seemed possible.

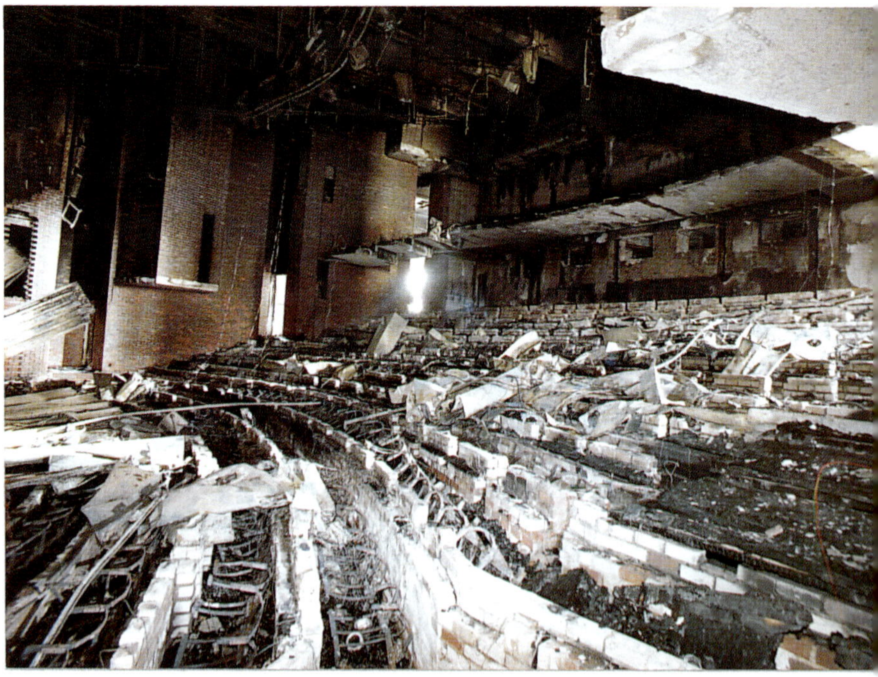

Only the month before the plushly orange auditorium had been filled with applauding Festival audiences. Now, literally not a seat in the house. Completely devastated by the inferno which raged through the early hours of August 13, 1994 — 20 years after the Monument's opening on July 13, 1974, the culmination of 20 years of planning.

Eye witnesses told of balls of flame shooting around the building, windows bursting, bricks popping, banisters burning from one floor to another. Soot everywhere. The souvenir shop nowhere— gone up in smoke. The floor of the largest lecture hall ridged in the tremendous heat.

The area round the fountain— centre of the golden scene at the beginning of this section— a charred mess. Surprisingly, the surrounding Cecil Skotnes panels and towering yellowwood sculpture survived comparatively unscathed.

After a benumbed, silent Saturday when even the weather went into melancholy mourning, a true Brit fighting spirit emerged as messages of support poured in. The Monument would be rebuilt, better than before. The Phoenix Fund was launched to help it rise from the ashes. As two comments in the hastily improvised visitors' book put it: "*The show must go on*" and immediately underneath, "*The show will go on*".

Not only the Standard Bank National Arts Festival and the Foundation's other special projects, but all the other events which take place here. Rhodes University graduation ceremonies, school prize givings, exams, exhibitions, conferences, concerts, seminars, wedding receptions (there was one planned the very day of the fire), formal dinners and dances.

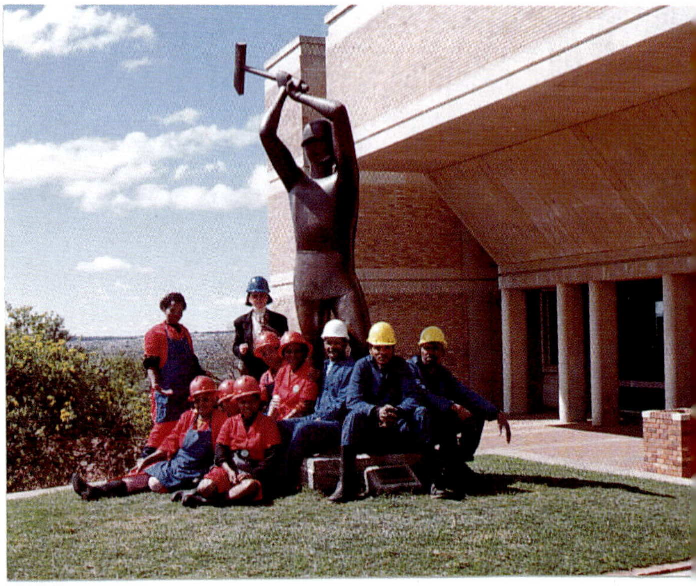

ABOVE: ***Inside, stark tragedy in the theatre; outside, Monument staff ready to swing into restoration action, backed by Bruce Arnott's blacksmith sculpture***

The depth of the widespread concern proved how meaningfully the Monument has integrated into both the community and the country's life. Over two decades it has grown into something great — exceeding the originators' most optimistic hopes. A platform for constructive exchange as well as for communication through the arts and education. Neutral ground where everyone can speak out.

Built primarily to commemorate the 1820 Settlers and other English-speaking pioneers who contributed to SA's development, to celebrate the English language and provide inspiration for the future, the main motivation has always been that the best form of commemoration is active. "While mindful of the past, to do things in the present which shape the future." Hence its design as a versatile venue instead of a mausoleum on the hill.

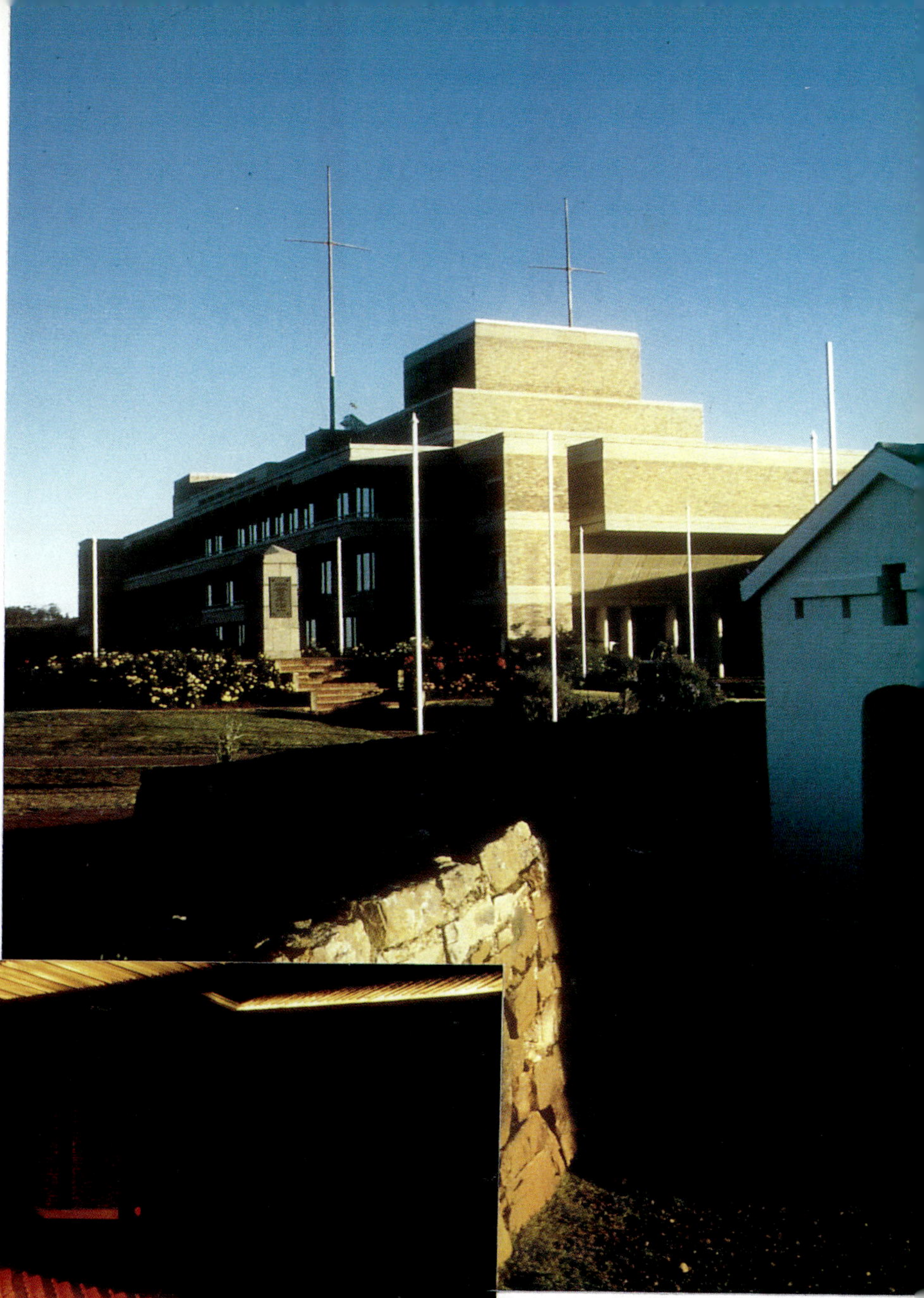

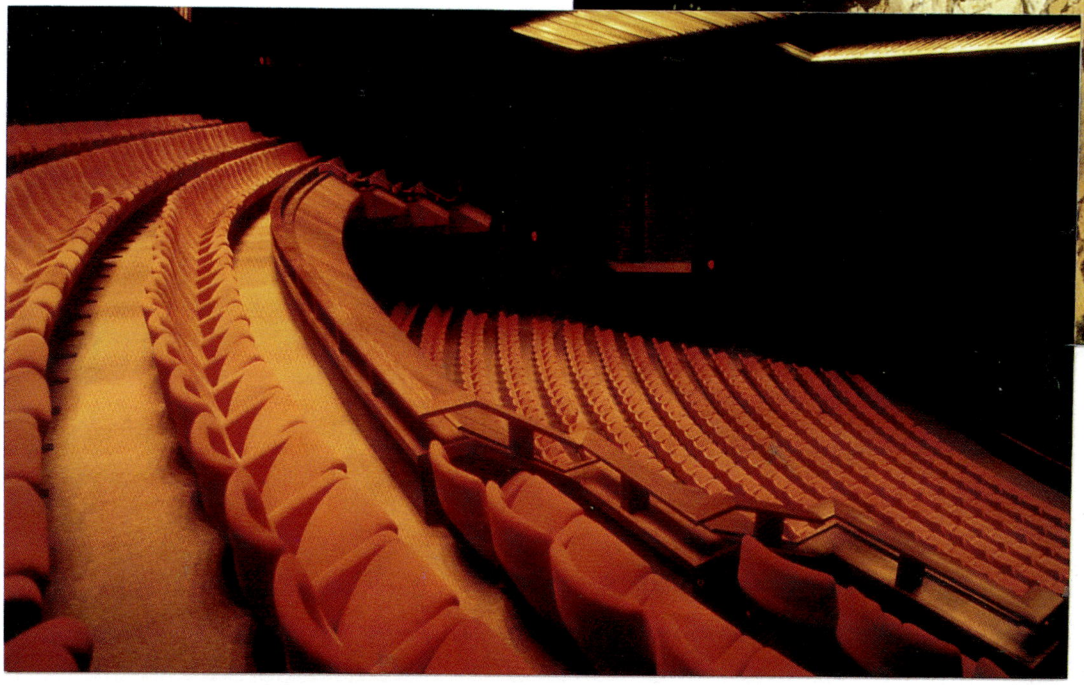

ABOVE AND LEFT: ***Glowing memories... Sun on the 1820 Monument and old stone wall of nearby Fort Selwyn — and theatre, the way it was and will be again***

Over the last years extraordinary things have happened, especially at the Festivals. Cultures have been shared, merged and forged. It has become a national monument in the widest sense. An ideal time for the phoenix— that legendary symbol of renewal — to spread its wings and fly high. Restoration plans include many improvements to take the Monument and all who gather here well into the next century — a whole new age.

A statement by a Council Chairman, made when the plans for the initial building were still on the drawing board, echoes with renewed relevance: *"Let us go forward into the future strengthened in the knowledge that we build not selfishly and that we are warmed and encouraged by the general goodwill of our countrymen. Let us never flag in our determination to make this Monument a shining success in the spirit in which it was conceived."*

WRITTEN IN STONE

ROCKS OF THE AGES

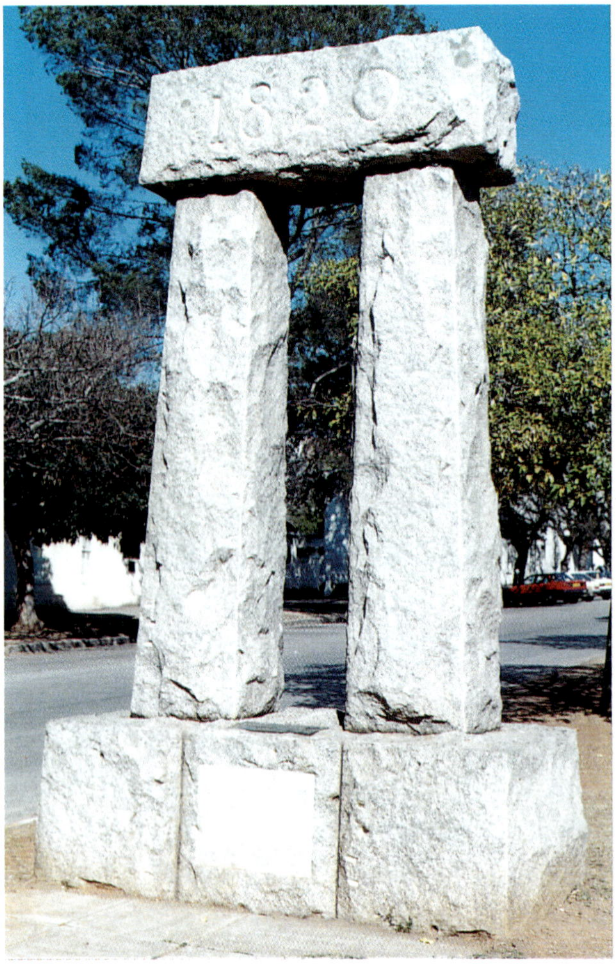

ABOVE: Shades of Stonehenge in High Street; a granite trilithon erected in 1953 by the 1820 Settlers Association of SA

GREAT slabs of 360-million-year-old quartzite rear round the 1820 Monument. Blasted from the hillside during the construction of the N2 bypass, they have not been raised at random. Some point to the future, like those at the turnoff — freedom of speech and worship, freedom from want and fear — unveiled in July, 1994, with directions for the new South Africa in view.

Others recall the past, bearing dates of events that caused significant increases of English-speaking immigrants: 1820, the Natal settlers of 1849-52, the 1867 diamond identification which foreshadowed the Kimberley rush, and the l886 Main Reef gold discovery in the Transvaal. In centuries to come, extraterrestrial tourists may be as puzzled by their purpose as we earthlings by mystifying mounds of ancient civilizations.

Or they might touch down on the astronomical toposcope viewing platform in front of the building and immediately get their bearings. Here carefully positioned rocks indicate the four points of the compass, the longest day (summer solstice, near December 22), the shortest day (winter solstice, near June 21), and the equinoxes which occur midway between the two.

In June the Pleiades, a cluster of seven stars, become visible in the early morning above the Precinct Stone. They are called *limela* (from *lima*— to dig) in Xhosa, and their rising marks the beginning of the Xhosa year. They also give their name to the month of June— *eyesiLimela*, when the young men (*abakhwethas*) return from the initiation ceremonies which mark their entry into adulthood.

Among the Thonga, the Pleiades are the only constellation which bears a name — *shrimelo*, the one which announces the tilling season. They bring the same message to the Khoi, Bambaras, Bapedis, and Zulus.

Obviously a perfect place for starry-eyed nights beneath the astrodome of the African sky. And on a clear day you can see forever, as well as the Winterberg and Hogsback mountain ranges.

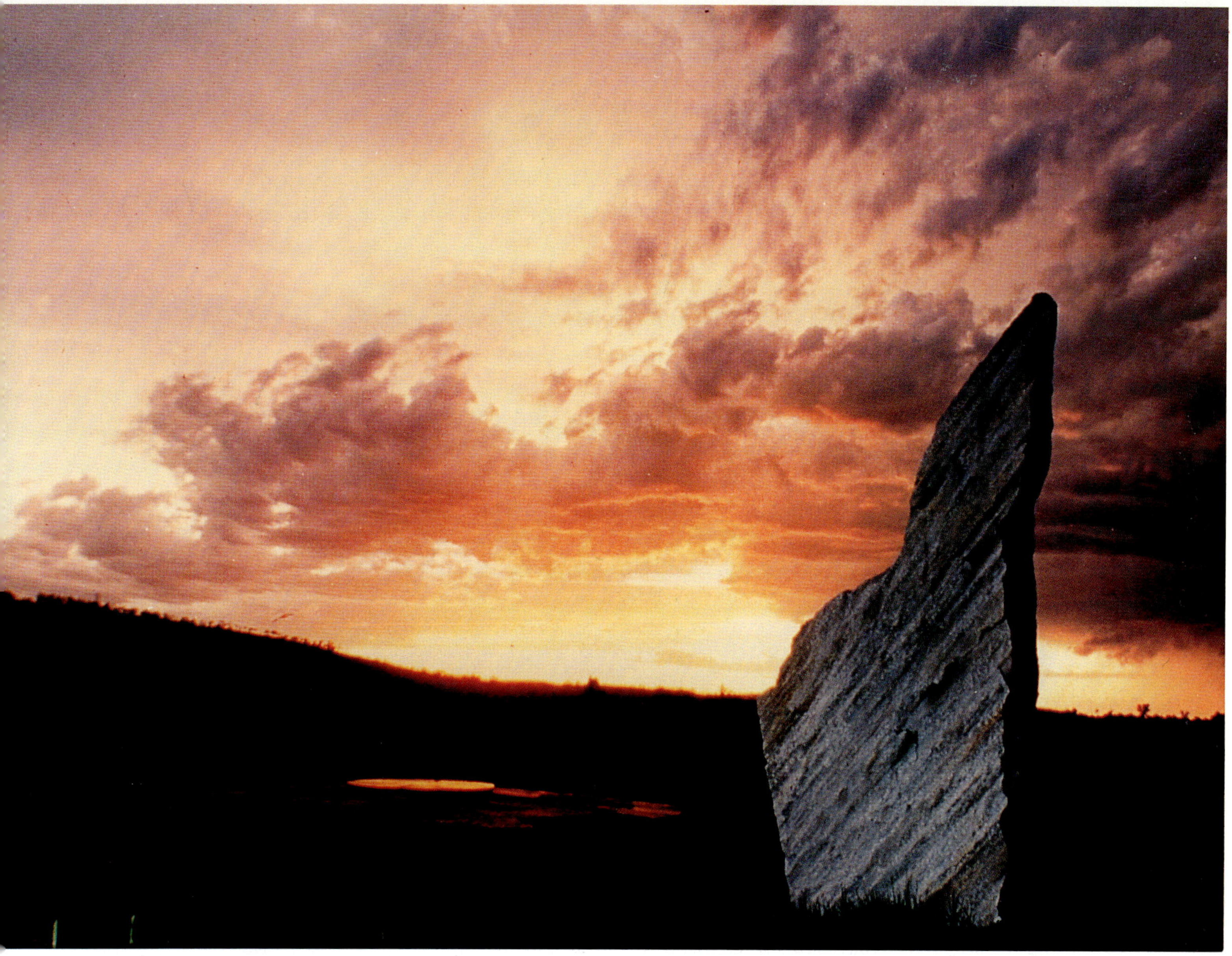

ABOVE: *Standing stone at 1820 Monument astronomical toposcope*

BELOW: *Wagon stone in Artificers' Square*

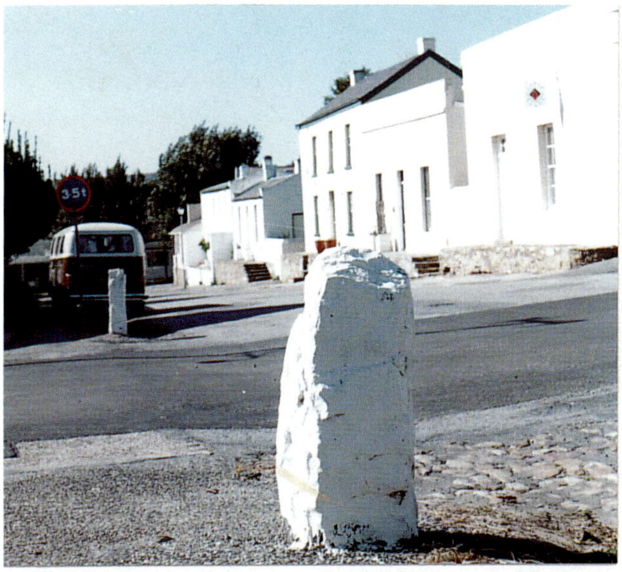

THE WAGON STONES

Mini monuments to a bygone era stand at the corners of streets in the oldest areas of Grahamstown. Usually painted a warning white to prevent unwary motorists from bashing into them, they date back to the days when wheels meant wagons, and they were erected to protect buildings from bumps by trailing vehicles drawn by spans of 8 to 12 oxen. At one stage Grahamstown held a premier position among the wagon-making centres in southern Africa. Many of the wagons used by Dutch farmers in the Great Trek were made here, and for decades after, the city continued to be the chief supplier to the North.

Also visible in the accompanying photograph is one of the few surviving cobblestone gutters. These originally separated the gravelled roadway from the natural earth of the pavement. Most have long since disappeared under successive layers of asphalt, but those which have reappeared are now left as their makers intended.

OLD BATTLES,

"A frontier, as I understand it, is not merely a military line; it is a zone of cultural contact and psychological adjustments. For generations men on a frontier seem to live confused and torn between two worlds."

— Prof Winifred Maxwell, in her presidential address to the Grahamstown Historical Society, 1972

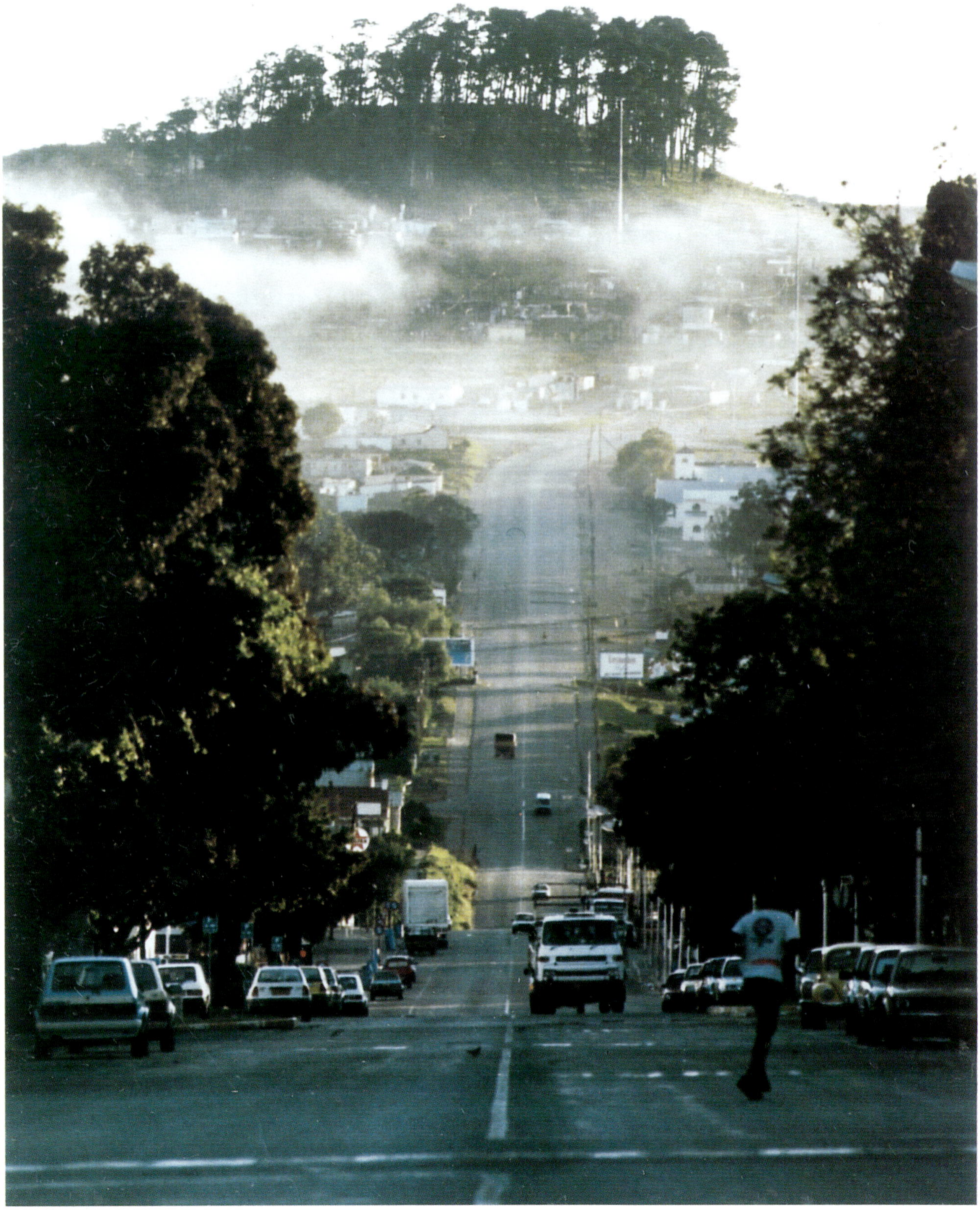

NEW DAWNS

THE hills on the Eastern side of Grahamstown presented a startling sight in the early afternoon of April 22, 1819. Thousands of Xhosa warriors, their bodies covered with red ochre, fringed oxtails round their legs, with plumes of eagles, cranes and other wild birds on their heads, and carrying strong oxhide shields and bundles of assegais, were massed on the slopes.

In the valley below, approximately where the Market Square shopping mall is today, some 350 defenders waited, the British troops sweltering in their tight-fitting scarlet tunics.

The Xhosa leader, the mystic Makana — also known as Nxele — made an impassioned speech in which he promised his followers that the bullets of the white men would turn into water. The warriors advanced, in their overconfidence breaking their throwing spears to improvise short stabbing-weapons.

The first musket and artillery volley was fired when they were about 36 metres from the troops. The devastating effect so terrified them that they milled around on the open ground. A further four volleys were fired into the confused mass, the grape-shot used by the artillery taking a terrible toll. The water in the nearby Kowie Ditch ran red with blood. The main attack was over in little more than an hour. Of the defenders, only three were killed and five wounded. Musket power had prevailed.

One of the stories to come out of what was henceforth called the Battle of Grahamstown was that of Elizabeth Salt. She reputedly carried a keg of gunpowder to the troops unmolested by the Xhosa, who did not harm women in battle. Although never verified, the legend is perpetuated in bronze on the city's centenary monument.

A far reaching result of the battle was that Secretary of State Lord Bathurst hastened the settlement scheme which the Cape Governor, Lord Charles Somerset, had been urging since 1817. Six months later the 1820 Settlers were on their way to form a human buffer to help hold the Eastern frontier of the colony. The settlers settled nothing. Four wars had already been fought, five more were to follow.

Grahamstown itself saw no further action, although as the military headquarters it was frequently full of troops on the move to forts and the fighting further forward. Reminders of these tumultuous times crop up in unexpected corners, especially on the Rhodes University campus, site of the Drostdy barracks.

As an old man, Dr W G Atherstone aptly said of Grahamstown: "She was cradled in bayonets. She is now a fair and beautiful city, and a centre of education." The same does not apply to the Greater Grahamstown townships on the slopes of Makana's Kop, the tree-topped hill, named after the warrior prophet, which dominates the Eastern skyline. But better days are dawning ...

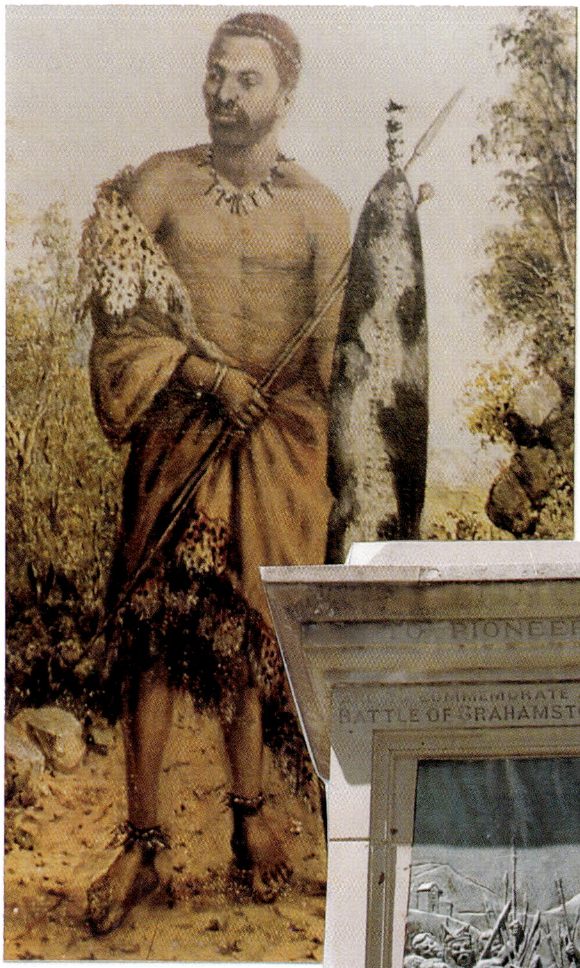

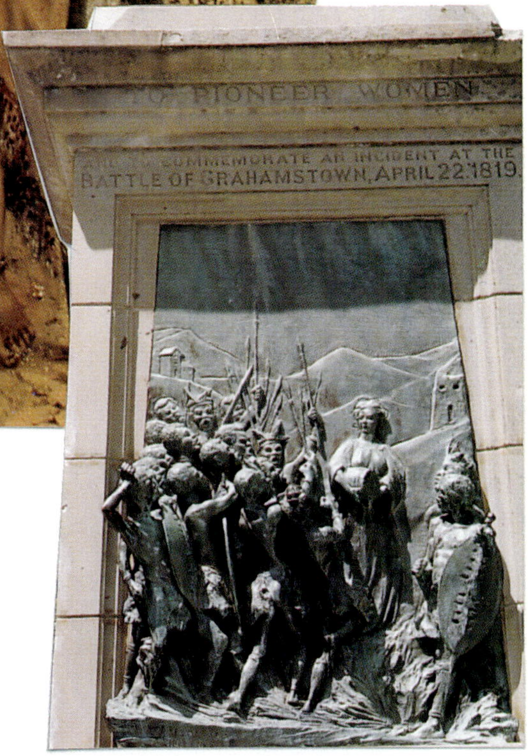

CLOCKWISE: *Daybreak on Makana's Kop; Makana painted by Frederick I'Ons; and centenary memorial plaque*

THE FINGO VILLAGE

DISTINCTLY dilapidated in parts, beset by grim, persistent poverty that cannot be denied, the Fingo Village is nonetheless vibrantly alive. To focus constantly on the down side somehow negates the spirit of the inhabitants, who have survived decade after decade of trials and tribulations and still managed to retain an innate dignity and gentleness, even joy. Be it ever so humble, there is no place like home, and hope springs eternal that better days are on the way. They have been a long time a-coming.

Part of Greater Grahamstown's wide township belt which girdles Makana's Kop and beyond, the Fingo Village is the oldest example in southern Africa of a Black settlement established under a European system of land ownership. Tradition has it that the grant of freehold titles was made in recognition of services performed in the defence of the Cape Colony by the Mfengu levies in the frontier wars of 1846 and 1850-53, but the first proposals for its establishment predate both.

As early as the 1830s Grahamstown had already developed its three-way split — the White town stretching between the Drostdy Gateway, the Cathedral, and the present Market Square; the beginnings of a 'Hottentot' settlement beyond the Old Cemetery, and over the Kowie spruit the Fingo area, largely to the right of what is now the main road to Bisho. Nobody knows just how much the Fingoes contributed to early Grahamstown as labourers of every description.

Controversy surrounds the identity of the Mfengu, as they were called. One version holds that they were initially refugees, small tribes fleeing from Natal, some driven out by Shaka Zulu in the 1820s. Many were given sanctuary by Hintsa, Chief of the Gcaleka Xhosa, and became known as Mfengu from the Xhosa *siyamfenguza* meaning "we are hungry". Broken and detribalized as a result of their experiences, they had a stronger

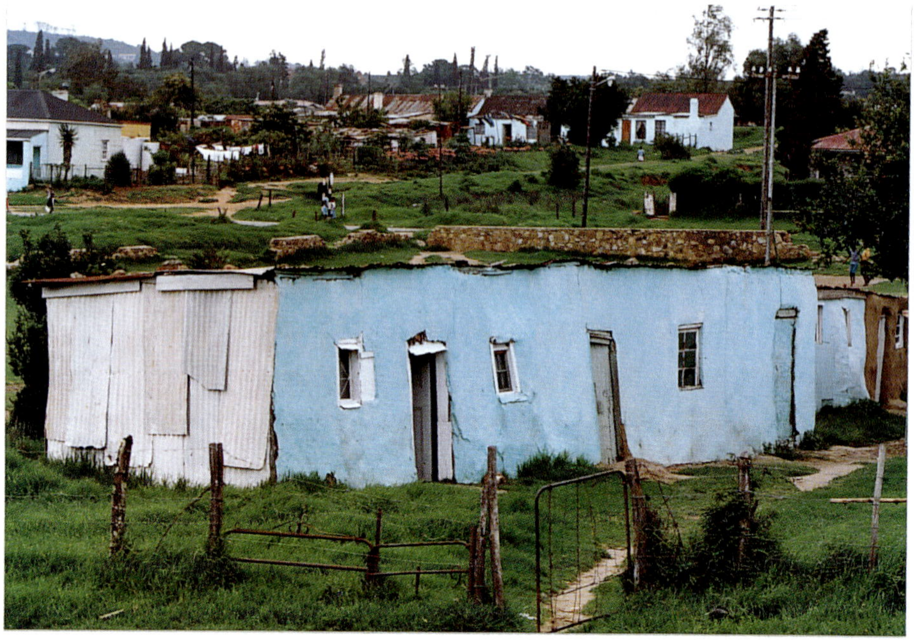

BELOW: St Philip's shortly after completion in 1867; and Lobengula grave

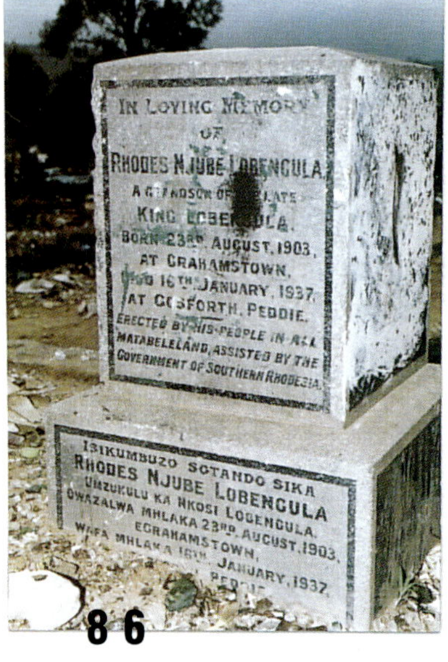

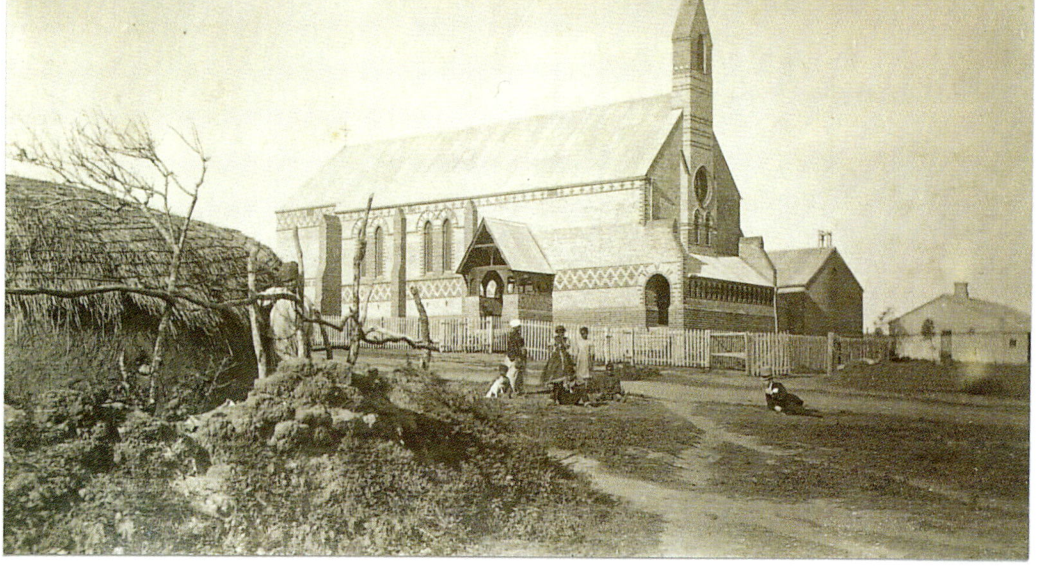

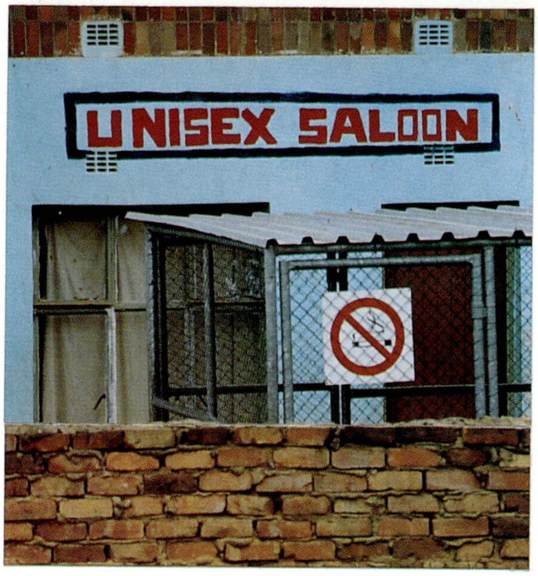

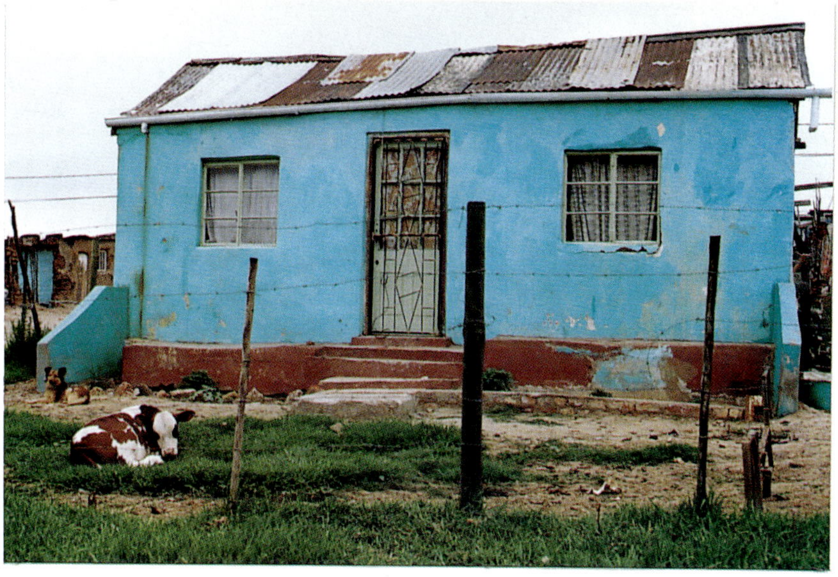

*CLOCKWISE: **Fingo Village blues and the green, green grass of home; the saloon is a hairdresser's — no smoking and no drinking either***

incentive than those bound by tradition to adopt the customs of the Whites with whom they came into contact.

They moved into the Cape Colony in 1835 and 1847 with the agreement of the Governor, Sir Benjamin D'Urban, and assisted the British in the wars against the Xhosa in 1846 and 1850 - 53. In the former, Grahamstonians had the bright idea of getting local Fingoes to defend their homes while they slept snugly in their beds at night. A body of 90 Fingoes was accordingly armed to form a ring of pickets round the town, relieving the slumbering citizens of "this irksome duty".

There is no evidence that freehold title deeds — issued in 1856 by the Governor acting "in the name and on behalf of her Majesty Victoria" — were for services rendered, but this belief continues today, and a number of village families treasure the original documents. Even though the Mfengu element in Grahamstown has been diluted over the years by inter-marriage, there is still a distinctive style about typical Fingo villagers and a special sort of relationship between them and the wider community.

St Philip's Church was consecrated in 1867 as part of the Anglican mission. A fine brick building, it formed a parallel parish to St Bartholomew's Church in Market Street. Both ran schools. Princess Emma, daughter of the Ngqika Chief Sandile, trained in Cape Town and taught at the Fikizolo ("arrived yesterday") School, the remains of which survive.

The Lobengula graves are stranded forlornly in a plot where pigs root and donkeys stray. The most legible headstone is that of Rhodes Njube Lobengula, a grandson of King Lobengula, Chief of the Ndebele of Zimbabwe, who was born in Grahamstown in 1903, and died at nearby Peddie in 1937.

Looking from here across towards Rhodes University, the other half of Greater Grahamstown is unbelievably pristine — a distant view vividly described by Township poet Lungile Lose:

"Foamy white clouds dance above town.
All the houses are white.
Did it snow over there?
I wish it would snow here too."

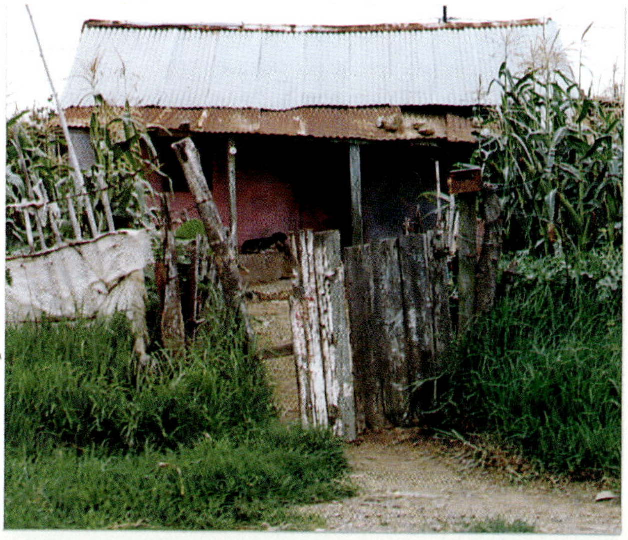

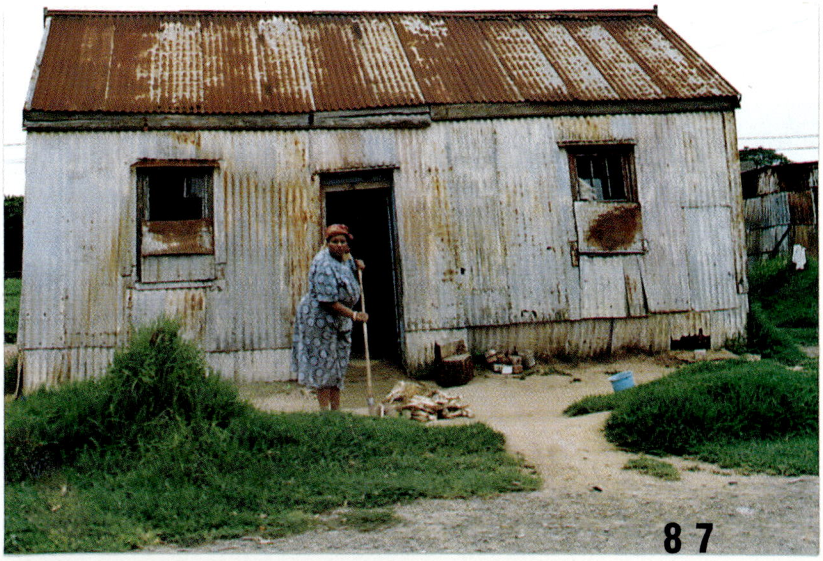

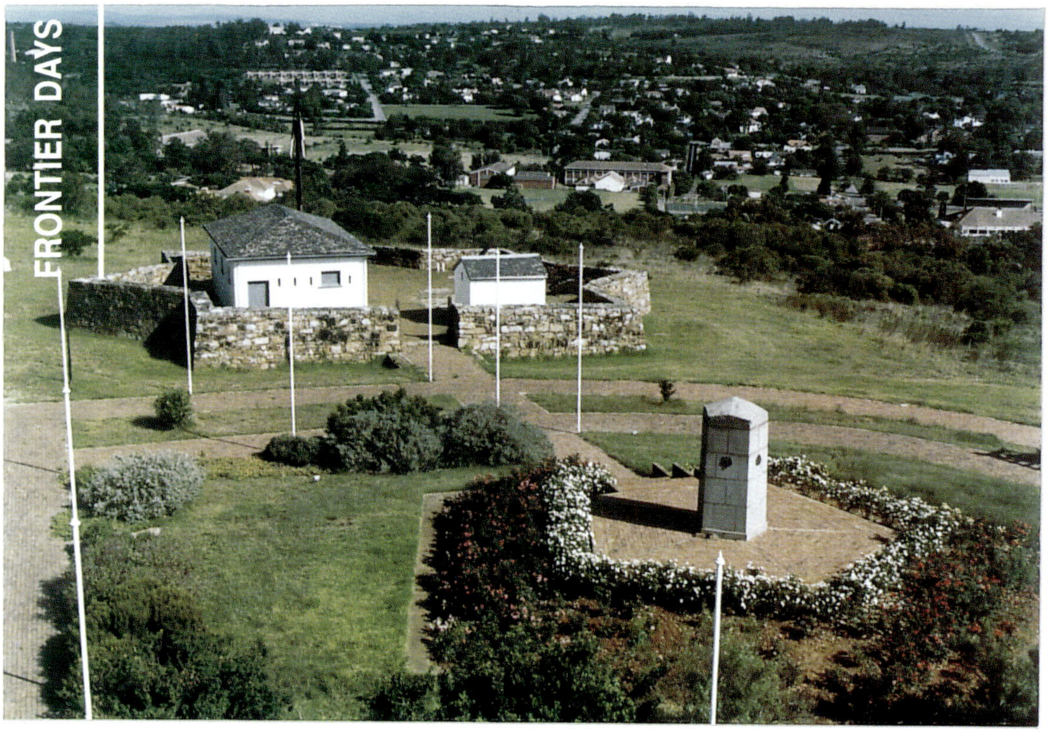

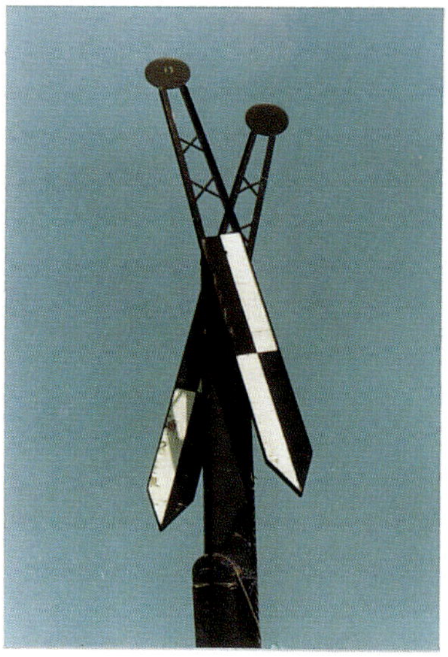

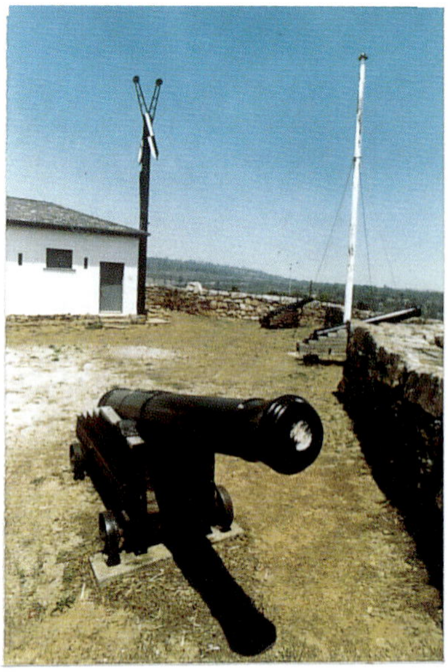

UP ON GUNFIRE HILL

CLOCKWISE: *Toy fort with ring of roses alongside; semaphore signal; and ex-naval nine-pounder*

LITTLE Fort Selwyn — smaller than ever next to the angular bulk of the 1820 Monument — looks like a toy fort, and in a sense always has been one. Never a shot fired in anger. The name Gunfire Hill comes from the 9 o'clock gun which used to be fired by the Royal Artillery each morning to alert citizens of the time (read from a sundial within the fort).

Some sticklers for time complained that "the sundial on Selwyn's Battery is moveable and twists about in a very eccentric manner", but an editorial in *The Grahamstown Journal* of December 15, 1849, declared "there is a charm in its very uncertainty ... As long as Selwyn's Battery crowns the rocky height, so long may our morning gun blaze forth from its battlements". It did so for the final time in September, 1870.

The star-shaped fort was named after Capt (later Maj) Charles Jasper Selwyn of the Corps of Royal Engineers, who was responsible for its design and construction. Primarily intended to protect the approaches to the town and its water supply, it was completed by the end of June, 1836, but has at no stage come under attack.

Manned again briefly during the Anglo-Boer War of 1899-1902, it then fell into disrepair, and in 1925 was converted into a private residence and tea garden. Old photographs show roses rambling peacefully over the gunpowder magazine.

The fort was declared a National Monument in 1936, was restored during the 1970s, and is now part of the Albany Museum.

The tall mast with crossed arms was a signal failure. In 1837 Lt Col Griffiths Lewis recommended that communications with Fort Beaufort and Peddie should be improved by building a series of signal towers based on Fort Selwyn, with a semaphore mounted on each.

However, it hardly mattered what positions the signalmen got the moveable arms into, as the telescopes supplied to read them were not sufficiently powerful, and the masts were usually obscured by haze or mist.

Today children delight in sliding down the guns and playing soldiers, which seems to have been the name of the game up here from the very beginning.

SOLDIERS OF THE EMPIRE

WHEN the mist swirls, the garrison ghosts stir. Especially in the Botanical Gardens where tall trees sigh over the Provost military prison. Close by is the oldest cemetery in Grahamstown.

Here lies Capt Robert Gethin of His Majesty's 72nd Regiment who, "after having by his gallantry highly distinguished himself in the army commanded by the Duke of Wellington", was killed near De Bruin's Drift on February 3, 1819. He was one of only three veterans of the Napoleonic Wars known to have died in action in Southern Africa.

Numbers of soldiers lived to tell their tales after a spell in the solidly built stone military hospital across the road, now the Department of Plant Sciences and Microbiology at Rhodes University. A medical aura is particularly pronounced in the high board-ceilinged main laboratory, once a ward.

The Eastern Cape was considered a better posting than many in the farflung British Empire.

Conditions varied, depending largely on the commanding officer, but from 1820 attempts to improve the lot of soldiers at regimental level were widespread.

Floggings for misdemeanours were, however, only abolished in the British army in 1881. In Grahamstown they took place in public on what is now the grassy stretch between the Drostdy Gateway and the towered Rhodes administration block — the old parade ground.

The poor wretch was fastened by his hands and feet to a triangular grating with his back exposed. The cat-o'-nine tails was then dipped in a bucket of salt water, and brought down on his bare back. The usual number of lashes was 39, but in practice this total was frequently exceeded.

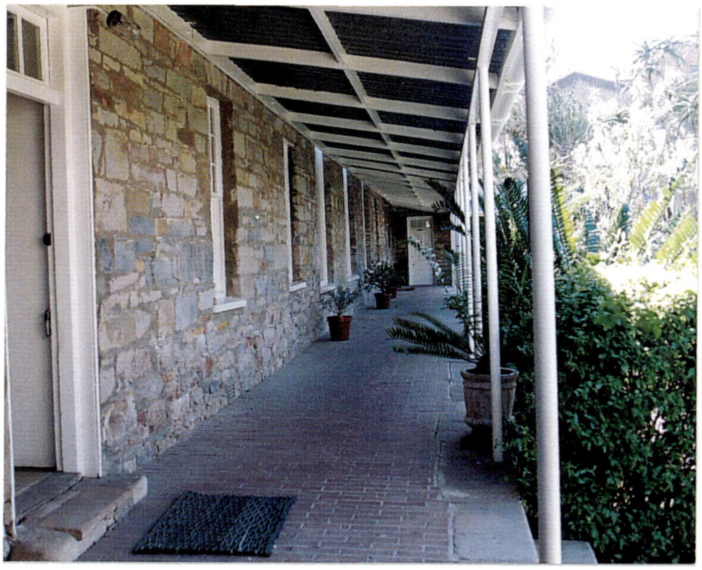

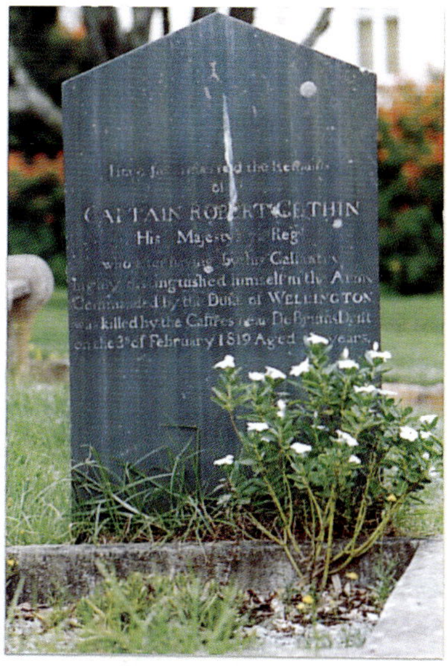

RIGHT: The Military hospital (now a Rhodes department); and Waterloo veteran's grave

BELOW: Horse artillery detachment in Drostdy quarters

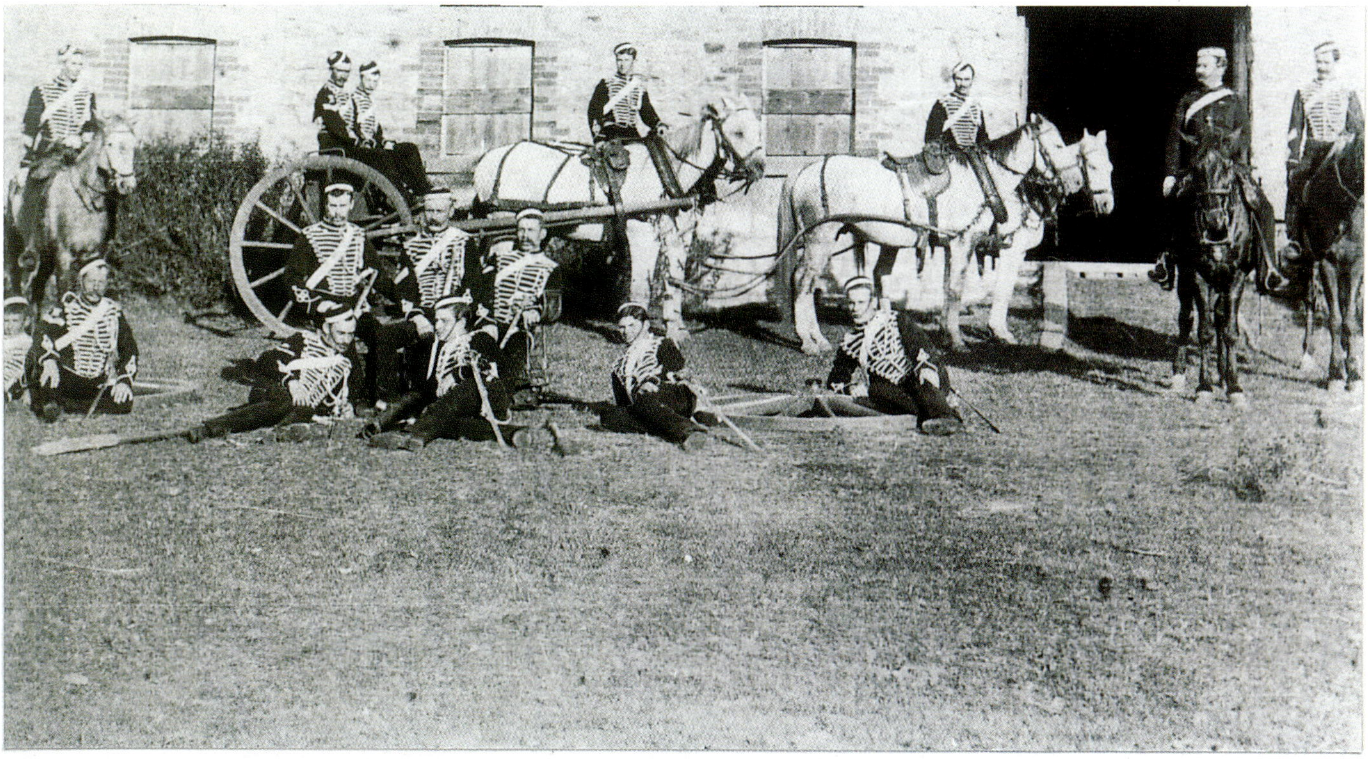

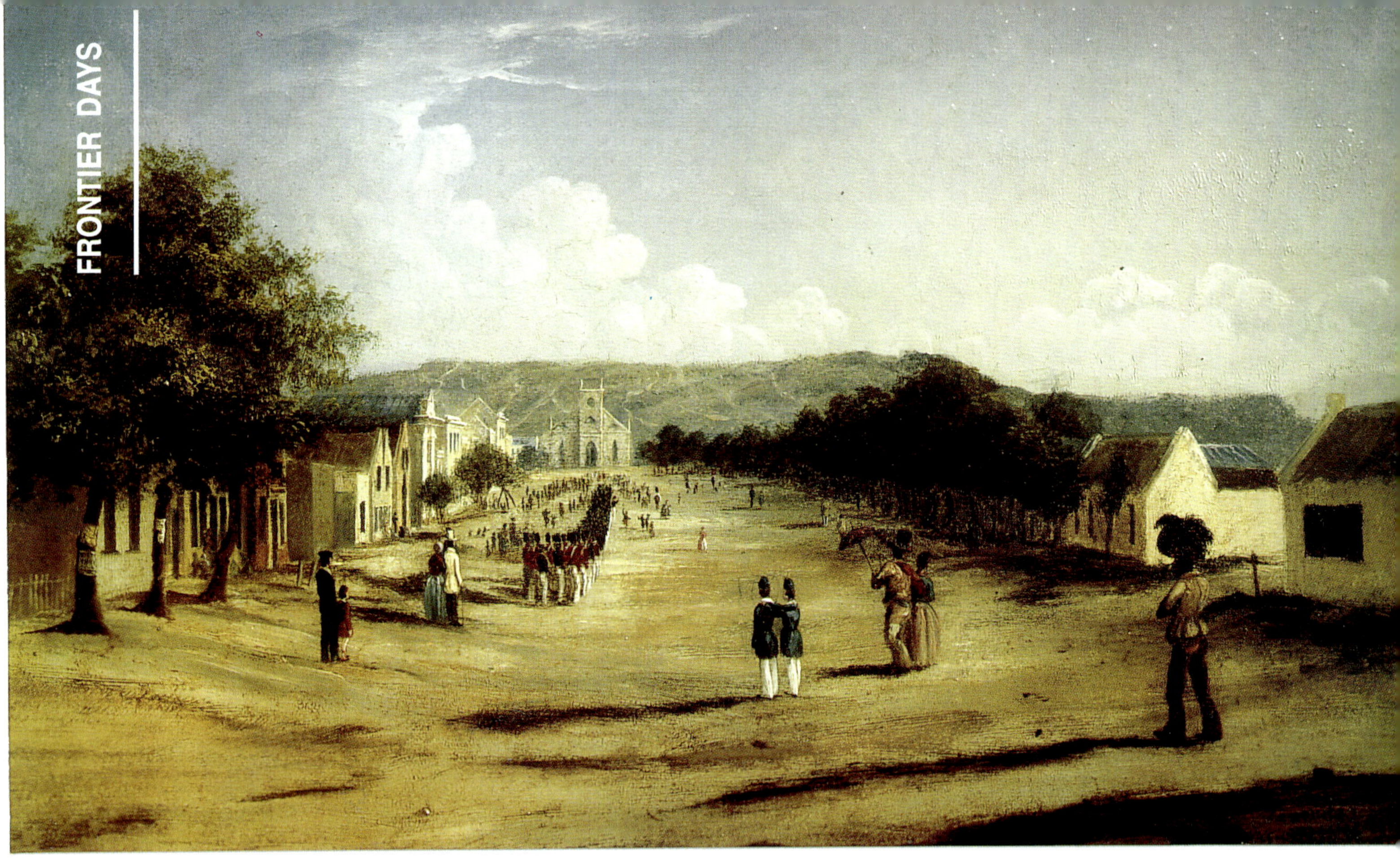

THE FRONTIER ARTISTS

HAVING admired works by Thomas Baines — the foremost mid-19th century painter of South African scenes — in a gracious gallery at the Albany Museum, you step straight out into them. Take High Street, for instance. Some changes obviously, but the light and spirit of place are uncannily the same.

If you pop into Naran & Son at the corner of Hill and New Streets for milk and a newspaper, you will be on the site of Potter's Inn where Baines lodged free of charge for months on end. He repaid the hospitality of the generous 1820 Settler proprietors with the very pictures you have just seen, plus a whole lot more.

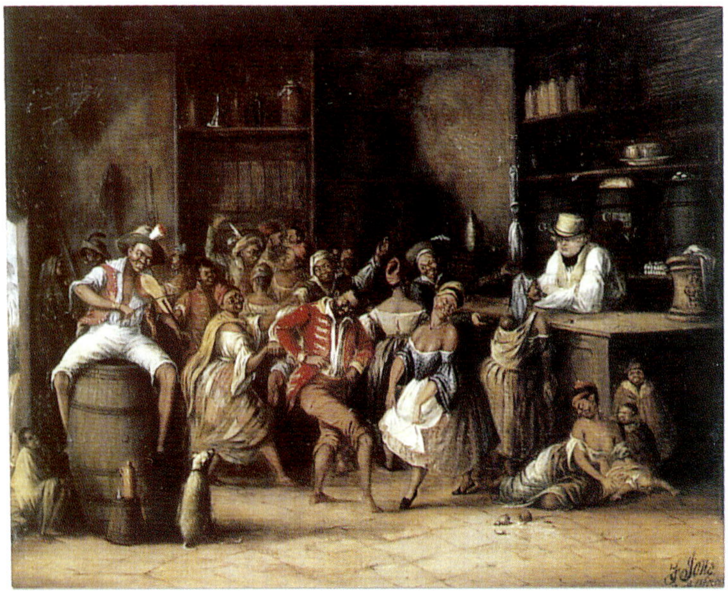

There is always a convivial feeling in this much altered family shop. Perhaps a hangover from the days when well-known frontier artist Frederick I'Ons depicted the revels in the inn's public canteen.

Both artists were British born. I'Ons arrived in Grahamstown in 1834 and died here in 1887, aged 85. Baines — ever on the move — made his first visit in 1848, and seems to have been instantly captivated by what he saw. Within days he had completed preliminary sketches and watercolours of views looking towards St George's Church (now the Cathedral) from the four points of the compass, later producing the finished oils, as was his custom.

I'Ons' portraits of Xhosa chiefs and tribal studies were much in demand as souvenirs by military men. His meticulous attention to details of clothing, personal ornaments and objects now provides invaluable reference sources.

Baines explored the entire area and later ventured deep into the interior for lengthy periods. Back on the frontier in 1851, he was appointed first official war artist in South Africa by Lt Col Sir Henry Somerset, commandant of the frontier forces, and went forward with the troops to the Amatolas.

He left the city in 1853, never to return, and died in poverty when only 55. Two fly-speckled works rescued from the top of a wardrobe in a Grahamstown home were recently valued by Sotheby's at close on half a million rands.

TOP: Sunday Morning, High Street, Graham's Town, December 28, 1848, by Thomas Baines (the troops marching to church); and LEFT: canteen scene by Frederick Timpson I'Ons

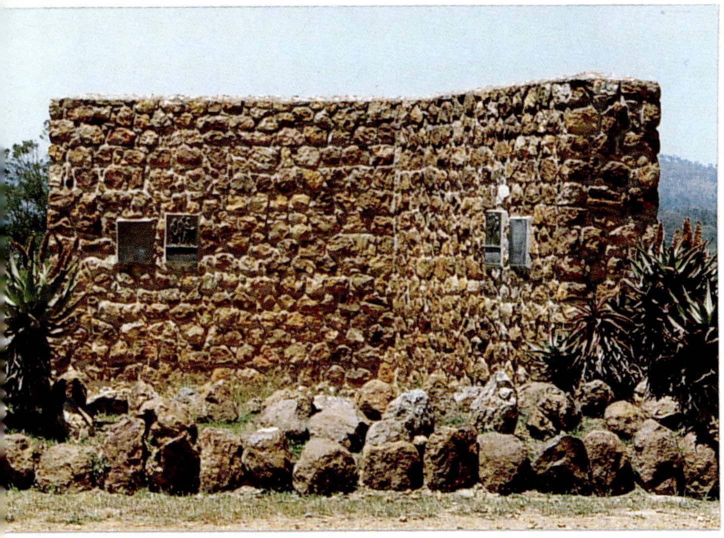

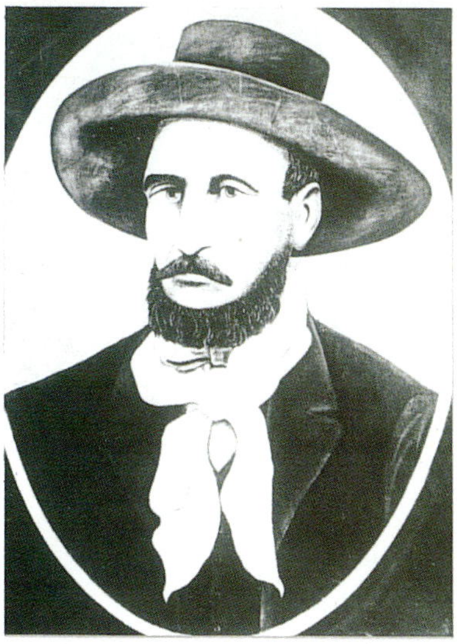

FAR LEFT: *Open book monument; and* BELOW: *Basil Mills, totally in command of South Africa's only military re-enactment group*

LEFT: *Posthumous portrait of Piet Retief*

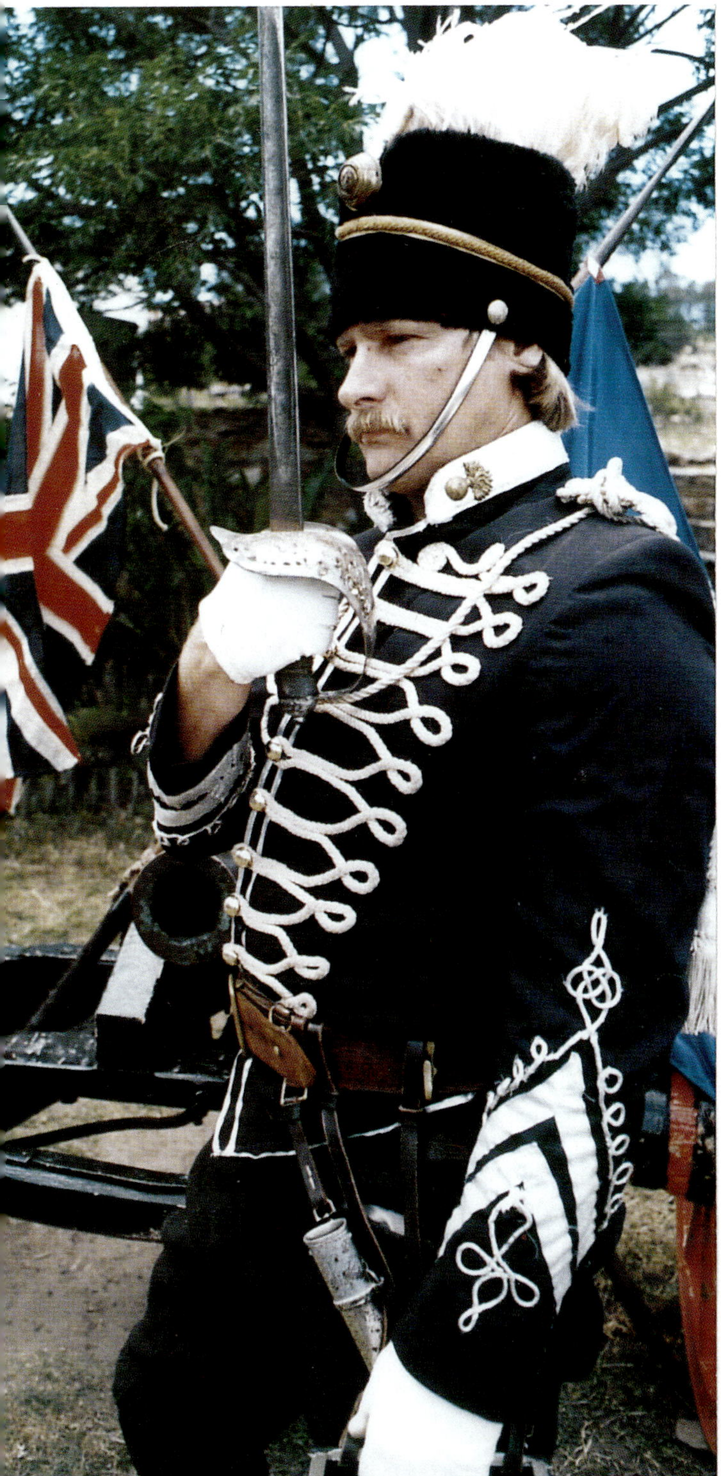

Piet Retief's Trading Store

BOER, BRIT (and Basil)

STRANGE to see Voortrekker Piet Retief's trading store at the top of High Street filled with fibre vibes and furnishings. From November, 1813, until he joined the Great Trek in February, 1837, Retief lived and worked in the Grahamstown area, having concluded an agreement with the Colonial Government to supply rations to the British troops on the frontier.

His windmill for grinding corn was near where St Aidan's now stands. He ran a bakery, butchery, and canteen, and acted as an auctioneer. He was involved in the buying and selling of no fewer than 24 plots, while his building operations included getting the Drostdy to roof height.

He owned several farms in the area and as Field-Commandant of the Albany Burghers was frequently caught up in frontier disputes. In February, 1837, he published his famous "Manifesto" in *The Graham's Town Journal,* setting out the reasons why certain farmers wished to leave the Cape Colony. That April his party joined the laager of Andries Potgieter and Gert Maritz beyond the Orange River.

The Bible Monument near the golf course marks the presentation of a Bible on April 23, 1837, "by the inhabitants of Graham's Town" to Pieter Uys and his party on their way to join the other trekkers, a token of the cordial relations between Boer and Brit.

Today, the only old battles which are re-fought are those mounted by the Grahamstown Military Re-enactment Volunteers under the enthusiastic command of founder Basil Mills. They specialize in the Crimean Charge of the Light Brigade, along with the Battle of Buffel's Kloof — mainly at agricultural shows, in uniforms meticulously made at home.

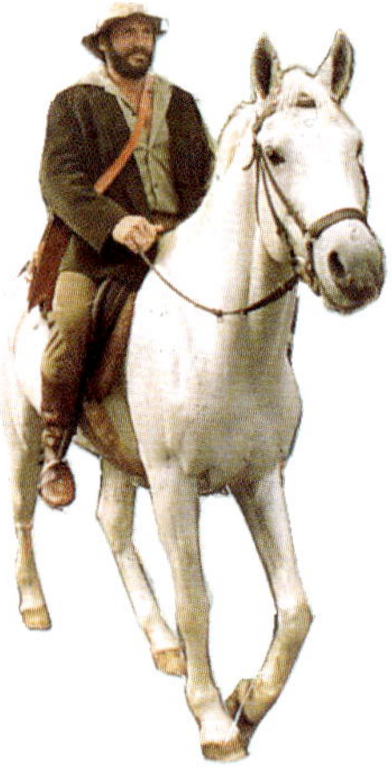

DICK KING RIDES AGAIN

WHEN it finally dawned on dozy Grahamstown that the 150th anniversary of Dick King's great gallop was coming up fast, they had already been pipped to the hitching post by some wide-awake Port Elizabethans champing at the bit to do the whole thing in reverse, a month early.

Whoa! What about the facts? Just for the record, on May 26, 1842, Dick King departed on horseback from Port Natal, where the 27th Inniskilling Regiment was besieged by the Boers in what is now Durban's Old Fort. On June 4, he delivered a despatch requesting reinforcements to Col John Hare, Commander of the Graham's Town Garrison, and later that month sailed from Algoa Bay with the relief troops.

Hailed as the saviour of Natal, his gruelling 960 km, 10-day journey has since become one of South Africa's most famous feats. It is commemorated on Durban's Victoria Embankment by an equestrian statue, and at Grahamstown's City Hall by a simple marble plaque, plus pylons along the way. There have been sundry repeat performances, most notably by Edwin Ferreira in 1967 at the 125-year mark, in conjunction with laying the foundation stone of the 1820 Monument. Then in 1992, rides in both directions. Talk about *Carry on King* — it was more like *Blazing Saddles*.

The far-sighted Fort Frederick Lions Club of PE proceeded as planned, and did their Grahamstown-to-Durban dash at the end of April to coincide with the 75th anniversary celebration there of the establishment of Lions International.

Grahamstown belatedly roared ahead by turning the clock back for a Durban-to-Grahamstown historic re-enactment on the actual dates, together with the Durban Publicity Association and the East London Endurance Club. Care of the horses was a top priority. The modern-day Dick King proved the ideal man for the job. Rugged endurance rider and veterinary surgeon Dr Coen de Bruin nursed them through by dismounting and walking up the inclines.

He also kept a watchful eye on young 'Ndongeni' (15-year-old Vincent Nkosi this time round), the Zulu lad who set out with Dick King but never got as far as Grahamstown. Vincent did, completing the last leg by bus in time to make a triumphal entry.

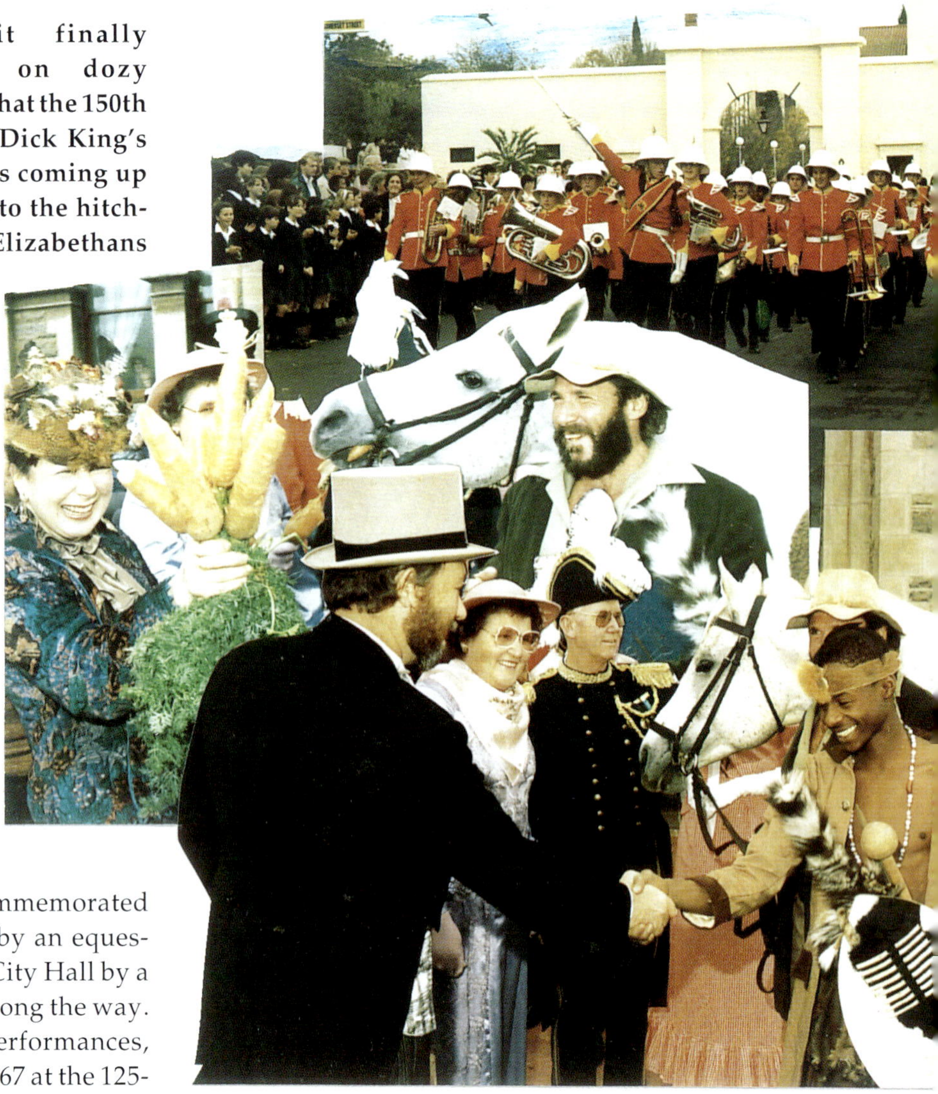

ABOVE: Everybody loves a parade: riders, redcoats and carrots captured the mood on June 4, 1992, with young 'Ndongeni' shyly shaking the Mayor's hand, and 'King' Coen de Bruin the central figure

& THE BALL THEREAFTER

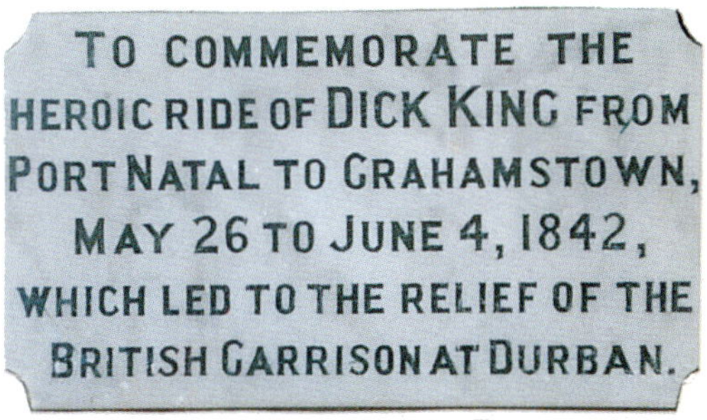

So much for the background nitty gritty. When Coen de Bruin cantered into town on his grey Arab stallion, Nourmahal Tabas ("Abode of Light" in Arabic), on June 4, 1992, the sun and the citizens came out to greet them. Not village pump but heart-warming pomp and ceremony, colour and pageantry.

Never mind that the ox-wagons, startled by the Highland pipers, took off like chariots of fire, literally leaving the coaches and pony traps standing. This was a proper parade, followed by an absolute ball. A Grand Victorian Military Ball, to be precise. Like something out of *Gone with the Wind*. The long entrance to the City Hall — officially opened 110 years ago that same month — was lined by potted palms and ramrod Redcoats plus every Union Jack the decorating committee could muster and metres of bunting from the 1947 Royal visit...

Victorian dress — or an approximation thereof — was obligatory. Birds became belles in lace curtains and ostrich feathers discreetly plucked from dusters. Even the television reporter demurely if somewhat surprisingly sported a boater. Officers wore scarlet uniforms borrowed from boys in the Kingswood College Band; gentlemen arrived in ancient tails and top hats.

A night that started out honouring an historic occasion ended up being one. Grahamstown's last Colonial whirl? Perhaps, but what a way to go!

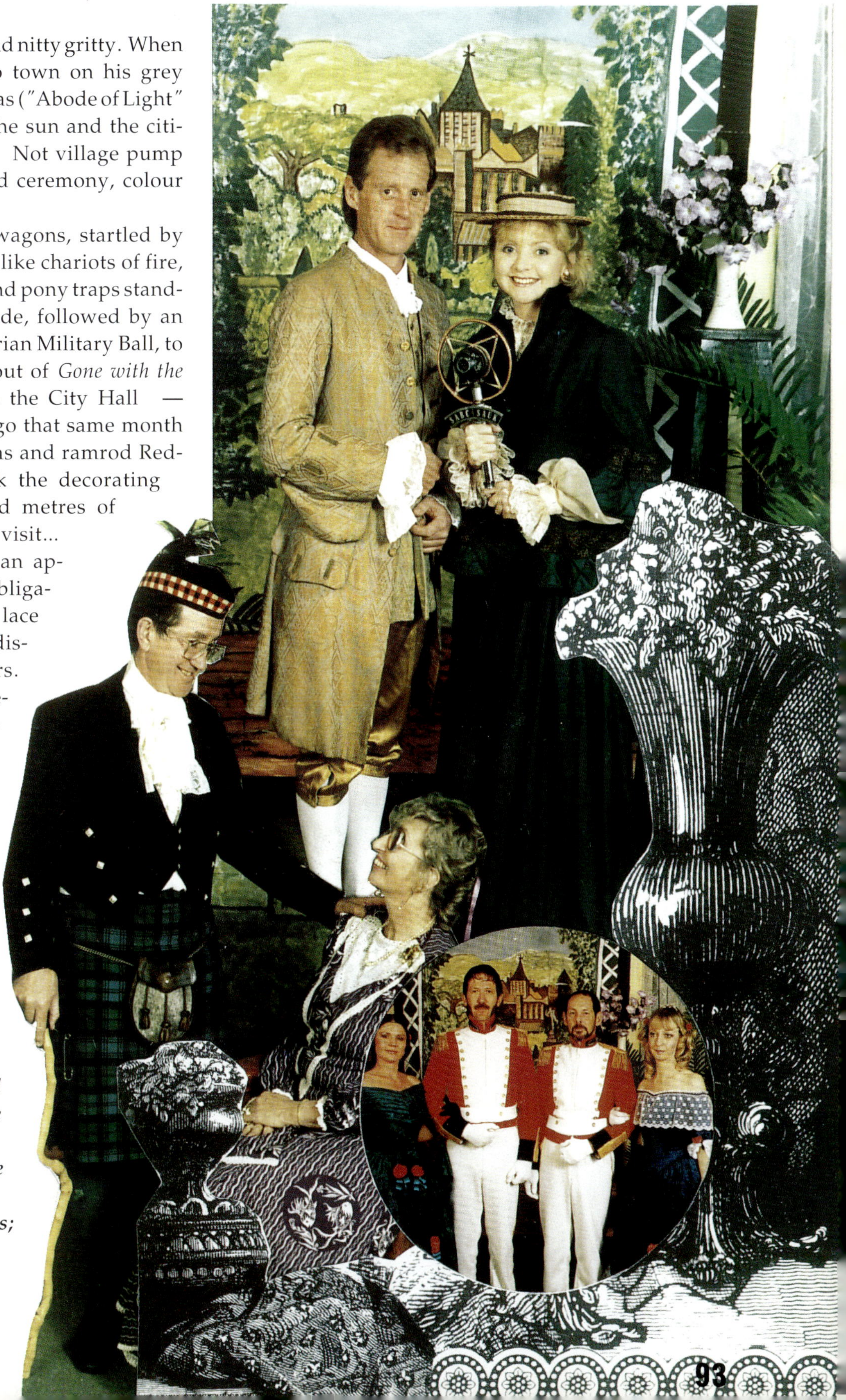

RIGHT: Marble memorial, and revellers all geared up for the Grand Victorian Military Ball: the quartet in the circle were absolutely spot on in specially made 1842 costumes; other blithe party spirits improvised outfits with whatever came to hand

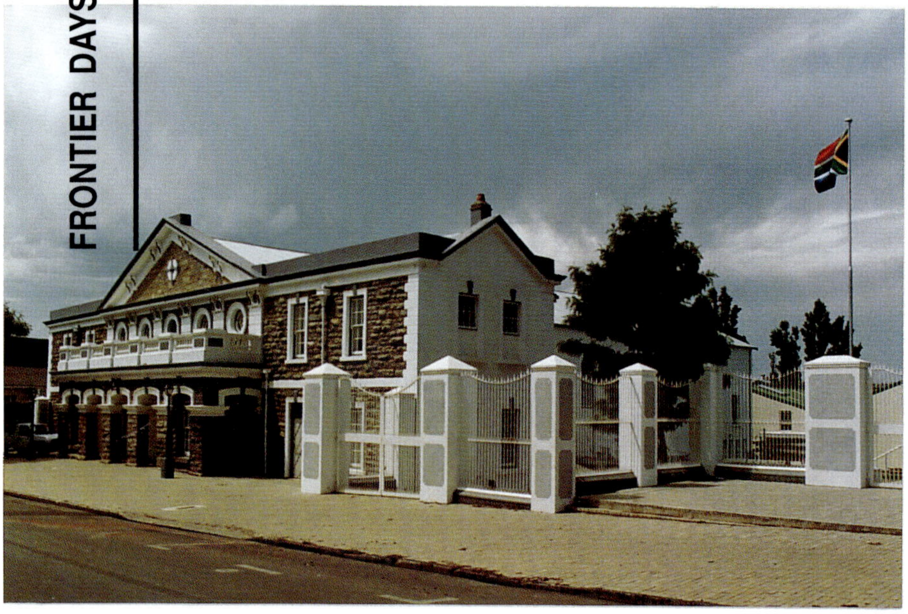

*"All through the Settlers' City is the tramp of marching feet:
They are swinging into order — hear the echoes in the street.
They are marching off to battle as their fathers marched before
At the ringing call of duty — 'tis the motto of the corps..."*

— **Extract from a First City marching song, 1939**

ABOVE: *Standing firm — Drill Hall headquarters of the First City Regiment*

DRUMS BEATING , COLOURS FLYING

TUNES of glory ... The swirl of blue and green Graham of Montrose tartan kilts, the skirl of bagpipes ...

First City — the oldest of South Africa's four Highland regiments — on parade, exercising its honorary freedom of entry into the city.

The Drill Hall in Hill Street — a handsome stone edifice erected in 1866 as the Albany Hall, and scene of numerous balls and theatrical performances, has been First City's headquarters since the turn of the century.

The dignified scarlet-carpeted officers' mess has a dramatic stage-set air about it. An atmosphere heightened by the array of gleaming sporting trophies — some the size of garden urns — ornately embossed award shields, leopard skins, rifles, maps, medals and massed memorabilia.

First City developed out of a volunteer corps, formed in 1875 and called the First City Volunteers, tracing its beginnings back to 1835. Photographs of former commanding officers line one wall. Beneath them, reminders of past engagements are safely behind glass.

Starting with swords and assegais from early clashes, then on to the Anglo-Boer War (1899-1902) when the regiment was divided into infantry and mounted sections. The infantry helped guard the rail link between the Cape and the Orange Free State, while the mounted men joined the anti-commando units. In 1904 First City was one of the colonial regiments to receive the King's colour for its part in the defence of the Empire.

The high tide of patriotism, an interval of peace, then World War I (1914-1918). Combined with the

Below: Bronze cast in Italy marks the alliance of First City and Cape Town Highlanders, 1943 - 1945 (on Graham of Montrose tartan)

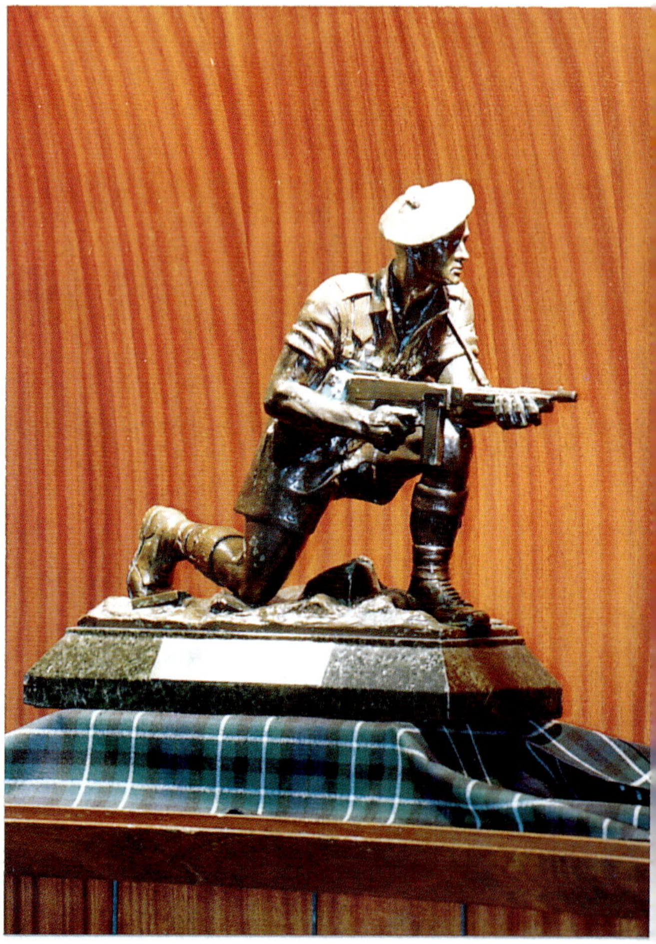

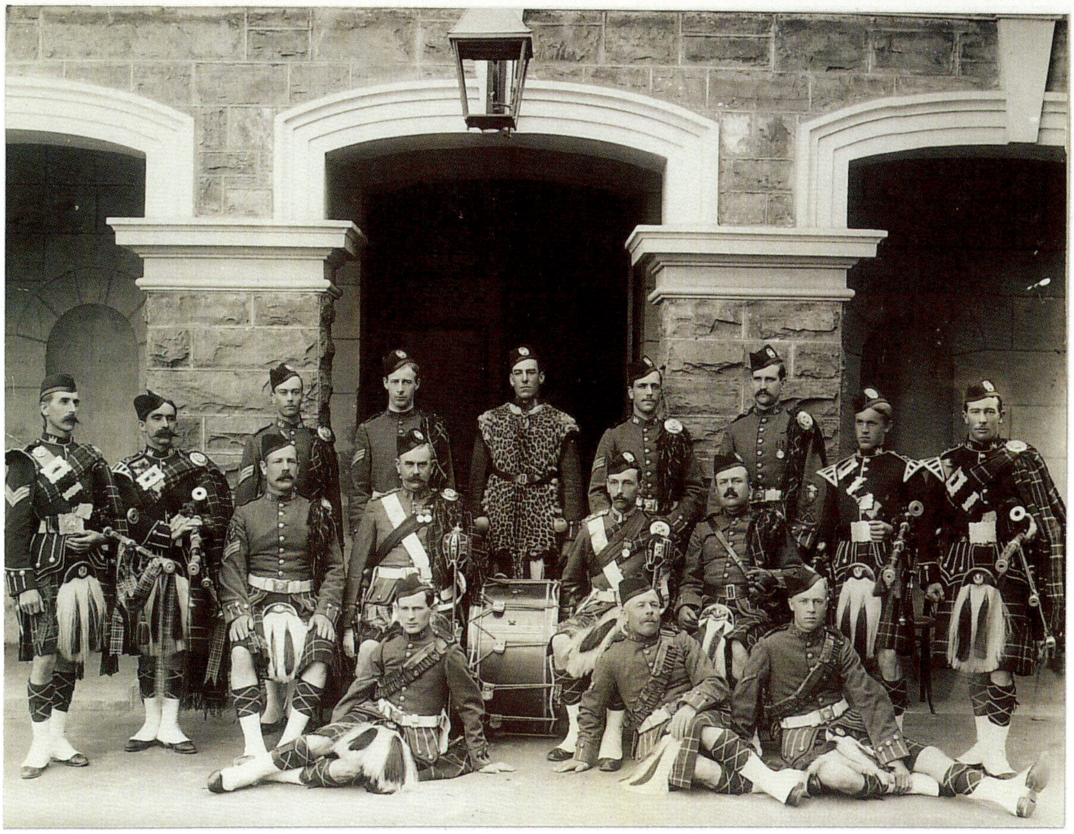

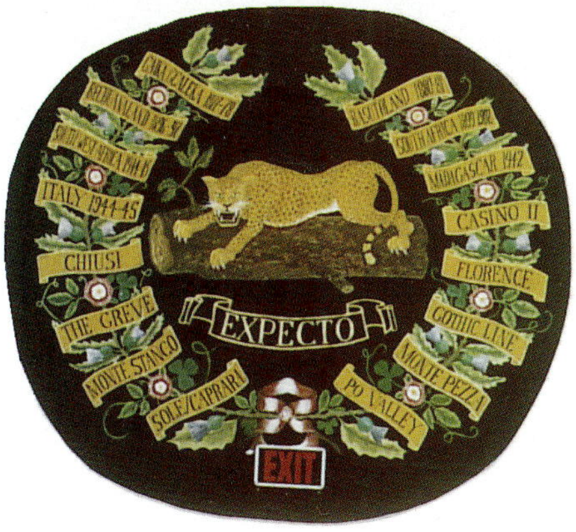

ABOVE: Albany leopard emblem on regimental colour, painted above the door. Expecto — not exit — is the motto, come what may

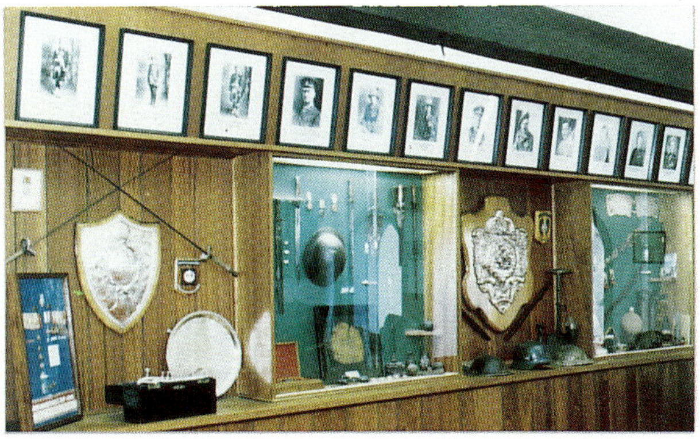

ABOVE: First City Regimental brass band in 1909; and LEFT: long march of military history in Officers' mess

Queenstown Volunteers to form the Eastern Rifles, members saw action in South West Africa. Letters home graphically described conditions:

"Just imagine bullets coming at you at the rate of 400-500 per minute, not per hour ... We were in dire straits for water, hours without a drink; your mouth stuck fast to the tongue and dry as hell. It was worse than that. At last someone discovered an old prospecting hole which contained water and very soon we were fit again. Only about 15 hours all told without water ..." And not a drop of the hard stuff either. Because of a temperance agitation, the customary issue of a twice-weekly tot of spirits was replaced with an issue of lime juice — certainly something to make up for at subsequent reunions in the mess.

Next, World War II (1939-1945). Initially deployed in Madagascar, by 1943 the regiment was part of the 6th Division in Egypt. Linked with the Cape Town Highlanders, it later took part in the bitter struggle up the spine of Italy — Monte Cassino, Chiusi, the Po Valley, Florence, Monte Pezza — foreign campaigns which sit strangely with Basutoland (1880-1881) and Bechuanaland (1897) on the regimental colour. Some did not return. Their names live on, on rolls of honour and war memorials.

Sweeping Defence Force changes after 1948 meant that the old army had to adapt to a new regime. When South Africa became a republic further adjustments had to be made. On May 30, 1961, at 23h59, with a fitting sense of the severance of an historic link, the officers of First City toasted Her Majesty, Queen of Great Britain and the Commonwealth, for the final time, and shattered their glasses.

By the mid-70s First City was a motorized infantry unit and its men were drawn from many areas. Now different times call for fresh approaches. *Expecto* — on the look out — continues to be the watchword.

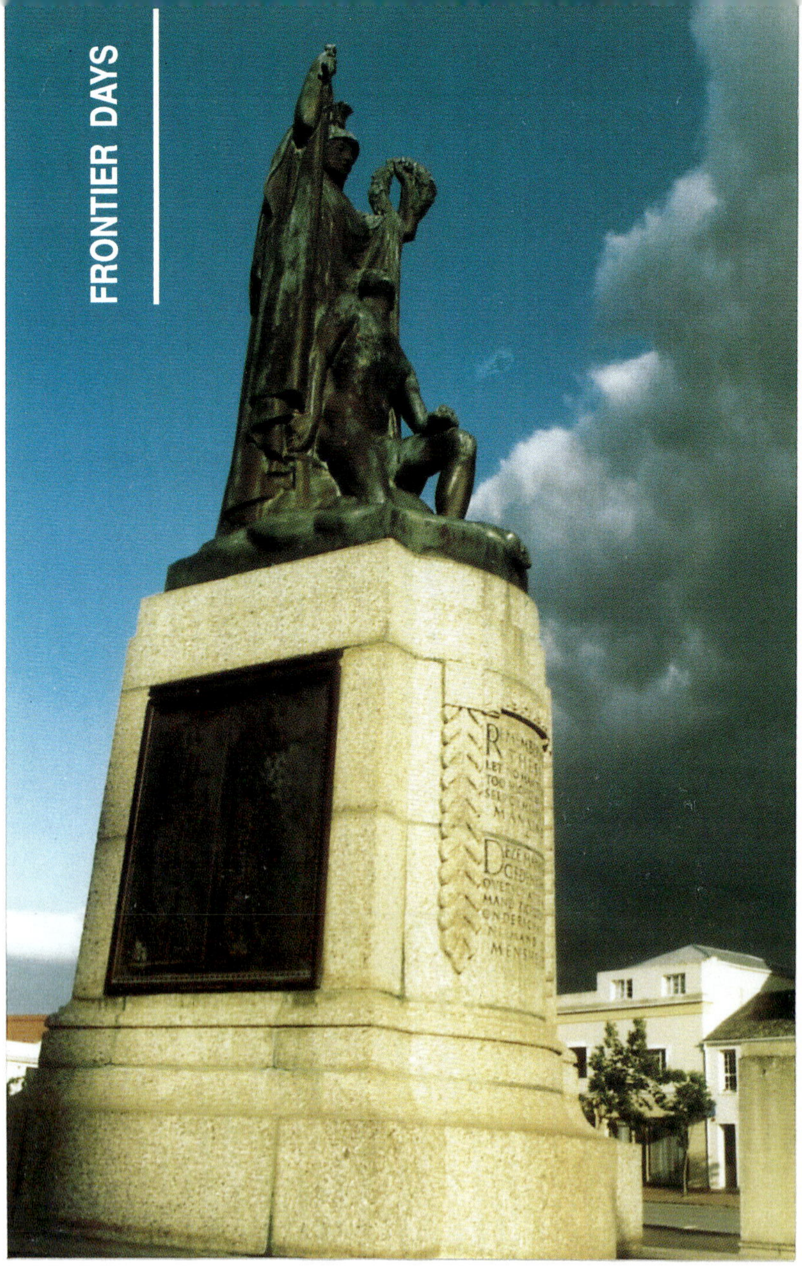

ABOVE: *To honour service and sacrifice*

1914 — 1918

"Remembering these let no man think too highly of himself or meanly of mankind."

— Inscription on World War One memorial by Prof Arthur Lord, Rhodes University

LEST WE FORGET

THE war to end all wars — World War I. Fought on fronts far removed from the frontier. Most visibly commemorated in Grahamstown by a bronze Britannia, companion to the figure of Peace on the opposite side of Church Square. Two statues with a single thought.

Strikingly silhouetted against the Cathedral's Gothic bulk, her arms aloft, one holding the sword of honour, the other the hard-won wreath of victory. In front, a man kneeling, a broken sword in his hand, typifying the fallen. Coiled about their feet, a vanquished serpent symbolizing the curse of war, its head drooping over the base.

The work of English sculptor Gilbert Ledward, who 10 years earlier had won a Royal Academy gold medal before going into the trenches himself.

Raised by public subscription "In memory of the men of Albany and Bathurst who on many fronts and in many units died for a great cause".

Unveiled with solemn ceremony in 1924 by Mr W R Meaker of the South African Infantry, who was blinded in the campaign overseas.

An occasion for some poetic oratory from Sir Thomas Graham, a descendant of Grahamstown's founder, who had lost a son in action:

"Whether they sleep in the warm soft sand of West Africa, or Palestine, or Mesopotamia or Egypt, or amid the jungles of East Africa, or amongst the rocky promontories of Gallipoli, or fathoms deep beneath the sea, or in the peaceful graveyards of Old England, or among the poppies and the cornflowers of Flanders, where death reaped her richest harvest, or wherever they lie, they have filled their names with imperishable glory. They were glorious in their generation and honoured in their time."

The wreaths were piled high. A yellowing record of the messages written on the accompanying cards brings home the personal poignancy of loss. *"In loving memory of dear Archie from his auntie, Mrs Keey, and Miss Keey."* *"In ever loving memory of my two sons Clem and George."* *"In fond remembrance of Aidan, Mandy and Henry Kelly from their pals."*

A little over 20 years later, two plinths were erected — one on each side. They list the names of the fallen in World War II, 1939 — 1945.

All continue to be honoured in our time. Officially at the Remembrance Day parade every November, and privately by passers-by who happen to read Prof Arthur Lord's dedicatory inscription and go on their way suitably chastened.

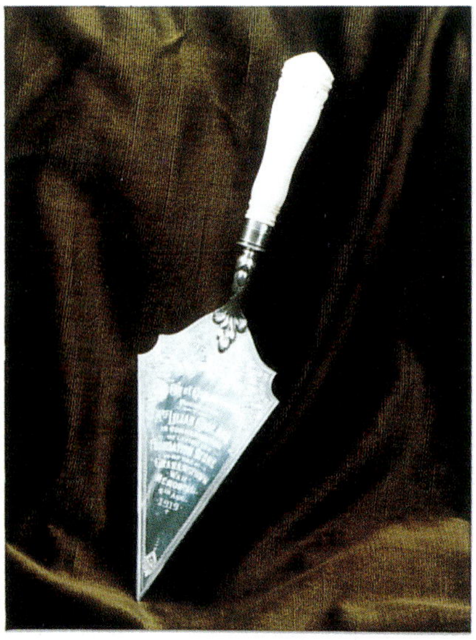

ABOVE: *From foundation-stone ceremony, silver trowel in Albany Museum*

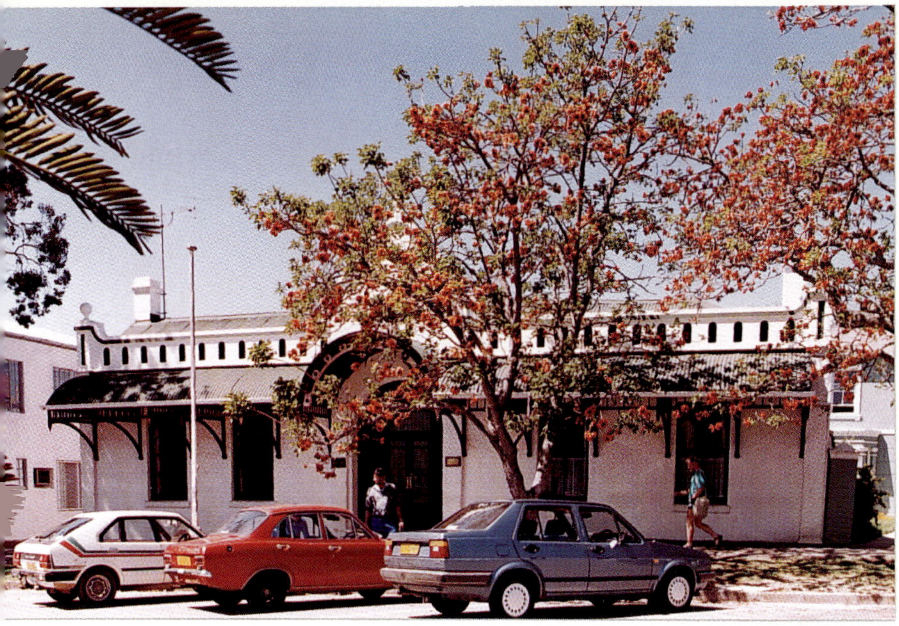

LEFT: Albany Club — High Street haven, matured in the wood

"In that part of the world which is called civilised there are only three places you can avoid women — the club, the monastery and the grave."

— Nathaniel Gubbins, English humorist

LAST MALE
STRONGHOLDS

GENTLEMEN, landed and otherwise, can go to ground in two comfortable bolt holes. Women in the club? The one stoutly maintains there is nothing in the rules which excludes them, the other that the possibility is being given lengthy consideration. Meanwhile they are all good fellows and jolly good company.

The Grahamstown Club is the oldest, officially founded in 1886 (some claim 1862, but the early records were lost). Décor is matter-of-fact masculine, with a stuffed crocodile in pride of place in the bar. Presented in 1906 by Fred Barber of Barberton gold-reef fame, it features on the maroon club tie and is an obvious conversation piece, though a brass plaque immediately below tactfully cautions:

"Let no one bear beyond this threshold hence
Words uttered here in friendly confidence."

A golf ball is suspended on a chain dangling from its upper jaw. A reminder of the days when the club was the golfers' 19th hole, and this particular trophy was fresh from a hole-in-one.

Billiards, darts and dominoes fill any gaps in the action, and the atmosphere is as relaxed as a double brandy. To echo the words of a speaker at its Diamond Jubilee in 1923, "*the Club has long been a refuge for unmarried men and a place where married men can escape the sweet perversity of womenfolk, find solace and get new courage to go home again*". Spoken in jest but an excellent excuse for another round of drinks. Cheers!

The Albany Club was started in 1896 and occupies the most eye-catching building in upper High Street. Inside it is a bit like something *Out of Africa*. Convivially colonial, particularly in the billiard room abutting the garden courtyard at the back.

The books on the library shelves in the committee room appear untouched by time — or anyone else. A diplomat's memoir of 1870, the Army List of 1873, dictionaries dated 1890, the South East African Year Book and Guide for 1934.

Past presidents' photographs are very much present, and legal personalities loom large — the courts being conveniently close by. Affiliated clubs range from Komgha to Kimberley, the Nairobi Safari Club to the Naval and Military Club in London.

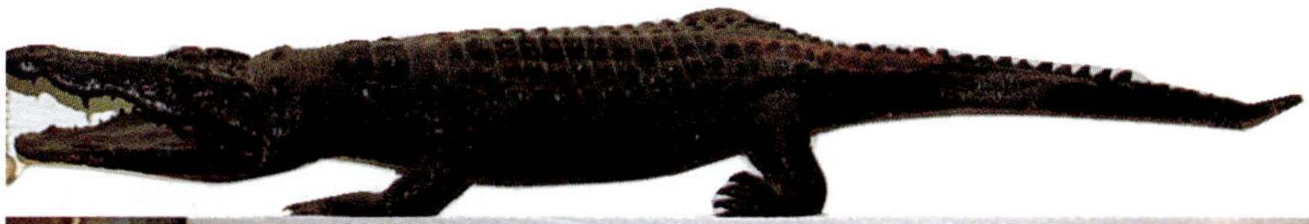

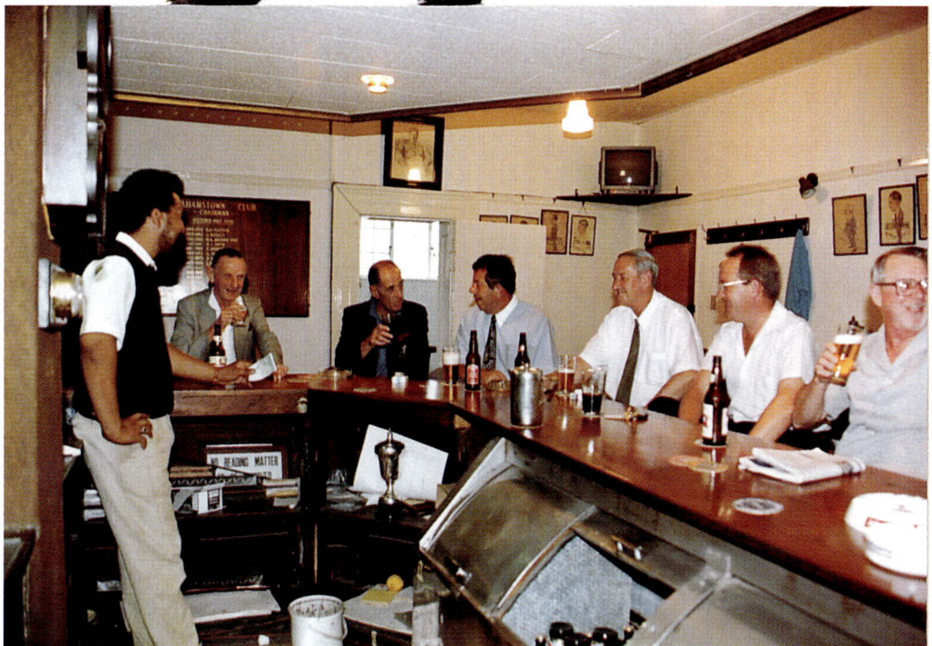

RIGHT: Grahamstown Club's watering hole, plus old croc

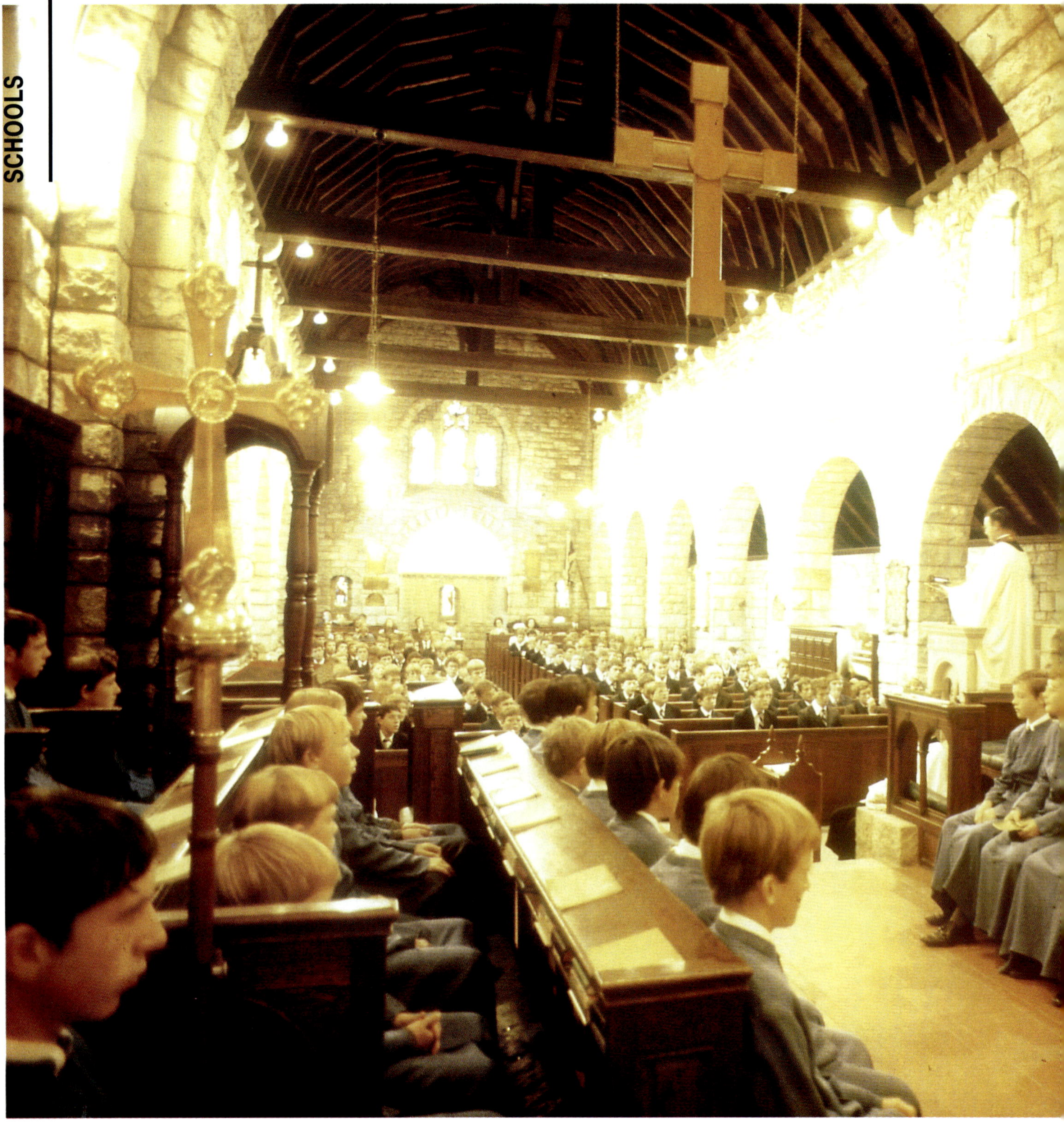

ABOVE: Choir boys and time-honoured traditions at a special service in the Herbert Baker-designed St Andrew's College chapel

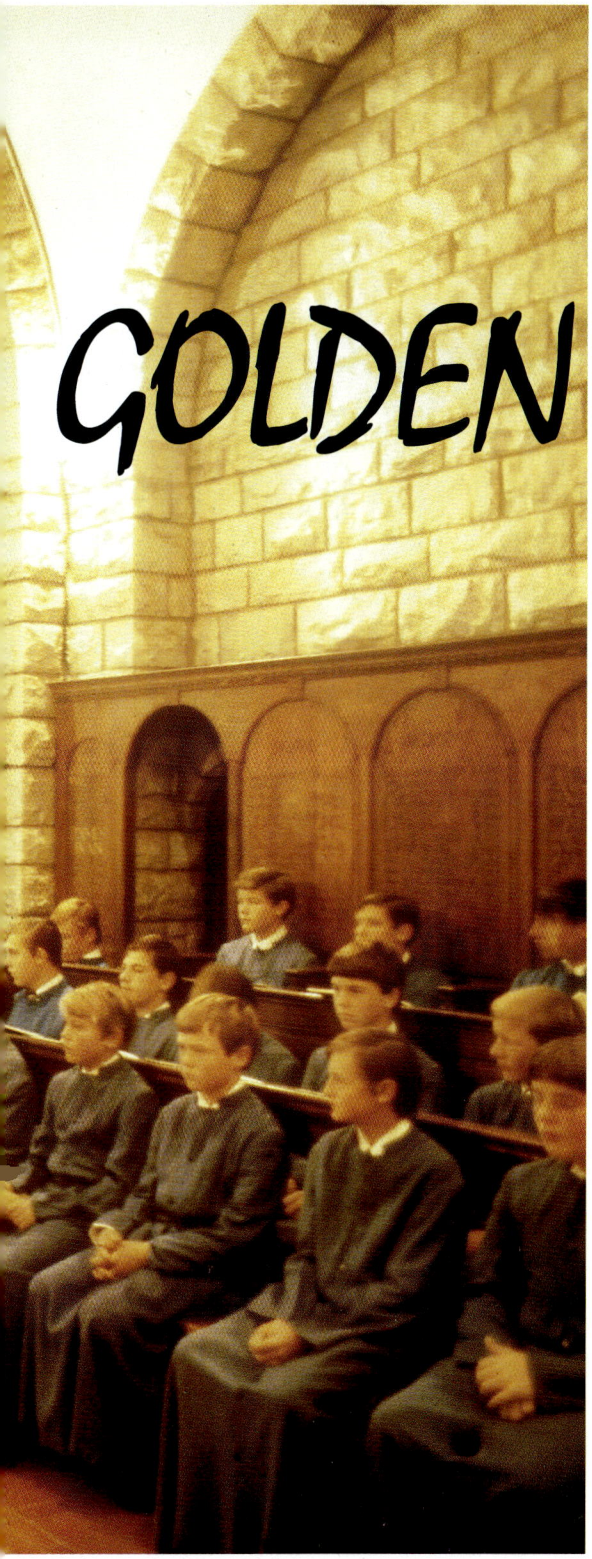

GOLDEN SCHOOL DAYS

THE need to provide educational facilities for the 1820 Settlers' children and garrison families got Grahamstown schooling off to an early start on traditional English lines. The first public free school was established in the former High Street gaol still called the Yellow House. Pupils from all races sat side by side and on one memorable morning managed to lock up their teacher in a cell formerly used for the incarceration of troublesome prisoners.

Later, with the development of the church-inspired schools, youngsters were sent to the little city from every corner of southern Africa. To this day it is the boarders who ensure its continued existence as an important educational centre, and give it that bumper school annual air. Old schools in the valley, new schools on the hills ...

Some are featured on the following pages, each and every one part of the learning process — a long lesson in progress.

"From this small Eastern Province town there has gone out for more than 100 years a stream of men and women trained in this city for the lives they are now leading; imbued with its spirit, they have passed to others what they have garnered here. It has not been a small or unworthy contribution to the life of our country."

— Ronald Currey, headmaster of St Andrew's College from 1939 to 1955

RIGHT: *Oldest Anglican school building in South Africa, dating back to 1844. St Andrew's started here— The Good Sheperd School, run by the Anglican Community of the Resurrection since 1916 continues...*

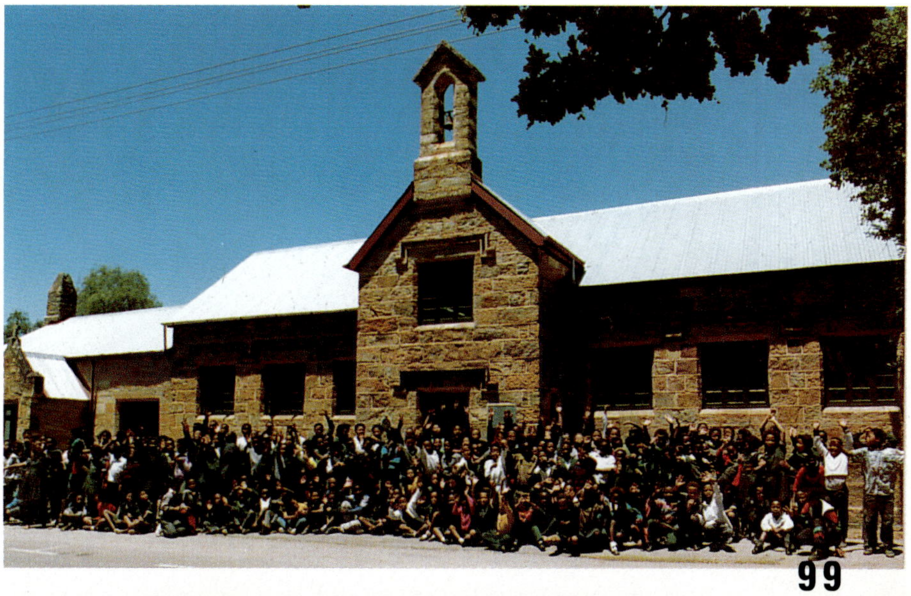

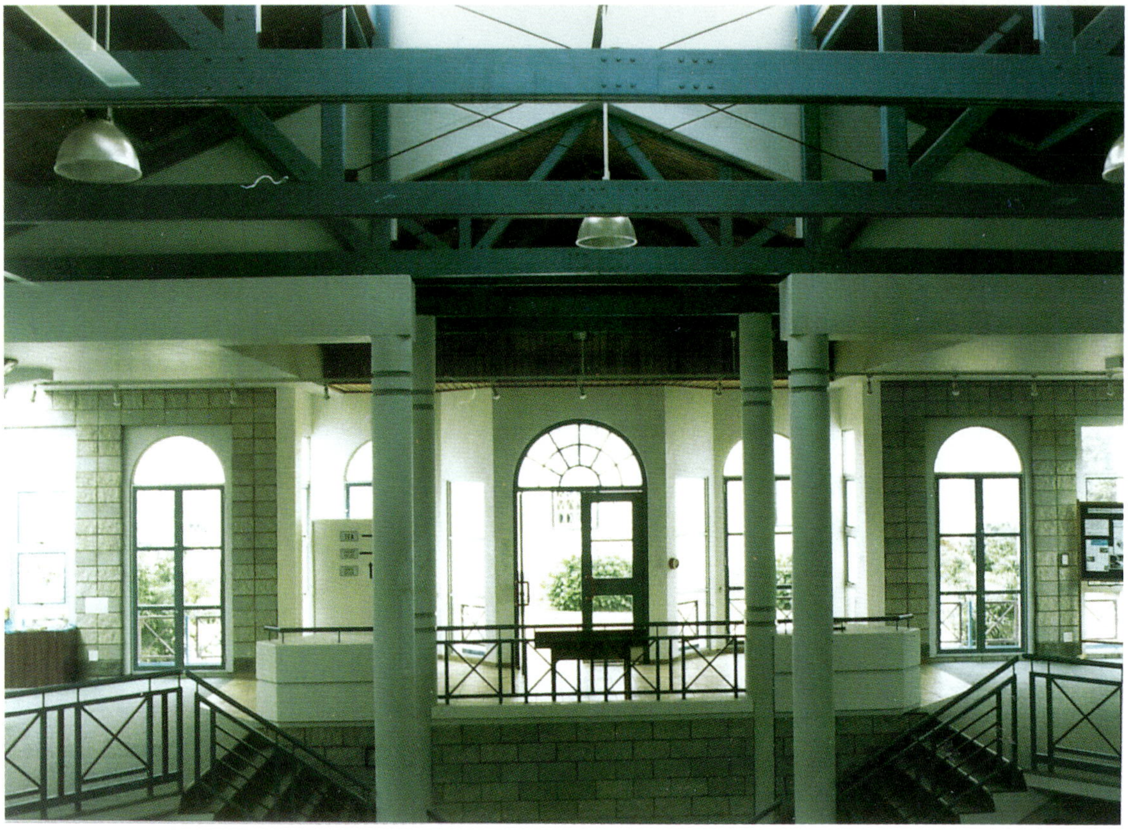

RIGHT: *Entrance to the future — design and technology centre at St Andrew's*
BELOW: *Piping up — first girl piper in St Andrew's band*
BELOW-RIGHT: *Towering memorial, new generations*

St Andrew's College and Diocesan School for Girls

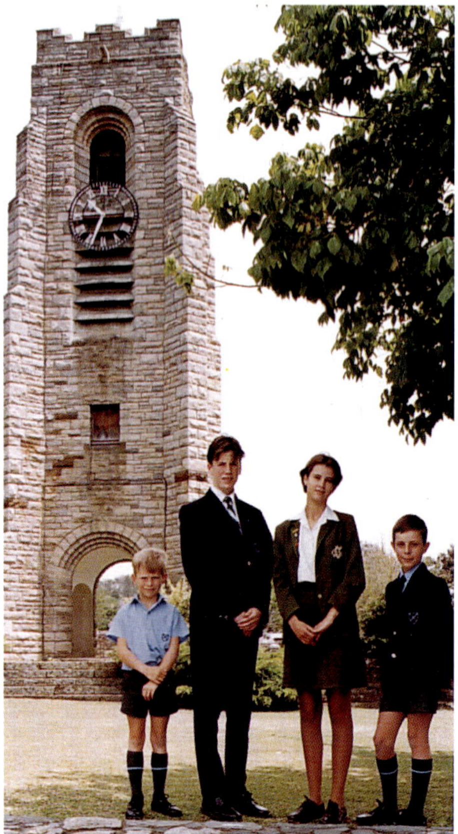

SOMETIMES at the end of serene summer afternoons, a lone piper walks back and forth across the cricket field terrace. His plaintive skirl hovers hauntingly in the hush of the approaching dusk and the sun ignites the sky behind the St Andrew's tower in a final blaze of glory. Memories are made of this. No wonder there is a place in every former St Andrean's heart that is forever Grahamstown.

Not that there are any ex-St Andreans. Once a St Andrew's boy, always a St Andrew's boy, age regardless."College" — so much part of the city that main roads run through it and motorists regularly stop to watch a few overs. A suburb in itself, together with the Diocesan School for Girls and "Prep" — a trio of schools in their own green belt, interlinked to form a supportive trio, sharing certain facilities and classes, yet each with its own distinctive character.

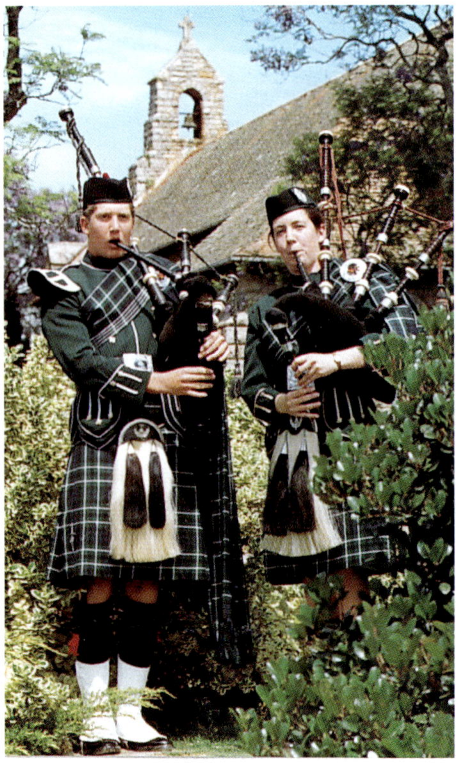

Housed in a harmonious variety of buildings — weathered stone, mellowed brick, white walls shade-dappled by venerable oaks. Right in the middle, the R2m Arthur Cotton Design and Technology Centre, which adds a 21st century dimension to education in South Africa.

Equipped with banks of computers, television and video editing facilities (much sought after by TV crews covering the National Arts Festival) and a variety of other work stations. Creative problem-solving is the core concept, preparation for ever increasing

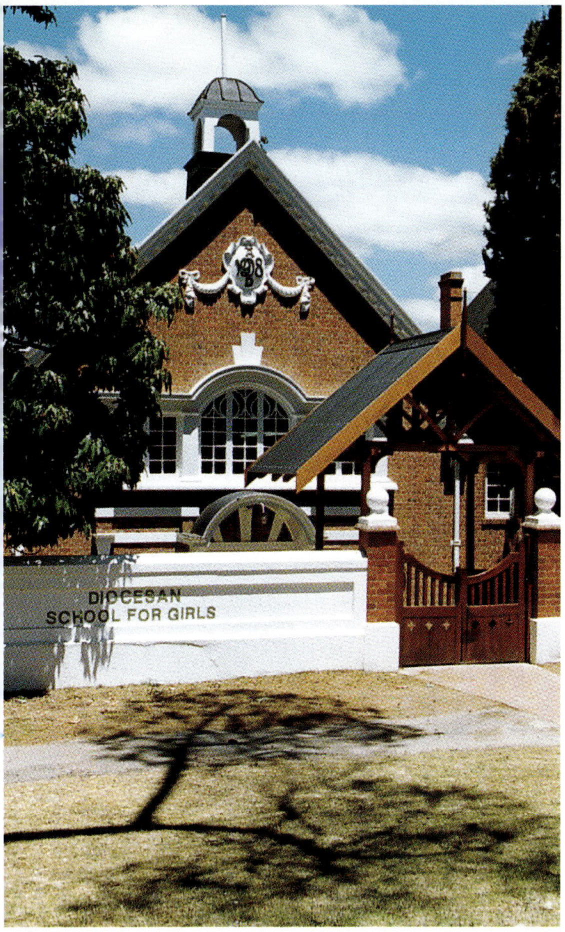

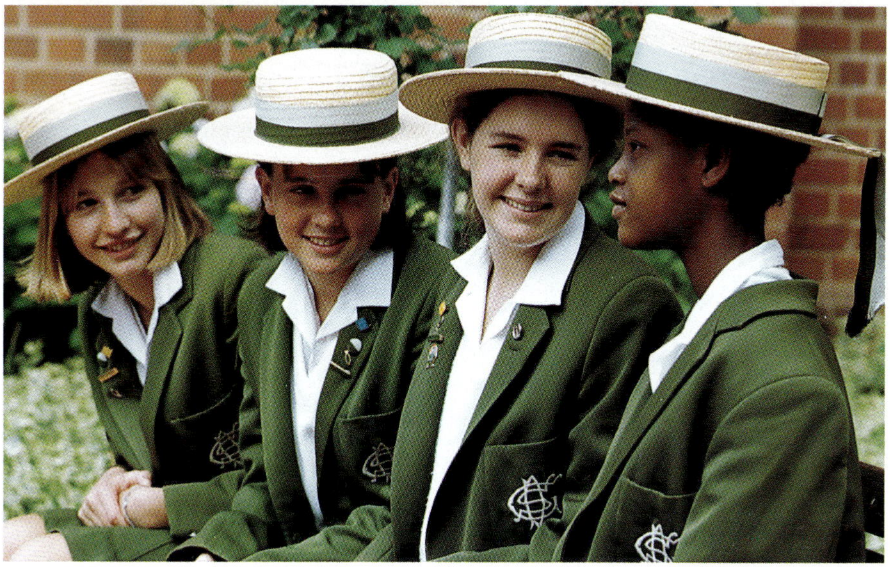

ABOVE: *Friendly foursome, boatered and blazered, at DSG*
Left: Library and lych-gate

technological challenges the aim. St Andrew's College was founded in 1855 by John Armstrong, the first Anglican Bishop of Grahamstown, "to provide sound Christian education for the sons of the frontier farmers". It continues to do so into the sixth generation, along with pupils from every part of SA and beyond.

The birthplace of Rhodes University, the school is one of only four in South Africa named in Cecil John Rhodes's will as having the right to elect its own Rhodes Scholar to Oxford annually. It also sends a student to Cambridge. Douglas Smith was the cricket professional at St Andrew's for close on half a century. A few years before he died in 1950, he walked into a Grahamstown solicitor's office and put a copy of Cecil Rhodes's will on the desk. "I am leaving all I have to St Andrew's", he announced. "Take this will and where it says Cecil Rhodes put Douglas Smith and where it says Oxford put in Cambridge instead." So every two years, a scholarship holder duly sets off, as did the present headmaster, Mr Antony Clark, who became head of Downing House while studying for a degree in history, and also played first class English county cricket.

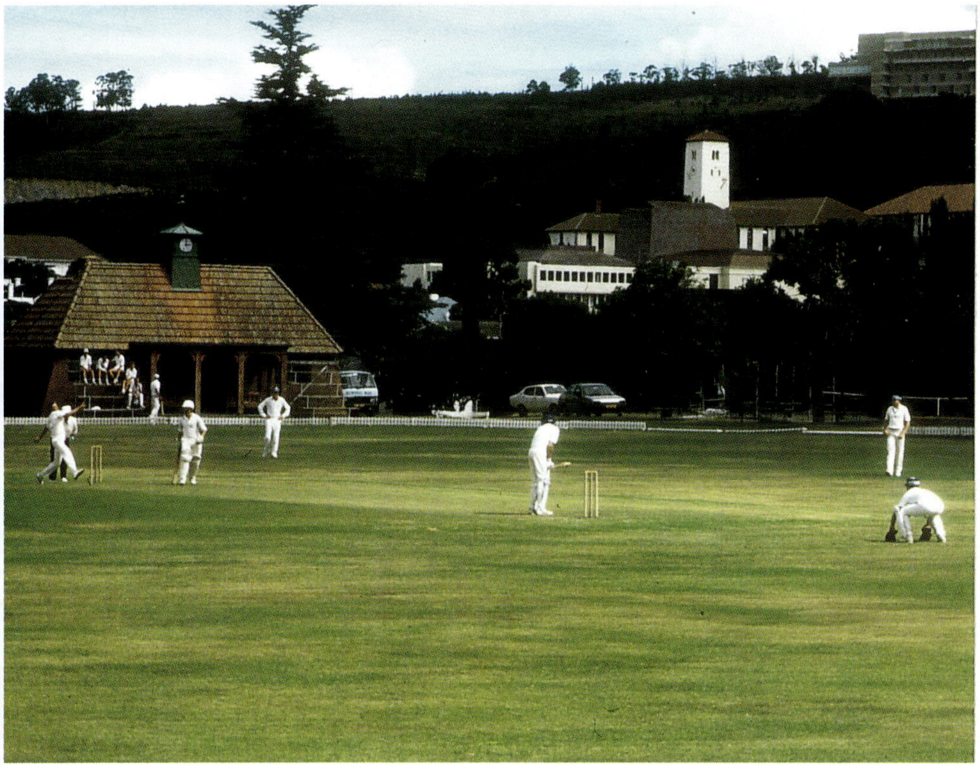

ABOVE: *Lower Field — " it's so much more than just a game that's played with bat and ball..."*

DSG dates back to 1874, when the first headmistress was Mrs John Espin, wife of Canon Espin, who was appointed the sixth headmaster of St Andrew's in 1882. Started in 1885, St Andrew's Preparatory School is the oldest independent "prep" school in South Africa. From 1888 right through to 1970, its headmasters were all members of the distinguished Mullins family. A group of schools where family values are prized: rooted in the past, reaching for the future.

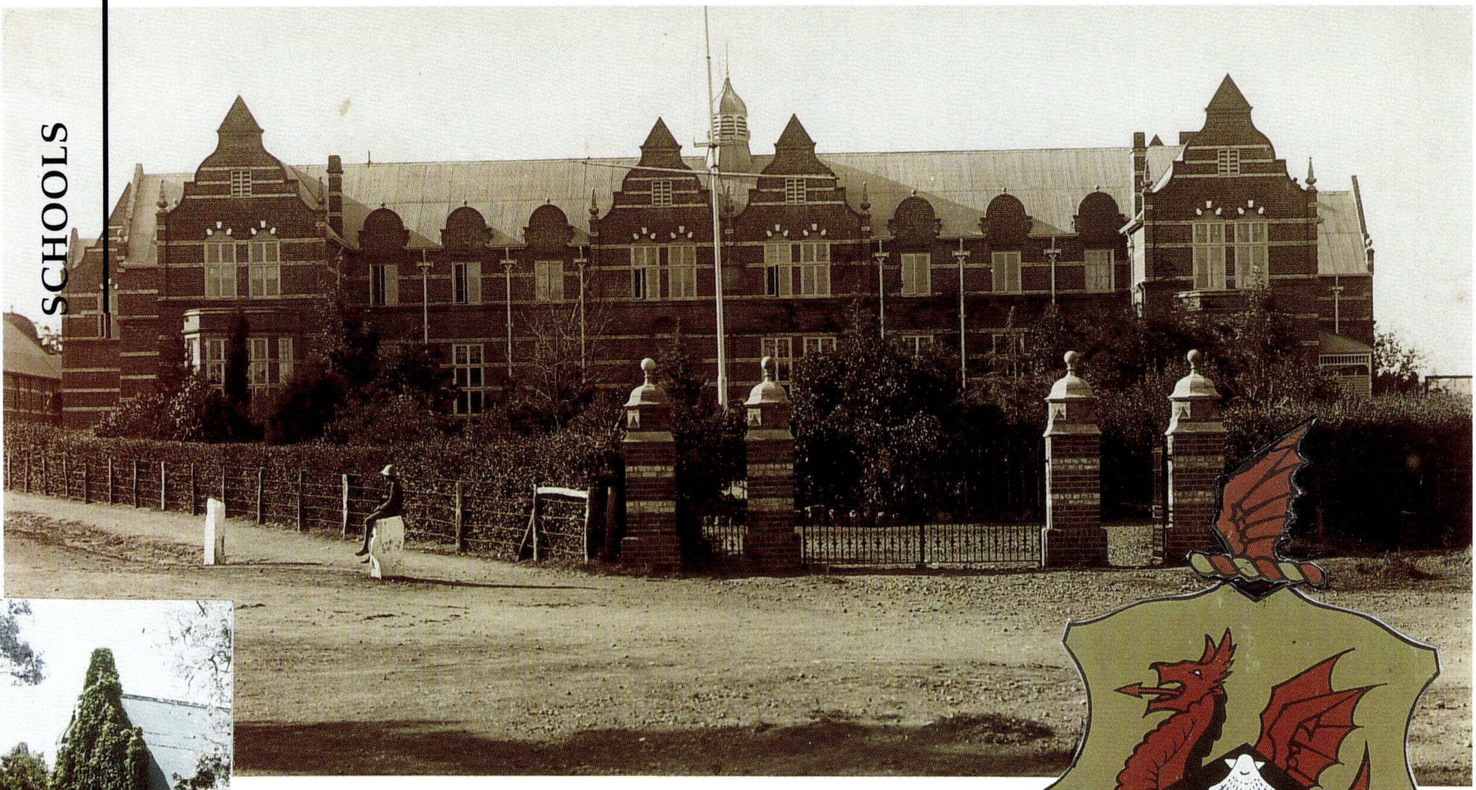

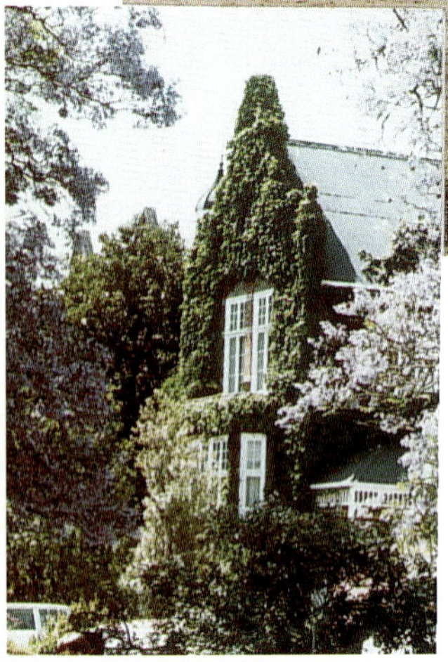

ABOVE: Hampton Court in "Darkest Africa" — the original Kingswood building now accommodates Chubb and Gane House boarders; the gates are also still there (see opposite)

KINGSWOOD

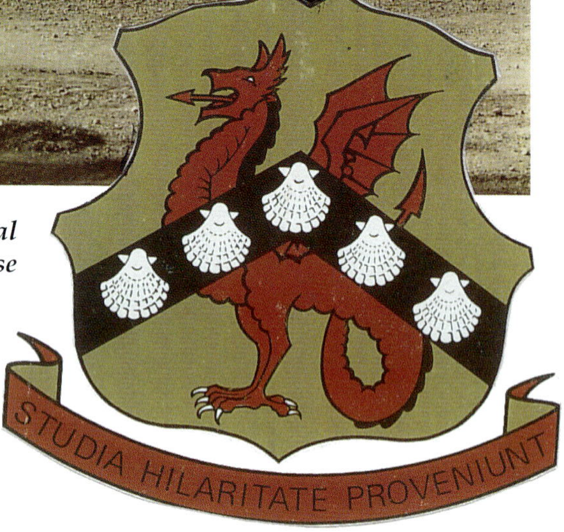

ABOVE: College badge features a watchful wyvern, a heraldic device from the knights of old

THE oldest Methodist school in South Africa, Kingswood College remains essentially young at heart, with a friendly feeling of fun and informality flourishing amid the traditions of 100 years.

Its Latin motto — *Studia Hilaritate Proveniunt* — means "With enthusiasm undertakings forge ahead". In pupils' parlance: "We give it stick."

Something always seems to be happening. Never more so than during its centenary in 1994, which was marked by everything from the ceremonial burial of a space capsule, a rousing reunion, and cricket tournaments, to the annual Kingswood Tattoo. (Rather different from Edinburgh's, with the drum majorettes well to the fore.)

Not forgetting the Big Brass Band. Be it the Bathurst Show or the Rand Show, Dick King's ride re-enactment or civic celebrations, the college redcoats march, their Flashman-style spiked helmets (cunningly moulded from fibreglass) snowy white, their instruments sparkling bright. Boys and girls together, making a magnificent sound.

The only major fully co-educational independent school in the country. Since the mid-1970s girls have been part of the big happy family environment which surrounds the youngsters from pre-primary to a university bridging year.

The wyvern on the school crest — a winged dragon, heraldic symbol of the overcoming of evil — also tops the weather-vane on the new sports pavilion, coping valiantly with the winds of change. Something Kingswood has done since its inception in 1894, when it derived both its name and ideals from the college established in England by John Wesley in 1748.

The memorial chapel built after World War II is the heart of the school and embraces all denominations. The first pew on the left aisle is permanently cordoned off as a reminder that if the 72 Old Kingswoodians commemorated had not died in action, their descendants might have sat there.

Across the road, the red brick gables of the original 1897 School House building, designed by William White-Cooper in a style described as "Hampton Court in Darkest Africa", have been cov-

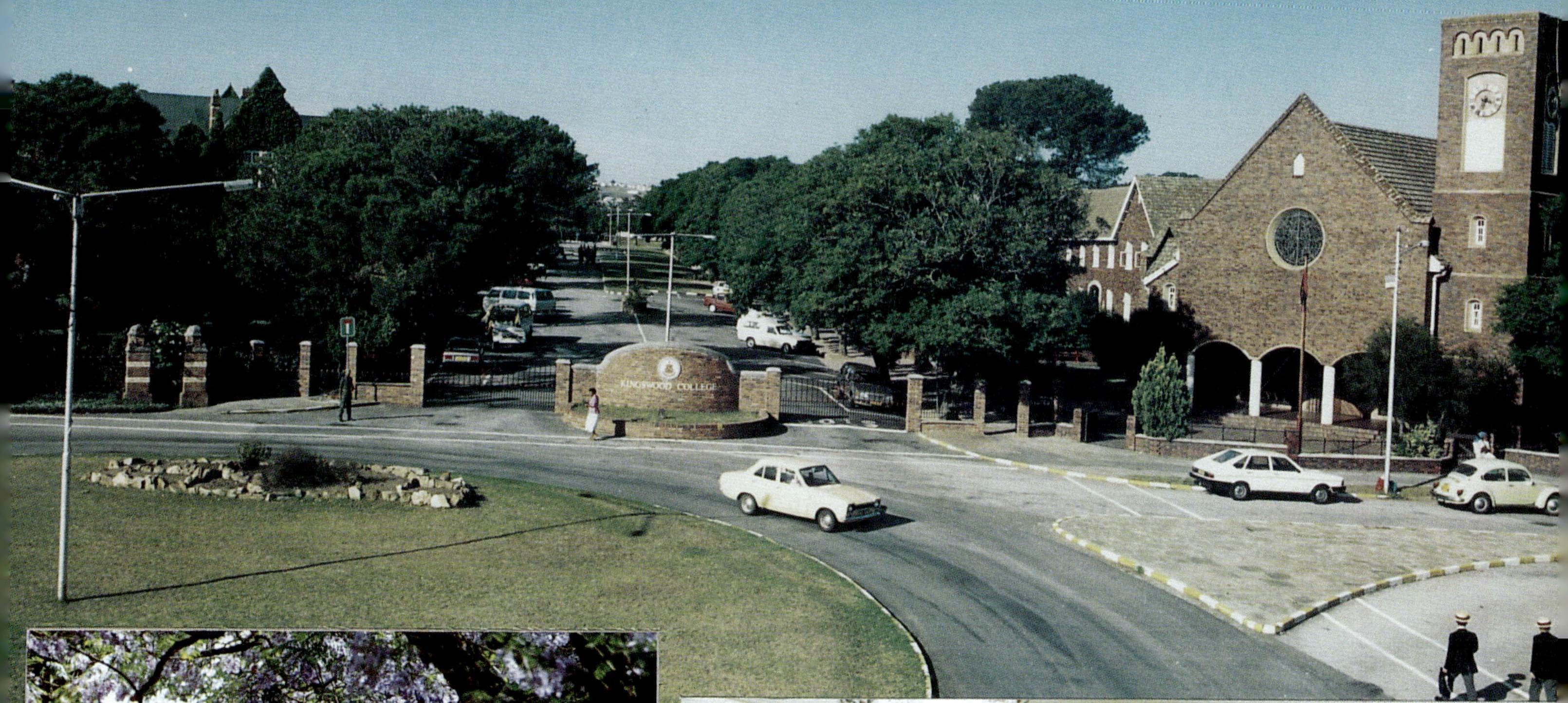

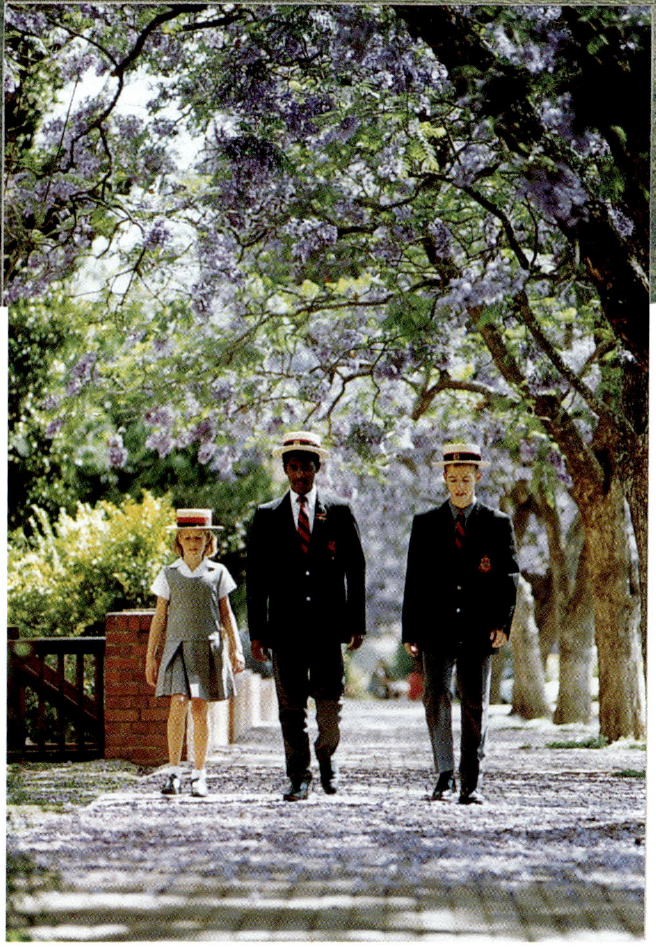

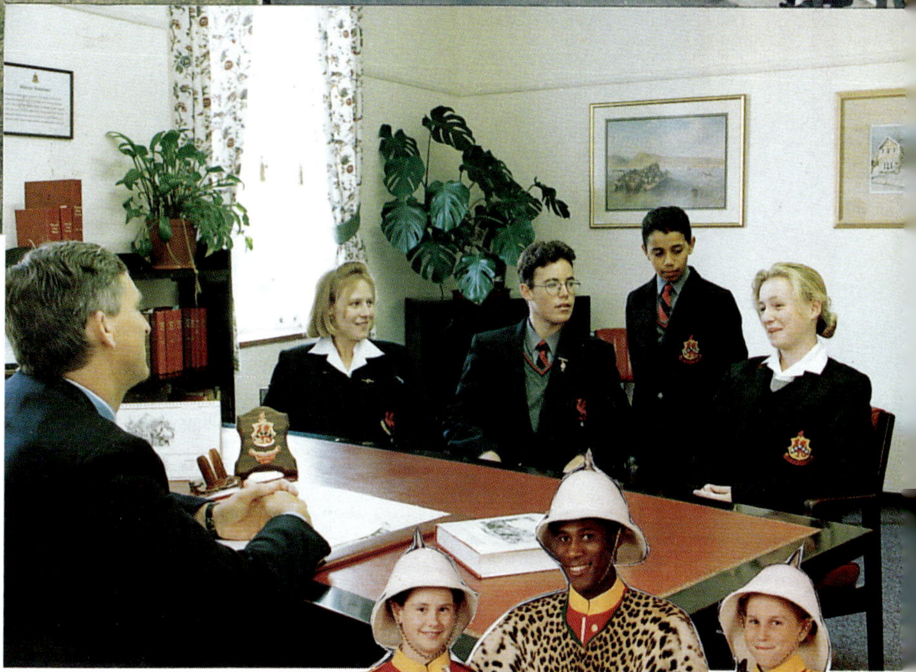

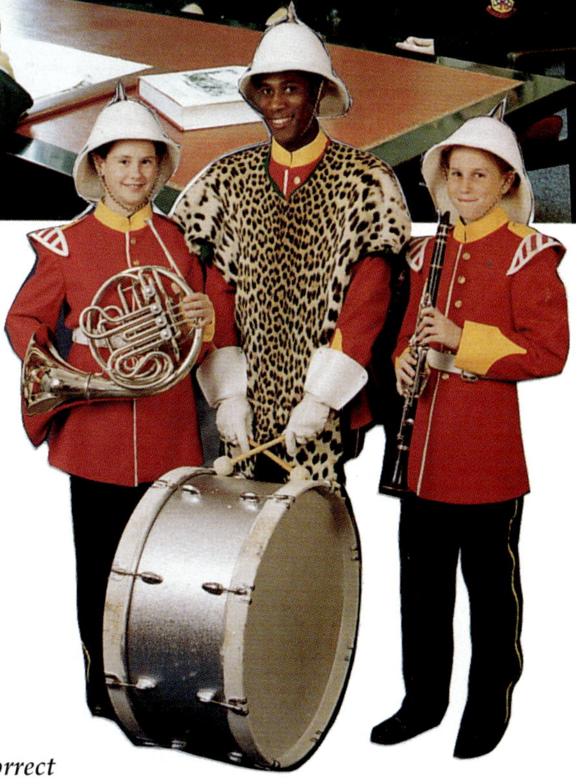

ered by vigorous Virginia creeper. New growth over firm foundations, suitably symbolic as Kingswood enthusiastically enters the next century, its ethos epitomized by this verse from the specially written centenary hymn:

> *"Pursued with zest and lively cheer,*
> *Our purposes and studies thrive.*
> *Help us to build each other up,*
> *To serve, to care, to grow, to strive."*

CLOCKWISE: ***Main entrance with 1962 chapel built on east-west axis, the correct traditional positioning of Christian churches; chatting to 'The Head'; band members pose proudly; and jacaranda time on campus***

VICTORIA GIRLS' AND GRAEME COLLEGE

GRAHAMSTOWN'S two nationally-known state-aided schools have not been built of bricks and mortar, but by the qualities of the teachers and pupils down the decades. Having acknowledged that, the first thing which strikes you about Victoria Girls' High School, stretching impressively along Beaufort Street, *is* the brick work.

More than a million, rosily red, each one individually tuck-jointed, the great gabled wing opened in 1986 in perfect harmony with the older core block which originally housed Graeme College.

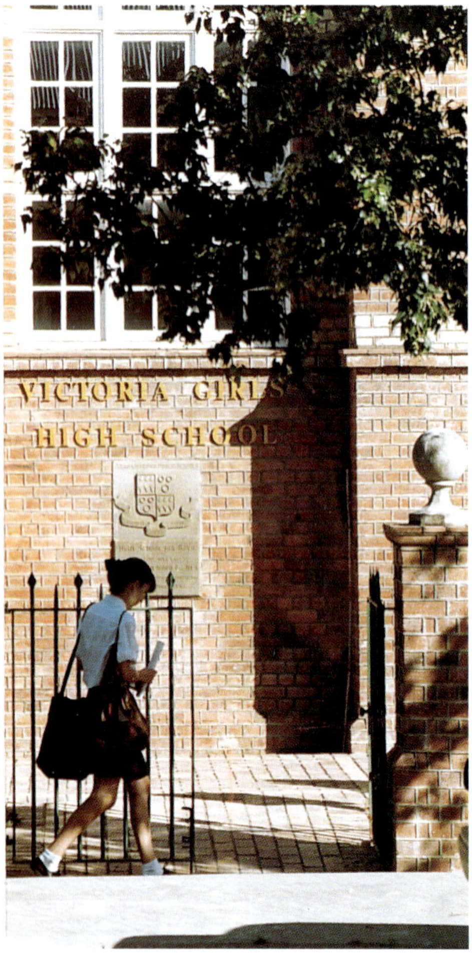

Figuratively speaking, some absolute bricks at the helm. In recent memory the last of the "old school" headmistresses (1950 - 1975), Miss 'Kitty' Richardson whose portrait hangs outside the hall called after her, with her faithful dog, Poppet, well to the fore. And for the past 20 years, the first headmaster of a state-aided girls' school in South Africa, Mr Trevor Long, ably steering it towards its centenary in 1997.

Founded in 1873, after an eventful history which started in the Drostdy Barracks in Somerset Street, Graeme College (for boys only) moved into its new golden brick complex way over in Somerset Heights in 1974. The school's motto is *Virtute et Opera* — by courage and toil, which can best be summed up in one word, grit. A quality that continues to be much in evidence.

"O, Courage and Toil was the watchword then!
'Tis the watchword now, and for days to come;
For courage and toil are the mark of men
On the fastest pitch, in the fiercest scrum,
At the hardest task when all goes wrong
And this is the Graemians' creed and song."

— **Third verse of Graeme school song**

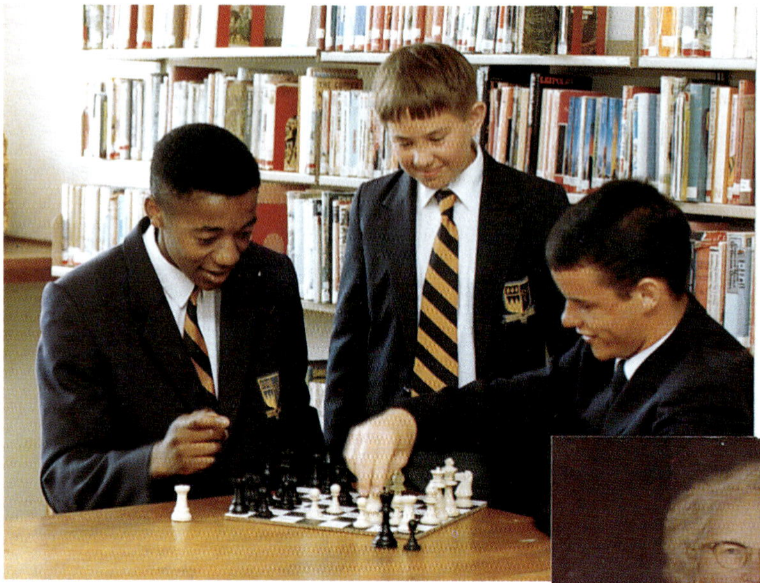

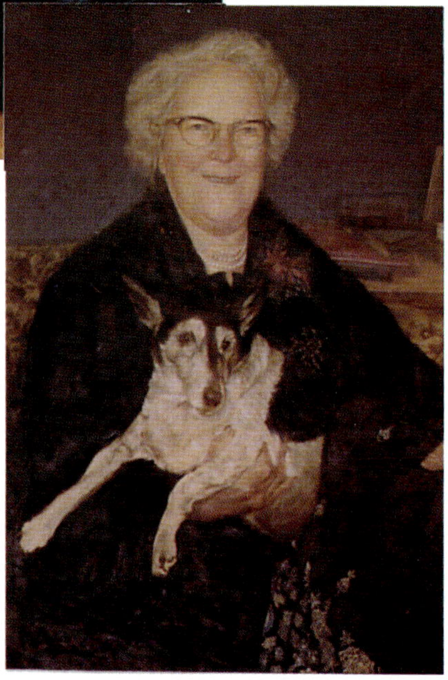

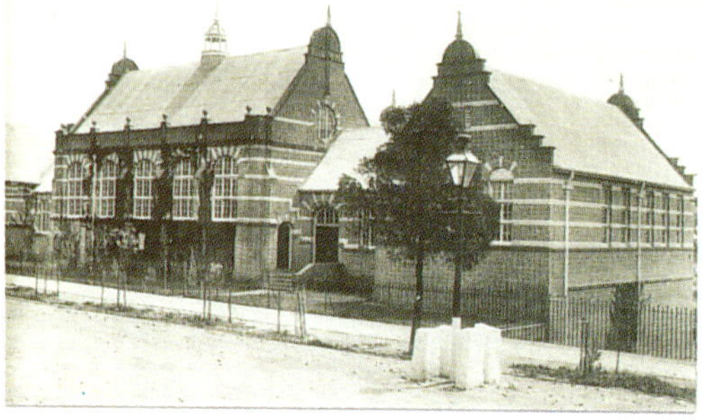

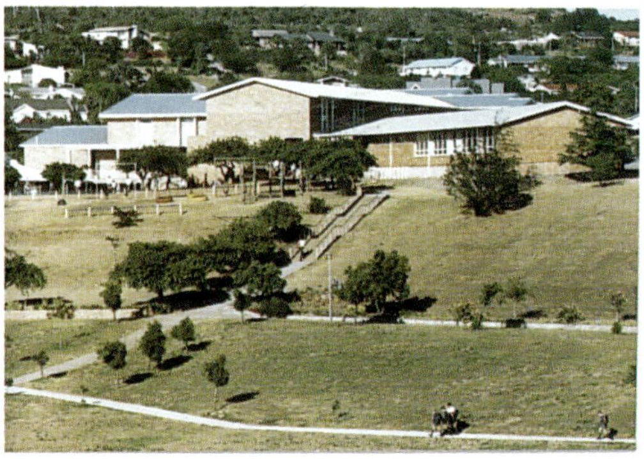

ABOVE AND BELOW; *Victoria girls and Graeme College boys with their respective buildings; and headmistress Kitty with canine companion, painted by Ken Robinson*

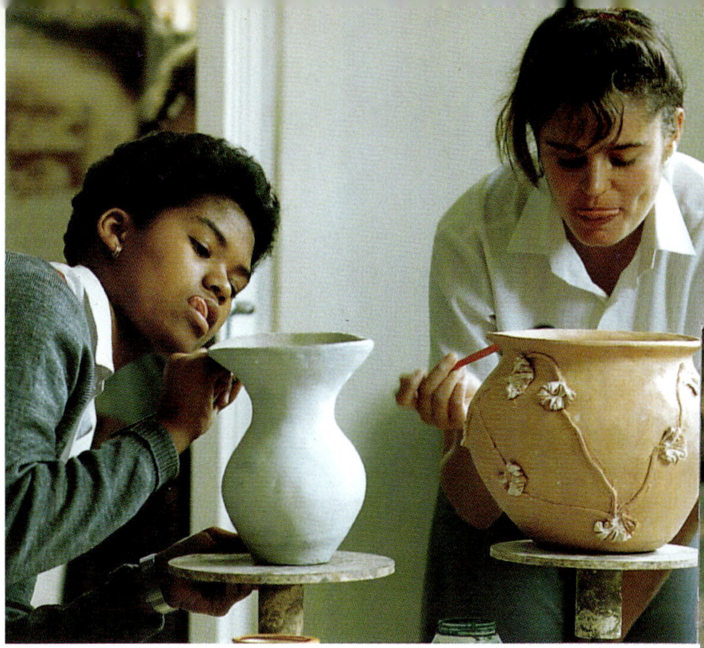

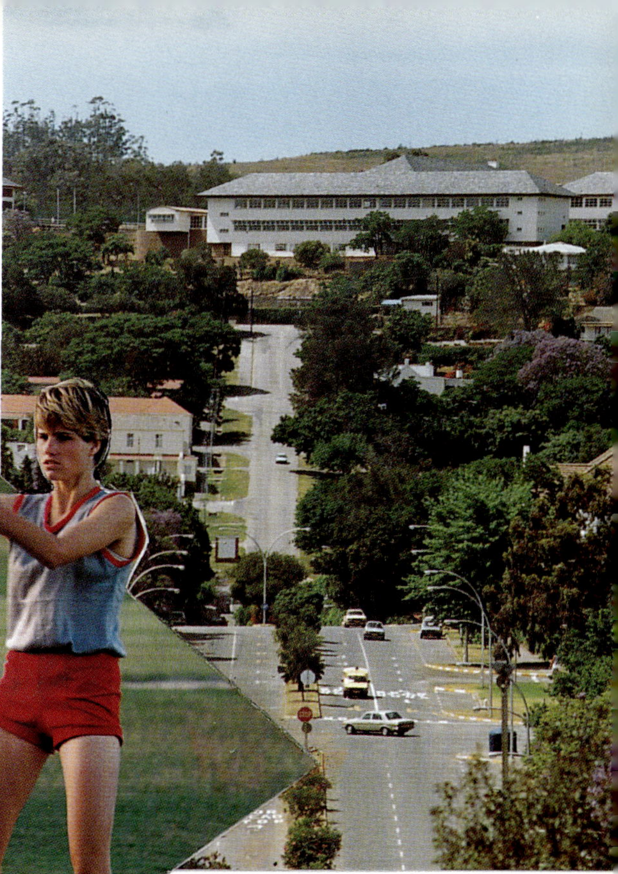

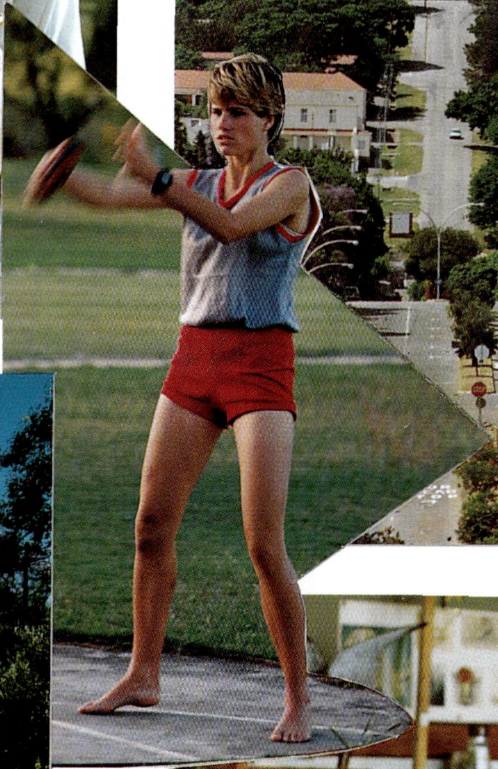

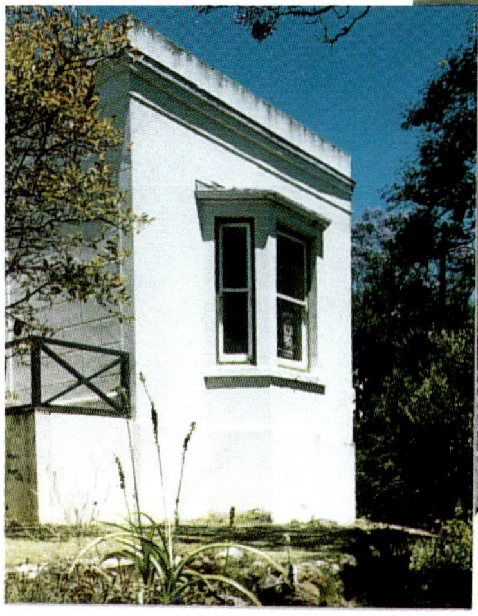

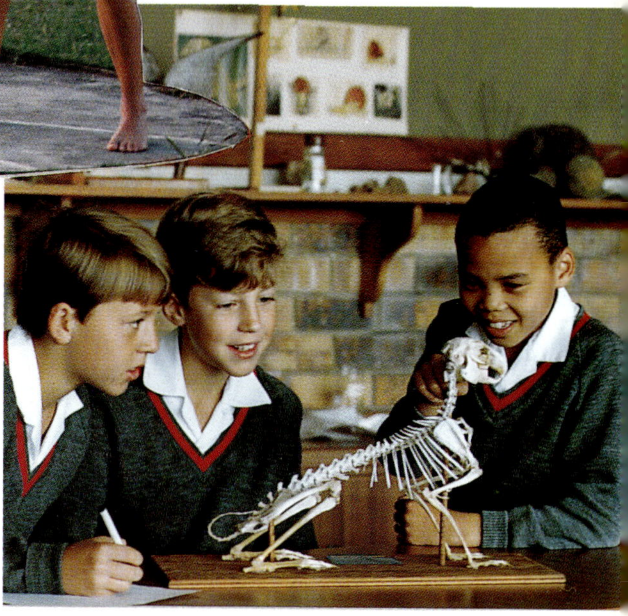

ABOVE: Potters at Carinus Art Centre (right)

FAR RIGHT: Hoërskool on the heights; shaping up on the track and boning up in class

PJ OLIVIER AND THE CARINUS ART CENTRE

CONTRACTORS did not have to move mountains to erect Hoërskool P J Olivier but they did flatten a hilltop. Sports fields were literally blasted out of solid rock, then covered with a layer of topsoil.

The high, wide and handsome buildings stand tall on a magnificent site at the head of Somerset Street, with a view guaranteed to broaden anyone's horizons.

The first and only Afrikaans-medium school in Grahamstown, it was opened in 1956 and also serves the surrounding district. Not an Afrikaans Eton as originally labelled, but an excellent state-aided school dedicated to bringing out the best in each and every pupil.

At the bottom of the hill, a rambling historical homestead has housed the Johan Carinus Art Centre since 1948. Some 800 pupils from different schools come here for lessons, sharing specialist teaching talents and facilities in a stimulating studio atmosphere.

Even exams are visual adventures. Like this test for Standard Eights with a choice of subjects, including:

"An iridescent bug, blue bottle red gold green, sat on my hamburger. I lost my appetite to marvel at its beauty."

After inwardly digesting this, pupils were required to: *"Begin with small sketches or arrange one. Collect objects, take photographs, make notes, pose models, iniate an actual life experience relevant to your choice of poem. DRAW, DRAW..."*

The results? Use your imagination! The young artists definitely did, rising to dizzy heights on the bottle fly's wings. It all depends on how you look at things ...

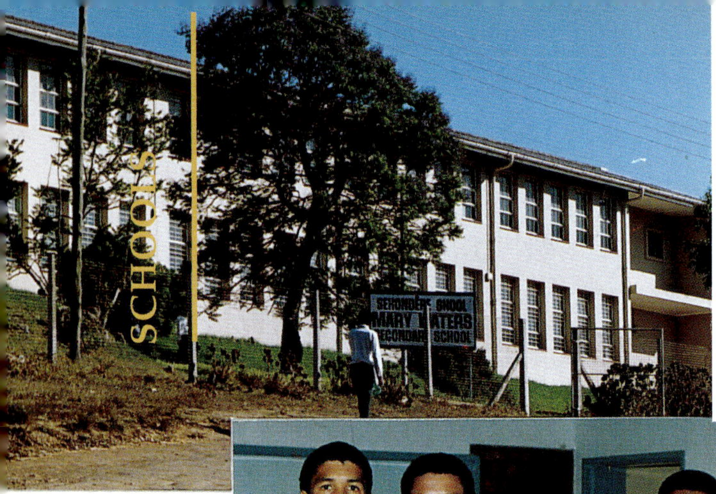

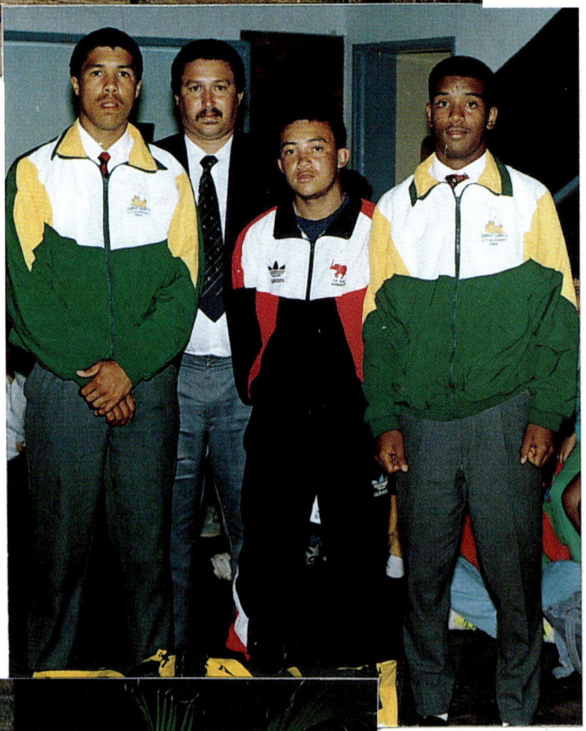

FRESH STARTS...

YOU see them stepping out in neat uniforms which hard-pressed parents have provided with pride and hope — the Township pupils. Their schools are on the rise. The desire to learn is welling up once more. Prize givings bring out the best, sport plays its part, and so increasingly does art.

Facilities are often far from adequate, classes much too large, instruction not always satisfactory. But new buildings are going up, teachers are enrolling for upgrading courses, and enrichment programmes and special coaching schemes are underway. After decades of disruption, miracles will not happen overnight.

As a leading educational centre, Grahamstown has a vital role to play in the new South Africa, and the Township schools are very much part of it. Scholars of different races and cultures are going forward together at schools all over the city. Rhodes University's enrolment is equally diverse. The future has begun ...

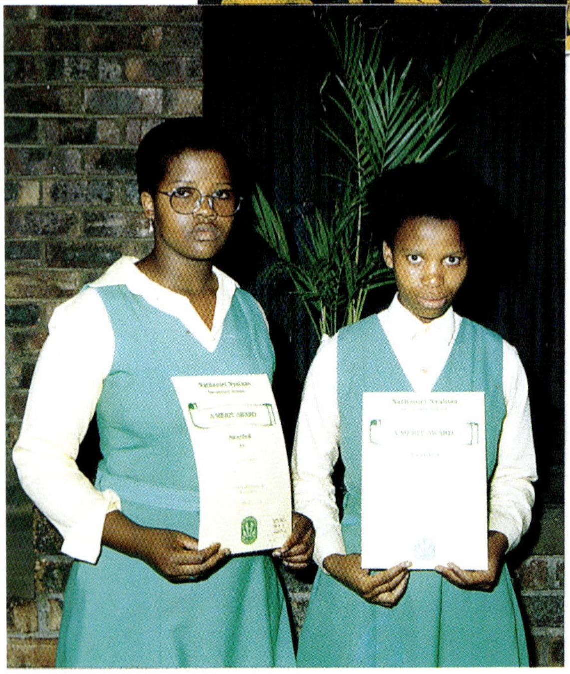

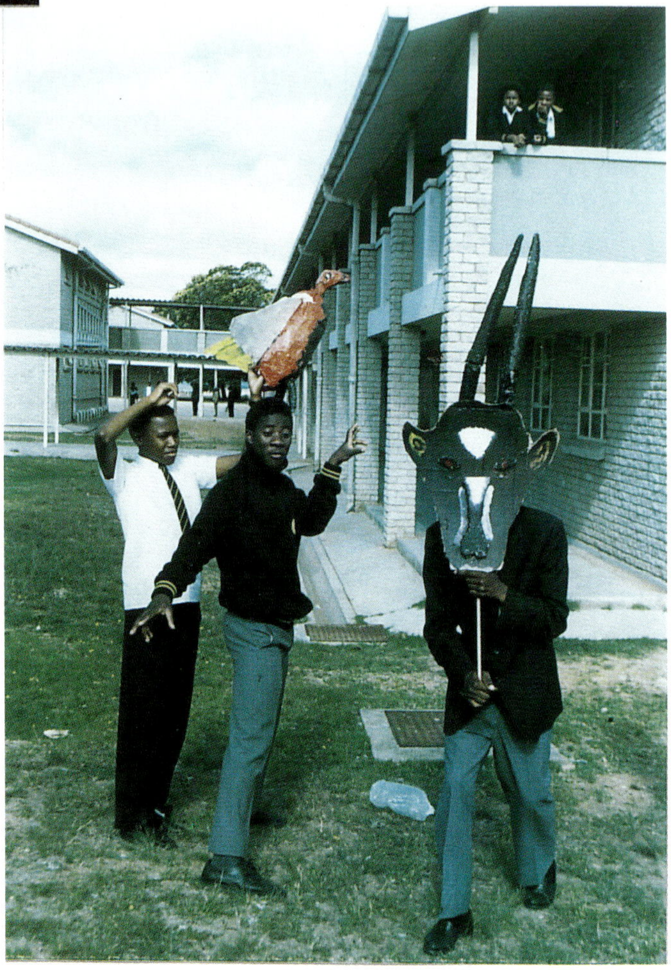

FROM THE TOP: *Sporting types at Mary Waters Secondary School selected for Eastern Province rugby academy teams; girls at Nathaniel Nyaluza merit their awards; and Nombulelo pupils strut their creative stuff*

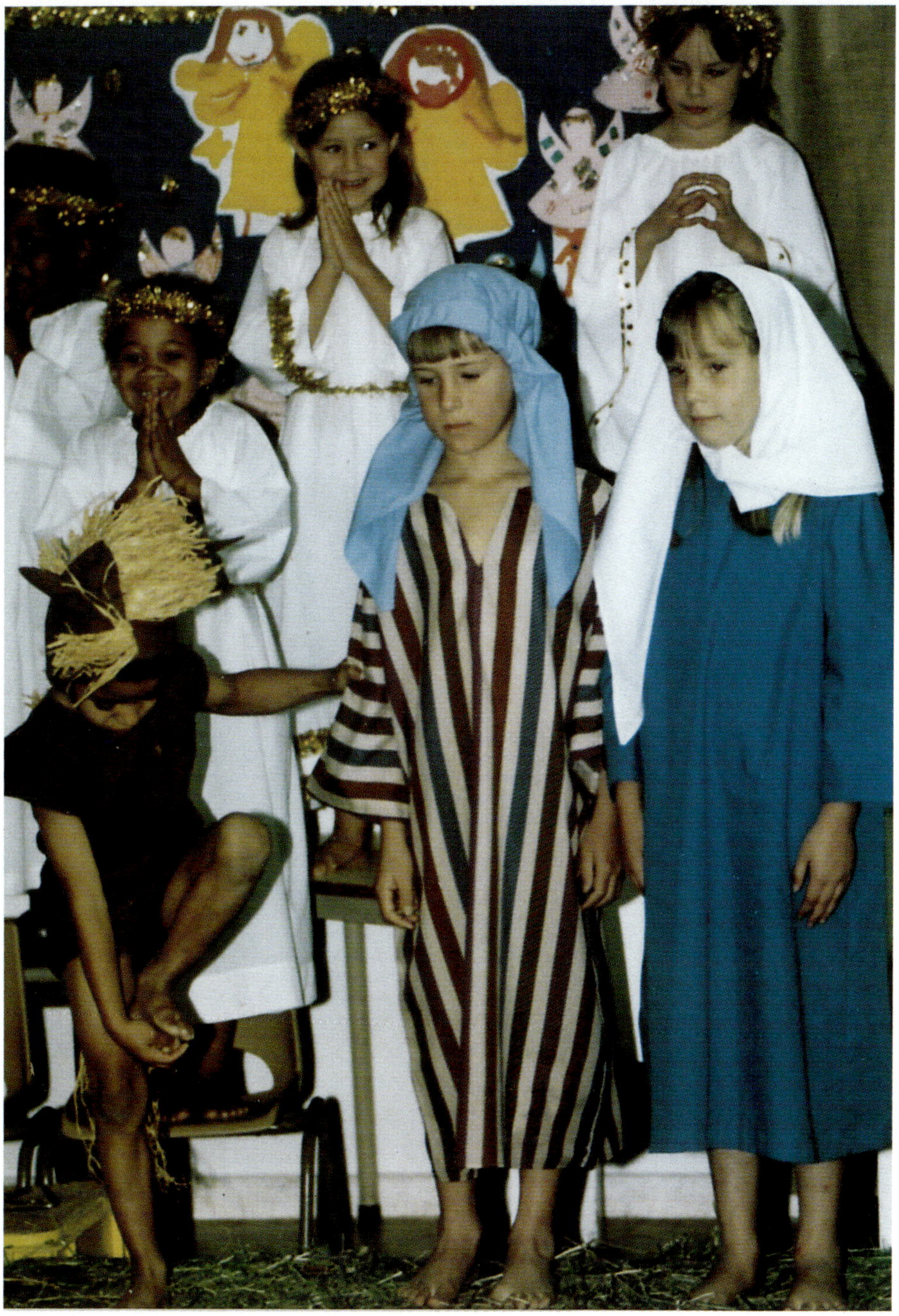

TRADITIONAL ENDINGS

THE donkey has a thorn in his foot, the smallest angel's halo is slipping, and Joseph and Mary are at a loss for words. The dilemmas and delights of Nativity plays, endearing and enduring.

Carefully rehearsed for weeks beforehand; but it is these unrehearsed incidents which make the age-old story ever new, and doubtless always have.

Especially in those early efforts staged by St Francis of Assisi in the 13th century, when he used real animals and a crib to teach people about the birth of Christ. (An Italian ass with a prickly problem would complain— fortissimo.)

As Christmas approaches, local nursery and primary schools become more Middle Eastern than Eastern Province.

Striped towels and dressing gowns abound, tinsel goes to tiny heads, and wise men faithfully follow that star of wonder, star of light, grandly garbed in velvet curtains and cardboard crowns.

A last carol, a final curtain call. Then, as the scholars of every age depart on holiday, the village curls up in a deep and dreamless sleep until the new terms start. All is peaceful and almost unnervingly quiet ...

ABAKHWETHAS

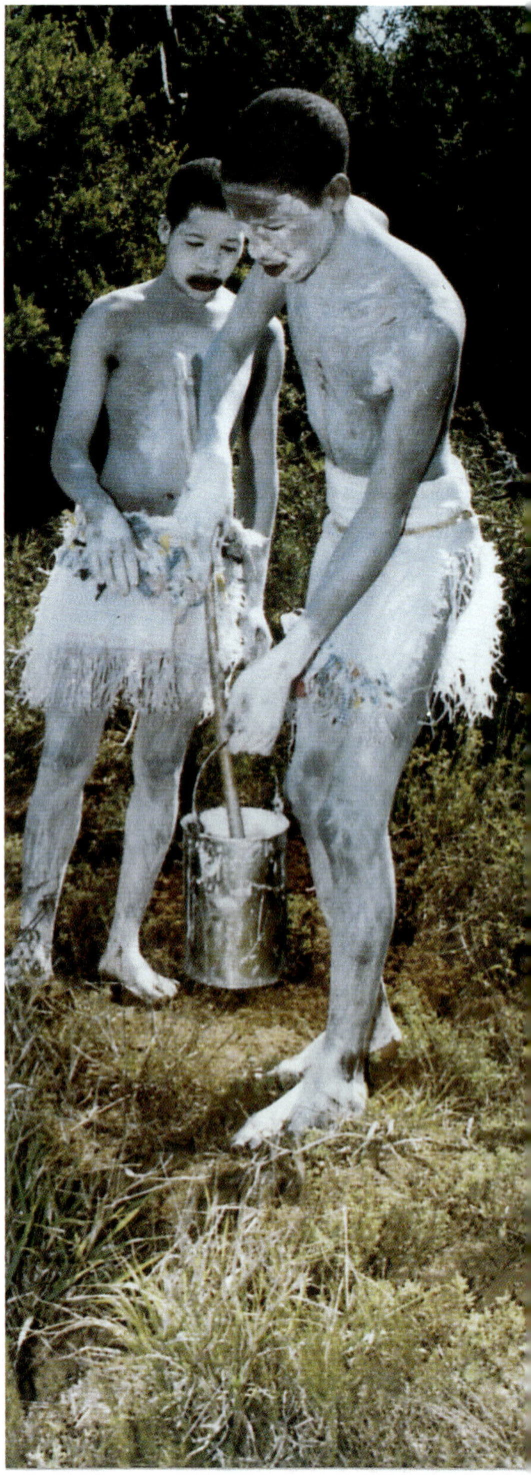

CLASSROOM lessons regardless, the traditional rites of passage to manhood continue to play a vital role in Xhosa culture. The white cliffs of Grahamstown lie just below Makana's Kop at the eastern entrance to the city. Chalky white clay called kaolinite, characteristic of the area, is collected here for *abakhwetha* initiation schools.

Down the scrubby incline opposite, floury figures loom eerily, spirits from another world. The *abakhwethas*. Only the transistor radios they occasionally carry indicate that they are tuned to modern times.

A closer look reveals that much else has changed as the distance from rural roots extends. Their loincloths are now of plastic sacking, their temporary huts or "lodges" likewise. Mattresses replace beds of branches. The deep seclusion of yesteryear with initiates literally "going to the bush" — hence the expression — is no longer always possible.

May, when the maize crop ripened, used to be the time. Now it is usually December, coinciding with long holidays — and warm nights, as firewood cannot be collected but must be bought, increasing costs. These already run at about R1 000 each for feasts, fees, and coming-out finery. The age of initiates varies from approximately 18 to 25 — depending on how quickly families can save the sum.

In Xhosa society, the male's transition from adolescence to adulthood is only achieved by the sacred rite of circumcision and special instruction in Xhosa traditions from the elders.

The "doctor" or *ingcibi* is appointed from these elders, and a feast held the night before the circumcision. The next morning, the operation is performed with a sharpened spear or even simply a knife made from an old file beaten flat. The clay-covered boys are put in the care of an elder or *ikhankatha* who dresses the wounds, sometimes still with the woolly grey leaf of the *Helichrysum pendunculatum* and the outer bulb layer of the beautiful *Boöphane disticha* — the idea being that these prevent serious inflammation.

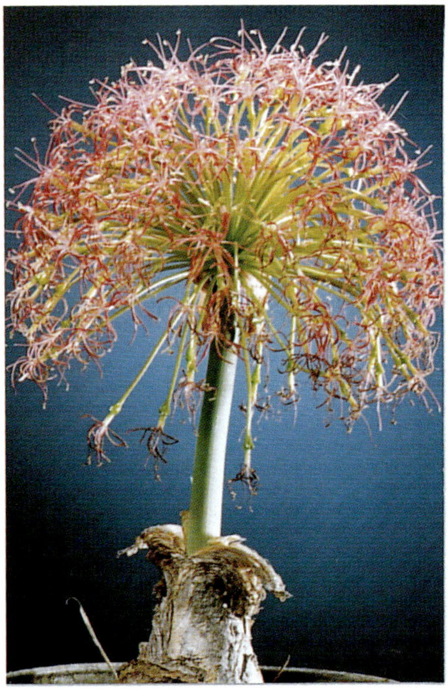

There is increasing medical concern about infection, but also an appreciation that there is much more to the entire experience than circumcision. Whatever the drawbacks, the young keep coming forward.

For the following three weeks the *abakhwethas* lie low. At first they live on a salt-free diet because they are allowed no water for seven days. This is thought to help the healing process. Small boys called *inqalathis* act as messengers, bringing them special food from home. Male visitors are received. No women are allowed. Long discussions take place.

Eventually the initiates emerge. Everything they used is burnt, symbolizing that the past is behind them. They are men, which calls for another celebration, plus complete new outfits, known as *ikhaki* — generally checked jackets, khaki trousers and shirts, cloth caps, and splendidly shiny shoes.

Out they step into the streets of Grahamstown, their faces glowing ruddily with ochre. Shy but dignified, highly conscious of their different status. A graduation of a different kind.

LEFT: ***Boöphane disticha* bulb in bloom**

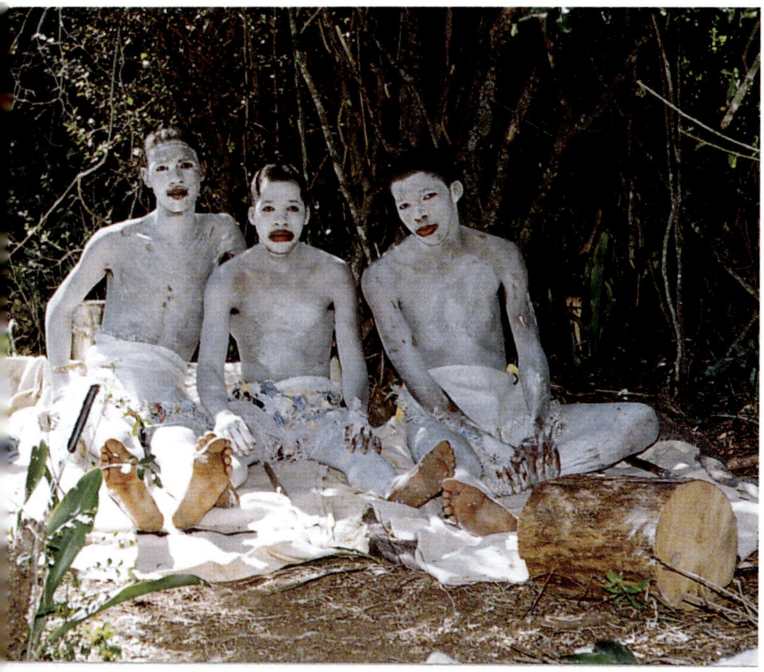

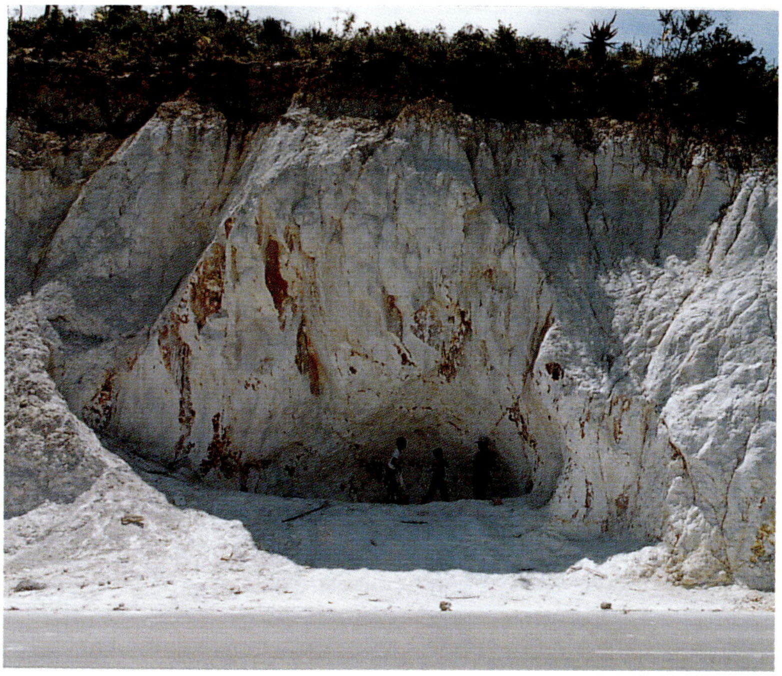

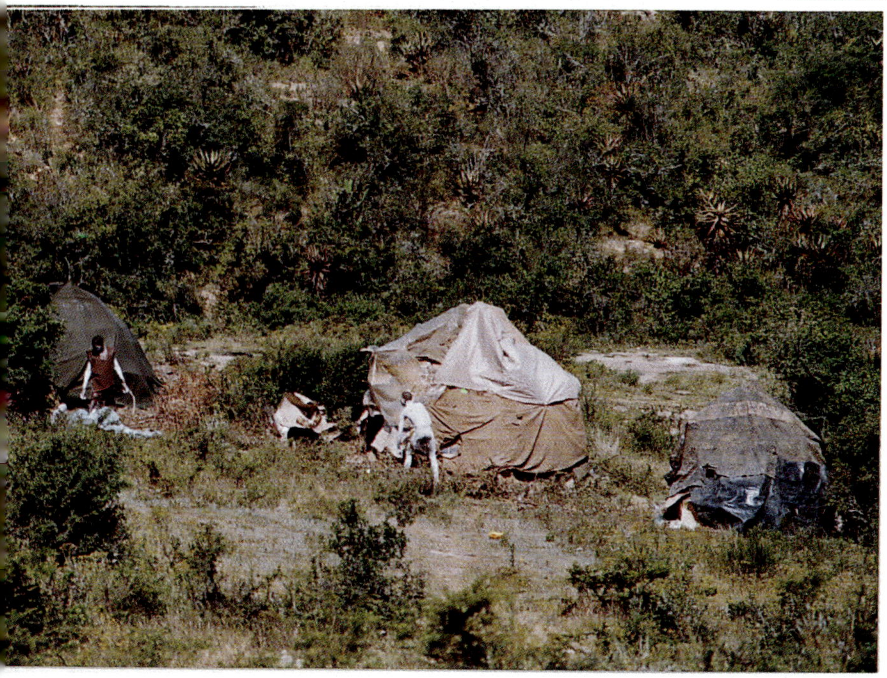

LEFT AND ABOVE: *White clay cliffs and days in the bush*

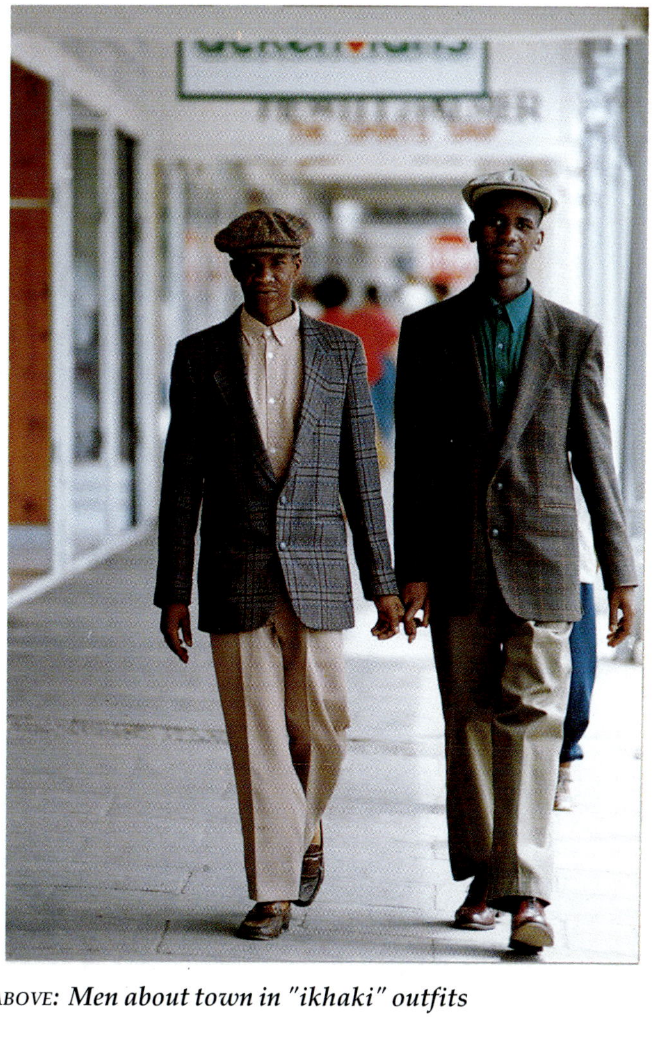

ABOVE: *Men about town in "ikhaki" outfits*

Rhodes

THE gowning glory of the Rhodes graduation ceremonies every April — an unforgettable experience for everyone from the blushing BA to the greying dignitary receiving an honorary doctorate in recognition of a lifetime's work.

The weekend when the university unites to see its ongoing purpose fulfilled by different degrees in an all-pervading glow of success.

Great golden spheres of flowers float above the 1820 Monument stage, a quartet plays, the Rhodes choir sings, and parents pack the auditorium with pride. The young batting about in basic black; the professors hardly recognizable in the medieval richness of their robes, some sporting mortar boards and floppy velvet bonnets at rather rakish angles.

Education is Grahamstown's main industry and Rhodes the major producer. Not assembly line think-alikes but individuals encouraged to shine in their own special way.

Established in 1904, it is widely considered the best small university on the African continent, and is the ninth oldest. Some 4 000 students study courses in more than 80 subjects, lectured by close on 300 academics in 38 departments in eight faculties. The university — which also has a divi-

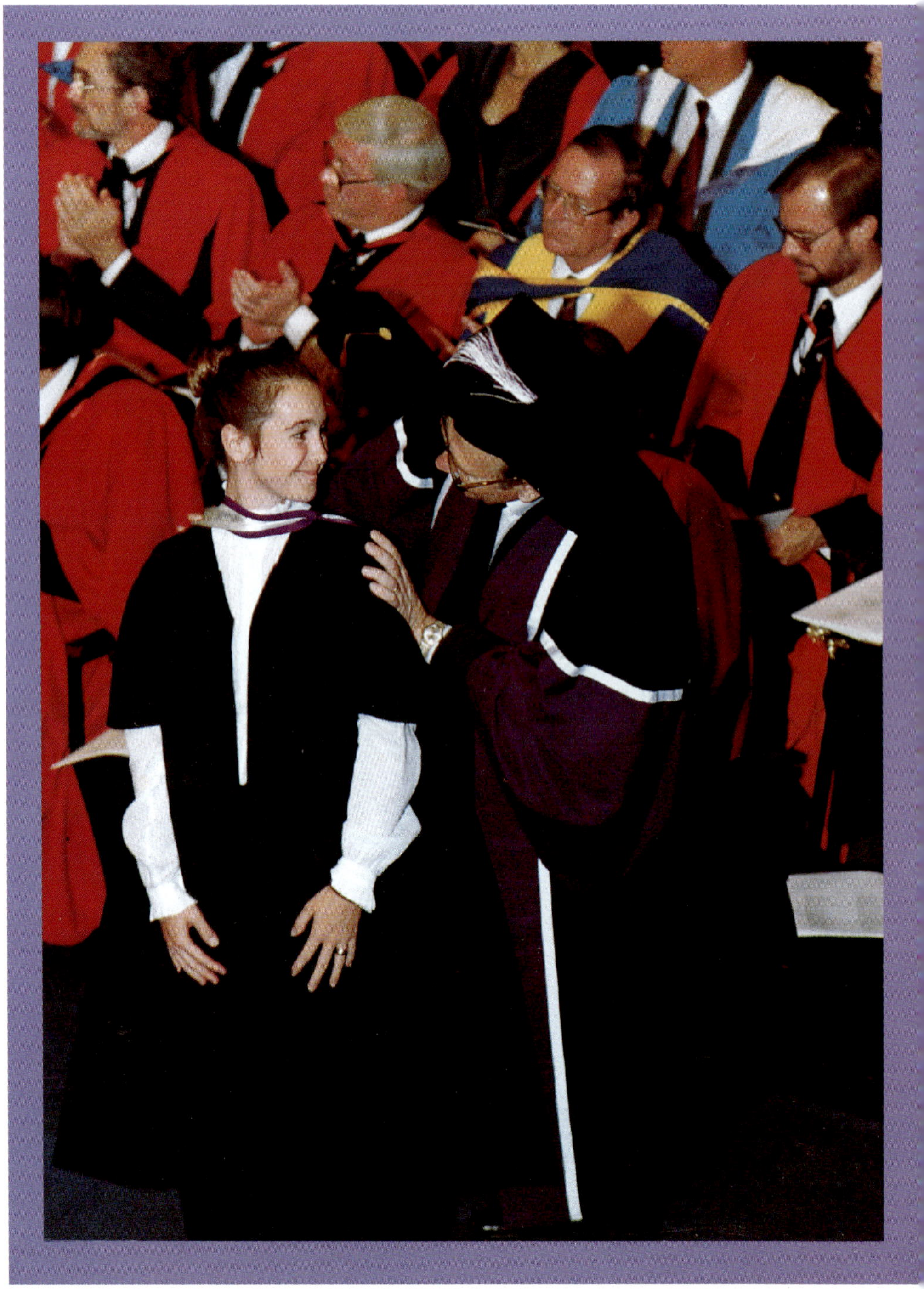

ABOVE: *That graduation glow...typified by a radiant BA with life opening up before her*

Below: Govan Mbeki, dignified recipient of an honorary degree of Doctor of Laws in recognition of the achievements of a lifetime

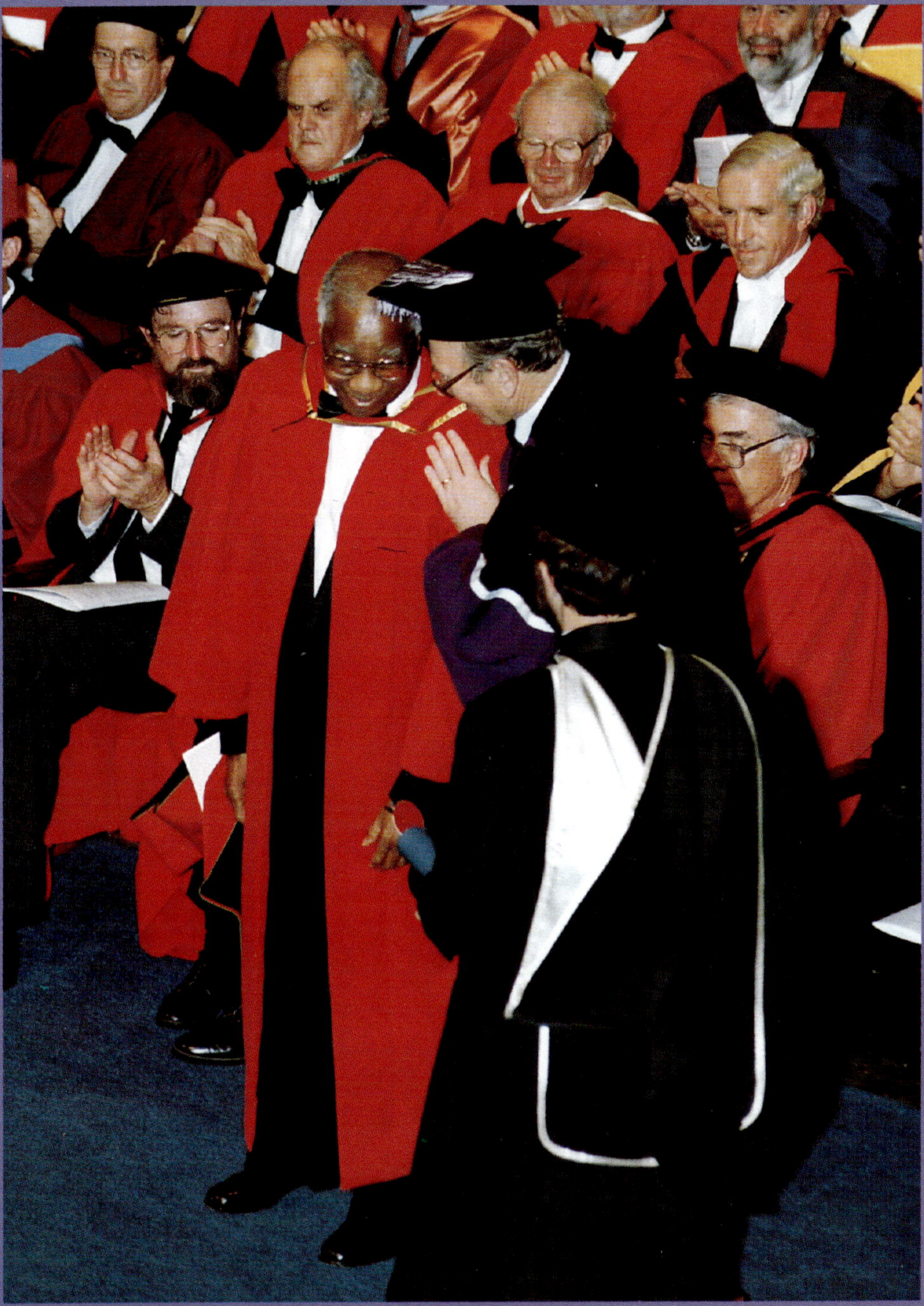

sion in East London — offers over 50 degrees and about half as many diplomas.

So much for statistics. It is the students who continue to count. Different but essentially the same. Young and comparatively carefree, though seemingly more serious of late. It is hard to believe that at graduations in the early 1950s they burst into boisterous song as the academic procession entered:

"The animals came in two by two,
parlez vous.
The elephant and the kangaroo,
parlez vous.
The animals came in two by two,
The Senate and Tom Alty too,
Inky pinky parlez vous."

The Rhodes choir still gives the lead with more inspiring anthems, including *The Purple and White*. Students and Senate suggested dark amethyst and white as the Rhodes colours way back in 1913. Council agreed, while drawing attention to the problem of "getting a fixed colour in that shade". Subsequent developments — especially synthetic fibre sports togs — have proved them right, with lilac and fuchsia blooming brightly on the fields. No shrinking violet, but then neither is Rhodes, which continues to live up to its motto *Vis, Virtus, Veritas* — Strength, courage, truth — as it plans ahead for its centenary in the year 2004.

University

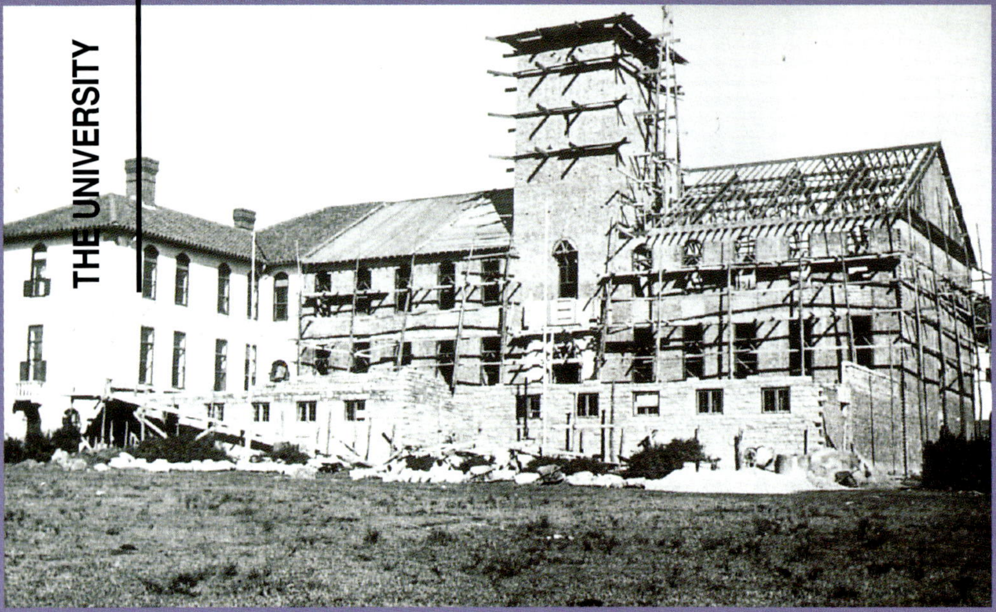

LEFT: *Rhodes's south side was completed as planned in 1914; the tower block only replaced the old Drostdy in 1937*

BELOW: *The indomitable Prof George Cory, equipped for any eventuality on one of his epic field trips*

GOING UP,

LIKE the students who fill its lecture rooms, Rhodes may not have grown up quite as expected, but it has turned out better than anyone could have dreamed.

University-level education has been available in Grahamstown since 1873, when the University of the Cape of Good Hope began degree courses through St Andrew's College. In 1878, St Andrew's started a government-subsidized College Department, and the first four professors were appointed.

An entirely separate establishment was the next step. With financial assistance from the Rhodes Trust — a generous parcel of De Beers preference shares — the Rhodes University College was founded by an Act of Parliament on March 31, 1904. (When Rhodes was inaugurated as an independent university on March 10, 1951, the remainder of the preference shares were pledged as part of its security.)

The four professors and their 50 students duly moved into the abandoned Drostdy buildings at the head of High Street, which dated back to 1827.

In 1910 the architectural firm run by Herbert Baker and Francis Kendall won a competition to design the new university buildings. Only part of their plan was executed owing to a lack of funds, painted plaster being used in most areas instead of the quartzite and Bathurst limestone originally specified.

An almost Mediterranean air resulted, enhanced by subsequent developments. Additions went up as finance allowed — including the trademark tower on the core block, which replaced the Drostdy itself.

Meanwhile, residences had been rising to the rear in the bare veld, vastly different from the present garden setting. Faded photographs reflect these earlier times when pleasures were simpler, love's first sweet song more bashful, and dress decidedly formal. Initially undergraduate gowns were worn to lectures, later only to evening meals, while ties took longer to disappear.

What of the professors? Always there, often under-appreciated, usually overworked. One of the original four continues to capture the imagination: Sir George Cory, perhaps the epitome of a real Rhodes professor — a far from dying breed.

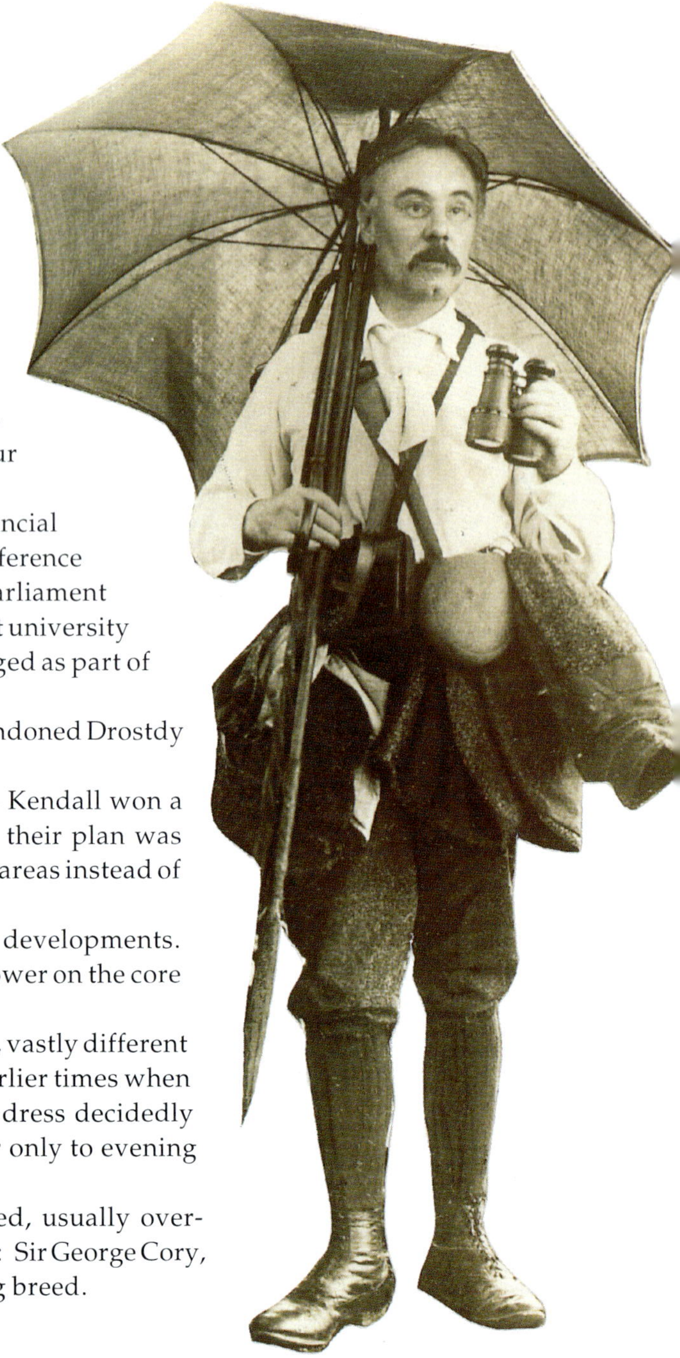

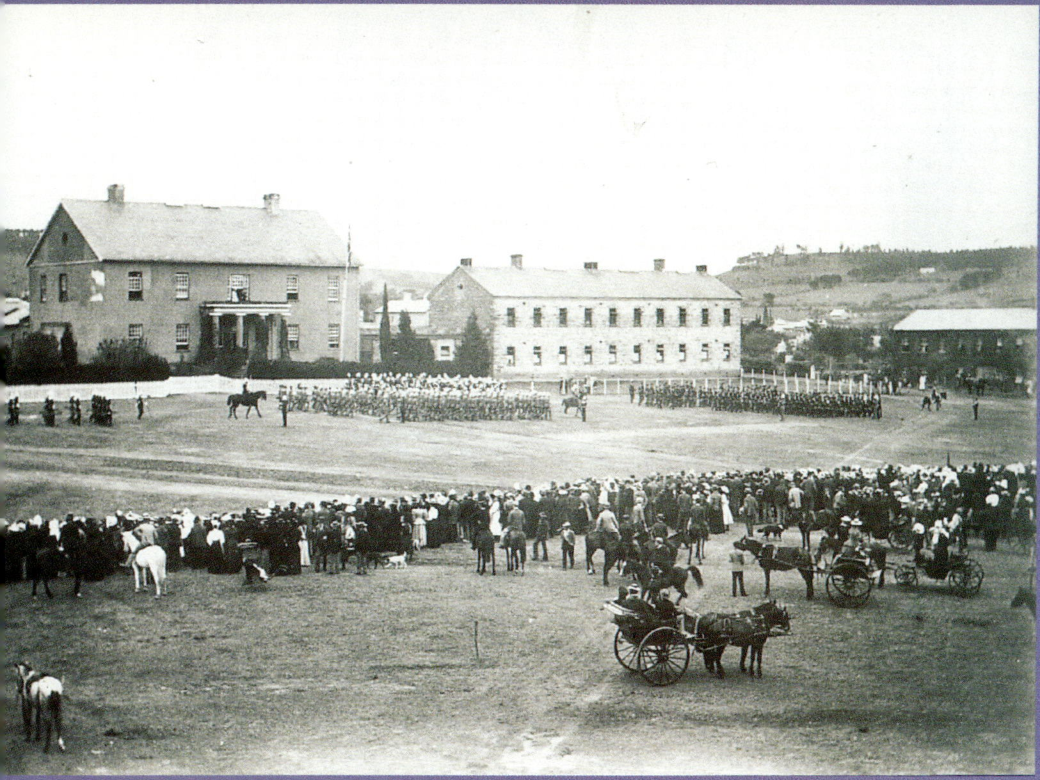

LEFT: *A military parade in front of the Drostdy, circa 1895; the barracks next to it now house the Linguistics Department; and the building to the right Mathematics*

GROWING UP

The first Professor of Chemistry, his interest in history resulted in his writing *The Rise of South Africa* and being knighted for it. A pioneer of oral history, he covered considerable distances on foot, gathering reminiscences from aged settlers and Xhosa chiefs, soldiers and Voortrekkers, farmers and townsfolk. The present Cory Library for Historical Research has as its foundation his collection of source material and documents.

A sometime City Councillor, popular singer of comic songs, and enthusiastic stamp-collector, he was ever willing to lend a helping hand. When no one could be found to re-gild the hands and figures on the Cathedral clock, during a university vacation he was seen daily perched up in a bosun's chair, getting on with the job, and — as he himself commented — scattering a far too liberal proportion of the gold leaf on the City of Saints below.

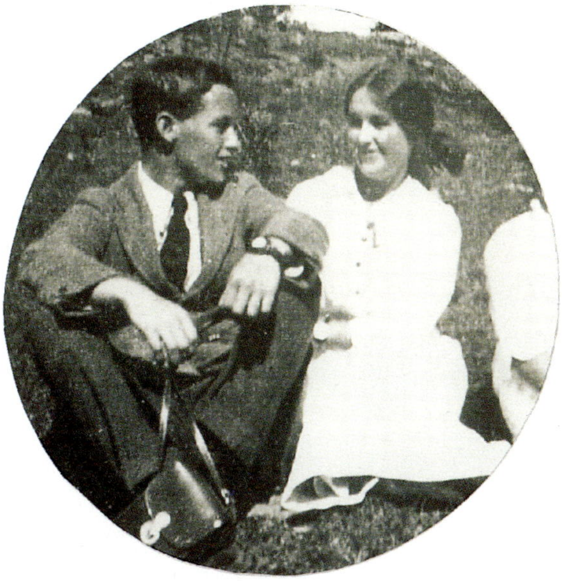

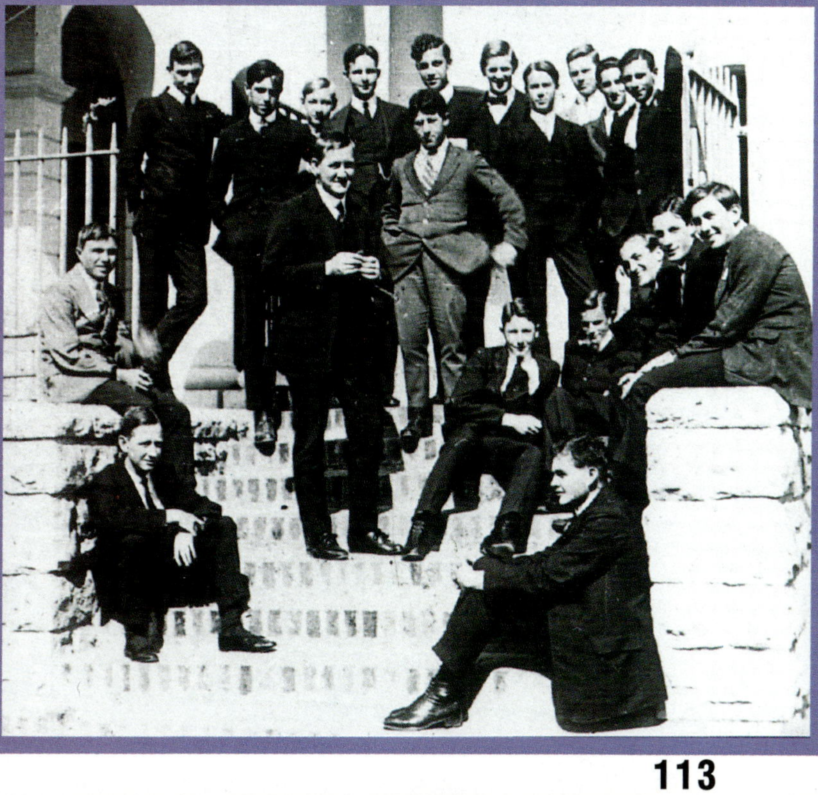

ABOVE: *Mutual adoration — from a 1915 Rhodian snapshot album; and* RIGHT: *a well-turned out class way back in the early 1940s*

THE WORLD

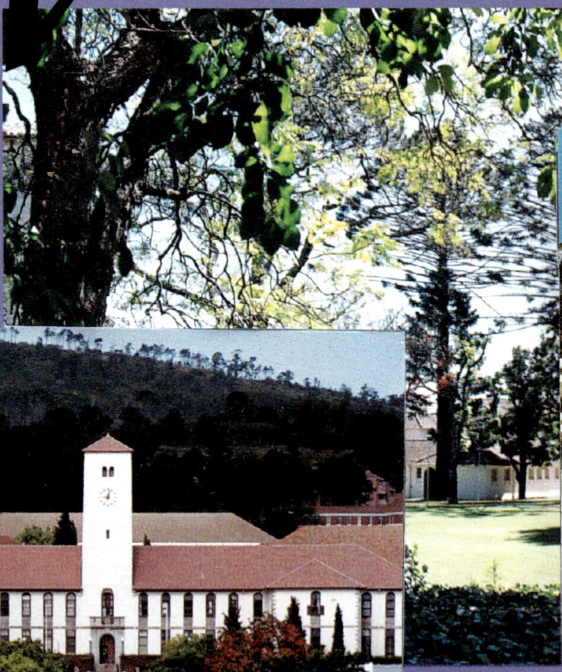

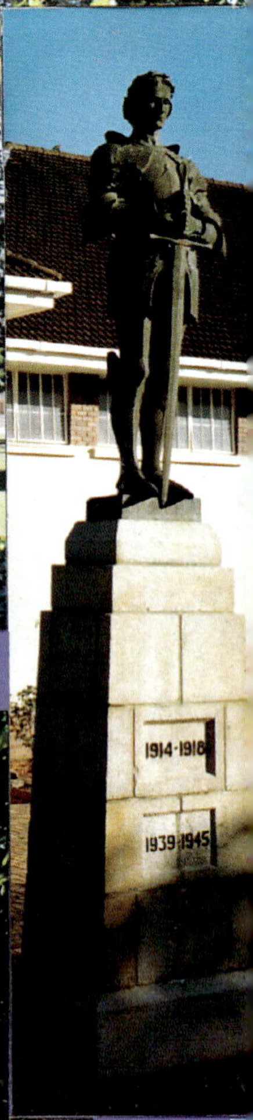

THE ivory tower of the university looks down the High Street towards the Cathedral and the little town looks up to it. Rhodes and Grahamstown — so synonymous, that as with a long and happily married couple, you seldom think of them apart.

But the university is a world of its own — a universe of knowledge in immaculately kept gardens. A young knight is eternally on guard, and the only silent hadedahs in the Albany area perch in a peaceful quad. Backed by pine-covered hills where the mist swirls and midsummer fires flare, filling the sky with ominous smoke signals.

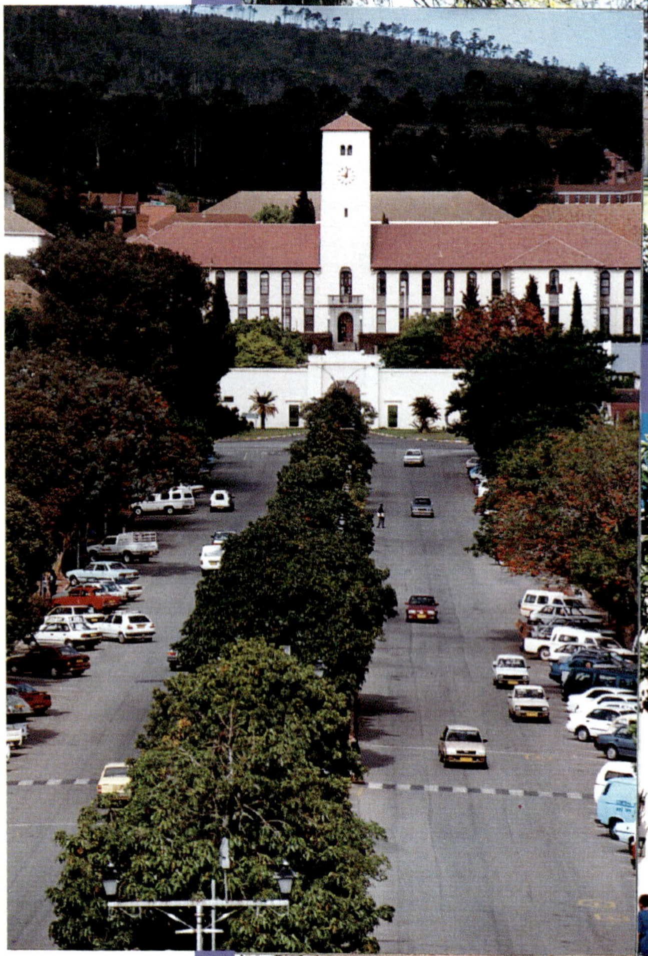

Behind the beguiling façades, be they late Victorian villas (Philosophy and the Institute of Social and Economic Research), historic stone barracks sporting National Monument plaques (Linguistics and Mathematics) or middle of the road modern (Pharmaceutical Sciences), each department and institute is like a foreign country, with a language and culture of its own. Their common bond is a dedication to learning and leading in their field.

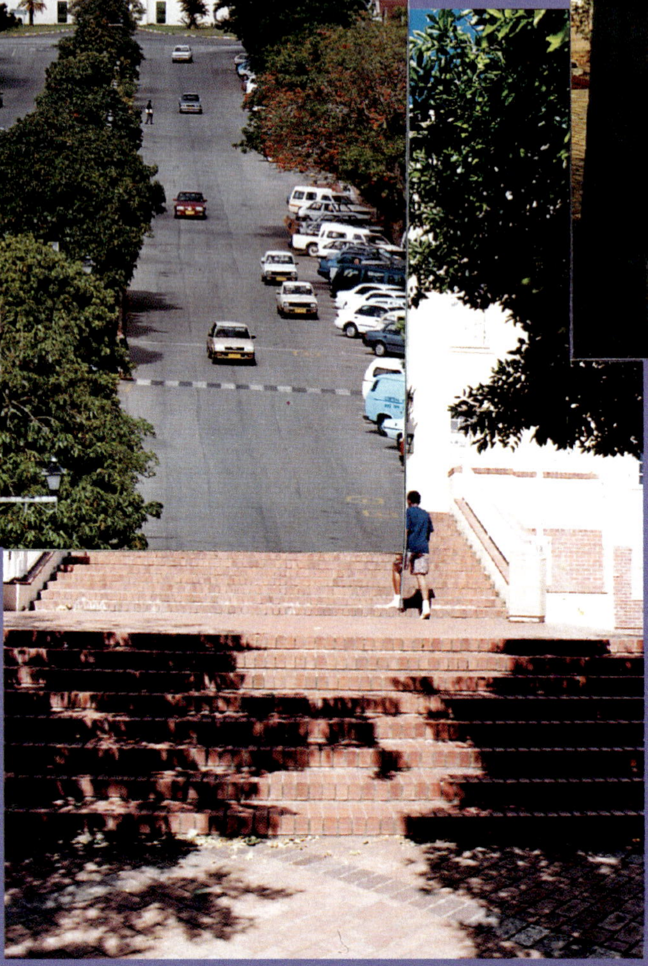

It has been calculated that given the city's diminutive dimensions, the concentration of brainpower is the most intense in the country. Be that as it may — and with only 22 and a bit pages in the telephone directory it could be true — it is always surprising to read reports in *Grocott's Mail* of the doings of the peripatetic academics who, when not teaching at home, are often similarly occupied abroad.

IN ONE CAMPUS

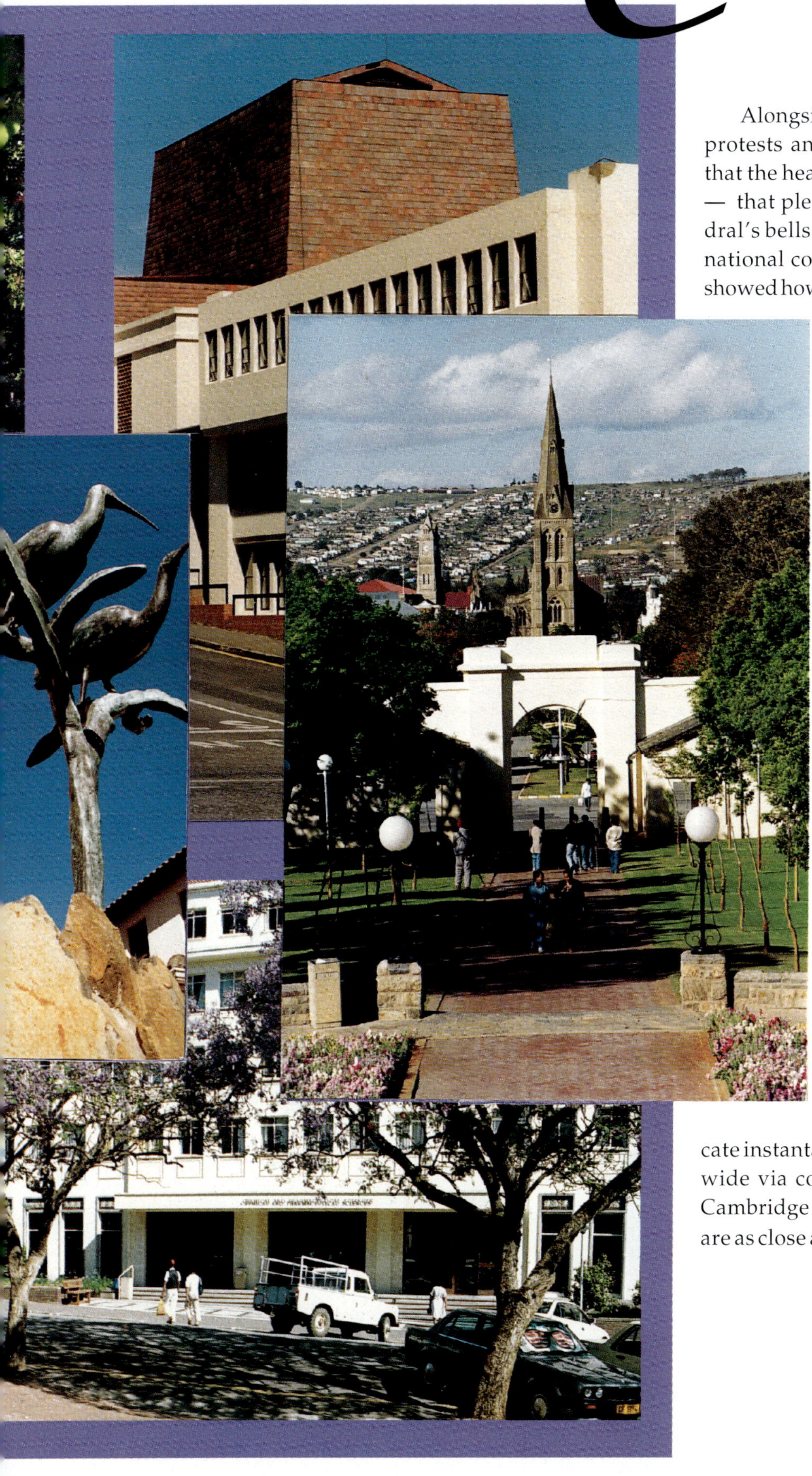

Alongside routine records of ratepayers' protests and mohair goat prices, you note that the head of the Geography Department — that pleasant fellow who got the Cathedral's bells restored — has been to an international conference in Argentina where he showed how evidence of permafrost in Southern Africa during the Last Glacial Maxim exists in the Eastern Cape Drakensberg.

The young chap in the Department of Ichthyology and Fisheries Science is back from Tasmania after presenting his findings on artificial food for abalone; the talented actor who lectures in the Drama Department has won a total of three awards at the Edinburgh Festival, and the distinguished Afrikaans novelist in the Department of Afrikaans and Nederlands had dinner with Queen Beatrix at the Royal Palace in Amsterdam while on a lecture tour of Holland.

Talk about the global village ... Grahamstown's where it's at. All the more so since Rhodes became the first academic institution in South Africa to establish a permanent link with the Internet. This enables academics throughout the country to communicate instantaneously with their peers worldwide via computers. Whether they are in Cambridge or Kyoto, Oxford or Ottawa, they are as close as colleagues across the corridor.

STUDENT

HERE'S to The Students — usually referred to collectively by locals as if a foreign breed but with a special place in the city's affections. Bless 'em all, the long-haired, the short and the tall (and they do seem taller every term). Without their zest, zaniness and zap, life in Grahamstown would be one long zizz ...

When all 4 000-plus push off on the lengthy end-of-year vac, the population ages visibly overnight and an unearthly hush descends. It is the tidal-wave of young eternally 'twixt 18 and 22 sweeping in every February which fosters the illusion of Shangri-lah.

Rhodes is unique among South African universities in that it has no natural urban hinterland from which to draw. Students come from elsewhere — every part of the country and further afield in southern Africa, including Botswana, Lesotho, Malawi, Namibia, Swaziland, Zambia, and Zimbabwe.

Approximately half are accommodated in halls of residence — as at Oxford and Cambridge, on which the Rhodes residential and academic system is based. Each hall comprises three or four residences of about 50 to 120 students, grouped round a central dining hall. Each of the eight halls has its own constitution, its own rules, and its own customs. Each residence has its own particular character, created by the students who live there. Those who do not live in, live out — in digs in the village, setting up their own communal houses.

Campus life is more concentrated than in big cities. Theoretically, studies are ditto. The lack of outside attractions does not mean there are no distractions. The endless round of student activities is faithfully reflected in a Church Square photographer's shop constantly crammed with leggy lovelies and their brawny swains inspecting happy snaps of the latest thrash or sports field clash.

Their lives are far from being one long party, however. They really do work hard. During exam times, the very air of Grahamstown becomes fraught with tension as so much mental muscle strains for lift-off in pursuit of excellence. The end result is that successive generations of

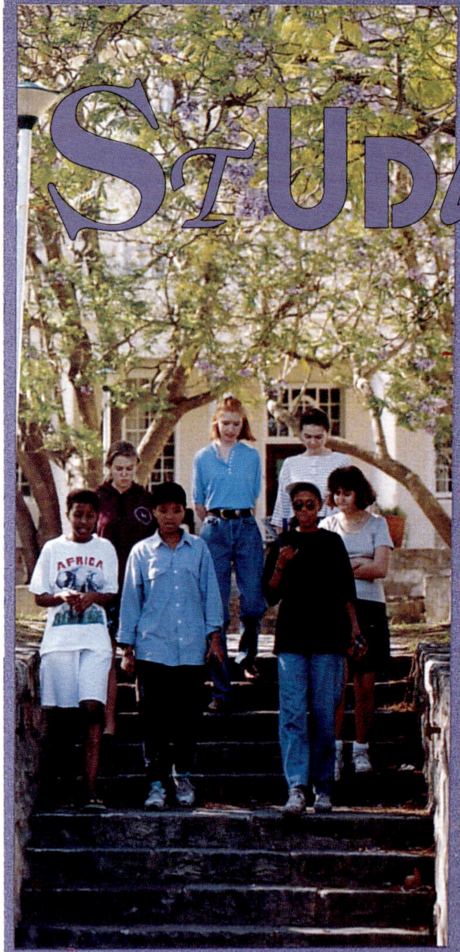

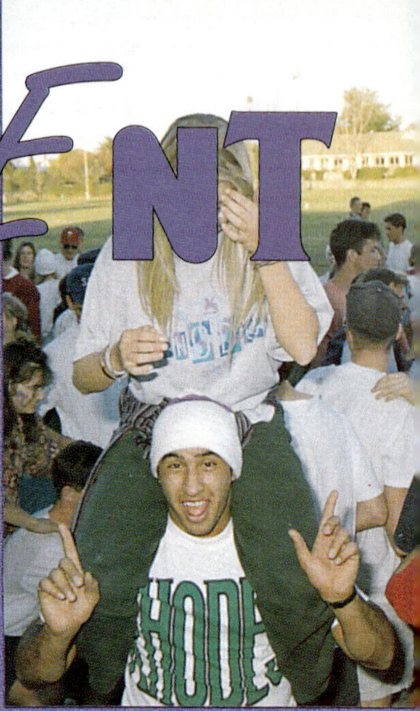

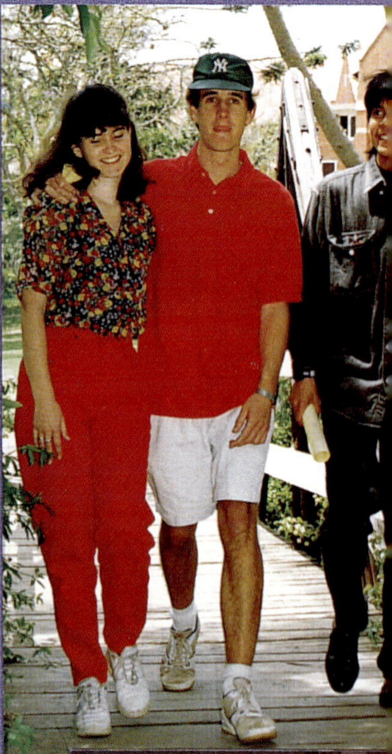

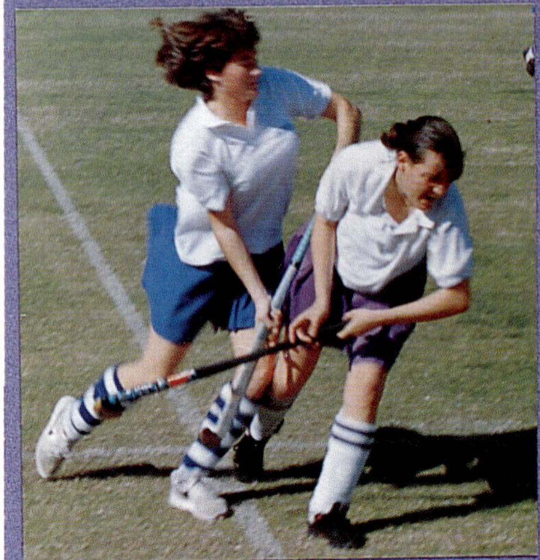

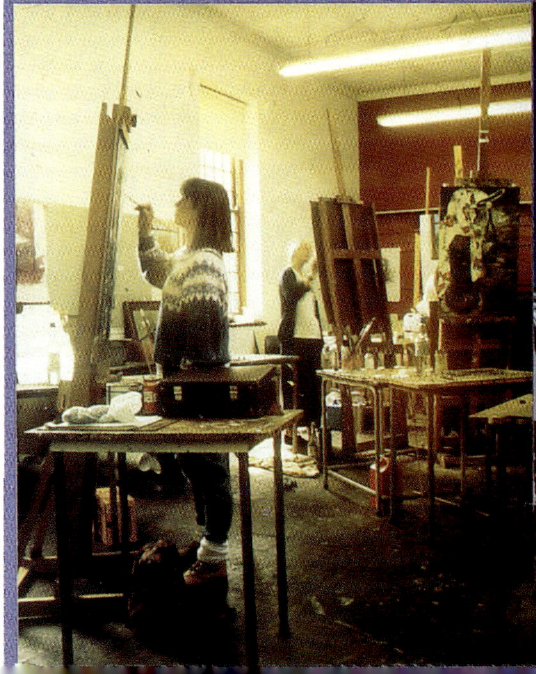

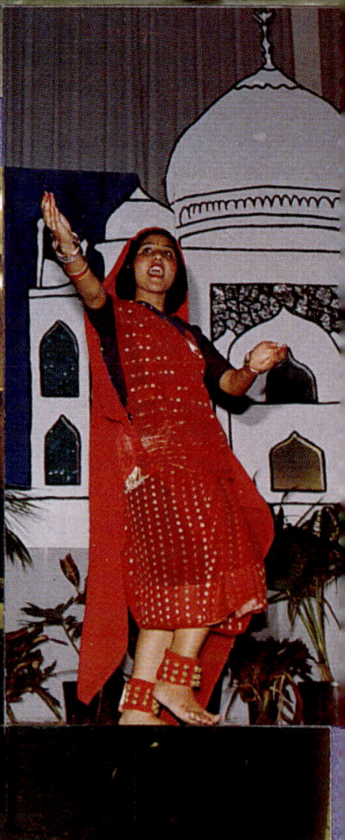

LIFE...

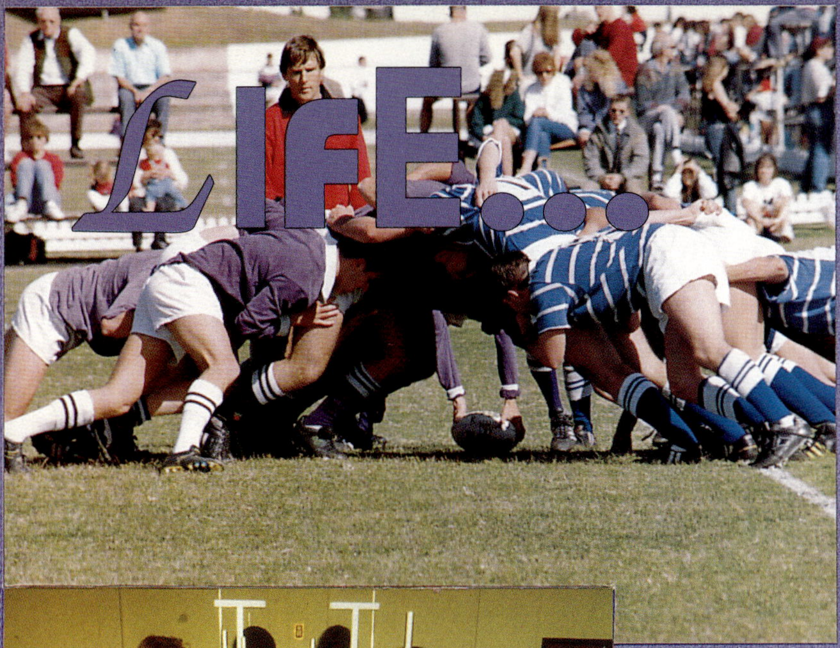

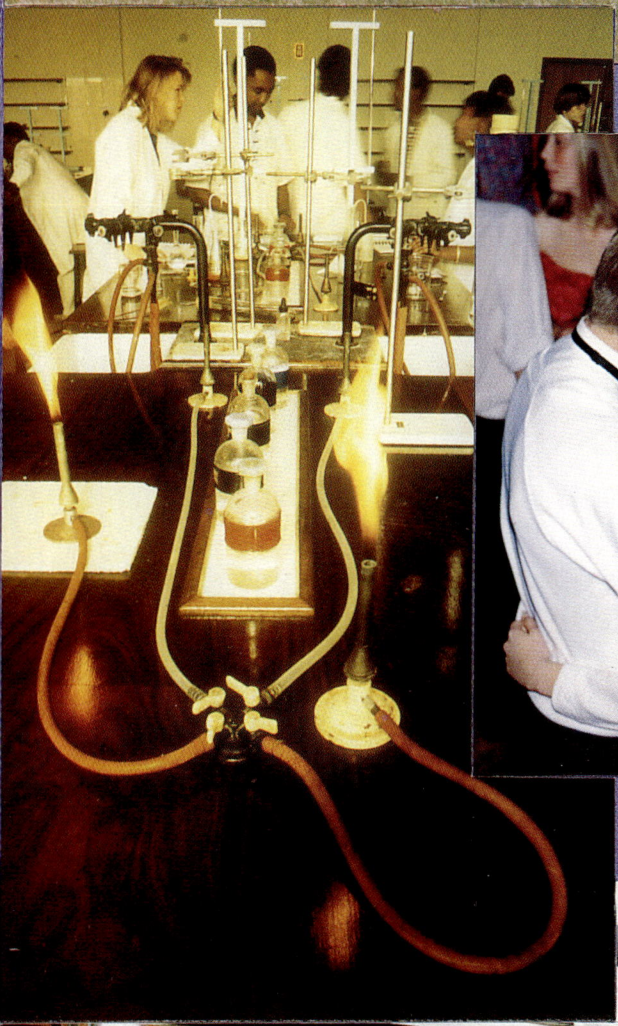

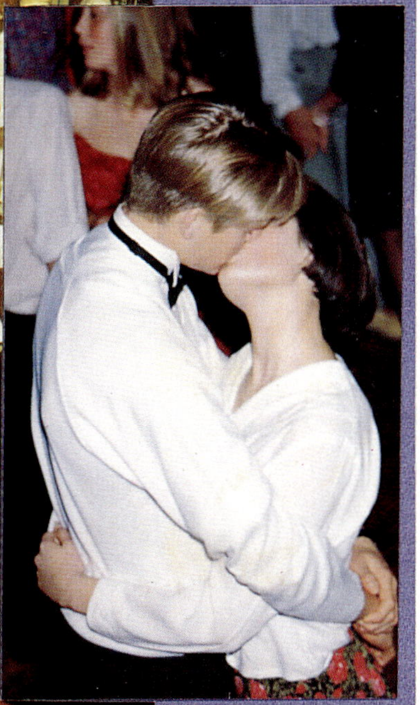

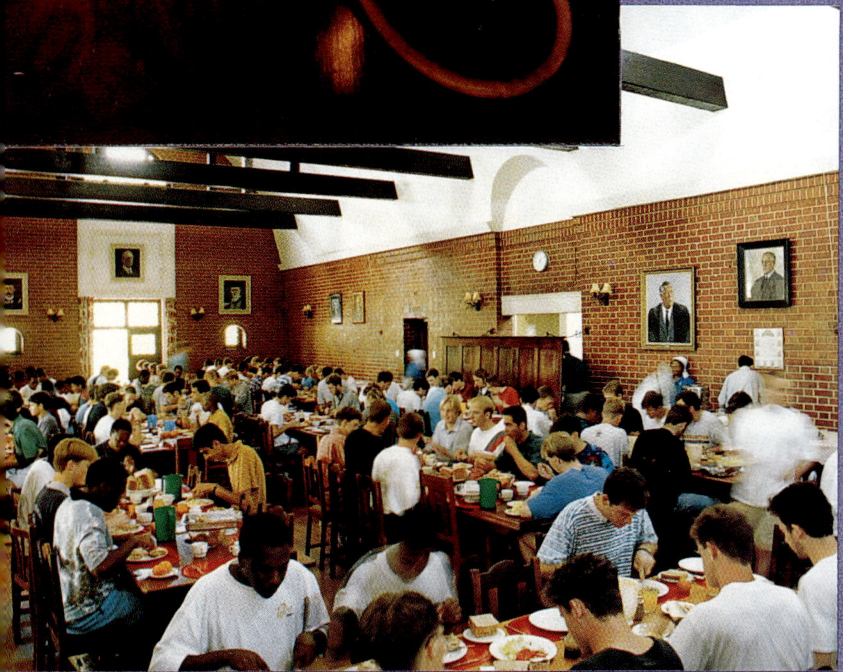

"I have yet to meet an Old Rhodian who was not happy in Grahamstown, who does not regard those three years as one of the great periods of his or her life."

— Graduate reminiscences in *Rhodes Review*

Rhodes graduates have risen to positions of influence quite out of proportion to their small numbers.

Of course each decade is different and its doings likewise. Or are they? In spite of outward appearances and obvious social changes, the life stage is the link, the rites of passage from late adolescence to early adulthood the inevitable journey. The route may alter, but not the direction.

Professors still keep their wit about them, in the understated style of one of the founding five, Prof A Stanley Kidd. When some pranksters drove a donkey into his lecture room, he merely said: "Will you and that new student sit in the front row" and proceeded as usual.

Wheels, women and song are another story entirely. In 1936, only three students owned cars, and had to get permission from Senate to do so. Today there is a parking problem.

Back in the early 1900s, a male student was called before the Senate for conduct calculated to show that mixed education was a dangerous experiment. He had habitually escorted a woman student along Somerset Street, and furthermore, had often carried her books.

Now it's no holds barred at technoraves. Oldies only know about them if they live within earshot (which most do, thanks to over-ample amplification). *Rhodeo*, the independent student newspaper, rivetingly reports:

"Relentless, the music is at most all bass — a boom da boom da boom cranked to marrow-boiling levels ... An incessant 118-126 beats per minute tickled incidentally by featureless vocals ..."

Students? Blast 'em all. Go home!

AMAZING DEVELOPMENT

NESTLED under ancient oaks on the Somerset Street side of the Rhodes campus is a compact cottage bearing yet another National Monuments Council plaque. So it should. For present achievements as well as past interest.

Since 1981 it has housed the Centre for Social Development. Run under the auspices of Rhodes University by its founder director Mrs Thelma Henderson, it is entirely self-supporting. Millions of rands have been received from South African and foreign donors suitably impressed by the range and effectiveness of its undertakings.

Many of today's community leaders were recipients of its assistance at some stage. The Grahamstown and Area Distress Relief Association's education division is administered by the centre. It provides bursaries which have enabled thousands of young people to further their studies at matric level, then university, technikons, or teacher training colleges.

Competent office workers are emerging from a commercial training centre. Adult education classes cover computer skills and basic book-keeping for treasurers, as well as committee procedure, childcare and cookery.

Beginning at the beginning, hundreds of little children caught in the poverty cycle are given a start which enables them to stay afloat when they enter the educational mainstream.

Seven major pre-school complexes have been built in the urban area. More than 36 have been set up in the surrounding rural district at the request of farmers and their workers. The centre provides the equipment, trains the staff and gives ongoing support. All pre-schoolers enjoy regular nutritious meals and their health improves noticeably.

The centre has also responded to other community needs, establishing a sports field for youngsters, service clubs for the aged, a school for mentally retarded children and vegetable garden schemes to supplement diets.

The wryly-named Sun City squatter camp was originally designated as a rubbish dump. As the centre's community project has progressed, a sense

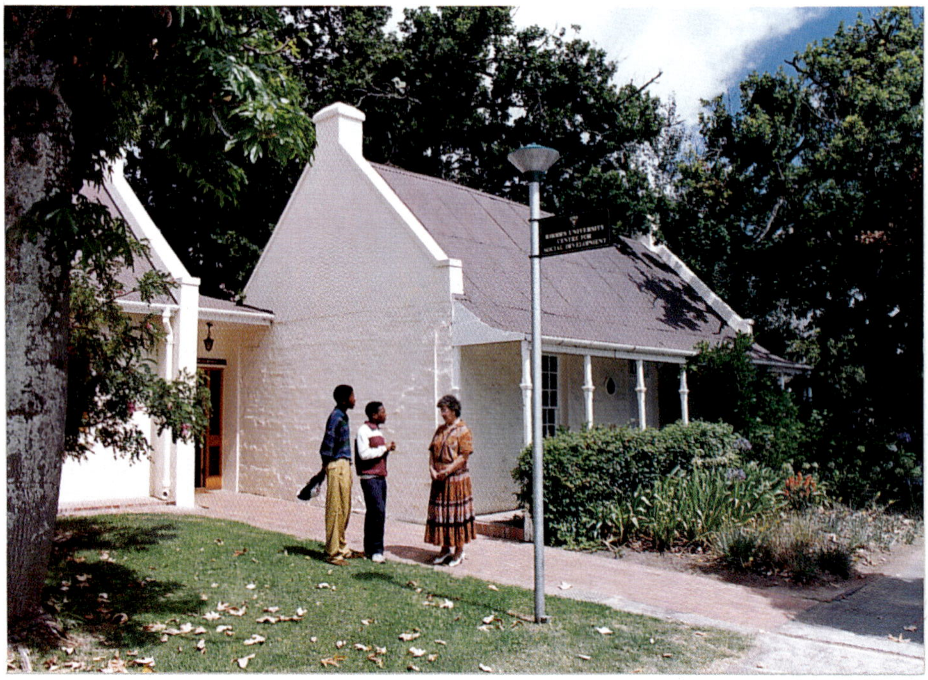

CLOCKWISE: Cottage at the centre; teachers who have learnt a lot; and director Thelma Henderson with a successful bursary student

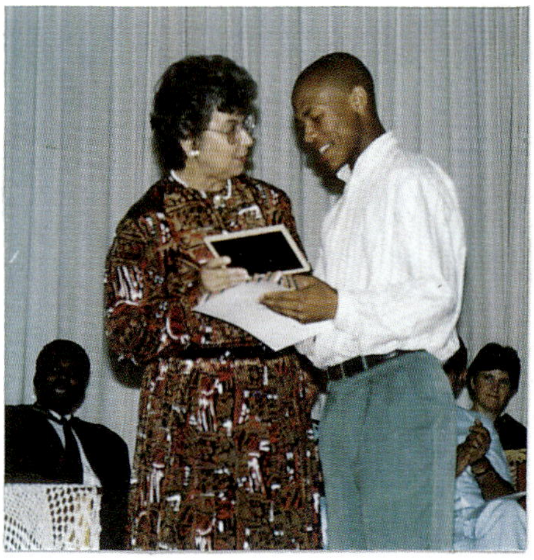

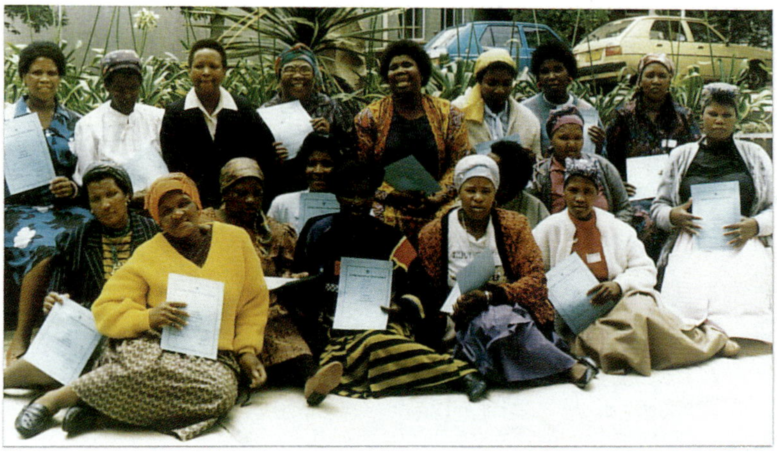

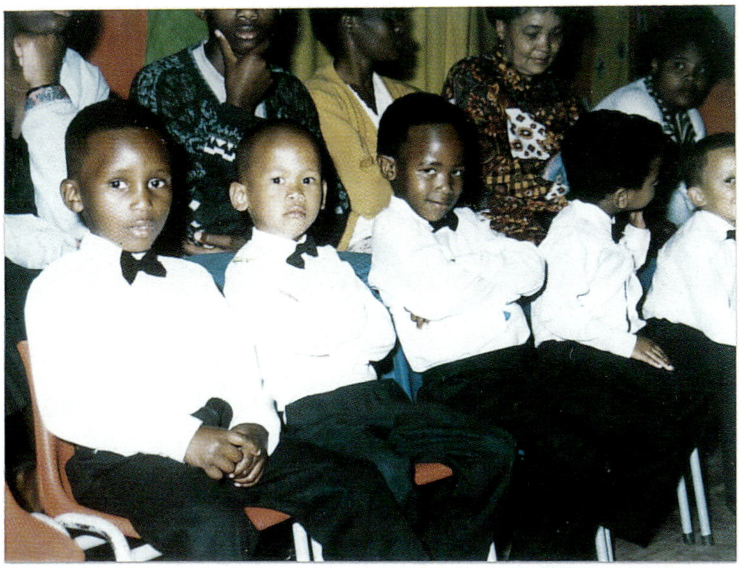

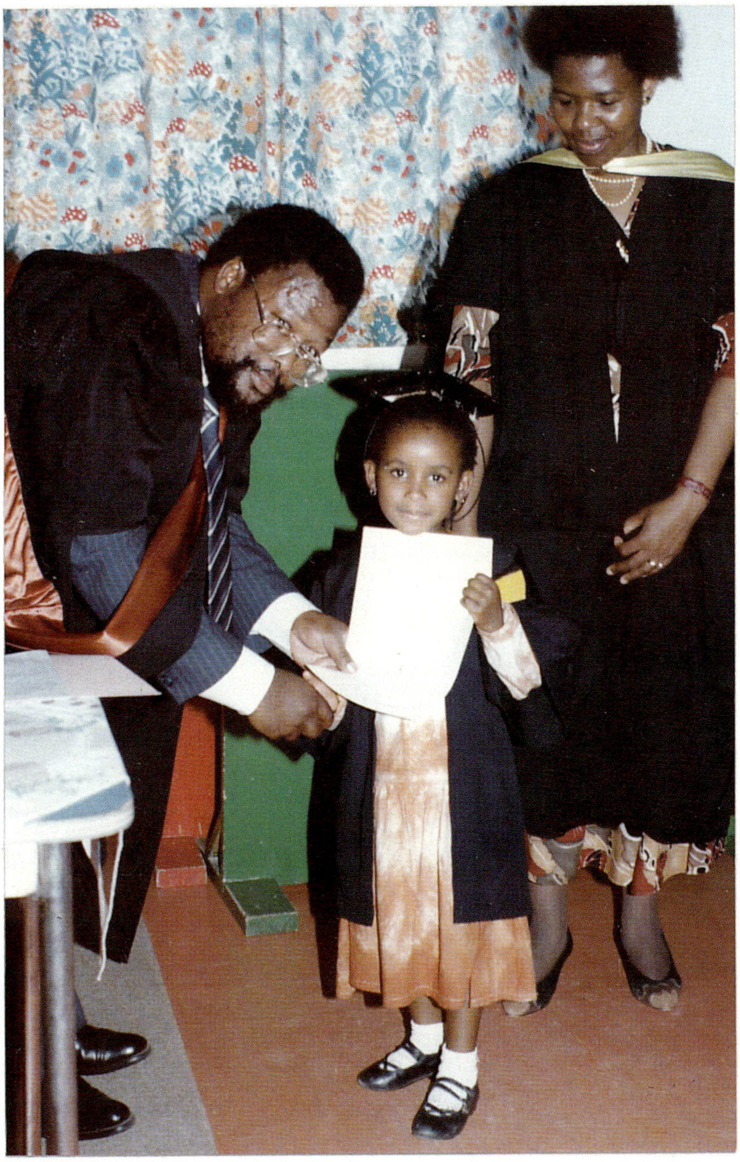

of purpose has emerged. In addition to a nursery school, a hall has been erected which is the focus of activities. Used for a clinic, church services, and gatherings, it is also the meeting place of a burgeoning Brownie pack. Numbers have increased to such an extent that two Brown Owls are necessary.

Helpers everywhere are fully involved in all aspects of each operation so that in time they are able to take over and run the schemes successfully themselves.

It is this participation which engenders the pride of achievement so evident at the end-of-year celebrations at the urban day-care centres. These have evolved into mini-graduations and coming out balls — which indeed they are. The first step into an infinitely more promising future.

The Centre for Social Development is the most visible aspect of Rhodes's involvement with Greater Grahamstown. The university does not stand remote in lofty academic isolation but channels its resources and expertise into the community in a number of meaningful ways.

TOP AND BOTTOM: Beaus and belles at Shaw Hall Day-Care Centre's debutante fund-raising ball
Centre: Proud moment at St Peter Claver's Nursery School mini-graduation

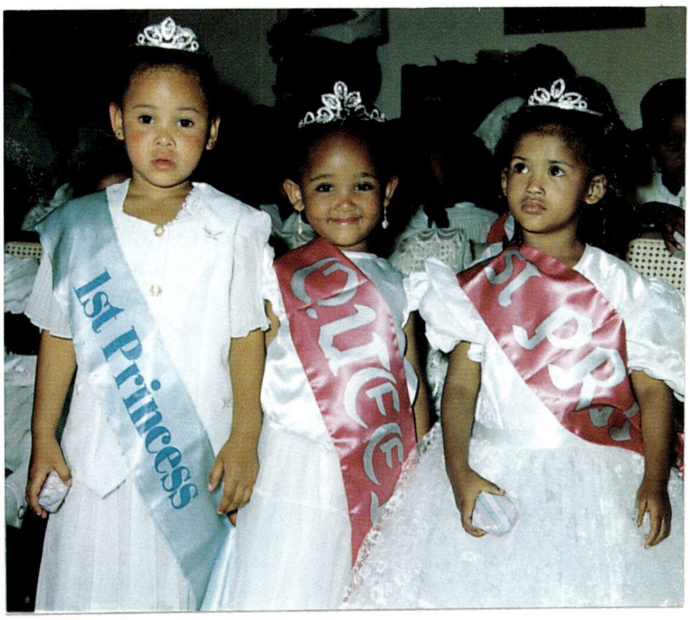

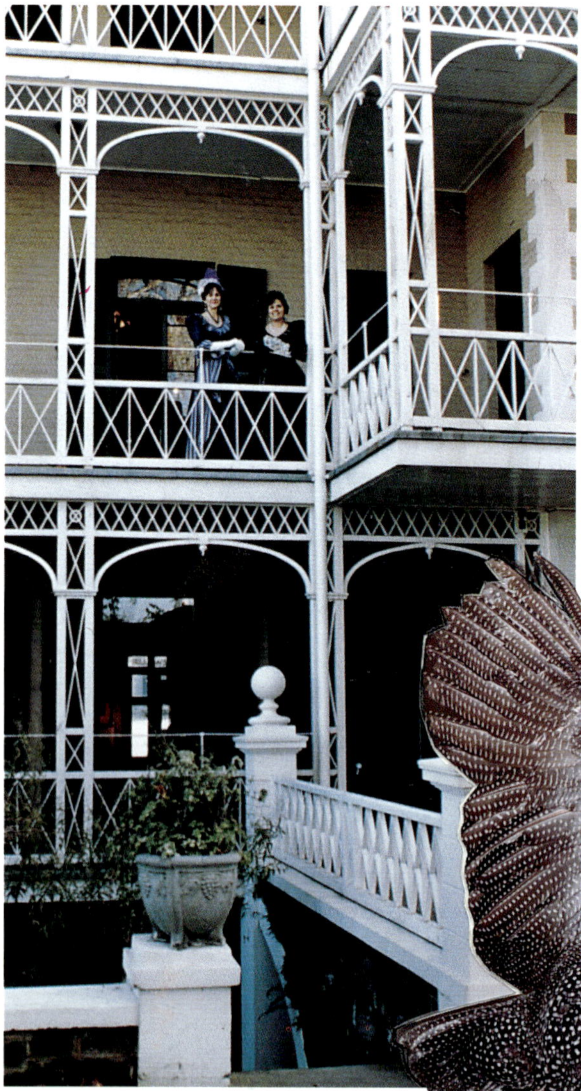

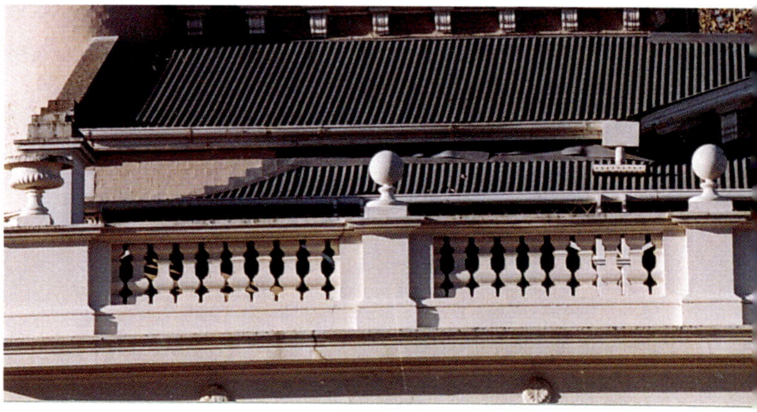

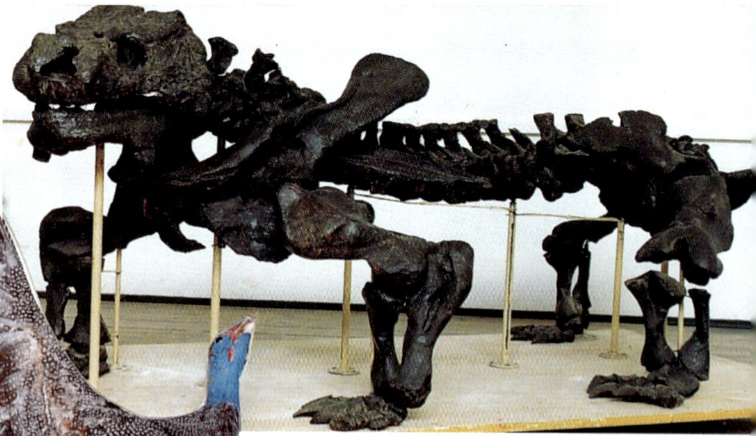

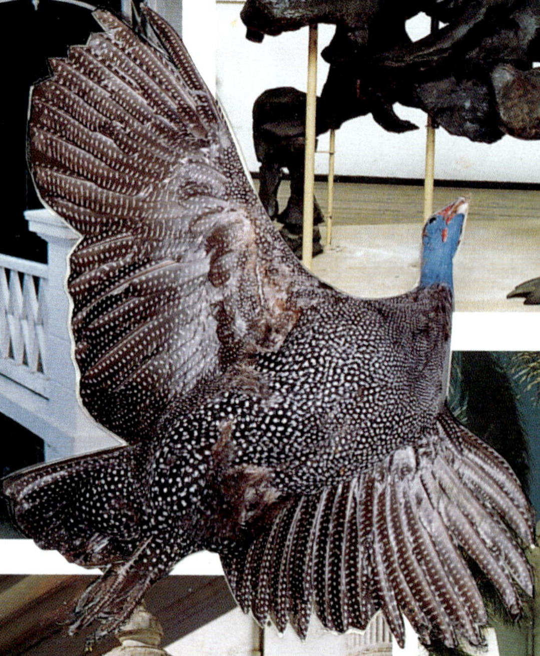

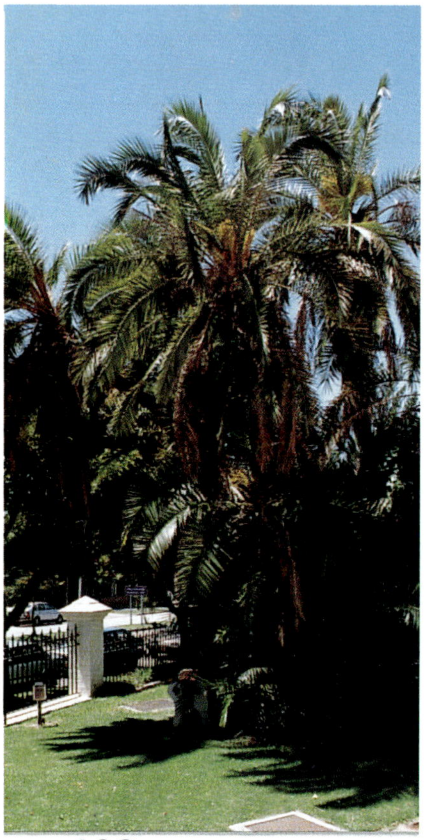

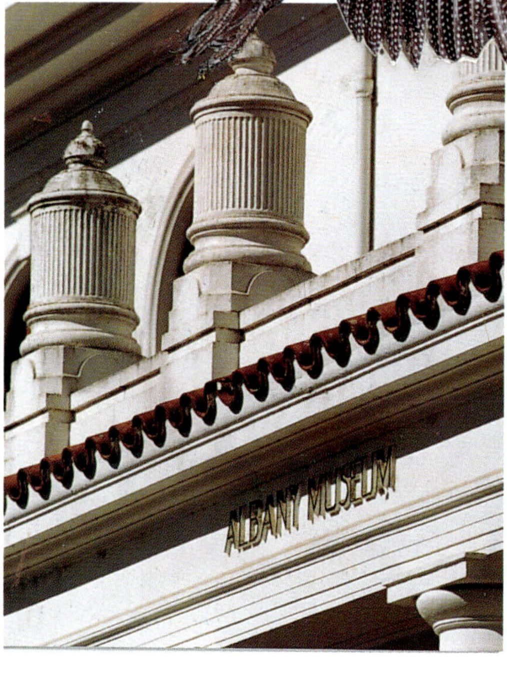

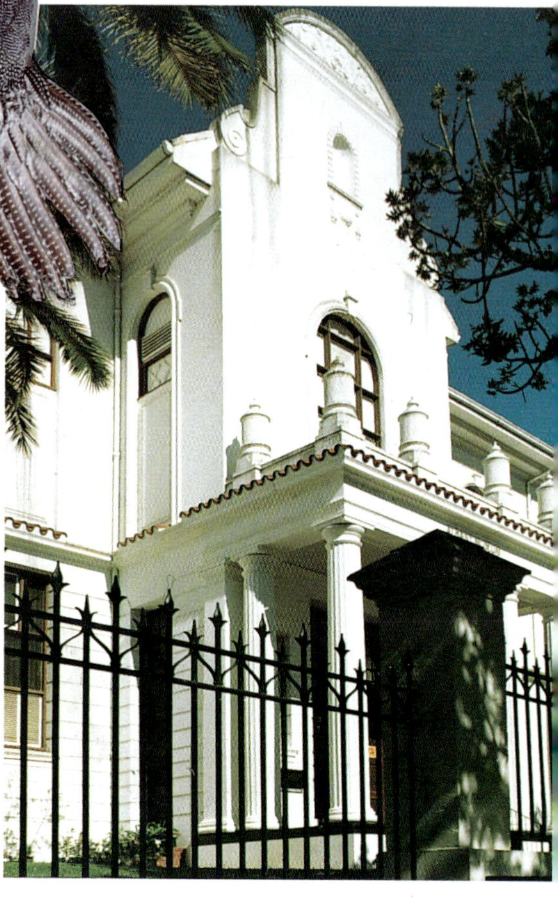

ALBANY MUSEUM MONTAGE: *The Observatory top left, the History Museum top right, gabled Natural Sciences core block, flanked by hers and his Phoenix reclinata palms*

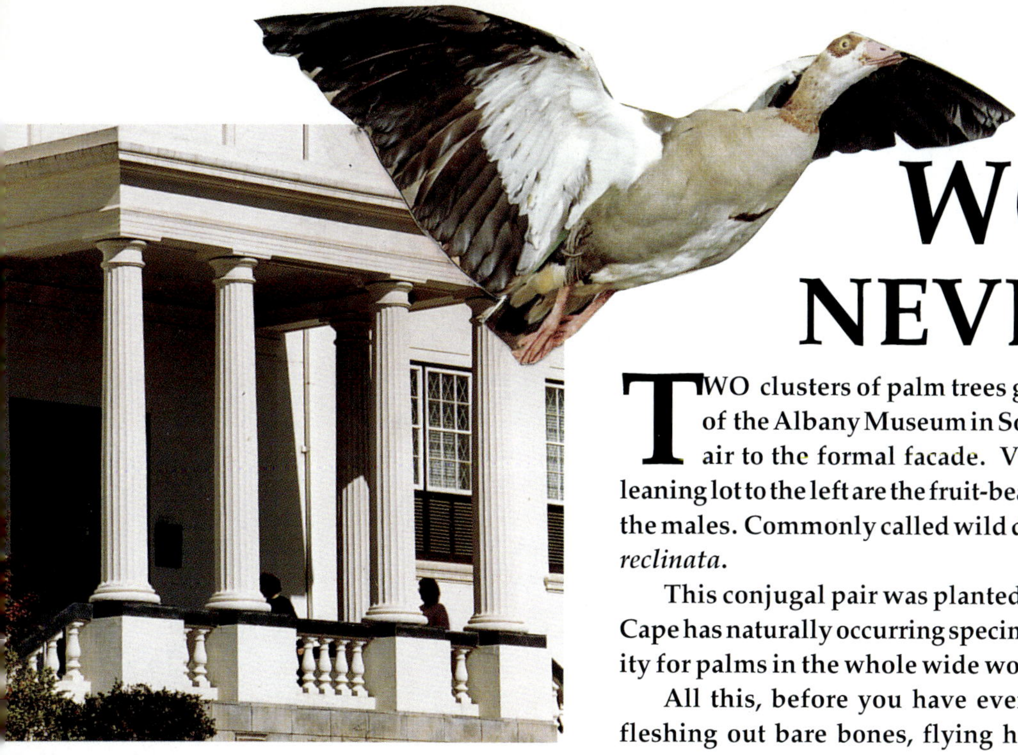

WONDERS NEVER CEASE...

TWO clusters of palm trees grow outside the Natural Sciences section of the Albany Museum in Somerset Street, lending a laid-back tropical air to the formal facade. Viewed from the pavement, the languidly leaning lot to the left are the fruit-bearing females, the stocky clump on the right the males. Commonly called wild date palms, their scientific name is *Phoenix reclinata*.

This conjugal pair was planted at the turn of the century, but the Eastern Cape has naturally occurring specimens, representing the southernmost locality for palms in the whole wide world.

All this, before you have even crossed the threshold. Opening eyes, fleshing out bare bones, flying high and branching wide — that is what Grahamstown's museums are about. An exceptionally good-looking bunch, much bigger than you would expect to find in any small town anywhere.

Founded in 1855, the Albany Museum is the second oldest museum in South Africa. It developed out of the Grahamstown Medical-Chirurgical Society and has kept going and growing, even though financial constraints keep it caged.

The History Museum is across the road in a classically pillared edifice. It has three additional novelty numbers under its wing— the Old Provost in the nearby Botanical Gardens, Fort Selwyn high up on Gunfire Hill, and The Observatory way down in Bathurst Street, gem of the city's tourist attractions. Not for star-gazing, but a beautifully balconied Victorian mansion, it bulges with bric-à-brac and scientific surprises — including the camera obscura, starting point of this book.

Still *more* museums ... Visitors often say the whole city centre seems like one, which most locals take as a compliment. The JLB Smith Institute for Ichthyology; the National English Literary Museum; libraries which are storehouses of different sorts of knowledge like the International Library of African Music at Rhodes University; and the Selmar Schönland Herbarium, a pressed plant library. Some are explored in this section, others elsewhere.

When curiosity flourishes, the world abounds with endless possibilities ...

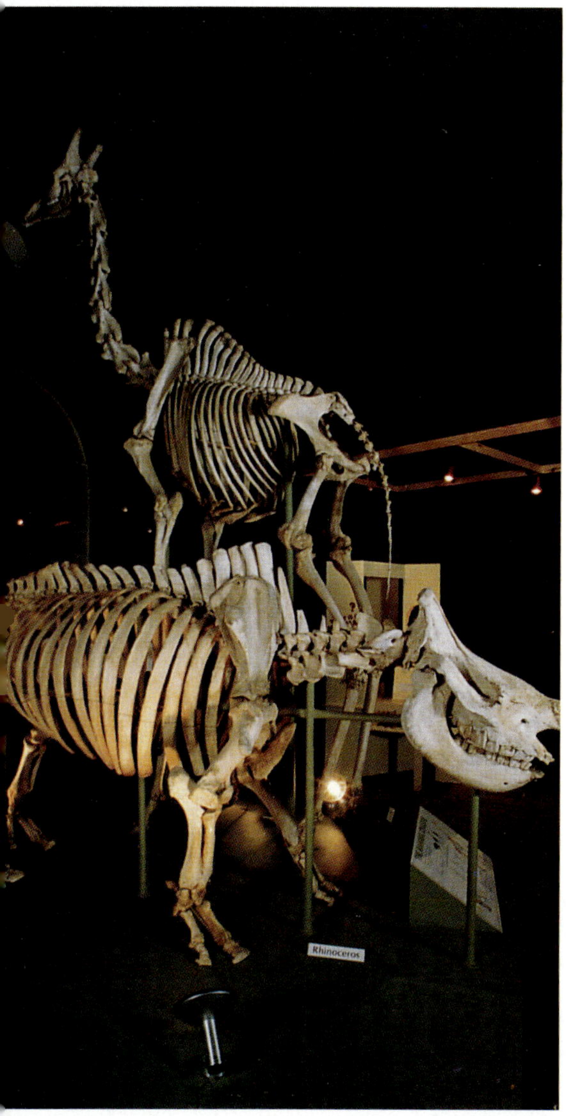

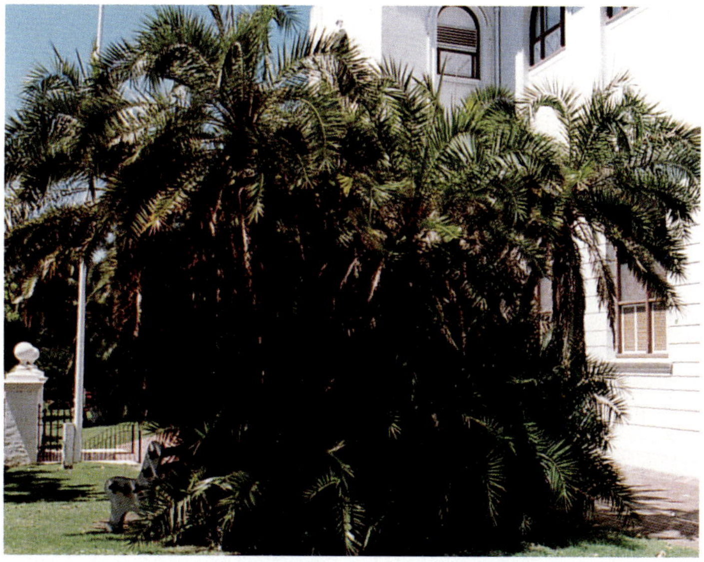

NATURAL SCIENCES MUSEUM

WALK ON THE WILD SIDE, WHIRL IN OUTER SPACE

WHAT? Why? How? WOW! The excitement of discovery, the revelations of the unexpected and the marvels of the mundane in that amazing mix which only museums can manage. One minute you are out in Grahamstown's tranquil tree-lined streets. The next, you are confronted by a life-sized pre-historic terror bird bestriding the entrance area of the Natural Sciences Museum.

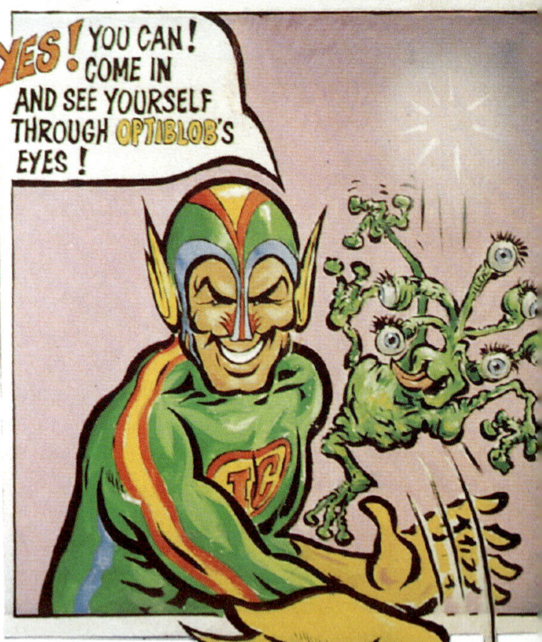

A few steps further — fast forward into outer space, gazing star-struck at whirling planets and a 330kg solid iron Gibeon meteorite, part of the largest shower of meteorites ever found, which fell in Namibia before 1836.

Then Captain I-C invites you to see yourself with Optiblob's many eyes. Not in a Bushman cave, which is round in the rear with actual drawings reproduced where they would have been *in situ*, but a multi-visual mirror adventure which reflects you into infinity from every angle. An image-shattering experience for the thirty-somethings, a total turn-on for the under-10s.

For a view of a different kind, an observation window looks into the cavernous gallery where a museum artist is at work on a series of enormous paintings of the weird and wonderful creatures which roamed the Eastern Cape some 360 million years ago.

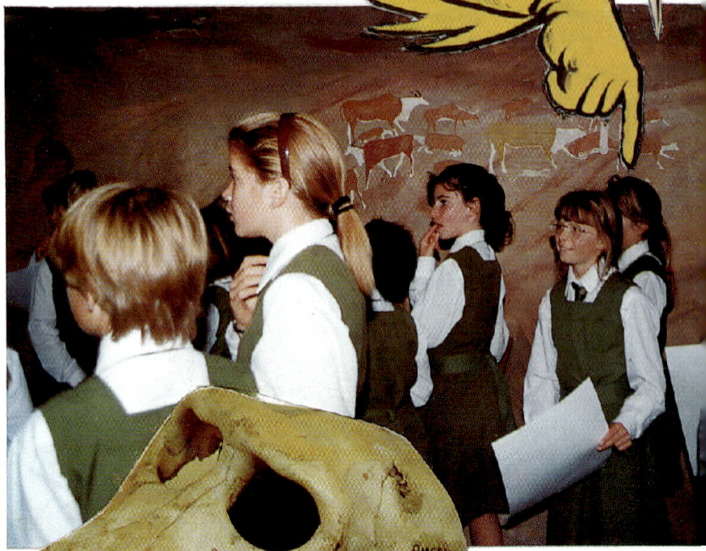

Upstairs to ancient Egypt. One of only three mummies in Southern Africa lies here serenely, a lady from Luxor, her mummified pet cat at her feet, badly burnt in the fire which destroyed many exhibits in 1941, but still a comfort in eternity.

A walk on the wild side coming up next. Animals large and small. A lion, and next to it a mouse. The baby elephant from Addo, rejected by its mother, is now the focus of endless loving attention. Beyond— strictly for the birds— wings over Africa, the miracle of flight made understandable, migrations, nests, eggs, and fine feathered specimens in natural settings. Casualties, not killed, superbly mounted by the museum's taxidermy department.

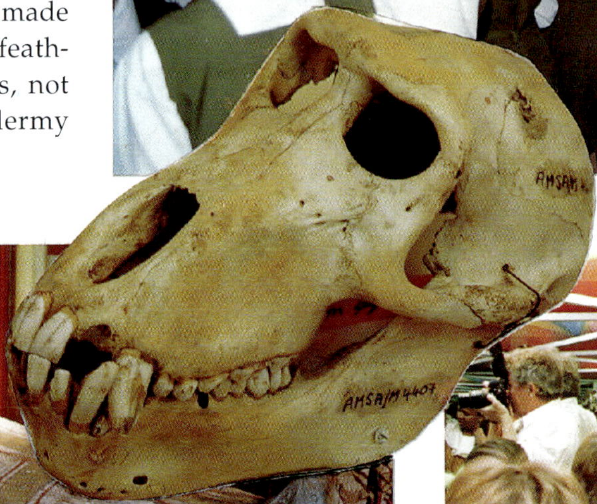

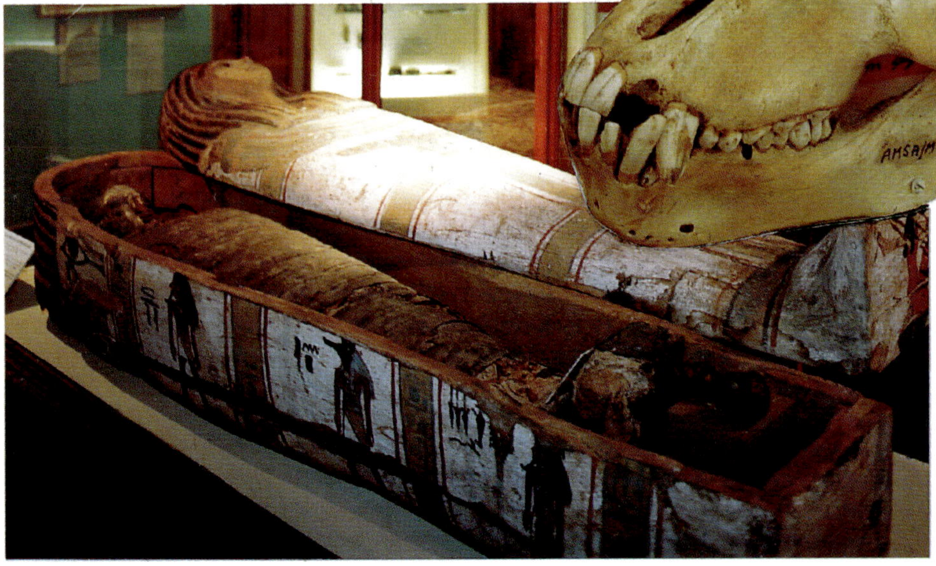

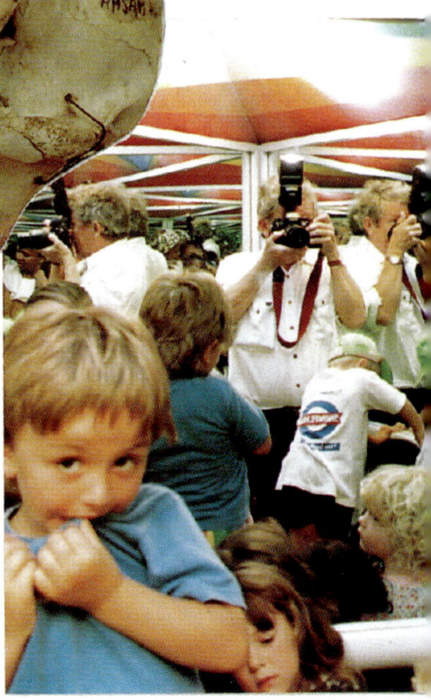

And an old-style exhibition hall crammed with curiosities, including the skull of Jack the Baboon who operated the railway signals to help his crippled master at Uitenhage Station in the 1880s and never made a mistake.

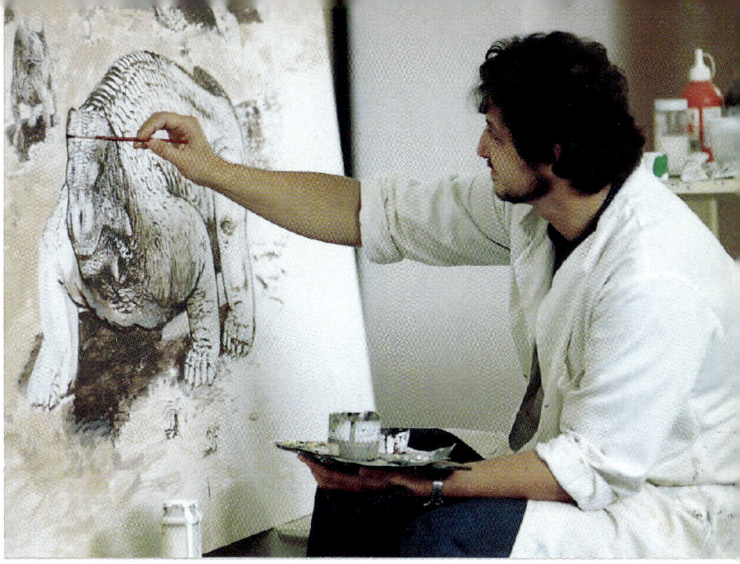

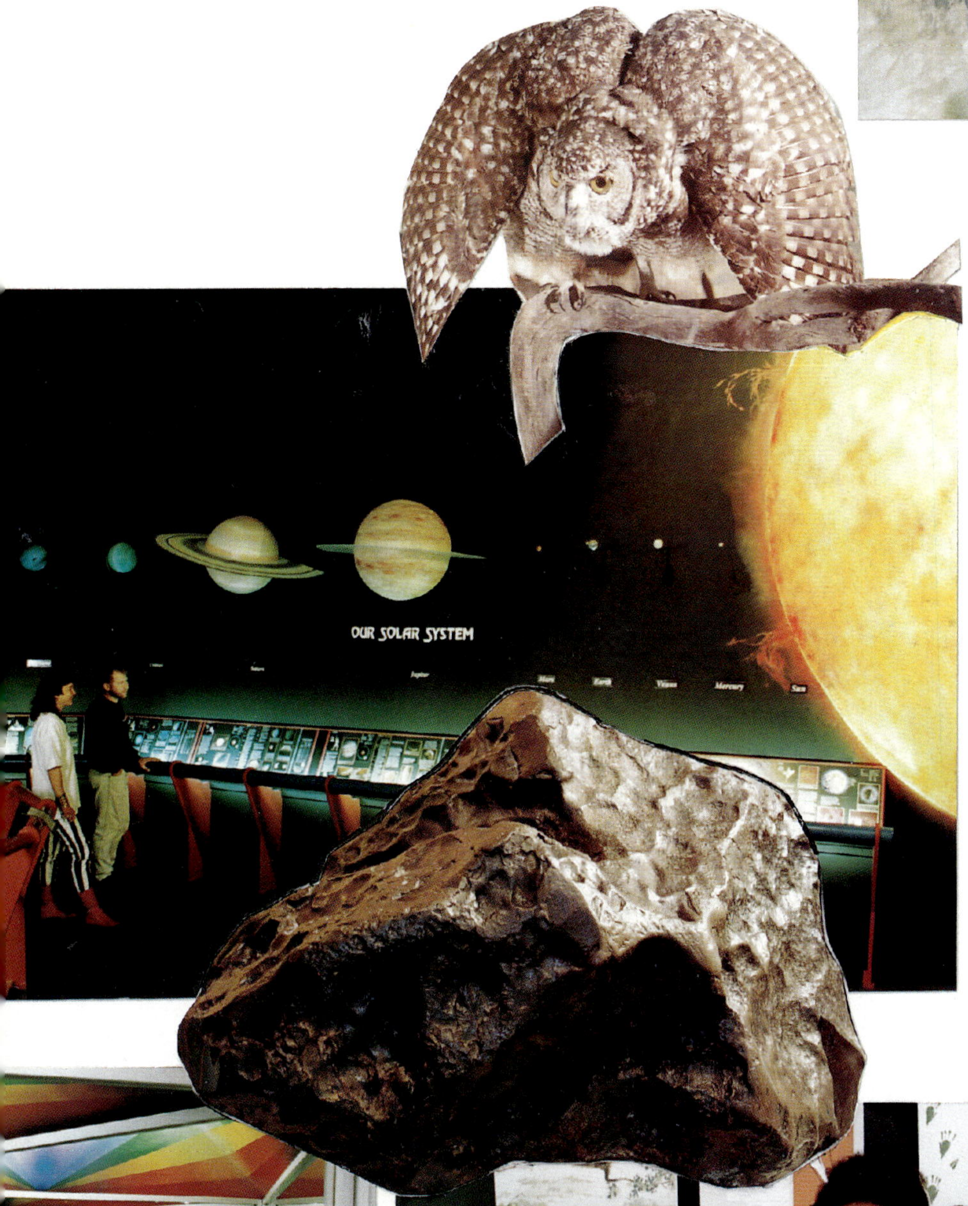

Well behind the scenes, the museum's research staff continue their studies of a number of unique collections — the National Collection of Freshwater Invertebrates (spineless wonders with considerable character), the oldest fossil collection in South Africa, the only collection of its kind of southern African wasps, important collections of freshwater fishes, fascinating archaeological finds from sites as varied as strandlopers' caves to local Victorian rubbish dumps ...

The museum's innovative education department arranges programmes for schools from both town and country. The briefest visit is a mind-expanding experience for visitors of any age.

ALBANY MUSEUM MONTAGE: Fun and facts in the Natural Sciences section where you can find anything from an Egyptian mummy to a wise old owl— and an artist at work

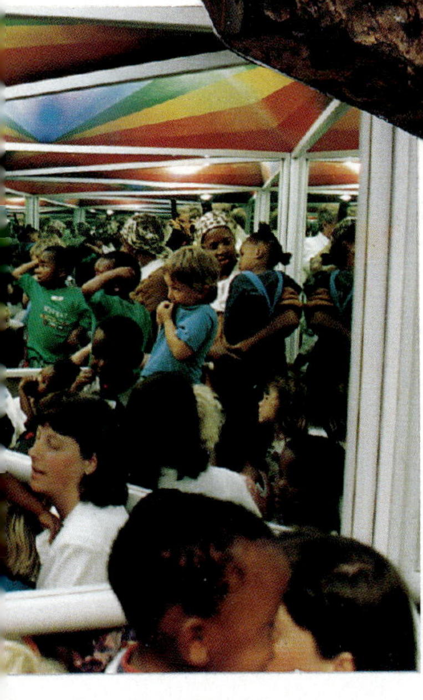

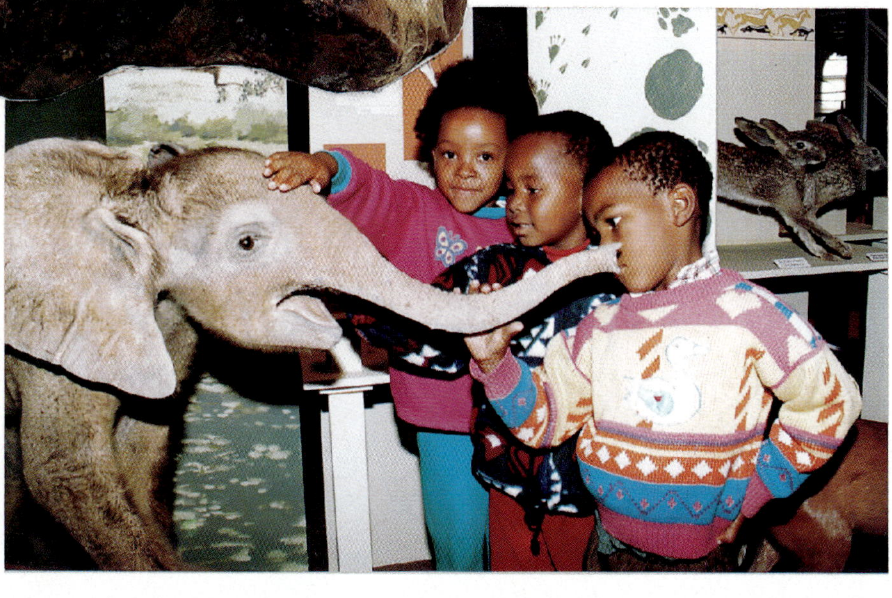

HISTORY MUSEUM

FAMILY TREES, GRASS ROOTS, AND NEW LEAVES...

All change at the History Museum! The focus is altering, the scope widening. Who knows — even the bland white entrance columns may soon take on a brighter hue to complement the vibrant blend of the various peoples, cultures, inevitable clashes, and common causes which give the Eastern Cape in general and Greater Grahamstown in particular its unique character.

Later Stone Age man, San hunter-gatherers, Khoi pastoralists, the Xhosa, explorers, missionaries, traders, Dutch farmers, military men, botanists, artists, educationists, 1820 Settler parties, political parties ... Far too many and far too much to try to fit in at any one time, so exhibitions are more fluid than fixed, with every section of the community getting involved. Travelling displays come from elsewhere, too. Like the Mayibuye Centre's informative photographic record of the African National Congress, shown with election souvenirs.

Objects from the collections — the basic evidence of the past — are being reassessed, mixed, matched, and added to in different ways to jolt viewers' preconceptions. To teach, to enthuse, but most of all to interest. Consider something basic like clay, for example.

The museum's geologist reveals how the rich clay deposits in and around Grahamstown were formed. The archaeologists dig out information on the impact of these deposits on successive layers of local life. Clay in housing, industry, sculpture, and pottery of every description — also cosmetics. Some Xhosa women still follow tribal face-painting traditions, with white indicating a change of status — an *intonjane* (young girl) growing up, or perhaps a nursing mother.

New approaches, old strengths. The widely used genealogical service continues, with an expert researcher tracking down clues for ever more creative family records. Not just lists of names and dates, but that elusive breath of personality in yellowing newspapers, diaries, and letters.

Every July, the spacious galleries on the upper floors accommodate prestigious exhibitions during the Standard Bank National Arts Festival. For the rest of the year, the central Grahamstown Gallery takes the visitor back into the city of the 19th century via paintings — an impressive number by Thomas Baines — and photographs. No other South African centre apart from Cape Town and possibly Port Elizabeth has such an abundant photographic record from so early a period.

The Rhodes Alumni Gallery features works by art students past and present. Bursting out of their frames with vitality, well worth viewing. The frequently seen ladder is not a modernistic sculpture but belongs to the maintenance staff who are constantly checking the roof for leaks. Resourceful

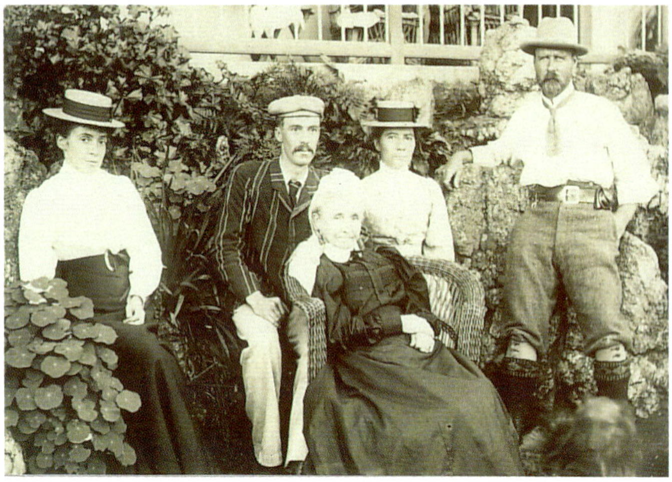

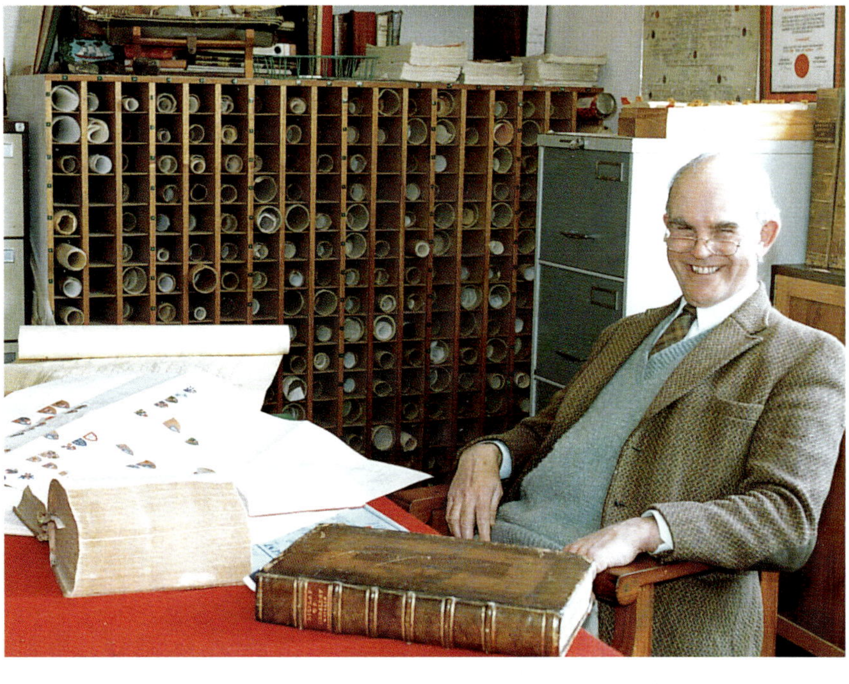

"The human spirit cannot do without a past, and unless it can feel itself putting its roots into its own past, rather as a tree grows deeper into the earth for every inch it grows, it cannot move into the future."
— **Laurens van der Post, writer**.

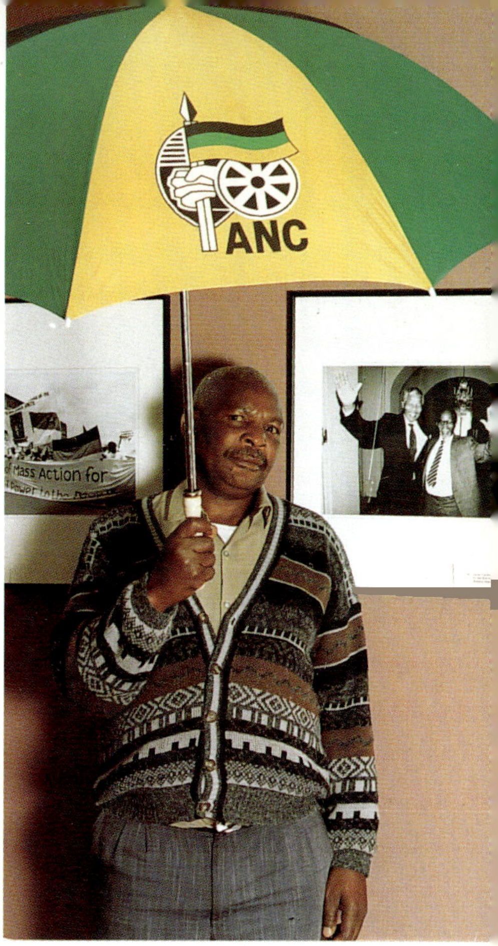

Rhodents surreptitiously added a life-sized figure which was initially thought to be a subtly original statement of angst and indecision. Going up, going down? Judgment suspended.

A popular saying puts people into three categories: those who make things happen, those to whom things happen, and those who never know what happened. An accurate description of human history.

The task of the historian has been defined as understanding the peoples of the past better than they understood themselves. With participation from the public it serves, this is the goal the Albany Museum's history team is aiming to achieve and share.

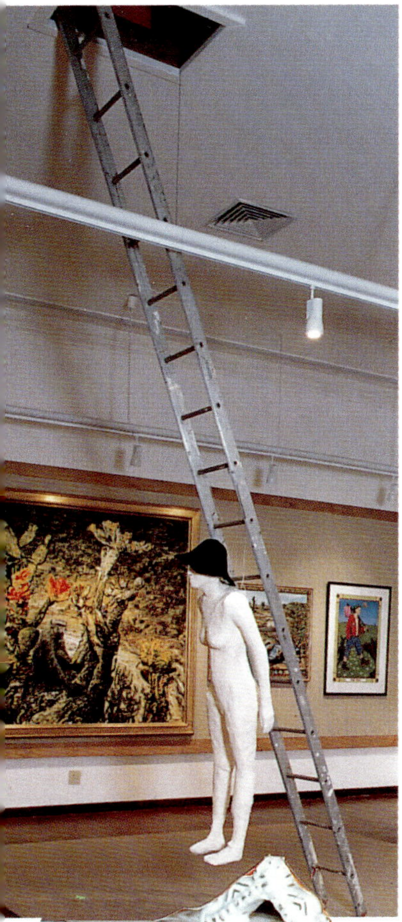

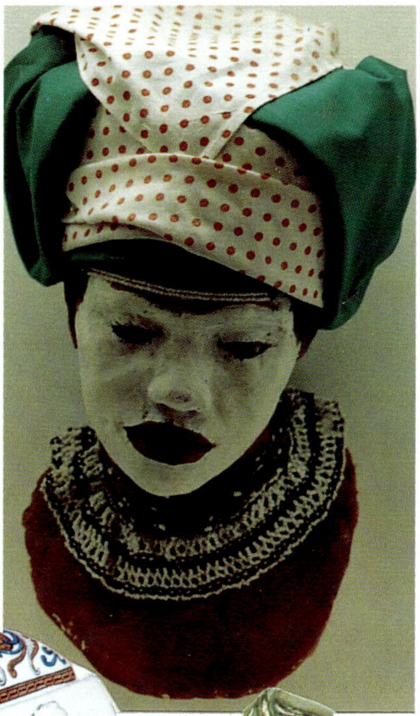

ALBANY MUSEUM MONTAGE: ***Everything has a place in the History section, from the genial genealogist to art gallery pranksters, customs and collections— and the story of the ANC***

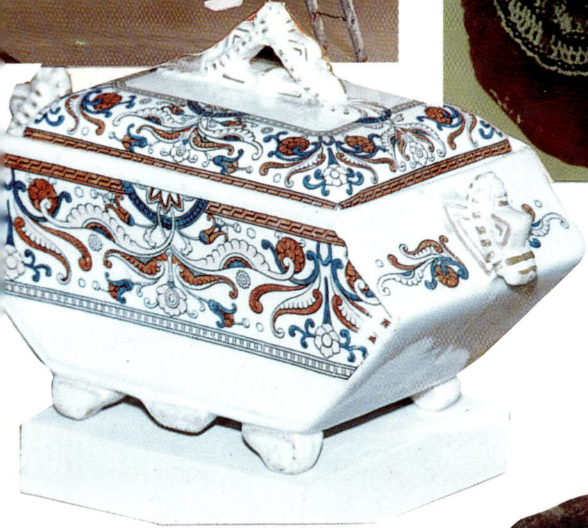

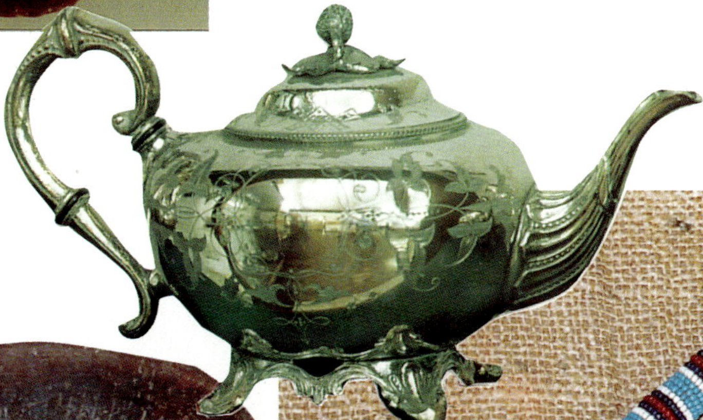

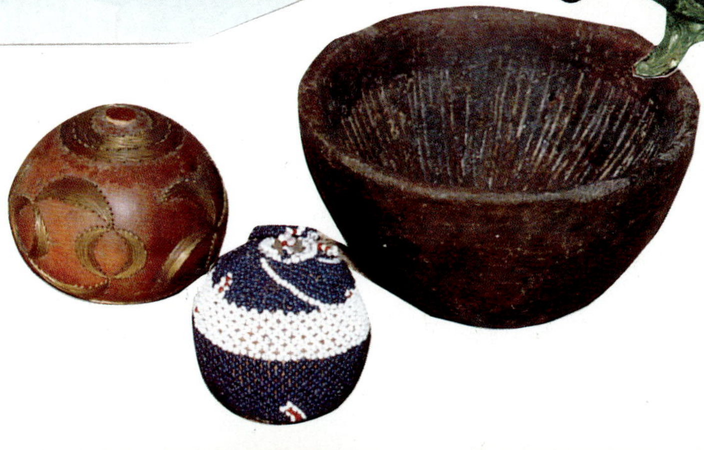

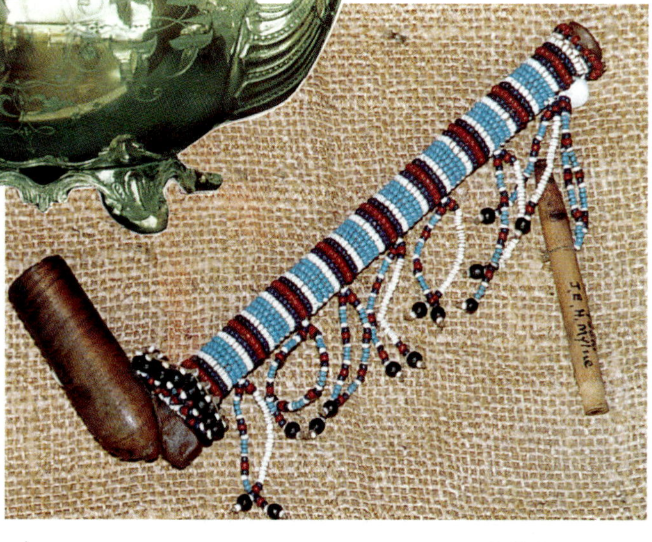

FISHY GOINGS ON AT THE JLB

Like most of Grahamstown's numerous experts, each so totally immersed in their particular subject that little else exists, the fish fundis at the JLB Smith Institute of Ichthyology find it impossible to believe that many people do not know exactly what ichthyology is, let alone how to spell it.

The study of fishes, to put it plainly. This does not even begin to give an idea of all that goes on at the JLB — much of it below ground level in an enormous temperature-controlled basement packed with pickled fish.

Here, more than 800 000 preserved specimens, some dating back to the year dot, others brought in yesterday, are carefully curated and made available for study. Freshwater and estuarine, as well as marine fishes from Southern Africa, Europe, Japan, Antarctica ... Suspended in propyl alcohol, with plasticised labels inside the containers so nothing goes adrift. Nearby, in what look like kingsize cool boxes — sharks, mantas, stingrays, skates, even a couple of baby coelacanths. The National Collection of Fish, a research "library" of a distinctly different kind.

Upstairs, the National Fish Library on more conventional lines is complemented by *Fishlit*. Not the paper used to wrap fish and chips as one wit put it, but a computerised database now available internationally on a CD that gives constantly updated access to the ever growing tidal wave of fish-related literature.

Staff are involved in projects as varied as measuring the impact of diamond dredging on the Western Cape coast and fish farming in rural areas, to conservation training in the Lake Malawi National Park and exhibitions at the institute's Angling Museum in Knysna. Enquiries and visits from the public are welcomed.

Scientists from foreign waters frequently surface at the JLB, which has developed into the leading centre in Africa for the study and management of fishes and aquatic environments.

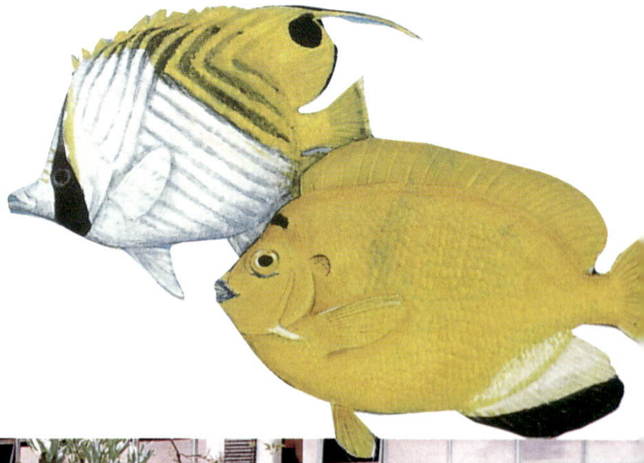

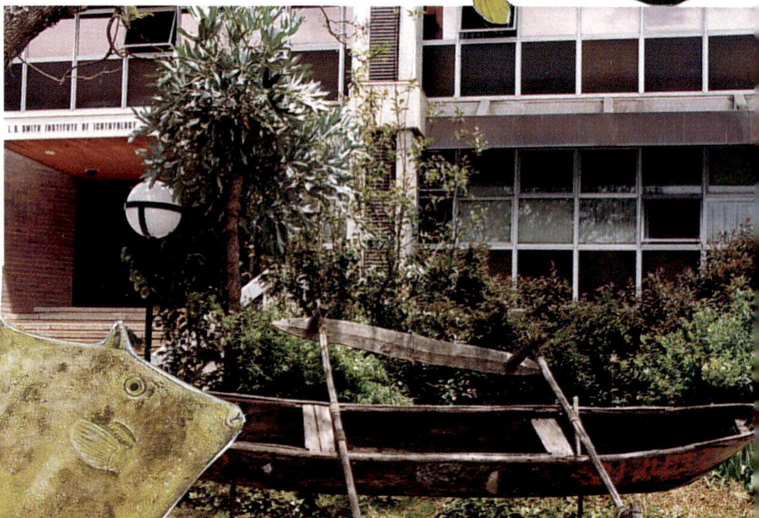

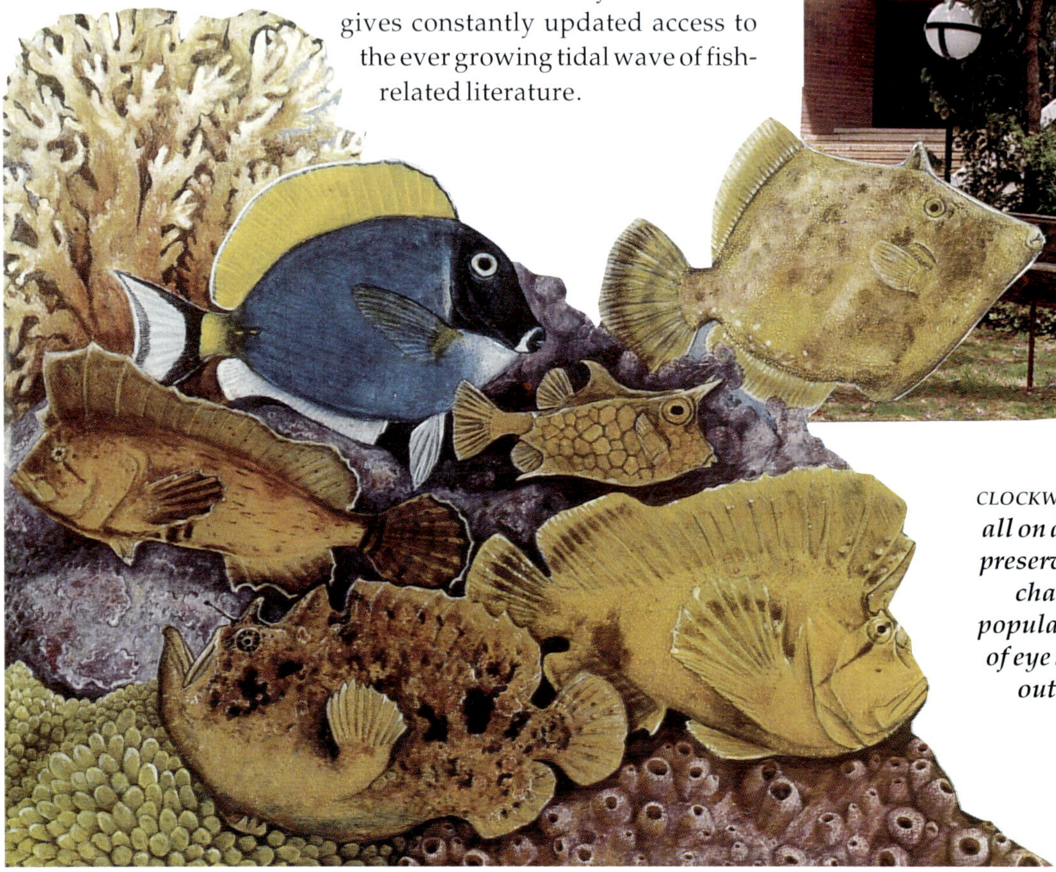

CLOCKWISE: *Info expert Margaret Crampton's got it all on disk; some ancient specimens still in original preservation jars; colourful South African coral reef characters congregate on one of Dave Voorvelt's popular posters, done in acrylic paints with a touch of eye shadow here and there; and a galawa or dug-out canoe from the Comores, home waters of the coelacanth, in front of JLB Smith Institute of Icththyology in Somerset Street*

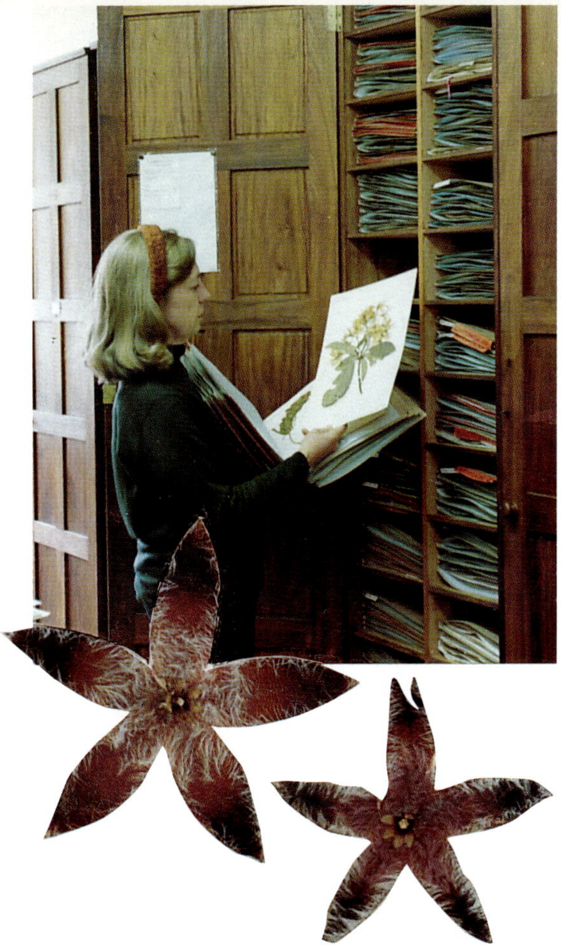

"What is a weed? A plant whose virtues have not been discovered."

— Ralph Waldo Emerson (1803-82)

GREEN MAGIC

SUBURBAN pavements turn into meadows starred with veld flowers after the summer rains. "I wonder what that is?", you think, gazing at a fragile white spire delicately striped with green. You can easily find out at the Selmar Schönland Herbarium in the Albany Museum, where the farmer ahead of you might have brought in the contents of a dead cow's stomach. Poisonous plants? The botanist's identification confirms the vet's diagnosis.

A local entrepreneur may be investigating the commercial possibilities of aloes. The medicinal uses of dried aloe sap were recorded in Egypt and Babylon as early as 3 000 BC. The giant *Ferox* which lights up the district with its fiery candelabras in June and July is a recognized source.

Or you could get caught up in a researcher's succulent euphorbia euphoria. There are more than 30 species within a 40 kilometer radius of Grahamstown, the richest concentration after Somalia, in the Horn of Africa. And you just wanted to identify what turns out to be a *Trachyandra asperata* (popular name Wilde Knoflok).

This is what happens when you enter the herbarium — open sesame to the secrets of the magical Green World. Not a place where herbs are cultivated but an enormous encyclopaedia consisting of some 200 000 sheets of dried plants. Three-dimensional specimens complete with the vital three Ws: when, where, and who collected them. Many of the same species— the research relevance is in the multiplicity.

A plant picked today can be compared with a specimen preserved by explorer William John Burchell who passed this way circa 1812-14, perhaps revealing changing conditions and distribution patterns, plus much else to the expert eye. Seaweeds, algae, fungi, seeds, wood, and early collections from other parts of the world are also available for study.

Selmar Schönland, who gave the herbarium its name, joined the Albany Museum in 1889, and was the first Professor of Botany at Rhodes in 1904. The museum and university's herbaria were amalgamated in 1993— a highly productive union of dried specimens with amazing private lives.

ABOVE LEFT: *Flower power on file; and* BELOW, *pressed specimens each tell their own story between the Herbarium sheets*

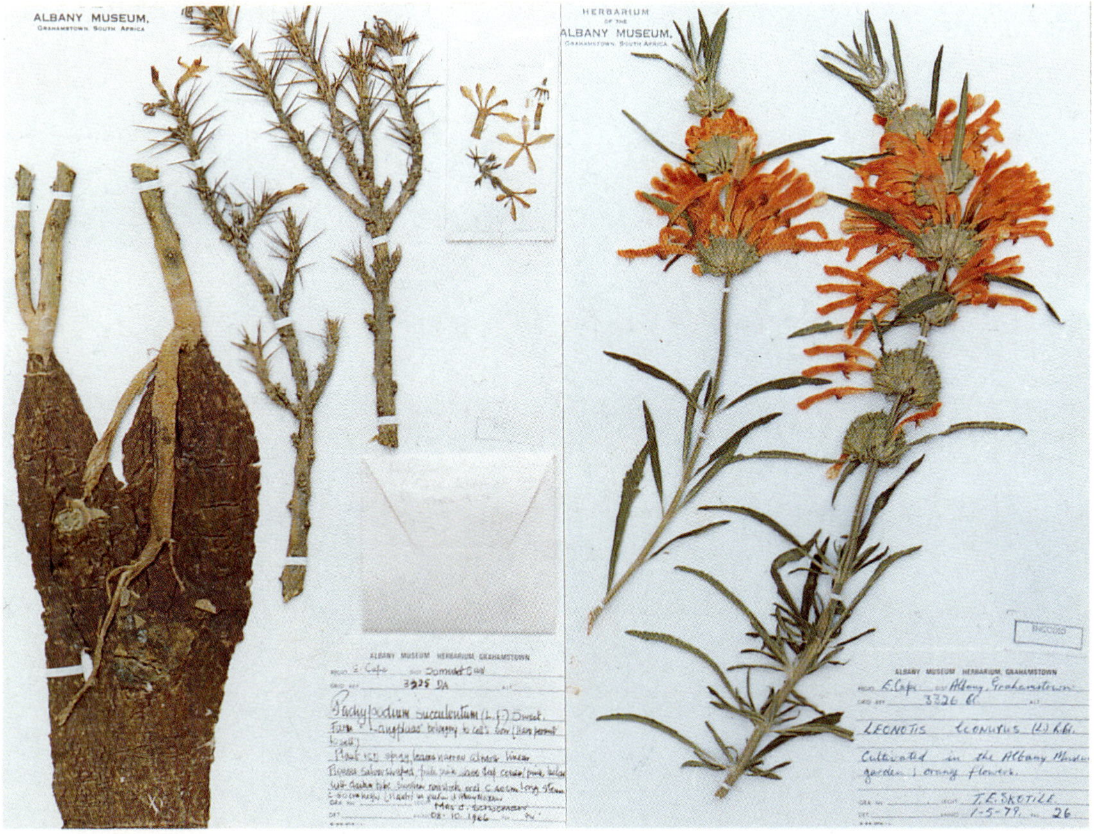

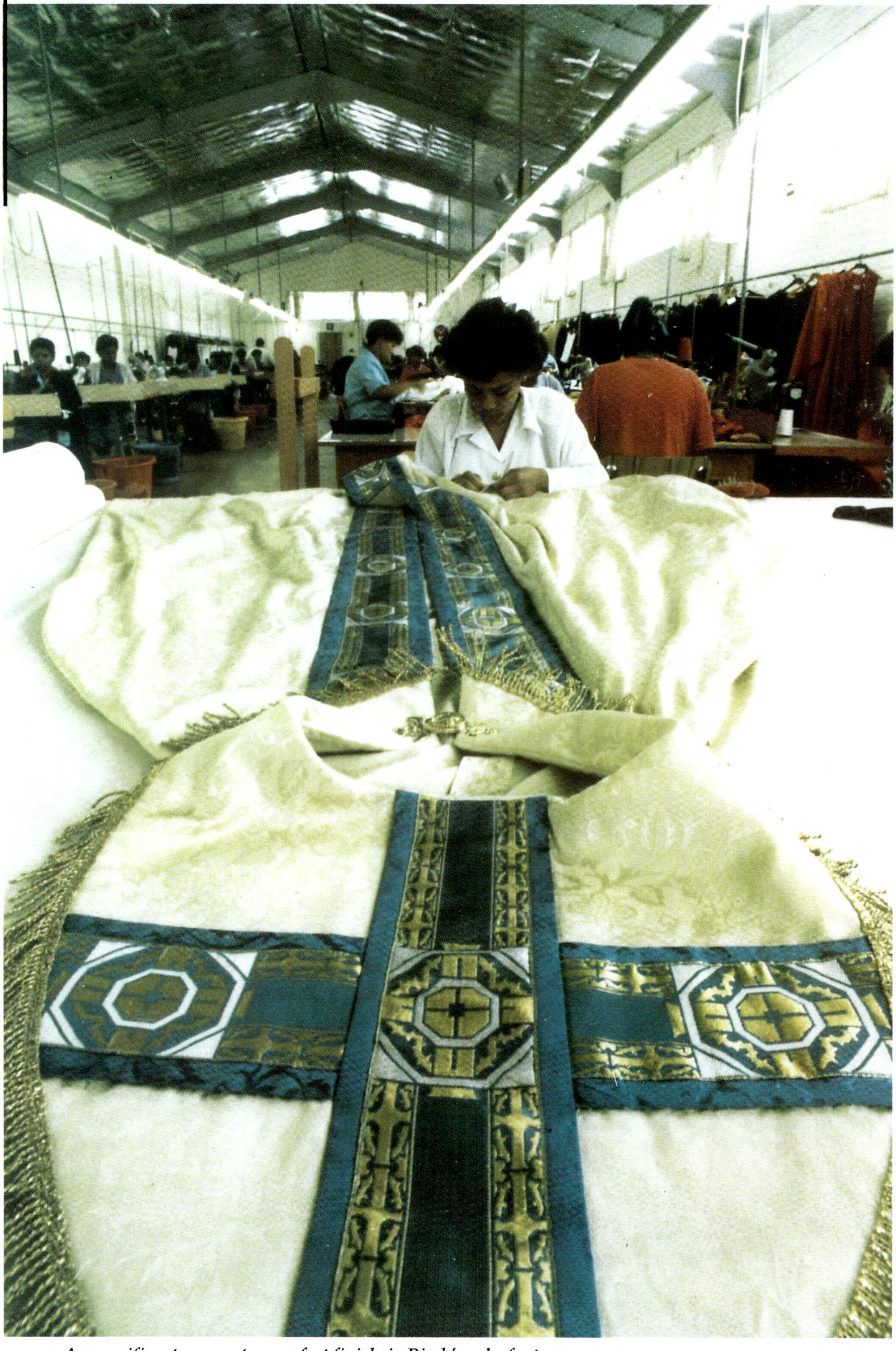

ABOVE: *A magnificent cope gets a perfect finish in Birch's robe factory*

MINDING OUR OWN BUSINESS

STUDIOUSLY industrious rather than industrialized, Grahamstown nonetheless contains some surprisingly enterprising business operations and always has. Seldom more so than the mid-19th century wigmaker who offered not only chignons, plaits, tails and coils, but also beards, whiskers and moustaches both for private use and theatrical companies. The explanation, perhaps, of those uniformly magnificent side-whiskers and luxuriant beards sported by even the weediest specimens in faded sepia photographs.

The Eastern Province Tobacco Works used to produce more than 900 kg of tobacco a week from imported American-grown leaf. The Grahamstown Tin-Plate Manufactury turned out hip-baths for the wholesale trade plus hot water incubators for chickens. In 1871 the Eastern Province Foundry began making a popular line of breech-loading rifles. For over a century Gowie's nurserymen and seed suppliers got much of Southern Africa growing, initially sending plants and fruit trees by ox wagon as far afield as Kimberley, Johannesburg, and even Rhodesia.

All long gone, as are the tanneries (one somewhat desperately called *The Forlorn Hope*), breweries, brickworks, soap factory, fizzy drink supplier, and Dicks' Bakery, best-known for its confectionery and Dixies — stripy bulls' eyes.

But Birch's — like *Grocott's Mail* — goes on forever. Founded in 1865 when the British Empire was expanding under the reign of Queen Victoria, before there was a railway line to Grahamstown and neither gold nor diamonds had been discovered in South Africa.

Its longevity might well puzzle the casual visitor who enters the delightfully dated departmental store on Church Square. Purchase money from each counter is still sent whizzing across wires in little canisters to a central cashier, who in turn despatches the change likewise. Male assistants have tape measures draped around their necks; fresh garden flowers on a crocheted doiley adorn the ladies' underwear counter. A potted aspidistra stands near the old school ties and new school uniforms for youngsters being clothed for the schools attended by their fathers, grandfathers, and great-grandfathers before them.

The secret of its survival is not out front but up top. Upstairs in an equally homely setting. Robes. Yes, robes. Birch's is the oldest and largest academic, judicial, civic, and ecclesiastical robe-making firm in southern Africa, if not the entire continent.

Orders for elaborate vestments are received from as far afield as Uganda, Malawi, Zambia, and Zimbabwe. Bishops' mitres are made to match.

Each garment has its own requirements, especially the church vestments. A traditional Latin cassock, for instance, has 51 hand-stitched button holes. South Africa's longest serving cassock maker, Mr Albert Peters, cannot even begin to guess the number he has stitched in more than 50 years.

Sometimes, a whole range of academic gowns has to be designed for everyone from the Chancellor down, as was done for the University of Namibia. The Orange Free State Technikon provided a similar assignment. All meticulously finished by highly skilled workers in the factory, which used to be "at the back" but has now moved to more spacious premises to cope with the ever-increasing demand. A Grahamstown success story, a fitting enterprise for the City of Saints and Scholars.

Now — on to some other local enterprises in the true sense of the dictionary definition: "bold spirit; force of character in launching out".

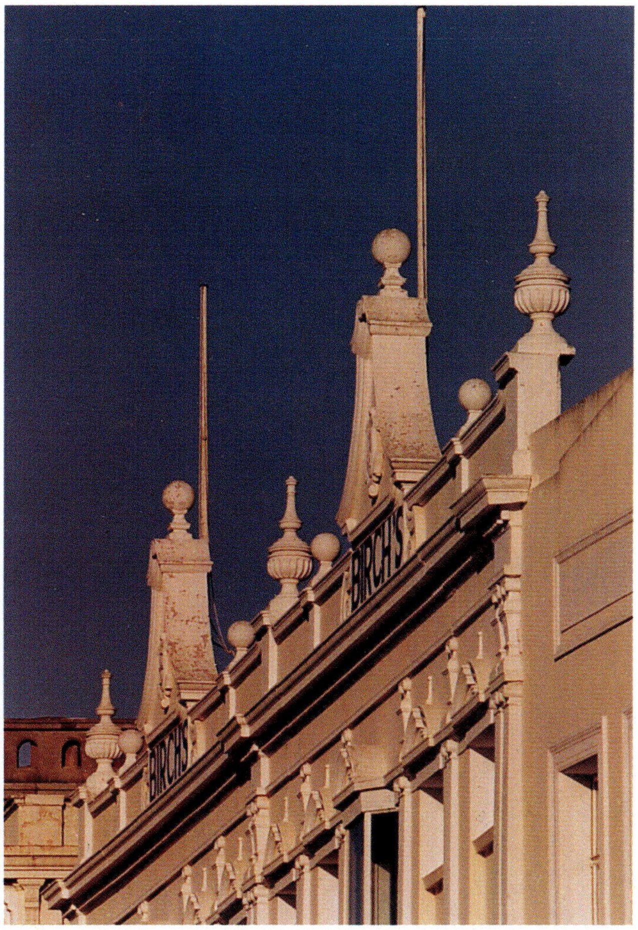

RIGHT: *Church Square store facade*

HOMELY INDUSTRIES

AND HAIRY FAIRIES...

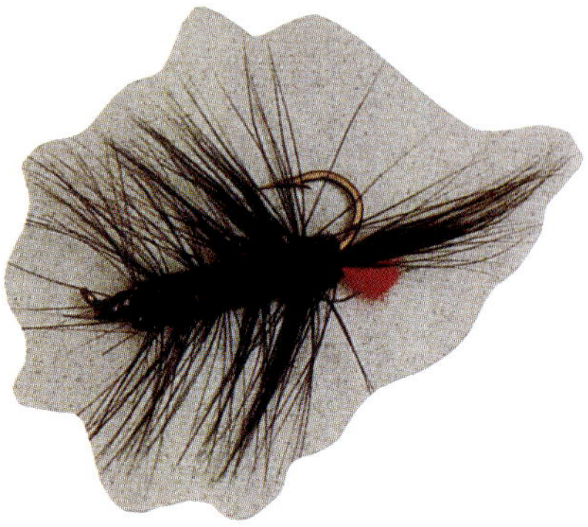

"THE Farmers' Wives" keep Grahamstown in cakes, cream cheese, and koeksisters— and butternuts, prickly pear syrup, chocolate cakes, pineapples, pumpkins, flowers (cut and dried), honey in the comb, venison pies or steak and kidney, rhubarb, marmalade, and new-laid eggs — free-range Henny Penny or ostrich.

Ostrich farming has recently been revived in the district and the home industries shop in Hill Street is fluffing up tail feathers into mini-dusters labelled with a sign of the times: "A present for Father, to use on his car or computer." Stir-fry strips, braai or fry patties, and recipe sheets for oven-baked ostrich (cut into cubes) are also on offer.

Feathers fly in nearby Bathurst Street, where the "Hairy Fairies" (registered trade name) maintain a low profile. Nymphs, Hackle Wet-Fuzzy Wuzzies, Matukas, and Muddlers. All fit to be tied by the oldest, biggest, and surely most modest trout-fly firm in the country. The miniscule masterpieces are created from feathers imported from the East, India, and the United Kingdom. Local guinea fowls put spots on some Matukas, and kudu tail-hairs occasionally come in handy.

Round the corner, the Phoenix Roller Mills in Dundas Street is still very much a going concern, though the first roller mill machinery to be installed in South Africa is no longer in operation. A magnificent construction, mainly of wood, on three levels, it continues to occupy the bulk of the building, and ran regularly up until the early 1980s. Now the huge sacks of meal and maize come from elsewhere, as do bags of stock feed supplements, artificial fertilizer, and old-fashioned bone meal. Seeds, dried beans, and pigeon and fowl food are in constant demand and so are the mill kittens, a small striped strain bred for 28 years, deadly mousers of wide renown.

Do not begrudge the few rands a pavement hawker may ask you to pay for a sturdy, serviceable broom. It is the result of hours of careful labour, an ingenious use of simple materials. Some broom reed, a piece of tin, a nail and wire plus binder twine to hold the sweeping part, and a Port Jackson willow pole, often cut in varying lengths to suit different customers' heights.

The bottle sellers, too, work hard for their stock, digging deep in old rubbish dumps, always hoping to strike it rich by unearthing a cache of the much prized "blues".

On to Ossher's at the Market Square, one of the last of the major Eastern Cape trading stores. The exterior is misleading — elegantly Edwardian, a

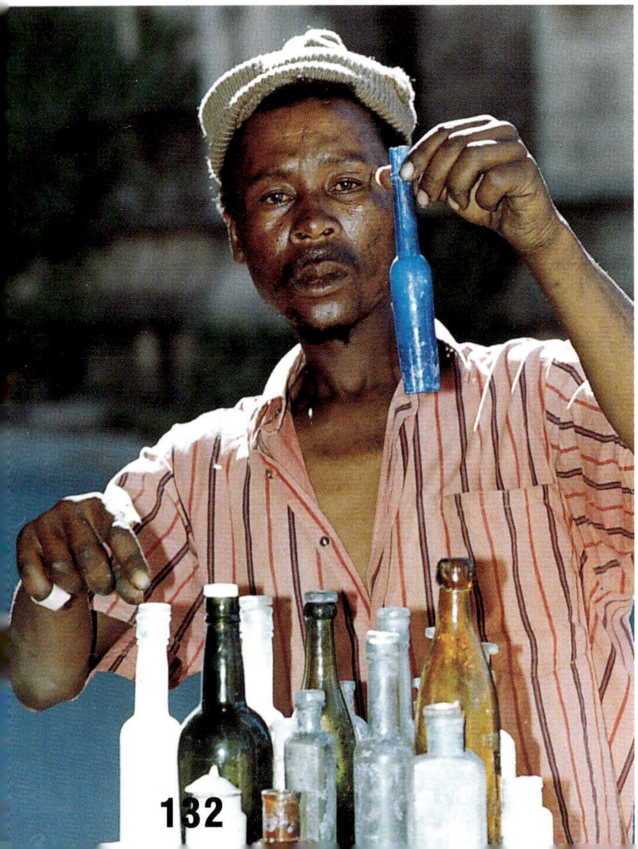

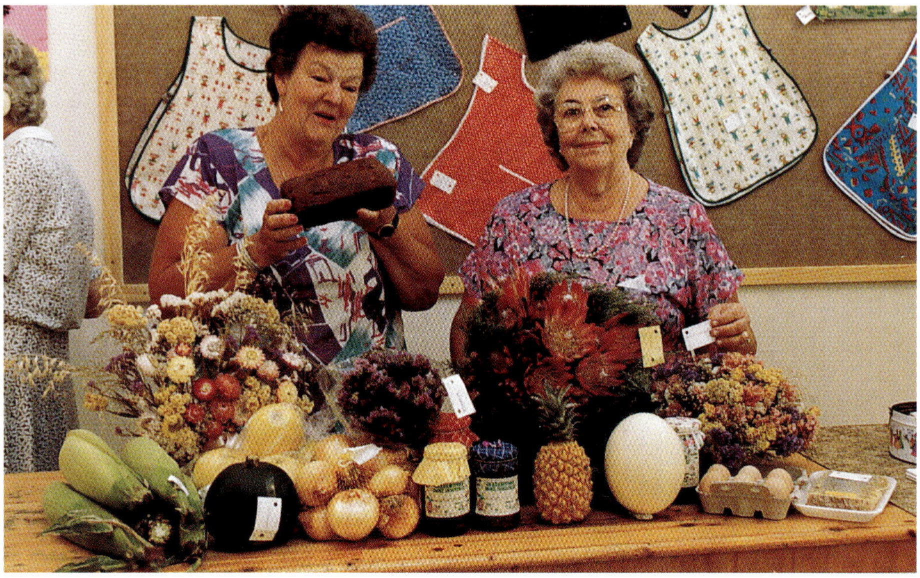

ABOVE: Wholesome taste of the country at Home Industries

LEFT: "Won't you buy my pretty bottles?"

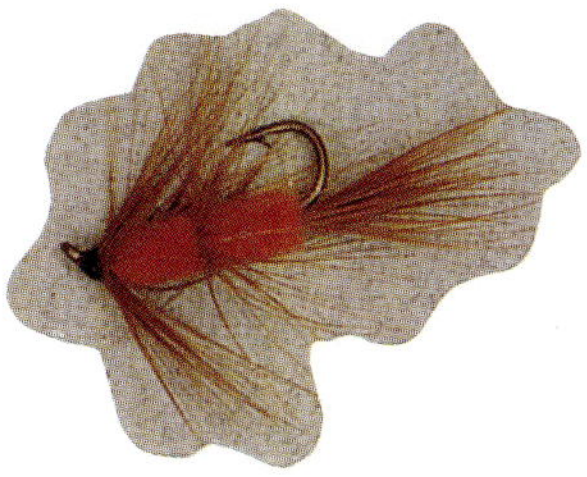

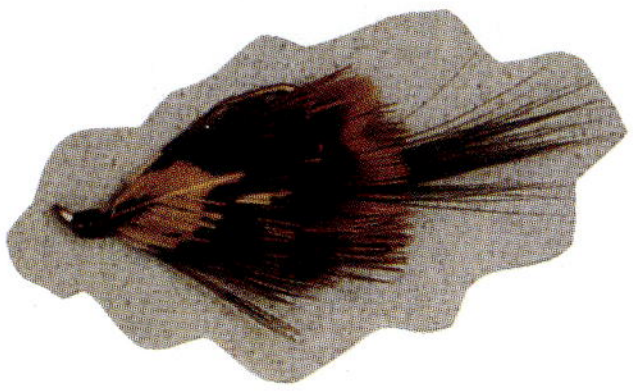

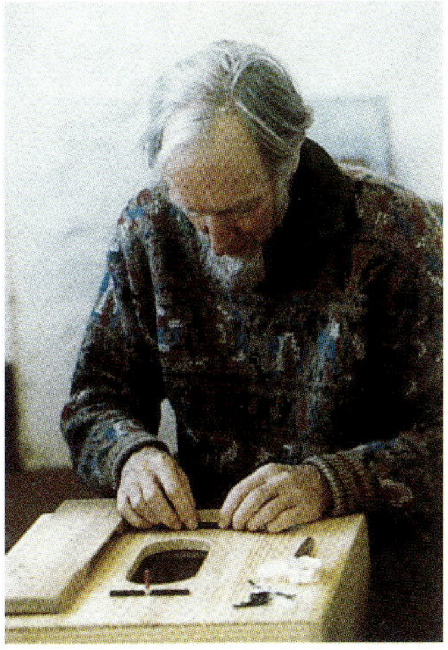

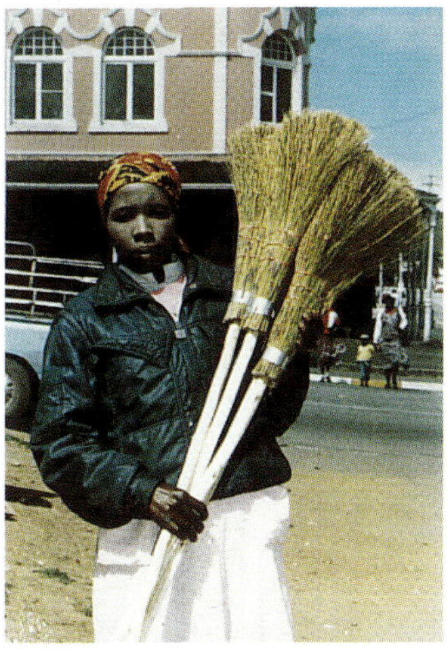

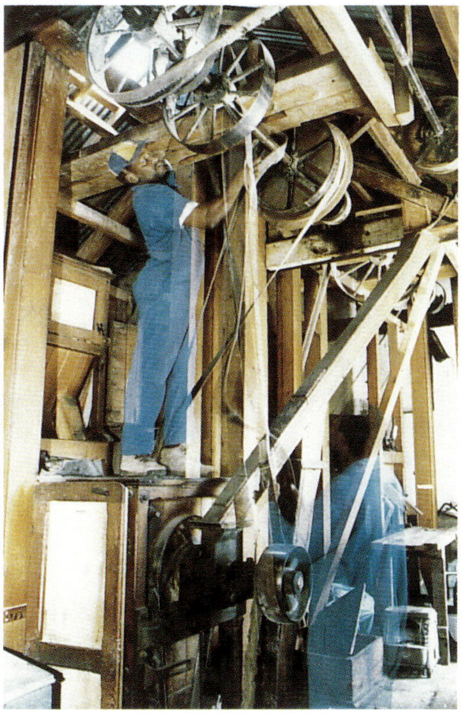

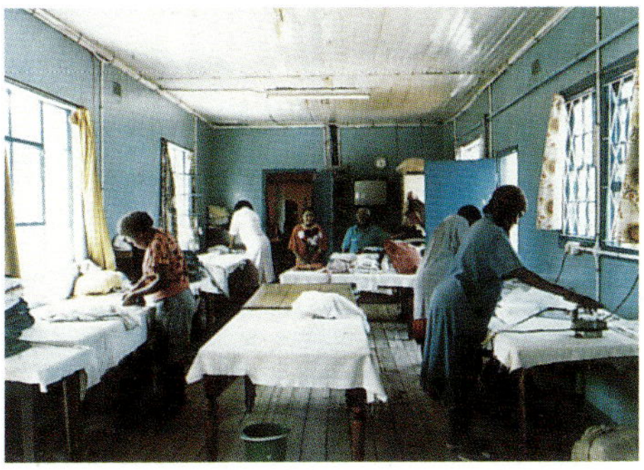

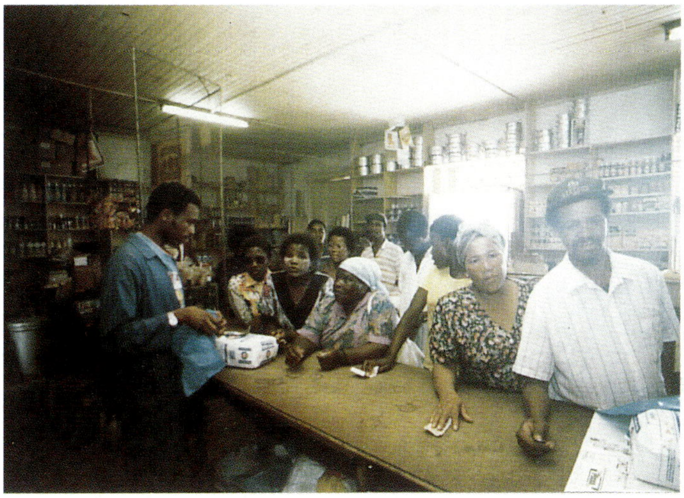

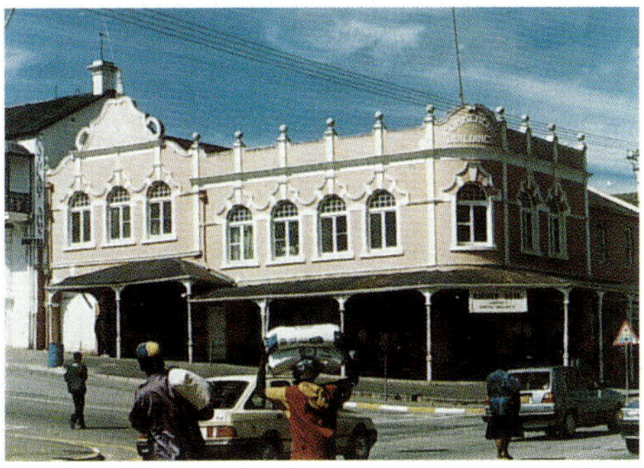

CLOCKWISE: *Crafting an instrument; broom lady; mill hands; Ossher's trading store — inside and out — and Charlie John's laundry; above it all, a trio of "Hairy Fairies"*

little pink palace from 1904. Inside, it is the genuine dusty article. Crammed with galvanized baths and buckets, big three-legged cooking pots, tin trunks, and blankets. Ethnic outfits made on the premises hang from ceiling rails, a fly-paper spirals stickily. Shelves are stacked with small packets of cheap tea and other groceries, as well as red ochre from the Transkei, chew tobacco, paraffin, and lamp wicks.

The sound of Africa is encapsulated in the *kalimbas* hand-crafted at African Musical Instruments. Basically *mbiras* or thumb pianos, small live things you can hold in your hands, tuned to the Western scale to allow musicians all over the world to enjoy their companionship.

Someone once commented that Grahamstonians seem to survive by taking in each others' washing. Maybe — but nobody does it better than the four meticulous Indian laundries, going way, way back, as does much of their equipment.

Finally, a nationally known financial institution, the Grahamstown Building Society — longest surviving building society in South Africa. Established in 1877, it recently became a mutual bank to comply with new legislation, but its signs are unchanged and are likely to remain so, at least until the next repainting, which could be in the next century.

SHINE, AFRICA, SHINE

VIVA DAKAWA

OUT of the blue, at the far end of Froude Street, the city's frayed suburban fringe suddenly gets knotted in a cluster of industrial buildings. Close by the dairy, slap bang in a former butter and ice factory, panel beating garage *et alles*, things have hotted up, melted down, and straightened out. Dakawa has happened.

The ANC Department of Art and Culture's dream which began in a refugee camp in Dakawa, Tanzania, is now a reality where fantasies find form. Torrents of glorious Afrocolour textiles spring from design boards. Graphic prints for the nation and weaving with designs on the future loom large. Kangas — those versatile wall hangings/bedspreads/table covers — make bold statements.

The impressively renovated and equipped complex was officially opened by Walter Sisulu in October, 1992. Funded by the Swedish International Development Agency and liberal donations from Norwegian Foreign Aid, it is run by an independent trust. Swedish instructors got the classes going; locals keep them on course. The aim is to offer top-level artistic and technical training to people with potential plus, but minus the basic education required by formal institutions. Time input varies from six months for individual skills to five years for the entire syllabus.

It is envisaged that the fully qualified trainees will contribute their knowledge to the upgrading and establishment of art and craft workshops through community organizations all over southern Africa, turning the Dakawa Ripple into a Mexican Wave. Meanwhile, their eye-widening work fills the spacious gallery with good vibrations which are spread near and far by enthusiastic purchasers.

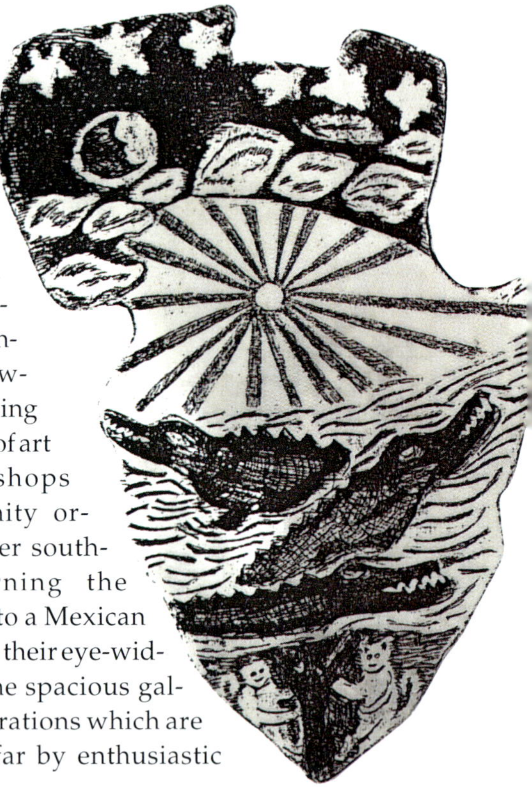

There is also a special project for school children, who are encouraged to broaden their horizons at drama, dance, music, ceramics, textile painting, weaving , and art sessions. A full programme for a more fulfilling life.

"It is a challenge to us to shed our past and claim the totality of South African experience, to make works that are not like over-chewed pieces of bubble-gum but which say distinctly I am proud to be South African."

— Wally Serote of the ANC at a Dakawa exhibition

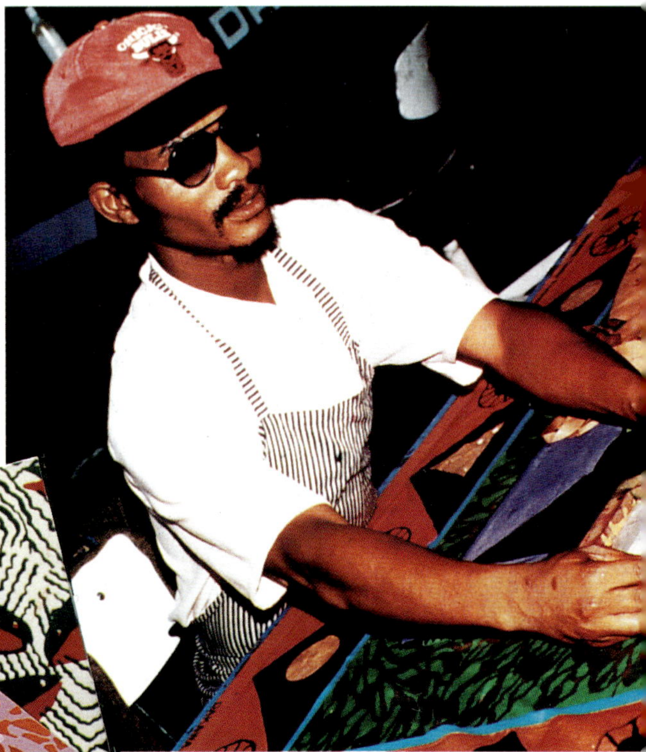

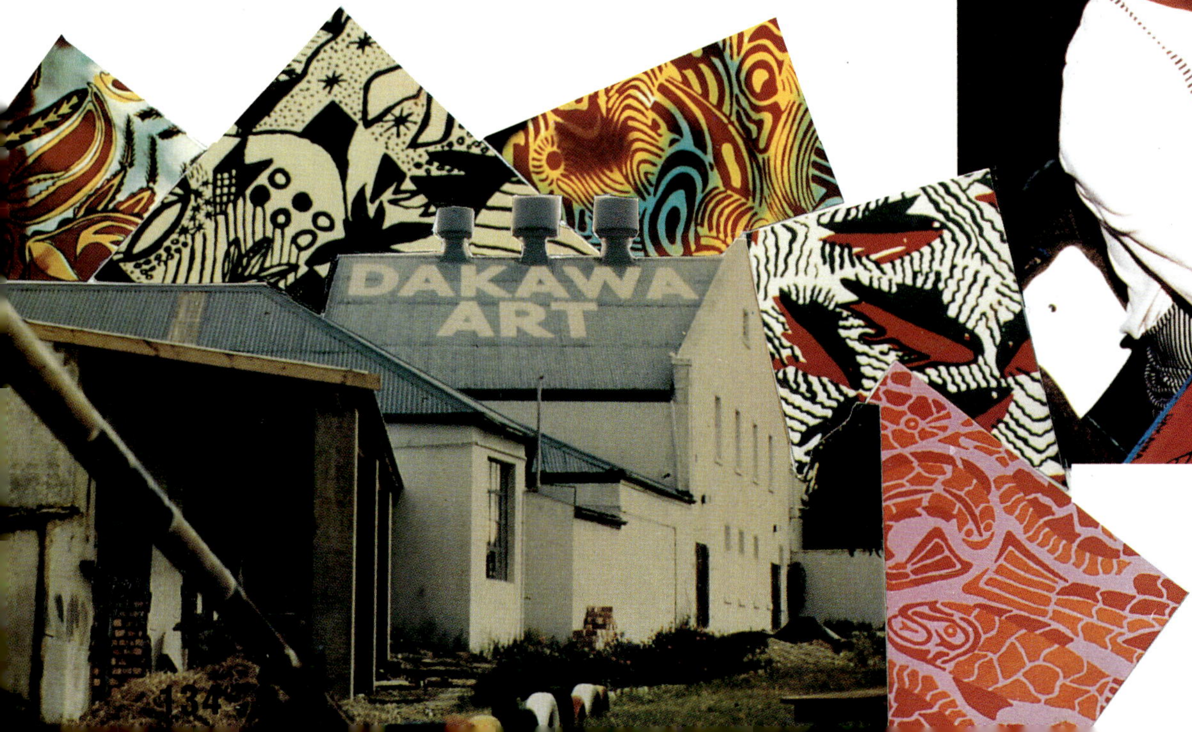

TOP: *"Big Bright Africa" Vulike Tem*

LEFT AND ABOVE: *Cooling turr on the roof, warm wonder colours ins*

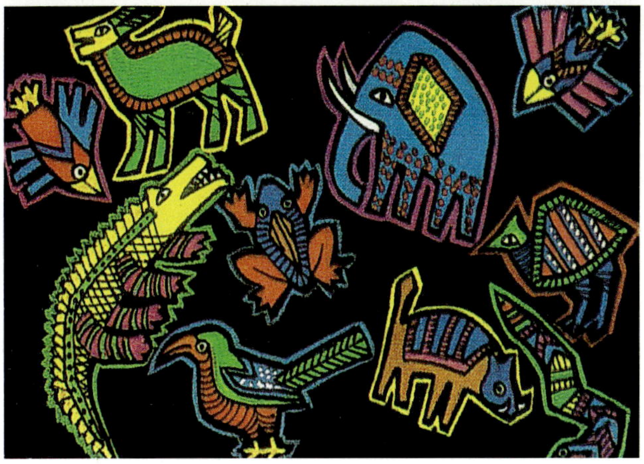

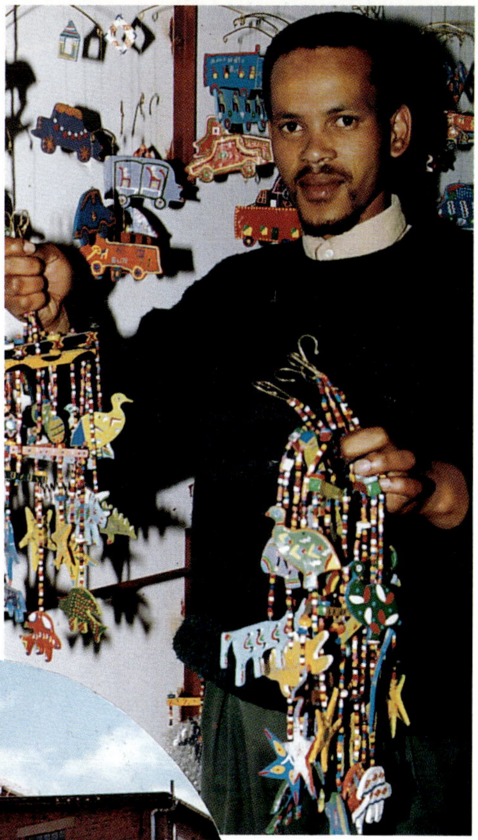

ALL SWITCHED ON
THE POWER STATION

THE report on the first decade of the Power Station co-operative scheme reads more like a riveting adventure saga than a routine round-up. In many ways it was.

It started with mechanical engineer Wally Gilbert exploring the dirt roads above Grahamstown on his motorbike and discovering the old Power Station in the industrial area, mouldering amid the bluegum trees.

He and his partner, Robert Berold, a chemical engineer turned poet— both escapees from the big city rat race — needed premises for their hand-crafted Tumblewood toy business. They promptly rented a section. Smothered in coal dust, the huge boilers and heat exchangers, unused for 20 years, were still in place. The concrete cooling ponds were for the birds.

They began work on April 1, 1984, strongly motivated by an idealistic goal of nurturing and training, employing and empowering unskilled people in a desperately impoverished area.

Other groups joined them. What developed was essentially an experiment in democracy, with all the attendant ups and some extremely discouraging downs. At one stage, everybody was totally switched off, but a vital few saw the light and pressed on.

Currently, export orders keep the Imizamo Yethu ceramics section fully stretched, while Mamba T-Shirts and Albany Placemats are in growing demand. Captivating brightly enamelled waste paper baskets made from old copies of *Grocott's Mail*, cake flour, and water have become top liners. The sound of marimbas is heard in the rear. Power Station products are once again heading for the best-seller lists.

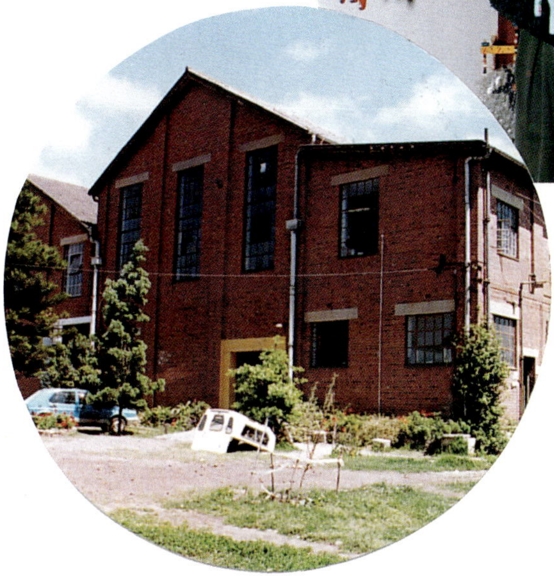

TOP LEFT AND ABOVE: ***Placemats for Africa and magical mobiles made from ceramic cut-outs at the old Power Station***

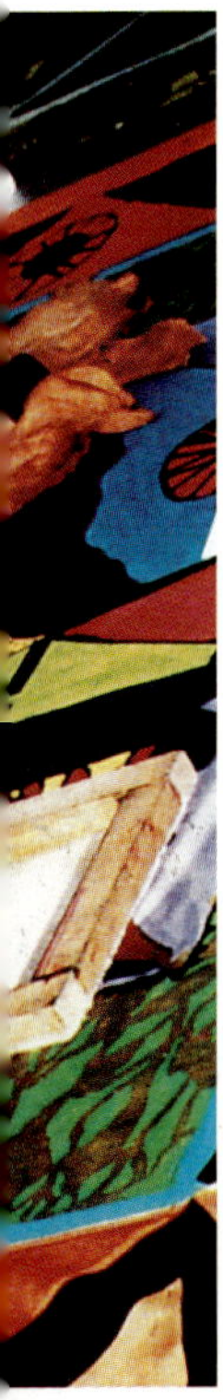

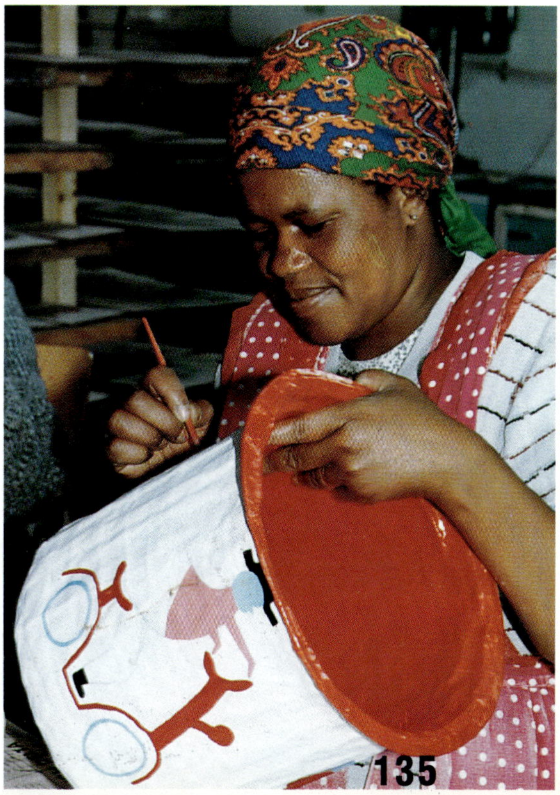

RIGHT: ***Transforming papier mâché moulds into covetable containers***

TRANSPORTS OF DELIGHT

STEAM trains have gone off the rails to become legends of a more romantic past. But right up to the 1980s, the daily appearance of these dragon-like locos snorting and grunting, belching clouds of smoke and whistling while they worked, echoed the excitement of the arrival of the first train in Grahamstown in 1879.

It joined up with another from Port Elizabeth, and the 25 dignatory-laden coaches, drawn by two engines and pushed by one, were welcomed by a crowd pressing forward so enthusiastically that it was a full 20 minutes before passengers could alight and proceed to tiffin in the goods shed.

The construction of the 57km branch line to Grahamstown from Alicedale on the main route north was extremely challenging because of difficult terrain. Deep cuttings had to be blasted through solid rock and three tunnels excavated.

It was largely these problems and not the protests of the city's many wagon builders that had so long delayed the link. They feared the iron horse would put paid to their trade. In fact, the ox-wagon's reign as the principal means of transport in rural areas continued for close on another 40 years.

Each maker had his own preferences and all possessed large stocks of wood, for the most part kept in their yards for seasoning. There was ironwood from the Pirie Bush for the frame, yellowwood from the Kat River for the naves, assegaiwood for the spokes, white pear for the outer circles of the wheels, and stinkwood from Knysna for the bed boards, side rails, and planks. Indian teak was popular with some, while others favoured

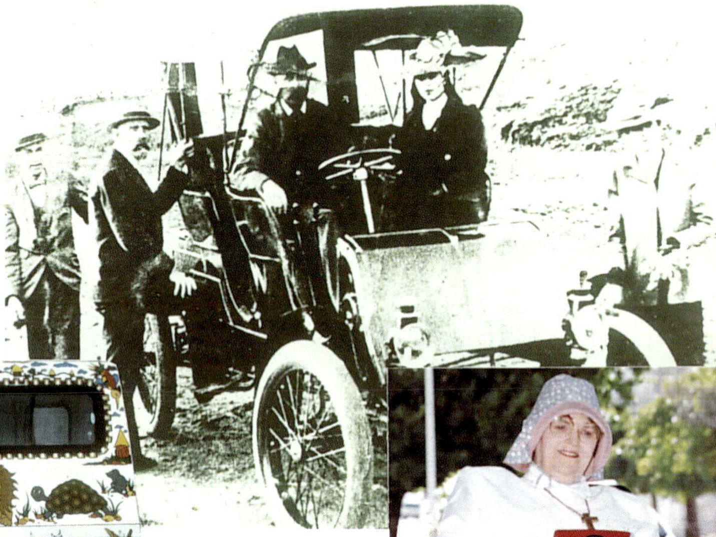

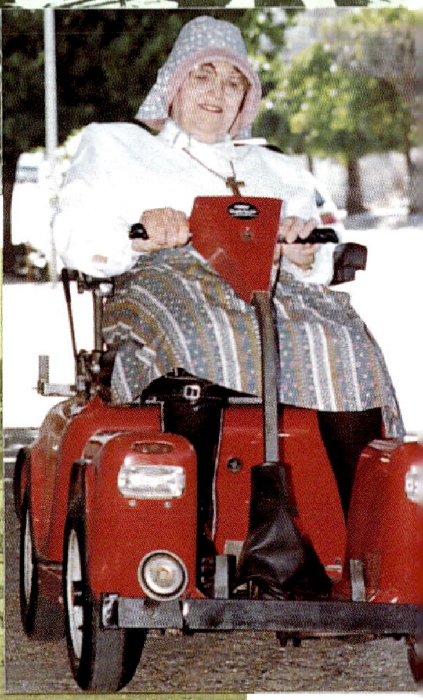

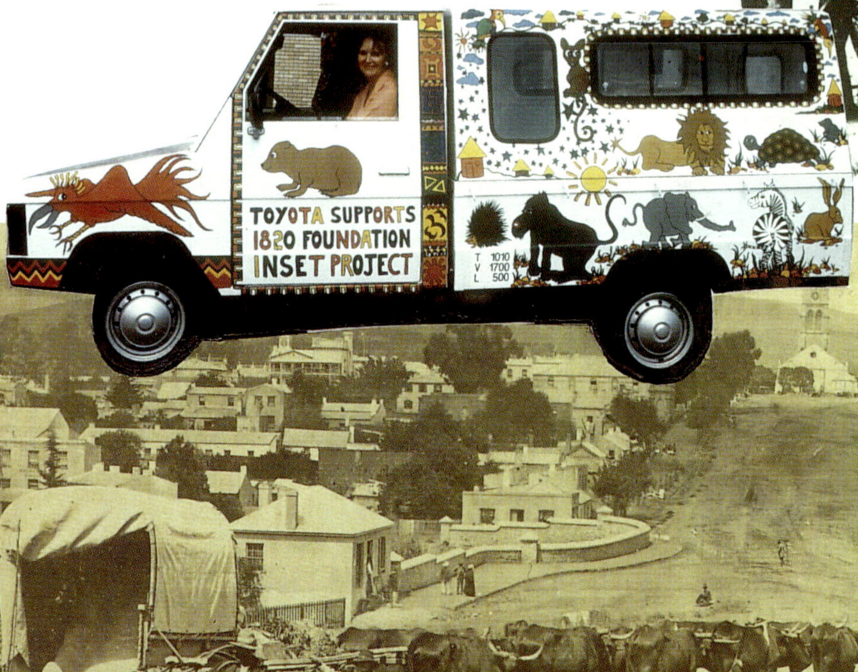

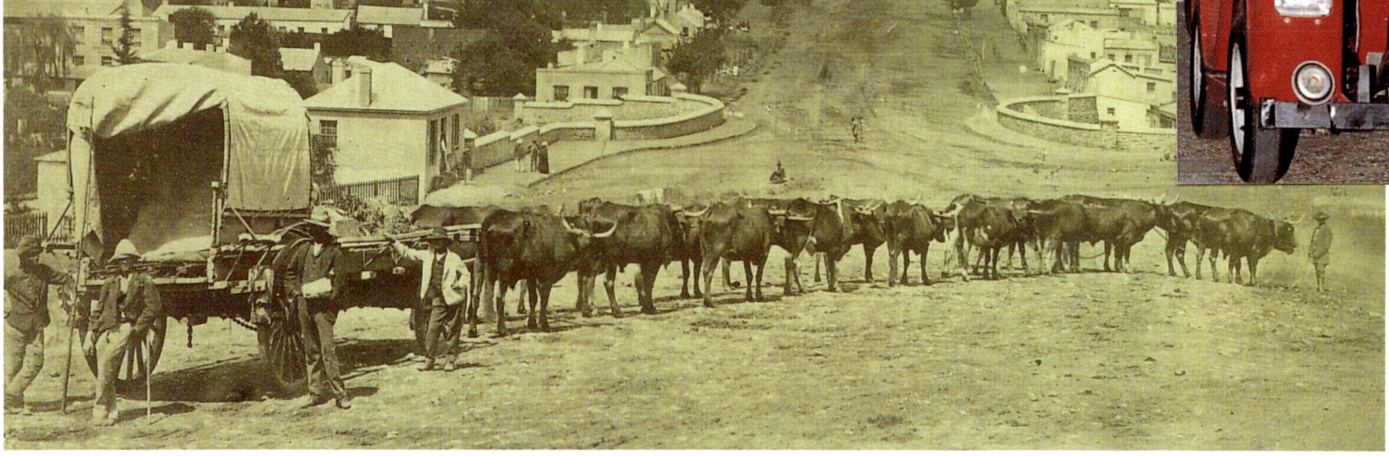

CLOCKWISE: *First car in Grahamstown; Maureen Pyott driving her red, red "Robin"; a typical ox-wagon turnout near Dundas Bridge in mid-1880's; and vibrant van for Inset education project*

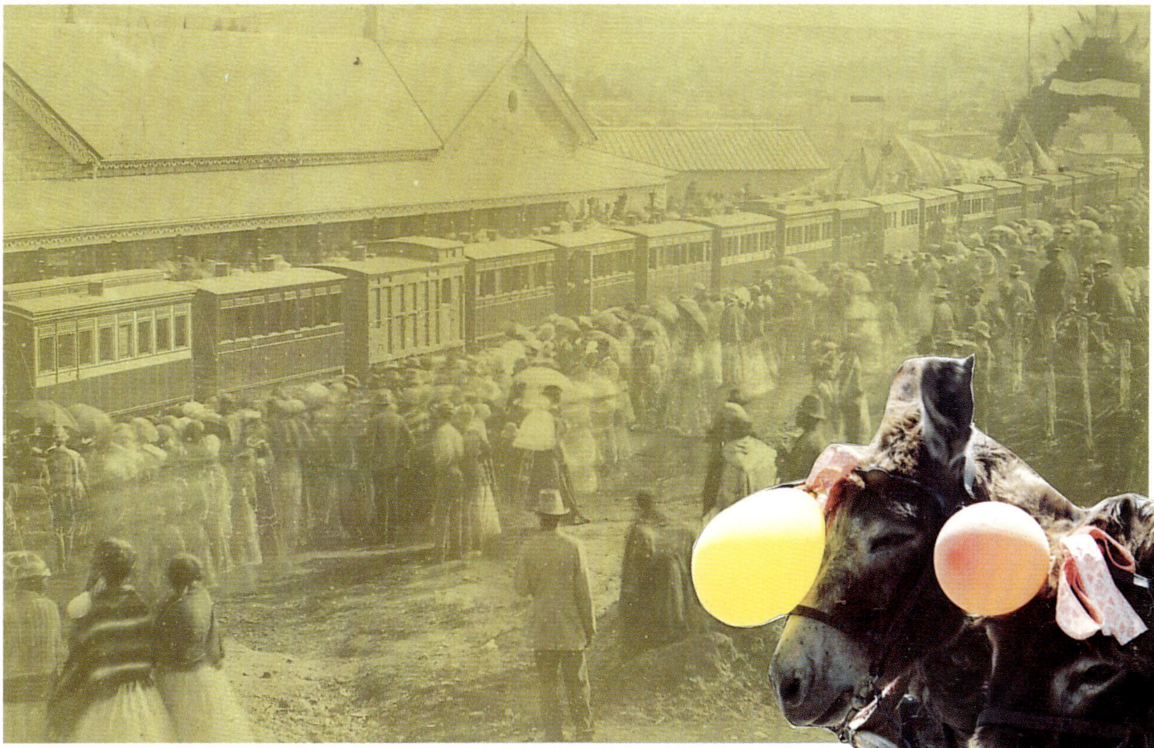

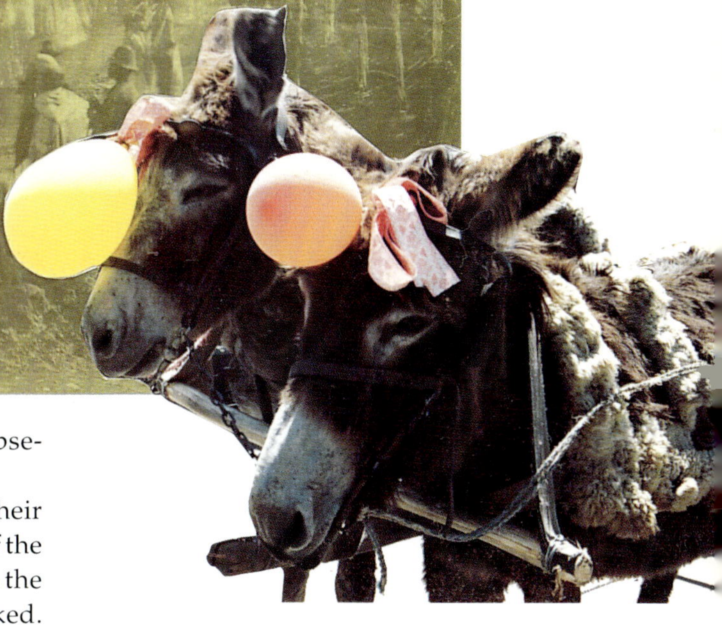

the white-and-red els from Drivers' Wood, where it was subsequently eradicated.

Horse-powered engines eventually put the final spoke in their wheels. The keenest motorist in town was Frank Galpin, son of the Observatory's inventive founder. He imported the first car in the Eastern Province, the forerunner of a string he drove and wrecked. A contemporary commented that "until his death, he remained the worst driver in the EP, perhaps in the world".

Invincible Maureen Pyott in her little battery-powered red runabout called "Robin" is the city's best-loved driver. As she wends her way blithely in and out of shops, sporting a perky motoring bonnet, she brings an Enid Blyton touch to the everyday.

Another transport of delight — and enlightenment — is the gaily decorated van of the Sakhisizwe In-Service Training for Teachers (Inset) project. By encouraging teachers, particularly on isolated farm schools, to improve language skills creatively, it opens the road to higher learning.

Grahamstown is the only centre in SA to hold an annual donkey-cart carnival. A fun way to educate owners, it is organized by the SPCA, suppliers of the fleecy harnesses which give their wearers a poodle cut. Local firms sponsor carts to defray maintenance costs, and generally the way ahead has brightened considerably for these patient beasts of burden.

The milktrain does not stop here anymore, but at National Arts Festival time the Grahamstown station is once again a popular destination. Transnet transforms the loco shed into a popular music venue called *The Crossing*.

CLOCKWISE: *First train steams into Grahamstown, Sept 3, 1879; every donkey has his day at SPCA carnival; and old locomotive shed is new theatre complex*

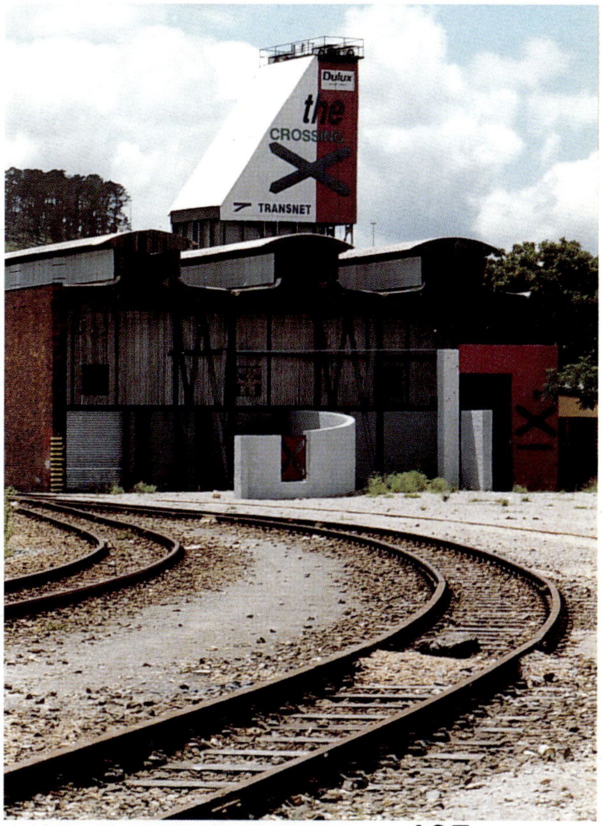

BELOW: *The Bowling Green, Grahamstown, painted by "Dummy" Brown, c 1916*

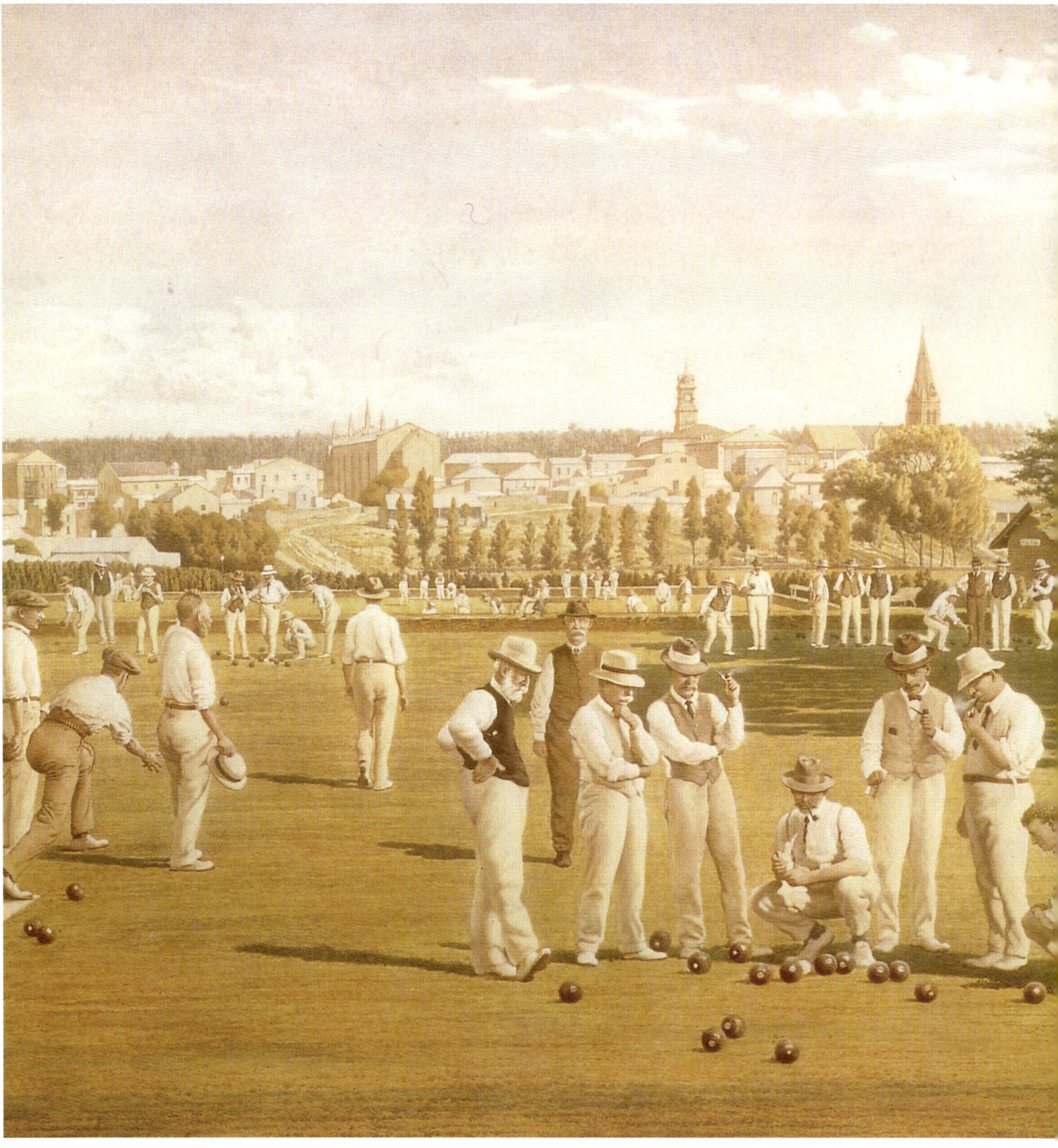

THE BOWLING CLUB

THE playing fields of Grahamstown are spread over the city like green tablecloths. Held in the hills, with a spire inevitably dreaming somewhere offsides, they make a perfect picture. Like the painting of the Grahamstown Bowling Club done by John Roland "Dummy" Brown.

A deaf mute, hence his nickname, he was born in Port Elizabeth in 1850. He trained at the Roeland Street Art School in Cape Town, and at 17 was sent to the Liverpool School of Art, where he won the Queen's medal and various scholarships. He taught in Liverpool for 30 years, then retired to Grahamstown.

Each of the players is identified in his preliminary sketch. Their counterparts may still be seen on Wednesday and Saturday afternoons, poses practically identical, the ritual the same, as is the distant skyline. Some noticeable changes have been chalked up, however. Ladies — demurely seated on benches in Brown's study — are out there bowling with the best. Casually dressed young members knock on wood at night under recently installed floodlights.

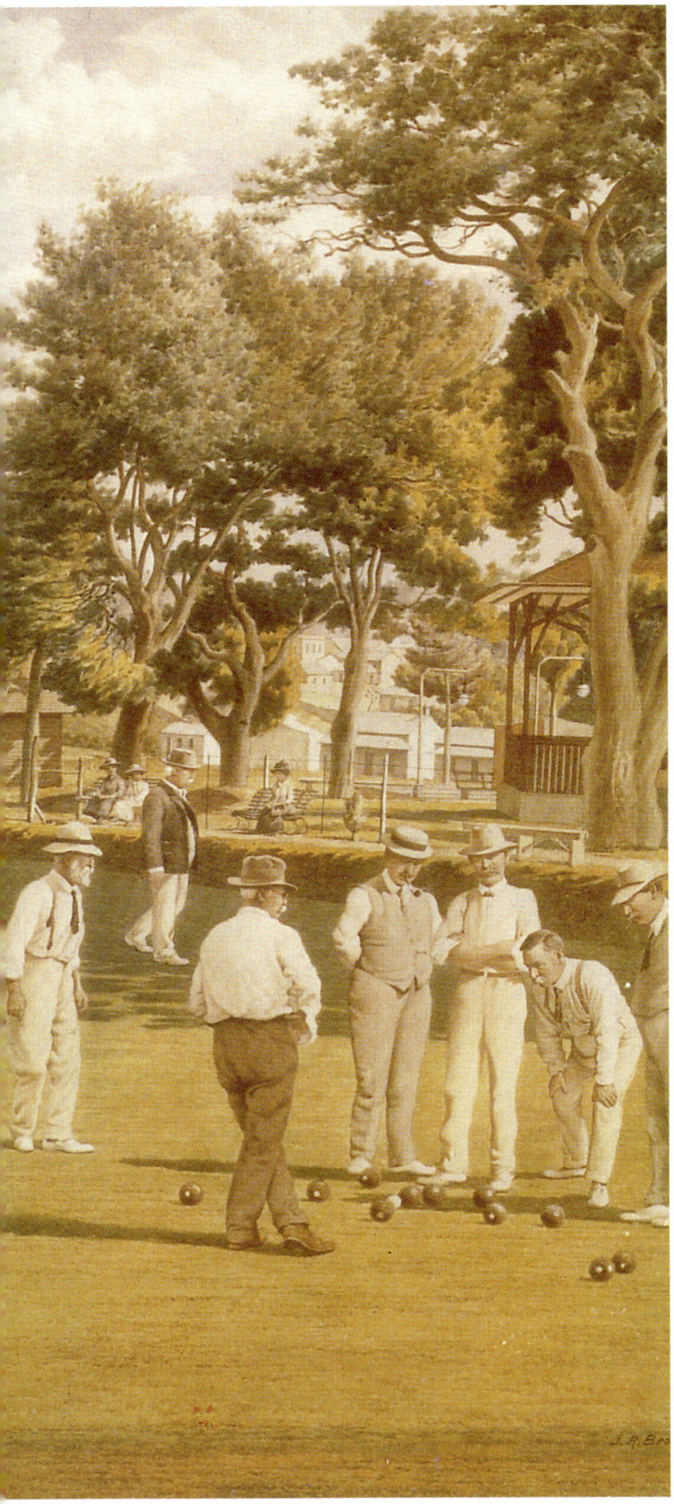

As with everything else in Grahamstown, the present sporting life has strong links with the past. A number of clubs have passed their centenaries and still have their eyes on the ball. Faded team photographs recall previous triumphs, new groups pose proudly every year. Boards record long lists of past presidents and champions in gleaming gilt — the same old family names crop up everywhere.

There are few cities in South Africa where sport has remained so truly recreational, retaining many of the attributes of amateurism. Access is so easy, fees so affordable, everyone seems to be playing their own little game.

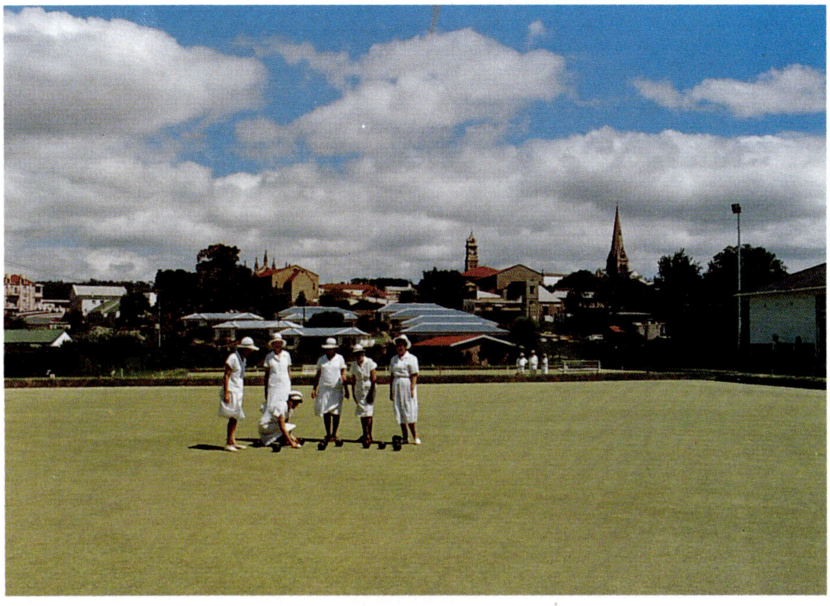

ABOVE: *Lady members on the same green today: only the trees have gone*

CLIMBING TO DIZZY HEIGHTS...

GOING OFF THE DEEP END...

GRAHAMSTOWN a climbing centre? Seems unlikely but perhaps not more so than much else that happens here. According to young Jeff Stevens, author of the *Grahamstown Crag Guide*, no other city in South Africa has such a wide variety of easily accessible crags and bouldering sites so close to town.

The New Wave boulders in the Botanical Gardens have been described as one of the top three training venues in the country — very popular in the evenings — with hundreds of variations traversing up and down the "wave".

The traverse along the stone walls of the General Lecture Theatre at

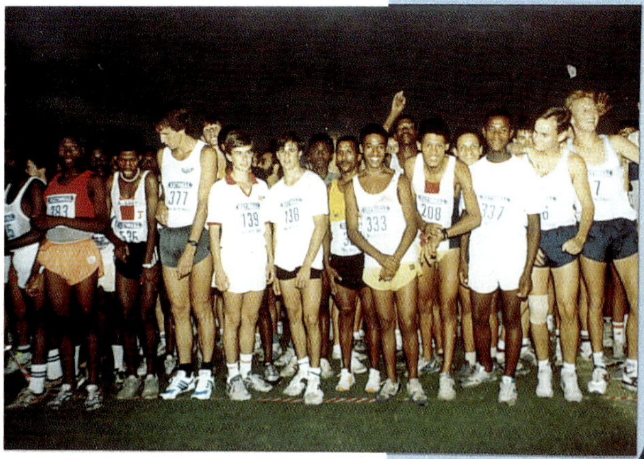

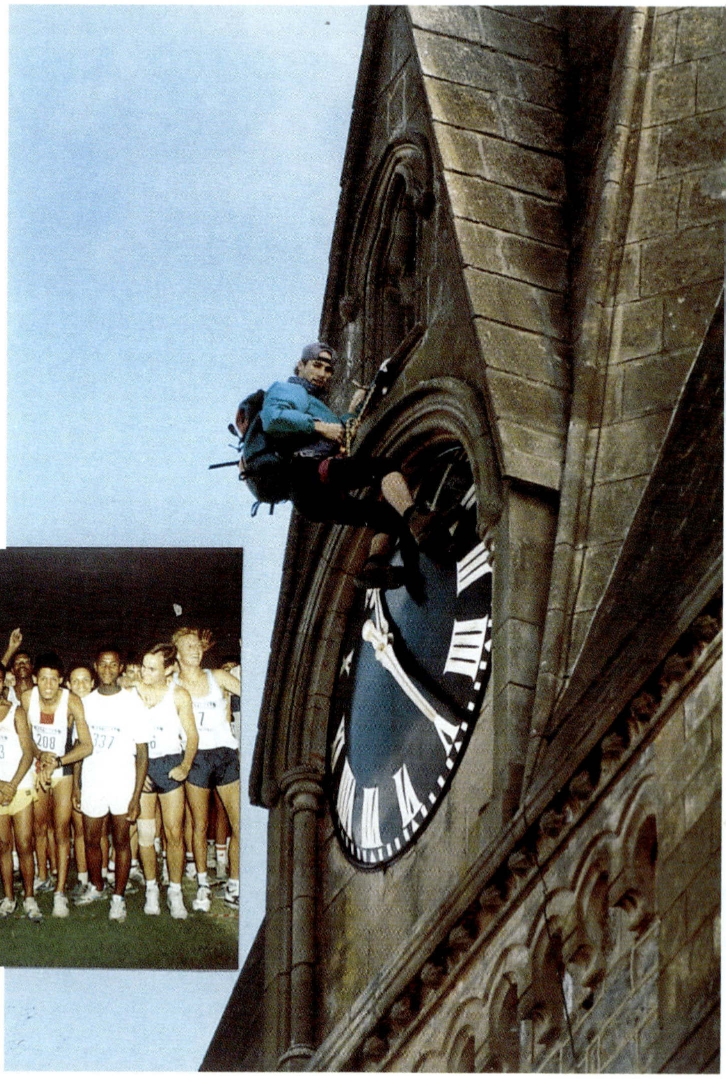

RIGHT AND BELOW: *Nite Race; high time; Graham's Town garrison cricket Team, 1867*

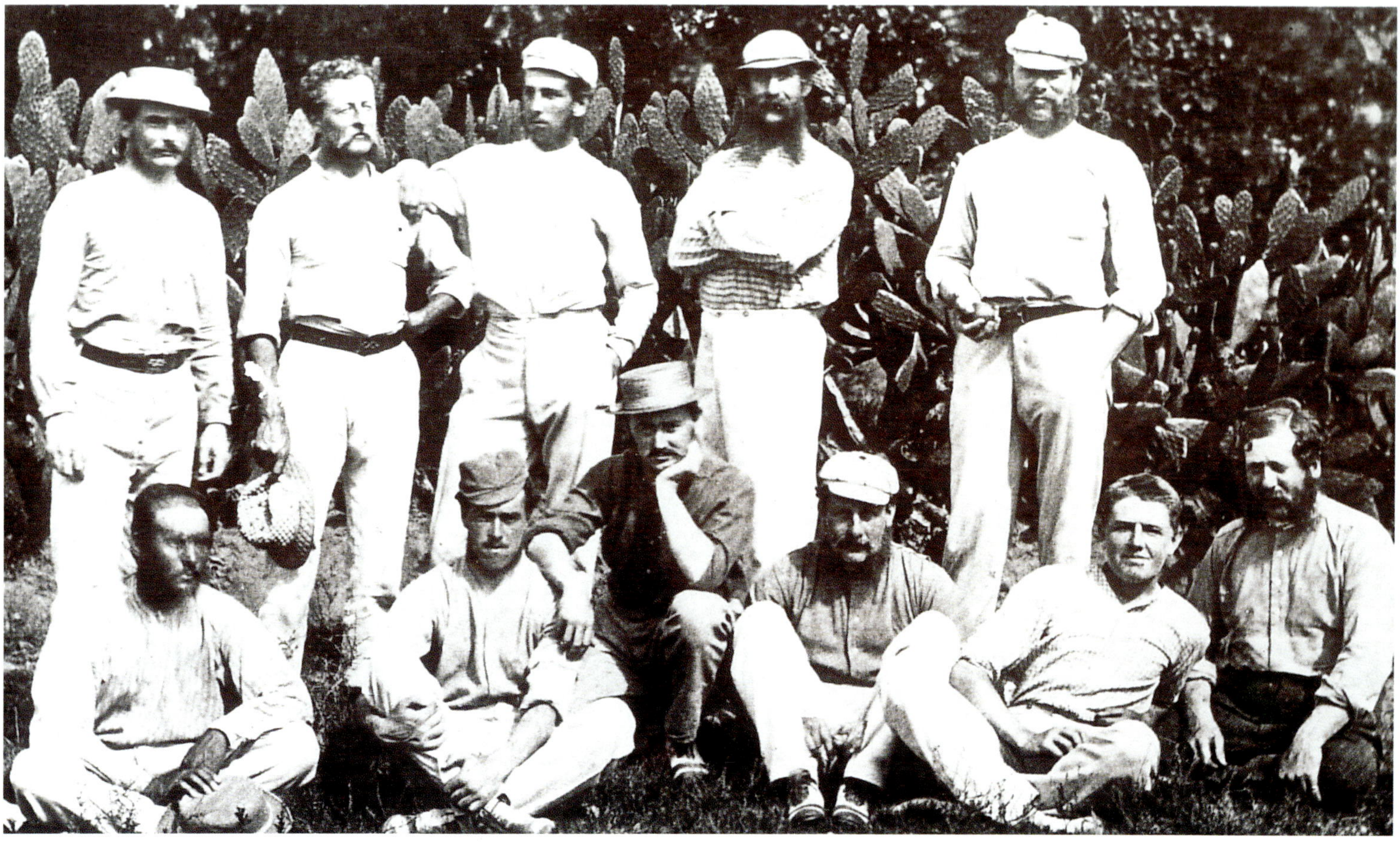

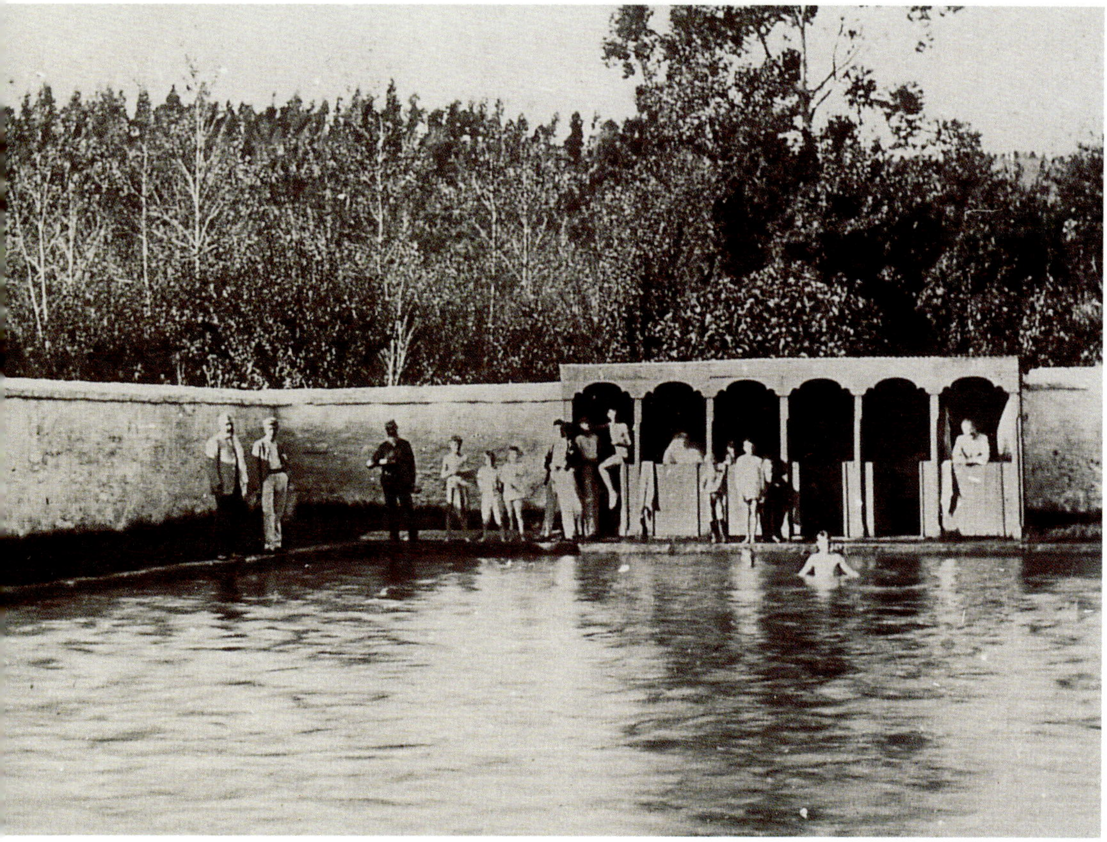

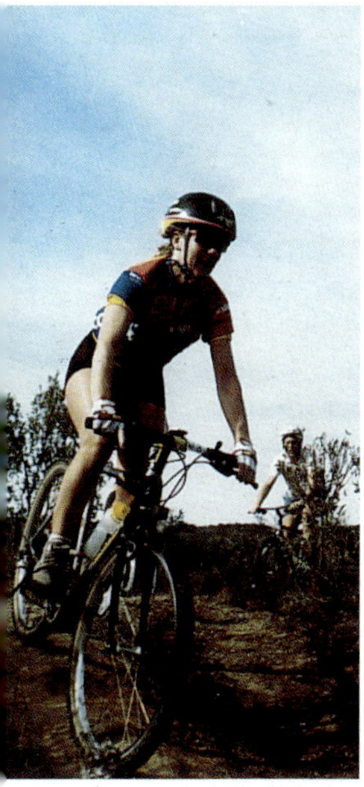

ABOVE: South Africa's first public pool
LEFT: Mountain bikers riding high

Rhodes University is probably Grahamstown's oldest training venue. The wall is inclined at 80 degrees and the holds are generally small. Training on this kind of medium is largely outdated, but many people feel that it is a great way to toughen fingertips and improve foot work. Exactly what was needed when intrepid Jeff ascended the Cathedral spire to remove a destructive wild fig which had taken root in a crevice and could cause cracking.

A down to earth game of cricket is more Grahamstown's style and has been since garrison days when, in true British regiment tradition, Soldiers v Civilians, Married v Single, and Colonial v Homeborn matches were arranged.

On May 24, 1862, the first match was played on "City Lords" — described as the best cricket ground in the Cape Colony and now part of Kingswood College.

Legendary cricket commentator Charles Fortune, who died in Johannesburg in 1994 at the age of 89, came to South Africa in 1935 on a teaching contract with St Andrew's College. He made his first freelance sports broadcast for the SABC from Grahamstown in 1939. In his heyday, during test matches he received as many as 1 000 letters a week, most of them complimentary, some of them violently abusive. Critics accused him of waffling and talking about irrelevant trivia instead of concentrating on the game. Fortune, however, blamed cricketers. He said they "dilly and dally and don't get on with the job".

Today Grahamstown has no public swimming bath, but back in 1853 the first in the Cape Colony was opened at the far end of the Botanical Gardens. For the next 80 years it was a much enjoyed amenity. Special hours were set apart for ladies in 1888, mixed bathing began in 1916. No filtration plant or tiles, and the water changed only once or twice each summer. In her evocative memoirs of the 1920s, May O'Shea recalls: "When Mother saw the green, slimy water and horror of horrors, frogs hopping in as we walked round the edge, she refused to allow us to proceed any further"

As schools and Rhodes built their own pools, the bath fell into disuse: empty and cracked, but with great accoustics. Up to the early 1980s Rhodes students threw dusk to dawn parties in the deep end, the perimeter lit by candles. Now it lies beneath the sports field to the left of the entrance road off the N2, never to surface again.

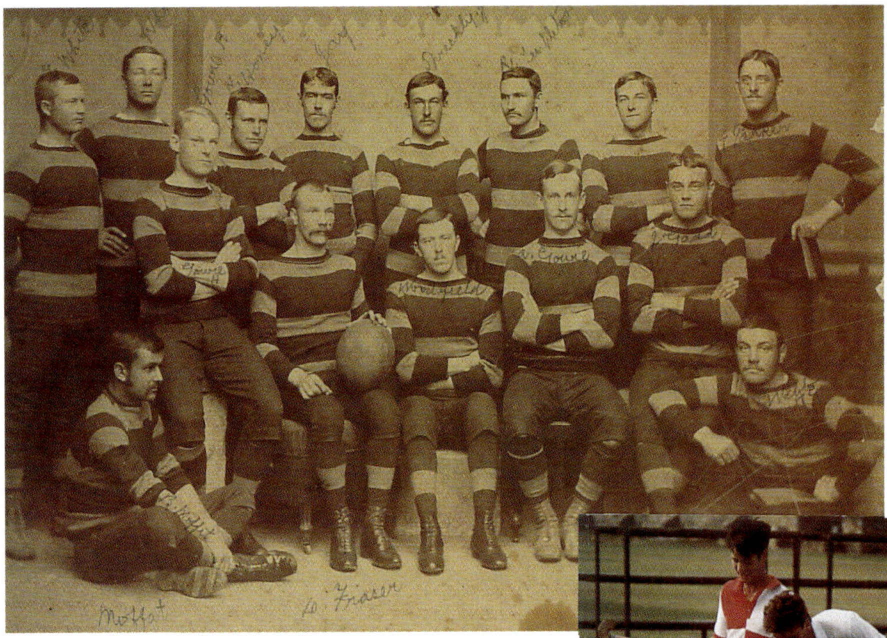

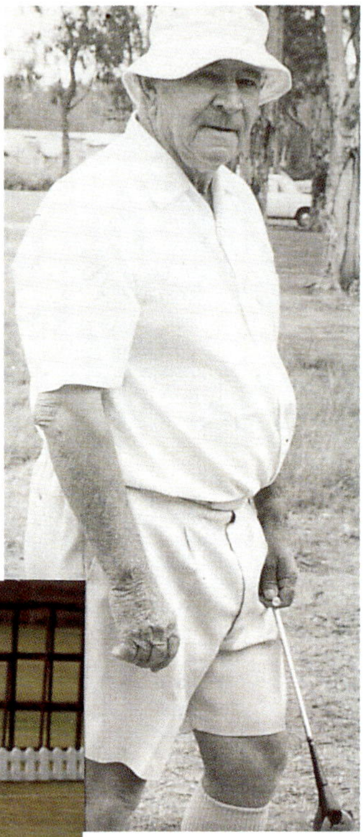

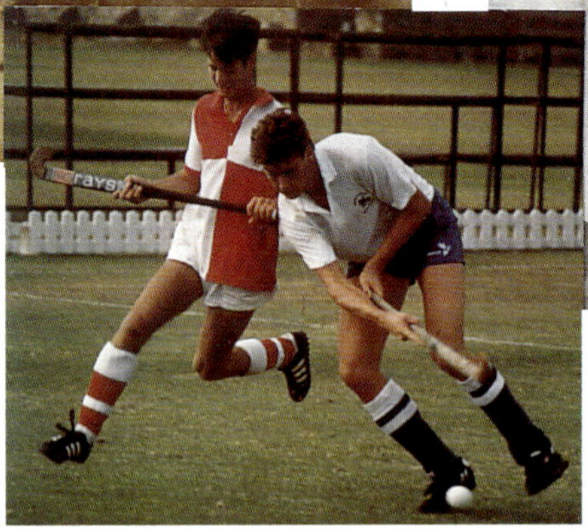

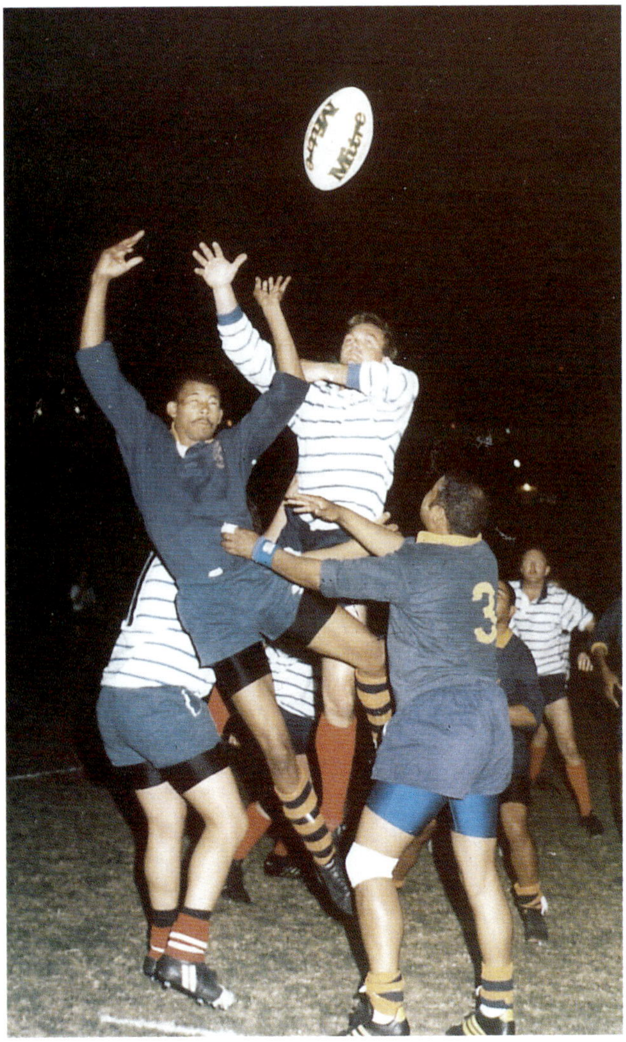

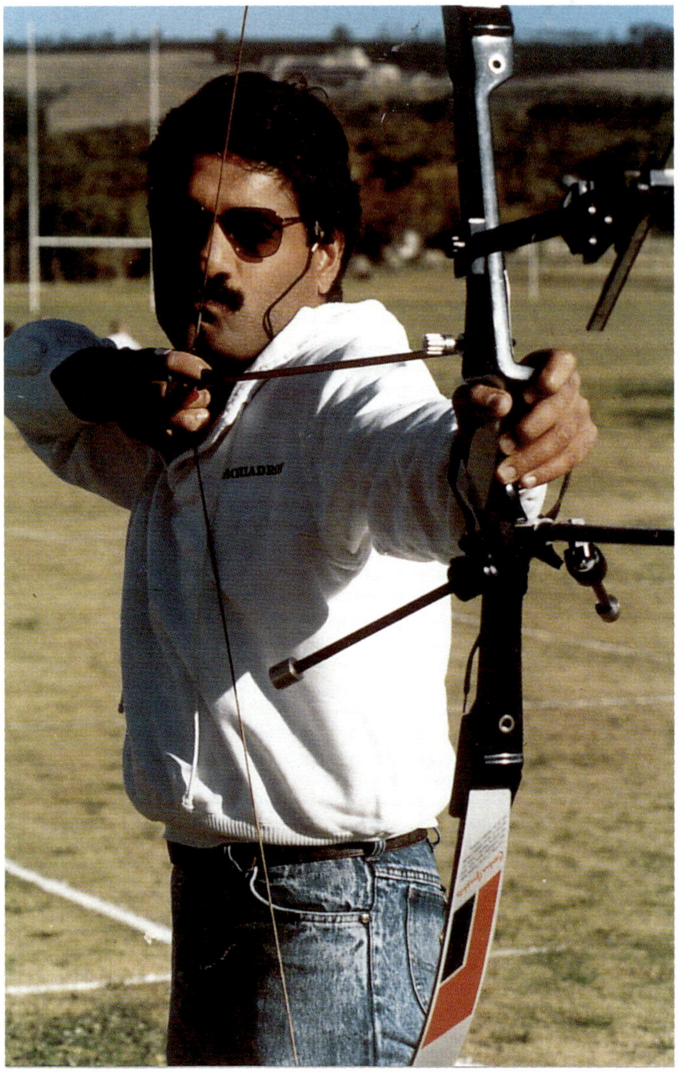

CLOCKWISE: *Albany Rugby Football Club team c 1888; George Pohl — still golf-clubbing in his 90s; hockey days; Mohammed Bassa takes aim; and back at the Albany for a night game*

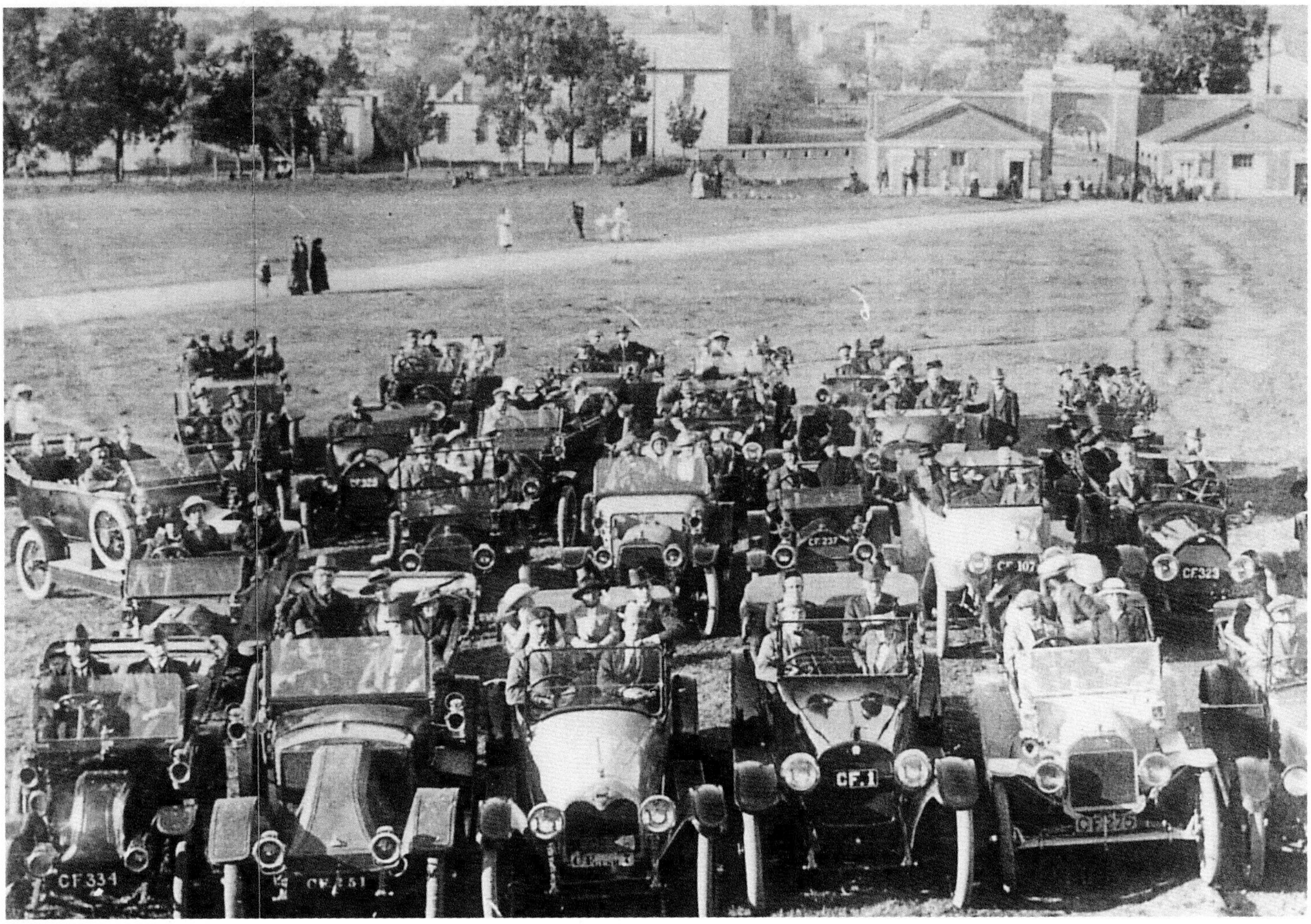

ABOVE: Rallying up, with the Drostdy Gateway in the background

HORSE POWER, ARROWS, TEES AND TENNIS...

IMPRESSIVE turnouts of magnificent men in their motoring machines, ready for rallies over dicey dirt roads, belong to the days when "wheels" were a novelty, not a necessity. The 1916 Hupmobile with the CF1 number plate in the photograph above was driven by the late Dr J D Louw, at one time chairman of the Rhodes University Council.

Horse racing — the sport of kings — has also disappeared from Grahamstown, but was immensely popular as early as 1823. Lt Col Henry Somerset, Commandant of the Eastern frontier, helped found the Albany Turf Club, and the first meeting took place in May that year on the flats above town, near the present golf course.

The Dutch farmers in the district thoroughly enjoyed the races. The future Great Trek leader, Piet Retief, became a steward, and many of his colleagues entered horses.

When the Governor of the Cape Colony, Lord Charles Somerset, came to visit his son in 1825, race meetings were held on three consecutive days. Lord Charles attended, astonishing the local populace by appearing in a blue coat and sash with a veil over his hat to protect him from the sun. He also carried a parasol.

Archers first took aim here in 1862. Members of the Albany Archers' Club continue the art, with vastly different bows.

The Grahamstown Golf Club was established in 1891. A crude course was hacked out of the bush in the valley alongside the Cradock Road. The City Fathers were somewhat alarmed by the initial application. It seems there was not a Scotsman among them for they warily acceded to the request, expressing concern about the holes: "Would they be dangerous to the public?" Nobody knew. The greens were made from blue ground from Kimberley, and a donga down the middle had to be negotiated several times.

The Albany Rugby Football Club celebrated its centenary in 1981, the Grahamstown Lawn Tennis and Croquet Club (the latter genteel occupation now defunct) in 1985, with gentlemen players appropriately clad in "Oxford bags" for the occasion.

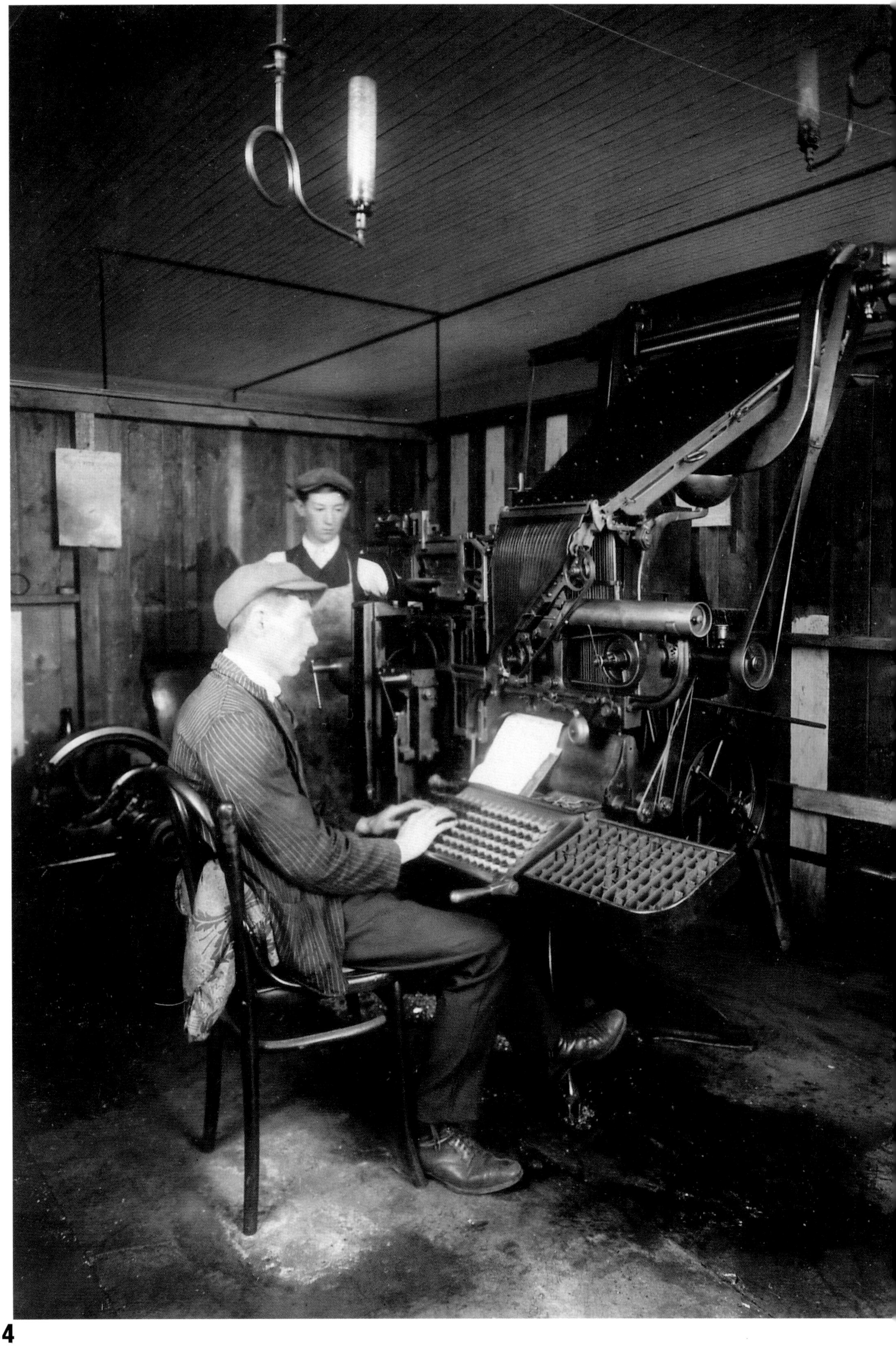

PRESS ON REGARDLESS

THE *Graham's Town Journal,* launched by Louis Meurant on November 22, 1831, was the first independent newspaper published outside Cape Town. Grahamstown editors were an enterprising breed. Between 1831 and 1871 they started no fewer than 11 papers. During one particular period, 1853-1859, five of these were in regular production at the same time.

Grahamstown printers also established newspapers in King William's Town, East London, Queenstown, Dordrecht, Kimberley, Bloemfontein and — the real scoop — Johannesburg, where *The Star* initially rose as *The Eastern Star* on January 6, 1871. The large Wharfedale press which still occasionally roars into life in the little museum in Anglo-African Street is a twin of the steam-driven original which was taken to the newly-discovered Witwatersrand Gold Fields — by train to the Kimberley railhead, then hauled the rest of the way by mule team and ox wagon. *The Eastern Star* appeared on the dusty Johannesburg mining camp streets on October 17, 1887, only removing *Eastern* from its masthead in 1889.

The office desk in the museum belonged to John Fairbairn, who, together with 1820 Settler Thomas Pringle and George Greig, did battle in Cape Town for South African press freedom, a goal which was enshrined in ordinance number 60 on May 8, 1829. Another historic date is November 27, 1882, when a congress in the Grahamstown City Hall saw the birth of the Newspaper Press Union.

Robert Godlonton — "Moral Bob" — became editor of *The Graham's Town Journal* in 1834, turning it into the influential mouthpiece of settler opinion over the next 32 years. So much so that it was nicknamed "the Settlers' Bible". Very different from Grahamstown's trio of notorious periodicals: *The Echo* (which specialized in spiteful riddles), *St George and the Dragon* (dedicated to persecuting the Dean), and the astounding *Comet*.

The latter was provokingly described by its founders as "the most libellous newspaper ever published". They stated that they would fight but never apologize. They never did, not even to *The Eastern Star's* editor, whom they called "a cad, cur and a coward" and "a malignant journalistic reptile".

All yellowing pages in the Albany Museum and Cory Library archives now, but literature and language are abiding passions in scholarly Grahamstown circles. The National English Literary Museum and the Dictionary Unit for South African English are filled with words, words, words. Rhodes has the only Journalism and Media Studies Department at an English language university in South Africa.

The Graham's Town Journal was incorporated into *Grocott's Mail* in 1920. Just four people on the much modernized technical side now — a far cry from the numerous compositors, linotype operators, and bustling machine-room of yore when it was *Grocott's Daily Mail.* A bi-weekly since 1965, it is essential reading on Tuesdays and Fridays.

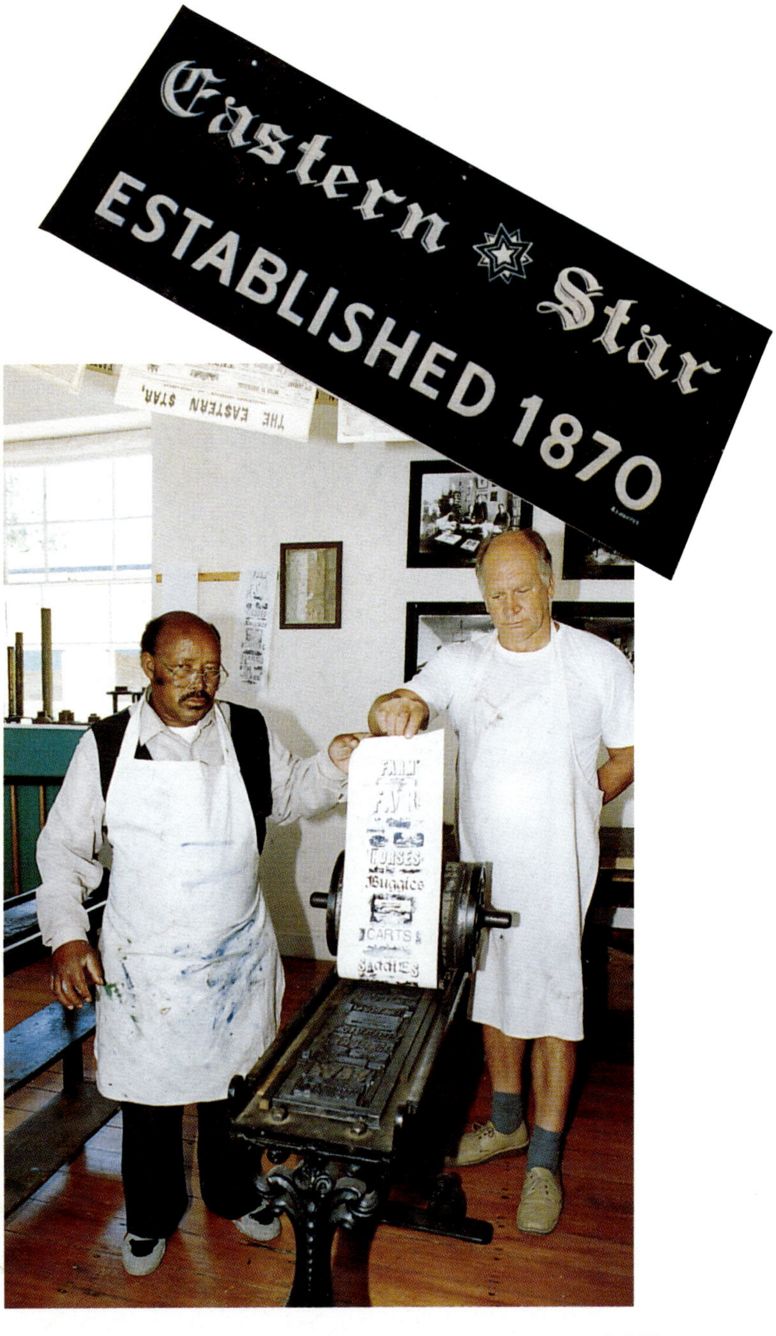

LEFT: Hot off the linotype press at Grocott's Daily Mail in 1909; and RIGHT, hands on the galley-proof press at The Eastern Star printing Museum

DEAR OLD GROCOTT'S

WHAT'S black and white and read all over? *Grocott's Mail*, of course, South Africa's oldest family-owned newspaper. Grahamstown could not function without it. Parish pump perhaps, but it keeps the entire community together, as welcome and informative as a letter from home. When long-time residents depart, they often take out subscriptions, and copies are eagerly perused from Cape Town to Kimberley, London to Los Angeles.

Newspaper production has been described as a daily miracle. At *Grocott's* it is a bi-weekly one, pulled off by a skeleton staff who work their fingers beyond the bone. Pressurized proof-reading leaves columns wide open to printers' devils. Everyone groans and giggles when they see yet another **CORRECTION**. For example, that Fisciano — Grahamstown's Italian twin city — has named an entire piazza after us, not just a pizza, as stated in the previous issue. Or — more mysteriously — "It was a collision with a cow that caused the accident, not as indicated in the headline: Police caused calamity".

The "Smalls" are big favourites, giving a total overview of what is really going on if you can put two and two together between the houses for sale, situations vacant, wanted known, marriages, and calls for baby carriages. Often brightened by gems in "Found" — false teeth in the Botanical Gardens, a gold chain in High Street — or requests from Rhodes student researchers: "I am collecting anecdotes about ghosts and hauntings in Grahamstown ..."; "I am conducting a survey on heavy metal and culture ..."

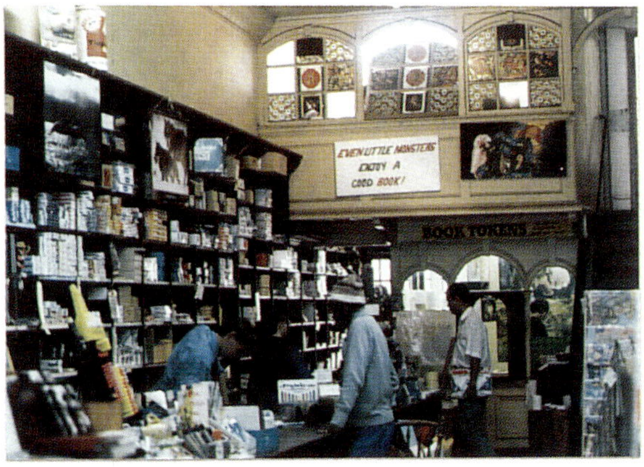

Hatched in 1869, launched in 1870 as *Grocott's Free Paper*, filled with advertisements. On January 2, 1872, it changed to *Grocott's Penny Mail* — the name still emblazoned on the frosted front door. The dates on the ornate bedstead-style gable record its birth and burnout. An earlier building was destroyed by fire in 1906 and promptly replaced by the present Edwardian delight, essentially the same ever since, both inside and out.

The editorial cubbyhole and printing works are in the rear, the long narrow stationery and book shop at street level where show tickets are reserved.

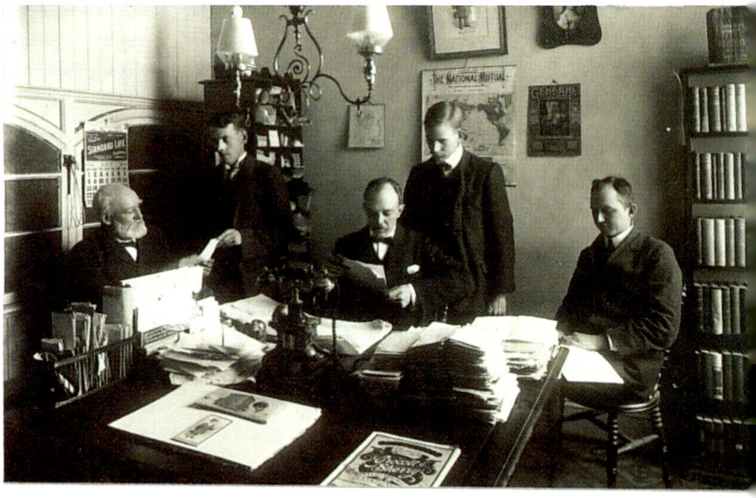

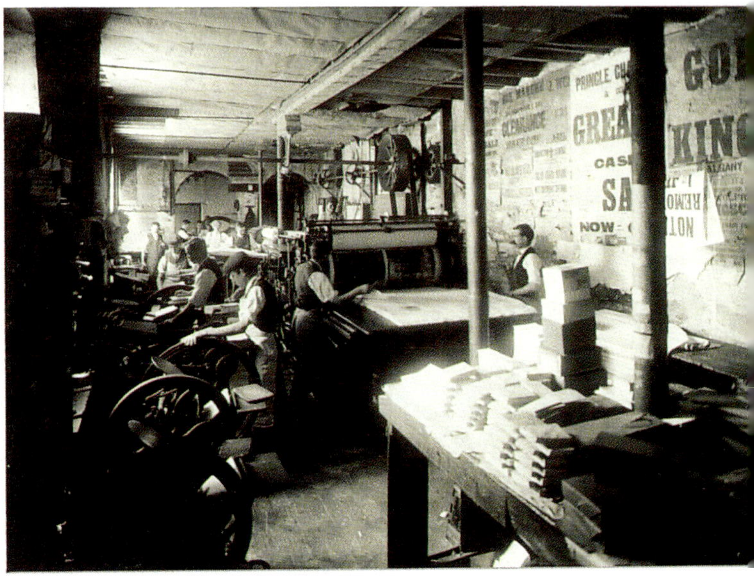

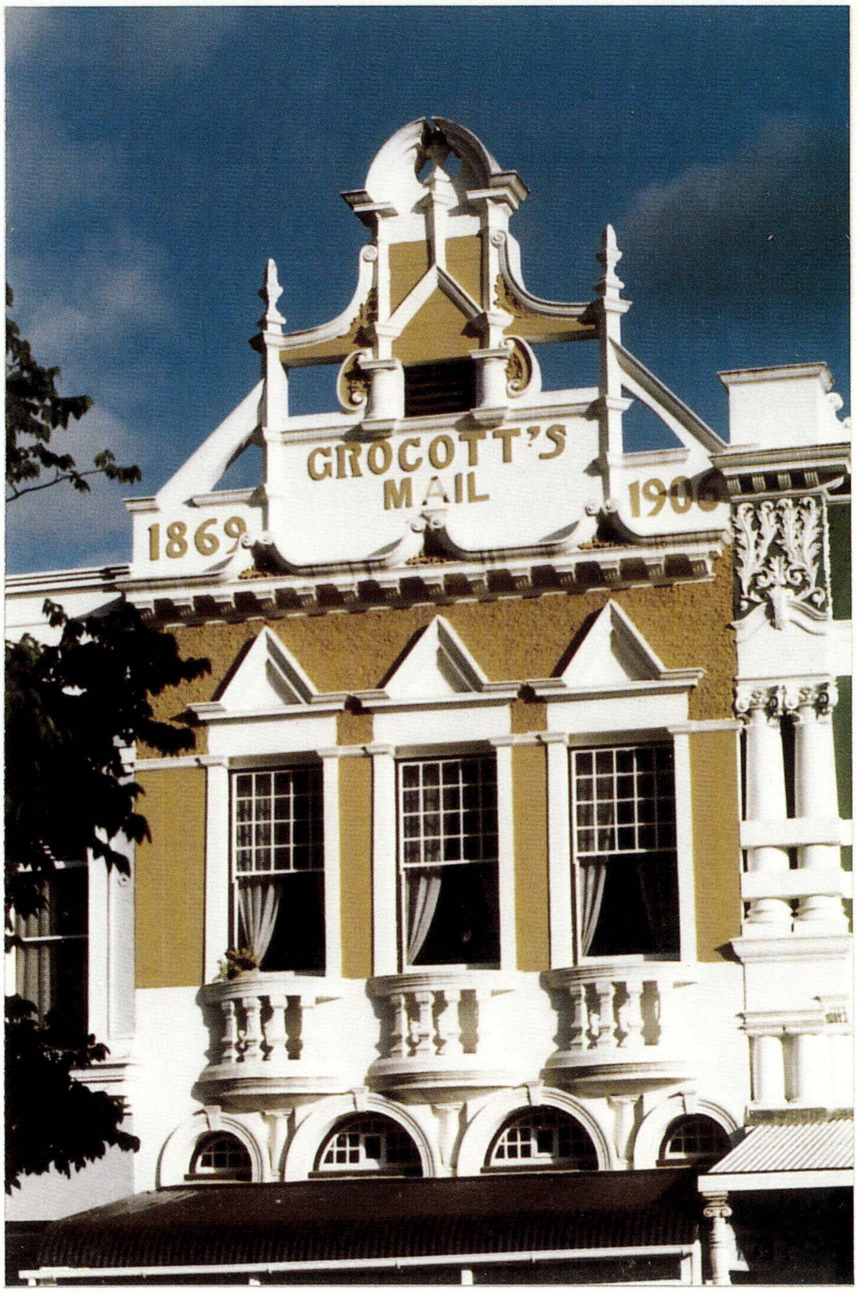

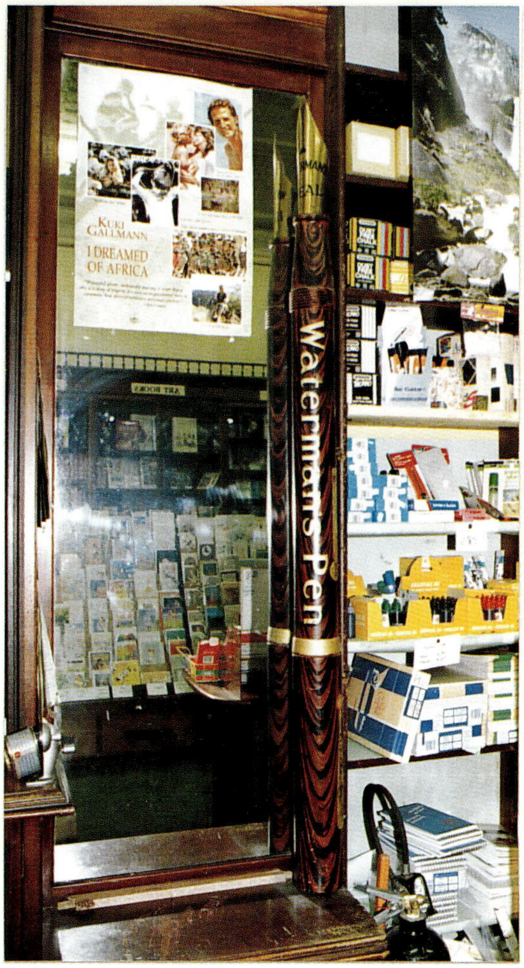

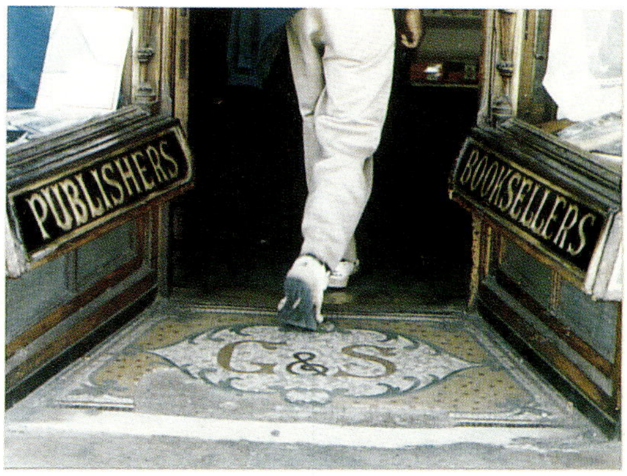

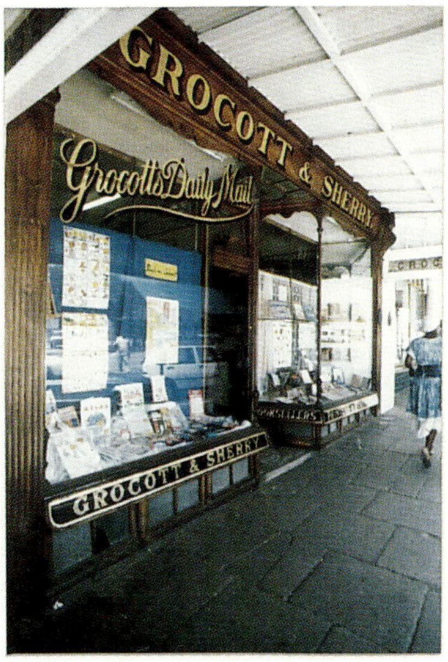

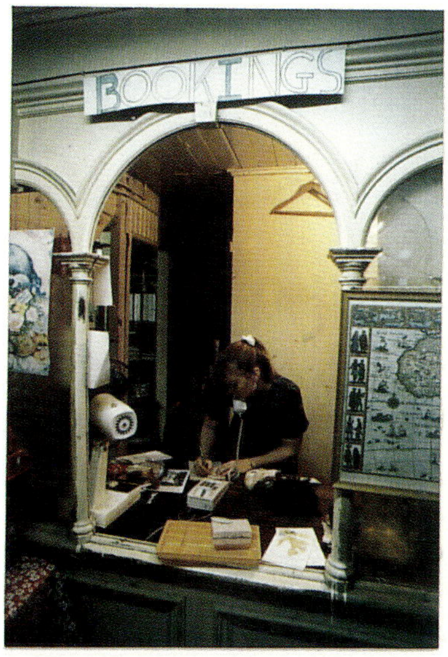

The staff of the accounts department above set up a kitchen amongst the ledgers during the National Arts Festival so that visitors can enjoy a traditional tea in the balconied front room.

The present proprietor is gentlemanly Jeff Grocott, son of Mr Vincent Grocott, nephew of Mr Hugh Grocott and great grandson of the founder, Mr Thomas Henry Grocott. Like them, he was educated at St Andrew's College. Like them, he sits at the huge double-fronted desk in the tiny office at the top of the stairs when he is not helping out behind the counter. Long live *Grocott's* and all who serve there!

LEFT AND ABOVE: *Step into Grocott's and you enter another era: only the printing works has changed. The stationary section never alters, the same leatherbound set of the complete works of Dickens is still on the office bookshelf. Dickensian is the word...*

NATIONAL ENGLISH LITERARY MUSEUM

"To love South Africa, one has to read her writers. There is no doubt they are the ones who have been crucified by this insatiable earth, this rawness, this experience of the elemental."

— Nadia Tazi, French writer

SOUTH AFRICAN writers include academics and housewives, businessmen and doctors, clergymen and clerks; the poor, the middle classes, the rich; atheists, Christians, Hindus, Jews, Muslims, and pagans; centrists, leftists, and rightists. They write for all possible tastes and from every conceivable angle.

Their mother-tongues range from Afrikaans to Zulu. What unifies many of them, and gives their work a common international accessibility, is their shared South Africanness and the fact that they write in English.

The mission of NELM— the National English Literary Museum — is to promote the reading and appreciation of all forms of imaginative South African literature written in English and to make this incredibly rich heritage available in one place. Two to be exact — for it has overflowed from the historic Priest's House to a Victorian villa across Beaufort Street.

It also has two satellites. One is *The Eastern Star* printing museum in Anglo-African Street. Here visitors gain hands-on experience of 19th century printing equipment. The other is the Schreiner House in the town of Cradock, where novelist Olive Schreiner lived as a young girl.

A constant fascination of literary study is the way an author's drafts reflect both the changes and growth of a work in progress. NELM's collection of original manuscripts — handwritten, typed and computer-printed—contains examples from world-famous playwright Athol Fugard, and well-known novelists Bessie Head, China Macphail, Stuart Cloete, Jack Cope, and Yvonne Burgess, to name but a few.

Poetry, too. From all over the country, with a strong input from Grahamstown, which has long been a nurturing ground for poets— starting with the leader of the Scottish Settler Party, Thomas Pringle, South Africa's first real poet in the English language.

Victorian botanist Mary Elizabeth Barber was another creative spirit inspired by local scenes, as

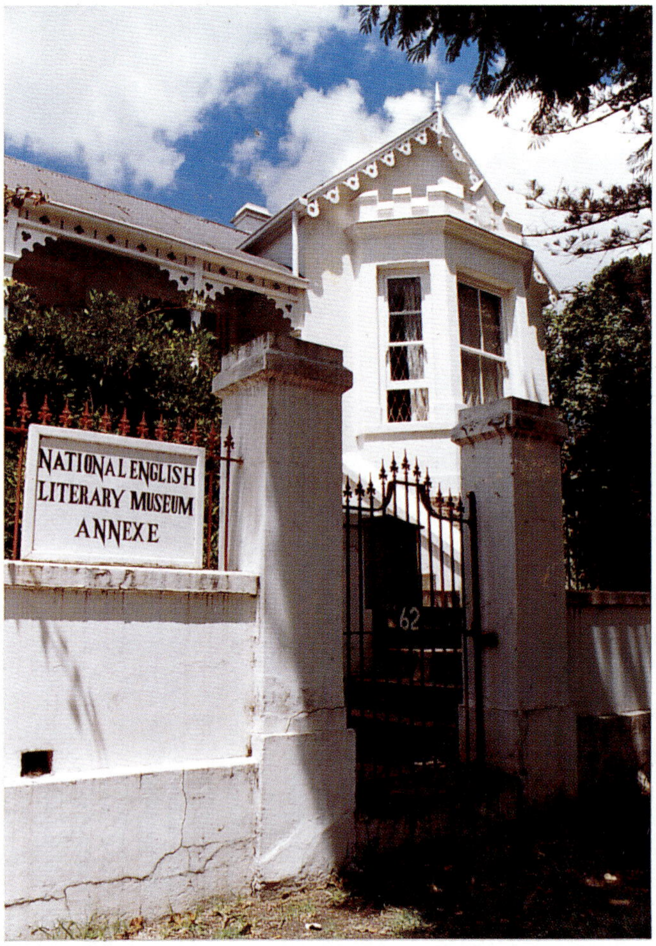

ABOVE: ***Victorian annexe, opposite the main building, has some of the best tiled fireplaces in town***

were Kingsley Fairbridge and Harold Sampson. Francis Carey Slater was here as a bank manager. Contemporary contributors include Don Maclennan, Chris Mann, Jenny Roberts, Rob Berold, and, of course, Guy Butler.

Guy Butler's poems, books, plays, and autobiographies have a special place at NELM. From the first he fought — and initially it was a lone battle — for the incorporation of the study of South African literature into schools and universities.

During his more than 50 years in Grahamstown, he has been a major influence in many spheres. He was appointed to the chair of English at Rhodes University in 1952 and held the post with great distinction. His enterprise led to the development

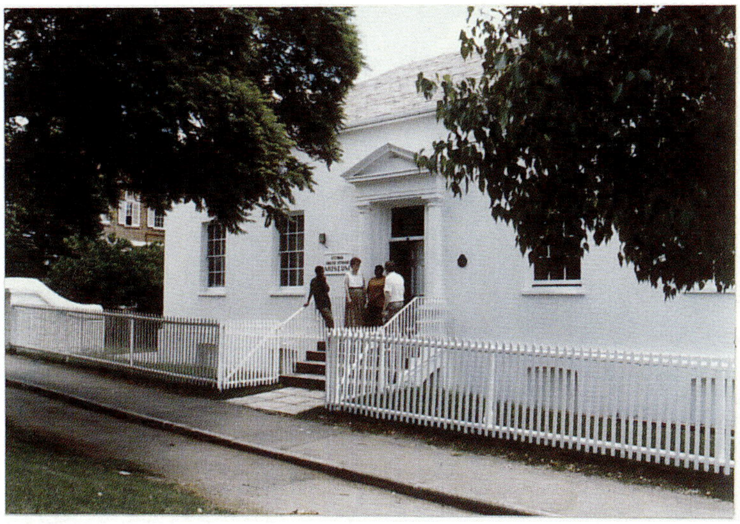

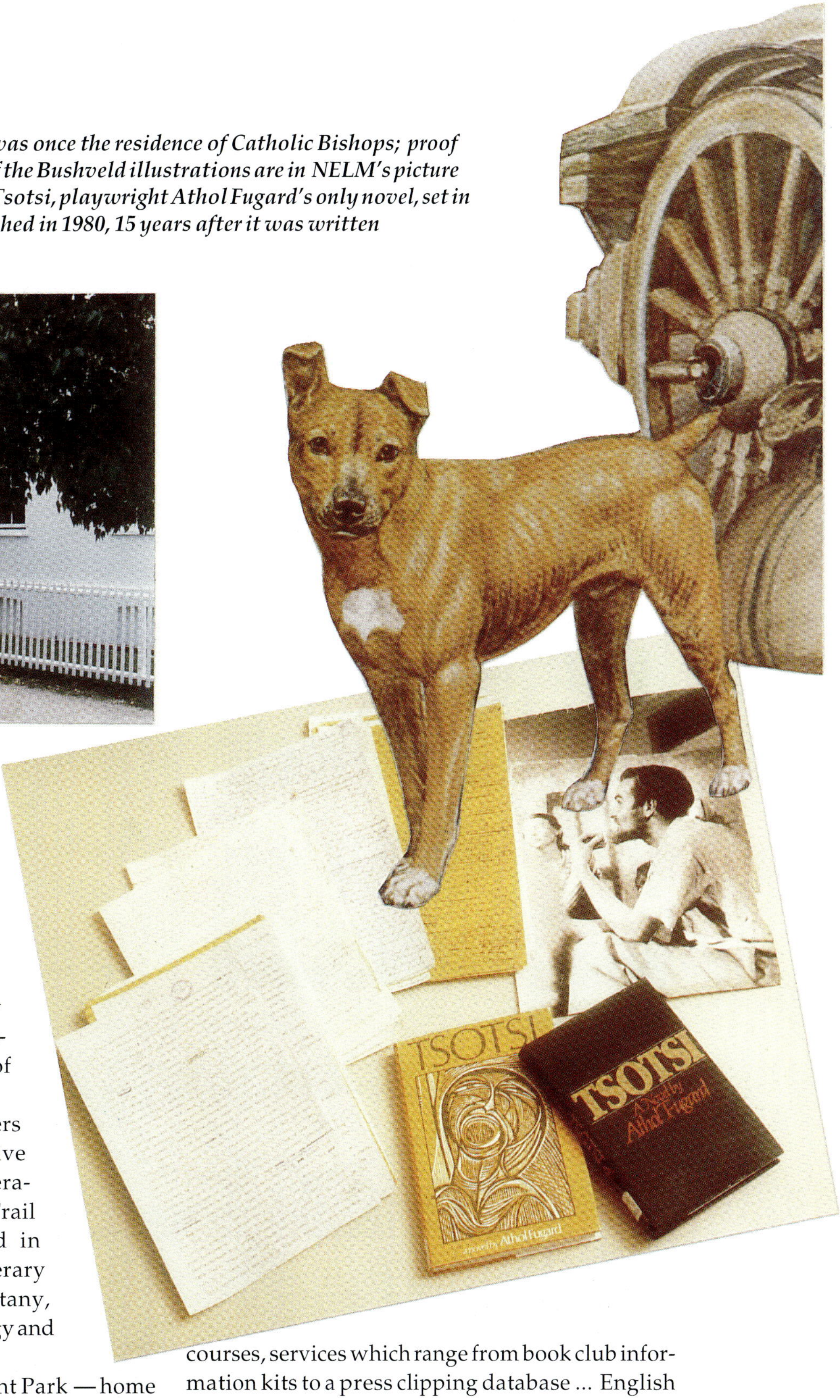

CLOCKWISE: *NELM's main building was once the residence of Catholic Bishops; proof copies of Edmund Caldwell's Jock of the Bushveld illustrations are in NELM's picture archives; and the original drafts of Tsotsi, playwright Athol Fugard's only novel, set in Sophiatown of the 1950s and published in 1980, 15 years after it was written*

of the Departments of Linguistics and English Language, Drama, and Journalism. He established the Institute for the Study of English in Africa, from which NELM grew.

A man of letters in the widest sense, he was honoured in 1994 for his immeasurable contributions by becoming the sixth individual to receive the Freedom of the City of Grahamstown.

Children, the readers and writers of the future, set off on imaginative NELM excursions which bring literature to life. The Schreiner Hiking Trail — a week-long exercise based in Cradock — not only looks at literary studies but includes talks on botany, geology, palaeontology, archaeology and the conservation of San art.

Amanzi near the Addo Elephant Park — home of Sir Percy Fitzpatrick, author of *Jock of the Bushveld* — is another literary venue in the area. NELM holds the manuscript, as well as boxes and boxes of "Fitz's" personal papers, plus proof copies of a special set of the famous *Jock* illustrations by Edmund Caldwell.

Research projects, loan exhibitions, school courses, services which range from book club information kits to a press clipping database ... English literature is alive and well and living in Grahamstown.

When the initial phase of the magnificent library planned to mark the centenary of Rhodes University in 2004 is completed, NELM and the Cory Library for Historical Research will be the first to move their collections into the new building.

"Writing a dictionary is a salutory and humbling experience. It makes you very aware of the extent of your ignorance in almost every field of human activity."

— **B T S Atkins, Oxford University Press**

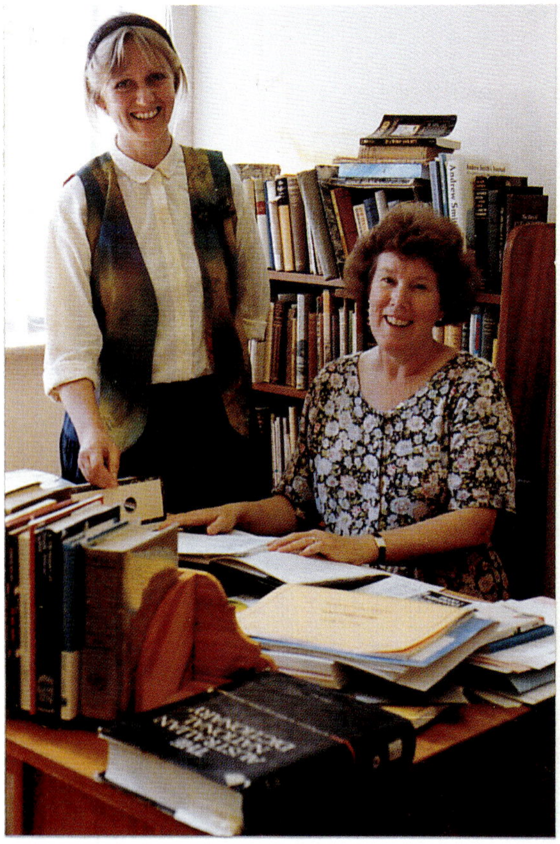

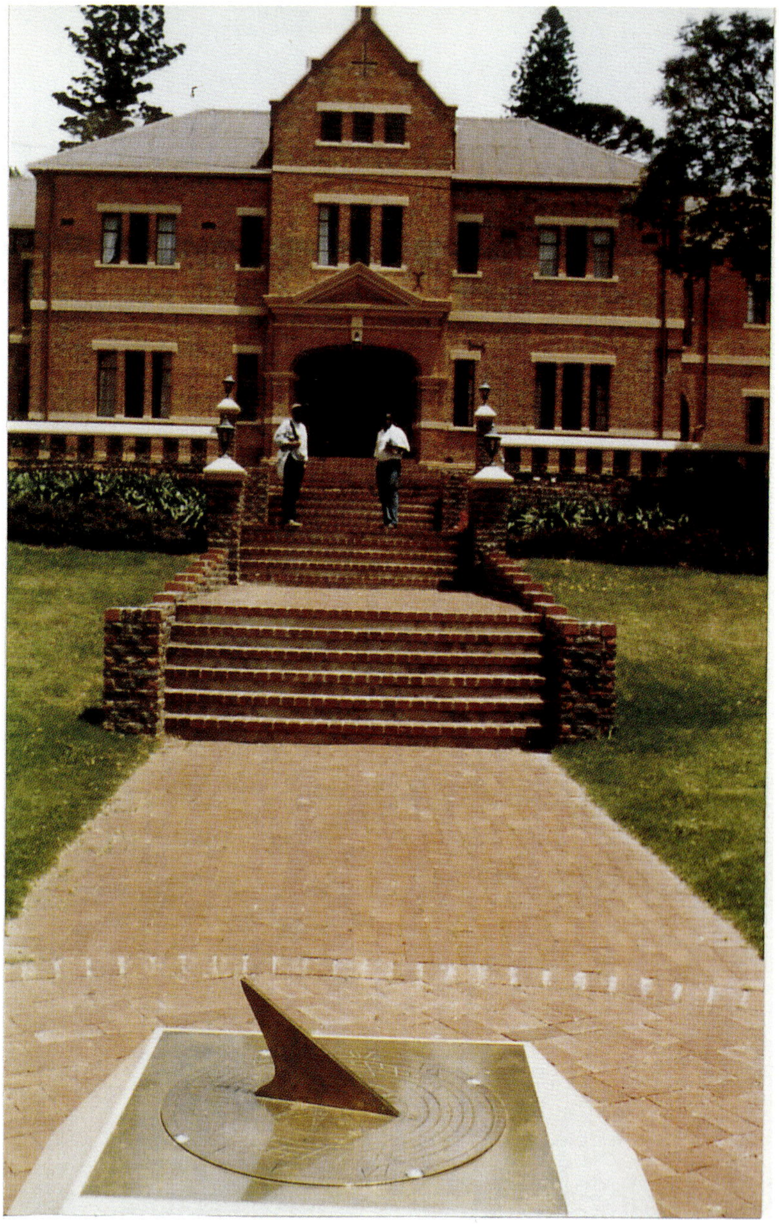

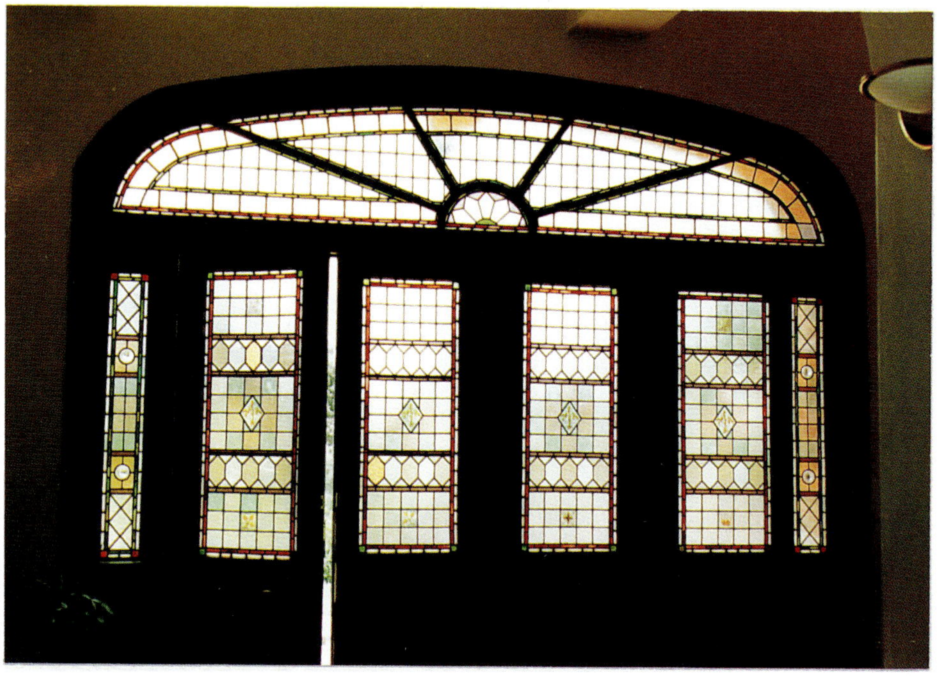

CLOCKWISE: ***Dictionary editors Penny Silva (seated) and Wendy Dore; sunny hours outside historic Gold Fields Centre for English, entered via a delicately tinted stained glass door***

RAINBOW NATION'S DICTIONARY

AARDVARK, aikona, bakkie, bonsella, biltong, dagga, doek, donga, dorp; mebos, mealie-meal, riempie, stinkwood, poegaai, vink, voetsek, shame, sies, hau!

"It's a *lovely* language we have!" declares Penny Silva, editor of the first ever *Dictionary of South African English on Historical Principles*. Compiled by the Dictionary Unit for South African English at Rhodes University, published by the Clarendon Press, printed in the Far East.

An enormous tome defining close on 10 000 words — each word's history being traced through time via snippets from personal letters, manuscripts, journals, historical texts, travel records, newspapers, political treatises, novels, and poetry. Spoken contributions too — from television, radio, even conversations overheard in the supermarket.

Take the affectionately remembered 'tickey' for example — the standard name for a small three-penny piece withdrawn from circulation in 1961. Five pages of densely packed source quotes are devoted to it. The first in 1855, with later additions such as *1955 WILLSLEY* ***Wagon on Fire*** *29 'It's God's trufe, Oom Frikkie, I don't make freppence a gallon on the stuff.' 'None of that nonsense, Ikay, ... You'd sell your soul for a tickey.'* Plus this sobering thought — *1989 B RONGE in* ***Flying Springbok*** *Nov. 13. Do you remember tickeys? Did you know the amount of precious metal they contained was worth more than a one rand coin today?*

The Dictionary Unit is on the first floor of the Gold Fields Centre for English, which has the most beautiful front door in Grahamstown. It was completed in the 1890s as a home for the Sisters of the Community of the Resurrection, and to house an orphanage and school.

Mother Cecile's favourite injunction to the Sisters was: "Thoroughness, sparkle." Attributes reflected in the dictionary, a painstaking work of immense scholarship produced with lively argument, some disagreement, and a great deal of fun and laughter. The book reworks data prepared by many people over 25 years — including the unit's founder, Prof William Branford, and his wife, Dr Jean Branford.

It fills a significant gap in world English lexicography, as there are already dictionaries of American, Canadian, Australian, Indian, and Jamaican English. South African English is probably the most complicated variant of English anywhere, interacting as it does with Dutch / Afrikaans, Malay, Black, and Indian languages.

Hardly Shakespearian English, which is made surprisingly accessible by the director of the Institute for the Study of English along the passage, who also happens to be the president of the Shakespeare Society of Southern Africa — a Grahamstown Foundation project. Yet even he could not resist *The Lonely Biltong*, an all time classic which he used to conclude the Gold Fields Centre's official brochure.

Penned in 1928 by B B Myers, for many years the man behind the *Beachcomber* column in the East London *Daily Dispatch*, it is only fully appreciated by Rainbow People, none more so than the dictionary compilers who once more brought it to light.

THE LONELY BILTONG

The sun shone out of the heavens,
The birds they all were still,
And only the song of the koppies
And the donga's bark so shrill
Broke the silence and heat of the noon day,
While under the summer sun
Two little mosbolletjies wandered
And laughed in childish fun.

Still were the tall maasbankers
And even the wild konfyt
Slept in the shade of the voorslags.
Although the hour was late,
Herds of beautiful voetsaks
Ate the succulent short green kloof;
While a couple of drunken disselbooms
Slept on the farmhouse roof.

Krantzes and veldskoens in hundreds
Scented the summer air;
The spruits were laden with berries,
Truly the world looked fair.
Over the gravelled naartjies,
A lonely biltong ran.
I gazed at it all in wonder,
And murmured "Ag, sis tog man!"

— **B B Myers**

THE WEATHER— enough to drive you bats

NO publication on Grahamstown would be complete without some mention of matters meteorological. In a class — and section — of their own.

Taking a global view, much depends on what is cooking up in the vicinity of Cook Island, as SA weather is influenced by a major atmospheric system controlled by sea surface temperatures in the middle of the Pacific Ocean. When these are high, it might mean rain stops play; low, dry gardens without a drop to drink.

Then there is the movement of depressions which come in from the Atlantic, and proceed towards the Indian Ocean and sometimes on to Australia. The onshore flow of air that may succeed them sometimes brings chilly low clouds billowing up the Blaauwkrantz Valley into the Grahamstown bowl. Why this invariably happens on a Sunday afternoon is anybody's guess. Depression is the word.

What really adds spice to the local mix is the fact that four very different SA climatic zones meet in the vicinity — the semi-arid Karoo, sub-tropical Natal coastal belt, Western Cape winter rainfall area, and inland summer rainfall region. The origin of the 'four-climates-in-a-day' description.

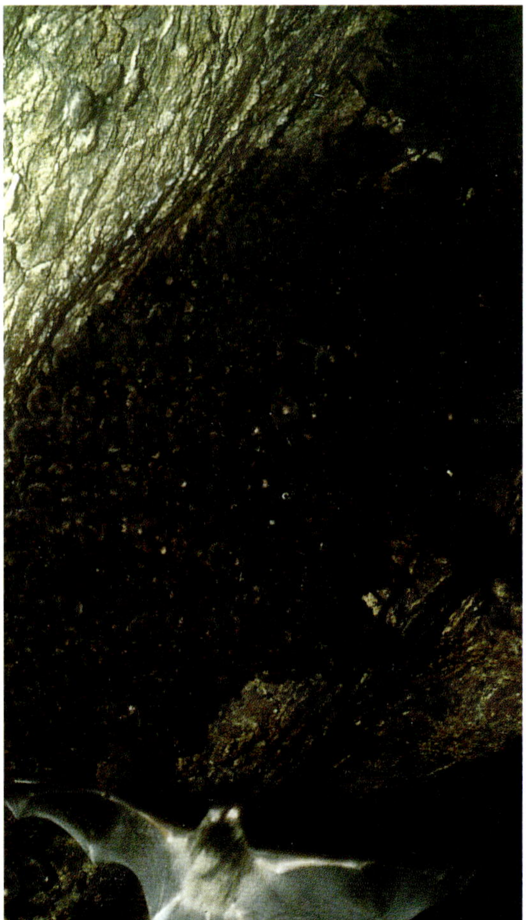

ABOVE: Batting about in storm water drain

Come what may, everyone has to adjust their internal thermostats as best they can, particularly the Grahamstown house bats. Extremely sensitive to temperature changes, these small creatures constantly alter their positions in rafter crevices, moving from one side of their lodgings to the other as things hot up or cool down. Fairly common in the Karoo district, where they live in rock cracks and survive extremes of heat and cold, they are totally at home in the galvanized iron roofs of settler cottages — and storm water drains.

A batman of repute in the Department of Zoology and Entomology at Rhodes puts forward the following three persuasive points in favour of the conservation of house bat populations.

Based on an examination of three large roosts (more than 2 000 bats each) and several smaller ones, it has been estimated that Grahamstown has a population of at least 10 000 insectivorous bats. At a conservative estimate they each consume about two grams of insects per night, removing at least 20kg from the environs.

Secondly, their faeces, which are dry and relatively odourless, have very good insulatory properties, and in England householders are being urged to retain bat colonies in their roofs for this reason. Finally, both the bats and their ectoparasites are, under normal circumstances, harmless to humans and not just fairweather friends.

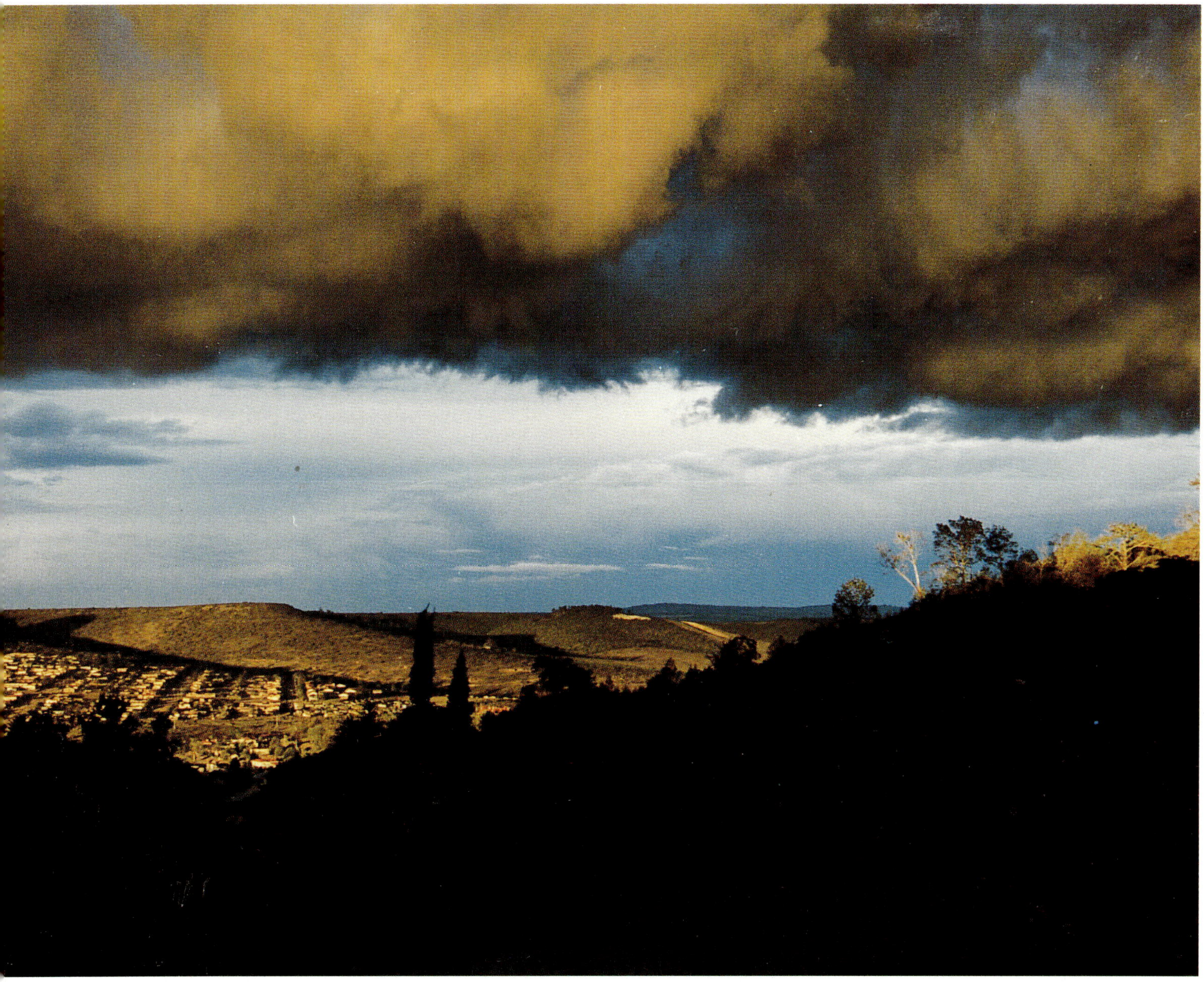

ABOVE: ***Stormy weather on the south side, sunshine over the Township slopes***

The sky over little lowrise Grahamstown seems particularly wide and open, ever changing, never still. The large fluffy white cumulus clouds so characteristic of the city's skyscape are due to the proximity of the coast. Drifting dreamily overhead, they bring to mind Constable's cathedral paintings. Sometimes they build up vertically into great anvil-topped cumulonimbus formations — thick, dark grey, and dramatic.

Feather-like high level cirrus clouds — appropriately called 'horse tails'— often herald the approach of hellish berg winds. It feels as if someone has left the Highveld oven door open when these fiery blasts blow seawards from the interior, hotting up by as much as one degree centigrade for every 100m of descent, and causing temperatures to rise by 10 degrees in the space of half an hour. Whew!

But relief is at hand. They normally develop one to two days before a cold front hits and cardigans come out again. It has been scientifically proved that, psychologically speaking, abrupt weather changes are preferable to a monotonously predictable climate, producing lively, interesting people who know how to adapt. A pretty fair description of Grahamstonians — in between sniffles.

"Graveyards, like churches, possess the strange power of excluding the everyday world. To enter is to abandon the bickering and small purpose of our everyday lives for a security and peace we seldom find elsewhere." — **Athol Fugard, playwright**

Fallen Angels, Wild Lilies

CARVED St Joseph lilies bloom on headstones, pale pink crinums flourish amid other flowers of the veld. Old fashioned roses ramble, starry jasmine scents the air. Doves roo-coo-coo consolingly. Occasionally, lively youngsters joust with lances made from rusty railings topped by *fleur-de-lis*. Only the Van Gogh cypresses stand sentinel.

Vestry minutes of St George's Church (later the Cathedral) in 1833 refer to the need to clear up what are now called the Old Cemeteries, indicating yet again that there is little new under the somnolent Grahamstown sun.

Over the decades, conscientious campaigns have been launched to cut back rampant growth, right leaning tombstones and remove lacy lichen. But these historic graveyards seem to have an independent afterlife of their own, and are soon mantled by poetic decay once more.

Time, the great healer, is also a stealthy destroyer. Vandalism too has taken its toll, accounting for fallen angels and broken ornamental urns. A grassy corner is reputed to have been a night hold for cart donkeys. At one stage, drunken revellers roistered regularly, especially when a Skokiaan Queen installed her brewing stills in some secluded tombs.

The earliest recorded grave is that of Lt Col George Sackville Fraser, who helped set up the military garrison in 1812 and departed this life on October 18, 1823. Extended in 1874 and closed in 1915 when the New Cemetery was opened on the city's outskirts, the cemeteries now see only the occasional burial in family or previously held plots.

There are close on 6 000 graves in this green peace between the railway station and Kingswood College. The main cemetery includes the Anglican, Baptist, Presbyterian, Coloured, Asian, and Military sections. Across a pine-lined avenue, the Roman Catholic part is dominated by the 54 Convent Sisters and 27 Jesuit Fathers who taught at St Aidan's. The Methodists fan out from the centre and the final resting place of those of the Jewish faith is further back.

The gravestones document bygone eras in the city and in South Africa. Some of Welsh slate were used as ballast in sailing ships. Jeremiah Goldswain, the well-known 1820 diarist, is among the 250 settlers at their journey's end. Many of the people mentioned in this book rest here, including Henry Carter Galpin of The Observatory and the admirable Dr William Guybon Atherstone.

Ordinary folk, explorers, missionaries, soldiers, civil dignitaries, legal men, scientific professionals, educationalists, and artists. Twenty-nine are listed in the *Dictionary of South African Biography*.

A rich research source for historians studying the institutions and social networks of the district. It is the human details which catch the casual stroller's attention. The babies' graves — "In heaven at rest, ere sin their souls had known" — mute testimony to the high infant mortality rate of the 19th century. The carefully chosen verses and quotations — "With Christ, which is far better" being a frequent choice.

And the changing fashions in Christian names. Violet Mabel, Bertha Winifred, Agnes Amelia, Harriet Cornelia, Mildred Alice, Myrtle Clare — what visions they conjure up of demure young creatures in high-collared blouses marrying Albert, Dudley, Frederick, Rupert or Obadiah "till death us do part", and now side by side again till Judgement Day.

The storms of grief long since over, an uncanny calm prevails. As you return to the ever-pressing present through a creaking turnstile, Spanish American philosopher George Santayana's wise words are worth pondering: "There is no cure for birth and death save to enjoy the interval. The dark background which death supplies brings out the tender colours of life in all their purity."

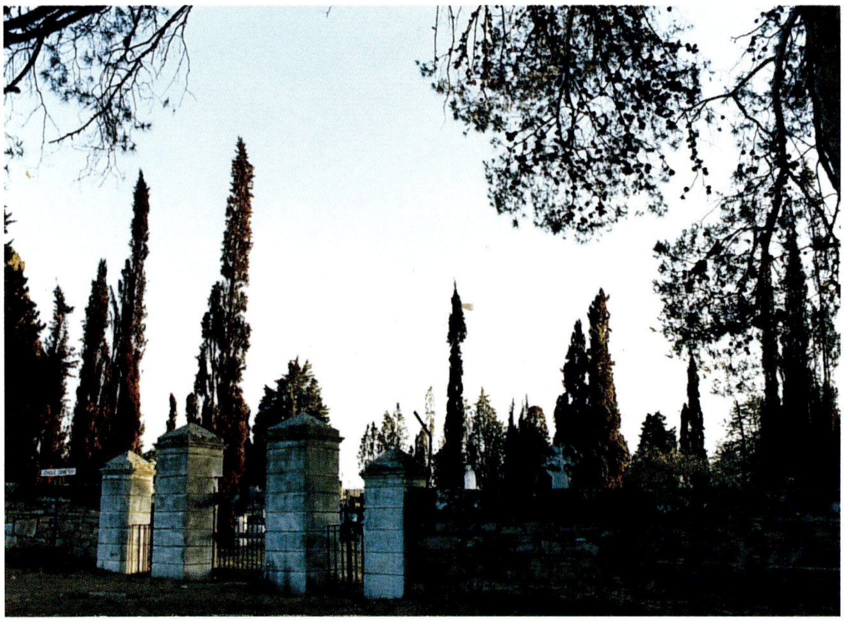

LEFT AND RIGHT: *The Old Cemeteries, where cypresses brood and tombstones tumble*

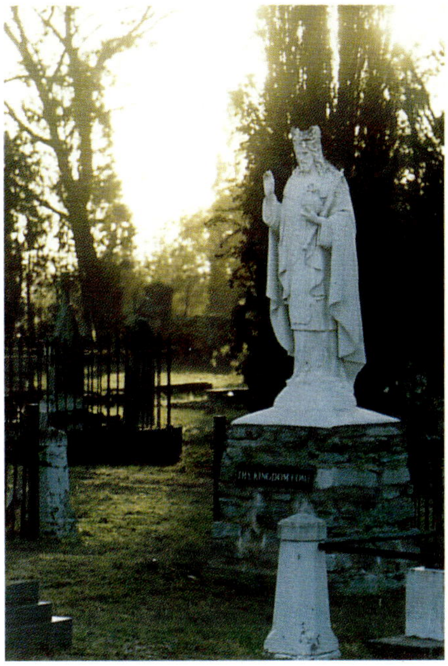

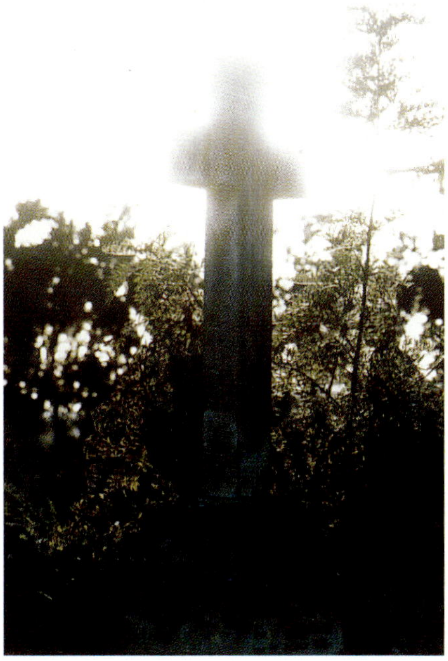

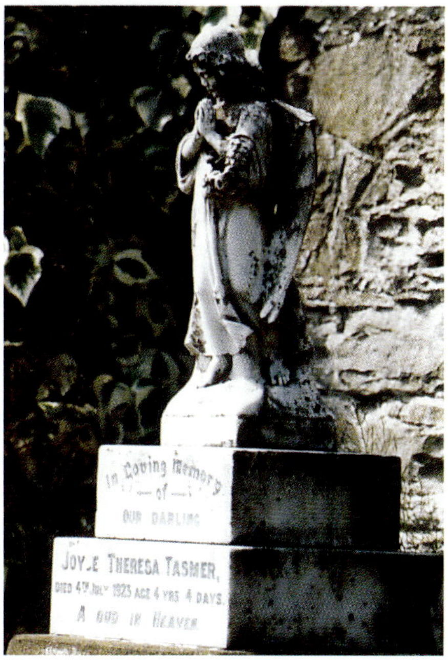
In Loving Memory
of
Our Darling
Joyce Theresa Tasmer,
Died 4th July 1923 Age 4 yrs 4 days.
A Bud in Heaven.

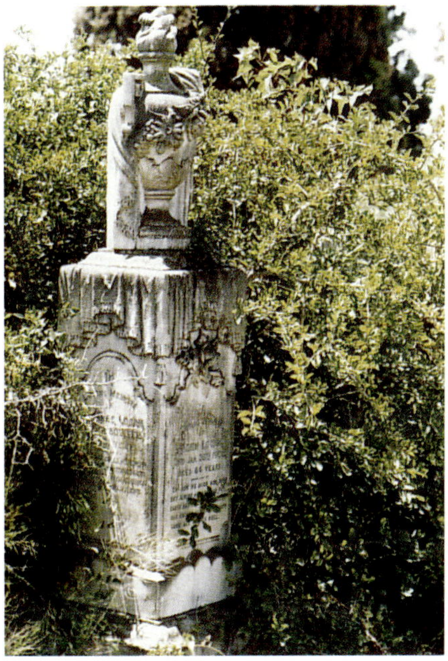

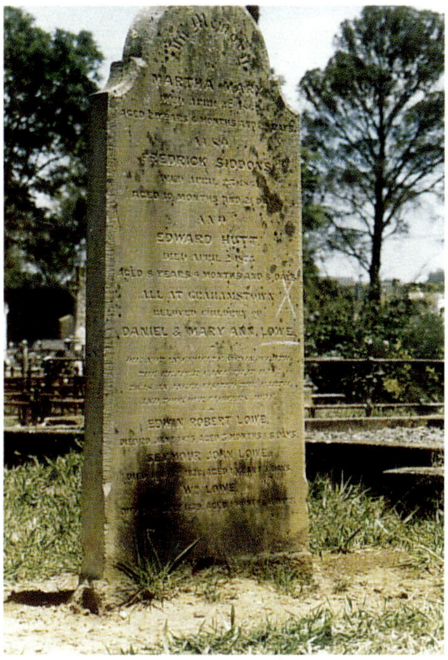
MARTHA MARY
FREDRICK SIDDONS
AND
EDWARD HUTT
ALL AT GRAHAMSTOWN
DANIEL & MARY ANN LOWE
EDWIN ROBERT LOWE
SEYMOUR JOHN LOWE
WM LOWE

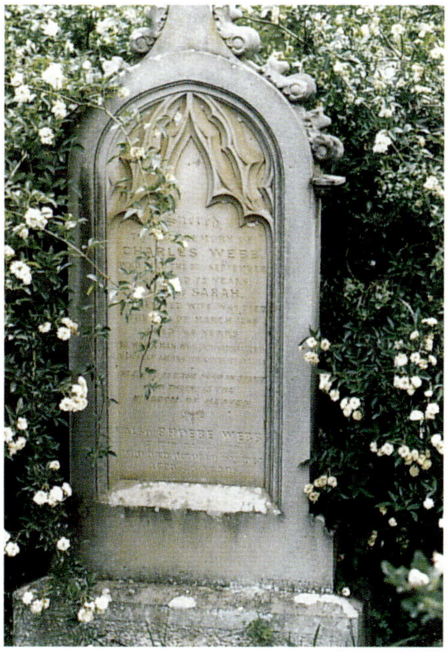
CHARLES WEBB
SARAH
PHOEBE WEBB

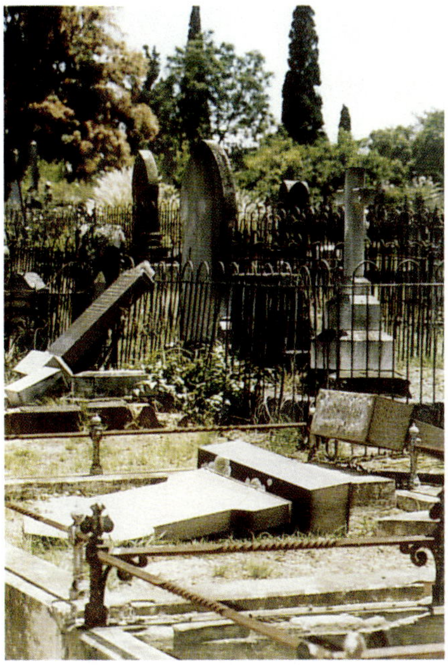

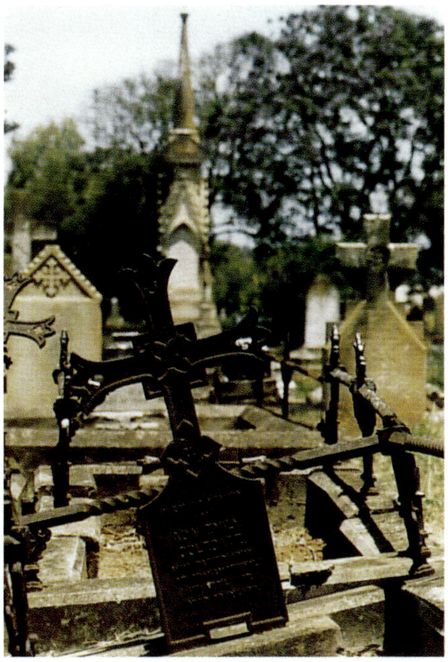

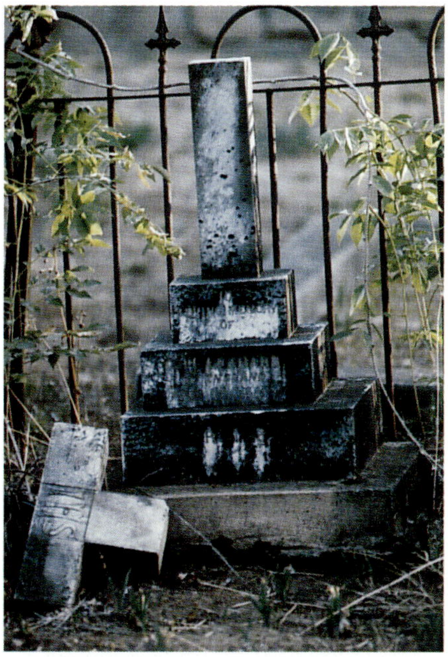

AIMING FOR THE STARS

Perhaps as a symbol of its high aspirations, Grahamstown continues to reach for the stars, looking to the future, building on the past. As did Henry Carter Galpin well over a century ago.

Always a poor sleeper, while other citizens snored he would be up in the Camera Obscura atop The Observatory Museum, where this book began. The camera table was shunted out of the way on a set of tracks, his 22cm reflector telescope rolled forward and focused on a heavenly body.

Galpin was an architect and surveyor by training; a watchmaker and jeweller by occupation, a versatile Victorian with a magnificent obsession — time and light. Having emigrated from England for health reasons, he arrived on the Eastern frontier in 1850, and later purchased a modest abode which he transformed into the first multi-storeyed building in the Eastern Cape. The house took its name from his observatory at its highest point.

He frequently used his starry-eyed observations to obtain Grahamstown's Mean Time — something he also did by day in the Meridian Room one floor down. At approximately 11.45 a sunbeam glides into the room through a carefully placed aperture and moves across the floor where Galpin marked a north-south line. By dint of sundry calculations, local noon was accurately established.

Before The Observatory's restoration in the early 1980s, students lodged in various roosts. A recent visitor to the museum nostalgically recalled his sojourn in the Meridian Room, when he used a ladder to get to his bed in the gallery.

Now Rhodes students aim for the stars on the other side of town. Rhodes's Astronomy and HAM Radio Society, *Astrosoc*, is one of the largest astronomical societies in Southern Africa. The observatory is situated on the roof of the Geography Department and utilizes the carefully restored 25cm Schwartz telescope built in 1880.

The main mirror, which is the heart of the telescope, was made by hand and is still in perfect condition. It reveals objects 4 000 times fainter than the unaided eye can see, and shows superb detail of the moon and planets. Viewers require a two metre ladder to look into the eyepiece.

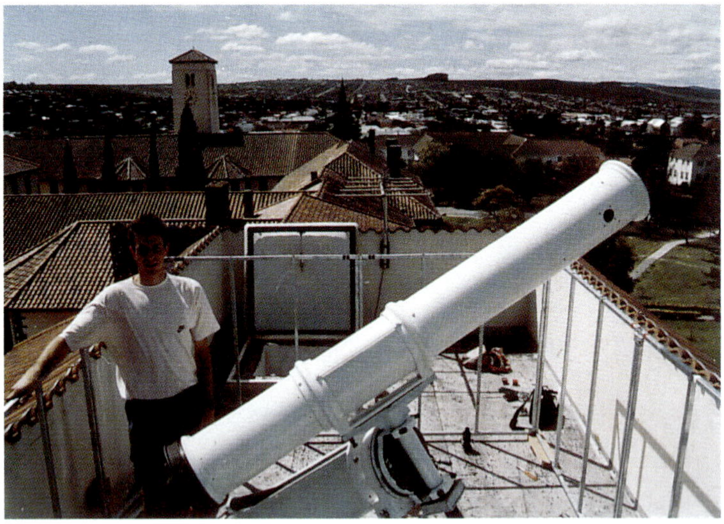

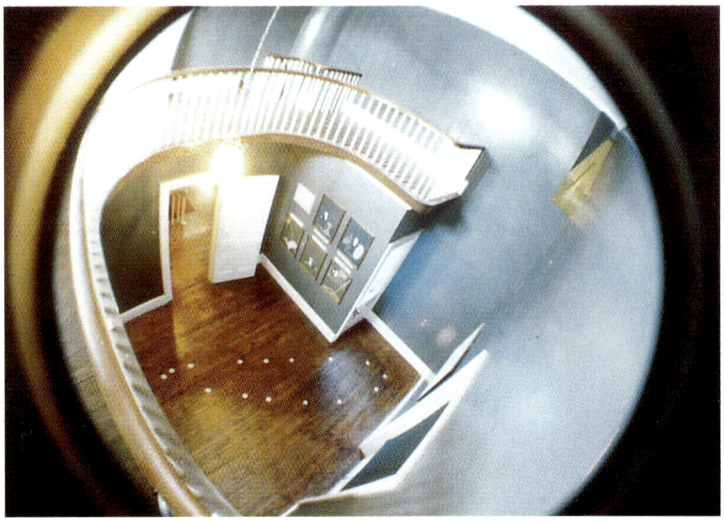

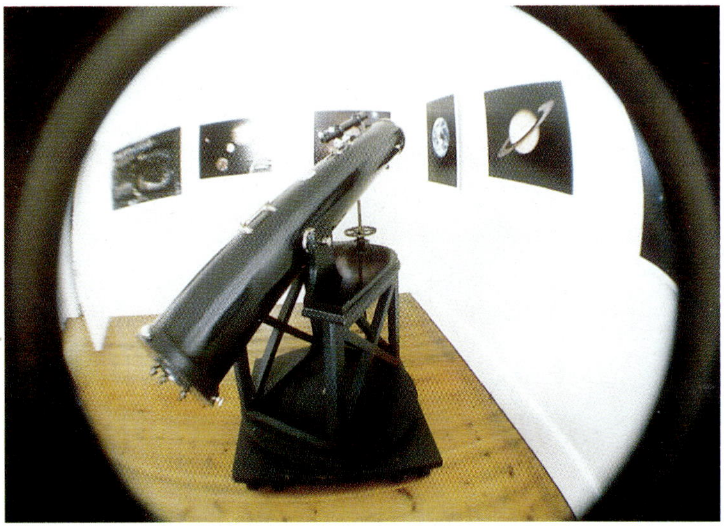

FROM TOP: *Pride of the Rhodes stargazers; Henry Galpin's ingenious Meridian Room; and his reflector telescope at rest*

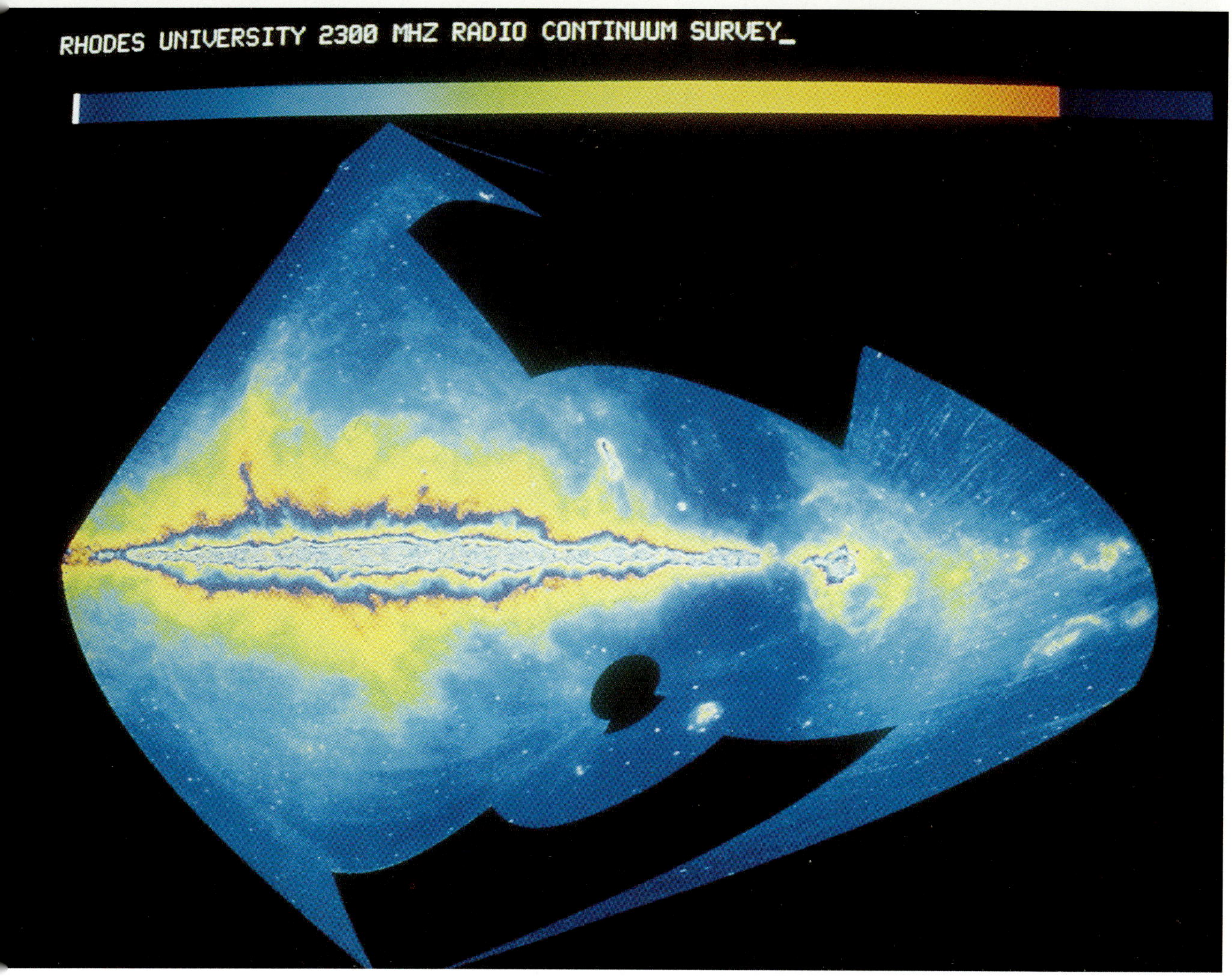

LEFT: The hisssss of the universe — colours of the image are coded to represent radio signal strength; and BELOW: the horn radio telescope that Justin built

Meanwhile, the hiss of the universe may be heard in the Department of Physics and Electronics. All objects in the universe emit radio waves, some weakly, some strongly. Radio astronomy is the study of these natural emissions of cosmic origin, which are detected as a radio noise or "hiss", using sensitive radio receivers. Out-of-this-world images are created by coding colours to represent radio signal strength.

Radio astronomers are able to determine the physical environment of objects such as newly born stars in their dusty cocoons, which are invisible to optical telescopes. They can detect emissions from galaxies and quasars at the very limits of the observable universe, and can measure the radio radiation field that is the afterglow of the "Big Bang".

The department was recently involved in mapping the entire Southern sky in a joint project with the Hartebeesthoek Radio Astronomy Observatory. For this, research officer Justin Jonas has built a portable horn radio telescope, mounted on a trailer so that it can be towed to places where conditions are best for observation purposes. Most other radio telescopes are too large to move. Because of the uniqueness of the survey, it has caused considerable interest abroad, and further collaborative efforts have been embarked upon with groups in the USA, England, and Germany.

Worlds away from Mr Galpin, but the spirit is the same. Ever upward and onward ...

"The past is but the beginning of a beginning, and all that is and has been is but the twilight of the dawn."

— H G Wells, English writer (1866-1946)

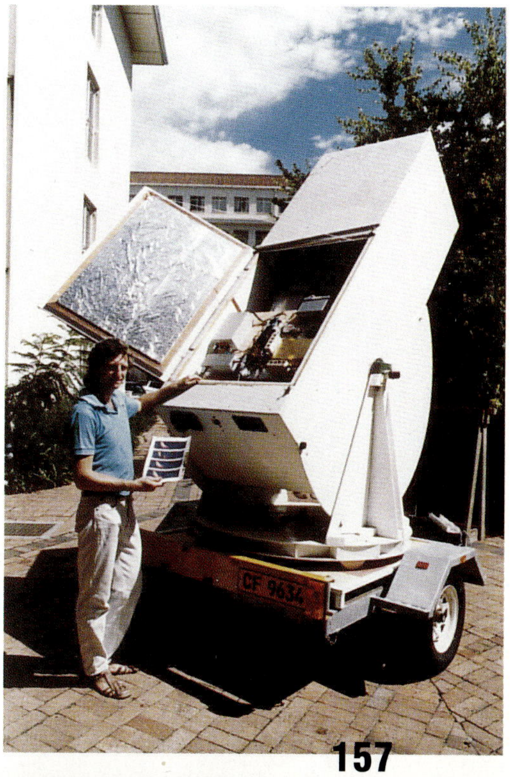

THE CREATIVE TRIO

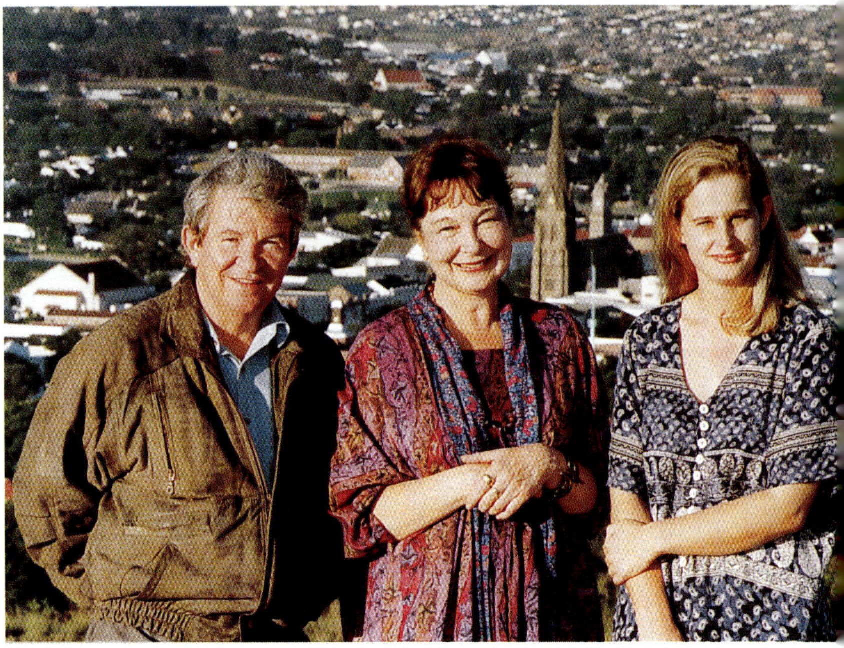

ABOVE: Book team — Duncan Greaves, Emily O'Meara and Lyn Tyler with Grahamstown behind them

Author **Emily O'Meara's** deep affection for Grahamstown is embodied in this book. During her 21 years with *The Star*, Johannesburg, special assignments took her to Paris and Mexico City, to London for a royal wedding, and to Grahamstown for an international conference. It was love at first sight. She returned for good as soon as she could, and devoted herself to serendipity: the art of making happy and unexpected discoveries. Her appointment as curator of The Observatory Museum, a Victorian house with a captivating camera obscura, has been perhaps the happiest of all. Philosopher poet Kahlil Gibran wrote "Work is love made visible". ***Grahamstown Reflected*** is just that and much more.

Creative designer **Lyn Tyler's** arrival in the right place at the right time was also pure serendipity. Having recently graduated from the University of Cape Town's Michaelis School of Fine Art, Lyn came to Grahamstown with her family in 1994. Her portfolio quickly revealed her fresh adventurous approach and she found herself a member of the team before she had a chance to unpack! Her youthfulness and love of life overflow on the pages of ***Grahamstown Reflected***.

Photographer **Duncan Greaves** has been getting things into focus for more than 40 years, and his eyes still click smiling. A coronation, heads of state from around the world, factories, ships at sea, the development of Richard's Bay Harbour, wildlife, and the mists and mellowness of early mornings and evenings have captured his imagination over the years. Duncan settled in Grahamstown in 1990. The epitome of a town photographer, he has dedicated himself to portraying the city, its people and their activities in his own special way, lending a lively air of the here and now to ***Grahamstown Reflected***.

GETTING GRAHAMSTOWN TOGETHER...

Assembling this jigsaw puzzle of a book was a fun exercise which sometimes left the team out of breath but never out of step. We hope it comes across as a happy book. It should, because it was compiled with genuine affection and enjoyment. Readers are seen as companions exploring the city with us, delighting in the magic of the everyday.

Occasionally we lost some pieces, only to find others exactly when we needed them. Like the *Boöphane disticha* lily (featured with the *abakhwethas*) that suddenly bloomed in a bucket behind the Albany Museum; the menacing anvil-shaped cloud looming dramatically on cue the morning Duncan Greaves photographed the World War I memorial; and his unscheduled shot of the Hospice Tree of Life. This inspired the tree spread — a particularly happy chance as Grahamstown has since received the National Arbor Award.

Initially the book was intended to be a booklet. Like so many Grahamstown projects, it grew and grew — at one time to more than 200 pages. Even then we had not covered everything on our list.

Designer Lyn Tyler cut it down to size, as she had to, because it was basically handmade — a home-knitted jersey full of character rather than a machine-perfect pullover. Only the copy was computer set; every image was reproduced to size and pasted down by hand.

The gallant Mr Greaves manfully dashed out on shoots slotted into his routine round of school sports days, Rhodes residence dinners, Nativity plays (at least a dozen), prize givings and THE WEATHER, which predictably went its own erratic way.

Author Emily O'Meara — temporarily transferred from The Observatory — started the book in a corner of the History Museum storeroom, with the convent's ancient harp to hand and a huge soap-pot as a wastepaper container. She finished her stint roosting alongside the stuffed owls in Natural Sciences.

Pat Black in the Albany Museum's Ichthyology Department fed the hand-written paragraphs through her computer in between feeding *Sandelia bainsii* larval fish, a species unique to the Grahamstown area. Madeleen Welman checked the pages of copy slipped two by two beneath her cottage door. Penny Silva, editor of the *Dictionary of South African English on Historical Principles*, was responsible for the final editing and proofreading. The team is deeply grateful for their practical input and ever-positive spirit which helped the vision unfurl ...

THANKS TO ONE AND ALL

This book has no dedication at the beginning. Here it is, at the end:

" *To Grahamstown, and all who have lived here, past and present.*"

The city is part of them, and they are part of it. They have all helped to turn this book into a celebration to share with friends and visitors.

Members of the team were warmly welcomed wherever they went. A routine list of people and organizations could not begin to convey the spirit of what was truly a combined effort.

Many supplied enough information for a book on their subject alone — and warranted one. In this light-hearted overview, they could only be given a few lines, but the interesting hours spent in their company were one of the pleasures of the project.

References consulted were wide and varied. Weightier tomes exist, scholarly research abounds. The Cory Library for Historical Research at Rhodes University and the Bowker Library at the Albany Museum contained the answers to most queries, and the assistants were endlessly obliging in finding them. The annals of the Grahamstown Historical Society provided a particularly rich resource, as did the handsomely-bound copies of old newspapers.

Many guides to Grahamstown have been compiled over the decades. Though the actors come and go, the stage remains much the same. Life's ever-changing drama has but one and the same background — the same central streets, the same eternal hills ... The team has simply re-arranged the pieces for a late 20th century production.

We express our appreciation to all the individuals and concerns represented in this version, and to those who are not, but who have assisted so generously. Thank you for making it possible.

PHOTOGRAPH AND PICTURE CREDITS

End papers: Duncan Greaves Early morning landscape of Grahamstown ; **John McKinnell** Church Square in the mist

In addition to the hundreds of photographs commissioned from Duncan Greaves specifically for this book, pictures were also used from the following sources:

Photographs

Albany Museum archives Changing the guard p14, Church Square 1903 p16, lamps on the Square p17, figure of Peace unveiled p19, laboratory p22, Marianne North p24, the Old Provost p25, JDR initials p28, WG Atherstone p28, Josie Wood p30, Cathedral 1824 p34, Rosa Wright p37, Mother Gertrude p39, convent interior p39, Supreme Court 1917 p45, St Aidan's staff p64, dormitory p64, Halley's Comet p65, rickshaws p72, St Philip's p86, Kingswood building p102, Victoria Girls' building p104, family group p124, rugby team 1888 p142; **Mohammed Bassa** archer p142; **Prof Ric Bernard, Zoology and Entomology, Rhodes University** Bats p152; **Centre for Social Development**, pp118-119; **Monty Cooper** Angel p18, organ p22, coelacanth p29, George St houses 59, trilithon p82, wagon stones p83, owl p123; **Cory Library for Historical Research, Rhodes** Mother Cecile p38, Commercial Hall p45, exhibition stands p72, soldiers p98, Rhodes pictures pp112-113, first car p136, ox-wagon p136, train p137, cricket team p140, swimming pool p141, rally p143; **De Beers** Eureka diamond p28; **Martin Ellenberger** Blaine's building burning (introduction) and p15; **Kate Farrington** Cathedral and tile (introduction), postbox p67, Dakawa p134; **First City Regiment** Band p95; **Grahamstown Foundation** (including photographs from **Conrad Cambray, Ruphen Coudyzer, Michael Hall, Deon Lottering, John McKinnell, Stephen Msikelelo, Cathy Pinnock, Susan Imrie Ross,** and **Sean Woods**) Modern dancers (introduction), fountain p70, Standard Bank balloon p73, arts festival scenes pp73-79, 1820 Monument pictures pp80-81, INSET van p136; **James Greaves** Donkeys p137, climber p140, telescope p156; **Grocott's** Linotype press p144, office and printing works p146; **JLB Smith Institute of Ichthyology** Coelacanth eggs p29; **Justin Jonas, Physics and Electronics, Rhodes** Hiss of the universe p157; **Anita Klingenberg** Nombulelo pupils p106; **Mary Waters Secondary School** Rugby players p106; **John McKinnell** Toposcope p83; **Military Re-enactment Group** Basil Mills p91; **NELM** Athol Fugard collage p149; **St Andrew's College** Chapel p98, cricket match p101; **Stephen Penney** Rugby game p142; **Syd Penney** Marathon runners p140, mountain bikers p141, hockey players and George Pohl p142; **Selmar Schönland Herbarium** Cape chestnut trees pp68-69; ***Women's Value*** / **Corrie Hansen** Church Square facades (forethought).

Drawings and Paintings

Albany Museum archives Fort Selwyn by Thomas Baines p13, Col John Graham p13, High Street 1877 by George Hawes p14, Gradwell's Mill by Francis Lewin Dashwood p20, Market Square by Thomas Baines p21, Opening of Parliament 1864 by Charles Jay p26, Grahamstown 1823 p47, Roman girl p72, Makana by Frederick I'Ons p85, High Street 1848 by Thomas Baines p90; **Marjorie Courtenay-Latimer** Sketch of coelacanth p29; **Dakawa** Textile designs p134, "Big Bright Africa" by Vulike Temise p134; **Douglas Galpin** The Old Well by Frederick I'Ons p19; **Grocott's** Hubble-bubble p23, balloon p72; **Gerhard Marx, Albany Museum** Fossil fish and map p12, dinosaur p28; **MuseumAfrica** Khoi chief p13, The Bowling Green by "Dummy" Brown p138; **National Cultural History Museum** Piet Retief p91; **NELM** Jock p149; **The Power Station** Table-mat design p135; **Private Collection, Johannesburg**, Canteen scene by Frederick I'Ons p90, **Lindsay Quirk** Schools' Festival poster p78; **Royal Botanic Gardens, Kew** Painting with kingfisher by Marianne North p24; **T Sheffield, *The Story of The Settlement*** bridge in "Bots" p25; **Victoria Girls'** Miss Kitty Richardson by Ken Robinson p105; **William Steyn** African mask p71, Eisteddfod poster p79; **Dave Voorvelt, JLB Smith Institute of Ichthyology** Fishes pp126-127.

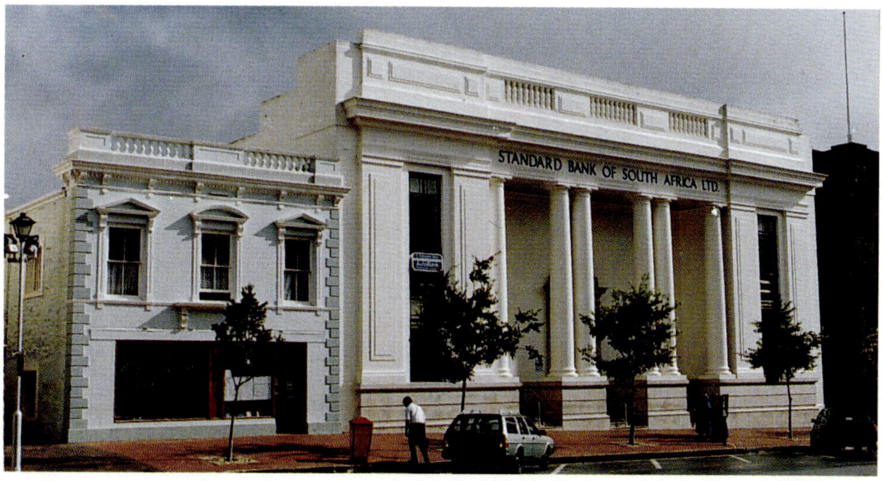

RIGHT: *Enquire within — Grahamstown Publicity Association next to Standard Bank on Church Square*

AN ALBANY MUSEUM PUBLICATION

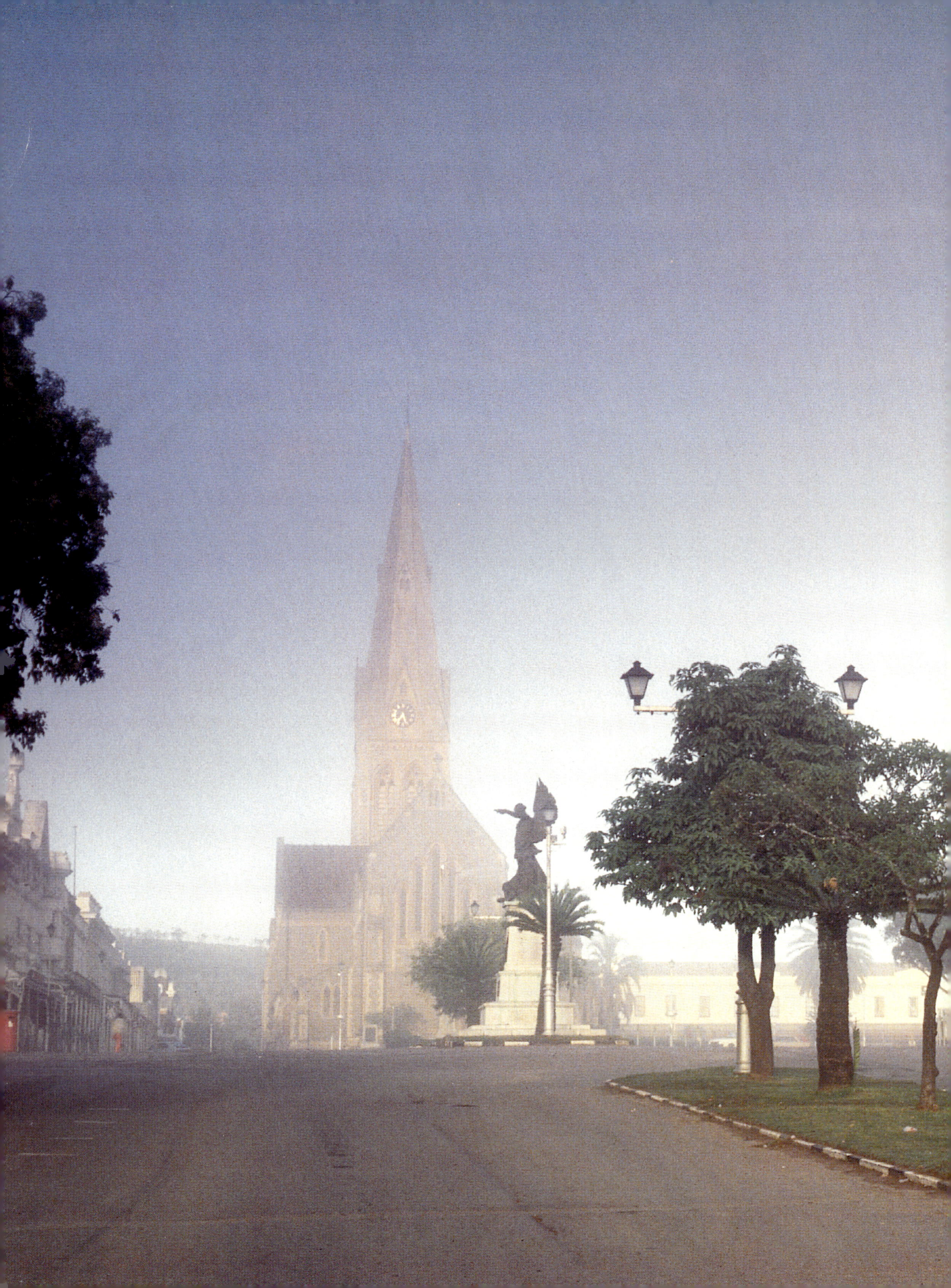